James Monroe

THE QUEST FOR NATIONAL IDENTITY

James Monroe

THE QUEST FOR NATIONAL IDENTITY

❧

Harry Ammon

McGraw-Hill Book Company

New York   St. Louis   San Francisco

Düsseldorf   London   Mexico   Panama

Sydney   Toronto

LIBRARY OF CONGRESS CATALOG CARD NUMBER: 78-141294
FIRST EDITION
07-001582-1

1 2 3 4 5 6 7 8 9 0 MAMM 7 9 8 7 6 5 4 3 2 1

CONTENTS

INTRODUCTION

"The Quest for National Identity," the subtitle I have chosen for this study of the fifth President of the United States, is particularly appropriate in that it not only epitomizes the goals which Monroe pursued throughout his half century in public life, but in that it also indicates his intimate involvement in the main trends of his own times. In a general way it can be said that nearly every leader of the revolutionary epoch whose active career extended beyond the establishment of the federal government in 1789 was engaged in the very same pursuit. The names of George Washington, John Adams and Alexander Hamilton come immediately to mind, as do those of Thomas Jefferson and James Madison, Monroe's fellow Virginians, with whom his life and career were so closely linked. In this connotation, the phrase—the quest for national identity—signifies the utopian aspirations of the revolutionary generation. The men of 1776 did not interpret the American Revolution purely in terms of a severance of the bond with Great Britain, but as a movement to create new institutions radically different from those of the past. They were keenly aware that the epoch about to begin was not only different from all that was past but that it was up to them to make it so. All felt a personal commitment to the ultimate objective of establishing in America a nation founded upon utterly different principles from those prevailing in the Old World and possessing a unique and unmistakable character.

The utopian vision of the revolutionary age cannot be reduced to a simple formula. Never spelled out in specifics, it was voiced in the form of broad maxims such as the belief that republican governments were superior to all others, that social institutions were subject to natural law, that all men were created equal and that the object of government was the preservation of liberty. To Monroe and his contemporaries these abstract principles seemed a sufficient foundation for the creation of a nation capable of guaranteeing liberty to all citizens. Even though these principles were deemed universally valid, the leaders of the revolutionary era never doubted that their implementation would have a peculiarly American aspect. To some this might mean only that America must be freed of the corruption inherent in European institutions, but to others, such as John Adams, it meant that "America was designed by Providence for the Theatre, on which Man was to make his true figure, on which science, Virtue, Liberty, Happiness and Glory were to exist in Peace." [1] Unlike the leaders of the French Revolution, American statesmen of Monroe's generation did not experience a call to redeem the world: their first duty was to reconstruct American institutions. Once this task had been completed then the United States would serve as an example to the world and exert a lasting moral influence. To these ideas which still play such a central role in American thinking, Monroe maintained a lifelong allegiance, and it is within this framework that his career can best be judged.

Apart from this generalized application "The Quest for National Identity" has a very particular meaning in relation to Monroe. He was the first President to enter office during an era of peace and internal economic stability. Every Chief Executive from Washington to Madison had been plagued by the complex problems facing a new and still weak nation in a world shattered by the wars set off by the French Revolution and by Napoleon's imperial ambitions. The War of 1812 did not bring a solid victory to the United States, yet, when it ended, not only was the world at peace, but the people had achieved a new awareness and a hitherto unknown feeling of self-confidence in themselves as a nation. The war had the effect of proving to Americans (and to the European powers) that the republican experiment was truly viable. Monroe's first term not only coincided with the restoration of peace, but his inauguration took place in an atmosphere of fiscal stability and seeming prosperity. Consequently, freed of the problems besetting his predecessors, Monroe had the unique opportunity of working in a positive way to realize the long-held aspirations of the nation. The republic was a going concern, and he was in a position to take bold steps to move the country forward.

What Monroe hoped to achieve during his presidency—and this could be said of all the offices which he held—was, to put it in its sim-

[1] Quoted in Gordon Wood, *The Creation of the American Republic* (University of North Carolina Press, 1969), 569.

plest form, to make America more *American* and to complete the emancipation of the nation from its dependence upon European practices and attitudes. Monroe pursued this goal, universally approved by his contemporaries, in a variety of ways. His greatest success lay in foreign affairs, where, ably backed by his Secretary of State, John Quincy Adams, he evolved new policy concepts which did have a uniquely American stamp. He failed notably, however, in his attempt to channel American political life in a direction which would render political parties obsolete. It was a cardinal doctrine of most of Monroe's generation that political parties were more typical of monarchies than of republics. The Era of Good Feelings, intended to usher in this new dispensation, terminated to his bewilderment in a chaos of contending factions. As has been frequently said, the decade after the War of 1812 should properly be labeled the Era of Bad Feelings.

How Monroe, who was an experienced and sensitive politician, could have misjudged the temper of the times makes an engrossing story. The explanation is a simple one—that of a political leader attempting to apply methods and theories developed to fit the circumstances of a vanished age. The America of his youth had been a unified and homogeneous nation, an agrarian country drawn together by the conflict with Great Britain. This unity had been eroded by many factors—the emergence of rival economic interests, the party quarrels of the 1790s, the disagreement over foreign policy after 1800, and, in his own administration, the bitter conflict over the status of slavery in Missouri. Under these circumstances his attempt to restore the former unanimity of purpose of the American people was doomed from the outset. Monroe did not grasp the fact that the essential problem of his day was not how to move forward a nation whose aims were clearly defined, but how to establish goals and ideals sufficiently compelling to draw together the clashing interests of a pluralistic society. His struggle to create harmony within the nation is an ever recurring theme in American history, and like all such attempts, even those which fail, provides a fuller understanding of the character of the American people.

II

In every historical investigation there are areas which the most persistent digging and probing cannot adequately illuminate. In writing about men of Monroe's generation, it is extremely difficult to penetrate the careful screen which they erected about private concerns. While there are quantities of material relating to public matters, personal data is indeed sparse. Like most Americans reaching maturity in the late eighteenth century before the romantics made self-revelation respectable, Monroe jealously screened his private thoughts and the intimate details of his family life from public scrutiny. Not only did he live in an age of reticence (and of much prudery as well) but the rationalist psychological theories of John Locke, which had been popularized by the *philosophes* of the Enlightenment, contradicted the notion that parental influence or childhood experiences offered a key to the understanding of adult personality. A man made himself what he was by the use, or abuse, of reason. From this point of view, a public man should only be judged in terms of service to the nation. Consequently, in Monroe's day it was customary for political figures to destroy papers of a personal character. Only one letter from Monroe to his wife survives, and the only specimens of her hand are in the form of signatures on legal documents. What is more, contemporaries accepted (and for the most part respected) this desire for privacy, for they also agreed that the details of private life were not a subject of public concern. In spite of the fact that Monroe lived for half a century in the glare of public life, gossip about him and his family was slight. There are just enough personal commentaries to offer tantalizing but incomplete glimpses behind the scenes.

While reticence was the prevailing rule, it was not universally observed. Exceptional circumstances led contemporaries to take a greater interest than usual in private behavior. The suspicion that Alexander Hamilton was using his knowledge of governmental fiscal operations to speculate in federal securities led a group of congressmen (among them Monroe) to conduct an unofficial inquiry into his conduct. Although they did not uncover any official malfeasance, they did expose his affair with Mrs. Reynolds. The widespread distrust of Aaron Burr's political integrity was responsible for much comment about his private character. In other instances, and here Jefferson is the most striking example, some men did voice their emotions and private thoughts with considerable freedom. Jefferson's case is outstanding, for historians know more about him than about any other man of the day. Not only was he an untiring letter writer, but he discussed such an incredible variety of subjects—there was literally nothing which failed to interest him—that we can take the full measure of the man. Of a rather mercurial temperament, Jefferson ordinarily said (often to his regret) in his letters what was on his mind at that time.

In mind and temperament Monroe differed completely from Jefferson, and this is reflected in his correspondence. Monroe, for example, almost never touched upon any subject in his letters except politics. We know that he had a large library (at least 3,000 volumes) and that he read widely, but except for one or two instances books and writers never figured in his letters. Consequently, almost nothing can be said about his intellectual development. He shared the common eighteenth-century interest in science, at least the titles in his library indicate that he did, but he never discussed such subjects in his letters. He was intensely interested in agricultural reform, yet we can only guess at his plantation activities, for none of his farm records survives. Monroe was a rather phlegmatic man, who tended to reflect before acting, therefore his letters lack the spontaneity so characteristic of Jefferson's correspondence. Frequently Monroe recast his letters several times before sending them.

As one reads Monroe's letters, one does not see the vast and exciting panorama of the contemporary world of science, politics, philosophy and social theory which one encounters in Jefferson's correspondence, but rather the narrower world of political affairs. Monroe's all-consuming interest (apart from farming) was a political one. Jefferson approached the ideal of the universal man established during the Renaissance. This was a rare achievement, of which only a man of genius was capable. It would not be correct to call Monroe, in contrast to Jefferson, an average man, for his talents were considerably above the ordinary, but like most men, his abilities were exercised in only one direction. In his case it was in politics, or to use a word with less unpleasant modern connotations, in the realm of statecraft. Therefore, a biography of Monroe must be essentially political in character, for it was only in this form of activity that he realized himself and gave expression to his inner being. Since he was a remarkably reticent man even in an age of reticence, he has to be defined in terms of what he did, what his relations were with other men, how he reacted under specific circumstances. In every stage of his career experience added new dimensions to his personality and point of view. Each one of these stages must be studied with care in order to evaluate its impact upon him. It is only in the total setting of the world of politics in his lifetime that we can begin to assess and understand Monroe.

CHAPTER 1

YOUTH AND EDUCATION

JAMES MONROE, the fifth President of the United States, was born in Westmoreland County, Virginia, on April 28, 1758. Today, apart from a few lively seaside resorts and lonely mansions standing in barren fields, there are scant hints of Westmoreland's once-great wealth. This county (one of the oldest settled areas in Virginia) was the birthplace of three Presidents: George Washington, James Madison and Monroe. Yet, although natives of Westmoreland, none of the three was associated with the county in adult life. The Washingtons, whose plantation was within five miles of the Monroe family estate, left the county in 1735, when Washington was three years old, to move to more fertile lands in King George County. Madison's connection with Westmoreland was slighter: he was born there when his mother was visiting her parents, but he grew to maturity in Orange County in the Piedmont. Monroe did not formally sever his ties with Westmoreland until he sold his property upon reaching his majority, but he never resided there after entering William and Mary College as a sixteen-year-old. The fact that its three most famous citizens had so little to do with the county of their birth was symptomatic of the general economic malaise afflicting Tidewater Virginia in the mid-eighteenth century. The once-rich alluvial soils were nearing exhaustion and ambitious men were transferring to the Piedmont. Only the great magnates of the county —families such as the Lees and the Carters—whose possessions there and elsewhere in the state were sufficiently enormous to sustain life in the grand style, continued on their ancestral estates.[1]

Monroe's decision to abandon the plantation held by his family for a century was influenced not only by the declining agricultural returns but also by a desire to improve his social and political standing. The

Monroes had been in the colony as long as the Washingtons, but they had never achieved either the wealth or the power of their neighbors. At the time of Monroe's birth his father, Spence Monroe, owned less than 500 acres of land in Westmoreland in contrast to the 6,000 held by the Washingtons. Spence Monroe's estate was sufficient to qualify him as a member of the gentry, but at the lower end of the scale.[2] His ancestors could not afford to educate their sons at William and Mary, let alone sustain the expense of a schooling in the mother country. In a society in which political power was firmly controlled by the great planters, it is not surprising that the Monroes held no significant offices. Until James Monroe's generation there was only one exception to this century-old record of respectable obscurity: his great-uncle Andrew had been a member of the House of Burgesses, a justice of the peace and a colonel in the militia.

Apart from a bare record of names gleaned from county archives little is known of the Monroe family other than the brief narrative in an autobiographical sketch written by Monroe after his retirement from the Presidency. He traced the family to Andrew Monroe (a member of the Monroe family of Fowlis in Scotland), who settled in the colony in 1650. The first settler, according to family tradition, had served on the Cavalier side in the Battle of Preston in 1648. Establishing himself on a small stream subsequently known as Monroe's Creek, Andrew patented 200 acres of land which in the next hundred years was augmented by his descendants into 1,100 acres on both sides of the creek. When James Monroe was born, the larger portion of the land was held by the elder branch of the family; the remainder, amounting to approximately 500 acres, by his father Spence Monroe, a descendant of a younger son of the first settler. It is quite in character with the age in which he grew to maturity that James Monroe's autobiographical sketch contained none of those intimate details of family life and youthful associations so much prized by subsequent generations. Of his father Monroe merely commented that he was a "worthy and respectable citizen possessed of good landed and other property." His account of Elizabeth Jones Monroe, his mother, was equally brief: she was pictured as "a very aimiable and respectable woman, possessing the best domestic qualities of a good wife, and a good parent." Her father, James Jones, was a Welsh immigrant, who acquired considerable property in King George County, a portion of which was inherited by Monroe's mother.[3]

Of his ancestral Westmoreland home—now long vanished—Monroe

did not record any memories. He cherished no sentimental attachment for the scenes of his youth in the humid Tidewater, where, like most plantation-bred young men, he was allowed great freedom, acquiring a lasting enthusiasm for such active pursuits as riding and hunting. He also developed a steady interest in the round of agricultural activities upon which the well-being of his family and of the colony had so long depended. Throughout his life, even while deeply involved in politics, he regarded himself a farmer by profession and, like his close friend Jefferson, experienced the greatest sense of contentment when engaged in the management of his lands. Monroe's formal education began at eleven, when he was enrolled as a day student at Campbelltown Academy, a school operated by the Rev. Archibald Campbell, rector of Washington Parish, in which the Monroe family lived. Campbelltown, considered the best school in the colony, was limited to twenty-five pupils. Here Monroe was so thoroughly drilled in Latin and mathematics that when he entered William and Mary in 1774 he was at once admitted into the upper or college division. At Campbelltown Monroe formed a close friendship with John Marshall, which lasted until the political animosities of the 1790s placed them in opposite camps.[4]

Monroe left Campbelltown Academy early in 1774 after the death of his father.[5] In addition to his eldest son James, Spence Monroe left two other sons, Andrew and Joseph Jones, and a daughter Elizabeth. In accordance with the prevailing custom James, as the eldest son, inherited all the family property. On his shoulders fell the burden of completing the education of his brothers and sister and seeing them established in life. In assuming this responsibility (which proved a lifetime obligation, for neither of his brothers was successful) Monroe was assisted by his uncle, Judge Joseph Jones of Fredericksburg, the executor of the estate. Judge Jones, who at that time had no heir, actively concerned himself with the welfare of his sister's family. The bond between uncle and nephew which developed at this time was far stronger than that inherent in the family tie. This relationship was all-important for Monroe, for his uncle now gave him (in addition to sound practical advice) something hitherto lacking in the family background—the patronage of a wealthy member of the ruling group within the colony. Born in Virginia in 1727, Monroe's uncle had been educated at the Inns of the Temple and was later appointed deputy king's attorney for Virginia. When he entered the House of Burgesses from King George County in 1772, he became one of the most important members of that body, working closely with Edmund Pendleton and George Mason of

Gunston Hall, two of the most influential colonial leaders. During the Revolution, Judge Jones served first as a member of the Committee of Public Safety and then as a member of the Virginia delegation to the Continental Congress. In 1789 he was appointed to the state supreme court, on which he served until his death in 1805. Highly esteemed by his contemporaries, he enjoyed the confidence of Washington, Jefferson and Madison, who prized him for the soundness of his counsel.

Whether it should be ascribed to family temperament or to the influence exerted by a distinguished relative on an impressionable sixteen-year-old, Monroe as an adult resembled his uncle in many ways—reflective, never rushing to conclusions but forming opinions deliberately. The same tact, warmth and patience in human relations, so pronounced in the Judge's character, were equally apparent in the nephew.[6]

Encouraged by his uncle, Monroe marked out his course for a political career. Following Jones' advice, he entered William and Mary College in June 1774, the first of his family to attend that institution. His preference (and that of his uncle) had been for a European education, but this was impossible in view of the disturbed political conditions at that time. He settled down as a boarding student in the large brick building housing the college, a structure Jefferson irreverently likened to a brick kiln with a roof. Here he formed an enduring friendship with his roommate, John F. Mercer, the fifteen-year-old son of a wealthy Stafford County planter. Monroe was not aware of it, but the quality of instruction at the college was undistinguished. The really significant thing about William and Mary (as Dumas Malone has aptly commented) was its location in Williamsburg, the colonial capital. If a sojourn at the college offered little in the way of intellectual stimulation, residence in Williamsburg gave plantation-reared young men a chance to observe the world of fashion and politics, for the sleepy town sprang to life once a year during the legislative sessions.[7]

II

The summer of 1774 was not the ideal time for a politically minded youth to concentrate on Latin grammar, for the long conflict between the crown and the colonists was reaching its climax. Monroe had been in Williamsburg only a few weeks when the town was shaken by the dramatic scene following the refusal of the members of the House of

Burgesses to obey the Governor's order of dissolution. Acting on their own, the Burgesses reconvened in the Raleigh Tavern and issued the call which culminated (in the spring of 1775) in the first Continental Congress.[8] As a leading member of the House, Monroe's uncle was a leading participant in these events. In August a second irregular meeting of the Burgesses took place in Williamsburg to draw up stringent non-importation agreements to be enforced by the local committees of correspondence. This form of reprisal was quite familiar to Monroe and other Virginians. Monroe's father had joined a hundred residents of Westmoreland in 1766 to organize a boycott to bring pressure on Parliament to repeal the Stamp Act.[9]

In the midst of all this excitement serious study was difficult, but after the August meeting of the Burgesses, the college seemed to settle back to a normal routine. The calm was shattered in April 1775, when Governor Dunmore, encouraged by the success of the moderate leaders in curbing the more radical spirits in the April meeting of the convention in Richmond, decided to reassert his authority. On April 20 he dispatched a detachment of marines to seize a small store of powder belonging to the city of Williamsburg. As the news of this outrage spread through the colony, the local committees of correspondence summoned militia units for an advance on Williamsburg to restore the powder to the municipal authorities. The most famous of these patriot bands, and the first to approach the capital, was that led by Patrick Henry. As he neared the city, he was met by an emissary from Governor Dunmore, who respectfully offered to pay for the powder. Henry, yielding to pressure from moderates, reluctantly agreed and disbanded his followers. Dunmore, badly shaken by this threat, sent his wife to the safety of a British frigate and fortified his residence.

These events had a most unsettling effect upon the college. The students, accustomed to taking a serious interest in politics, now became directly involved in the everyday turbulence convulsing the capital. The faculty was powerless to prevent these youths from joining the townspeople in their frequent meetings or from drilling boldly on the college grounds. The principal fomenter of student action was James Innes, the "gentleman usher" of the grammar school. The twenty-year-old Innes, who had considerable talents as a leader and orator, not only organized a military unit among the student body but also found time to be active in the city militia. Very much a campus hero, he was emulated by the younger students, including Monroe, who purchased

a rifle and joined the ranks of the college patriots. The relief of the
faculty was evident when Innes departed without leave for military
service in the summer of 1775.[10]

Monroe's hero worship of Innes involved him in a minor altercation
with the college authorities in the spring of 1775, when he and seven
other students (including Innes) signed a petition complaining about
the quality of the food served by Maria Digges, the "Mistress of the
College." They also charged that she neglected sick boys in the grammar
school, sold college stores, showed favoritism to her brothers and was
rude to the students. When the professors summoned the petitioners
and questioned them on each charge, it was immediately evident
that Innes was the instigator, for he alone was bold enough to particu-
larize upon each point. In his testimony Monroe made the rather
startling response: "That he had never read the petition and consequently could not undertake to prove a single article." With such
inadequate substantiation of the charges the faculty had no difficulty
in upholding the established order and in unanimously acquitting Mrs.
Digges. Innes was singled out for reprimand and warned to control
his passionate temper. The professors took the occasion to reprove
Innes for keeping students out in a tavern "at unreasonable hours until
they were drunk, which occasioned a midnight disturbance at the
College." The students were again reminded that they could best serve
their own interest, that of the college and of their country by attending
to their studies. All these admonitions were quite useless; the young
men, chafing over the narrow Tory orientation of the school, ignored
the orders forbidding them to bring firearms into their rooms.

In June 1775 the attention of all Virginia was focused on Williamsburg, where the Burgesses had been summoned to consider Lord North's
conciliatory resolves. The membership of this final assembly held under
royal authority was much the same as that of the previous year and
just as intractable. Shortly after the legislature convened, Dunmore destroyed his influence with the Burgesses by withdrawing to a warship.
Undaunted by this intimidating gesture, the Burgesses immediately
rejected the conciliatory resolves and set up a Committee of Public
Safety to assume governmental power. The breach with England was
now complete; hostilities broke out between the Governor's forces and
those of the colony and within a year the Patriots were in control of
Virginia.

The seventeen-year-old Monroe was quickly drawn into the tide of patriotic enthusiasm which burgeoned out of the conflict between the Governor and the Burgesses. To prove his devotion with deeds rather than words, on June 24, 1775, he joined a group of twenty-four men under the command of Theodorick Bland, Jr., in a surprise attack on the Governor's palace. Bland's force, which met no opposition, removed 200 muskets and 300 swords stored at the palace and turned them over to the Williamsburg militia. Monroe was the youngest member of the party, which included such important figures as George Nicholas, Harrison Randolph, and Jefferson's friend the Italian *philosophe* Philip Mazzei.[11]

III

In the spring of 1776 Monroe and his roommate, John F. Mercer, unable to endure the stultifying routine of college life, enlisted as cadets in the Third Virginia Infantry, commanded by Colonel Hugh Mercer, a Fredericksburg neighbor and friend of Monroe's uncle, but not related to Monroe's college friend. Since the ranks of the regiment filled quickly, they were soon commissioned lieutenants.[12] Monroe was assigned to the company of Captain John Thornton, with whom he served until August 1777.[13] During the spring and summer the Third Virginia trained at Williamsburg with other regiments under the command of General Andrew Lewis, a successful Indian fighter. The training which the Third Virginia received under Lewis was well above the usual standards of the day. Considerable emphasis was placed upon discipline and drill, and awkward squads were formed for those recruits who needed special attention. On Lewis' orders all officers were required to wear short-fringed hunting shirts—a costume worn by Washington in the field.[14]

The midsummer march from Virginia to New York was the least of the hardships Monroe was to endure during the next two years. Fortunately his rugged constitution fitted him well for the rigors of military life. Slightly over six feet tall, broad-shouldered, with a massive if somewhat rawboned frame, he was an impressive figure. By no means handsome—his face plain, the nose large although regular—his wide-set eyes were his most striking feature. They reflected a warmth confirmed by his smile. The grave and sober mien so characteristic of Monroe in later life was not apparent in this enthusiastic eighteen-year-old recruit who was so passionately caught up by the fervor of the revolutionary

cause. It is true that he was inclined to be overly serious and modest
to the point of shyness, but he was neither cold nor unapproachable.
Without facile brilliance and tending to be slow in thought, Monroe
possessed substantial qualities of judgment which earned him the lasting
respect of far more talented men. His personal attraction rested on his
sensitivity and his generosity of spirit and in an innate benevolence
which made men of all sorts feel at ease. Even as a young man he had
an ability to create an understanding and a sympathetic atmosphere
through genuine warmth, guilelessness and his total want of malice.[15]

The long-anticipated day, when the routine of drilling was translated
into action, arrived at last: in August the Third and Ninth Virginia
regiments were ordered to join Washington's army on Long Island.
During the long northward march in the August heat, Mercer (now a
brigadier general) was replaced as commander of the Third Virginia
by Colonel George Weedon, a Fredericksburg tavernkeeper who was
promptly dubbed "Old Joe Gourd" by his men, since he was reputed
to serve punch from such a ladle. Weedon proved an able if not brilliant
field commander, ultimately achieving the rank of brigadier in recognition of his efforts at Harlem Heights. After a fatiguing march the 700
officers and men of the Third arrived at Washington's headquarters on
Manhattan on September 12 "in good spirits and generally healthy."
They were greeted with "great joy" by the other units in camp, who
expected much from the Virginians.[16] To Washington, whose army was
constantly dwindling as militia terms expired and the "Long Faces"
(as the deserters were dubbed) silently stole away in the night, the sight
of well-trained troops was heartening.[17] Assigned a campsite near King's
Bridge 14 miles north of the city, Monroe's company could hear the
sound of British cannonading from the batteries across the river,
although out of range. During their first days on Manhattan the men of
the Third had no chance to rest, since they were called out frequently
during the night by false reports of enemy movements. The intelligence
service was so inadequate that it was impossible to distinguish rumors
from valid reports.

When the British began their invasion of Manhattan on September
16, Monroe's unit was far distant from the landing at Kip's Bay (near
present-day East 34th Street). Washington, expecting the main British
thrust to be to the northward, had stationed the larger part of his
forces at Harlem (110th Street), some six miles from Kip's Bay. Consequently, the brunt of the invasion fell on poorly disciplined Connecticut

militia never before exposed to enemy fire. As soon as the British landed, the militia fled without firing once. Washington and his aides, attempting to rally the retreating militia, were left in such an exposed position that they had to flee ignominiously before the advancing red-coats. When the news of the militia's "disgraceful and dastardly" behavior reached Monroe and the Virginians as they stood in battle formation, they furiously denounced those who had "shamefully abandoned their posts without exchanging fire." They loudly proclaimed, according to Captain Chilton of the Third, that they would behave quite differently, fighting "to the last for their country." [18] That these were no empty boasts Monroe and his comrades proved fully on the following day.

During the night of the sixteenth, the Third Virginia was stationed at the edge of woods overlooking a low-lying meadow which separated Harlem from the opposing heights, known as Vandevanter's Heights, along which the British were expected to move. Early the next morning, Captain Chilton reported, the men "discovered the enemy peeking from their Heights over the fencings and rocks and running backwards and forwards." Small parties of the British began to advance slowly, opening fire from about 300 yards, too distant a range to be effective. The Virginia regiments had been ordered to hold their fire, but goaded by the sight of the hated redcoats, a young officer (of whom, Captain Chilton caustically remarked, "we have too many") opened fire, and soon all the men were firing. Colonel Weedon finally stopped the waste. For the next hour the Virginians sat and withheld their fire, constantly exposed to that of the enemy and exhibiting a firmness of discipline then a rarity in Washington's army.

While the Virginians waited, Colonel Thomas Knowlton led a detachment of 150 Connecticut rangers into a hollow between the heights, where he was involved in a hot skirmish with an advance British unit concealed in a thicket. Washington, who rode up to investigate the reports of this engagement, was urged to send support to Knowlton, on the assumption that the British force numbered not more than 300 or 400. As he considered this proposal, the sound of British bugles rang out from the opposing heights. The call was not a military one, but the famous hunting call—the chase is ended and the fox is dead. Hearing this derisive tune, which seemed to cap the American disgrace, Washington promptly ordered reinforcements to Knowlton.[19]

Furious over the British contempt, Monroe and members of the

Third Virginia prepared for their first contact with the enemy. Three companies of the Third Virginia, including Captain Thornton's company—in which Monroe was a subaltern—were sent under the command of Major Andrew Leitch to join Knowlton's detachment.[20] Meeting the British head-on, the Virginians discovered that the enemy force was far stronger than had been anticipated, numbering nearly 1,500. Nonetheless, the smaller American contingent, suffering heavy casualties (Knowlton and Leitch were killed), held its ground until reinforcements arrived. The British soon withdrew, and Washington had the happy but then rather rare experience of seeing British regulars running from American troops. After the engagement Monroe and his comrades gloried in their achievement, bragging that they had at last shown the enemy that not all Washington's soldiers were Connecticut men—temporarily forgetting that Knowlton's small unit came from this maligned state. The next day Monroe savored the delight of hearing his regiment singled out for special praise for bravery in commander's orders of the day.[21]

Heartening as this victory was, it did not work any miraculous change in the morale of the army or improve the military position of the American forces. Washington still commanded an army he could not fully trust and hence dared not risk a battle except under highly advantageous circumstances. Consequently, he had to confine himself to defensive action, letting his movements depend on those of the British. Since Lord William Howe, commander of the British forces, was majestically slow in his operations, the position of the Continental army remained unchanged for nearly a month. The respite was welcome to the Virginians, who had been subjected to heavy duty after a fatiguing march. Tired as they were, their commander was able to report that the morale of his regiment was excellent. In mid-October, with Howe threatening to flank his position, Washington withdrew northward to the vicinity of White Plains, a position which left him the choice of a confrontation or a clear road for retreat. By the twenty-sixth the Third Virginia was at White Plains but did not take part in the main engagement on October 28. However, two days earlier Monroe's company was involved in a moonlit skirmish in which twenty of the enemy were killed and thirty-six prisoners taken without a single loss to the Virginians.[22]

Since the positions occupied by the Americans were considered too strong to assault, Howe moved his army westward in the direction of

New Jersey.[23] Suspecting that this might be a feint, Washington's war council adopted the dangerous expedient of dividing the army into four detachments: 7,000 to be left under General Charles Lee at White Plains with orders to move into New Jersey should that prove Howe's destination; 4,000 men with General William Heath at Peekskill to check any projected northern movement; and a total of 3,800 at Forts Lee and Washington to check a move southward. The balance of slightly over 3,000 men was assigned to accompany the commander in chief into New Jersey. In making these arrangements it was assumed that the forces with Washington could be rapidly augmented by Lee's command and by militia levies. The dispersal of an army considered too unreliable to fight a major engagement was a questionable measure, but unavoidable until Howe's objectives were clear.

As an officer in the Third Virginia, Monroe was with Washington's army when it crossed the Hudson early in November. This withdrawal was shortly followed by news of a major disaster: Forts Lee and Washington, upon whose resistance so much reliance had been placed, had been lost with an enormous cost to the American army in men and supplies. Washington of necessity could only retreat before the advancing British while he waited for Lee to join him. Unfortunately Lee, convinced that the proper strategy was for him to remain behind the British as a threat to Howe's rear, made no effort to rejoin the commander in chief. During the next three weeks, as Howe continued his steady advance, Lee and Washington exchanged a series of remarkable letters in which the commander in chief urged Lee to join him without categorically ordering him to do so and in which Lee never indicated that he was doing anything but hastening to Washington. Indeed, historians have criticized Washington on this occasion (and also at Monmouth) for failing to issue firm orders to General Lee. Instead he permitted Lee a freedom of action which the General exercised with unfortunate consequences. Throughout the three-week march through New Jersey Washington's anger steadily mounted over Lee's inexplicable delay.

By the time the army reached the Delaware early in December Monroe's regiment was sadly depleted. At the start of the retreat into New Jersey a third of the men were absent because of sickness; by the end of the long march still another third had fallen ill, leaving the number of actives at slightly over 200. Of the seventeen officers present and fit for duty early in November only Monroe and four others were

still with the regiment at Christmas.[24] Monroe was one of the few
officers fit for duty at the battle of Trenton. The plight of the ill-shod,
poorly fed and inadequately clothed army presented a discouraging
prospect as the men plodded southward along the muddy roads in the
unceasing rains of the bitter November weather. A half-century later,
as he recalled the days of his revolutionary service in his memoirs,
Monroe still vividly remembered the day when, as a member of the rear
guard, he had watched the army file through Newark. He had then
somberly reflected on how much depended on this shabby and worn
band of 3,000 men. As the Continental troops left the town, a British
advance guard appeared but made no attempt to harass the retreating
Americans.[25]

IV

Early in December Washington crossed the Delaware, after taking the
precaution of collecting all the small craft within a 35-mile radius—a
task carried out so efficiently that no transport was available to the
British, who were obliged to delay their advance until the river froze.
Ten days later, on December 15, as Washington continued his wait
for Lee, a messenger rode into camp with the incredible news that
the absent general had been captured through his own carelessness two
days earlier. Lee's detention had one great advantage in that it removed
the major obstacle to the reunion of the two armies, which was accomplished on December 20. With his forces substantially augmented Washington turned his thoughts to the possibility of exploiting his control
of water transport by assuming the offensive. Howe, having little reason
to expect an attack, had dispersed his army in comfortable quarters
provided by Princeton, Trenton and other nearby towns. With less
discussion with his generals than had been his habit, Washington
decided to launch a surprise attack on the Hessian garrison at Trenton,
which was believed to be about 3,000 strong. His plan was a simple one:
starting at sunset on Christmas Day, 2,400 Continentals would be
quietly ferried across the river to move on to Trenton by dawn.[26]

As the army massed at McKonkey's Ferry, Monroe was not at his
regular post with the Third Virginia. He was already on his way across
the river. Captain William Washington, a kinsman of the commander
in chief, had been detailed to take a detachment of fifty men in advance
of the main army with the specific mission of mounting guard at the

junction of the Pennington and Lawrenceville roads to prevent any warning from reaching the British. Since Captain Washington had no subalterns fit for duty, Monroe had offered his services as a volunteer officer.[27] When he arrived at the junction of the two roads, Captain Washington sent Monroe and a platoon to mount guard farther along the road in the direction of Trenton.[28] During the bitterly cold night with its alternating snow and sleet, a minor incident occurred at Monroe's post which he never forgot. During that night he met Dr. Riker, the physician he credited with saving his life at the ensuing battle of Trenton. Riker, whose house was close to the road, was roused by his dogs when Monroe and his men took their stations. Angered by this uproar, Riker went out to investigate, greeting the interlopers with violent and profane language until he realized they were American soldiers. As soon as Monroe had calmed Riker, the doctor invited the men to his house to eat and to warm themselves. Monroe had to decline the offer, but the doctor, determined to make a contribution to the cause, not only brought food out to the hungry men, but volunteered to go with them as a surgeon.[29]

Although the attack was delayed until after daybreak, since it had taken much longer to cross the river than anticipated, the element of surprise was not completely lost. In view of the excessively bad weather the Hessians had neglected to send out their usual patrols; consequently the Continental army was within a half-mile of the town before they encountered the first pickets, who gave the alarm just as the first soldiers entered Trenton. In wild confusion the Hessians attempted to form ranks, while the sleeping commander (it was a little after eight) had to be routed from his bed. With Captain Washington's little company in the lead, followed by the Third Virginia, the Continentals approached the town along the Pennington Road which entered Trenton at the V-shaped junction of the two principal thoroughfares, King and Queen streets. At the junction of these streets, the Hessians were trying to mount two cannons to command the American approach. If brought into action, the cannons would expose the Americans to deadly fire at point-blank range. To prevent this operation Captain Washington and Lieutenant Monroe led the company in a charge, driving the Hessians back and capturing the field pieces. Both officers were severely wounded and had to be carried from the field. Fortunately for Monroe, Dr. Riker managed to "take up an artery" severed by the bullet which entered his shoulder. Without this immediate medical assistance

Monroe would have bled to death on the field.[30] Both Monroe and Captain Washington were rewarded for their conspicuous gallantry; Monroe was promoted to the rank of captain in a company to be raised by Colonel John Thornton and Captain Washington was elevated to the rank of major. Monroe's convalescence was slow. Not until three months later was he able to leave the home of Henry Wyncoop in Bucks County, where he was nursed by the family.[31]

CHAPTER 2

AIDE TO
LORD STIRLING

A S SOON AS he had recovered, Monroe hastened to Virginia to assist the other officers in recruiting, which hitherto had not been successful. With the backing of his uncle and influential friends, Monroe joined energetically in the task, making two trips into the outlying districts of King George County, but all his efforts were unavailing; not a single man enlisted. Monroe was shocked to discover that recruiting officers were held in contempt as indolent and insignificant men even when they bore the scars of battle. Lacking private means to offer cash bounties, he could not compete with the state line, which offered higher bounties and shorter enlistments than the Continental army. When the other officers were unable to raise more than fifteen men, Monroe, convinced that further recruiting was useless, set out for Washington's headquarters.[1] On his way he paused in Philadelphia to visit his uncle, then a member of the Virginia delegation in Congress. Sympathizing with his nephew's disappointment over his failure and concerned lest Washington feel that insufficient efforts had been made to raise recruits, Jones gave his nephew a letter for the commander in chief explaining that the inadequacy of the Continental bounty had rendered recruiting an impossibility. As Jones told his old friend, the only effective methods of enlistment Monroe might have used were of a kind ill befitting the character of a gentleman and also ones he would not have wished his nephew to employ.[2]

When Monroe arrived at the Continental encampment near the Neshaminy Bridge in Bucks County, Washington, who fully understood the difficulties encountered in raising new regiments, readily granted him permission to remain in camp, although there was no command available at the moment. At the commander in chief's request Monroe wrote the officers in Virginia urging them to continue recruiting. In high spirits at being back with the army, Monroe happily wrote Major Thornton: "Let me assure you . . . that nothing would afford greater pleasure than having you with me, the expence [sic] would be nothing, for as long as I have a Biscuit, half should be at your service. Your brother George this day made his appearance in camp as fat as a porpoise. He dines with me today. I wish you were here, to test the old copper bowl, which is to be filled." [3]

Like all the young officers, Monroe, eager for glory and advancement, preferred a field command. Since none was available, he accepted the post of additional aide-de-camp with the rank of major to William Alexander, Lord Stirling, one of Washington's brigade commanders. This titled gentleman was the American-born claimant to a Scottish earldom, whose rights had been recognized in British courts but rejected by the House of Lords. Nonetheless he continued to bear the title, and in the army was always addressed as Lord Stirling. Although proud of his rank, he was neither vain nor pretentious. A rather bluff and hearty man of strong social inclinations, Stirling was fond of convivial sessions over a punch bowl. Indeed, many felt that he was somewhat too attached to the bowl. However, his indulgence never interfered with his duties. Stirling's once-considerable fortune was now much reduced, but he continued to live in the grand style at his handsome country place, "Basking Ridge," not far from Elizabeth, New Jersey. In his own right and as the brother-in-law of Governor William Livingston of New Jersey, Stirling was a man of influence. Valued as a brave and reliable if unimaginative field commander, he was famed for his habit of riding along the lines during battles shouting encouragement to his men in vociferous tones. This bellicose behavior was in marked contrast to the mildness of Stirling's speech and manner in private. Of all Washington's subordinates none was more loyal than "His Lordship." [4]

In later years, as Monroe looked back on this epoch in his life, he felt that service under Stirling had been especially valuable in giving him military experience most useful when he was Secretary of War in 1812. As a lieutenant he had only been aware of the affairs of a small detachment, whereas he now participated in large-scale operations. He took full advantage of the opportunities offered by Stirling, who freely discussed over-all problems with his aides. Monroe also felt that the friendships with officers from Europe and from other sections of the United States were a more than adequate substitute for the formal education he was missing, for these contacts broadened his knowledge of the world and eradicated the provincialism inherent in his Virginia upbringing.[5]

Monroe met all the brigade commanders in the army, but the only one he knew well was General Charles Lee, on whose staff his former roommate was serving. The friendship with Lee, commencing after the general's release by the British in April 1778, was an exciting experience for the twenty-year-old Virginian. Lee, whose true character still remains enigmatic, possessed a charm which had won him many friends among the officers who delighted in his caustic wit and his colorful tales of adventure in faroff Poland, Hungary and Constantinople. Lee's appearance was not prepossessing—thin as a match with an ugly face dominated by an aquiline nose. The singularity of his looks was not enhanced by the carelessness of his dress. His extensive European military career had given him a reputation as the ablest and most experienced officer in the army—an opinion Lee fully endorsed. Taking an avuncular interest in the shy young Virginian, Lee encouraged Monroe to overcome his *"mauvaise honte,"* which he felt was preventing the young officer from displaying his real talents.[6] Behind the hesitant manner Lee sensed abilities of the first order. Monroe's friendship and admiration for Lee were not affected by the general's disgrace after Monmouth. He continued to correspond with Lee until the latter's death in 1783. Lee's conduct at Monmouth has been more harshly judged in modern times than it was in 1778: many of Washington's most devoted friends felt that Lee had been too severely treated.[7]

Among the young aides, who constituted a lively group at the camp, Monroe numbered many friends—including Alexander Hamilton, Richard Kidder Meade, and his former roommate Mercer. John Marshall was also present, having been appointed judge advocate on the same day (November 20, 1777) Monroe was made permanent aide-de-camp.[8] It was at this time that Monroe first met Colonel Aaron Burr, who was attached to Stirling's brigade. Among the foreign officers, Monroe became especially intimate with two—the Marquis de Lafayette and Pierre S. DuPonceau. Lafayette, who had joined the army in the summer of 1777, was the first French officer to be liked by the other commanders, for American officers resented the high ranks Congress handed out so freely to foreigners. Lafayette's extreme youth (he was only twenty-one) might have rendered his position most unpleasant had it not been for his great personal charm, which disarmed the most hostile, and his ability to speak English, a skill lacked by most of the foreign officers.[9]

Monroe's closest friend was his contemporary in age, eighteen-year-old Pierre S. DuPonceau, whom he met in February 1778. The two became inseparable—exchanging letters on the days on which they did not see one another.[10] DuPonceau, in contrast to the dashing Lafayette, was an intellectual, whose nearsightedness and weak lungs ill qualified him for a military life. As a young boy he had demonstrated a precocious talent for languages, and it was the ability to speak fluent English which had brought him to America as the secretary of Baron Steuben, on whose staff he was serving. DuPonceau (later a distinguished Philadelphia-based international lawyer and pioneer student of American Indian languages) brought Monroe into direct contact, for the first time, with the world of the *philosophes*. The young Frenchman was an enthusiastic supporter of the Revolution, which he viewed in terms of the liberal theories of the Enlightenment rather than as a local quarrel between England and her colonies. For DuPonceau the American conflict was but the first step in a great movement which would liberate the peoples of the world from tyranny. The two young men shared many common tastes in reading and when camp duties were not pressing discussed the books they lent each other. In April 1778, while at Valley Forge, Monroe borrowed the plays of Nicholas Rowe, more renowned for his mixing of sentiment and pure Whig politics than for his power as a dramatist. DuPonceau also lent Monroe James Watson's then-popular sermons, in which historic Christianity was presented as consistent with deistic principles. Watson's widely quoted remark—"Where mystery begins, religion ends"—fully epitomizes the tone of his writings. Monroe and DuPonceau shared an appreciation for another writer whose deistic views were less extreme than those of the French *philosophes,* Mark Akenside, a now forgotten but once widely read eighteenth-century poet. In a long poem, "Pleasures of the Imagination," Akenside not only expressed deistic concepts but also defended the superior virtues of the ancient Stoic philosophy, a point of view with a strong appeal for Monroe. Like many extremely shy yet ambitious men, Monroe was hypersensitive to criticism and overly concerned that failure to achieve his goals might be attributed to a lack of ability. Stoicism offered a refuge from these self-doubts. This philosophical predilection, later strengthened by Jefferson, built a habit of reserve in Monroe that became more marked as he grew older.[11] From his reading and his correspondence with DuPonceau (meager as this record is), it is evident that Monroe no longer thought of the Revolution in the narrow terms of a family quarrel between George III and his American subjects. He now viewed the conflict—and this was a widely shared attitude—as the first step in a world-wide struggle to liberate mankind from the baneful effects of despotism. This sense of commitment to a movement for political freedom with world-wide implications had a profound effect upon Monroe and his contemporaries. This identification with a force greater than themselves gave a particular stamp to every aspect of their later careers. In its simplest form it could be called a sense of mission—they felt themselves called upon to achieve something previously unattainable in human experience. Thus Monroe, for the rest of his life, worked to convert the ideals of the Revolution (expressed only in the most general terms) into a basic reality of American life—a reality which would serve as a model and as an example to the rest of the world.

These pleasant hours with DuPonceau and his books gave Monroe a brief respite from the tedious duties of an aide-de-camp—delivering messages, keeping muster records, transmitting the general's orders and accompanying Lord Stirling on his rounds. Although often dull, it was by no means a safe occupation. During battles the aides, who rode about the field with messages, were constantly exposed to enemy fire. Since Lord Stirling liked to remain close to his lines, his aides usually found themselves in an equally exposed position. It was while standing near Lord Stirling at Brandywine that Lafayette was wounded.[12]

Stirling's solid virtues as a commander were amply demonstrated on September 11 at Brandywine. His brigade bore the main brunt of the enemy attack there, holding fast in face of a totally unexpected British onslaught. Had General John Sullivan been able to shift his men to support Stirling and the other commanders pressed by the British, the engagement might have had a much different outcome. A month later at Germantown, Stirling, who had been stationed in the rear, held his brigade firm as the panic-stricken militia rushed by in the all-enveloping early morning fog. The stiff resistance offered by Stirling's brigade enabled Washington to retire without additional losses.[13] For weeks after Germantown the army buzzed with heated discussions of the engagement as a succession of commanders were court-martialed for their responsibility in losing an engagement before the battle had really commenced. The most serious blame fell on General Adam Stephen, who was believed to have given the order to retreat; he was dismissed for drunkenness on the field.

While Howe settled into the comforts of Philadelphia, now abandoned by Congress, the dispirited Continental army lingered at White
Marsh, some 13 miles from Philadelphia, waiting to see if Howe contemplated another campaign before winter. Monroe, however, was
not at the encampment but at Reading, where Stirling had gone to
recuperate from an injury received when he fell from his horse.[14] It
was here that Monroe first heard the rumors of a plot to replace Washington, when Major James Wilkinson arrived in town on November 1
bearing dispatches from General Horatio Gates announcing the victory
at Saratoga. Wilkinson, basking in the reflected glow of the American
triumph, was persuaded to linger in Reading to dine with Lord Stirling.
After dinner as the aides gathered about the usual punch bowl, Wilkinson took on a confidential tone, repeating current criticism of the commander in chief. In particular he quoted a portion of a letter from
General Thomas Conway to Gates, in which Conway had declared that
heaven alone had saved the country from ruin by a weak general and
bad counselors. The following day Stirling's aide, Major William Mc-
Williams (who was either the sole recipient of the information or the
only one to recall it) informed his commander of Wilkinson's comments.
Stirling at once reported them to Washington. The repercussions of
this convivial evening gave rise to the much-celebrated and equally
doubted plot (known as the Conway Cabal) to deprive Washington of
his command. Although there never seems to have been an organized
drive to remove the commander in chief, there was unquestionably
much criticism both in the army and in Congress of his conduct of the
war. Wilkinson's challenges to Stirling and Gates gave the whole affair
a much greater notoriety than it merited.[15]

As soon as it was certain that Howe had settled in for the winter,
Washington considered locations for winter quarters. Comfort and ease
would have dictated York or any of the larger towns, but such a choice
involved ceding Howe full control of a fertile region with freedom
to move about at will. Only by remaining close to Philadelphia could
Washington hope to inhibit the movements of the enemy. He chose
as the site of his camp Valley Forge, a few miles northwest of Philadelphia. This location offered excellent natural fortifications easily
strengthened by redoubts and entrenchments. The position proved to
be such a strong one that Howe, who was aware of the weakened condition of the Continental army, made no effort to attack. Since there were
but few houses (the town had been burned by a British party in September) winter shelters had to be built. At the commander in chief's direc-

tion the men constructed log huts 16 by 14 feet with walls 6 feet high, stopping the cracks with mud. Saplings covered by mud and straw provided an imperfect roofing, which leaked during thaws and rains. The brigade commanders were allotted two huts each—one for their own use, the other for the aides. Except that their quarters were less crowded, Monroe and the other aides fared little better than the rank and file. Washington, with that superb sense of what was right and proper which won him the devotion of his men in spite of his aloofness, lived in his homespun tent until the huts were nearly finished. He then moved into one of the few houses still standing; here he was only more comfortably housed than his generals in that he had two rooms.[16]

The sufferings of the courageous band wintering at Valley Forge have become legendary. The officers, men of means, normally fared better than the enlisted men, but at Valley Forge there was little of the general distress they did not share—the hunger, ragged clothes, the suffering from exposure to the cold, typhus and body lice were common to all ranks. The officers had to be content with the same ration of wet flour issued during the worst weeks of shortage. It was not unusual to see officers mounting guard wearing old dressing gowns or wrapped in blankets in place of cloaks.[17] Yet these hardships did not suppress the vein of humor so characteristic of Americans under difficult circumstances. Nearly sixty years after the winter of Valley Forge DuPonceau vividly recalled a moment when self-mockery effectively destroyed self-pity:

Once with the Baron's permission, his aides invited a number of young officers, to dine at our quarters; on condition that none should be admitted, that had on a whole pair of breeches. This was of course, understood as *pars pro toto;* but torn clothes were an indispensable requisite for admission; and in this the guests were sure not to fail ... the guests clubbed their rations, and we feasted sumptuously on tough beef-steaks and potatoes, with hickory nuts for our dessert. In lieu of wine, we had some kind of spirits, with which we made *Salamanders;* that is to say, after filling our glasses, we set the liquor on fire, and drank it up, flame and all. Such a set of ragged, and at the same time merry fellows, were never brought together. The Baron loved to speak of that dinner, and of his *Sans-Coulottes* [*sic*], as he called us.[18]

In February the masculine monotony of the officers' messes was relieved by the arrival of the wives of the higher-ranking officers—Mrs. Washington, Mrs. Knox, Mrs. Greene, Mrs. Clement Biddle, Lady Stirling and her daughter, Lady Kitty. Social life, which was now more organized and less rowdy, retained a Spartan character, following the example set by Martha Washington. The young officers customarily called upon her in the evenings, where in a hut built for the aides she maintained the atmosphere of a "domesticated family" [19] The usual upper-class amusements—card playing and dancing—were avoided, since they suggested an indulgence in luxury and frivolity during a time of stress. The guests were served tea and coffee, while the officers provided the entertainment. The gatherings were probably livelier at Mrs. Knox's, for she was esteemed as a wit, and more elegant at Mrs. Greene's, the only officer's wife to speak French.[20]

The most memorable day at Valley Forge was May 6, 1778, when the commander in chief mustered all the pomp and ceremony from the limited resources of the camp to celebrate the recently signed treaty with France. At nine all brigades assembled for a reading of the official proclamation. After suitable remarks by the chaplains the troops were inspected under the command of DeKalb, Lafayette, Lord Stirling and their aides. The parade culminated with a thirteen-gun salute followed by a *feu de joi*—a running musket fire from right to left down the first line of the ranks and in reverse direction down the second. The parade and the *feu de joi* were executed with a remarkable precision, which was entirely the result of Steuben's painstaking drilling during the winter. After the King of France and the American states had been cheered, the men were dismissed to celebrate more informally, assisted by a double ration of rum. Washington, followed by his officers marching thirteen abreast, led the visitors—in all more than a thousand persons— to a marquee where a buffet had been arranged, consisting of (as one of the guests recalled) a "profusion of fat meat, strong wine and other liquors." [21] During the rest of the day the Americans vied with one another in demonstrating their affection for the French officers, many of whom for the first time received a friendly greeting from their American colleagues.[22] Endless toasts were drunk to the alliance, to the union of the states and to independence.

Monroe, an ardent admirer of France, was utterly caught up in the spirit of the celebration. This mood of excitement was still with him the next day when he answered DuPonceau's request for some books:

Affection, gratitude and every motive which can weigh on the feeling mind induce me to write you a long letter; extreme fatigue, the stubborn labor of yesterday, the real inability interposed powerful obstacles. They are insuperable. I rely on your candor, let my unfeigned congratulations on the joyful cause which produced yesterday's event plead my pardon. I cannot answer each part of your letter, such a practical or rather prosaic flight. "for each seems either;" the language is prose but the thoughts are poetry. I have only to commit you to the guidance of your favorite she saint; hand in hand walk thro the celestial bowers of happy Paridise [sic]; fondest pair! most desirable state!

but pure eloquence is more sublime than the parade and rapsody [sic] of language; then in plain language so towering are your thoughts, so great your expectations that I fear sending you any of our books. A plain and simple collection only well adapted to a retir'd clergyman; come in when at leasure [sic] and you shall chuse [sic] for yourself; they are all at your service.[23]

The most immediate effect of the alliance was an improvement in the morale of the army and the nation. In June, when the ranks of the army had risen to 12,000 actives, Washington was eager to assume the offensive by pursuing Howe's successor, Sir George Clinton, when he evacuated Philadelphia. However, most of the brigade commanders, including Charles Lee, preferred a cautious policy until French aid arrived. In the face of this opposition Washington temporized by placing Lafayette, who had supported the proposals for an attack, in command of a force of 1,500 men to harass Clinton on his northward march through New Jersey. Deciding that this force was inadequate, Washington augmented Lafayette's forces until the French commander had nearly half the army at his disposal. When Lee realized that something more than a limited operation was under way, he asserted his seniority, insisting that he be placed in command. Washington yielded, thus placing in command the general most opposed to offensive action— a decision subsequently much criticized.[24]

Thus it was Lee who launched the attack on the British rear guard as it left Monmouth Court House under the command of Lord Cornwallis on June 28. When the firing started Monroe was several miles distant moving with the main body of the army, which had been marching all night toward Monmouth. At noon, as Washington was hastening toward Monmouth, he was stunned to encounter units from Lee's command in full retreat. The first confused reports indicated that Lee had ordered a withdrawal for no apparent reason, since his army had not been in danger, and in fact had been in command of the field. The subsequent meeting between Lee and Washington on the road to Monmouth has been the subject of nearly two centuries of controversy over the exact nature of the remarks exchanged by the two generals. Whatever was said, there can be no doubt of Washington's anger at Lee. Since Cornwallis' advance forces were fifteen minutes behind Lee's retreating columns, Washington had no time to make further inquiries—all his energies were devoted to the problem of arranging his forces to withstand this advance.

The first British attack was directed at the American left wing commanded by Lord Stirling, assisted by Major Monroe, who was temporarily functioning in the important capacity of adjutant. After a hot fight lasting an hour, the British relaxed their onslaught. During this respite Monroe took out a scouting party of seventy men to observe the enemy movements. Approaching close to the British lines, he saw that the enemy troops were being shifted to the British left in preparation for a thrust at Washington's right. Monroe's prompt warning to the commander in chief enabled Washington to make arrangements to strengthen the right wing, which held firm.[25] After five assaults with heavy casualties the British succeeded in forcing General Anthony Wayne, who was in the center, to withdraw to a more sheltered position. At five in the afternoon, having failed to rout the Continental forces, the British withdrew to a fixed position. Although his men were exhausted from the forced march and the long engagement, Washington hoped to renew the battle, but night fell before he could make arrangements. Under cover of darkness the British quietly decamped, leaving Washington technically in command of the field. Monmouth was not a satisfactory victory, since the enemy escaped intact, but at least it proved that the army was a far better disciplined instrument than ever before.[26]

This was the last engagement in which Monroe participated. Washington made no further contact with the enemy before Monroe left Stirling's service at the end of the year. In the weeks after Monmouth, once the simultaneous celebration of the victory and the Fourth of July staged in New Brunswick was over, the court-martial on Lee's conduct began its sittings. Lord Stirling, a friend of both Lee and the commander in chief, presided at the trial. Among the few witnesses brought forward in Lee's behalf was Monroe's friend Mercer, who testified with conviction on Lee's bravery, a circumstance not really to the point since Lee's conduct, rather than his courage, was at issue. After listening to a long series of witnesses many of whom were clearly biased against Lee, the court found him guilty on three counts: disobedience to orders, misbehavior before the enemy and disrespect to the commander in chief. He was suspended from his command for twelve months—a punishment which seemed too light if he were really guilty and hence by its mildness raised doubts about the justness of the verdict. Lee never again held a command, but he was by no means disgraced. Although they deplored Lee's rudeness to Washington, many of Lee's fellow officers considered his withdrawal at Monmouth fully justified. Monroe was one of the many who remained friendly with Lee. Mercer, angered by the verdict, resigned from the service.[27]

In the late summer Monroe accompanied Stirling to Elizabethtown, a site chosen for the brigade headquarters because of its proximity to "Liberty Hall," the town house of Governor Livingston, and "Basking Ridge," Stirling's country residence. These two handsome establishments were the focal points for a brilliant round of social activities. Monroe probably felt more at home in the less magnificent and more relaxed surroundings of the "Hermitage" in nearby Paramus, where Mrs. Theodosia Prevost (later Mrs. Aaron Burr) resided. Mrs. Prevost was the wife of a British officer stationed in the West Indies, but, since her sympathies were entirely with the American cause, she continued to reside in New Jersey. Although it was technically illegal for the wife of a British citizen to remain behind the American lines, Monroe and other friends used their influence to prevent her evacuation.[28] The thirty-five-year-old Mrs. Prevost was the center of a lively and fascinating social group that included Burr. Educated far beyond the average for women of her time, she bore her learning gracefully, retaining such an essential femininity of manner that none regarded her as a blue-stocking. Her intellectual interests, her knowledge of the world and the freedom of her conversation, so markedly in contrast to the conventional attitudes and near-illiteracy of contemporary women, won her a host of admirers, including Major Monroe. Here at the "Hermitage" the young officers, as James McHenry fondly remembered, "talked and walked and laughed—and frolicked and gallanted" away the time.[29]

While he was reveling in this agreeable society Monroe fell in love for the first time, or perhaps more accurately it should be said that he indulged in a sentimental *affaire de cœur* with one of the young ladies he met at Mrs. Prevost's. Of this attachment and its complexities he confided to Mrs. Prevost in a half-serious, half-humorous vein:

A young lady who either is, or pretends to be, in love, is as you know, my dear Mrs. Prevost, the most unreasonable creature in existence. If she looks a smile or a frown, which does not immediately give or deprive you of

happiness (at least to appearance), your company soon becomes very in-
sipid. Each feature has its beauty, and each attitude the graces, or you have
no judgment. But if you are so stupidly insensible of her charms as to deprive your tongue and eyes of every expression of admiration, and not only
to be silent respecting her, but devote them to an absent object, she cannot
receive a higher insult; nor would she, if not restrained by politeness refrain
from open resentment.[30]

The young lady in question, who remains unknown, had objected to
Monroe's intention of studying in France. When Monroe had last
seen her at "Basking Ridge," he had attempted to convince her that
it was not unreasonable that he should go abroad by reminding her
of the fortitude Mrs. Prevost was displaying during the long separation
from her husband. This recital touched the young lady, and Monroe
begged Mrs. Prevost to forgive him for speaking so freely of her difficulties:

  I hope you will forgive me, my dear little friend, if I produced you to give
life to the image. The instance, she owned, was applicable. She felt for you
from her heart, and she has a heart capable of feeling. She wished not a
misfortune similar to yours; but, if I was resolved to make it so, she would
strive to imitate your example. I have now permission to go where I please,
but you must not forget her. . . . Encourage her, and represent the advantage
I shall gain from travel. But why should I desire you to do what I know
your own heart will dictate? For a heart so capable of friendship feels its
own pain alleviated by alleviating that of others.[31]

There is so much of the fashionable sensibility in Monroe's letter that
it is difficult to tell just how deeply his emotions were involved.
  After two years as an aide Monroe was growing impatient with the
boring routine of his duties. A field command proved impossible in
view of the surplus of officers. The fact that he was a Virginian was
an additional handicap, for the commander in chief, sensitive to criticism that he favored his compatriots, sought to be more that just in
distributing the few commissions available. As an alternative Monroe
attempted to secure a diplomatic appointment. Although he made a
special trip to Philadelphia and had the assistance of General Charles
Lee, who presented Monroe to his many friends, he was again unsuccessful. He now turned to the last remaining possibility. Resigning
from Stirling's staff on December 20, 1778, he returned to Virginia
to apply for a rank in the state line. Here he met further disappoint-

ment; there were no vacancies in the state regiments nor could he obtain a militia appointment. The latter units elected their own officers, and, since Monroe had been so long out of the state, he was quite unknown to the men in the ranks. Monroe now conceived the idea of attempting to raise a corps in the state to take southward where the war was raging. To secure support for his project he returned to Washington's headquarters at Middlebrook in May 1779, receiving strong letters of recommendation from the commander in chief and from Lord Stirling.[32]

In addition to these important letters he obtained a less formal one from Alexander Hamilton, then one of Washington's aides, to John Laurens. Hamilton, himself chafing for a field command, suggested to Monroe that if he could find no other opening he might be interested in joining Laurens, who was planning to raise a Negro regiment by offering freedom to slave volunteers.[33] Although Henry Laurens' father John had persuaded Congress to approve the scheme with the recommendation that the owners of the slaves be compensated, it was summarily rejected by the state legislature. Monroe was warmly recommended by Hamilton, who wrote:

D'r Laurens: Monroe is just setting out from Head Quarters and proposes to go in quest of adventures to the Southward. He seems to be as much of a knight errant as your worship; but as he is an honest fellow, I shall be glad he may find some employment, that will enable him to be knocked in the head in an honorable way. He will relish your black scheme if any thing handsome can be done for him in that line. You know him to be a man of honor a sensible man and a soldier. This makes it unnecessary to me to say anything to interest your friendship for him. You love your country too and he has the zeal and capacity to serve it.[34]

Washington's letter of recommendation was addressed to his close personal friend, the wealthy Archibald Cary, one of the most influential members of the Virginia legislature. The commander in chief did not write letters of recommendation casually, and that he did so for Monroe was a mark of the sincere esteem he had for Stirling's former aide. In carefully considered phrases Washington put forward Monroe's qualifications:

I very sincerely lament that the situation of our service will not permit us to do justice to the merits of Major Monroe, who will deliver you this, by placing him in the army upon some satisfactory footing. But as he is on the point of leaving us and expressed an intention of going to the Southward, where a new scene has opened, it is with pleasure I take occasion to express to you the high opinion I have of his worth. The zeal he discovered by entering the service at an early period, the character he supported in his regiment, and the manner in which he distinguished himself at Trenton, when he received a wound, induced me to appoint him to a Captaincy in one of the additional regiments. This regiment failing from the difficulty of recruiting, he entered into Lord Stirling's family, and has served two campaigns as a volunteer aide to his Lordship. He has, in every instance, maintained the reputation of a brave, active, and sensible officer. As we cannot introduce him into the Continental line, it were to be wished that the State could do something for him to enable him to follow the bent of his military inclination, and render service to his country. If an event of this kind could take place, it would give me particular pleasure; as the esteem I have for him, and a regard for his merit, conspire to make me earnestly wish to see him provided for in some handsome way.[35]

Washington's endorsement was sufficient to obtain from the legislature an appointment as lieutenant-colonel in a regiment, which he was to raise. Unfortunately recruiting proved even more difficult than it had two years earlier, and at the end of the year Monroe was still without a command.[36]

CHAPTER 3

POLITICAL APPRENTICESHIP

THE TRANSITION from military to civilian life was not easy for Monroe. With the outcome of the Revolution still in doubt, it was deeply frustrating for a young man dedicated to the American cause to be forced to sit idly on the sidelines. Although only twenty-one, he felt that his dreams of future distinction could never be realized, for the main road to glory—military achievement—seemed permanently closed. Morosely he talked of giving up public life in favor of farming. His sense of discouragement was aggravated by a major personal disappointment. Although he was ordinarily reticent in his letters about his innermost feelings, his distress was so great that he unburdened himself to Thomas Jefferson, a new but most trusted friend: "A variety of disappointments with respect to ye prospects of my private fortune previous to my acquaintance with your Excellency, upon w'ch I had built as on a ground w'ch could not deceive me and w'ch failed in a manner w'ch could not have been expected perplexed my plan of life and expos'd me to inconveniences w'ch have nearly destroyed me." [1] Apart from telling Jefferson that the injury had been caused by a relative upon whose support he had relied for advancement, Monroe did not elaborate on his personal problem. The only person to whom his words seem applicable was his uncle Judge Jones; yet, if there was a breach between them, it was brief. By the spring of 1780 uncle and nephew were corresponding on the same basis as in the past.

The sympathetic understanding Monroe received from Jefferson, whom he had recently met in Williamsburg, helped him greatly in overcoming his depressed feeling. The attention of the Governor of Virginia, who was fifteen years older than Monroe and internationally

celebrated as the author of the Declaration of Independence, was deeply
flattering to the younger man. Although Monroe was quite aware that
the patronage of the Governor could be most useful, his friendship did
not rest merely on self-seeking ambition. Interested as Monroe was in
the philosophical and political concepts of the Enlightenment, he could
not but eagerly respond to the opportunity of an intimate association
with one of the most brilliant, well-informed and lively minds of the
day. Jefferson also had a capacity for friendship—a capacity rare in any
day, but all the more unusual in the formal world of the late eighteenth
century. Ever sympathetic with the aspirations of his younger contemporaries, Jefferson, who had something of the pedagogue in him, was
always eager to aid those who seemed to possess extraordinary talents.
Of all the many protégés he sponsored Monroe alone achieved true
greatness. On his part, Monroe could not offer Jefferson the same degree
of intellectual stimulation he received. The appeal of the young Virginian rested upon quite different grounds. Jefferson, like all Monroe's
friends, cherished him for the tremendous warmth of his personality,
his innate goodness and his ready response to the feelings of others.
These particular qualities were summed up by Jefferson when he commented to Madison in 1787: "Turn his soul wrong side outwards and
there is not a speck on it." [2] In a half-century of close friendship Jefferson never had occasion to modify this unstinting praise.

Jefferson, as he was to do on many subsequent occasions, exerted a
decisive influence on Monroe's life. At this time, Monroe, who was
floundering about and had no idea what to do with himself, badly
needed advice and encouragement. The Governor provided exactly
the right tonic, administered with tact, understanding, and a very real
personal concern about the young man's fate. He advised his protégé
to prepare for a career in politics by studying law. Following Jefferson's
advice, Monroe re-entered William and Mary early in 1780 and joined
William Short and Mercer in reading law under Jefferson's direction.[3]
Monroe's association with the college was probably nominal, for the
course of study proposed by Jefferson was far more exciting. Jefferson
disapproved of the current habit of utilizing apprentices to the law
as clerical drudges. He believed that they should not only study law, but
also read those books which illuminated the fundamental principles
of the social order and gave meaning to the law. His pupils mastered
the thorny but liberal Coke, followed by the more graceful but Tory-
minded Blackstone. Jefferson further assigned the statutes of Virginia,
of which he had one of the few complete collections. As an advocate

of the case method in an age in which law cases were rarely reported, he made his own extensive compilation available to his students. As the crowning glory to the course of study he added what might be termed the "Great Books" as viewed by an American *philosophe*—a catalogue from which St. Thomas and Aristotle were excluded with the same impartial rigor with which they are now included. The list Jefferson prepared for Monroe was probably much like the one he sent to Fulwar Skipwith a decade earlier. It included Locke, Bolingbroke, Rousseau, Montesquieu, Algernon Sidney and Hume, among the moderns. To represent the ancients he recommended Plutarch, Tacitus, Cicero, and his own favorite Epictetus, who appealed equally to Monroe. As a man of sensibility as well as sense, Jefferson did not omit the most characteristic novelists of the age—Smollett, Richardson and Sterne.[4]

In the spring of 1780, when the state capital was about to be transferred to Richmond, Jefferson suggested that Monroe go with him to continue his law studies there. Somewhat hesitant to leave the college and thus forego the opportunity of studying law under the celebrated George Wythe, who had just been appointed the first law professor at William and Mary, Monroe turned to his uncle for advice. Jones' reply was replete with the practical wisdom which made him such a valued counselor:

If Mr. Wythe means to pursue Mr. Blackstone's method, I should think you ought to attend him from the commencement of his course, if at all . . . indeed I incline to think Mr. Wythe under the present state of our laws will be much embarrassed to deliver lectures with that perspicuity and precision which might be expected from him under a more established and settled state of them. The undertaking is arduous and the subject intricate at the best. . . . Whichever method he may like, or whatever plan he may lay down to govern him, I doubt not it will be executed with credit to himself and benefit to his auditors. . . . I have no intimate acquaintance with Mr. Jefferson, but from the knowledge I have of him, he is in my opinion as proper a man as can be put into office, having the requisites of ability, firmness and diligence. You do well to cultivate his friendship, and cannot fail to entertain a grateful sense of the favors he has conferred upon you, and while you continue to deserve his esteem he will not withdraw his countenance. If, therefore, upon conferring with him upon the subject, he wishes or shows a desire that you go with him, I would gratify him. Should you remain to attend Mr. Wythe, I would do it with his approbation, and under the expectation that when you come to Richmond you shall hope for the continuance of his friendship and assistance.[5]

Jones also reminded his nephew that by remaining with Jefferson he might have a chance to further his military career in the event that the Governor should assume active command of the militia. From a practical point of view Jones considered the patronage of Jefferson far more relevant to his nephew's advancement than lectures by George Wythe. Following his uncle's advice and his own inclinations, Monroe joined Jefferson in Richmond.

He chose this time to carry out a plan he had long been considering—the sale of his property in Westmoreland. As soon as he could, he intended to locate in the Piedmont. This was an essential step for his political advancement, for as a small planter in a county dominated by great landowners he would find it difficult to exert a significant influence in either local or state affairs. By moving to a new area, where the scale of landholding was not so large, he would have enough property to be on a par with other planters.

II

Jefferson never assumed command of the militia, but in the summer of 1780 he had an unexpected opportunity to gratify his protégé's military ambition with a temporary assignment. In May 1780, after the surrender of Charleston to the British, the South was faced with the prospect of a major British invasion. The reports reaching Richmond about the efforts of the governors of North and South Carolina to raise troops and collect supplies to assist the small and ill-equipped army under DeKalb were confused and fragmentary. In order to obtain information needed to prepare the state, if a large-scale invasion were under way, Jefferson and his Council decided to send Monroe to North Carolina as a special military agent. He was instructed to establish a system of expresses 40 miles apart along the course of his route to transmit messages to Richmond at the rate of 120 miles a day. His main objective was to report on the plans already under way for repulsing the British.[6]

Monroe set out in the middle of June, traveling by way of Halifax, North Carolina. On his southward journey he was shocked at the poverty of the country, so thoroughly stripped of supplies for the army that he had difficulty finding corn for his horse. Instead of proceeding directly to DeKalb's headquarters in Hillsboro in the north-central portion of the state, Monroe decided to go to Cross Creek, on the Cape Fear River about a hundred miles from Wilmington, to confer with Governor Nash of North Carolina and General Richard Caswell, who commanded

a force of 1,500 militia. From here he notified Jefferson of a large
British fleet reportedly bound for Virginia. It was some weeks before
the alarm which this report aroused was quieted by the news that the
fleet had gone to New York. More reliable were his reports on the
numbers and disposition of the American forces in North Carolina.
His expresses operated so efficiently that his first communication
traversed the 200 miles to Richmond within two days.[7] Unfortunately
all but one of Monroe's dispatches vanished along with many of Jefferson's official papers during the British invasion of 1781.

Having sent off his first dispatches, Monroe proceeded to DeKalb's
headquarters. During the next month he accompanied the army on its
marches, reveling in the physical activity after six months of sedentary
life. The best-remembered hours were those he spent with Captain
Thomas Pinckney of South Carolina, who was also present as an observer. The two men were attracted to one another and agreed to share
quarters and mess together. Pinckney, who was then ten years older
than Monroe, was a charming and urbane man of the world. Educated
in England, he had returned to America just before the Revolution
after completing the Grand Tour. Like Monroe, he was a passionate
enthusiast for the revolutionary cause, and the two men spent many
hours speculating about the future which awaited the new nation.[8]
His self-confidence now fully restored, Monroe returned to Virginia
late in August in a much happier frame of mind. He declined all recompense for his services, as he had done throughout most of the Revolution. His fortune was small, he told Jefferson, but he looked upon it
as his duty to make this contribution to the common cause.[9] He settled
down contentedly on a small estate which he owned in King George
County to complete his law studies.[10]

Except for a month in a volunteer unit formed among his neighbors
during General Alexander Leslie's invasion in November 1780, Monroe
remained on his farm during the next year.[11] Jefferson could do nothing
for his protégé, since even in the face of a massive British invasion in
December the Governor had been unable to raise additional units in
the state line. In June 1781, however, Monroe went to Lafayette's headquarters to offer his services in the army being gathered for the siege
of Yorktown. Again he came away empty-handed; all the regiments
had full complements of officers. Equally vain was his application to
Jefferson's successor, Governor Thomas Nelson, for a commission
in the recent Virginia levies. In the face of this unwelcome idleness
during the last months of the war, Monroe displayed greater equanimity

than he had in 1779. He consoled himself with the knowledge that with 15,000 regulars in Virginia there could be no doubt of the eventual defeat of Cornwallis and the imminent termination of the war.[12] His last military service during the Revolution was a minor charge entrusted to him by his former commander, General Weedon, whom Monroe encountered while he was en route to Lafayette's camp in June. At Weedon's request Monroe acted as the officer in charge of the truce flag given to the British ship *Riediesel* to pass through the American lines with a cargo of tobacco for the American prisoners of war at Charleston.[13]

With the American victory near at hand, Monroe felt free to complete his education abroad. Early in October 1781, having tentatively engaged passage, he turned to Jefferson for additional suggestions in order to continue his "studies on the most liberal plan," which would not only qualify him for public office but also enable him "to bear prosperity and adversity in the capricious turns of fortune, with greater magnanimity and fortitude, by giving him resources within himself, of pleasure and content w'ch otherwise he wo'd look in vain from others." [14] Jefferson ordinarily did not favor European education for Americans, but gave his approval to Monroe's plan, since a sojourn in Europe would implement his protégé's knowledge of the world and give him further time to recover from recent disappointments. Counseling Monroe against studying law at the Temple, Jefferson recommended instead that he attend the sessions of the courts and of Parliament. Since Monroe would be in Europe and hence in a better position to keep abreast of new publications, there seemed no need for adding to the list of books he had given his friend. Generously Jefferson forwarded a gift of forty volumes of the debates of Parliament and of the *Historical Register,* which he trusted might "be of use when you shall become a Parliamentary man, which for my country and not for your sake, I shall wish to see you." Jefferson's letters of introduction to the American Peace Commissioners in Paris presented Monroe as a man of "abilities, merit and fortune" and his "particular friend," but these were never used, for it proved impossible to obtain passage.[15] This plan for an extended European residence was to remain a cherished dream not to be realized until a decade later, when Monroe became Minister to France.[16]

III

No time was lost brooding over this setback, for Monroe immediately embarked upon the first stage of the political career he had long had in mind. In the spring of 1782 he was elected a member of the House of Delegates from King George County in the place of his uncle, recently named a delegate to the Continental Congress. In his campaign, which involved visits to all parts of the country, Monroe found the letters of recommendation from Washington and Lord Stirling, which had been of such little use in advancing his military career, to be most helpful in winning support from influential residents.[17] He sought a seat in the lower house not because it was financially remunerative (the delegates received only a small *per diem* allowance, which merely covered their expenses) but because membership in the legislature was essential for a young man anxious to advance his fortune and his career. Here the talents of a young lawyer like Monroe would be observed by the most powerful men in the state—men in a position to recommend clients to him and to grant him entry into their own ranks, which in itself would attract clients. In important cases no one cared to be represented by a county-court lawyer who was neither familiar with the usages of the superior courts nor personally acquainted with the judges. As valuable as the patronage of Jones and Jefferson had been, Monroe also needed the good opinion of such established leaders as George Mason, Richard Henry Lee, Edmund Pendleton and Edmund Randolph. When his election took place, he had already acquired some fame. Edmund Pendleton, noticing that Monroe and John F. Mercer had been elected, commented to Madison that both were "said to be very clever." [18] Obviously Monroe was looked upon as a rising figure.

The legislature at this time was divided into two loose and shifting factions which historians have labeled "conservative" and "radical," although this usage implies a more rigid differentiation than was actually the case. Neither group can be defined on the basis of a set of principles, but only in relation to specific issues. The conservatives, who dominated the state government during the post-Revolutionary era, were by no means a rigidly aligned group. On the contrary, they frequently disagreed among themselves. They constituted a power establishment whose pre-eminence was challenged from time to time by the radicals. In general it can be said that most of the conservatives were much concerned with strengthening the Union created by the Articles of Confederation, whereas the radicals were either indifferent or openly hostile to the central government. Although this was by no means the only issue separating the factions, it can be used to describe one phase of the conflict between them. The most important members of the legislature—George Mason, Edmund Pendleton, Judge Jones, James

Madison, George Nicholas and Edmund Randolph—tended to be conservatives. The radical element was dominated by one leader of quite exceptional power—Patrick Henry, whose immense influence stemmed both from his reputation as a firebrand of the Revolution and from his remarkable oratorical gifts, which enabled him to sway the uncommitted, inexperienced members of the lower house. Frequently, with sudden bursts of magnificent eloquence, he defeated measures that had seemed certain of approval. Henry, however, had one striking defect which diminished his effectiveness as a leader; naturally indolent, he had no taste for the grueling committee work essential to maintaining power.

Legislation was controlled by four great standing committees (every member served on at least one and the more active legislators on several) and by select committees which drafted reports and worked out the details of bills. The dominant members of the House of Burgesses were those who worked steadily on these committees and who kept themselves informed of the work of other committees. Since many of the younger members, choosing to regard membership in the House merely as the finishing touch to a gentlemanly education, preferred playing cards and enjoying idle flirtations to these tedious duties, they had little or no idea of the contents of measures before the House. It was over this ill-informed mass that Henry exerted an enormous if rather spasmodic influence. Given to transitory enthusiasms, he never hesitated to leave a session to attend to private affairs. During these frequent absences the conservatives usually had no difficulty in maintaining control. Until the formation of the federal government, when this division in state politics vanished, Monroe was associated with the conservative faction. This affiliation was logical for Monroe, who, as his conduct during the next decade amply demonstrated, shared the convictions of those who sought to strengthen the Union. Moreover, his closest personal ties were with the conservatives, for both Judge Jones and Jefferson were usually allied to this faction. It should also be noted that the best path to political advancement for an ambitious young man lay in winning the approval of the dominant power group and securing admission to its ranks.

During the brief spring session Monroe was able to make some return to Jefferson, now in retirement at Monticello, for the many kindnesses received during the past two years. Jefferson's withdrawal from public life had been precipitated by two factors. He had been hurt by the allegation that as governor he had failed to take adequate steps to repulse the British invasion. It is true that he had been vindicated by a subsequent legislative investigation, but the suggestion that he had been incompetent still rankled. A second and more compelling reason was his wish to remain with his wife, who was fatally ill. Consequently, when elected to the House of Delegates from Albemarle in the spring of 1782 he declined to serve. When he informed the speaker of the House of Delegates that he would not attend, Jefferson gave no reason, thus giving rise to comments that he was shirking his responsibilities at a time of public crisis. Distressed at hearing the motives of his friend questioned, Monroe wrote Jefferson urging him to attend and silence his critics.[19] Jefferson replied at length, asserting the right of every citizen to devote a proper amount of time to his private affairs and pointing out that after ten years in public life he had fully earned this privilege. He challenged the right of the state to force a citizen to hold an office he had not sought. Only incidentally did Jefferson allude to the illness of his wife—a subject on which he felt so much anguish that he could not bring himself to write about it at length. Monroe silenced Jefferson's severest critics by showing them this letter.[20] In replying to Jefferson, Monroe tactfully pushed politics aside to offer consolation.[21]

IV

Monroe's contributions to the spring session cannot be assessed since the journals have not been preserved, but he made a sufficient impression on the delegates to be elected to the Governor's Council. This body, still frequently called the Privy Council, was a vestigial survival of the royal Governor's Council. Unlike its ancestor it possessed few significant powers. The Council, consisting of eight councilors and the governor, functioned as the executive of the state. Without the approval of the majority of the council the governor (who had no vote) could not act. In the colonial era appointments as councilors had been highly valued, but the post-Revolutionary impotence of the executive rendered the office less attractive. Since the older and more experienced political leaders no longer found it advantageous to serve on the Council, the legislature was turning to much younger men. While Monroe was on the Council, William Short, Samuel Hardy, John Marshall and Beverley Randolph—all nearly his age—were also members. Not all the older generation approved of this rapid advancement of the younger leaders. Edmund Pendleton, for example, let it be known that he not only considered John Marshall too young, but that he also thought the office of councilor incompatible with the activities of a young attorney at the Richmond bar. Not daring to risk offending the Chancellor of the Court of Appeals, Marshall promptly resigned.[22] Pendleton raised no objection to Monroe, who was not as yet launched on a law career. Not until June 1782 did he qualify to appear before the county and other inferior courts.[23]

The duties of a councilor were largely routine, but required constant residence in Richmond. The Council usually met daily and the salary was based on the number of meetings attended. During the next year Monroe remained in Richmond, scarcely more than a village of fewer than three hundred houses, mostly of frame construction. Public buildings were makeshift—the capitol a former warehouse, one of the few large buildings not destroyed during the British invasion. Streets were unpaved and the town had a raw and unkempt appearance. Accommodations were most inadequate; delegates either boarded at private homes or stayed at Formicola's, the only tavern in the city. The tavern, which had only two rooms on each of its two floors, was so jammed during legislative sessions that the delegates slept in upstairs rooms in beds packed in side by side. These discomforts were relieved by the presence of many of Monroe's friends, including John Marshall, with whom he spent many hours at cards in the tavern or attending the theater improvised for touring companies.[24]

While a member of the Council, Monroe gave special attention to the development of the region west of the Alleghenies, then considered an important source of future revenue for the state as well as an important area of private investment. The Revolution had not only swept away the restrictions imposed by the Proclamation of 1763 on western expansion but had also terminated the tight monopoly exercised by the royal governor and his circle over land grants. Like many of his contemporaries, Monroe had seized the opportunity to make extensive investments in western lands, for which he used some of the proceeds from his Westmoreland property. As an officer serving for three years he had received a land bounty of 5,333⅓ acres of land in Kentucky.[25] In all he succeeded in patenting more than 100,000 acres of land, largely in Fayette and Lincoln counties, Kentucky.[26] He had more extensive claims, but inaccurate surveys and improper entries in the land records made it impossible for him to validate these grants. The investments which he made in the West substantially increased the modest fortune he had inherited. Although Monroe was on the whole a cautious investor, he somewhat overextended himself and during the next decade he was frequently short of ready money. In 1785 he had to withdraw from a joint purchase with Madison of Genesee Valley lands for the simple reason that he did not have enough ready money to keep up his share of the payments.[27]

As a councilor Monroe had to concern himself with the West, where Virginia was maintaining an army under the command of George Rogers Clark, who was attempting to subdue the Indians. Monroe, anxious to improve his knowledge of the West, turned directly to Clark for information. Although he did not know Clark, he wrote the General asking him to correspond about military operations, conditions of settlement, the prospects for trade and the outlook for the eventual independence of this region. Monroe promised to do everything he could to advance the interests of the Westerners, since he had a "particular respect for the exertions of these people & admire & esteem them for that spirit of enterprise" which they had shown in defending themselves.[28] Clark, delighted to have a spokesman in the Council, responded at once. Their friendship developed rapidly with Clark advising Monroe on land purchases. In January 1783 Monroe felt he knew Clark well enough to warn the General that he must be careful in supervising the expenditures of his officers and be prepared to defend himself against charges of speculation and drunkenness. Such reports, Monroe told Clark, were injurious to Virginia's interests, since it gave ground to the assertions in Congress that Virginia was mismanaging her western affairs and thus could be used as a justification for congressional action in assuming jurisdiction over the West.[29]

Early in 1783 Monroe considered going to France with Jefferson. Although greatly tempted by this offer to join the newly appointed peace commissioner, the plan was abandoned when Congress withdrew Jefferson's appointment upon learning that peace negotiations were so far advanced that his services would not be required.[30] Any disappointment felt by Monroe was softened by the honor conferred on him in June, when the legislature chose him to represent the state in Congress. As other members of the delegation the Assembly elected Jefferson, Arthur Lee, Samuel Hardy and John F. Mercer. This delegation, including distinguished older leaders as well as younger men of promise, was typical of those sent by Virginia to Congress at this time. During the next three years, while Monroe served in Congress, the replacements were equally outstanding; among them were Richard Henry Lee, Edward Carrington and William Grayson. Grayson, regarded as one of the best-educated and wittiest men of his day, was Monroe's cousin. With all his colleagues except Arthur Lee and Richard Henry Lee, Monroe was on friendly terms. The Virginia delegation as a whole distrusted Arthur Lee because of his involvement in confused Revollutionary financial transactions and his monomaniacal hatred of Silas Deane. Richard Henry Lee, at odds with the nationalist aspirations of the majority of the Virginia delegation, held himself at a distance from his colleagues.

Since his term did not begin until November, Monroe continued to sit on the Council until late October.[31] During July and August, while visiting Jefferson at Monticello, he looked about the county for property, for he wished to establish himself permanently near his closest friend. He located a suitable tract, but relinquished his claims when he learned that Colonel Harvie, who was acting as his agent, wished to purchase it himself. He felt this to be a small recompense to Harvie, also an old friend of Jefferson, who had done him many favors in the past.[32]

CHAPTER 4

THE CONFEDERATION CONGRESS, 1783-1786

WHEN MONROE took his seat on December 13, 1783, Congress was then in Annapolis, where the delegates had located after fleeing from Philadelphia earlier in the year in the face of an incipient mutiny among unpaid troops. It had settled on the banks of the Severn in quest of comfort and security after a brief sojourn at Princeton, where the accommodations proved inadequate. At this time its members were divided into two loosely defined factions: the nationalists, who wished to strengthen the central government, and those who, for want of a better term, are usually labeled the antinationalists. Neither constituted a firm party unit, for each tended to fragment on specific issues, such as that presented by the Jay–Gardoqui proposals of 1786, when the North–South division cut across all other affiliations.

Monroe's congressional career was launched at a moment when the prestige of Congress was at its lowest ebb.[1] The end of the war, by lessening the need to rely on the Union for self-preservation, had given new authority to leaders, such as Samuel Adams and Patrick Henry, who considered the states the proper vehicles of sovereign power. Many Americans, accustomed to regard centralized power as the first step on the road to tyranny, were distrustful of every measure emerging from Congress. Widespread indifference to the future of the central government led not only to excessive absenteeism but also to the selection of second-rate delegations. After the dislocations of the war, most Americans were more concerned with paying taxes (often ten years in arrears) and recouping financial losses than with the considerations of national welfare which preoccupied Congress. Consequently the nationalists, who had struggled so long to increase the effectiveness of the central government, lost ground. As a committed nationalist Monroe devoted his energies during his three-year term in Congress to revitalizing the movement to strengthen the Confederation government.

Monroe's service in Congress was of fundamental importance in shaping his later attitudes and at the same time in giving him a better understanding of the complex forces contending for power on the national scene. In particular he acquired an awareness of the sectional character of the divisions within the nation. It seemed to him that all elements in the nation must be guaranteed a fair share in the benefits of republican government. If this could not be done, the Union would surely perish. Far more open-minded than most of his contemporaries with rather similar agrarian backgrounds, Monroe at this early stage of his career demonstrated an unusual degree of sympathy for the aspirations of the mercantile community. This willingness to respond to the aims of radically different groups proved to be one of the greatest assets in his subsequent career.

One might have expected the excitement of victory sufficient reason to bring delegates flocking to Annapolis to ratify the treaty in time to meet the March 3 deadline for the exchange of ratifications, but apathy was so great that more than a month elapsed after Monroe took his seat before the necessary nine states were present. The anxiety of those delegates sufficiently concerned to arrive promptly was only partially eased by the agreeable social life of Annapolis—a wealthy and cultivated town, many of whose 300 houses were as splendid as any in Philadelphia. It is true that the New Englanders were shocked at the idleness of the inhabitants and at the uncultivated state of the surrounding fields. To the Southerners, accustomed to the ungroomed appearances of their towns, these shortcomings were not apparent. Plays were performed twice a week; balls, horse races and tea parties were almost daily affairs.[2] At twenty-five, Monroe, after his long rustication in Virginia, was still young enough to welcome these diversions. He felt sufficiently lighthearted to indulge in a mild flirtation, which gave rise to rumors of a more serious attachment than he contemplated.[3]

Far more delightful than the casual entertainments of the city was the solid pleasure of sharing lodgings with Jefferson, whose French cook not only provided remarkable dinners but also gave Monroe a chance to practice his still-rudimentary French. As they waited for the delegates to arrive the two Virginians had ample opportunity to canvass every phase of public policy. Characteristically, Jefferson had brought along a rather sizable private library, including works by leading *philosophes*—Helvetius, Diderot, Tissot and Chastellux. Monroe and other congressmen freely used this collection, and when Jefferson departed for France in the spring Monroe purchased most of these works, including a French manual on chess. Jefferson also left his cook for his colleague; by this time Monroe had made such an advance in French that he rarely had any difficulty in conversing with him.[4] Jefferson's most important legacy to his friend, however, was to place him on a confidential footing with Madison. Monroe and Madison had undoubtedly met, but they had not been on intimate terms. This friendship with Jefferson's most trusted political confidant cemented Monroe's bond with the nationalists. In presenting his colleague to Madison, Jefferson was unstinting in his praise: "The scrupulousness of his honor will make you safe in the most confidential communications. A better man cannot be." [5] During Jefferson's absence in France, Monroe and Madison remained in close touch except for one brief interval.

As the weeks dragged by without a nine-state quorum, the delegates grew more and more anxious that Great Britain might repudiate the treaty if ratification were delayed beyond March 3. Consequently, as soon as seven states were present an effort was made to put the treaty to an immediate vote on the grounds that treaties became valid as soon as they were signed. Jefferson (this was before he departed for France) and Monroe were as concerned as the other members about the fate of the treaty, but they blocked the vote, since treaties, as they pointed out, did not become effective until officially ratified.[6]

Not until January 14, 1784, when nine states had assembled, was the treaty approved by unanimous vote. Almost at once attendance fell off, forcing the postponement of vital matters until the session was nearly over. During these months Monroe, as a junior member, was an observer rather than a leader. He supported Jefferson's Land Ordinance of 1784, which included a provision prohibiting slavery in the Northwest Territory, and joined the rest of the Virginia delegation in voting for John Jay's appointment as Secretary of Foreign Affairs.[7] Not until spring was Monroe given an important committee assignment, when he became a member of the committee to examine a site for the permanent location of the capital near the Falls of the Potomac. After visiting Georgetown in May, Monroe and his colleagues reported in favor of a tract a mile and a half below the town, but sectional rivalries in Congress were much too sharp at that time to permit a decision on such a southerly location.[8]

While Monroe was absent on committee business, the usually placid atmosphere of Congress was shattered by a series of fierce debates which, in character with the evident demoralization of that body, were over a matter of only secondary importance. The conflict centered around the discovery that the commissions of the Rhode Island delegates had expired, rendering them technically ineligible to sit in Congress. Although irrelevant to the main questions before Congress, the issue had serious implications: formal disqualification of the Rhode Islanders would leave only six states legally represented, thus forcing the suspension of all business. Monroe's old friend Mercer, who, according to Jefferson, was "afflicted with the morbid rage of debate," was a prime mover in demanding the expulsion of the Rhode Island delegates.[9] Monroe was shocked by this senseless wrangle—the "most indecent conduct" he had ever witnessed in a legislative body.[10] As a result of his thoughtless conduct, Mercer lost the esteem of Jefferson and the more responsible leaders and momentarily was deprived of any hope for further advancement.[11]

Faced by the need to make essential arrangements before the adjournment scheduled for June 3, the effort to unseat the Rhode Islanders was abandoned. With only a month of the session remaining, Congress turned to the long-postponed question of garrisoning the Northwest posts, which it was expected Britain would yield in compliance with the provisions of the treaty of peace. Monroe's active role in these discussions left no doubt that he had long since formulated clear-cut opinions on the issues involved. His solution—the creation of a permanent military force under the control of Congress—was highly unpalatable to many delegates, who saw the specter of tyranny in the formation of a standing army in peacetime. Monroe was not unsympathetic with this apprehension, but he considered a standing army indispensable as long as any European power held possessions on the North American continent. Even if it were granted that the states could provide adequate defenses against the Indians, the problem presented by the presence of European powers was beyond the scope of any one state.[12] Monroe did everything he could to promote the adoption of a measure calling for a force of 450 men enlisted for three years, which David Howell of Rhode Island had introduced. This modest scheme was so alarming that only three states approved and even the Virginia delegation was inimical. For two weeks Howell and Monroe struggled vainly to preserve the principle of a national army controlled by Congress. They managed only a token victory in the form of an army of

700 men recruited for one year by the states on a quota basis but subject to the regulations employed in the Continental army.[13]

Although the adjournment (the first since 1775) had been long planned, it was not until a few days before the date fixed for ending the session that arrangements were made for an interim executive in the form of a Committee of States with a member from each state. The nationalists had hoped that the committee might open the way to improving the executive functions of Congress. Unfortunately, rather than providing for the election of committee members by a vote of Congress —as the nationalists wished—each state delegation chose its own member, thus giving the antinationalists an edge. As Monroe predicted, the antinationalists acted as obstructionists by absenting themselves from the committee meetings to prevent the necessary quorum for transacting business. So unsuccessful was the experiment that it was not again attempted.[14] Before disbanding it was agreed to reconvene that fall in Trenton.

II

As soon as the session ended, in June 1784, Monroe returned to Virginia. After a short visit with his uncle in Fredericksburg, he went to Albemarle to inspect some plantations offered for sale, then on to Richmond for a few days with Madison, William Short and John Marshall. The latter, who had been most helpful during the winter by raising money on Monroe's state treasury warrants, was at this time a particularly close friend.[15] Late in July Monroe left for an extensive tour of the West, an undertaking not without considerable risk in view of the inability of the United States to assert its jurisdiction over the Indians north of the Ohio River. Originally planned as a joint enterprise with Jefferson before the latter's departure for France, the tour was a logical outgrowth of Jefferson's general interest in the West and Monroe's own involvement in land speculation. Both realized that firsthand knowledge of the region was necessary to frame sound measures for its future development.[16] When offered the chance to accompany Indian commissioners bound for Fort Schuyler in New York, Monroe reversed the route he and Jefferson had planned, for they intended entering the West via Pittsburgh. The New York commissioners had been appointed by Governor George Clinton, who was attempting to assert state control over the Indians in defiance of Congress' recent declaration that it alone could negotiate with the Indians. Monroe sailed from New York with the commissioners in a sloop which had among its passengers Catherine Livingston, the daughter of the Governor of New Jersey, and several other ladies bound for Albany on a summer outing.

With the native courtesy of a well-bred Virginian Monroe sought to be agreeable to the young ladies, whose reactions varied from amusement to mild infatuation. Among those who found conversation with the serious-minded Colonel Monroe less entertaining than the polite banter of the Philadelphia beaux was Miss Sarah Vaughan, who made some rather tart comments after her return home:

Poor Col. Monroe! The man is in despair he has written a letter to Gen. Gates telling him that he has lost his heart on board the Albany sloop, and fills the sheet with a panegyric upon his fair one. I fear his love did not meet with a return, but we were blind and not acquainted with one half his perfections of person or mind, they were sumed [sic] up to me this day and amounted to eight which includes every perfection that a female can wish or a man envy. He is a member of Congress, rich, young, sensible, well read, lively, and handsome. I forget the other accomplishment, and will not subscribe to the last unless you prove the dimple on his chin to be what constitutes beauty, and I have a doubt about the sixth unless it is agreed that affording [a] subject for gaiety and liveliness to the company you are in, is the same thing as being gay and lively yourself. If you are the goddess at whose shrine he worships inform me of it that I may think higher of his perfection. His being your choice will have great influence upon me, and stop me when I might be saucily inclined, for at present he is more the object of my diversion [sic] than admiration.[17]

Apparently Monroe had not entirely shaken off the *mauvaise honte* for which Charles Lee had once chided him.

In Albany he heard the disturbing news that in order to pass Oswego he would need the permission of the British commander. From this and other reports he concluded that the British had no intention of relinquishing their control over the Northwest.[18] This news was of far more concern to him than the rumors of Indian unrest. With a rare flippancy he dismissed the Indian danger with the remark that he hoped to escape safely by "either a little fighting or a great deal of running. . . ." [19] Although only an observer at the conferences between the Indians and the commissioners, the fact that he was a member of Congress led the Indian chieftains to be particularly attentive to him.[20] Monroe was most impressed by Colonel Joseph Brant, a Mohawk chief with the rank of colonel in the British army, whose Indian forces had been the terror of the northern frontier during the Revolution. Later that year Monroe received a request from Brant for assistance in securing the release of Indian hostages.[21]

From Fort Schuyler Monroe continued his journey with a party bound for Detroit by way of Canada under the leadership of a Mr. Taylor of Schenectady, who was familiar with the interior. Embarking in "batteaux" at Oswego, the party reached Fort Niagara, where Monroe was courteously received by the British officers. The commander of the fort, who invited Monroe to dine, was so convincing in his warnings of the impossibility of traveling on the Canadian side without a strong armed guard that Monroe separated from Taylor's party. Accompanied by an Indian guard provided by the commander of the fort, he continued on the American side to Fort Erie. On arrival at the fort he was dismayed to learn that most of Taylor's party had been killed by Indians while camped on the Canadian side of the lake. In view of the extensive Indian disturbances, Monroe reluctantly turned back. After resting a week with the hospitable officers at Fort Niagara, he embarked for Montreal on a British sloop, on which he again encountered Colonel Brant.[22] Since Monroe's primary interests were political it is not surprising that he made no comment in his letters on the scenic splendors of the wilderness, although he was sufficiently interested to view the falls. He was much more concerned with assessing the economic potential of Canada. He was particularly aware of this question, for Pitt's attempts to relax the British colonial system in favor of the United States had been defeated by arguments such as those presented in Lord Sheffield's celebrated pamphlet, *Observations on the Commerce of the American States*. Sheffield had maintained that Canada could supply the timber needed in the mother country and the foodstuffs essential for the West Indian colonies if restrictions were continued on the United States in order to foster Canadian enterprise. As he sailed down the river Monroe found the stands of timber impressive, but when he reached the rapids near Montreal, he realized that the cost of shipping the timber prevented Canadian forests from becoming a ready source of supply. The country between Montreal and Lake Champlain was more fertile than he expected, but he still considered Lord Sheffield's contention that Canada could supply all the grain needed in the West Indies "visionary." [23] His conclusions were most important, for a cardinal aim of the nationalists was to empower Congress to regulate trade so that restrictive legislation could be imposed on English commerce to force Great Britain to make concessions to the

United States. Only if the West Indies were dependent on supplies from the United States could such a policy succeed.

III

More promptly than the majority of the delegates, who had remained quietly at home, Monroe reached Trenton on October 19, the day before the beginning of the session, to find only six other members present. The town stirred memories of the battle in which he had been so seriously wounded, and he could make only a painful comparison between the ardor of the patriots of 1776 and the apathy which now seemed to grip the nation.[24] Three weeks elapsed before a quorum was was present; not a delegate appeared from New England during the first two weeks of the session. Understandably, an atmosphere of melancholy settled over Congress. The delegates were not only bored by their idleness; they were also suffering from the physical discomforts of meeting in a town without adequate accommodations. During the first weeks of the session they talked fitfully of summoning a convention to remedy the defects of the Articles, but the failure of past efforts made such a venture seem hopeless. Making good use of the enforced leisure, Monroe relayed to his correspondents the conclusions derived from his recent tour. The outlook he portrayed was gloomy: Great Britain would continue to occupy the posts on the convenient pretext that the Americans had failed to pay their prewar debts as required in the treaty of peace. Although his friends responded to his pleas to seek to remove the obstacles to the payment of the debts, all the measures proposed in the Virginia legislature failed.[25] Since the United States could not assert its territorial claims by force, Monroe considered that it might be possible to apply pressure through the enactment of restrictions on Canadian commerce.[26]

Monroe's spirits rose as the delegates slowly assembled, for the new members seemed abler than their predecessors. In December he felt sufficiently optimistic to predict to Jefferson that much good could be expected during the session, since the delegates seemed seriously concerned with the welfare of the union.[27] Unquestionably the decision to move to New York after the first of the year improved the morale of the members and encouraged more regular attendance. Here Monroe lived more comfortably than in Trenton, renting a house with two members of his delegation, William Grayson and Samuel Hardy. Although more expensive than lodgings, it spared them, as Grayson observed, the inconvenience of a common boardinghouse where it was necessary to mix with the "landlady, her aunts, cousins and acquaintances [and] all other sorts of company. . . ." [28] Although few of its streets were paved and pigs still roamed freely as scavengers, New York was a luxurious and elegant city with a tradition of rich display in dress and lavish entertainment. The merchants gladly provided the congressmen a tempting round of balls, tea parties and dinners. Taverns and coffee houses gave a cosmopolitan air to which the local gentry added as they rode in handsome carriages every afternoon on Broadway, then the principal thoroughfare. For the young bachelor members of Congress the accomplished young ladies with their rather grand "New York" manner exercised a notable attraction. As William Grayson observed, New York proved to be a veritable "Calypso's Island," for during the first year after the move Rufus King, Samuel Osgood, Eldridge Gerry and Monroe all married New Yorkers. [29]

From the beginning of the session of 1784–1785 Monroe emerged as a leading figure with a seat (and frequently the chairmanship) on the most important committees. His position as a member of the first rank led to his appointment to a committee to adjudicate a boundary dispute between New York and Massachusetts. It was largely an honorary appointment, but it linked his name with such distinguished elder statesmen as George Wythe, John Rutledge and William Paterson. [30] Still closely allied to the nationalists, Monroe supported every measure designed to strengthen the Confederation. He remained in close touch with Madison, who was then seeking to implement the same objectives as a member of the Virginia House of Burgesses. [31] In their regular correspondence they frequently resorted to cipher, since they did not wish to entrust their confidences "to chance & the curiosity of idle or vicious people." [32]

Perhaps in no area was his influence as strong or his interest as great as in foreign affairs. Early in the session he was deeply involved in a confused conflict over the organization of the diplomatic service precipitated by the news that Franklin wished to retire as Minister to France. At once a powerful group of delegates, having convinced themselves that the replacement of individual ministers by a single general commission would diminish the authority of the central government, blocked the nomination of ministers. They were joined by the "place seekers" who lobbied for favorite candidates. Monroe, convinced that the United States could not protect its interests or secure the respect of the European powers unless it adhered to the customary pattern of individual representation, vigorously opposed the commission system. Not until March 1785, after much intrigue and bargaining, was John Adams appointed Minister to London and Jefferson named Franklin's successor.[33]

While the ministerial appointments were pending, a number of committees were set up to draft instructions for foreign missions. As chairman of several of the more important committees, Monroe helped prepare reports which reflected his interest in the West and his desire to secure advantages for American commerce. Most important was the report on instructions for a projected mission for Spain. In this report, which formulated the policy followed during the Confederation, he recommended that the *sine qua non* of any treaty negotiated with Spain must be recognition of the thirty-first parallel as the boundary of Florida and an absolute guarantee of the free navigation of the Mississippi.[34]

Monroe also served as chairman of a committee established at his request to consider the Northwest posts, which the British had not yet surrendered. The committee report (never acted upon by Congress) recommended that the Minister in London be instructed to express the dissatisfaction of the United States over continued British occupation.[35] In February, in order to do something he felt would be more effective than diplomatic protests, Monroe introduced a resolution to impose prohibitive duties on all goods imported from Canada and to exclude Canadian trade from any treaty made with Great Britain.[36] However, he decided not to press for approval. It was, he thought, a sound measure, but one impossible to execute as long as the British still held the posts. How could the United States enforce commercial restrictions when it was not in control of its own frontier? He was also deterred by the possibility that Britain might use American restrictions as further pretext for retaining the posts.[37]

As chairman of a committee on commercial treaties Monroe submitted a report in April condemning the negotiation of additional trade treaties until Congress was given the power to regulate commerce. Without this authority the Confederation government could not impose the retaliatory measures needed to force concession from colonial powers. It was his conclusion that treaties were not needed with countries lacking colonies, for these nations, which desired American trade, had already granted favorable terms.[38] Monroe's policy differed radically from that outlined by Jefferson, who in December 1783 had recommended negotiating commercial treaties with all nations on the assumption that through the use of the treaty-making power Congress could enforce a uniform system of regulations on the states—a loose construction of the Articles not generally accepted.[39] Monroe's report was framed primarily with an eye to promoting the nationalist drive to persuade the states to grant Congress the power to regulate commerce by amending article nine of the Articles of Confederation. In December Monroe had managed to obtain the appointment of a committee to propose such a revision only after "infinite difficulty" [40] and had also secured as members a number of nationalists, including Rufus King. In February the committee had reported in favor of amending article nine and a month later had submitted a circular letter to be sent the state legislatures in behalf of the revision.[41] It was undoubtedly to heighten the sense of urgency that Monroe framed his report on commercial treaties. What could be more convincing than to show that the United States would never obtain a trade many deemed vital unless the Articles were amended?

The proposal to revise article nine was coolly received. Months after the original recommendation had been submitted Monroe pessimistically wrote Jefferson: "The importance of the subject and the deep and radical change it will create in the bond of the Union together with the conviction that something must be done, seems to create an aversion, or rather a fear of acting on it." Yet, if it was adopted, the amendment would "form the most permanent and powerful principle in the confederation" and hold the Union together more effectively than any other bond.[42] New Englanders sympathetic to the revision sought postponement in order to have time to overcome the fear of centralization current in the North. Even in his own delegation Monroe had only Hardy's support, for R. H. Lee and Grayson were in opposition.[43] The response in Virginia was just as unfavorable. Jones and Madison sought to enlist support, but found that the Virginians, who enjoyed a direct trade with Great Britain, could not be convinced that the revision of article nine would benefit them, since they suffered little from British restrictions.[44] Aware that these nationalist aspirations were ahead of the times, Monroe acknowledged that the matter must rest until continued injury to American commerce convinced the nation of the necessity of reform.[45]

Monroe was too deeply engrossed in foreign affairs and the revision of article nine to participate in the drafting of the Land Ordinance of 1785. Although William Grayson was the Virginia representative on the thirteen-state committee, Monroe was not aware of the provisions of the ordinance until it was submitted on April 12. As reported, the ordinance strongly reflected the views of New England, which Rufus King (himself the intermediary for the absent Timothy Pickering) had pressed upon the committee. While the delegates agreed on preserving the rectilinear system of survey used by Jefferson the year before, they differed sharply over the arrangements for the sale of land at auction. Monroe and the Southerners strenuously objected to the 30,000-acre minimum established by the committee. They argued that this restriction would deter both the individual settler and the speculator, neither of whom would be able to purchase such a large amount. The New Englanders had fixed upon this figure hoping to promote settlement in groups and thus duplicate the township method with which they were familiar. When the ordinance was before the house Monroe joined Grayson and James McHenry of Maryland to amend the bill to permit a more flexible system of sale. As a result of their efforts the ordinance was altered to provide that every alternate township could be sold in sections of 640 acres each. Far less time was devoted to a potentially much more explosive provision of the ordinance. At Pickering's suggestion King had incorporated in the original measure a provision that one section in every township be set aside for the support of religion. It required a curious bit of parliamentary maneuvering to delete this proviso, which few of the delegates favored but none of whom wished to oppose openly. Instead of taking a vote on a resolve to delete the passage, the delegates acted on a resolution asking the question: shall the provision for the support of religion be allowed to stand? In the roll call five states voted for retention, two against and two divided; consequently the measure, lacking a majority of seven states, was dropped. If the resolution had been put in the original form —that is, to strike out the words—the passage would have been retained and a provision supporting religion included in the Ordinance of 1785. For reasons they never explained Monroe and the Virginia delegates were among those voting to retain the passage. Madison, then struggling in Virginia to prevent the enactment of a tax for the support of religion, was horrified that such an illiberal measure should have emerged from a congressional committee. Monroe, to whom Madison expressed his astonishment, does not seem to have volunteered an explanation.[46]

After continuous attendance at the sessions since the preceding October, Monroe departed for a well-earned vacation in August 1785. Again he toured the West, but combining personal as well as public interests he included Kentucky (where he checked on his land holdings) in his itinerary. Madison had intended joining him, but as a result of a misunderstanding arrived in New York after Monroe had set out. For the first portion of his tour Monroe accompanied the Indian commissioners sent to Ohio by Congress. They traveled by way of Pittsburgh and then down the Ohio to Limestone, where Monroe parted from his companions to go on to Kentucky to have his lands surveyed. Returning to Richmond by way of Lexington and the Wilderness Trace, he lingered in the capital for several days in the congenial company of Mercer, Peyton Skipwith, Beverley Randolph, Wilson Cary Nicholas and other friends.[47]

Monroe's second western tour significantly altered his thinking about the political organization and future development of the Northwest. His tour made him aware of the feeling in the West that the eastern states were not just indifferent but were in fact actively hostile to the interests of the area. The inhabitants, unable to use the Mississippi to export their products, were increasingly dissatisfied. Attributing much of this distrust to the uncertain policies of the Confederation, Monroe was convinced that Congress must promptly set up a governmental system and establish clear rules for the admission of new states. Since he deemed a "great part of the territory . . . miserably poor, especially that near Lakes Michigan & Erie & upon the Mississippi & the Illinois [which] consists of extensive plains which have not had from appearances & will not have a single bush on them for ages," he concluded that the Northwest would be too sparsely populated to justify the creation of the ten states contemplated in Jefferson's ordinance of 1784. Even though he was sympathetic to western demands, he still considered it unwise to give too much power to a region whose interests were antithetical to those of the older states.[48]

IV

As soon as he returned to Congress in the fall, Monroe secured the appointment of a committee to revise Jefferson's ordinance of 1784. The committee, of which he was chairman, was an able one, composed of William Samuel Johnson of Connecticut (who replaced Monroe as chairman in 1786), Rufus King and two South Carolinians, John Kean and Charles Pinckney.[49] Monroe's familiarity with the region and his established position of leadership was sufficient to produce a report adhering closely to his views. From Jefferson's draft ordinance two basic principles were retained: first, that the new states be admitted on an equal footing with the old ones; second, that a state might be admitted when its population equaled that of the least populous state. The most radical departure from the earlier plan lay in the reduction of the number of projected states from ten to five and in the elimination of the vaguely worded principle that territorial governments should have a democratic basis. The provision excluding slavery, struck out in 1784, was not restored. Monroe's draft ordinance created a temporary government composed of a governor and a council chosen by Congress. As soon as the population should be sufficient a territorial legislature elected on a basis of free manhood suffrage would be established. Considering it impractical to grant autonomy to the inhabitants of the territories, Monroe preferred to adopt a "Colonial Govt. similar to that which prevail'd in these States previous to the revolution. . . ." [50]

Jefferson, understandably somewhat critical of this plan, still regarded small states as more in accordance with the republican nature of the American government. Although it was difficult for him to admire a scheme which seemed to treat the Westerners as subjects rather than as citizens, he readily admitted that Monroe's familiarity with the West tended to lessen his confidence in his own plan.[51] Jefferson made no comment about the omission of the section prohibiting slavery. Monroe never explained why he did not incorporate this provision, to which Jefferson had attached so much importance.

Monroe's ordinance was still pending when his term ended in the fall of 1786. The Ordinance of 1787, as the bill was called when it passed the following year, adhered very closely to Monroe's original except for two important changes. First, the ban on slavery was restored by Rufus King, an ardent antislavery spokesman.[52] Second, it contained sections regulating inheritances and protecting contract obligations. Monroe's most important contribution—the structure of territorial government—was left unaltered.

The progress of the ordinance had been impeded in 1786 by a variety of factors. The New England delegates consumed considerable time in a fruitless effort to inhibit the development of the West as a political force by raising the minimum population requirement for statehood.[53] The measure was also held up as Congress waited for Virginia to modify the act of cession to permit the reduction of the number of states from ten to five. The greatest delay was caused by the lengthy debate over the Jay–Gardoqui negotiations during the summer of 1786. In this dispute—the bitterest to rock Congress since the end of the war—

Monroe played a central role. The conflict originated over proposals made by Don Diego de Gardoqui, the first Spanish Minister to the United States, who had arrived in New York in the summer of 1785 bearing instructions to secure American acquiescence to the closing of the Mississippi. At the time Congress, approving recommendations made by a committee chaired by Monroe, granted Jay power to negotiate with Gardoqui subject to the important limitation that the free navigation of the Mississippi and the territorial rights of the United States must be guaranteed.[54] In imposing these restrictions Congress was merely continuing a policy first formulated six months earlier by another committee under Monroe's chairmanship. Since Jay had served on this first committee and hence was fully familiar with the issue, Monroe had no hesitation in allowing the Secretary of Foreign Affairs to negotiate without constant consultation with Congress.[55]

Gardoqui, who at first impressed Monroe as "polite and sensible," quickly proved to be an astute and perceptive diplomat.[56] In spite of the rigid instructions imposed on Jay, he soon discovered that many delegates were quite willing to let the river be closed indefinitely. Gardoqui, whose English was fluent, entertained congressmen lavishly at his splendid residence on Broadway. He cultivated Jay with care, for he knew from previous association in Spain of the Secretary's vanity and love of flattery.[57] With the groundwork established, Gardoqui easily drew Jay into discussing a general treaty project. By the early spring of 1786 they had agreed in substance that the United States would "forbear" the navigation of the Mississippi for thirty years in return for substantial trade concessions in Spain. Each power was to guarantee the territorial possessions of the other. To obtain the necessary modification of his instructions Jay applied to Congress in late May for the appointment of a committee to confer with him. Monroe at once understood that the Secretary wanted to be "relieved of his instructions," for Jay had approached Monroe earlier in the year outlining Gardoqui's proposals.[58] Monroe had then reminded the Secretary of the binding character of his instructions.[59] Such a sacrifice as Jay contemplated was unthinkable for Monroe. He stated his objections cogently in a cipher letter to Madison: "From the best opinion that I have been able to give the subject I am of opinion that it will be for the benefit of the U. S. that the river shod. be opened, that although we may not be in situation . . . to contest it, yet, if we enter'd into engagements to the contrary, we separate these people,—I mean all those westd. of the mountains from the federal government & perhaps throw

them into the hands eventually of a foreign power. . . ." Such a concession was rendered quite unnecessary in view of the fact that Spain
of "all the powers of Europe is the most in our hands." [60]

The Secretary's request was turned over to a committee composed of
Monroe (chairman), Rufus King and Charles Pettit of Pennsylvania.
These associates, who favored Gardoqui's scheme, were not at all
pleasing to Monroe. Pettit, he thought, had no better reason for favoring Jay than a deep-seated hostility to Virginia derived from a conviction that Virginians were inimical to a sound public credit. King
was judged even more harshly as a New Englander willing to sacrifice
the West to obtain a market for fish. King was no more complimentary
in commenting on the committee's chairman, whom he thought concerned solely with maintaining a high price for western lands. Although
King maintained it was absurd to insist on a right we could not obtain
either by negotiation or force, it was apparent that he felt deeply
antagonistic to the West: as he noted to Gerry, every immigrant to the
West was a resident lost forever to the East.[61] Although the committee
called upon Jay at once, disagreement between the chairman and his
confreres delayed its report for two months. The deadlock was broken
when King suggested that the committee ask to be discharged, and thus
allow Congress to decide whether a conference committee should be
appointed. To this Monroe readily agreed, since it would open the way
to a public airing of the proposals.[62] On August 3 Secretary Jay read
Congress a long statement asking that his instructions be revoked so
that Gardoqui's offer could be accepted.[63] This revelation, for the exact
nature of Gardoqui's offer had not been generally known, precipitated
a month-long debate which brought to the surface more sharply than
any other issue the conflict of interests between the northern and southern states. As tension mounted some New England delegates began to
discuss forming a northern confederation. Vague rumors of these conferences disturbed Monroe, who would have been truly alarmed had
he known that a few had even talked of creating a monarchy.[64]

From the beginning of the debate the contest assumed a sectional
character—the five southern states irrevocably opposing any change
in the original instructions, and the seven northern states (Delaware
was not represented) ready to barter the navigation of the Mississippi
for trade concessions. Throughout the debates this alignment never
varied. Madison (then in Philadelphia) was called upon to sound out
two absent Pennsylvania delegates whose votes were sufficient to alter
the alignment of that state. If they favored the original instructions,

then he was to press them to attend the session.[65] In his drive against Gardoqui's proposals Monroe was ably supported by his cousin, William Grayson, and by Charles Pinckney, one of the most effective speakers in the house. Their major attack was directed against the contention made by King and other New Englanders that the value of the trade was more than sufficient to justify closing the river. Indeed, Monroe contended that trade might well decline since tobacco had been specifically excluded from the proposed treaty. Monroe and the anti-Jay speakers also laid heavy stress upon the fact that Spain was the one European power from which the United States had nothing to fear—her extended frontiers with weak defenses made her dependent upon the good will of the United States, whether Congress consented to close the Mississippi or not. Knowing the states-rights proclivities of many New Englanders, Monroe momentarily laid aside his nationalism to emphasize the point that the treaty would create regulations infringing on the power of the states to regulate commerce.[66]

With little hope of defeating Jay's proposal by a frontal assault, Monroe, Grayson and Edward Carrington (also a member of the Virginia delegation) drew up a substitute proposal recommending the transfer of the negotiations to Madrid in the charge of John Adams and Thomas Jefferson, who would be authorized to close the river to imports if Spain would allow the export of American goods subject to a three per cent duty. Madison, when told of this alternative, was not much impressed; sensibly he pointed out that even a minor concession on the navigation of the Mississippi was to give ground. On the practical side he doubted that Spain would consider such terms.[67] Nonetheless, Monroe laid the proposal before the Committee of the Whole on August 18.[68] He now attempted to enlist Washington's support in behalf of the substitute proposal. Washington, already favorable to the concessions recommended by Jay, made no reply to Monroe's letter. The former commander in chief cannot have been pleased at seeing his old friend Jay accused of intriguing with members of Congress to repeal the previous instructions. Monroe's language in his letter to Washington was far more temperate than that used to other correspondents. Jay, he told Jefferson, had managed the negotiations "dishonestly." His comment to Patrick Henry was even blunter, when he accused the Secretary of "seducing" delegates by a "long train of intrigue and management." [69] It was at this time that Monroe acquired a lasting distrust of John Jay. In vain Monroe appealed directly to Congressmen Arthur St. Clair of Pennsylvania and Lambert Cadwalder of New Jersey, who were both in a position to deadlock their delegations.[70] Before the proposals were brought to a vote one more stratagem was attempted. Monroe and several colleagues called on the French chargé, Louis B. Otto, known to be well disposed to the United States, to enlist France's support for American claims to the Mississippi. If it could be announced that France, which possessed great influence over Spain through the Family Compact, approved the American cause, then Congress might transfer the negotiations to Madrid. Otto, who lacked authority to make such a pledge, simply promised to communicate the proposition to his government.[71] With all possibilities exhausted, further delay was pointless. On August 29 the compromise was rejected by a seven-to-five vote. At once Congress agreed to rescind Jay's instructions by exactly the same division.[72]

Technically, the original restrictions on Jay were now withdrawn, but Monroe and Pinckney discharged one last shot. The day after the repeal they presented a resolution raising the question whether instructions approved by nine states (a two-thirds majority) could be revoked by the votes of only seven states. The question could not be answered in view of the seven-to-five division, but it made one point clear: since a treaty required a nine-state majority, the rigid alignment in Congress rendered further negotiations useless. Nonetheless, the two factions continued to spar futilely for several days.[73] When Monroe was obliged to go to Philadelphia on official business early in September, he was still so fearful that the pro-Jay element might take advantage of his absence to renew the struggle that he extracted a pledge from his opponents that nothing would be attempted until he returned.[74]

This promise had been readily given, since Monroe was to be accompanied by Rufus King, Jay's main defender. During the debates Monroe had privately described King as one of the most "illiberal" delegates ever sent from Massachusetts, but the recent animosities did not impair their cooperation on a mission both deemed vitally important to the future of the Confederation.[75] They had been sent to persuade the Pennsylvania legislature to broaden its recent act granting Congress the power to levy import duties. The measure had started its career in April 1783, when Congress (prodded by Madison) requested from the states the right to impose a five per cent duty on specified goods for purposes of revenue only. This, of course, was a far more limited proposal than that advanced by Monroe in 1785 to amend article nine. Although most of the states had granted this five per cent duty by 1786, some had so hedged their consent that the project was imperiled. As

Monroe and King prepared to plead with the legislature, King, a polished and experienced orator, rose to speak first, but he became so nervous that Monroe had to take over from his faltering colleague.[76] Their intercession proved fruitless. The project received a further setback when Governor Clinton, in spite of a direct appeal from Monroe, declined to use his influence to modify the New York act.[77]

Late in September, when Monroe returned to New York, an effort was made to discredit Jay by releasing the journals of Congress. As usual this was voted down by seven to five.[78] To calm the Southerners, who still suspected Jay might continue negotiations, Charles Thomson, Secretary of Congress, showed the journals to the Secretary.[79] Although the public was not generally aware of the details, the Gardoqui proposals were not a well-kept secret, for the delegates had commented freely upon the proceedings in their letters. The members of the Virginia legislature were sufficiently well informed to resolve unanimously that the free navigation of the Mississippi be preserved.[80]

V

As his term drew to a close, Monroe's view of the future of the Confederation was not hopeful: yet, as he observed to Patrick Henry, it required nothing "but common sense and common honesty" to remedy the defects of the government. Unfortunately, these were qualities in which "we are, it is to be lamented, very defective." [81] By this time Monroe, like so many other nationalists, was ready to seek remedies outside Congress. Thus he looked on the approaching Annapolis Convention, arranged for September by Madison, as a stepping stone to a general governmental reform.[82] Monroe did everything in his power to promote the success of the conference at Annapolis. When he learned that New Hampshire did not intend to send delegates, he promptly wrote Governor John Sullivan to convince him of the importance of full representation from all the states. "I have looked forward," Monroe told his old revolutionary comrade, "to that convention as the source of infinite blessings to this country. However expedient it may be to extend the powers of Congress, yet recommendations from that body are received by such suspicion by the states that their success . . . is always doubted." Perhaps proposals by an independent agency might meet with a better reception from the states.[83] As soon as he received from Annapolis the appeal to Congress to summon a special convention to revise the articles, Monroe moved the appointment of a committee to report on the request. The committee was appointed on October 11, just a few days before he left Congress, but it did not submit its report approving the convention until long after Monroe had returned home.[84]

As Monroe was preparing to leave for Virginia after three years of service in Congress, weariness over the fruitless exertions of recent months led him to take a dim view of his achievements. "It has been," he informed Jefferson, "a year of excessive labor & fatigue & unprofitably so." [85] Yet he had achieved more than he fully appreciated. Blocking Jay's attempt to close the Mississippi and laying the groundwork for future territorial government were no slight accomplishments. Equally notable was his contribution to the nationalist cause by highlighting one of the major defects of the confederation government in his report on commercial treaties. He had not only gained a vast amount of experience but had also made a name for himself as a leader of outstanding abilities. The revelation of the full details of the Jay–Gardoqui proposals during the debates over the ratification of the Constitution in Virginia elevated him to the first rank in the estimation of the Westerners. Indeed, until a generation of native western leaders emerged just before the War of 1812, Monroe was looked upon as the only national figure identified with the aims of the West. The Continental Congress had provided an advantageous theater for Monroe to display his talents. In a body in which action was suspended for months and even years, and where there was a constantly fluctuating membership, those delegates who kept themselves better informed than their colleagues were in a position to exert extraordinary influence. Monroe, never a ready speaker, owed much of his success to his steady attention to the business of Congress, as well as to his ability to grasp the broader aspects of the problems of the day. It was a combination of political insight and diligence which singled him out from the mass of the delegates.

CHAPTER 5

LAWYER AND FARMER
1786-1790

WHEN MONROE left New York for Virginia on October 13, 1786, he was no longer a solitary traveler; beside him in in his chariot was his twenty-year-old bride of eight months, the former Elizabeth Kortright.[1] The wedding had taken place on February 16, after which (according to one of Monroe's colleagues) he had "decamp'd for Long Island with the little smiling Venus in his arms, where they have taken house, to avoid the fulsome Compliments during the first Transports and we have not yet seen him in Town. . . ." [2] Perhaps Monroe also wished to avoid for the moment the rather blunt humor he could expect from his friends. He did not escape entirely, for Gerry (at whose wedding Monroe had been best man) drove a rather obvious point a few months later:

How are your matrimonial prospects?—*fertile,* I presume for southern soil is almost spontaneous. Mine are not yet promising for after the loss of one harvest a little time is requisite to prepare another. Does brother King make disposition for a summer crop? or does he propose to put in winter grain: as to Friend Osgood's field, I somewhat expect it is run out, unless by being unimproved, it is become enriched.[3]

After several days in the country the newlyweds returned to New York, to live with Mrs. Monroe's father until Monroe's term ended.[4]

Elizabeth Kortright was the daughter of Laurence Kortright, a once-wealthy West Indian merchant long resident in New York, whose fortune had been largely destroyed during the Revolution. She was a remarkably beautiful woman, with a much-admired taste in dress

and decoration. In public her formal manners left an impression
of coldness and reserve, but in private she was a devoted wife and a
doting mother, possessing to the full the domestic virtues then so highly
prized—a complete absorption in the affairs of her family and household and a total detachment from the world of politics and business.
She was in many ways the image of the conventionally reared eighteenth-century woman, corresponding admirably to the ideal wife
pictured by Monroe's uncle when he learned that his nephew was to be
married. Jones' formula was a simple one: "sensibility and kindness of
heart—good nature without levity—a modest share of good sense with
some portions of domestic experience and economy will generally if
united in the female character produce that happiness and benefit which
results from the married state...." [5] Monroe, like so many of his contemporaries, considered the only substantial happiness to be that of
the domestic circle; only then did a man acquire a sense of security
and stability not to be obtained otherwise.[6] All this Monroe now found
in his marriage. The bond which united the Monroes was a remarkably
close one, rendering every separation painful.

From his friends Monroe received warm congratulations, but none
wrote with such fineness of feeling as Jefferson, whose attitude toward
family life was much like that cherished by his younger friend. With
that sensitivity which was such a large part of his charm, Jefferson
realized that life in Virginia might seem tedious and lonely to a young
lady accustomed to the comfort, luxury and social life of New York.
In one of his letters to Monroe, Jefferson included a passage as much
for the eyes of the bride as for the husband:

> I am in hopes that Mrs. Munroe will soon have on her hands domestic
> cares of the dearest kind, sufficient to fill her time and ensure her against the
> tedium vitae; that she will find that the distractions of a town, and waste of
> life under these, can bear no comparison with the tranquil happiness of
> domestic life. If her own experience has not yet taught her this truth, she
> has in it's [sic] favor the testimony of one who has gone through the various
> scenes of business, of bustle, of office, of rambling, and of quiet retirement,
> and who can assure her that the latter is the only point upon which the
> mind can settle at rest.... But I must not philosophize too much with her
> lest I give her too serious apprehensions of a friendship I shall impose on
> her.[7]

Mrs. Monroe, her husband reported, was "very sensibly impressed"
with Jefferson's kind attention to her.[8] Adjusting rapidly to life in
Virginia, she was indeed fully occupied with those domestic cares so

firmly recommended by Jefferson after the birth of their first child, Eliza, in December 1786.[9]

In the months following his marriage Monroe's thoughts were occupied with the problem of increasing his income in order to provide adequately for his family. Since he had not yet acquired an estate on which to settle, he reluctantly turned to the law—a profession which did not interest him greatly—as offering the most immediate rewards. Although he preferred the attractions of urban life in Richmond, where the superior courts provided the most lucrative practice, and had asked Jefferson to send him plans for a town house to cost between three and four thousand dollars, he ultimately ruled out the capital city.[10] In reaching this decision he was influenced by the advice of both his uncle and his old friend Mercer, who warned him that the returns from the law in a city, where there were many well-established lawyers, would not be sufficient for several years to compensate him for the high cost of living in Richmond. Jones urged on Monroe the many advantages of putting up his shingle in Frederickburg, where he not only had many friends but would also not encounter any significant rivals at the bar. Knowing his nephew's abiding interest in politics, Jones also stressed the difficulty of running for the legislature in Richmond, whereas he could easily be elected from Fredericksburg. In the event that Monroe chose the latter town his uncle offered to let him have a house on his own terms.[11]

To all these arguments was added an even more cogent one—Monroe was extremely short of money in the months after his marriage. Although he possessed considerable property, it was largely in the form of western lands which could not readily be converted into cash. His immediate distress, however, stemmed from the difficulty of collecting debts in Virginia, where conditions were then bad. To his embarrassment, he was so short of funds that he could not forward money to Jefferson for the installments of the *Encyclopédie* which his friend was purchasing for him in Paris.[12] Just before he left New York his problems were aggravated by the bankruptcy of a New York broker who held a bill of exchange in Monroe's favor for $530.[13] Under these circumstances there seemed no alternative but to begin his married life by opening a law office in Fredericksburg. He and his wife moved into a simple but comfortable two-story house owned by Joseph Jones a few squares from the one-story building in which his law office was located. These were temporary arrangements, for he planned to move to Albemarle, where Judge Jones intended to join him.[14]

Nonetheless, Monroe fretted that his financial difficulties were causing his wife so much inconvenience. When he went to Richmond on business in April 1787, he did not have sufficient funds to take her along and had to leave her with friends. From Richmond he sent his wife an affectionate letter (the only one to her which has survived) which makes it possible, if only for a moment, to measure the quality of their relationship. Without salutation, the letter began:

I arriv'd here the evening after you left me and I have since been in health. I lodge and dine with Mr. Jones. I hope to hear from you by the post this morning. I have the utmost anxiety to know that your self and our little Eliza are well, and that you are well rec'd and kindly treated by Mrs. Lewis. Of this I have no doubt but shall be happy to hear it from yourself. Has [Eliza] . . . grown any, and is there any perceptible alteration in her. Mr. Madison writes me that some time will elapse before our furniture will reach Fredericksbg. . . . Have you heard how Peter proceeds in the garden and what is the state of everything [at home]. . . . I was sorry that you had not with you the article you mentioned as necessary for the little monkey. I hope she suffers no inconvenience from it. I have engag'd Lucy of Mr. Jones and shall upon our return home dismiss Priss and her family. I shod. be happy to keep her cod. it be done with propriety but as it cannot be done for reasons that I am persuaded will be satisfactory to you, we had better dismiss her. It is however as you please. I hope you use much exercise. I am satisfied the pain you complain of in your breast arises from this source. Let me instruct you not to neglect it—it will also contribute much to secure you from the disease of this country, the ague and fever. Quarrier [?] has engag'd to begin a carriage for us—he objects to making it perfectly flat or straight before—he says it will sink and be apt to leak, that they might also be out of fashion—be so kind as to inform me in what style you wish it and the color you prefer.

I find it impossible to make arrangements for your reception here during the term of the c[our]t. Mr. Randolph hath not mention'd it and I have no money. I have partly arranged with Mr. [Edward] Carrington that we shall get a house together this fall and bring yourself and his lady down for the court. . . . His lady will be content to live on very little during the court . . . and I have assured him you will be as easily satisfied. Such difficulties as are insurmountable shod. be submitted to with fortitude and patience however painful or afflicting they may be. In future I trust we shall have little occasion to exercise this kind of fortitude for I hope we shall be able to surmount those difficulties which the severities of fortune had impos'd on us in our commencement as to avoid separation for such [a] length of time.[15]

He ended his letter with phrases considered quite appropriate between man and wife in the eighteenth century: "Believe me my dear Eliza, most affectionately yours. Jas. Monroe." Below his signature he added a postscript: "Kiss the little babe for me and take care of yourself and her."

His financial difficulties were further complicated later in the year when his brother Andrew nearly went bankrupt. Monroe was so short of money that he had to sell several slaves to meet his brother's needs.[16] Money was not the only worry harassing the newlyweds during the first year in Virginia. Before leaving New York they had ordered some furniture from a cabinetmaker which, they later learned from Mrs. Monroe's sister, looked "vile." Madison, who obligingly agreed to examine the work (he took Grayson and William Bingham with him for moral support), reported that they could find no specific objection to the workmanship. Since the cabinetmaker assured him that mahogany always looked bad when new, Madison advised Monroe to accept it. It was finally shipped in April 1787, but in June the Monroes were still anxiously awaiting its arrival.[17]

II

During the first six months after his return to Virginia Monroe's time was completely taken up with settling into a new home and launching his career as a lawyer. Not until the summer of 1787 did he find time to tell Jefferson that "Mrs. Monroe hath added a daughter to our society, who tho' noisy, contributes greatly to its amus'ment." [18] A fledgling lawyer embarking on a country practice had to spend much time from home attending the courts in the adjacent counties as well as appearing for the sessions of the superior courts in Richmond. It was not that he had many cases, but it was essential that he prove himself seriously engaged in his profession in order to nullify the reports that he intended to move to New York. Naturally, he resented this incessant round, traveling over miserable roads and sleeping in wretched inns, for he felt with some justification that his congressional career had demonstrated both the steadiness of his character and his ability to apply himself to business.[19] During his first year home he did not hold public office—not through choice, but because he lost the spring election for the House of Delegates in King George in 1786.[20] He blamed his defeat on his inability to leave Congress in order to reassure the voters in person that his marriage did not mean permanent residence in the North.[21] He was more fortunate in the spring of 1787, when he was elected to the House of Delegates from Spotsylvania County through the help of John Taliafero, a relative of Jones' first wife and the most influential man in the county. Madison and other conservative leaders were delighted at this new addition to the forces seeking to check Patrick Henry's paper money party.[22]

Membership in the legislature was gratifying, but it did not entirely alleviate the disappointment he experienced when he was not included in the delegation sent to the Philadelphia Convention in 1787. It is not at all clear why he should have been omitted, but it was certainly unfortunate that he was not present during the session of 1786–1787 when the delegates were named. With some justice he felt that his record as a nationalist leader entitled him to participate in the drafting of a new constitution. Monroe, who was basically kind and good-natured, frequently blamed setbacks to his ambitions on personal hostility. Instead of venting his anger by directly confronting his supposed opponent, he usually withdrew into himself, quietly brooding over the injury. Consequently, those whom he regarded as responsible rarely knew that he had been offended. Fortunately this extreme sensitivity did not make him vindictive. Once an explanation had been made or when he discovered that no slight had been intended, he usually forgot the whole matter. This magnanimity of spirit was surely one of the traits Jefferson had in mind, when, in the same year, he said of Monroe: "Turn his soul wrong side outwards and there is not a speck on it." [23]

On this occasion Monroe, blaming Randolph and Madison, unburdened himself to Jefferson:

The Governor [Randolph] I have reason to believe is *unfriendly to me* and hath shewn (If I am well inform'd) *a disposition to thwart me;* and *Madison,* upon whose friendship I have calculated, whose views I have favored, and with whom I have held the most confidential correspondence since you left the continent, is in strict league *with him* and hath I have reason to believe concurr'd in *arrangements* unfavorable *to me;* a suspicion supported by some strong circumstances, that this is the case, hath given me much uneasiness. However in this I may be disappointed and I wish it may be so.[24]

Since he had previously sensed a certain coolness toward him on Randolph's part, the circumstances surrounding the selection of the Virginia delegation gave him grounds for thinking that he had been deliberately passed over. Originally the legislature had chosen George Washington, George Mason, James Madison, George Wythe, John Blair, Edmund Randolph and Patrick Henry. Henry, who had long opposed any strengthening of the central government, declined in order to be free to oppose the work of the convention—at least this was the interpretation Madison placed on his resignation.[25] When Henry withdrew the Governor and council (with Governor Randolph casting the deciding vote) turned to Richard Henry Lee, who was as hostile to a strong central government as Henry.[26] When Lee in turn rejected the appointment, Randolph and the council chose Dr. James McClurg, a wealthy Richmonder with considerable local influence but lacking Monroe's experience in national politics. Understandably Monroe felt that even if he could not be the first choice, he should have been chosen as a replacement. The slight was unintentional and the parties involved had no idea that he had been offended. Undoubtedly they assumed that Monroe's financial embarrassment would make him prefer to avoid a costly journey to Philadelphia. They did not realize that an appeal to Monroe's sense of public duty would have been sufficient to induce him to leave home on such an important occasion no matter how great the personal sacrifice. There was certainly no coolness on Randolph's part, for he sent Monroe a copy of the Constitution as soon as it was completed.[27] Monroe continued to correspond with Madison, although their letters were not as frequent during the summer when Madison was bound by a pledge of secrecy not to discuss the proceedings while the convention was in session.[28] Outwardly there was no rift in their friendship.

III

In the December 1787 session of the legislature Monroe usually worked closely with the conservative leaders George Nicholas and George Mason in opposition to Patrick Henry. Under the patronage of Nicholas and Mason resolutions were introduced early in the session providing for the repeal of all laws impeding the collection of British debts. The fate of this measure, which Monroe had long promoted, was disappointing. Just before the proposal was brought to a vote Nicholas suddenly shifted his position to join Henry in supporting an amended version which authorized the suspension of the measure until Great Britain had restored the frontier posts. The emendation made the proposition worthless.[29] In view of the loose character of factional alliances, it is not surprising that Monroe was not always in the ranks of the conservatives. Thus, when a bill was submitted requiring all freed slaves to leave the state within twelve months after manumission or be sold at auction, he joined the majority in voting it down, although both Mason and Nicholas had endorsed it.[30]

During the session one topic took primacy over all others—the Constitution drafted in Philadelphia, which, as Monroe observed, was creating a greater disagreement "among people of character" than any issue since the Revolution. His attitude when he arrived in Richmond had been favorable to the proposed government. True, it had many serious defects, but in view of the pressing need for strengthening the Union, there seemed no other course but to accept it.[31] However, as he listened to the discussions in Richmond and read the innumerable essays in the press, he became more and more critical of the Constitution. The tone of the legislature, which had been chosen in the spring of 1787 (long before the Philadelphia convention assembled), was strongly antifederal. Indeed, George Nicholas was the only prominent federalist in the legislature; most of the influential leaders in Richmond that winter —Mason, Henry, Benjamin Harrison and Governor Randolph—were outspokenly hostile. To this list of critics should be added the names of some of Monroe's closest friends—Beverley Randolph, John Dawson, William Grayson and Joseph Jones.[32] Moving in this critical atmosphere, it is not surprising that Monroe's doubts increased; by April, as Madison noted, he had become distinctly "cool" toward the results of the Philadelphia convention.[33]

In the spring of 1788 Monroe was put forward by the antifederalists in King George County as a delegate to the ratifying convention, although he had not publicly announced his opposition. When Washington's influence brought victory to the federalist candidate, he was at once entered in neighboring Spotsylvania County, where the support of John Taliafero again proved all-important. He was easily elected when Major John Willis, the antifederal candidate, willingly stepped down in Monroe's behalf at the request of Taliafero.[34] After the election Monroe drafted a pamphlet explaining his objections to the Constitution, but he never published it, since the printer was slow and inaccurate. Only a few copies were distributed to friends.[35]

Monroe's pamphlet was a curious work, more of a record of the debate he waged with himself over the merits of the Constitution than a direct attack on the document.[36] Indeed, three-fourths of this lengthy essay was devoted to presenting the reasons the Articles of Confederation had proved inadequate. They had failed, in his judgment, not only because Congress lacked essential powers, but they would also remain unworkable as long as each state had one vote. From his point of view the arrangement worked out in Philadelphia was an effective compromise between local and national interests, since there was no possibility of eliminating the state governments. Yet in spite of this broad approval of the structure of the government, he felt that certain specific provisions made the whole unacceptable unless they were modified. In the first place he took strong exception to the Senate, which seemed to preserve one of the most unsatisfactory features of the old government—the principle of state equality. Thus, as in the old Congress, state jealousies would paralyze the government. To correct this defect, he urged apportionment of the Senate according to population and direct election by the people. It also seemed unwise to violate the principle of separation of powers by permitting the Senate to share in executive powers. In common with nearly all the critics of the Constitution, Monroe condemned the grant of power to levy direct taxes as an interference with purely local matters.[37] In spite of experience to the contrary during the Confederation, he insisted that any deficiency in revenue from the tariff could be supplied by requisitions. Monroe, however, was almost alone among the antifederalists in recommending that the federal government be given direct control over the militia as a means of eliminating the need for a standing army. He was also exceptional in that he had no fear of executive power. Most antifederalists, including his uncle, thought the executive much too strong and independent; Monroe on the other hand approved the veto power.[38] He was much closer to John Adams than the antifederalists in his conception of the executive as an arbiter between the sections and interests in the country, but he believed that the President must be popularly elected to carry out his role effectively. In view of his own experience in Congress it is not surprising that he advocated strict limitation on the treaty-making power: a mere two-thirds vote was insufficient unless a quorum was established in the Constitution. He concluded by repeating the general antifederal protest over the omission of a Bill of Rights.

Monroe's opinions placed him in the most moderate circle of antifederalists. He not only presented cogent arguments for a stronger government, he posed far less sweeping objections than those advanced by Richard Henry Lee. Indeed, he saw more good than evil in the document, and raised points easily modified. Consequently, in the ratifying convention he was much closer to George Mason than to Patrick Henry, who was inveterately hostile to a stronger central government. For Monroe the antifederal strategy of demanding amendments prior to ratification was not a useful tactic for defeating the Constitution, but a means of improving it and creating a government more in harmony with the republican ideal.

IV

The ratifying convention which met in Richmond on June 2 was the most distinguished body ever to assemble in Virginia, numbering among its 173 members the outstanding leaders of the past generation.[39] Of the great men of the state only three were absent: Washington, who preferred to exert his influence from a distance; Jefferson, who was absent in France; and Richard Henry Lee, who had been defeated by a federalist candidate. For Monroe, as for many Virginians, the convention offered the last opportunity to observe the elder statesmen of the revolutionary epoch. Such large numbers of spectators appeared in Richmond that the sessions of the convention had to be shifted from the still unfinished capitol to the larger quarters provided by a newly constructed academy on Shockoe Hill. Monroe was especially moved at the appearance of the aged and infirm Edmund Pendleton, whose influence rivaled that of Washington. "Pendleton," Monroe commented, "tho' much impaired in health and in every respect in the decline of life shewed as much zeal to carry [the Constitution] . . . as if he had been a young man." Although Pendleton, then president of the Court of Appeals, was unanimously chosen to preside over the convention, he spoke frequently, since the proceedings were conducted in the committee of the whole. Whenever he stood to address the convention, bracing himself on his crutches, the audience was deeply affected. The post of chairman of the committee of the whole fell to Pendleton's colleague on the Court of Appeals, George Wythe, who took little part in the debate. Slight of figure but brisk in manner, the balding Wythe was widely respected for both his past services and the breadth of his legal knowledge. Much younger than these elder statesmen, but attracting just as much attention, was the handsome and eloquent governor, Edmund Randolph, who at thirty-seven ranked as one of the first lawyers of the state. Attention was drawn to him not just because of his brilliance, but, as Monroe told Jefferson, because he "exhibited a curious spectacle to view." Having refused to sign the Constitution in Philadelphia, he now arose in the convention and announced that he intended to vote for ratification. The loss of such a prominent figure was a serious blow to the antifederalists. With

Pendleton and Randolph as his associates Madison undertook the burden of defending the Constitution with able support from James Innes, Henry (Light Horse Harry) Lee, John Marshall, Francis Corbin and George Nicholas.[40] Compared to this distinguished roster the antifederalists were far less impressive. They had to rely almost entirely on Mason, Henry, William Grayson and Monroe. It is true that Henry was a host in himself, speaking on all but five of the twenty days when the convention was in session. He alone among the speakers always received the undivided attention of a full house, and he could undo in a word, Madison declared, what had taken an hour's work to establish.[41] Day after day Henry lashed out with biting sarcasm as he painted the menace presented by the Constitution to individual liberty and to the sovereignty of the states. Far less violent was George Mason, who presented the moderate antifederalist position. Mason, an impressive figure at sixty-two with snow-white hair and clad in a black silk suit, spoke slowly with a clear voice, making an appeal to reason rather than the passions. Mason and Henry, who had so frequently been in opposing camps during the past decade, were now bound together in an uncomfortable alliance. Mason, in contrast to Henry, was genuinely convinced that the Constitution was acceptable if revised. Consequently, his advocacy of amendments prior to ratification was quite sincere. Henry, on the other hand, merely accepted prior amendment as a strategy useful in preventing the inauguration of a strong government. This diversity of aims was apparent at the opening session, when Mason proposed that the discussion proceed article by article rather than in a general and uncontrolled fashion. Anxious to restrain Henry, who would not be as effective in a close analysis of detailed provisions, the federalists readily agreed to Mason's suggestion. Although the federalists were believed to have a slight majority in the convention, the margin was too close to allow either party to relax. The debates, as all realized, were crucial to the final outcome.

Among so many notable orators Monroe played a lesser role suited to his moderate abilities as a speaker. Yet Monroe, unlike most of the delegates (only twenty-three members spoke), was not a silent observer, but arose to speak on four occasions.[42] His speeches were not the slashing attacks Henry delivered, but were restricted to specific points in which he had taken particular interest. Monroe's first speech (June 10), a reply to the federalist contention that the choice before the convention was that of union or disunion, was a strong plea for prior amendment. In view of the absence of any serious conflicts between the states or danger of foreign invasion, he considered the federalist assertion wildly exaggerated. There was ample time for the nation to "calmly and dispassionately examine the defects of our government and apply such remedies as we shall find necessary." Why must it be assumed that the union would perish if ratification were made conditional upon prior amendments? On the contrary, a reasonable delay to correct the defects would result in a far stronger union. He then singled out those provisions most in need of alteration. First on his list was the elimination of the direct tax. An equally serious objection was the failure to fix an exact quorum for the Senate action on treaties. To ratify the Constitution as it stood was "dangerous," for it would "neither secure our interests nor the rights of our countrymen." "We have," he concluded, "struggled long to bring about this revolution, by which we enjoy our present freedom and security. Why, then, this haste—this wild precipitation?" [43]

Three days later Monroe spoke again on a topic for which Henry had carefully paved the way. Henry was anxious to expose the full details of the Jay–Gardoqui negotiations in order to crystalize the antifederal views of fourteen delegates from Kentucky. Moreover, since Monroe had already raised the point that the Senate could easily be dominated by a handful of states, the full story of the Gardoqui proposals would effectively dramatize this danger. Henry also wished to undo the effect of Madison's reassurances that the West had nothing to fear from the eastern states.[44] After describing the negotiations in some detail, Monroe maintained that the danger to the West would be greater in the new government, since in the absence of a fixed quorum seven states would suffice to close the Mississippi, whereas in the Confederation nine states had been required to ratify treaties. Madison, in his reply, insisted that the rights of the West were far safer under the Constitution, for now treaties would require the participation of both the Senate and the President. Moreover, he considered it absurd that attendance in the Senate would be so uneven that seven states could control proceedings.[45] It is difficult to assess the influence of Monroe's revelations on the final vote, but all except two Kentuckians voted with the antifederalists.[46]

After this digression the convention (now in the twelfth day of its sessions) resumed the examination of the Constitution article by article as provided by the rules. On June 18 Monroe subjected the electoral college to severe criticism, not only as contrary to republican ideals, but as creating an election system rendering the President subservient to state interests. The electoral college held still another shortcoming: it opened the door to the danger of manipulation and bribery by ambitious individuals or foreign powers seeking to control the government. If the President was to protect the interests of the people, he must be directly elected.[47]

On the last day of the convention, in a brief speech Monroe again pleaded for amendments prior to ratification. There was greater danger of disunion "from the adoption of a system reprobated by some, and allowed by all to be defective" than from suspension of ratification until the document had been modified. On this point the federalists had the last word, when Governor Randolph announced that eight states had ratified. The choice before Virginia was now clearly one of "Union or no Union." The vote was then taken bringing victory to the federalists by a margin of 89 to 79. One concession was granted the antifederalists. The convention approved twenty amendments and a Bill of Rights to be submitted to Congress for addition to the Constitution. As a member of the committee drafting the amendments Monroe undoubtedly was responsible for two directly related to objections he had raised during the debates. The first of these exempted states from direct taxes if they raised quotas assigned them; the second declared that no commercial treaty could be made without the consent of two-thirds of the whole number of the Senate and that no treaty yielding territorial or navigational rights could be ratified without the approval of three-fourths of the whole number of both houses.[48]

V

The convention over, Monroe had to stay in Richmond to attend the special session of the legislature called to reconsider the district court bill adopted at the previous session, but which the justices of the Virginia higher courts had refused to implement on the grounds that it was unconstitutional. Impatient to be home for the harvest, the delegates (most of whom had been members of the ratifying convention), simply suspended the bill until the next session. Not until he returned to Fredericksburg did he find time to send Jefferson his comments on the convention. It struck Monroe as significant that at the end of the convention there had been no trace of "depression" among the antifederalists. He ascribed this calm reaction to the temperate conduct of both parties, to the restraint shown by the victors to their adversaries, and to the all-important fact that both parties had been motivated by principles and not by trivial or transitory interests. There was no doubt, he told Jefferson, that Washington's influence had been the decisive factor in ratification. Although he had implicit confidence in Washington's personal integrity, he expressed misgivings (particularly interesting in view of charges later made in the 1790s) about the anticipated re-entry of the former general into public life. "More is to be apprehended," he confided to Jefferson, "if he takes part in public councils again, as he advances in age, from the designs of those around him than from any disposition of his own." [49]

In the autumn Madison and Monroe renewed their regular exchange of letters, but avoided all reference to their disagreement over the Constitution. For the moment personal interests took precedence over public concerns. It was with obvious pleasure that Monroe was able to inform Madison in October of the realization of a long-cherished dream: the purchase of an estate in Albemarle. He had acquired 800 acres of land (the present site of the University of Virginia) and a house in Charlottesville from George Nicholas, a purchase made possible by the willingness of Nicholas, who was moving west, to accept Kentucky lands in lieu of the price of £2500. Monroe had little money, but an ample quantity of land.[50]

The demands of his law practice made Monroe late for the opening of the 1788–1789 legislative session.[51] In Richmond he found a majority of the delegates, all of whom had been elected in the spring before the ratifying convention, decidedly antifederal.[52] Although Edward Carrington may have exaggerated in reporting that the legislators were meeting in a "phrenzy" of hostility toward the Constitution, neither he nor other worried federalists understood the nature of this animosity.[53] It is true the delegates were indignant over Edmund Randolph's failure to inform the ratifying convention of a letter from Governor George Clinton of New York calling on Virginia to join New York in refusing to ratify without previous amendment. Many believed that the suppression of this letter (Randolph held it back on the technicality that it was addressed to him as governor and not as a convention delegate) had kept Virginia in the federalist ranks. Henry at once introduced measures, requesting Congress to call a second convention, which were approved by a large majority in the House of Delegates. Monroe, faithful to the opinions expressed in the convention, voted for these resolutions.[54] What the federalists failed to grasp (and hence their excessive alarm) was that the majority of the antifederalists wanted the Constitution amended but not destroyed. It was for this reason that Richard Henry

Lee, for example, reluctantly emerged from retirement to enter the Senate of the United States.[55] Had the antifederalists—as some suspected —sought to destroy the government, the means were readily at hand. When the session began Henry had a two-to-one majority on his side, yet he made no effort to prevent the inauguration of the new government by blocking bills to choose electors or to hold elections for representatives. Both these measures went through the legislature without difficulty.[56]

Henry and the antifederalists were prepared to let the federal government begin operations unimpeded, but they were determined that the first senators would be antifederalists, and in particular that Madison should not be chosen. Consequently William Grayson and Richard Henry Lee, two notable opponents of the Constitution, were sent to the Senate. The dismay of the federalists over this choice was somewhat diminished by reports that the Senators-elect were willing to give the new government a fair try.[57] Not content with excluding Madison from the Senate, Henry sought to keep him out of the House of Representatives by so arranging his district that it would contain an antifederal majority.[58] In shaping Madison's district Henry took pains to see that it included Monroe's home county. Once the bill passed, rumors began to circulate that Monroe would run against Madison. Edward Carrington, a friend of both men, was exasperated and spoke harshly to Madison of Monroe's defection: "Let me assure you that you can upon no occasion of public nature expect favors from this Gentleman." [59] In spite of the anticipation that the antifederalists would attempt something more than requesting Congress to summon a second convention, the legislature settled down to state concerns, enacting a new judiciary bill which finally satisfied the presiding judges.[60] At the end of the session the federalists could complain of nothing more odious than a measure to prevent state officials from holding federal posts, which federalist George Nicholas promptly concluded was intended to "destroy" the new government by doubling the cost of operation. Joseph Jones, an antifederalist, was equally critical of the measure on the same grounds—that it would increase the cost of government.[61] Clearly it had no partisan aspects.

Before the session ended, the rumor Carrington had heard was confirmed—Monroe was running against Madison for Congress.[62] He had agreed reluctantly after considerable pressure from the antifederalists.[63] As he explained to Jefferson, "Those to whom my conduct in public life had been acceptable, press'd me to come forward in this government on its commencement; and that I might not loose [*sic*] an opportunity of contributing my feeble efforts in forwarding an amendment of its defects, nor shrink from the station those who confided in me would wish to place me, I yielded." [64] His friends never doubted for a moment the integrity of Monroe's motives; there was not the slightest suggestion that he was influenced by private animosities. Throughout his career Monroe cherished an intense, self-sacrificing acceptance of the obligations of public service, and no argument was so effective in enlisting his aid as that stressing the needs of the public. In 1788 Monroe clearly felt that refusal to run against Madison would seem to be a betrayal of a public trust in order to gratify private friendship. He believed it his duty to continue the struggle for amendments. Between Madison and Monroe there was no breach: Madison understood the reasons for his friend's conduct and did not interpret Monroe's action as a personal affront.[65]

Madison's friends, fearing that he might lose his election to a rival powerfully backed by the Cabell family in Amherst and by French Strother in Culpeper, considered running him in another district. This plan was rejected lest it arouse a public outcry that he was violating the state law requiring congressmen to reside in their districts, even though the validity of this act was questioned.[66] They finally persuaded Madison, who had never been obliged to campaign in the past, to leave New York in order to canvass his district. Monroe was presented to the voters as the candidate whose constant support of amendments entitled him to the confidence of the people. The point was well put by French Strother:

> I hope you will consider the necessity of uniting in favor of a Gentleman who has been uniformly in favor of Amendments. I mean James Monroe Esq. a man who possesses great abilities integrity and a most amiable Character who has been many years a member of Congress of the House of Delegates and of the Privy Council and whom I have prevailed on to offer in our District: Considering him as being able to render his Country Great Services on this important occasion.[67]

Since amending the Constitution was the central issue in the campaign, much would depend on Madison's attitude toward revision. Without informing Monroe, his backers spread reports that Madison was hostile to the amendments proposed in the ratifying convention. Madison countered with a public statement expressing his conviction that the time had now arrived to consider amendments which would satisfy the critics of the Constitution and provide additional safeguards for liberty.[68]

Both candidates made considerable efforts to capture the important Baptist vote. When the Baptists were reminded that Madison had at one time voted against the sale of the glebe lands of the Episcopal Church, Madison's friends were ready with the reply that Monroe had himself voted the same way on another occasion.[69] In the final weeks before the election the candidates toured together, appearing at courthouses and churches, each speaking in turn.[70] The victory went to Madison by the substantial margin of 330 votes, with Monroe carrying only Spotsylvania. The Baptists, who esteemed Madison because of his long advocacy of religious liberty, were undoubtedly responsible for his success. Monroe, without any real wish to supplant his friend, expressed relief over the outcome.[71] The election over, the two friends resumed their correspondence, writing freely about politics and rendering friendly services for each other.[72]

In the spring, the busiest season in the life of a country lawyer, Monroe took his wife and daughter with him on his rounds. Mrs. Monroe now had her first opportunity to see the Albemarle countryside, which she found much to her liking.[73] When he returned to Fredericksburg in late April, Monroe, having learned that Jefferson had applied for leave from his post in France, decided to move to his new farm near Charlottesville somewhat earlier than he had originally planned. The additional expenses entailed by this move as well as the intense heat compelled him to abandon a vacation trip to New York arranged to permit his wife to visit her father.[74] Mrs. Monroe still missed her family, who neglected to write her regularly, leaving her dependent on Madison and other friends in New York for news.[75] Although Monroe did settle in Albemarle late in August, he had already started farming operations by sending servants, horses and other equipment to his farm in March.[76] The farming activities which he began so hopefully in 1788 proved most unrewarding. During the next two years he gradually realized that his original estimate of the productivity of the Albemarle property had been erroneous.[77] At the end of the third season, after heavy expenditure on improvements, he was bitterly disappointed in the yield of his land. He summarized the situation to Madison in 1792:

At best but little can be said in its [the estate's] favor, but less industry had been used to improve its natural deformities or make it yield what it is really capable of, than might have been. Time and patience have been immemorially prescribed, as the only source or relief in difficult cases. Whether the practice of these virtues will produce in the present in-

stance the desired effect, is questionable. Admit it might, it would notwith-
standing be infinitely more agreeable independent of the profit, to apply the
same labour to a more grateful soil.[78]

The cost of the improvements obliged Monroe to withdraw from a
joint investment with Madison in Genesee Valley lands. Madison, assuming the whole obligation, repaid Monroe his principal plus a generous return on the estimated profits.[79] To supplement his income
Monroe redoubled his efforts to extend his rapidly growing law practice.
The year he moved to Albemarle he was one of four lawyers chosen
by John Taylor of Caroline to take over pending cases on Taylor's
retirement from the law in favor of farming. During his first two years
in Albemarle Monroe did not feel that his private commitments permitted the luxury of holding public office: he had not offered himself as
a delegate from Spotsylvania in 1789, since he was leaving the county;
in 1790 when the citizens of Albemarle asked him to run for the House
of Delegates, he declined.[80]

Just a few days before Christmas 1789 there was a most welcome arrival in Albemarle—Thomas Jefferson returned to Monticello. Jefferson, pleased that one of his closest friends had responded to his plea to
reside in Albemarle, delightedly reported to Short that the neighborhood was much improved now that Monroe was in the county.[81] During
the first month after his return Jefferson was so involved with his private
affairs and in preparing for the wedding of his daughter Martha that
there was no opportunity for Mrs. Monroe to become closely acquainted
with the Jefferson family.[82] Not until 1791 did his younger daughter
come to know Mrs. Monroe at all well, when she stayed at Monticello
while her husband was in Williamsburg. After the visit, thirteen-year-
old Maria Jefferson pronounced Mrs. Monroe to be a "charming
woman." [83] Jefferson, however, did find some time for political affairs.
Shortly after his return he welcomed Madison, who had delayed setting
out for Congress to visit his long-absent friend, hoping to persuade
Jefferson to accept Washington's offer of the Secretaryship of State.
During Madison's visit conferences took place with Monroe, the Nicholases, John Breckinridge and others. Jefferson's friends jointly drafted
a welcoming address to the returning Minister in which they delicately
exerted pressure on him to remain in public office. Monroe, who helped
prepare the address, transmitted it to Jefferson nearly a month before it
was formally presented in order to give his friend ample time to frame
a reply.[84]

VI

When Jefferson returned to America he found Monroe changed in many ways. In place of the shy and inexperienced youth he now saw a married man of thirty-one, whose ability had established him as a major political figure in the state. The promise Jefferson had seen in his protégé a decade earlier had been fully realized. Yet the change was more in externals than an inward one, for Monroe had retained all those qualities of warmth, sincerity and kindness which had led Jefferson to value his friendship. These attributes were now enriched by a mature judgment based on an extensive knowledge of public affairs. Monroe was not merely esteemed as an agreeable member of Jefferson's social circle but as a colleague whose views merited serious consideration. Thus the association between them underwent a change—Monroe was no longer a protégé but a coworker dedicated to the same goals as his friend. Jefferson's return inevitably altered the relationship between Monroe and Madison. Their friendship (not formed until after Jefferson's departure for France) had flourished quite independently of the friendship each had had with Jefferson in the past. Under such circumstances it would not be unusual for the two younger men to become rivals for the attention of the older and more famous of the trio. Although some writers have asserted this to be the case, there is no indication that Monroe and Madison vied with one another for primacy in Jefferson's friendship. Each had a profound admiration, a deep affection and sincere respect for Jefferson, and both Monroe and Madison found in his company a friendship and an understanding they experienced with no one else. Undoubtedly the bond which each had with Jefferson was stronger than the tie which bound the two younger men together.

Although Jefferson made no distinction between his two friends, confiding in them and seeking their advice, there is no doubt that the bond with Madison was much closer than with Monroe—or, to put it more accurately, it was a friendship based upon more complex elements. Not only did Madison share Jefferson's interest in politics, he was also a participant in the theoretical speculation about government, society, the nature of man and all those elevated themes to which Jefferson devoted so much thought. Madison's original and logical mind readily grasped these concepts in a way completely alien to Monroe, who had no talent for abstract thinking. Monroe was essentially rooted in the pragmatic and was more sensitive to political movements than either of his friends. In all the letters exchanged between Jefferson and Monroe over four decades there is not one which can be said to deal exclusively or even at any length with philosophical or scientific pursuits. On the contrary, their letters deal with the world of practical action, whether it be in Congress, in international affairs or in the Cabinet. Their correspondence is that of two close friends whose common point of interest was political and not theoretical. This contrasts markedly with the letters Jefferson and Madison exchanged, in which an unending stream of philosophical discussion merges with the world of practical politics. Although each of these three men differed from one another in temperament and habit of thought, they worked together with a degree of understanding and harmony without parallel in American history. There was no need for lengthy argument or explanation among them; for one to suggest a point of view or a plan of approach was enough for the others to act. It was a unique collaboration, which exerted a decisive influence on American political developments in the 1790s.

CHAPTER 6

SENATOR AND
PARTY LEADER
1790-1794

I N THE SPRING of 1790 Monroe was unaware that he had nar-
rowly missed election to the United States Senate, when the Governor and Council, voting on an interim successor for the recently
deceased William Grayson, had selected Jefferson's one-time close
friend John Walker over Monroe in a decision that hinged on one vote.[1]
This choice was not pleasing to Jefferson, and in June 1790, when Monroe made a business trip to Richmond, several state leaders urged him
to become a candidate in the fall.[2] In spite of a strong interest in returning to active political life Monroe hesitated, since it seemed essential to put his finances on a more secure footing before resuming his
career. Reluctantly—"really against his will," according to Jefferson—
he consented to allow his name to be brought forward.[3] His backing
came from moderate elements who wished to prevent the election of
either obdurate antifederalists, such as the first two senators, or of an
extreme federalist. In his decision one personal factor played an important role: residence in Philadelphia, the temporary capital, would
enable Mrs. Monroe to visit her family for the first time since her marriage.[4] In addition to Jefferson's support Monroe enjoyed the active
backing of George Mason of Gunston Hall, who wrote to his friend
Zachariah Johnson, a member of the House of Delegates, urging that
Monroe, a "man of Integrity, Abilities, and firmly attached to his
Country's Interest," be elected.[5] Even with these influential supporters
Monroe felt uncertain of victory. Not only did federalists like Henry
Lee and John Marshall (whose close friendship with Monroe seems

81

to have cooled after the ratifying convention of 1788) oppose him, but the titan of the antifederalists, Patrick Henry, refused to endorse his candidacy. These misgivings proved groundless, for he easily defeated the federalist candidate.[6]

During the month after his election Monroe devoted himself to clearing up as many of his pending law cases as possible. His clients were notified that he would continue his practice when Congress was not in session. Late in November he started out for Philadelphia with his wife and daughter, arriving in time for the opening of the session. Mrs. Monroe lingered in the city just long enough to have four-year-old Eliza inoculated for smallpox; then, as soon as the child had recovered from the mild case she had contracted, mother and daughter went on to New York for a long visit with the Kortright family.[7] Monroe was greeted eagerly in Philadelphia by Jefferson and Madison, who invited him to lodge with them at the boardinghouse kept by Eliza Trist's mother.[8]

In December 1790, when Monroe (now thirty-two) took his seat in the Senate, the upper house could aptly be described as a graveyard of talents. Although its twenty-four members included some of the most distinguished figures of the revolutionary epoch—Charles Carroll of Carrollton, Rufus King of New York, Ralph Izard and Pierce Butler of South Carolina and Oliver Ellsworth of Connecticut—it deliberated in relative obscurity. Like the Confederation Congress the Senate held its sessions behind closed doors under a self-imposed rule of secrecy. The public knew little of what went on other than the meager information garnered from the bare record of the journal. Since the members had no opportunity to dazzle the people with their oratory, attention was concentrated on the House of Representatives, where full publicity was given to proceedings. The meetings of the Senate were held in Congress Hall at Sixth and Chestnut streets in a chamber on the south end of the second floor. Here Vice-President John Adams presided at a plain mahogany table with the chairs of the Senators arranged in a semicircle before him. The proceedings were dignified but surprisingly informal with few set speeches. On cold days the Senators frequently left their seats to cluster about the fireplace.[9] It was in this room that Monroe listened to the President's annual message. In a short address Washington reported favorably on the state of public finances and credit, and briefly announced that disturbances on the frontier had made it necessary for him to summon the militia. He also warned the legislators that the unstable situation in Europe following the French Revolution might require special measures to protect American commerce. Apart from calling attention to the need for measures to regulate the militia, the mint and the post office he made no legislative recommendations.[10]

In 1790 most of the business of the Senate was transacted in the committee of the whole with select committees appointed to make reports on specific matters. As yet there were no standing committees. Under these circumstances the prestige and power of a Senator depended very much on his willingness to work and his familiarity with the measures under consideration. Unlike many Senators who rarely served on committees, Monroe's experience and diligence brought him rapidly to the fore. During his first session he and ten other members held nearly all the important committee assignments. He served regularly with Rufus King, Philip Schuyler, Oliver Ellsworth and Caleb Strong, then the outstanding leaders in the Senate. As a newcomer Monroe held only one chairmanship, of a committee appointed to consider a request by the Virginia legislature that Congress approve settlements for bounty and pension claims of Virginians who had served in the Continental line. His committee recommended that Virginia's request be denied on the grounds that existing federal laws were adequate to provide for the settlement of all claims. The committee further pointed out that the claimant and not the state should appeal to Congress in the event a claim was not approved. By appealing on behalf of individuals, states were in effect prejudging the validity of claims pending against the United States.[11]

For most of the session, a tranquil one free from the sharp conflict raging in the House, Monroe was the sole Senator from Virginia. His colleague, Richard Henry Lee, was in poor health and unable to come to Philadelphia until February.[12] The bill to charter the Bank of the United States, which aroused such notable opposition in the lower house, encountered no serious obstacle in the Senate. Although Monroe and five Southern Senators were the only members to vote against the measure, it cannot be said that they constituted a sectional bloc since an equal number of Southern Senators voted on the other side. The Senate did not yet exhibit the factional alignments apparent in the lower house.[13] However, strong feelings were aroused late in February 1791, when Monroe introduced a bill (in accordance with resolves of the Virginia legislature) to open the doors of the Senate to the public. This proposal was decisively rejected by a vote of seventeen to nine. In subsequent sessions, as Monroe persisted, the majority opposed gradually dwindled, but it was not until February 1794 that the Senate agreed to open its doors.[14] Those wishing to exclude the public maintained that secrecy was the sole means of insuring freedom and independence of discussion in the Senate; once the public was admitted the Senators, seeking popularity in rhetorical displays, would no longer scrutinize public measures calmly and judiciously. In a carefully drafted speech—the only one Monroe delivered in the Senate to be preserved— he took the position that the Senate, as a representative body in a republican government, should be subject at all times to public scrutiny. How could the people protect their liberties unless they were fully aware of the operations of the government? Experience, he continued, had shown that bodies with delegated powers, but operating secretly, tended to extend their powers. Only by exposing "the trustees of the publick . . . confidence to the publick view" could the people prevent the adoption of measures "dangerous to the publick liberty." With an impassioned flourish he concluded:

Let the jealous, the prying eye of their constituents uphold their proceedings, mark their conduct, and the tone of the body will be changed. Many a person whose heart was devoted and whose mind pursued with unceasing ardor the establishment of arbitrary power; whilst he supposed his movements were unseen . . . wod. change his style and from motives of private interest become the fervent patron of the publick liberty. I could wish for the honor of humanity that good actions might always proceed from good motives but to the public 'tis altogether immaterial—with them the end only is important and wise is that political arrangement that so operates on the principles of human action, as to make men, bad men, faithful publick servants.[15]

These arguments echoed both his own observation of the danger of secrecy during the Jay–Gardoqui negotiations and the mounting uneasiness he shared with Jefferson and Madison that Hamilton was seeking (in Joseph Jones' words) "to establish the government on the principles of consolidation." [16] To expose these designs the operations of government must be made public.

II

As soon as Congress adjourned in March Monroe and his family returned to Virginia. The demands of his law practice and his farm did not permit him the indulgence of a vacation such as Madison and

Jefferson's joint spring tour of New York state. His homecoming was not a happy one. An exasperating but minor inconvenience was the necessity of leaving his wife and daughter in Fredericksburg, since the house under construction on his Albemarle land was not ready for occupancy. Much more distressing to Monroe was the discovery that his younger brother Joseph had married the daughter of James Kerr of Charlottesville without consulting him. Although Kerr was a social acquaintance of the Monroes, the Kerr family standing in the community was not such as to make the match desirable. Monroe was particularly annoyed that Kerr, whom he had aided in the past, should have concealed the marriage plans from him. His anger was all the greater since the marriage made it unlikely that his brother (still a minor) would make a name for himself. Although Monroe had sent his younger brother to the University of Edinburgh, Joseph had wasted his time, preferring dissipation to study. An attempt to remedy Joseph's educational shortcomings on his return to Virginia in 1789 by arranging a program of law studies had failed. Monroe was particularly disappointed, for he had hoped that his brother might be able to provide a secure haven for his own family in case of need. Jefferson, who appreciated his friend's distress, wrote sympathetically but urged him to moderate his anger. The thing was done, and the only question to consider was "what is to be done to make the best of it in respect to his and your happiness." He reminded Monroe that his brother's behavior indicated no other "vice" than that "of following too hastily the movements of a warm heart." Not one to cherish a grudge, Monroe was soon reconciled with his brother, whose continued improvidence remained a lasting source of concern.[17]

While Monroe looked after his private affairs, Madison and Jefferson were progressing slowly on their northward tour in the summer of 1791. Although it is incorrect to see this journey as the starting point of political parties, there can be no doubt that the observations of public opinion and the meetings with prominent New Yorkers constituted an important element in the development of parties. At this time the opposition to the administration was still confined to questioning the tendencies of the program embodied in Hamilton's fiscal system. From the start of the federal government the measures proposed by the Secretary of the Treasury had been regarded in Virginia with disapproval, but not until the passage of the bill assuming state debts in 1790 was this dissatisfaction openly expressed. Monroe was indeed rather surprised by the intensity of the reaction to this measure:

he knew it was unpopular, but he expected that the arrangement to locate the capital on the Potomac would mitigate the antagonism.[18] Virginia's hostility was made explicit when the legislature late in 1790 overwhelmingly approved Henry's resolutions, condemning assumption as tending to create a "monied interest," which would prostrate agriculture, and as an unconstitutional exercise of powers not granted to the federal government.[19] In these resolves the agrarian and states' rights principles that governed Virginia's thinking for the next half-century received their first official statement.

The criticism of the fiscal system mounted when, after the chartering of the Bank of the United States early in 1791, a wave of speculation in public securities developed. The Hamiltonian program, as Henry firmly told Monroe, was a "consistent part of a system which I have ever dreaded—subserviency of Southern to N——n Interests." [20] This had also been the first reaction of Jefferson, Madison and Monroe, but by the summer of 1791 they no longer interpreted Hamilton's financial policies in narrow sectional terms; they now saw these measures masking a movement which was fundamentally antirepublican and promonarchical in aim. The furor aroused in the spring of 1791 over the publication of Paine's *Rights of Man* prefaced by Jefferson's commendatory letter was taken as further proof of the correctness of their conclusions. The essays of "Publicola," attacking Paine and praising Burke, written by John Quincy Adams but erroneously ascribed to his father, seemed to offer additional confirmation that high administration officials held antirepublican views.[21] The three Virginians, who had ample time to discuss these issues during the winter in Philadelphia, were not only in full agreement about the trends of the times but were also equally convinced of the need to alert the people to the dangers facing them. In midsummer Monroe summed up their conclusions in a letter to Jefferson:

Upon political subjects we perfectly agree, and particularly in the reprobation of all measures that may be calculated to elevate the government above the people, or place it in any respect without its natural boundary. To keep it there nothing is necessary but virtue in a part only (for in the whole it cannot be expected) of the high publick servants, and a true development of the principles of those acts wh. have a contrary tendency. The bulk of the people are for democracy, and if they are well informed the risk of such enterprizes will infallibly follow. I shall however see you in Sep[tembe]r at wh. time we will confer more fully on these subjects.[22]

The growing perturbation of Monroe and his friends was rooted in their sensitivity to the impact the French Revolution was having upon American political thinking. The affirmative response given to Burke's condemnation of the Revolution strongly suggested the existence of a monarchical element in America and raised the threat of an antirepublican movement. Hence those most dedicated to the ideal of a republican government were deeply suspicious of the slightest moves of men known to be less than enthusiastic in their approval of the French Revolution. Concern over this development induced Monroe to publish three essays over the signature "Aratus" in Freneau's *National Gazette* shortly after Congress assembled in 1791.[23] In these essays he warned Americans against the danger of joining in the general panic sweeping Europe on the heels of the revolution in France. The monarchs in whose realms oppression still flourished, and where men were deprived of their natural rights, had every reason to be alarmed, but why should a revolution confined to France and designed to replace tyranny with liberty in that nation alone arouse such dismay among certain circles in this country? Were not the revolutions in France and America founded on the same principles? Indeed, in America, where the "tyranny was in embryo only and at a distance, we considered ourselves authorized to apply timely force to prevent its establishment"; whereas in France the oppression was at its height and bore directly on the people. "In both instances," Monroe asserted, "the power which belonged to the body of the people ... was resumed. It now rests where it should be.... Whoever owns the principles of one revolution must cherish those of the other; and the person who draws a distinction between them is either blinded by prejudice, or boldly denies what at the bar of reason he cannot refute." Monroe did not elaborate upon the character of those writers hostile to France, merely declaring that in his opinion they were monarchists whose goal was the destruction of liberty. Aratus left no doubt of his views on the responsibility of Americans toward the revolution in France:

Authors of a great revolution, which has operated like a first cause upon the proudest and most enlightened nations of the earth, they owe it to Him who gave them comfort in the day of their distress—they owe it to themselves and to the cause of humanity, to cherish the principle upon which they acted. And deservedly degraded would they be in the common estimation of the world, if after having roused their fellow men in other countries ... whilst the conflict was at the height and the prospect of a brilliant achievement

within their reach, they should by a neglect of their duty, as an abandonment of their principles, be the first to yield the ground which had been
with such difficulty acquired.[24]

These essays are most significant, because they reveal that Monroe
and his associates at this very early date were seeing American politics
in terms of the issue which was to be the center of political conflict
during the next decade—the charge that the enemies of France at home
(as well as abroad) were monarchists determined to uproot republican
institutions. "As a friend of humanity," Aratus told his readers, "I rejoice in the French revolution, but as a citizen of America, the gratification is greatly increased. . . ." Let Americans remember that the two
revolutions were intimately linked and dependent upon each other;
failure in France would endanger liberty in America.[25] These essays
also mark a significant reinterpretation of the American Revolution
in the light of the upheaval in France, a point of view which gave
powerful impetus to the Jeffersonian movement.

The Aratus series, which constituted Monroe's debut as a polemicist,
did not arouse the furor which had raged over Publicola, nor were they
intended to do so. Aratus was not replying directly to any particular
critic of France, but rather engaged in pointing out the dangerous
implications of the current condemnations of the revolutionary developments in France. Aratus was characteristic of Monroe's political
style: never a sprightly writer, he adhered to the prevalent *Spectator*
manner with arguments stated forthrightly and succinctly. As a political essayist he had one virtue: he rarely fell into the habit of turgid
legalistic argumentation, a fault marring the essays of some of the ablest
polemicists of the day, including those of Hamilton and Madison. This
ability to present a clear and factual case was prized by Jefferson and
Madison, who made frequent use of his skill.

III

Monroe and his wife reached Philadelphia in October 1791 several
days after the new session had commenced and settled into lodgings
Jefferson had engaged for them.[26] Most of the members of the Senate
were familiar faces from the last session, but among the newcomers
was Aaron Burr, an acquaintance since 1779, who had been chosen
to succeed Philip Schuyler of New York. Burr's position was then rather
equivocal, since he avoided committing himself to either faction. Not
until the following session did he ally himself with the "republican"

element. In the Senate Monroe's role was similar to that of Madison in the House: organizer and leader of the "republican" faction. The session of 1791–1792 was prolonged for seven months as the result of a deadlock between the two houses over a bill apportioning representation to conform with the census of 1790. The New England senators, aided by those from the small states, reworked the House bill to allow New England greater representation than could be strictly justified on the basis of population. Virginia, on the other hand, lost two representatives to whom she was entitled according to the census returns. Washington's veto of the measure was praised by Monroe as an "act of decision, firmness and independence" that presented a "ray of hope to the desponding mind of the republican party ... inspiring within them a confidence that the government contains within itself a resource capable of resisting every encroachment of the public right." [27]

The conflict over apportionment had been largely sectional and did not impinge directly upon the conviction of the republican element that an effort was being made to subvert the government. However, the nomination of Gouverneur Morris as Minister to France aroused all of Monroe's apprehensions on this score. Declaring his opposition on the ground that both Morris' mercantile associations and his well-known monarchical views made him unsuited for the post, Monroe further recalled to the memory of the senators (many of whom had been members of the old Congress) that Morris' reputation for indiscretion had at one time prevented his election to the Treasury Board. The fight against Morris was supported by a number of senators usually favorable to the administration (like Roger Sherman of Connecticut) who objected to Morris because they considered him a profane and immoral character.[28] The issue was further complicated by the fact that Morris' appointment was linked with the proposed establishment of permanent diplomatic missions at The Hague and London. With the aid of a handful of senators opposed to the establishment of permanent missions, Monroe delayed Morris' confirmation by putting through a resolution calling for additional information about the need for permanent diplomatic establishments. A Senate committee (Monroe was not a member) conferred with Jefferson, who presented cogent arguments for the three projected missions. The Secretary of State had no affection for Morris, but he thought the missions so essential that he refrained from voicing any doubts about the pending nomination.[29] Moreover, only by accepting Morris could he insure the approval of his protégé, William Short, as Minister to The Hague. On January 12 Morris was finally confirmed by a vote of sixteen to eleven, with Monroe in the opposition. This appointment was followed four days later by the confirmation of Short. The widespread suspicion that Morris held views hostile to republican institutions originated in part from remarks, made during the constitutional convention, which George Mason and others clearly recalled.[30] Washington deemed the objections raised in the Senate sufficiently significant to tell Morris bluntly to be more discreet.[31]

Monroe's effectiveness in organizing the forces opposed to Morris was fully appreciated by the administration. Later in the session, when Washington was about to nominate General Anthony Wayne to replace Arthur St. Clair (who had been catastrophically defeated by the Indians in Ohio) he consulted Monroe in advance. Although Wayne had many friends among administration supporters in Congress, it was anticipated that some of these would receive the nomination coolly, since Wayne had just been deprived of his seat in the House of Representatives on charges of fraud arising from his election in Georgia. In view of these circumstances opposition by the "republican interest" would lead to his rejection and further embarrass the administration. At the President's request Jefferson asked Monroe whether he would be willing to approve Wayne's nomination. Monroe replied that he did not like the choice, but he would not raise any objections since there seemed to be no other suitable candidate. As soon as he received Monroe's response Washington submitted Wayne's name; he was promptly confirmed.[32]

Monroe's complaisance in accepting Wayne did not extend to other military arrangements sought by the President. Although Monroe throughout the Confederation era had favored the creation of a permanent military establishment as the only practicable means of defending the frontier, he now made a determined effort to block administration plans to enlarge the Army for the protection of the West. In February Monroe, whose interest in the West and in military concerns was well known, was named to a select committee under the chairmanship of Caleb Strong of Massachusetts to report on an administration-sponsored House bill for frontier defense. Within the week the committee was discharged and an entirely new one appointed, apparently because a majority of its members—Strong, Monroe and Stephen Bradley of Vermont (who later became a Republican)—opposed the administration bill. The new committee (Burr was chairman) produced a report in accordance with administration wishes. When the measure came before the Senate, Monroe, perhaps recalling the strategy used against him on a similar occasion in the old Congress, attempted to weaken the bill by amendments to restrict the length of service and reduce the number of men. His efforts were unavailing, and the bill passed by a small majority.[33] This reversal of his former stand was not the result of any change in his views on the proper organization of frontier defense, but sprang from a reluctance to entrust a larger military force to a government he distrusted.

IV

In mid-May, when the session finally ended, the Monroes—accompanied by Madison—set out for Virginia.[34] Mrs. Monroe, having tired of city life, was anticipating her return to the tranquility of the country with greater pleasure than in former years.[35] Monroe, who always looked forward so eagerly to the resumption of his farm activities, was much disappointed at the condition of his plantation. His first inspection reinforced his conviction that the property was unfruitful. Unless he could find more time to supervise its improvement, it seemed wiser to relocate on more productive land. He may have been unduly pessimistic in attributing the "miserable" condition of the farm to neglect, for the spring of 1792 had been excessively dry and all crops had been injured.[36] In spite of his concern over his plantation, Monroe could not linger in Albemarle: he had to leave immediately for Richmond to try cases before the Court of Appeals. After the prolonged congressional session it was apparent that in the future he must limit his practice to the county courts, lest his long absences damage the interest of his clients. In Richmond he replaced his carriage, which had proved unsatisfactory for long journeys, with a lightweight phaeton. To provide a conveyance for his family in Philadelphia he asked Jefferson to supervise the construction of a post chariot similar to the one used by Jefferson in town.[37]

During his sojourn in Richmond, Monroe expected to attend a meeting of the committee on the revision of the laws, to which he had been appointed the year before by his friend Governor Beverley Randolph when Edmund Pendleton had resigned.[38] However, when several members who preferred to meet in Williamsburg failed to appear, it was necessary to adjourn to the latter city. To avoid a long separation from his family, Monroe returned to Albemarle for his wife and daughter. Eliza had been ill but had recovered sufficiently to accompany her parents. Not until the middle of August was Monroe able to leave the sultry Williamsburg climate for the cooler air of Albemarle County. The Committee on Revision was the fourth such body to be set up since 1776. The earlier committees had had limited success, in part because the first committee (under the chairmanship of Jefferson) had attempted a thorough reform of the legal system, an undertaking not contemplated by the legislature. In 1792 the committee members included St. George Tucker, Henry Tazewell (both Monroe's close friends), Arthur Lee, Joseph Prentis and William Nelson, Jr. Operating on a more limited scale than its predecessors and assisted by a compilation prepared by the judges of the High Court of Chancery, the Committee on Revision soon drafted a compilation of all laws then in effect, which the legislature subsequently approved.[39]

Monroe was still away from home when he heard the results of the gubernatorial election in New York, where the incumbent Governor Clinton had been victorious over John Jay only because the election board (which Clinton controlled) threw out the votes of one county on a dubious technicality. The Virginia leaders, accustomed to more genteel political behavior, were dismayed at the undisguised ambition of Clinton and embarrassed that they had agreed to support him for Vice-President in the approaching election. Jefferson, believing that Jay had a real majority, felt that Clinton would have behaved more honorably if he had permitted the validation of the rejected votes. At the very least, he wrote Monroe, Clinton should have sought a fair majority in a new election.[40] Monroe had only harsh words for Clinton's conduct: "Certain it is with respect to this gentn., that altho' as a center of Union to the republican party in that State it may be necessary to support him yet there are traits in his character and particularly that of extreme parsimony which are highly exceptionable. No one wd. point to him as a model for imitation. . . ." Yet, admitting his conduct on this occasion to be "vicious," Monroe felt the danger was minimized by the possibility of anticipating what Clinton would do in any given situation, and guarding against it.[41] The Virginians clearly understood that the alliance with Clinton was not based upon a common ground of concern for the welfare of the nation. It was a marriage of convenience in which Clinton found the support of the Virginia leaders useful in his battle for state power, while the Virginians utilized the New Yorker to achieve their national goals. Firmly but politely Monroe declined Burr's request that he write a letter for publication expressing approval of Clinton's conduct.[42]

A few days after Monroe returned to Albemarle from his sessions with the revisors, he was invited to Monticello to confer with Madison and Jefferson about Hamilton's anonymous accusation that Jefferson, in giving Freneau a post in the State Department, was subsidizing the editor of an antiadministration newspaper. Hamilton's opening attack had been followed by other letters elaborating on this theme and portraying Jefferson as the sworn enemy of the Constitution. In spite of pressing private affairs the three Virginians agreed that these attacks must be answered at once to prevent the destruction of the republican opposition by a campaign of personal vilification. To let the charges stand would tacitly invite the triumph of Hamiltonian principles. The labor of rebuttal was divided between Madison and Monroe with the bulk of the task assumed by Monroe. During the next few weeks there was a bustle of activity as messengers hastened between Charlottesville and Montpelier bearing documents and drafts for revision. Between September 26 and December 31, 1792, a series of six essays entitled "Vindication of Mr. Jefferson" appeared in the Philadelphia *Dunlap's American Daily Advertiser*. Madison's contribution was the third article, which dealt in a rather gingerly fashion with his own relationship with Freneau.[43]

Monroe's first essay, a reply to the charge that Jefferson had been hostile to the Constitution, was based on letters Madison had received from Jefferson in 1787 and 1788, in which Jefferson, indicating a general approval of the Constitution, had also expressed reservations about certain features, such as the absence of a bill of rights. The second essay (probably revised by Madison) was a vigorous defense of the right of Cabinet members to express views on public measures. These two essays and Madison's third were undoubtedly all that had been originally planned. However, when Monroe arrived in Philadelphia in mid-October he discovered that Hamilton had made further charges over the signature "Catullus." Catullus first claimed that the letters included in the "Vindication" were not authentic. Second, he raised a completely new and irrelevant issue by attempting to prove that Jefferson had never looked upon the public debt as a binding obligation. Delving into State Department files Hamilton misleadingly quoted a letter written by Jefferson to Jay in 1786 concerning a proposed transfer to Dutch bankers of the debt that the United States owed France. Hamilton so used the letter that Jefferson seemed to be advocating the transfer of the debt only to avoid the anger of France when the nation repudiated it. All that Jefferson had in fact done in the letter was to inform Jay of the proposal without any comment. Monroe answered the first charge by offering to let Catullus or his representative examine Jefferson's original letter, a suggestion ignored by Catullus, since it would draw him into the open. To refute the second charge he used a copy of the original letter to Jay, which Jefferson supplied him. Shrewdly, Monroe did not print the text of the letter but presented a careful summary which left no doubt that Jefferson had not originated the proposal. Hamilton's slip in using a letter from the secret files of the government was exploited to the full, since this proved that Catullus obviously held a high post in the administration.

Most unwisely Hamilton attempted to gloss over his use of departmental files by maintaining that he had received a copy of the letter in 1787 when he had not been in office and stubbornly adhered to his original interpretation of the letter. Monroe, in the most vigorous and sharply worded essay in the series, replied bluntly with the declaration that Catullus had printed a *"false, deceptive* and mutilated" extract of the original letter. Hamilton, now named as the author of Catullus, was accused of abusing his official position to obtain confidential documents with the sole object of destroying the influence of a man who stood as a major obstacle to the creation of a monarchy. As a final goad Monroe offered to reveal his identity—if Catullus would follow suit. Hamilton was not yet routed. In an effort to involve Jefferson in the controversy Hamilton challenged the author of the "Vindication" to produce the original of Jefferson's letter to Jay. Monroe, in what proved to be the final essay in the dispute, pointed out that it would scarcely be proper for the Secretary of State to publish a confidential document in his own defense; would it not, he queried sarcastically, subject Jefferson to the "imputation urged with such propriety against the Secretary of the Treasury, in case these publications have proceeded from him." Such an indiscretion, Monroe continued, was exactly what Catullus hoped to provoke. After a long section in which Monroe argued that there had been nothing improper in the proposal to transfer the French debt—it had been desired by France, sought by the Dutch bankers and would have extended the due date—Monroe struck out: "I shall conclude this paper by observing, how much it is to be wished, this writer would exhibit himself to the public view, that we might behold in him a living monument to that immaculate purity, to which he pretends, and which ought to distinguish so bold and arrogant a censor of others." This effectively silenced Hamilton, who must have regretted his decision to cite Jefferson's letter to Jay, and thus submerge his major charge in irrelevancies. Hamilton's withdrawal from the contest was undoubtedly prompted by the veiled threat in Monroe's last essay. The Secretary of the Treasury had no wish to continue a conflict which might produce some unpleasant personal revelations. Although it seems unlikely that Hamilton suspected that the Senator from Virginia was the author of the "Vindication," he surely understood the hint about his own vulnerability.

The running conflict between the Hamiltonians and the republican interest for which Monroe was emerging as a notable spokesman had a profound effect upon current political trends. What had been a disagreement between two loosely defined factions was assuming much sharper contours. It was at this point that the two parties which dominated the life of the nation for the next two decades began to take shape, the republican interest coalescing as the Republican Party, while the pro-Hamilton faction was identified as the Federalist Party. It was only during the next few years that the final alignments took place under the pressure of the issues presented by the French Revolution. In this movement to create a political force capable of blocking the ambitions of the Federalists, Monroe continued to play a central role.

V

The Secretary of the Treasury was peculiarly vulnerable in December 1792, for it was at this time that the untidy details of the Reynolds affair were brought to light by a handful of Republicans, among them Senator Monroe. A few days after his arrival in Philadelphia in October, John Beckley had recounted some unusual circumstances which seemed to implicate Hamilton as a speculator in the public funds. Beckley, a Virginian by birth, long the clerk of the Virginia House of Delegates and now clerk of the House of Representatives, was one of those not-uncommon individuals who can be described as hangers-on of great men.[44] A personal friend of Jefferson, Monroe and Madison (and indeed of many prominent Republicans) Beckley was always to be found on the periphery of great events but was never really an active figure in promoting them. He functioned for some twenty years after the organization of the new government as a general busybody and purveyor of highly questionable gossip. His surviving letters leave the impression of a man who sought (without deserving it) the confidence of the great. He was at best a useful middleman, but in view of his limited advancement in public life he cannot have been highly regarded by those he served. From Beckley Monroe learned that Jacob Clingman, a former clerk of Representative Frederick A. Muhlenberg of Pennsylvania, had charged Hamilton with using James Reynolds of New York as a confidential agent for purposes of speculation.[45] Clingman and Reynolds, both in prison under charges of attempted subornation of a witness in a Treasury case, apparently hoped to use this accusation as a means of blackmailing Hamilton into dropping the case against them. Monroe, Muhlenberg and Representative Abraham Venable of Virginia, after hearing Reynolds' dark hints of grave wrongdoing on the part of the Secretary of the Treasury, called on Mrs. Reynolds, who seemed to add substance to the charges by producing letters showing that Hamilton had given money to her husband. On the basis of this limited evidence the three congressmen visited Hamilton in his office on December 15. The Secretary of the Treasury asked them to postpone the discussion of the matter until that evening, when he would receive them at home and produce documents fully establishing his innocence. To this request, and to the proposal that Oliver Wolcott be present as a witness, the unofficial investigators agreed. That evening Hamilton related a shocking tale, which must have been a great disappointment to the three congressmen, since it revealed that the Secretary of the Treasury was guilty of nothing more serious than adultery followed by blackmail. The embarrassed delegation agreed to keep the affair confidential. This, then, was the secret Hamilton dreaded having exposed. Ultimately the whole affair was made public in 1797, when party passions rose to a point at which gentlemanly restraints were abandoned.[46]

VI

Heavy commitments in Richmond and Williamsburg during the summer of 1792 allowed Monroe little more than a month for plantation activities before returning to Philadelphia. En route he paused at Montpelier and arranged to meet Madison in Fredericksburg some ten days later for a leisurely journey northward. No sooner had Monroe arrived at his uncle's than a messenger arrived bearing a most startling letter addressed jointly to him and to Madison, written by two of Aaron Burr's devoted followers in New York, Melancthon Smith and Marinus Willett, who now proposed that the Virginians should supplant Burr as vice-presidential candidate in place of Clinton.[47] Willett and Smith, proclaiming themselves friends of both Burr and Clinton, rested their case for Burr upon the report that Clinton had frequently disclaimed any wish to be a candidate, since he considered the governorship of New York of greater importance. Earlier in the year the New York and Virginia leaders had agreed not to oppose the re-election of Washington, but to express dissatisfaction with the administration by advancing Clinton for the Vice-Presidency. By October the Virginians had so thoroughly laid the groundwork for this arrangement among state leaders that any change would result in confusion.[48] The proposal to substitute Burr for Clinton not only aroused the same distaste in Monroe that Clinton's behavior in the gubernatorial election had evoked earlier in the year, it also served to raise lasting doubts about Burr's integrity. As soon as Monroe read the letter he forwarded it to Madison with a covering letter expressing strong disapproval of this "injudicious and improper" suggestion. It was, he thought, an attempt to make the interests of the nation subservient to the ambitions of the New Yorkers. Although he gave Madison blanket approval to frame a reply, Madison preferred to wait until he joined Monroe in Fredericksburg.[49] In a carefully worded joint response offense to Burr was avoided by resting the refusal on the impossibility of making a change at such a late date.[50] Burr's motivation for becoming involved in this curious intrigue is characteristically obscure. The best explanation is that advanced by Jabez Hammond, a contemporary New Yorker, who concluded that Burr—whose party affiliations were not as yet fixed—looked upon both Hamilton and Clinton as rivals and hence had no compunction about advancing his career at Clinton's expense.[51]

Having dispatched their letter, Madison and the Monroes departed for Philadelphia, where they arrived on November 1, four days before the opening of the session. Monroe was again without a colleague for some weeks, since Richard Henry Lee had resigned and his replacement, John Taylor of Caroline, had not yet taken his seat. It was most agreeable for the senior Virginia Senator to have as his associate a close friend who shared his political views. The Virginia senators, courtly and formal, made a distinguished pair—both were tall men: Monroe large and muscular, Taylor slender with red hair. In temperament, however, they contrasted strongly: Taylor, by nature a scholar with an abiding passion for agriculture, disliked the routine demanded by public office. A rigid purist in his political views, he could not tolerate the compromises necessary in the world of politics. Ultimately Taylor withdrew completely from active politics to become a leading

Republican theorist and writer. Monroe, one of the first to recognize Taylor's unusual abilities as a writer on political topics, enlisted his pen in the party struggle.

The second session of the second Congress was no more fruitful than the first, but at least it was short, lasting but four months. Few measures of importance were considered in either house. Indeed, business was impeded in the lower house by a prolonged drive to investigate the conduct of the Secretary of the Treasury. While the House debates raged on, a torpid atmosphere settled over the Senate: even on minor questions it was difficult to secure action. A bill introduced by Monroe to aid soldiers of the Virginia line in taking out land in Ohio was tabled after a second reading. Equally unsuccessful was his attempt to secure approval of Jefferson's longstanding report on weights and measures. As usual the proposal to open the doors of the Senate was presented and again rejected by a large majority.[52]

VII

The shortness of the session enabled Monroe to return home much earlier than in previous years. By the end of March he was in Fredericksburg catching up on his law business. This year he made no complaints about the condition of his estate. Not only was he on hand to supervise the spring planting, but the weather, as favorable as it had been disastrous the year before, also produced a bumper crop. Since the construction of his residence had gone as planned, he could now also offer proper accommodations to his guests.[53] As Monroe made the rounds of the county courts in the summer of 1793, he listened closely to conversations on the courthouse steps and in the taverns. Everywhere he found the radical turn of the revolution in France following the execution of the king a subject of general discussion. It was pleasing to note that few were unfriendly to the revolution except in Alexandria and Richmond, towns "containing no enlightened men." Although many regretted the unhappy fate of Lafayette and the execution of the king, they seemed "to consider these events as incidents to a much greater one . . . which they wish to see accomplished." He was not in the least astonished to observe that those loudest in the praise of the policies of the Secretary of the Treasury were those most vigorous in their condemnation of France.[54] These reports reassured Jefferson, who, as he read the newspapers and listened to Cabinet discussions about American policy, was becoming more and more apprehensive that the President might be influenced to adopt an anti-French program. Such a decision was dreaded not merely because of its international implications but because it might well presage a move to curtail the liberties enjoyed by the people in America. In the spring Jefferson anxiously sought some means of demonstrating to the President that public opinion was solidly pro-French although fully in accord with a policy of neutrality. It was hoped that the public enthusiasm lavished on Citizen Edmond Genet, the first Minister from the French Republic, who was journeying to Philadelphia from Charleston, would have this effect. Monroe, who passed Genet on the road to Fredericksburg, was able to report that the French Minister was making a most favorable impression, which augured well for the effect he would have in the more prejudiced atmosphere of Philadelphia. In spite of his Francophilism Monroe did not misread public enthusiasm for Genet: he clearly understood that the sentiment of the people, while strongly sympathetic to France, was equally firm in support of American neutrality.[55]

Regarding neutrality as a policy in accord with the wishes of the nation and also the one most advantageous to France, since it would insure her the benefits of American neutral commerce, Monroe did not at first see anything objectionable in Washington's celebrated April proclamation of neutrality, which carefully avoided the use of that word in deference to Jefferson's sensibilities. It seemed but a harmless if unnecessary admonition to the people to mind their own business.[56] By the end of June, however, Monroe viewed it in a rather different light as Jefferson filled him in on the Cabinet discussions. Moreover, he also learned that prosecutions of offenders taking place under the proclamation left no doubt that it had the force of law. He now joined Madison in condemning the measure as an unconstitutional invasion of the power of Congress to declare war. By refusing to allow citizens to accept commissions in foreign armies, the proclamation contradicted a principle universally accepted by European powers. Monroe was particularly critical of the administration for issuing it gratuitously without seeking adequate returns from the belligerent powers who would benefit from our neutrality.[57] Once convinced of the impropriety of the proclamation, Monroe worked to convert other Virginians who had accepted the measure without protest.[58] His revised view received Jefferson's full endorsement: ". . . you have," he wrote, "most perfectly seized the *original* idea of the proclamation." [59] In Jefferson's opinion the furor stirred up and the arrival of Genet had at least one beneficial

effect—for the first time parties had emerged sufficiently into the open
for it to be possible to assess the relative strength of each.[60] Until 1793
the emergent parties were really little more than congressional factions,
operating only during sessions of Congress without any effective organization capable of furthering party aims during the recesses. Although
the leaders kept in contact with one another, they had no effective
rapport with the public at large. Agitation over France was shaping
political alignments more distinctly, yet there had been no progress
in forming a party organization beyond the rather nebulous association
between the New Yorkers and the Virginians; nor had any serious effort
been made to involve the public in party affairs.

The question of public opinion in relation to policymaking assumed
a new significance in the spring and summer of 1793, when the President
discovered that his Cabinet was sharply divided over the direction to
be taken by American foreign policy in relation to France. Both Hamilton and Jefferson in presenting their arguments to the President
relied heavily upon conflicting interpretations of public attitudes to
support their contentions. The President, seeking an impartial view,
beheld only confusion and disagreement. The press was just as divided,
since party writers advocated divergent policies. Hamilton, drawn into
the newspaper polemics as "Pacificus," undertook to defend the proclamation and to prove that the treaty obligations with France were no
longer valid. At Jefferson's behest Madison (disguised as "Helvedius")
reluctantly undertook a reply. To resolve the uncertainty in his Cabinet Washington sent Attorney General Edmund Randolph to Virginia
in the spring for a firsthand report on public opinion. Randolph, to
the disbelief of Jefferson and Madison, who kept a close eye on his
movements, told the President that there was no real opposition to his
policies except of a personal nature—a manifestly inaccurate report.[61]
By the time Randolph returned to Philadelphia the whole question of
public opinion had assumed a more immediate aspect as a result of
the Genet affair, which brought into play new forces and led to an
effort on the part of both parties to organize public opinion as a means
of shaping presidential policy. In this new development Monroe and
Madison played central roles in galvanizing public support in behalf
of the Republicans.

Shortly after the first of July Hamilton had discovered that Genet
was equipping a French prize, the *Little Sarah* (appropriately renamed
La Petite Democrate), as a privateer in violation of Washington's proclamation.[62] Hamilton at once informed Jefferson, but before the Sec-

retary of State could get to Philadelphia from his country residence, Governor Thomas Mifflin of Pennsylvania intervened. He sent his secretary of state, Alexander J. Dallas, to obtain Genet's pledge that the ship would not sail before Washington, then vacationing at Mount Vernon, returned to the capital. Although Dallas was a close friend of Genet, he failed completely. In an interview on July 6 Genet, rebuffing him harshly, threatened to appeal from the President to the people if his plans were thwarted. Jefferson, in a meeting with Genet the next day, found the Minister still greatly agitated. However, Genet did not address the Secretary of State in such blunt terms as he had used with Dallas. Complaining bitterly about the American disregard of obligations toward France, he did not repeat his threat to appeal to the people. When the interview ended Jefferson felt that he had calmed Genet and secured an understanding (although there was no explicit pledge) that the ship would not sail prior to Washington's return.[63] Secretary of War John Knox and Hamilton heard the details of both these conferences from Governor Mifflin. When Washington arrived in Philadelphia on the eleventh, Jefferson laid the whole matter before him in a report written the day before.[64] The President at once instructed Jefferson to notify the French Minister that the *Little Sarah* was not to sail. Genet, impervious to the warnings of Jefferson and his other Republican friends, permitted the privateer to sail in defiance of the President's orders. His fate was settled; three weeks later, on August 1, the President decided to request his recall.

As usual the Cabinet was divided—not over the recall but over the proposal that the news be released immediately together with the circumstances leading to the decision. Hamilton, supported by Knox, used every argument he could muster to persuade the President to publish the full story. Genet had presented Hamilton with what seemed the perfect weapon for destroying the influence of the Republicans and at the same time for embarking the administration on a course hostile to France. On his part, Jefferson made no attempt to defend Genet, but endeavored to hold the administration to its policy of noninvolvement. The Secretary of State reminded the President that public repudiation of Genet might well provoke a rupture with France. Discouraged by the united front which Hamilton and Knox were presenting, and perhaps as a means of putting pressure on Washington, Jefferson on July 31 (while the decision on Genet was still pending) informed the President that he intended to resign at the end of September. On the sixth of August, after Washington had decided to withhold

the news, Jefferson agreed to remain in the Cabinet until the end of
the year.[65]

At this point Hamilton, frustrated in his efforts to alter administration policy through the Cabinet, sought to arouse public opinion by
spreading reports that Genet had insulted both the President and the
nation. He also planned a series of public meetings to denounce Genet
and endorse the proclamation. In this project Hamilton worked closely
with Rufus King and Chief Justice John Jay, who undertook much
of the organizational work. On August 12 Jay and King published a
letter in the New York press accusing Genet of having threatened to
appeal to the people. At the same time they busied themselves in
promoting a succession of public meetings at which resolutions were
adopted condemning all attempts by foreign Ministers to communicate
with the people except through the Executive and strongly endorsing
the April proclamation.[66] The most celebrated of all the meetings was
the one arranged by John Marshall in Richmond on August 17, 1793.
It was presided over by George Wythe, an old friend of Jefferson and
a Republican sympathizer. Like many other Virginians Wythe was not
aware of the unfavorable reaction of the Republican leaders to the
proclamation. Under Marshall's capable management the meeting unanimously adopted resolutions approving the proclamation and affirming the confidence of the people in the integrity and patriotism of the
President. The final resolution, which condemned Genet without
mentioning him by name, declared that all communications by a foreign
Minister through any but the Executive channel were violations of
the law and an indignity to the people. The resolve concluded with
a warning to the people that such actions might open the way for
foreign intervention in the affairs of the United States. Before adjourning, the meeting approved an address to the President praising
him for his past services and for his devotion to the cause of peace.
These resolves were typical of those adopted elsewhere and marked
a real coup for the Federalists, since Virginia was a center of pro-French
feeling.

The Republicans, rendered somewhat complacent by the favorable
reception given Genet, were completely unprepared for this massive
onslaught. For several months Monroe and Madison had been deeply
engrossed in their private affairs, and hence somewhat isolated from
the mainstream of events. Jefferson, who had been in Philadelphia
during the summer, had endeavored to keep his Virginia friends informed about major developments. Although he warned them early

in July that Genet's activities were threatening to wreck the Republican cause, he had not been successful in communicating to either Madison or Monroe the extent of the danger or the urgency of the situation. On July 7 Jefferson had written Madison that the Genet appointment was "calamitous," adding that the Minister had been "disrespectful and even indecent towards the P.[resident] in his written as well as his verbal communications, talking of appeals from him to Congress, from them to the people. . . ." Madison agreed that Jefferson's account was dreadful, but only made the rather mild suggestion that someone should be found to put the Minister right.[67] Monroe, far more ardently francophile than Madison, took the matter even more lightly, confidently assuring Jefferson that the people would pardon Genet's errors and attribute them to the "effect of an honest heart active in the support of the best of causes. . . ." [68]

On August 21, when Monroe wrote this letter, his thoughts were only superficially engaged with Genet, about whose conduct he had no details. He was much more interested in resuming discussions with Madison, who had arrived at Monroe's farm on the edge of Charlottesville a few days before. Madison's visit had been long postponed, since the matter which brought them together was not pressing. They met to prepare for publication in the fall a pamphlet John Taylor had forwarded to Madison earlier in the year at Monroe's suggestion.[69] The leisurely editorial work planned by Monroe and Madison was abruptly terminated by the arrival of a batch of Philadelphia papers and the Richmond papers of August 21, containing reports of the meetings held in Richmond and elsewhere. As soon as they had read these accounts and the letter of Jay and King accusing Genet of threatening to appeal to the people, they knew at once that they were confronted with a campaign conducted by the "cabal" in Philadelphia.[70] It was clear that prompt action was necessary to correct any impression that the Richmond resolutions were approved by the Republicans, since Wythe's association with the proceedings might easily have that effect. Pending the outcome of their deliberations, Monroe dashed off notes to distant friends to put them on guard. To John Breckinridge in Kentucky he wrote an urgent warning:

The monarchy party among [us] has seized a new ground whereon to advance their fortunes. The French minister has been guilty, in the vehemence of his zeal, of some indiscretions, slighting the President of the U. States, and instead of healing the breach, this party have brought it into the public

view & are labouring to turn the popularity of this respectable citizen against
the French revolution, thinking to separate us from France & pave the way
for an unnatural connection with Great Britain. Jay and King have certified
the indiscretion charged to the minister, & handed it to the public printers. I
have time only to suggest the idea, to enable you to understand what you
may see in relation to this object, & put the friends of republican government on their guard.[71]

Monroe and Madison, unable to consult Jefferson, quickly agreed
that the effect of the Richmond resolutions could be neutralized only
by holding similar meetings of a contrary tone throughout the state
under the "auspices of respectable names." [72] Working steadily during
the next few days, they drafted a set of resolutions to be distributed to
Republican friends throughout Virginia. In preparing this draft they
worked under the considerable handicap of not knowing about either
the decision to recall Genet or the full extent of his misconduct. Madison, it is true, had in his possession a letter written by Jefferson on
August 3 relating the Cabinet decision to recall Genet and summarizing
Hamilton's attempts to persuade the President to release the full story
to the public. Genet, Jefferson cautioned Madison, would *"sink the
republican interest* if they do not *abandon him."* Unfortunately the
critical passages (in italics) were in cipher, and Madison, who had left his
key in Fredericksburg, was unable to decode the letter.[73]

The draft resolutions began with a preamble stressing the need for
meetings to express the popular sentiment and to demonstrate that the
views of the people in the country differed from those previously formulated in towns where citizens could more easily assemble. After praising
the President for his services to the nation, his patriotism and his devotion to peace, the resolutions expressed gratitude to France for her
aid during the American Revolution, extending the sympathy of the
people in her struggle for liberty. All attempts to alienate the two nations at a time when France was struggling to preserve her freedom
against the onslaughts of the "Priests and Nobles" were denounced.
The draft concluded with a resolution asserting that the object of the
recent meeting in Richmond had been to destroy the bond between
France and the United States in order to connect the nation more closely
with Great Britain and to convert the government into a monarchy. Of
the truth of this last assertion the resolves proclaimed there could be
no doubt in view of the "active zeal displayed by persons . . . of known
monarchical principles" in seeking to arouse prejudice against the

French Revolution.[74] The draft had no sooner been completed than a letter arrived by private messenger from Jefferson, making it necessary for Monroe and Madison to reconsider their draft.[75] In view of the seriousness of the situation revealed by Jefferson, it now seemed imperative for the Republicans to disengage themselves from the French Minister. As to the best means of accomplishing this Monroe and Madison disagreed. Madison preferred a blunt repudiation, but Monroe hesitated, fearing that an open break would not only create confusion in the public mind but also appear an attack on France. As Madison commented, Monroe could "hardly bring himself absolutely and *openly*" to abandon Genet.[76] Under the aegis of Monroe's sense of caution they avoided a specific denunciation of Genet, adding instead a statement (similar to that put forth by the Federalists) affirming the general principle that all foreign Ministers should negotiate with the Executive and condemning all appeals to the people. This passage was further qualified (in line with Monroe's thinking) by a clause stating that, if the French Minister should make such an appeal, the act would be regarded as a reflection on him and not on France. On August 30, their work completed, Madison left Charlottesville. A few days later Monroe hastened to Staunton to attend the county court, bearing a copy of the resolutions and a covering letter from Madison soliciting Archibald Stuart's aid in securing the adoption of the resolutions.[77] Monroe arrived in Staunton just in time to check a movement to adopt resolutions in harmony with those approved in Richmond. With Stuart's cooperation the first set of Republican resolves was adopted on September 3. The second set to be approved was that sent to John Taylor of Caroline, who organized a meeting on September 10 with his uncle, Edmund Pendleton, in the chair. Both these sets were widely reprinted and were used as models in other counties.[78] The resolutions drafted by Madison and Monroe differed from those submitted by the Federalists in that the latter praised the proclamation but ignored France, whereas the Republicans treated the proclamation with silence while vigorously affirming friendship with France. By echoing the Federalist condemnation of Genet in a gentler and less specific fashion the Monroe–Madison resolves dissociated the Republicans from the French Minister without directly repudiating him.

Monroe and Madison were anxious to have the resolutions adopted widely in the state, but they found themselves circumscribed by their unfamiliarity with trustworthy men in all the counties.[79] To stimulate action on the resolutions and to alert the Republicans of the danger facing them, Monroe in the last weeks of August, as he prepared for his journey to Staunton, hastily wrote an essay for publication in Richmond. In this letter, which appeared on September 4 over the signature "Agricola," he called on the citizens of the state to affirm their affection for France.[80] In making this appeal he did not question the accuracy of the charges made by Jay and King, but took the offensive by impugning the motives of those who sought to discredit the French Minister. They were "enemies of the French revolution, who are likewise the partisans for monarchy," whose sole object was a closer union with Britain and a complete rupture with France. Following the outline of the draft he and Madison had just completed, Monroe supplied a summary of the points to be covered in meetings. During the next three months Monroe published three additional letters identifying the critics of Genet as members of a pro-British monarchical faction. Constantly he stressed the importance of continued friendship with France as essential for the preservation of liberty at home. These essays, presenting the Republican point of view in a vigorous manner, were answered by John Marshall, who replied in four essays under the pseudonyms "Aristides" and "Gracchus." Marshall's replies were couched in sharply satirical terms, but their effectiveness was impaired by his decision to assume a defensive position. Instead of hammering away at Genet's indiscretions, he took the less satisfactory ground of attempting to defend Genet's critics from the charge of being monarchists and Anglophiles.

It is difficult to assess the ultimate effect of the propaganda warfare over Genet. The outbreak of yellow fever in Philadelphia in the late summer of 1793 prevented both campaigns from reaching the intended climax. This epidemic, which ran on through November, not only disrupted the operations of the government but impeded communications, since the all-important Philadelphia papers (with one exception) suspended publications for several months. Certainly from the Federalist point of view the campaign was a failure: they had been unable to force the revelation of the full details about Genet and thus discredit the pro-French element. On the whole the Republican counteroffensive seems to have neutralized the impact of the Federalist campaign. When the President notified Congress in December of the request for Genet's recall, he did not submit some of the ruder letters written by the French Minister. Jefferson also gained a point in that the President in his message merely described the proclamation as a declaration of the existing state of affairs, thereby avoiding the implication that it represented a new policy toward France.

When the Federalist leaders realized that the President was not going to release the details of Genet's iniquity, they made one last attempt to force a complete disclosure. On December 5, the same day the President's message went to Congress, Jay and King published a summary of what Hamilton had told them about the remarks Genet had reportedly made in his interview with Dallas and Jefferson. A few days later Dallas, assisted by Monroe, published a long account of his interview with Genet. This statement (Jay rightly called it "artful") left the matter in some doubt. Although Dallas denied that Genet had threatened to appeal to the people, he did admit that the Minister had used the word *appeal,* which Dallas now declared he had understood to mean that Genet would appeal to Congress by publishing his correspondence with the Executive. Dallas' letter also left the impression that Hamilton and Knox had deliberately circulated an inaccurate version of facts received indirectly from Mifflin, rather than seeking a verification from Dallas—whom they saw every day. Jefferson was then planning to release his report to Washington of July 10, but he withheld it when Monroe reminded him that it was to the advantage of the Republicans to let the case rest entirely on Mifflin's verbal statement to Knox and Hamilton. As long as there was no additional confirmation, which Jefferson's report might provide, the charges against Genet remained unsubstantiated.[81] Under the guidance of Monroe and Madison the Republicans had not only weathered the storm over the Genet affair but had also succeeded in preserving the bond with France. From this episode the Republicans learned the importance of organizing public opinion and in the future they made notable use of public meetings to advance the party program. To facilitate collaboration, interstate ties were now strengthened. Certainly the Federalists in 1793 had shown themselves superior to their rivals in both respects.

CHAPTER 7

MINISTER TO FRANCE

THE THIRD CONGRESS, which assembled in December 1793, was the scene of a sharply intensified party conflict when Monroe arrived for what proved his last session as a member. Although the drama was largely centered in the House, where the Republicans had a majority, Monroe was immediately drawn into the Anti-Federalist campaign planned by the Republican leadership. At the start of the session the Republicans labored to exploit the public resentment stirred up by recent British commercial restrictions. For this purpose Madison presented a series of resolutions recommending commercial reprisals against Great Britain with the expectation that Federalist opposition would convince the public of the sinister designs of that party. Monroe was enthusiastic about this move—which, he felt, left the door open for negotiations, yet, if war ensued, would place the blame squarely on Great Britain. Madison's resolves were well received in the House, but the vote was postponed at the request of Northern representatives to allow time for the people to endorse the proposed restrictions. Public meetings on the model of those of the previous year were arranged in the major cities. The most spectacular rally (attended by nearly 2,000 persons) was organized at Monroe's request by Robert Livingston in New York.[1]

In spite of the success of the public meetings, the decision to postpone the vote, which Monroe had approved as sound strategy, proved unfortunate. New developments now enabled the Federalists to launch a bold counterstroke. Since the introduction of Madison's resolves, public rage at Britain had been further exacerbated in February by the report that the Governor-General of Canada had asserted in a speech to an Indian delegation that a rupture was imminent between

Great Britain and the United States. Capitalizing on this alarming news, the Federalists presented a bill to authorize the President to raise 15,000 auxiliary troops if he felt the nation threatened by an invasion. In view of this recent provocation the Republicans, as advocates of a firmer policy toward Britain, could not oppose military preparations; yet, as Monroe noted, if they acceded and embarked upon a war while the government was in the hands of the "enemy of publick liberty," they ran a far greater risk than from a putative attack from Canada. Much as he abominated the "pusillanimity" of the administration, any increase in the military establishment was unthinkable.[2] When it became known that Hamilton would be placed in command of these forces, the Republican opposition became even more determined.[3] Skillfully the Republicans in the House transformed the original bill into a harmless measure that empowered the President to summon 80,000 militia if he deemed it necessary. As Monroe commented with gratification, this maneuver enabled the Republicans to claim credit for supporting defense measures and yet avoid the danger of placing military power in the hands of the British party.[4] At the same time a Federalist-sponsored one-month embargo on all American ports was approved.

As Madison marshaled his forces in the House, Monroe waged another battle on behalf of the Republicans in the Senate. In January the Senate Republicans, hoping to expose the administration's supposed anti-French sentiments, called on the President to submit the dispatches received from Gouverneur Morris. The results were disappointing, for the letters contained little that was damaging, nor was Monroe correct in concluding that the President had held back damaging portions. In fact, the President retained only one letter.[5] The Republicans had been able to put this hostile resolution through the Senate by a two-vote majority that depended on the votes of John Langdon, an uncommitted Senator, and of Albert Gallatin, the newly elected Republican Senator from Pennsylvania. Determined to destroy this momentary Republican advantage, the Federalists moved to unseat Gallatin on the technicality that he was not eligible since he had not been an American citizen for the nine-year period required by law. Although Gallatin's qualifications had been challenged earlier in the session, action had been postponed until the Federalists felt certain of victory. Monroe, Taylor and Aaron Burr conducted a ten-day fight on Gallatin's behalf, losing by a vote of fourteen to twelve. The defeat was a blow to Monroe; he had anticipated a tie which the Vice-President would not be able to break, since his vote could not be used to displace a sitting member. However, Benjamin Hawkins of North Carolina, who usually voted with the Republicans, refused to support Gallatin's claim. Monroe also erred in assuming that Robert Morris, Gallatin's Federalist colleague from Pennsylvania, would abstain from voting; at the last minute Morris changed his mind.[6] The ejection of Gallatin, who had been permitted to vote and serve on committees, substantially strengthened the Federalist position. A month later Monroe repaid the Federalists in their own coin. On March 24, 1794, Kensey Johns, who had been appointed by the Federalist governor of Delaware to fill a vacancy, appeared to take his seat. Just as Johns was about to be sworn in by Adams, Monroe arose to object that the appointment was invalid, observing that a session of the legislature had intervened after the vacancy, and hence the governor had no power to make an interim appointment. By a one-vote margin Johns' credentials were referred to a committee, which verified Monroe's statement, costing Johns his seat and depriving the Federalists of a reinforcement.[7]

Although the most important Republican leader in the Senate, Monroe did not accept assignments on committees until late in the session so he could be free to join his wife in New York, where her father was fatally ill. Early in February he was summoned by his sister-in-law, Maria Knox, who asked his help in arranging Mr. Kortright's business affairs. There he found his father-in-law's affairs in great confusion, with little prospect of any return from a once-substantial estate. Laurence Kortright's death in February severed the strongest tie binding Mrs. Monroe to New York and removed the last impediment to a permanent residence in Albemarle.[8]

The turn of events after Monroe's return did not favor Republican plans. When it was learned that the British had repealed the restrictive measures, the Republicans abandoned Madison's resolutions in favor of a measure introduced by Abraham Clark of New Jersey proposing an embargo on commerce with Great Britain until she paid indemnities for her depredations and surrendered the posts.[9] Monroe approved this shift, which allowed the Republicans to back a resolution fundamentally consistent with their aims but sponsored by a member of Congress not identified with their party.[10] Clark's resolution passed the House by a large majority, but was checked in the Senate, when John Jay was nominated Minister Extraordinary to Great Britain. This "executive maneuver" (as Monroe termed the appointment) opened the prospect of a settlement and thus Clark's bill was rejected by the vote of Vice-President Adams. "Thus," Monroe wrote Jefferson, "you find

nothing has been carried agnst. that nation, but on the contrary the
most submissive measures adopted that cod. be devised, to court her
favor and degrade our character." [11]

Shortly after the rejection of Clark's proposal, Monroe and Taylor—
at the request of the legislature of Virginia—introduced a proposal to
suspend the collection of debts due British merchants until Great Britain should comply with the terms of the treaty of 1783. In the light of
recent court decisions many Virginians were faced with the prospect
of paying these debts, which many considered canceled by a state law
allowing them to pay the sum of their debts into the state treasury in
depreciated currency. Monroe probably had little sympathy with the
resolution he now introduced, and the other Republicans had even
less, for only the Virginia senators voted in its favor. The other Republicans absented themselves out of courtesy to their colleagues.[12] The
Federalists naturally saw sinister motives in this Virginia-sponsored
resolution, but Fisher Ames' acid comment—"Thus, murder, at last
is out"—seems exaggerated.[13]

Monroe was not only critical of the plan to send an emissary to England, but reports that Hamilton might be chosen disturbed him
greatly.[14] When these rumors became current in April, he wrote the
President a letter of protest offering to state his objections in a personal
interview.[15] Washington, forgetting that he had consulted Monroe two
years earlier before appointing Wayne, was indignant over this senatorial presumption. Although Secretary of State Randolph thought that
Monroe deserved the courtesy of an interview, the President coldly
refused, penning a chilly response:

In reply to your letter of yesterday, I can assure you, with the utmost truth,
that I have no object in nominating men to offices than to fill them with
such characters as in my judgment . . . are best qualified to answer the purposes of their appointment.[16]

If the Senator "had any facts or information, which would disqualify
Colo. Hamilton for the mission" then they should be submitted in
writing. "No one," the President continued, ". . . is yet absolutely
decided on in my mind; but as much will depend, among other things,
upon the abilities of the person sent, and his knowledge of the affairs
of this country, and as I *alone* am responsible for a proper nomination
it certainly behooves me to name such an one as in my judgment com-
bines the requisites of a mission so peculiarly interesting to the *peace*

and happiness of the country." Monroe responded, stating that his objections were founded on Hamilton's well-known affection for Britain and his open admiration of monarchical government. To name Hamilton would merely "furnish an opportunity for political intrigue against republicanism here and against our connection with France. . . ." It would surely alienate France and deprive the United States of the support of a friendly power.[17] The President, who had long since eliminated Hamilton, did not reply.

Monroe considered Jay just as undesirable as Hamilton for the English mission. Not only was Jay a staunch Federalist, but his conduct during the Jay–Gardoqui negotiations in 1786 had undermined Monroe's confidence in his integrity. With Taylor's assistance Monroe rallied the weakened Republican forces in a futile effort to prevent Jay's confirmation. In a lengthy speech Monroe reviewed the Gardoqui proposals, which he considered particularly relevant, since it was generally believed that Spain had a secret treaty with England.[18] If this were true, sending Jay to England would again jeopardize America's western interests. In an effort to convict Jay of pro-English sentiments, Monroe recalled a report to the old Congress in which Jay had argued the justice of paying interest on the debts owed British merchants, since the United States had committed the first infractions of the treaty of peace.[19] Monroe and Taylor maneuvered to block the appointment by introducing a resolution declaring that it was contrary to the spirit of the Constitution for judges to hold any other office while on the bench—a proposal voted down seventeen to four, with four Republicans joining the majority. Monroe did not consider Jay's confirmation by a vote of eighteen to eight a true measure of the opposition strength, since many opposed voted affirmatively when they saw that confirmation was certain.[20] The conviction, shared by all Republicans, that closer ties with England meant the destruction of representative government in America led Monroe to resort to a drastic measure. He called on Jean Fauchet, Genet's successor, to inquire whether the French Minister could negotiate a settlement of all the outstanding disputes and thus neutralize the effect of Jay's mission. Fauchet, who had no such power, declined to act.[21]

II

Although Washington had not relished Monroe's blunt comments on Hamilton and Jay, a few months later he offered him the post of Minister to France to replace Gouverneur Morris, recently recalled at the request of the French government. The demand for Morris' recall, following so soon after the Genet affair, had placed the relations between the two countries on a precarious footing, which Jay's appointment would aggravate. It seemed quite logical to Washington, who still considered himself a neutral force in the party struggle, that he could best conciliate France and minimize resentment over Jay's mission by sending a Republican to replace Morris. Monroe was not the President's first choice, however. Washington had at first considered shifting Thomas Pinckney from London to Paris, but abandoned this plan when Jay declined to become resident Minister to Great Britain.[22] After refusals from both Robert R. Livingston and Madison, Washington then turned to the Republican leaders in Philadelphia, who recommended Aaron Burr.[23] Burr, eager for the appointment, rounded up some Federalist support, a circumstance Monroe considered ill calculated to inspire confidence in the "steadiness" of the New Yorker's "political tenets." [24] Nonetheless, Monroe expected the President to name Burr in spite of Washington's known personal objections to the New York Senator. Monroe had just posted these comments in a letter to Jefferson on the morning of May 26 when the Secretary of State came in to offer him the French Mission, requesting an immediate reply. Fully expecting Burr to be chosen, Monroe naturally was astonished. When he reminded Randolph that he could scarcely accept in view of his support of Burr, the Secretary assured him that Washington would never appoint Burr. Randolph did not tell him that the President's objections to Burr, which rested entirely on the New Yorker's private character (he had a reputation as an intriguer and also as being entirely too fond of associating with ladies of easy virtue), were so strong that Washington refused to consider him for a moment. Instead, Randolph assured the Senator that the President, in view of Jay's recent appointment, did not wish to appear to be favoring New Yorkers. To Monroe's comment that this seemed strange, since the post had been offered to Livingston, Randolph replied that the New Yorker's former service in the Department of Foreign Affairs had overridden this objection.[25] Randolph, who seems to have been responsible for proposing Monroe's name to the President, pressed for an answer within the hour, indicating that if he declined the appointment would be conferred on a figure with little national standing.[26] Unable to leave the Senate floor, where a bill involving balances due to the states was pending, Monroe sent a note to Madison asking him to canvass the Republicans and then notify Randolph of their decision. Madison, quickly ascertaining that the Republicans were in full accord, informed Randolph of Monroe's acceptance. Without delay the Senate confirmed Monroe.[27] Burr was disappointed, but he bore his Virginia colleague no ill will, writing to congratulate the new Minister and asking that his stepson, John B. Prevost, be appointed secretary. In the interest of harmony Monroe acceded to this request, but with misgivings about Prevost's character—which reflected his distrust of Burr rather than any known shortcoming in the stepson.[28] Monroe did not regret leaving the Senate, where—in spite of "systematic efforts" on the part of the Republicans—nothing had been accomplished to "vindicate the honor or advance the prosperity of the country." [29]

In accepting the mission to France, a decision which nearly wrecked his career, Monroe displayed less caution than Livingston—who, as he told Monroe, had declined lest he be required to violate his principles or risk his reputation should hè find himself in disagreement with the administration.[30] Monroe was not unaware of these perils, but Randolph's assurance that he had been chosen as the best person to give France unequivocal proof of American friendship appealed directly to his high sense of public duty. That it was his duty Monroe never doubted: indeed all the Republicans concurred in the premise that a rupture with France could only be prevented by a member of their own party. This view was succinctly stated by Jefferson in 1796, when he wrote urging Monroe to stay on in France in a "post which the public good requires to be filled by a Republican." [31] Who but a Republican could inspire in the French a confidence in the continued affection and friendship of the people of the United States? This conviction ultimately led Monroe in his dealings with the French government to make a distinction between the views of the people and those of the administration in power. Although Washington never knew the full extent of the impact of Monroe's partisanship upon his diplomatic conduct, the suspicion that he was acting as an agent for his party rather than for his government was largely responsible for his recall in 1796. If Monroe, on the eve of his departure, had any intimation of the difficulties of his position, he would not have been able to offer the President the ready assurance that he looked to the guidance of the Executive to compensate for his own deficiencies.[32]

Deeming the relations with France to be in a critical state, the new Minister, in accordance with the President's wishes, prepared to sail at once; he did not take time to go to Virginia to arrange his private affairs, but within ten days after his confirmation he was on the road to Baltimore to arrange passage. Considering the importance the administration seemed to attach to the mission, the preparations were somewhat casual. The newly appointed Minister was not accorded an interview with the President, nor were his conferences with the Secretary of State of much value. Whatever logical powers Randolph had previously shown at the bar, they were singularly absent during his tenure in the State Department. His dispatches leave an impression of carelessness, of counting too much on a mood or a momentary inspiration; they tend to be chaotic, ill-organized effusions with the major points obscured under a mass of trivia. His letters to Monroe were often ambiguous and contradictory. As a result of this inattentiveness to detail, Monroe began his mission with a fundamental misapprehension about the nature of Jay's mission. The Secretary of State failed to make it clear to the new Minister that Jay was authorized to discuss commercial affairs with Great Britain, leaving Monroe under the impression that Jay was strictly limited by his instructions to settling the disputes arising from the Treaty of 1783. Most surprisingly, in view of the relevance of Jay's mission to his own task, Monroe was not shown Jay's instructions. Had he seen these he would undoubtedly have conducted himself quite differently in his representations to the French government concerning the character of Jay's mission.

As he waited for the ship to sail Monroe hastily arranged for Madison and Joseph Jones to look after his personal affairs. Although Jones agreed to keep an eye on Monroe's plantation, which was to be left in charge of an overseer, his plan of residing on his nephew's property was never carried out, for Monroe's brother Joseph, who was living on the estate, resented the arrangement. Joseph's affairs were uppermost in Monroe's thoughts during the few days he spent in Baltimore. Expecting his brother to begin practicing law in Charlottesville, he arranged for Joseph to receive a stock of household goods and regular supplies from the farm. However, Joseph, as improvident as ever, continued to live on the plantation and made no attempt to establish himself at the bar. A most unpleasant shock was the discovery that Joseph still had debts in Scotland for which the departing Minister now had to find funds. Since Monroe used his ready cash for the voyage, he was unable to leave sufficient money to meet his share of the first installment on a 5,000-acre tract of land they had purchased in Loudoun County for three dollars per acre. Arrangements also had to be made for the care of a 3,500-acre tract of land adjacent to Monticello, which he had acquired the year before. Although this new property in Albemarle was intended as a permanent residence, he had not as yet begun to construct a house. During his absence he had planned for Jones to draw on his salary, but due to some misunderstanding Randolph declined to make advances until he heard from Monroe, thus complicating Jones' task. An alternate plan of selling lands in Kentucky to meet the payments proved unworkable, since Jones could not find buyers at the price indicated by his nephew.[33]

On June 18, less than three weeks after his appointment, Monroe, his wife and eight-year-old daughter sailed from Baltimore on the *Cincinnatus,* commanded by Captain Joshua Barney, who was bound for France with his son to press commercial claims. The passage cost the substantial sum of $700–$400 for the cabin and $300 for supplies. Before sailing Monroe prudently purchased sugar, hams and other provisions, anticipating scarcity in Paris. With the Monroes were two white servants—Michael, who acted as major-domo in Paris, and Polly. Also on board the *Cincinnatus* were Fulwar Skipwith, Joseph Jones, Jr., and M. LeBlanc, Secretary of the French legation. Skipwith, a young Virginian related to Jefferson, had been engaged as Secretary of Legation. Joseph Jones, Jr., the fifteen-year-old son of Monroe's uncle, was being sent to France to complete his education.[34]

During the month-long crossing, an exceptionally calm one, the new Minister had ample time to study Randolph's instructions, which remained effective throughout his mission.[35] Randolph began by authorizing Monroe to express the deep interest of the President in the French Revolution and his "immutable" wish for its success: at the same time he was also to impress on France the commercial benefits she derived from American neutrality—benefits which would be lost if the United States were involved in the European conflict. Since it was expected that Jay's mission would cause uneasiness in France, Monroe was instructed to assure the French that Jay had been forbidden to make any arrangements tending to weaken the obligations of the United States to her ally. Should questions arise concerning Jay's objectives, France was to be informed that Jay had been sent to "obtain immediate compensation for our plundered property and restitution of the posts," a passage Monroe interpreted to mean that Jay had no power to treat on commercial matters. Randolph also touched on a variety of claims which included compensation for captures and spoliation of American property as a result of illegal seizures, compensation for damages arising under the embargo placed on all American ships in Bordeaux in 1793, and reimbursement for money advanced to Santo Domingan refugees and for supplies ordered by French agents. These instructions specifically denied the Minister power to enter into discussions relevant to a treaty of commerce; any such proposals must be referred to Philadelphia. To provide information for the President, Monroe was asked to write regularly, reporting fully on economic and political conditions in France. In a final paragraph Randolph summed up the major objectives of the mission to France:

> You go, Sir, to France, to strengthen our friendship with that country.... You will show our confidence in the French Republic, without betraying the most remote mark of undue complaisance. *You will let it be seen that in case of war, with any nation on earth, we shall consider France as our first and natural ally.* You may dwell *upon the sense which we entertain of their past services.*...[36]

The italics (inserted by Monroe when he published this letter in 1797) indicate his understanding of the primary purpose of his mission. This interpretation was also supported by pro-French resolutions of the House and Senate and a friendly letter from Randolph to the Committee of Public Safety, all to be transmitted to the French government. A strong predilection for the revolutionary cause led Monroe to place a greater emphasis upon the literal meaning of Randolph's words than the administration had anticipated.

III

As the *Cincinnatus* entered the harbor at Le Havre on July 31, Monroe was stirred by the sight of the massive fortifications dominating the port, where great warships rode at anchor and others lay half-completed in the stocks. He was, of course, pleased over the realization of his long-cherished ambition to visit France, but most of all he was excited by the prospect of observing at first hand the Revolution he had so long admired from a distance. Even before his ship dropped anchor he learned of the recent unheavals in Paris, culminating in the overthrow of Robespierre. As he disembarked, he received a foretaste of the ambivalent attitude of the French toward the United States. Although respectfully greeted by the city officials, he was astonished by the violation of his diplomatic status when his trunks were opened and his provisions impounded. After resting briefly in Le Havre, the Monroes set out for Paris, where they arrived on August 2, five days after the execution of Robespierre.[37]

At the moment of his arrival in France conditions seemed favorable for a restoration of amicable relations: the regime identified with the hostile policy toward the United States had just collapsed, and Robert Morris, whose antagonism to the Revolution had rendered him *persona non grata,* was being replaced by a Minister of unquestioned republican sympathies. Although both nations were in a position to make a fresh start, the first step was difficult. Robespierre had been eliminated, but the Committee of Public Safety, which conducted foreign affairs, was still at the mercy of the Paris mob and fearful of introducing policies of uncertain popularity.[38]

As the Convention gradually reasserted its control the powers of the Committee were reduced, and in August a rule was adopted requiring that one fourth of the members of the Committee be replaced every month. It is true that there was some continuity in membership—the names of Reubell, Merlin de Douai, Cambacérès, Treilhard and Sieyès frequently occur—but the steady turnover was not favorable for shaping new policies. Most French leaders were unfamiliar with the issues involving France and the United States: of all the diplomatic problems facing the Committee that presented by America was the least significant. Thus a combination of fear and inattention led the Committee to resort to temporizing measures. By and large the Committee members continued to cherish the distrust of the United States formed during the Terror. The arrival of the American Minister presented the Committee with a problem not anticipated in Philadelphia. How much, the members wondered, could they trust Monroe? Could a Republican enjoy the confidence of a Federalist President? Such an appointment was inconceivable in France, and inevitably they suspected he might not be aware of the real objectives of the American government. Unpromising as this situation seemed, it had one advantage: since the Committee had no fixed policy, the Minister had a rare opportunity to influence decisions, if he could win the confidence of French officials. To this task Monroe now directed his efforts.

At first, however, the outlook was discouraging. He was presented to the foreign affairs representative of the Committee by Gouverneur Morris, who hastened to Paris as soon as he heard of the arrival of his successor. Not at all happy at a presentation arranged by a discredited emissary, Monroe had no choice but to accept Morris' agency. Although the reception was polite, he was given only the vaguest assurance that he would be officially received as soon as his credentials could be examined. Through Louis G. Otto, former secretary of the French legation in America, he learned that uncertainty about public response might delay his reception indefinitely. Otto, who headed one of the Committee's diplomatic bureaus, suggested that Monroe apply directly to the National Convention. The members of the Committee of Public Safety readily approved a plan absolving them of responsibility. It was equally welcome to the leaders of the Convention, who wished to symbolize in the dramatic fashion then so popular that they were reasserting the sovereign authority usurped by Robespierre. Convinced that the "connection between the two countries . . . hung upon a thread," Monroe accepted Otto's advice—there seemed no other way to obtain recognition. He realized that such unorthodox conduct would be used against him by the antirepublican elements at home, but this seemed unimportant in view of the opportunity offered to display to the world the continuing friendship between the two republics. A public reception would prove that the recent misunderstanding between France and the United States had been caused by inept diplomatic agents.[39]

On August 13 (just eleven days after his arrival in Paris), Monroe wrote Merlin de Douai, the president of the Convention, asking that arrangements be made for the reception of the representative of the "ally and sister Republic" of France. Since the very next day was chosen, there was not time to prepare an address with any care. Hastily, with Otto translating, the American Minister drafted an address lauding France's contribution to liberty, but, in line with the example set by the House and Senate resolves, without using the word *revolution*.[40] At two on the afternoon of the fourteenth he entered the chamber of the 700-member Convention after making his way through a friendly throng of several thousand spectators gathered outside. As he entered the hall he was greeted with clapping and loud cries of "Long live the Convention, long live the United States of America, our brave brothers." As Captain Barney, who was present, observed, they were received "more like beings of a superior nature than men." The Minister then addressed the Convention, affirming his conviction that the reception accorded him was but a new proof of the friendship France had always shown her ally. In phrases well-suited to the sense of the occasion and the French love of grandiloquence, Monroe declaimed:

Republics should approach near to each other. . . . This is more especially the case with the American and French Republics: their governments are similar; they both cherish the same principles and rest on the same basis, the equal and unalienable rights of men. The recollection too of common dangers and difficulties will increase their harmony, and cement their Union. America had her day of oppression, difficulty and war, but her sons were virtuous and brave and the storm which long clouded her political horizon has passed and left them in the enjoyment of peace, liberty and independence. France . . . has now embarked in the same noble career; and I am happy to add that whilst the fortitude, magnanimity and heroic valor of her troops command the admiration and applause of the astonished world, the wisdom and firmness of her councils unite equally in securing the happiest result.

As further proof that America was not an unfeeling spectator of France's valiant struggle, he submitted the resolutions of both Houses of Congress and Randolph's letter, adding on his own authority that the President had requested him to inform France that Washington also shared these sentiments. If he could promote harmony between the two nations, Monroe would deem it the "happiest event of my life, and return hereafter with a consolation, which those who mean well and have served the cause of liberty [,] alone can feel." [41] These were no empty phrases. Not until he read this address did Washington begin to comprehend the gulf which separated the administration from the Republican opposition. The tone of revolutionary amity struck by Merlin de Douai in his reply was even less welcome in Philadelphia:

How then should . . . [we] not be friends? Why should we not associate the mutual means of prosperity that our commerce and navigation offer to two people freed by each other? But it is not merely a diplomatic alliance: It is the sweetest fraternity, and the most frank at the same time, that must unite us; this it is that indeed unites us; and this union shall be forever indissoluble, as it will be forever the dread of tyrants, the safeguard of the liberty of the world, and the preserver of all the social and philanthropic virtues.

He then gave Monroe the fraternal embrace as a sign of the union between two peoples who would "complete the annihilation of an impious coalition of tyrants." The Minister was seated opposite the President, as the Convention enacted decrees recognizing him as Minister of the United States and ordering that the proceedings be printed in both English and French in the official records of the Convention. A third resolution provided that an American flag should be displayed in the chamber next to the flag of France.[42] At his own expense he purchased a silk flag with silver stars and a fine gold fringe which was presented by Captain Barney to the Convention a month later.[43] Monroe was much impressed by this emotionally charged ceremony, a kind of public drama novel to him: it was, as he told Madison, an affair of "distressing sensibility." Important as the action of the Convention was, he considered the friendly reception given him by the crowd the decisive factor in persuading the Committee of Public Safety to display a friendlier attitude toward him.[44]

As he had correctly gauged, his address and reception found little favor among the Federalists, who would have preferred to see the resolutions of the two houses and Randolph's letter "smuggled in and as secretly deposited." [45] He was not surprised at Madison's report that his speech had been "very grating to the ears of many," who only refrained from open condemnation because to do so would be an attack on the administration.[46] No one was more critical than Jay, who protested from London that these ill-considered remarks had jeopardized his negotiations. He was especially aggrieved that Monroe had not considered the effect his remarks would have on public opinion in England.[47] The Republicans were understandably delighted at the reception. "Your address," wrote Senator John Brown of Kentucky, "has been read with enthusiasm and approbation by every friend of the Rights of Man, as breathing the genuine sentiments of Republicanism, and as expressing the sense of nineteen twentieths of the Citizens of the Union." [48] The chorus of praise from the Republicans dimmed the voices of the critics and strengthened Monroe's belief in the rightness of his conduct.

As a result of the slow transatlantic communications (now disrupted by the war) American diplomats not only suffered the handicap of operating without regular contact with the administration but faced the additional hazard that long-delayed dispatches might create serious misunderstanding. From the outset of his mission Monroe's standing with the administration was damaged by the late arrival of the account of his reception by the Convention. Although he had written promptly stating the reasons for his action, the dispatch did not reach Philadelphia until long after later communications, in which he alluded to his reception without explaining his motives. Assuming that Monroe was avoiding an explanation, Washington instructed Randolph to express his disapproval. Accordingly, in a strongly worded letter the Secretary rebuked the Minister in Paris for not insisting on a private reception which would have spared the nation the embarrassment of seeing Monroe's address assailed in the press of the allied powers. He also took the

Minister to task for remarks which seemed to raise doubts about American neutrality. Cautioning him to be careful not to let his private views color public statements lest he be disavowed, Randolph reminded him that he still had it "in charge to cultivate the French republic with zeal, but without any unnecessary *éclat....*"[49] Several days later when Monroe's earlier explanatory dispatch arrived, Randolph wrote removing some of the sting from his reprimand, admitting that the explanations removed all improper impressions. In this second letter Randolph characteristically shifted his emphasis from the restrained language of his rebuke to the openly pro-French tone of his instructions, ending his letter with the charge: "Remember to remove every suspicion of our preferring a connexion with Great Britain, or in any manner weakening our old attachment to France."[50] Small wonder that Monroe continued to regard the tightening of Franco-American relations as the primary objective of his mission, whereas the President wished only to preserve the status quo. Although Washington officially accepted Monroe's explanations, privately he expressed the opinion that the address to the Convention had not been "well devised" in view of America's proclaimed neutrality. He did not, however, share Jay's conviction that Monroe had damaged the prospect of a favorable settlement with Great Britain. As the President shrewdly pointed out, Monroe's remarks could alarm the Ministry as well as merely offend it.[51] For the moment at least, Washington was content to continue Monroe in Paris, as the best means of preventing a rupture pending the outcome of Jay's negotiations.

IV

Quite unaware of the developments at home (Randolph's reprimand did not reach him until February), Monroe eagerly turned to the specific objects of his mission, encouraged by the new friendliness of the Committee, which now released his impounded supplies and offered him a carriage and horses. He accepted the use of the carriage only until he could purchase his own equipage. He was also offered a residence in Paris, but this he declined, since such gifts were forbidden by the Constitution.[52] Working rapidly to take advantage of the "thaw," he submitted on September 3 a note reviewing the major grievances of the United States.[53] First, he raised the question of indemnities arising from the embargo imposed on American ships at Bordeaux, which had been in effect from August 12, 1793, until April 10, 1794.

Although the order had been rescinded, no adjustment had ever been made for the losses sustained by the owners of the ships held in port. Second, he presented a demand for the payment of supplies sent to Santo Domingo by American merchants on orders from the French Minister to the United States, for which shippers had never been paid. This, like the embargo claims, was a minor issue, for which France acknowledged responsibility. Far more significant were the complaints arising from damages to American commerce as a result of French violation of Articles 23 and 24 of the Treaty of 1778, in which France had accepted the principle that free ships made free goods (except for contraband of war). Since the outbreak of the war these provisions had been ignored, as France seized American cargoes, contrary to the stipulations of the treaty. In response to the argument advanced by French officials that they were only following British practices, Monroe rightly asked why France, with whom the United States had a treaty defining these rights, should fail to adhere to principles which were at once beneficial to the United States and in harmony with France's treaty obligations. "Will our ally contend with England . . . in rivalship, which shall harrass [sic] our commerce most and do us the greatest detriment?" Moreover, France gained nothing from such restrictions. In pressing for the repeal of these orders he made it clear that he was not presenting a formal demand for the enforcement of the Treaty of 1778, but that he was recommending revocation as a policy highly advantageous to France: repeal of the orders would not only encourage American trade, it would also remove a major cause of friction between the two powers. With greater frankness than the occasion required, he told the Committee that he had not been instructed to press these particular issues. Nor was it wise of him to comment that, if France was convinced of the necessity of these restrictions, Americans would endure them "not only with patience but with pleasure." In the dispatch enclosing a copy of the note of September 3 Monroe explicitly stated the reasons for his approach: first, it seemed more conciliatory to rest his appeal on the basis of friendship; second, he felt that it might be embarrassing for the United States to insist on the enforcement of the treaty, for France then might demand rights under the treaty, which the administration would prefer not to grant.[54] When Monroe, somewhat later, received supplementary instructions from Randolph directing him to request the repeal of the French restrictions, he saw no reason to shift his ground: Randolph said nothing about basing the American case on the enforcement of the Treaty of 1778.[55]

Monroe's note of September 3 brought another rebuke from Randolph, who protested that the Minister's approach rendered it impossible in the future to rest the case for repeal on the basis of a violation of treaty obligations. Admitting that he had not written specifically on this point, Randolph insisted that it should have been evident that the administration would not waive its rights under the treaty: ". . . was it necessary to intimate that an indifference prevailed in our government as to these articles, by a declaration that you were not instructed to complain of the decree?" [56] By the time the reprimand reached Paris the issue had been rendered academic with the repeal of the offensive decrees. The success of his representations seemed sufficient proof to Monroe that his course had been the proper one to follow. Not only did the outcome increase his confidence in his judgment, but it also encouraged him to act independently when the occasion warranted it. [57]

As he waited for a reply to the note of September 3, Monroe inaugurated changes in the consular service in accordance with his instructions. His first measure was to appoint Fulwar Skipwith Acting Consul General, a choice pleasing to the French in view of Skipwith's open republican enthusiasm. Skipwith was installed, although it was known that Washington had appointed a French citizen, Alexander Duvernat, who had not yet arrived in Paris. However, a resident consul was needed immediately to process the claims of Americans flocking to Paris in the expectation that the favorable reception accorded the new Minister presaged a favorable settlement of all claims. The appointment was also designed to reduce the influence of self-appointed agents such as James Swan, whose political contacts enabled them to charge handsome fees for assisting claimants. The President, accepting the validity of Monroe's contention that in the tense political atmosphere of Paris no French citizen could hope to enjoy the confidence of the Committee, withdrew Duvernat's commission in favor of Skipwith. [58]

Perhaps no problem was as annoying as the validation of passports, which were ordinarily issued by the Minister or the consuls. Shortly after his arrival the Committee of Public Safety had complained about Morris' carelessness, asserting that he had granted papers to British spies. The French were baffled that merchants who had not resided in the United States since 1776 carried American passports; some indeed, claiming double citizenship, also held British passports. To improve this situation the consuls were instructed not to issue papers unless the applicants proved actual citizenship. However, ownership of property was not in itself sufficient evidence. Not long after this, when the

French arrested a spy with American credentials, Monroe restricted the issuance of passports to his office.[59] Punctiliously he fulfilled the tedious duty of sending to the Committee a monthly list of all Americans in Paris together with their reasons for being in the city.[60] Although he made every effort to accommodate reasonable complaints, he steadfastly refused to make concessions when the grievances were invalid. Thus he successfully protested the French assertion that resident Ministers could only extend their protection to native-born citizens. In the summer of 1795 he refused to order the consuls to restrain American ships from engaging in trade between France and England, pointing out that he was being asked to repress a trade not contrary to French law. All he could do was require that American shippers abide by the laws of France.[61]

V

One of the first duties assigned to Skipwith was the preparation of a report on the seizures made by the French. Since Morris had kept no records, the consuls were summoned to Paris to assist Skipwith and to provide information on trade problems in general.[62] In mid-October, when Monroe submitted the report to the Committee, he was granted an interview on the same day. Whether sincere or not, the Committee members professed themselves shocked at the extent of the seizures, assuring the Minister that they were totally unaware of the extent of depredations authorized by local authorities. A few days later (October 18) he followed up this interview with an additional note and a separate document entitled "Supplemental observations to the note of 3d. of September, upon the American commerce." [63] The note of October 18 was designed to prod the Committee to act on his earlier protest by warning that commerce between the two countries would soon cease unless the restrictions were lifted. As an additional stimulant the Committee was reminded that prompt action would enable him to send the news to America in time for the opening of Congress, when it was customary for the President to report on the disposition of foreign powers toward the United States.

The "Supplemental Observations" fell into the framework of Monroe's program of exerting every possible pressure upon the Committee to repeal the restrictive orders. In this paper he appealed to French self-interest, by arguing that the continued use of purchasing agents operated to the detriment of France, since France paid higher prices and received fewer shipments than would be the case if competitive bidding were permitted. Moreover, goods purchased by agents were French property and thus subject to seizure, whereas, as long as they were shipped by American merchants on their own account, they enjoyed the status of neutral property. As things now stood, American merchants had no interest in trading with France. The agents, with a vested interest in the restrictive system, acted as a powerful obstacle to a complete reform of France's commercial policy. They alone stood to lose by a system of trade which encouraged independent shipments. In delivering this attack on the purchasing agents, Monroe was echoing the rising tide of criticism in France against the centralized economic policies instituted by the Jacobins. He was aware that French officials were deeply concerned about the prospects of famine in the wake of the poor harvest of 1794.[64] The deliberations of the Committee were a well-kept secret; consequently, when Monroe met with the diplomatic members of the Committee not long after submitting his "Observations," he had no intimation that a drastic change in policy was in the offing. Therefore, he was completely at a loss when Merlin de Douai abruptly queried: "Do you insist upon our executing the treaty?" When Monroe evaded by replying that he had nothing to add to what he had previously stated, the question was reiterated. Suspecting that the sole purpose was to extract a formal statement from him, Monroe repeated his former declaration that he had no instructions. He was, he told the Committee, advocating measures which would not only benefit the United States but serve the true interests of France as well. The meeting ended with some random comments from the members concerning the delicacy of adopting a policy which many would construe as favorable to England. In retrospect Monroe could not decide whether the Committee was searching for an easier ground upon which to rest a repeal of the orders or was attempting to force the United States to comply with the treaty.[65] He had no idea that he had given the exact reply sought by the Committee, which had before it a report prepared by Otto recommending that American demands (which were in accordance with France's treaty obligations) be granted. Otto had suggested that the way might be paved for a commercial treaty favorable to France, if the United States were not forced to insist upon repeal as a matter of right. After this enigmatic interview Monroe debated appealing to the Convention, but he ruled this out, since it might seem to be a denunciation of the Committee and jeopardize his standing with that body.[66]

Although the Committee had in fact decided to repeal the orders, nothing was said to the American Minister, who now fretted that French apprehensions about the objectives of Jay's mission might prevent a decision in his favor. His first opportunity to reduce French anxiety over Jay's negotiations came in November, when he informed the Committee of recent instructions authorizing him to offer the services of the United States in restoring peace between France and England. The offer, as expected, was courteously declined. A query about Jay gave him a chance to declare that the envoy to England had been sent on "especial business" under specific instructions to "demand reparations of injuries . . . to which his authority was strictly limited." [67] His narrow understanding of Jay's mission was apparently confirmed a few days later by a dispatch from Randolph dated September 25, warning him to take steps to counteract the unfavorable impression of American policy Fauchet was supposedly transmitting to his government. In pointed terms the Secretary had written:

One thing is certain: that he [Fauchet] supposes a British tendency to prevail in some members of our Government. . . . You are possessed of all the means of confronting this idea. *You know how Mr. Jay is restricted* [italics are Monroe's] and I must acknowledge to you, that not withstanding the pompous expectations announced in the Gazettes of compensation to the merchants, the prospect of it is in my Judgement illusory; and I do not entertain the most distant hope of the surrender of the Western Posts. Thus the old exasperations continue; and new ones are daily added. Judge then how indispensable it is, that you should keep the French Republic in good humor with us.[68]

What else could Monroe conclude from this amazing letter but that he must at all costs preserve friendship with France, since, as Randolph intimated, Jay was not expected to succeed. He was quite unaware that the Secretary was veering away from the Federalist position and was in fact expressing his own opinions rather than those of the administration. In making his comments to the Committee about Jay, Monroe had some reservations about how his remarks would be received in Philadelphia; consequently, he said nothing about the exchange with the Committee in his next dispatch. Randolph's letter removed his hesitations, and only after receiving it did he belatedly inform the Secretary about the details of the conference.

The American Minister was given another insight into the mysterious operations of the Committee later in November during a conference about communications he had received from Don Diego de Gardoqui, onetime Minister to the United States and now Minister of Finances in Spain. Gardoqui, presuming on an old but distant acquaintance, had written asking the American Minister to help him obtain permission to take the waters at Bagnères and to deliver an enclosed letter to Otto. Suspecting that this was a thinly disguised peace overture, Monroe neither replied nor delivered the enclosure. After a second letter arrived he felt that silence on his part would be misunderstood, if the Committee became aware of Gardoqui's letters. Much gratified by the Minister's frankness, the Committee asked him to inform Gardoqui to write directly for permission to enter France. The Committee members then introduced an entirely unexpected topic: Monroe was asked whether France could float a loan in the United States. Concerned that an outright rejection might prejudice the Committee against American claims, Monroe temporized, offering to refer the matter to his government. However, he expressed as a personal opinion his own belief that the United States would do everything possible to aid France. At this conference Monroe (in accordance with his instructions) pressed the Committee to support America's claims against Spain and Great Britain.[69] Recent rumors that peace negotiations were imminent made this question more urgent than it had been. He followed up this conference with a note stressing that France could hope to raise a much larger sum if it were known that she was supporting American claims in the peace negotiations.[70] In private Monroe was far more confident that France could float a substantial loan—perhaps as much as $10,000,000— than he indicated in his conversations with the Committee.[71] Although he raised the matter, he did not expect much tangible assistance from France in advancing American interests in the peace negotiations. He really felt, as he told Randolph, that the United States would best serve its own interests by taking advantage of the deep involvement of the European powers in the war to seize the posts and to open the Mississippi by force; neither Spain nor England was in a position to retaliate.[72]

In June of the following year, while Jay's Treaty was pending, he reiterated this advice in stronger terms, telling Randolph that the time had finally come "when the duty we owe to ourselves, and the respect which is due to the opinion of the world, admonish us that the insults and injuries of Britain are to be no longer borne, and that we ought to seek redress by again appealing to arms...."[73] A few months later he suggested to Madison that the United States should seize the posts, invade Canada and occupy the Bermudas as a means of forcing Britain to acknowledge American claims: "... this would be acting like a nation, and we should then be respected as such here and in England." [74] This vigorous approach, which did not strike a responsive chord in Philadelphia, became a cardinal principle in his view of American foreign policy. Again and again he was to restate these conclusions during the next two decades, only to find that such aggressive counsel was no more to the liking of his Republican associates than it had been to Washington and the Federalists. As Samuel Flagg Bemis observed some years ago, Monroe is unique among the early national leaders in that his writings are free from those constant affirmations that the true policy of the United States was to steer clear of European politics.[75] From a very early date Monroe envisaged a far more active role for the United States in the world scene as the sole way of safeguarding American interests.

The belated request for aid in raising a loan seems to have been nothing more than an attempt to extract some exchange for the projected repeal of France's commercial restrictions. Although nothing was said to Monroe hinting at a change of policy, the Committee had already recommended to the Convention that neutrals be granted free entry to French ports and that the provisions of the Treaty of 1778 be observed. Not until some weeks later, on November 21, was the American Minister informed of this decision.[76] The news was immensely gratifying, for it meant that in less than four months he had achieved the main objectives (as he understood them) of his mission—the restoration of amicable relations and the cancellation of the objectionable trade regulations. Certainly he owed much of his success to the excellent personal rapport he had established with French public officials. The fact that he created such confidence in himself was important, for Frenchmen as a rule saw little significance in American trade as a source of supply for essential foodstuffs, but rather looked to the Baltic market now being reopened. Thus from a practical point of view there was little impetus to favor American trade. Moreover, in making this reversal, the Committee members were not insensitive to the argument that a natural affinity existed between the only two republican governments in the world, a point of view skillfully developed by Monroe. It must be remembered, too, that he was the beneficiary of the determination to liquidate the Jacobin economic policies now blamed for the famine and fiscal collapse facing France. Not only were the restrictions lifted but new instructions penned for Fauchet in October 1794 reflected a mild and friendly tone. Unfortunately, the Washington administration did not place a high value on the results of Monroe's

labors or regard trade with France as of much importance. So fearful
were the Federalists of the consequences of his open declarations of
friendship for France that they could not appreciate the tangible benefits of his mission. Only if Jay had failed to conclude a treaty would
Monroe's achievements have been prized.[77]

CHAPTER 8

THERMIDORIAN FRANCE

ONROE, for whom politics was a consuming interest, was intensely interested in the complex events he witnessed during his two-year sojourn in France. Although he arrived after the most spectacular scenes of the Revolution, the process by which the Thermidorians established a stable regime in the face of threats from both the right and the left nonetheless offered a fascinating study. The labyrinth of French politics was by no means easy to penetrate: not only did factions shift constantly, but the Thermidorians, behind a great show of Jacobin ideology, also enacted measures flatly contradicting these principles. On the whole Monroe's letters revealed an excellent understanding of the course of events, considering that his information was derived solely from the press and conversations with members of the government without the benefit of an inside source. Undoubtedly Thomas Paine, who had been a member of the Convention, supplied him with useful background material, yet the letters written before Paine's release from prison showed a full grasp of the circumstances leading to Robespierre's fall. Thus on the basis of his own observations Monroe correctly discounted the reports that Robespierre's removal had been necessary to circumvent a Jacobin purge of the Convention.[1]

His chief limitation sprang from his own tendency (one not uncommon with Americans) to take a generalized view of events, seeking to attribute political actions to broad principles rather than to personalities or private ambitions. He consequently ignored the enormous role played by personal relations in the Thermidorian movement; there is almost no commentary in his letters about the major figures he came to know. Moreover, in terms of his American experience he did not understand the extent to which the Thermidorians were motivated by both fear of renewed violence and a quest for personal security. His emphasis upon the seemingly moderate republicanism of the Thermidorian movement led him seriously to underestimate the power of rightist elements.[2] Nonetheless, in spite of his enthusiasm for the cause of liberty, he was sufficiently realistic to acknowledge the necessity of repressive measures, such as the suppression of the Jacobin club in 1795, if France were to achieve political stability. During the political turmoil of these years he was careful to remain completely detached. His belief in the superiority of American institutions led him to hope that the committee appointed to draft a new constitution in 1796 might be moved to imitate the Constitution of the United States. He saw no objection in supplying the committee with a summary of the Constitution of the United States. The French constitution of 1796, which bore no resemblance to that of the United States, was disappointing, but he felt that at least it provided adequate safeguards against the greatest threat to liberty in France—executive domination.[3]

Monroe's earliest private and public letters were replete with lengthy analyses of French politics. Not only had he been instructed to report on political and economic developments in France, but he wished to present a correct view of the Revolution to his fellow countrymen, who were largely dependent upon hostile accounts taken from the British press. However, after the summer of 1795 he became much more reserved in his official correspondence, for he was annoyed over the release to the press of a portion of one of his dispatches containing a critical account of the Jacobin society.[4] Washington, who had publicly censured the new democratic republican societies appearing in America in imitation of the French political clubs, had considered the letter an apt demonstration of the dangers against which he had warned the nation. Although the extracts of this dispatch did not appear over Monroe's name, he was immediately identified as the author.[5] It was indeed painful for the Republicans to see one of the Minister's official communications used to injure his own party.[6]

So completely was Monroe's interest confined to politics that his letters contained few references either to his life in Paris or to general conditions in France. When he arrived with his family, he entered a city still in the shadow of the Terror—anxiety and fear had not dissipated. Paris bore visible scars not only of the austerity of the Jacobin years, but also of the neglect and decay that followed the Revolution. Buildings were everywhere in a dilapidated condition, the streets filthy, the shops empty; nowhere was there evidence of the famed elegance and luxury of the city. The Monroes possessed one of the few carriages to be seen in Paris during the first winter of their residence, which was one of the coldest of the century. Not only was fuel scarce and costly, but food supplies were so inadequate that rationing was necessary. The Minister was allowed only two pounds of bread a day for an establishment of fourteen persons. Fortunately, with foreign credit at his disposal, Monroe was able to purchase flour at the exorbitant price of forty dollars per barrel.[7] Although there was some renewal of social life that winter, most of it was not the sort in which the Minister and his family could join. He could not without jeopardizing his mission frequent the newly opened salons of Mmes. Tallien and Hamelin, for these ladies were too deeply involved in the precariously shifting politics of the day. Nor could he with propriety attend the public balls which now became the rage of all classes.[8] During this first winter, the Monroes had little social diversion—even official entertaining had ceased.[9] As long as French policy toward the United States remained undefined, the members of the Committee of Public Safety hesitated to appear overly friendly to the American Minister. Consequently, when he invited the members of the Committee to dinner in September 1794, not one attended, and only a few bothered to acknowledge the invitation. Of the few Americans in Paris that winter the Minister had a low opinion. Most were New Englanders with strong pro-British sentiments, who were in France to press claims against the government.[10]

II

After France abandoned her anti-American policy late in 1794 the social scene brightened considerably for the Monroes as French public leaders not only accepted invitations from the American Minister and his wife but also began to entertain. At first the Monroes lived in the house occupied by Gouverneur Morris, but early in the summer of 1795 they moved to an elegant residence known as the Folie de la Bouexière on the rue de Clichy. Although the Folie was small, with only six principal rooms, it was a sumptuous structure in the fashionable style of a one-story pavilion. Set in the midst of superb gardens laid out by Chevaulet, the Folie had been constructed by a wealthy farmer-general as a pleasure retreat. The rococo interior was elaborately embellished with a profusion of gilded ornamentation, bronze statuary, mirrors and richly painted ceilings. In furnishing the Folie, the Minis-

ter, in preference to the usual painted furniture found in houses of
this style, chose pieces of simpler design in natural woods. It was at this
time that Monroe purchased the splendid Louis XVI pieces now in
Fredericksburg. In purchasing the Folie, which cost only 73,000 livres
(about $15,000), Monroe intended to sell it at cost to the United States
as a permanent residence for the American Ministers, an arrangement
rendered impossible by his subsequent estrangement from the administration. The fact that at the end of his mission he disposed of the house
for $20,000 led to reports that he had speculated in French real estate.
The profit, if any, was nominal, for he had spent substantial sums in repairs and in replanting the neglected garden.[11] His purchase was not to
be compared to that of such active speculators as Jonathan Russell, who
acquired just outside Paris a forty-room chateau with eighteen acres of
land for a thousand guineas—a fraction of the original cost.[12]

In this handsome residence on the outskirts of Paris (but still within
the walls) the Monroes drew together a social circle composed of visiting
Americans, French officials and personal friends. With a staff of only
seven servants, including a gardener, a cook and a coachman, entertaining was simple but generous. At their dinner table could be seen
members of the Convention, of the Committee of Public Safety and
later members of the Directory, for Monroe regarded personal contacts
with French officials the key to the success of his mission. He was on
excellent terms with Merlin de Thionville, Tallien, Thibaudeau and
Reubell, all highly influential during the Thermidorian reaction.[13]
Reubell, later a member of the Directory, was a dominant figure in
foreign relations at this time. A warm welcome was extended to visiting
Americans, among them many Federalists, who later repaid the Minister's hospitality by spreading reports that he was a speculator and that
his home was a center of antiadministration sentiment.

Far more important to the Monroe circle than these casual profit-
seekers were those visitors whose enthusiasm for the revolutionary
cause had drawn them to France. Prominent among these republican
zealots during the winter of 1795–1796 was Dr. Enoch Edwards, a
wealthy Philadelphian introduced to Monroe by both Jefferson and
Madison. Edwards enjoyed the confidence of the Minister, who talked
rather too freely with him, for Edwards was inclined to be indiscreet.[14]
Joel Barlow, who had originally gone to Europe in connection with
the sale of the Scioto Company lands but had remained to give his
aid to the revolutionary movement in France, was also a frequent

visitor at the Folie. His activities had earned him the reward of French citizenship, thus placing him in the select company of Paine, Washington, Hamilton, and Madison, all of whom had been honored in this fashion. Barlow and his charming wife were the center of a stimulating group of American and European radicals, some of whom had been members of the Godwin circle in England. Perhaps Monroe may not have known Mary Wollstonecraft and her American lover, the adventurer Gilbert Imlay, or the redoutable Godwinite Hester Maria Williams, but he did form a close friendship with Benjamin Vaughan, a former member of Parliament and intimate of Joseph Priestley who had fled England to avoid trial for treason as a result of his open pro-French sympathies. With Vaughan, who later emigrated to America, Monroe maintained a correspondence lasting until his retirement from the Presidency.[15] Another English visitor at the Minister's residence was Sir Robert Smith, an English banker of radical views who had renounced his title to stay in France during the Revolution. If friendship with such advanced spirits was not calculated to be well received in Philadelphia, the Minister's association with the Irish revolutionaries Alexander H. Rowan and Wolfe Tone, who were in Paris to seek French aid, was greeted with positive horror by the Federalists. When Rowan went to America, Monroe gave him a letter of introduction to Randolph, an act the President considered a "premeditated" effort to embarrass the administration by officially presenting a person who had been convicted of sedition in England.[16] Although Monroe did not aid Tone officially, he allowed the use of his name for the "authenticity of what you may advance, and you may add that you have reason to think that I am in a degree, apprised of your business." Tone had no success in his plans, but Monroe's name opened many doors for him.[17] Still another revolutionary exile welcomed at the Folie was van Staphorst, a member of the Dutch banking family which rendered such useful services to the United States.[18] Accepting the premise that the survival of freedom in America was dependent upon the advancement of republicanism in Europe, Monroe saw no impropriety in these friendships.

The most celebrated radical in the Minister's circle was Thomas Paine, whose intimacy with Monroe scandalized the Federalists. When Monroe landed in France, Paine had been incarcerated for more than nine months. Gouverneur Morris, who abominated Paine's principles, had not intervened on the ground that Paine, as a French citizen, was not within his protection. Monroe (who had no instructions on this point) secured Paine's release by insisting to the Committee that he was still an American citizen and as such should either be brought to trial or discharged.[19] At the time of his release Paine was so ill that the American Minister took him to the Folie to nurse him and to protect him from further arrest. Paine's sojourn at the Folie from November 1794 until the spring of 1796 was not only longer than the Minister anticipated but ultimately a source of embarrassment. Paine had not been at the Folie long before Monroe learned that his guest was drafting a bitter attack on Washington, whom he blamed for Morris' failure to intervene on his behalf. Only after considerable persuasion did Paine grudgingly agree to refrain from polemics while at the Folie.[20]

In sheltering Paine, Monroe was not merely performing an act of piety toward this hero of two revolutions, but he was welcoming a guest whose charm, knowledge and fascinating conversation were much appreciated. As yet Paine's excessive drinking had not reached the disastrous level of his later years; true, as Wolfe Tone noted, he "drank like a fish," but admirers thought brandy only made him more eloquent.[21] The Minister probably found Paine's knowledge of French politics useful, but there is no indication that Paine exerted much influence on his host, whose attitudes toward the Revolution were formed before Paine's release. Not until after the formation of the Directory in 1796 did Paine present his views to the Foreign Office, and then his advice merely reinforced the decision to follow the British lead in imposing commercial restrictions on the United States. Nor does it appear (as some of Paine's biographers have asserted) that it was only through Paine's protective friendship that Monroe was able to remain in Paris in 1796 after the rupture produced by Jay's Treaty. On the contrary, the Directors—who had no affection for radicals like Paine— had a personal regard for Monroe quite unrelated to his association with the author of *Common Sense*.[22]

Much as he admired the hero of two revolutions, Monroe's guest was a political liability. After a lifetime of pamphleteering it was too much to expect Paine not to air his grievance against Washington just to avoid embarrassment to his host. In the spring of 1796, when Monroe discovered that his guest was again readying a denunciation of the President, he objected. Unwilling to yield to Monroe's wishes, Paine preferred to leave the comforts of the Folie. The fruit of his labors was a vituperative open letter to Washington, published first in England, then in Philadelphia by that staunch Republican, Benjamin F.

Bache.[23] This tract did not appear until Monroe had been recalled, but the Minister had been implicated by reports concerning Paine's comments about Washington's ingratitude.[24]

Monroe was not at all pleased when he heard that Paine wished to return with him to the United States. To land in America in the company of a notorious critic of the President would jeopardize his political future. He disapproved of many administration policies, but he did not wish to be identified as personally hostile to the all-popular Washington. At Monroe's request, Benjamin Vaughan dissuaded Paine from crossing with the Minister by pointing out that this exposed him to great risk of capture, for the British would surely make every attempt to seize him and bring him to trial for treason. Vaughan was careful not to let Paine know that he was Monroe's agent, lest Paine elevate the Minister to the first rank of his enemies.[25] When Paine returned to America some years later, Monroe, like so many of the revolutionary pamphleteer's friends, avoided intimate association with him. Americans had become uneasy about the radical character of Paine's later writings, especially his attack on Christianity in the *Age of Reason*.

Paine was but one of many persons aided by the Minister, who received appeals from Americans, Englishmen and Frenchmen. Perhaps his most notable achievement was securing the release in February 1795 of all the Americans still in prison.[26] Normally he could do little for French citizens, but he took particular interest in the plight of one: Madame Lafayette, still in prison and in danger of execution. However, he dared not act in her behalf until he had won the confidence of the Committee of Public Safety lest a premature move increase her danger. In order to lay the groundwork for an appeal and to place her as much as he could under his protection, Monroe utilized the one force to which the French leaders were always responsive—public opinion. The story of his intervention as related by Monroe in his autobiography has a quality of drama rare in his writings:

There were then no private carriages in Paris and the hacks were generally in the worst state. Mr. Monroe procured a carriage of his own as soon as he could, had it put in the best order, and his servants dressed in like manner. In this carriage Mrs. Monroe drove directly to the prison. . . . As soon as she entered the street, the public attention was drawn to it, and at the prison gate the crowd gathered round it. Inquiry was made, whose carriage was it? The answer given was, that of the American Minister. Who is in it? His wife. What brought her here? To see Madame LaFayette. The concierge . . . brought her to the iron railing in which the gate was fixed. A short time before, her mother and grandmother had been taken from the same prison and beheaded, and she expected from the first summons to her to experience the same fate. On hearing that the wife of the American Minister had called with the most friendly motives to see her, she became frantic, and in that state they met. The scene was most affecting. The sensibility of all the beholders was deeply excited. The report of the interview spread through Paris and had the happiest effect. Informal communications took place in consequence between Mr. Monroe and the members of the Committee, and the liberation of Madame LaFayette soon followed.

After she had been released the American Minister obtained a passport enabling her to join her husband at Olmutz, where he had been imprisoned by the allies.[27]

A number of Jefferson's friends (many of whom had been in prison during the Terror) were welcomed at the Folie. Madame de Corny, wife of a close associate of Lafayette's and one of Jefferson's dearest friends, was a frequent visitor, although she declined to dine when other guests were present. A much more celebrated figure out of the past was Madame de Vallette, Voltaire's protegée, whom he had so fondly called "La Belle et La Bonne." The eighty-year-old Mr. Thomas Gem, an expatriate English physician whose advanced ideas (he was a friend of D'Holbach) had once delighted Jefferson, still managed to walk a good league to breakfast with the American Minister.[28]

During their sojourn in France the Monroes developed a lasting predilection for both French decorative arts and for French social usages. It was here that Mrs. Monroe adopted the rule that visiting strangers must pay the first call. When Mrs. Monroe was in the White House her rigorous application of this rule, contrary to American usage (which required the resident to call on visiting strangers), stirred up a tempest of major proportions in Washington social circles.[29] All the members of the Minister's family learned to speak French fluently; by 1796 Monroe was sufficiently at ease to dispense with an interpreter at official interviews.[30] His open enthusiasm for the Revolution, the obvious admiration for French taste, which he shared with his wife, and the grace and beauty of Mrs. Monroe all contributed to make him a personal success among French political leaders. Eliza, now eight, received a thoroughly French education at the school operated by Mme. Campan, a former lady-in-wating to Marie Antoinette. Her school, located a short distance from Paris at St. Germain-en-Laye, became the most fashionable girls' school in France during the Directory and Empire. The new political leaders, who were for the most part parvenus, considered it essential that their daughters acquire the polish and manners of the *ancien régime,* which were instilled with authority by Mme. Campan. Unfortunately, this aristocratic polish was accompanied by a large measure of snobbery. Her pupils, including Eliza Monroe, tended to develop exaggerated notions of their own importance, whatever their origins. Eliza, at this time an only child much indulged by her parents, emerged from Mme. Campan's school a vain young lady who never forgot (and gladly reminded all and sundry) that Hortense de Beauharnais had been a friend of her schooldays. Such open snobbery made her highly unpopular with her contemporaries. Monroe also enrolled Joseph Jones, Jr. (his tutors were unable to control him), in another school in St. Germain. In order to visit Eliza and Joseph and also to escape from Paris during the summer, the Monroes rented a house at St. Germain. Apart from a visit to Versailles in September 1794, the summer days at St. Germain constituted the only excursions from Paris until after the Minister's recall.[31]

The public entertainments arranged by the Minister were of a kind to gratify the French taste for ceremonial affairs with symbolic overtones. On July 4, 1795, Monroe, hoping that a public celebration of Independence Day might advance American interests by reminding the French of the common nature of the two revolutions, invited the Americans in Paris, the members of the diplomatic corps, members of the Committee of Public Safety and members of the Convention— some two hundred in all—to dinner at the Folie. To accommodate the guests a dozen marquees, borrowed from the war ministry, were decorated with wreaths of roses and extended over a long table set up in an alley in the garden. Music, fine food and patriotic toasts created a mood of revolutionary sentiment which was obviously highly pleasing to the French officials present, who found the new Minister's courtesy to the representatives of republican France an agreeable contrast to the distance maintained by Morris.[32]

A similar celebration the following year was attended by rather unhappy repercussions. In 1796 the Americans in Paris decided to return the Minister's hospitality by organizing a public dinner. The promoters—all zealous Republicans—tactlessly omitted from the printed list the customary toast to the President. Since this open neglect would compromise Monroe, he arranged through Dr. Edwards that the first volunteer toast be to the President. Although by no means happy with this solution, Monroe attended the dinner lest his absence from a gathering attended by other members of the diplomatic corps and such prominent Frenchmen as Tallien and Barbé-Marbois should cause a greater scandal. As soon as the gentleman selected to deliver the voluntary toast to Washington arose, Monroe also stood up raising his glass and cheering three times after the toast had been completed. While the toast was being delivered several guests hissed and a brief scuffle ensued between Republican enthusiasts and those resentful of this public disrespect toward Washington. The episode embarrassed the Minister, who knew that it would be used against him at home. To minimize the harm, he sent Madison a full account of the affair. Hostile reports elevated the scuffle into a full-fledged brawl with the Minister bearing the blame for omitting the toast to Washington. Although the incident took place after his recall had been decided upon, it was used as an additional proof of the wisdom of the President's action.[33]

On several occasions the American Minister participated in the rather theatrical public ceremonies so dear to the revolutionary leaders in France. Not long after his arrival he marched in a procession of members of the Convention accompanying the removal of Marat's body to the Panthéon. As he walked next to Merlin de Thionville, Monroe asked frankly if Marat was really as much admired as this honor would indicate. With equal frankness Merlin de Thionville replied that not only was Marat universally execrated, but within three months his body would be removed; the only reason for the present reburial was to allay suspicions that the Thermidorians contemplated repressive measures against former Jacobins. Merlin proved to be correct; in February 1795, during a procession accompanying the remains of Voltaire and Rousseau to the Panthéon, Monroe noted that the bodies of Marat and Mirabeau had been discreetly removed. On this second occasion the Americans, now that France had lifted all her restrictions, were given a prominent position in the line of march before the members of the Convention. Monroe's cousin and Captain Barney's son bore the flag which the Minister had presented to the Convention.[34]

An inevitable obligation assumed by American diplomats at this time was the duty of executing commissions for friends and acquaintances. Not only did Monroe have his young cousin in charge, but former senatorial colleagues from South Carolina, Ralph Izard and John Rutledge, asked him to place their sons in French schools.[35] Most gratifying was the opportunity to repay Madison and Jefferson for their many favors. For Madison he shopped for used furniture, securing excellent bargains in a set of bed curtains with matching draperies, carpets and a china tea set. For Jefferson he searched out books, purchasing for himself the complete works of Voltaire, Rousseau, Helvétius, Crébillon and Buffon. He also advanced money to Jefferson's friends who were in need. Perhaps the most unusual commission was a request from Elbridge Gerry for "balm of Fioraventi" to use in treating his wife's eyes.[36] The Minister also arranged for the completion of Houdon's bust of Washington, commissioned by the state of Virginia when Jefferson had been Minister in Paris. At the request of the Secretary of War he purchased a quantity of books and scientific instruments and recruited a badly needed cannon founder.[37]

The Franco-American amity which he had re-established with such care lasted but a year. Indeed, in the very letter informing the Secretary of State that the restrictions had been lifted, he had voiced uneasiness about the future: "I am very sorry, however, to add that latterly this prospect has been somewhat clouded by accounts from England, that Mr. Jay had not only adjusted the points in controversy, but concluded a treaty of commerce with that government: some of those accounts state that he also concluded a treaty of alliance, offensive and defensive." [38] Although publicly discrediting these rumors, he was far less certain in private. His conviction that Jay's "principles and crooked policy ... [were] disguised under the appearance of great sanctity and decorum" gave him no reason to doubt these reports. Monroe was too harsh in his judgment. The treaty, far from containing any suggestion of an alliance, merely provided for the British evacuation of the Northwest posts, the creation of joint commissions to settle the irritating questions of British debts and boundary conflicts and a few unimportant trade provisions. When the treaty was made public, it was discovered, however, that it put forth on two points an interpretation of neutral rights somewhat different from that included in the treaty with France. Although these were essentially minor points, the French latched onto them as a justification for reimposing severe commercial restrictions on the United States. In order to prevent the ratification of a treaty which he believed to contain commercial provisions objectionable to France, Monroe resorted to the unusual expedient of a private letter to Randolph in December 1794, which he first sent to Madison, leaving it to the latter's judgment whether it should be forwarded to the Secretary of State. Madison, who shared Monroe's opinion (although he had not yet seen the treaty), promptly sent the letter to Randolph. Why, Monroe asked the Secretary, should approval be given a treaty which granted nothing except that which belonged to the nation by right, when the United States had only to wait until England had been defeated to make all its claims good? Jay, he maintained, had allowed himself to be made an instrument of Pitt's determination to produce a rupture between France and the United States, for it could not be doubted that ratification of the treaty would renew the hostility of recent years.[39] Although Randolph was himself opposed to the treaty, he made no reply, nor did he show the letter to the President as Monroe had hoped.

In view of these circumstances Monroe was not surprised that the French were resentful. Late in December 1794 he received a letter from the Committee asking him to transmit a copy of the treaty as soon as possible to avoid misunderstanding. Since he had not yet received the text from Jay, he could only repeat the assurance just received from the special envoy in England that the treaty contained nothing contrary to existing obligations. Unfortunately for Monroe, this statement (which was included in the treaty as a specific restriction) was short of the truth, for Jay's Treaty included provisions affecting several articles of the Treaty of 1778. Although these modifications were distinctly minor, they were deemed sufficient to give substance to France's charge that America was abandoning her ally. In the first draft of his letter to the Committee, Monroe had considered expressing his distrust of Jay, but he eventually deleted this telling sentence: "Mr. Jay has not informed me of a single article the treaty contains, nor even the title of it—perhaps because that Gentleman and myself are not in the habits of intimacy nor always united in our politics." He replaced this tart comment with the positive (if untrue) affirmation that he did not "believe an American Minister would ever forget the connections between the United States and France, which every day's experience demonstrates to be the interest of both Republics still further to cement." [40]

In promising to communicate the treaty as soon as he received it, Monroe created needless difficulties for himself. In spite of the Committee's bland assumption that the treaty would be promptly submitted, France had no right to see an agreement still not ratified. The Minister made this commitment in the unshakable belief that there should be no secrets between nations sharing the same republican principles. It was a dangerous step in view of his admitted doubts about Jay, and it is difficult to avoid the suspicion that he intended to use French reaction to compel the administration to reject the treaty. Jay, however, turned the tables on Monroe by refusing to communicate the results of his negotiations. A few weeks after Monroe's promise to the Committee, Jay arrogantly informed his colleague in Paris that he would shortly communicate the principal heads of the treaty "confidentially" in cipher.[41] This offer was valueless to Monroe: in the first place he had no cipher, since Morris had taken it with all the official papers in his office. Moreover, under the seal of a confidential communication, he could not impart the contents of the treaty to the French government. When Monroe sent his secretary, John Purviance, to London for a copy of the treaty, Jay, refusing to release it except in the "strictest confidence," gratuitously reminded his colleague that the United States as a sovereign nation could make any agreements it wished, and that no nation had a right to inspect them before ratification.[42] This response made it obvious that Jay not only lacked confidence in his colleague's judgment but that he also considered France's reaction of little consequence. The Minister to England was in fact arrogating to himself a decision which lay within the authority of his colleague. Since Monroe was willing to assume the consequences of divulging the treaty, he could only interpret Jay's refusal as proof of an intent to jeopardize Franco-American relations.

In the next month Jay's attitude became more exasperating. In March Colonel John Trumbull came to Paris bearing a letter from Jay to inform Monroe that Trumbull, who had memorized the treaty, would communicate it confidentially. Furious that Jay was willing to grant a private citizen access to information denied a colleague, he refused the offer. Since the French soon learned the nature of Trumbull's mission (he seems to have talked freely), Monroe became concerned that continued silence might destroy the Committee's confidence in him. Consequently he undertook the "painful task" of informing the Committee that Jay had refused to divulge the contents of the treaty. To the Committee's terse reply that a treaty supposedly innocent scarcely required such secrecy, Monroe could only offer his assurance that it would be rejected at home if it contained anything hostile to France. This was close to a tacit admission that it might in fact contain such provisions.[43]

With the help of Benjamin Hichborn (an American then in Paris) Monroe finally obtained a summary of the contents of the treaty. When Hichborn told Trumbull that continued secrecy might have serious consequences, the latter, welcoming the opportunity to unburden himself to an unofficial emissary of the American Minister, provided a complete résumé omitting only those provisions containing concessions to the British interpretation of neutral rights, and hence in conflict with portions of the Treaty of 1778. Monroe at once passed this limited information on to the Committee of Public Safety.[44] It was to be many months before the Minister had a more detailed account of the treaty, for Washington, who hesitated to ratify, withheld it from the public. The text was not released until July 1795. The first relatively complete account to reach the Minister was that received from Madison in June, more than six months after Jay had completed his negotiations. Fully expecting that the Federalists would exploit the disagreement with Jay to damage his reputation, Monroe carefully sent Madison copies of all the relevant correspondence to use in his defense. This was an unnecessary precaution, since it was not until after his recall that details of the conflict appeared in the press.[45]

The American Minister's anxiety to keep the good will of the Committee of Public Safety in the spring of 1795 had been more than a matter of Franco-American harmony—he was then seeking the support of the Committee for the American claim to the free navigation of the Mississippi in the peace negotiations under way with Spain. He had also been instructed to enlist French aid in obtaining a treaty with Algiers in order to end the seizure of American ships and the enslavement of their crews. When Colonel David Humphreys, to whom Washington had entrusted the Algerian affair, arrived in Paris early in 1795 the Committee, in a seemingly cooperative mood, had issued papers conferring on the American negotiator what was in effect the status of a French agent. Before Monroe and Humphreys could send Barlow (their choice as American negotiator) to Algiers, they learned that an agent left there by Humphreys had concluded a treaty. Nonetheless, they decided to allow Barlow to go to Algiers, where he discovered that the Dey, prodded by the French consul, was seeking to circumvent the treaty. Without any support from the French consul, who had apparently never received orders to assist the Americans, Barlow renegotiated the treaty and ransomed the prisoners.[46] Monroe received some vague promises of French assistance in connection with the navigation of the Mississippi, but nothing was ever done to carry them out.[47]

The text of Jay's Treaty, when it finally reached him, confirmed Monroe's own suspicions, for Jay had "obtained nothing which he ought to have obtained." Moreover, Jay had agreed to many things which he ought not have conceded on any consideration.[48] As soon as he read the treaty, he realized that the provisions relating to neutral rights would be seized upon by France as a violation of the spirit, if not the letter, of the Treaty of 1778. In his opinion, Jay's Treaty performed one useful function: "It fully explains the views of its author

and his political associates; views which were long known to many. . . ." [49]
From now on the public could no longer doubt the Anglophile tendencies of the Federalists. He summed up for Madison his reasons for condemning the treaty:

If it is to be ratified, it may be deemed one of the most afflicting events that ever befell our country. Our connection here will certainly be weakened by it, altho the British violation be deemed a sufficient ground to set it aside. . . . I mean by this that the pure and delicate tie of antient [sic] amity will be weakened & wh. was a tie of affection, of gratitude & of sentiment, deeply fixed in the hearts of the people. . . . To bear the British aggressions and spoliations without resentment was one thing, but to make this treaty is another. . . . It is impossible for me to describe the mortification I daily undergo on this respect. The opinion which is gone forth to the world . . . is that we are reduced by it to the condition of British colonies—an opinion undoubtedly untrue, abhorrent as the treaty is, but yet that is the state of things. . . . [50]

Monroe's reaction was quite typical of the Republicans—and indeed of many Federalists, who could see no merit in this relatively harmless treaty. They were not so much disappointed by what the treaty did as by what it failed to do. None could complain that at last the posts were to be surrendered or that the debts owed to British merchants were now to be paid, but many had rather unreasonably hoped for substantial trade concessions and for a recognition of American principles of neutral rights.

As soon as the text of the treaty was known in France, Monroe sensed a coolness toward him in official circles. It is true that he was still received courteously, but he now had to listen to many uncomplimentary remarks about the United States.[51] The French were not only annoyed over Jay's Treaty but, according to one Frenchman well disposed to America, there was also considerable resentment over the speculating activities of Americans in Paris, the bad faith of representatives of land companies and the greed and occasional dishonesty of American merchants.[52] Yet in spite of these dissatisfactions, for several reasons, no official protest was made during 1795. First, even after the Senate had ratified, it was by no means certain that the treaty would be implemented. Monroe's correspondents (including Secretary Randolph) led him to believe that the treaty might not receive the President's signature; or, in the event that he signed, the Republicans in the House would defeat the measures necessary to carry the treaty into effect. Naturally, the American Minister actively disseminated these reports, which were also transmitted by the French Minister in the United States.[53] Nor was the Committee of Public Safety prepared to undertake any major policy decisions after the middle of the year, since the Directory was to be installed in November. Even when the new regime was established, there was still further delay while French foreign policy toward America was given a thorough study—its first re-evaluation since 1789.

During the first year of the Directory foreign affairs were supervised by Jean François Reubell, who had acted as a specialist on diplomatic matters while a member of the Committee of Public Safety. To what extent this Alsatian lawyer and radical republican was familiar with American affairs cannot be said, but it seems unlikely that his total pre-occupation with the extension of France's boundaries to the Rhine allowed much time for such minor problems as those presented by the United States. His representative in dealing with foreign ministers was Charles Delacroix, a onetime secretary to Turgot and a former supporter of Robespierre. Bearing the title of Minister of Foreign Affairs, Delacroix was ordinarily little more than the spokesman for the Directors, but he exerted considerable influence in American policy.[54]

After three months of consideration, the Directors emerged with an American policy which again turned France in the direction followed by the Jacobins, and, like the earlier policy, was based on nothing more substantial than irritation, ignorance and an inability to assess the importance of American trade in the future of France. Although the full rationale behind this policy shift remains obscure, a few things are fairly clear. For one thing the Girondists, long advocates of a generous mercantile program, were fading into the background. Thus Otto, who had been arrested again late in 1795, was no longer in a position to exert any influence. Perhaps, too, the advice of Talleyrand (not yet a Director, but a power to be reckoned with) was carrying weight with the new regime. Not only had he acquired a distaste for America during his exile in Philadelphia, but he was also convinced of the impossibility of deflecting American trade from Great Britain. From this point of view a policy of moderation promised no rewards for France. In taking a firm line with the United States the Directors could always adopt the pose of devoted republicans who were seeking to prevent the United States from falling into the hands of the monarchists. From its inception the Directory was faced with a myriad of problems: runaway inflation, food shortages and military reverses. Thus every possible avenue of popularity was exploited. It could not harm the government to show the people that it opposed the reactionaries wherever they might be found, including distant America. The Directors might benefit, as had the Jacobins, from harsh treatment of an ungrateful ally.[55]

The American policy of the Directory was formulated on the basis of a report submitted in January 1796 by Delacroix, who defined France's primary objective as the dissolution of the bond between the United States and Great Britain. Apparently unconvinced by the errors of the past, he contended that this aim could best be achieved by inciting those known to be hostile to England to repudiate the Washington administration. Once again France was to intervene in American domestic politics on the misguided assumption that a Republican victory would attach the United States closely to France. Although Delacroix recognized the potential of American shipping as a source of supply, he did not see it as a means of drawing the United States to France, but recommended commercial reprisal to punish the Federalists and bring the Americans to their senses. His report had some resemblance to an earlier *Mémoire* submitted by Fauchet, whom Monroe wrongly regarded as the evil genius of Directorial policy. Fauchet's *Mémoire,* while presenting the view that France must work with the Republican party to overthrow the Federalists, did make a plea for recognition of the commercial importance of the United States, which he felt was not properly understood in France. It was his opinion that trade restrictions only drove the Americans closer to Britain, hence a moderate policy was advisable. Unfortunately, the Directors were apparently impressed only by those portions advocating continued interference in American domestic politics and ignored the suggestion that American trade relations be fostered.[56]

Although the full implementation of the harsh policy recommended by the Minister of Foreign Affairs was postponed pending the action of the House of Representatives on Jay's Treaty, Monroe had a foretaste of the new turn of events in February 1796 during the course of a routine conference, which he had requested to present complaints of American merchants over France's failure to pay for goods purchased by French agents. At the end of the meeting Delacroix bluntly informed his caller that Jay's Treaty had the practical effect of canceling the Treaty of 1778 and placing the United States on the allied side. When Monroe replied that he could scarcely refute this charge without specific complaints, he was told that a formal note would soon be presented. He was even more disconcerted to learn that Adet was to be replaced by an envoy extraordinary sent to demand explanations of Jay's Treaty. This news brought to the surface the conflict implicit in his mission: as a diplomat Monroe was a split personality, attempting at one and the same time to serve as a spokesman for his government and to act as a political leader seeking victory for his party. If this special mission, as was probable, culminated in a rupture, the Federalist position would be vastly strengthened. Convinced that the Directory was acting in a "passion" without a full understanding of American conditions, Monroe mobilized all his powers of persuasion to prevent the execution of the plan.[57] It was thus in the twofold capacity of Minister and party leader that he wrote Delacroix a few days later. Speaking first as a diplomat, he pointed out that sending a special envoy would advertise to the world the disagreement between the two republics—a state of affairs only pleasing to the enemies of the two nations. Moreover, it was a dangerous move, for much would be expected from the mission, and France might be tempted to make demands of such a nature that war would be the only alternative. Shifting to arguments stemming from his political affiliations, he warned the Directors that the proposed mission, by reviving memories of the Genet affair, would fatally handicap the Republicans in their effort to preserve friendship between the two nations. Only the party in power would benefit from outside interference in American affairs. His advice was simple:

Left to ourselves everything will I think be satisfactorily arranged and perhaps in the course of the year: and it is always more grateful to make such arrangements ourselves than to be pressed into them.

He ended his letter with the assurance that his object was not to prevent the presentation of well-founded objections to the treaty, but merely to avoid the unusual means of protest contemplated by the Directory. The Directors, reared in the cynical school of French politics, were at a loss to decide whether this frankness was a mark of imprudence or a deliberate effort to deceive them about the real objectives of American policy.[58] It goes without saying that Monroe never transmitted a copy of this letter to Washington, nor was it included in the documents later published in his defense. It was only to Madison that he hinted at this unorthodox approach. Monroe's counsel had no effect upon a government which had already given its blessing to the interference in American politics undertaken by Adet on his own initiative.[59]

Since the implementation of the Directory's policy depended entirely upon news from America, Delacroix did not concern himself greatly with preparing the formal statement of grievances against the treaty. Not until March did Monroe have his first glimpse of the specific complaints, when he was inquiring about the accuracy of reports that the Directory was contemplating severe reprisals against American shipping. After reassuring him that this was not the case, Delacroix read a list of seven specific charges. Asking for a formal presentation in writing, the American Minister extended his personal assurance that he would be the first to urge his government to render justice to France, if it could be shown that the United States had injured its ally. Again letting partisanship overcome diplomatic discretion, he declared that as a representative of the "American Nation" he was bound to observe the President's instructions as long as he served as Minister, but he would not remain in office for a moment if he were required to promote a measure contrary to his principles.[60] This exchange was not reported to his superiors. Monroe was quite unaware that these remarks, which were intended to sway the Directors in a moderate direction, had quite the opposite effect. Any suggestion that the people were hostile to the administration was taken as a confirmation of Delacroix's own views and those advanced by Adet, that direct pressure must be exerted upon the American people to induce them to repudiate the Federalists.

The formal statement submitted a few days later was not an alarming document in spite of its length and complexity. The Directors, raking together every conceivable grievance, had allowed subsidiary questions to push major issues into the background.[61] This approach offered an opportunity, which Monroe readily seized, of prolonging the argument in order to postpone a rupture. First, the French charged that the United States had violated the Treaty of 1778 by letting its courts assume jurisdiction over prizes seized by French ships and permitting British ships to enter American ports with their prizes. Monroe easily disposed of these contentions, pointing out that prizes seized within the jurisdiction of the United States were fully within the authority of American courts. This was a sovereign right, which the French themselves acknowledged. As far as he knew, no American court had ever adjudicated prizes captured on the high seas, nor had the United States ever permitted a British ship to bring a prize into port. Under neither head, as he noted, had the French cited specific cases.

The Directors also raised the confused issue of consular rights under the old consular convention—a problem not at all relevant to the current difficulties. This convention had been ambiguous on several points, but, as Monroe reminded the Directors, France in implementing the agreement in 1792 had enacted legislation favoring the American interpretation of the treaty. He sensibly suggested that the whole question be made a subject of future negotiation. To the insignificant charge that the United States had illegally detained the French frigate *Cassius* for alleged violations of American neutrality, he declined to make a reply without a detailed account of the affair either from his government or from France. In regard to the British attempt to intercept the homeward-bound Fauchet while he was still in American waters, Monroe firmly insisted that the strong protest made by his government had been sufficient redress.

The final and all-important grievance related to Jay's Treaty, which the French asserted contained a definition of neutral rights in articles eighteen and twenty-five contrary to the Treaty of 1778, which had specifically exempted both items from seizure. In his reply Monroe admitted the correctness of the facts, but denied that the new provisions could in any way be interpreted as hostile to France. All that the United States had done in this matter was to accept the principles of international law generally held in Europe. The United States, he maintained, deemed it better to have a treaty short of the concessions, which France had given, rather than have no agreement at all. Monroe emphasized that the treaty gave England rights which were merely a recognition of current international practices. In spite of this modification, he contended that France could expect to derive considerable benefits from Jay's Treaty, for Americans would be all the more willing to risk cargoes to France, now that they were guaranteed reimbursement in Jay's Treaty for cargoes seized by England. Although Pickering had outlined this point of view in a dispatch on September 12, 1795, Monroe had also long doubted the validity of the doctrine "free ships make free goods." Looking upon the British position as essentially correct, he felt that any change in the doctrine would require the consent of all powers.[62]

III

Monroe began these critical discussions at the very time the administration no longer regarded his mission as of prime importance. Not only had the ratification of Jay's Treaty, in spite of its general unpopularity, lessened anxiety about France's hostility but Randolph's downfall in August 1795 had also removed the only pro-French member of the Cabinet. Timothy Pickering, the new Secretary of State and a spokesman for the most extreme Federalists, considered the continuation of a Republican in such a crucial post as the French ministry both a danger to the United States and a threat to Federalist supremacy. From the moment he entered office Pickering and his cohorts planned Monroe's removal.[63] Reports unfavorable to the Minister were put in circulation and every dispatch was minutely scrutinized to draw out points calculated to prejudice the President. The moment to act came when Pickering received Monroe's dispatch of March 25, 1796, summarizing his reply to French complaints.[64] Unfortunately this dispatch, which was not accompanied by either the French note or Monroe's written response, left the impression that Monroe had not been very effective. Both documents had originally been enclosed, but just before Monroe sent his dispatch Delacroix asked to have the French note returned for redrafting. In the interest of Franco-American amity Monroe consented, agreeing to modify his original in light of the French revision.

It was on the basis of this incomplete evidence that Pickering on June 13 informed the Minister of the President's dissatisfaction in a harshly worded dispatch which Monroe likened to a letter sent by an "overseer on the farm to one of his gang." [65] The Secretary's dispatch (antedating the decision to recall Monroe by a month) is of considerable importance in that it remained the only official statement of the reasons for the Minister's recall. The Secretary left no doubt as to the extent of the President's displeasure:

It has, therefore, been a matter of no small surprise to the President, that, during so long a period you contented yourself merely with having those means [of satisfying French objections to Jay's Treaty] in your possession without applying them to the object for which they were transmitted.

In not presenting these arguments promptly the Minister had placed the "justice, honor, and the faith of the country" in question. Monroe was angered by this letter—the first from Pickering in six months, since nothing he had previously received from the Secretary had intimated that he was expected to state the American case before the French formally complained. Had he spoken prematurely, the Directors would have concluded that France was indeed justified in resenting the treaty.[66]

With the dispatch of March 25 in hand Pickering first discussed re-

moving Monroe with his colleagues in the Cabinet and with Hamilton
and Jay. All were in agreement that the Minister should be recalled
in spite of the outcry which would ensue. Hamilton undertook to
broach the matter to the President. With Hamilton's query (how could
an open Francophile be allowed to represent the administration in this
sensitive post) the President agreed, but he hesitated to remove the
Minister on such slender grounds.[67] His counterproposal of sending an
envoy extraordinary was opposed by the Cabinet, which questioned the
power of the President to create a new diplomatic post without congressional approval; only by a removal could he create a vacancy. Pickering now produced a letter written a year earlier by Monroe to Dr.
George Logan, which the Secretary ingenuously maintained had been
found in the dead letter office. Although the bulk of the letter and a
lengthy enclosure (intended for publication) was mainly a favorable
account of the progress of the French Revolution, it contained an offensively explicit condemnation of Jay's Treaty.[68] Only one voice in
the administration was raised in Monroe's defense: Tench Coxe, Commissioner for the Revenue, forwarded to the President a letter from
Rochambeau, praising the American Minister's adroit diplomacy,
which had earned him the highest regard in France. This did not alter
the President's decision. Early in July, Washington instructed Pickering
to notify Monroe of his recall. Now that he had succeeded, Pickering
calmly waited six weeks before writing Monroe in order to prevent
the Minister from reaching the United States before the Presidential
election.[69] When Pickering finally did write, he ignored Washington's
suggestion (it was not an order) that it would be "candid" to let the
Minister know the reasons for his recall.[70]

Before Pickering drafted the letter of recall he received the delayed
French note and the Minister's reply. Pickering presented these documents, which conceivably might have altered the President's decision,
in the worst possible light. He characterized French complaints as "feeble" ones, which confirmed "the suspicions some months entertained
that the ominous letters of Mr. Monroe composed a part of a solemn
farce to answer certain party purposes in the U. States." Even if it were
granted that his answers to the complaints had been "sufficient to ob-
viate" the grievances, the fact remained that the Minister had been
supplied "facts and arguments" authorizing "on some points a more
forcible explanation." If this were not enough to condemn the Minister, Pickering alleged that he had been reliably informed that it was

not the French who reprobated Jay's Treaty, but the Americans in
Paris. From this point of view Monroe's dispatches were tissues of mis-
information.[71]

What were the "facts and arguments" supposedly ignored by the
Minister? They comprised various dispatches from Randolph and Pick-
ering defending Jay's Treaty in anticipation of French complaints.
The most important document was a copy of Randolph's lengthy re-
sponse to Adet's protest that the treaty was in conflict with the Franco-
American alliance. This note, expounding the same interpretation of
neutral rights which Monroe had included in his reply to the Directory, had indeed been submitted to Delacroix in October 1795, when
Monroe learned that a copy of Randolph's note had not arrived in
Paris. Unfortunately he had not mentioned this in his dispatches.[72]
Second, Pickering maintained that Monroe had ignored suggestions
sent him on September 12, 1795, which had reached Paris in December,
well in advance of the French protests. In this note Pickering restated
the American interpretation of international law governing the rights
of neutrals, an argument fully explored by Monroe in his reply to the
Directory. About all that Pickering could cite in complaint was the
Minister's failure to remind France that the United States, as an independent power, was sole judge of its interest, and hence could allow no
interference by a foreign state.

While his destruction was being engineered in Philadelphia, the
Minister was fighting a futile delaying action in Paris. His hopes of
mollifying the Directory vanished in July after the arrival of the news
that the House had failed to obstruct Jay's Treaty. He was then notified that France was suspending the provisions affecting neutrals in the
Treaty of 1778. Henceforth American vessels would be accorded the
same treatment as that meted out by Great Britain. His restatement of
the American position on these treaty rights was without effect on the
Directory, nor was his polite reminder to the Directors, who were pursuing imaginary grievances, that the United States had never received
any satisfaction for France's past violation of the treaty—not one of the
claims for damages admitted as valid had yet been paid.[73] In order to
ease the French resentment over the failure of the Republicans to block
the execution of Jay's Treaty in the House, Monroe prepared a *mémoire*
defending his party. The Republicans, he explained, had not only been
concerned about the constitutional question, since the House had no
share in the treaty-making power, but also by the very practical con-

sideration that they would bear the onus if rejection of the treaty were to result in further depredations on the high seas and in the continued retention of the posts. This was never submitted, but it effectively summed up the verbal arguments he used with Delacroix, who retired behind a screen of ambiguously phrased complaints.[74]

The announcement at the end of August 1796 that Mangourit, formerly consul at Charleston, would succeed Adet in Philadelphia was a clear indication of rapidly deteriorating relations. The selection of Mangourit, who had aroused Washington's official disapproval during the Genet affair, at a rank lower than that of Minister was a calculated insult. Monroe promptly remonstrated against the appointment of a diplomat known to be *persona non grata* to the President. In presenting his objections to this choice, he also queried Delacroix about reports in the Swiss press announcing a French decree ordering the seizure of enemy goods on neutral ships. On receiving an assurance that this was not true and that Mangourit's appointment had been canceled, he felt a momentary surge of hope, but within two weeks this illusion was dispelled when he learned that the withdrawal of Mangourit had nothing to do with his representations, but resulted from the decision to suspend relations with the United States. The worst was yet to come: in October he learned that the decree announced in the Swiss press was indeed a fact.[75] From this point ships carrying British goods or touching at British ports were subject to seizure. For the next two years France rigidly adhered to this policy, which not only deprived her of a major source of needed goods but also drove American shippers into the port of her enemy.[76] Yet Monroe's own partisanship had so dulled his perceptions that he blamed the Federalists rather than the French for this reversal. His sole satisfaction now that his mission was ended (for the news of his recall had reached Paris, although he did not receive official notice until November) lay in his conviction that his efforts had "detained . . . [the French] seven months from doing what they ought to have done at once." [77] Monroe can be excused for assuming so much credit, for it did seem on the surface that his representations had prevented the execution of various measures of reprisal. He had no way of knowing, so deeply veiled were the Directory's policy decisions, that the measure finally adopted had only been held up until news of the outcome of the House's deliberations on Jay's Treaty reached France. Once the treaty had been implemented there was no reason for restraint; Americans must be taught the consequences of offending France.

Many Frenchmen certainly regretted the recall of a well-liked minister, who was esteemed for his republican principles, although admittedly these now received little but lip service in France; but few would have agreed with Otto (now released from prison) that his recall was the most unpardonable of blunders made by both nations since the Revolution. The Directors obviously did not regard it as an error to revert to the Jacobin practice of influencing American affairs by intimidation. When Monroe's successor, Charles C. Pinckney, arrived in Paris early in December, the Directory announced that no minister would be received until the United States had satisfactorily answered French complaints.[78] In this final breach Monroe saw no French defects, but blamed Washington's farewell address, which seemed to repudiate the American tie with France. Of the President he commented bitterly:

Most of the monarchs of the earth practice ingratitude in their transactions with other powers . . . but Mr. Washington has the merit of transcending, not the great men of the antient [sic] republicks, but the little monarchs of the present day in preaching it as a publick virtue. God only knows, but such a collection of vain, superficial blunderers, to say no worse of them, were never . . . before placed at the head of any respectable state.[79]

The American Minister took his leave on December 30 in an official ceremony, which, if not as significant as his reception, gave rise to the same impassioned rhetoric. Monroe, to the distress of the Federalists, saw fit to reaffirm his faith in the common basis of the two revolutions:

I was a witness to a Revolution in my own country. I was deeply penetrated with its principles, which are the same with those of your Revolution. I saw, too, its difficulties and remembering these, and the important services rendered us by France upon that occasion, I have partaken with you in all the perilous and trying situations in which you have been placed. It was my fortune to arrive among you in a moment of complicated danger from within and from without; and it is with the most heartfelt satisfaction that in taking my leave, I behold victory and the dawn of prosperity upon the point of realizing all the great objects for which . . . you have . . . so nobly contended.[80]

In a speech of fulsome compliment to the retiring Minister the President of the Directory left no doubt of the partisan implications of the refusal to receive Pinckney: ". . . you have known," he proclaimed, "the true interests of your country—depart without regret. We restore in you a representative of America; and we preserve the memories of a citizen whose personal qualities did honor to that title." The President of the Convention added his own wish that Americans would never forget their debt to France, nor that the French, like the Americans, "adore liberty." Pickering had only one comment on Monroe's address —"unpardonable." [81]

CHAPTER 9

A DIPLOMAT RETURNS

AFTER TAKING formal leave on December 30, 1796, Monroe postponed his departure until spring, preferring to cross the Atlantic in a milder season. To prevent displays of friendship from French officials which might be embarrassing to him and to Pinckney, he took his family to Holland.[1] Not long before he sailed his partisan interests led to a curious attempt on his part to obtain evidence to lend substance to the charge that the Federalist leaders had long plotted a close liaison with Great Britain. On the basis of information received from Paine, Monroe sent his private secretary to see Francisco de Miranda, an early leader in the Latin American independence movement, then in Paris, on a quest for documents believed to implicate Hamilton and Knox in secret negotiations with Pitt in 1784.[2] At that time they had listened sympathetically to Miranda's scheme for recruiting troops in New England to be employed in the wars for liberation in South America, but had refused to countenance the plan when Miranda failed to obtain a guarantee of British naval support. Miranda, who had no fondness for extreme republicans (such as he classified Monroe), refused the request and promptly notified Hamilton of the inquiry.[3]

Almost three years to the day of their departure the Monroes returned to America, arriving in Philadelphia on the *Amity* on June 27. Before they could disembark, Jefferson, Burr and Gallatin came aboard to welcome them and obtain a firsthand account of events in France. If his friends entertained any doubts about the rectitude of the Minister's behavior, these quickly vanished. After talking to Monroe, Gallatin wrote glowingly of the returned diplomat as an exemplar of integrity, honor and patriotism, whose success in delaying French re-

prisals had been a *tour de force*.[4] In view of the importance attached
to Monroe as a party leader and the emphasis placed on Franco-American
amity, the Republicans considered it essential to demonstrate their approval of his conduct. Within five days after his arrival he was honored at a public dinner at Oeller's Hotel with Vice-President Jefferson,
Senator Henry Tazewell of Virginia, William Branch Giles and fifty
members of Congress among the guests. It was rather unusual for so
many legislators to be in the capital late in June, but the circumstances
were exceptional. President John Adams, in office since March, had
summoned Congress into special session to consider measures to be
taken in response to the French refusal to receive Pinckney. The legislators, unwilling to take rash action, declined to enact the extensive
defense program sought by the administration, substituting far milder
measures. Naturally, the Republicans welcomed the opportunity to further embarrass the administration by conspicuously honoring a diplomat so lavishly admired by the French. Jefferson, although a Republican, was serving as Vice-President in a Federalist administration
because internal dissensions in the Federalist ranks had prevented its
leaders from uniting behind a common candidate.

The testimonial dinner was most gratifying to Monroe, for it was
open proof of the esteem he still enjoyed among the Republicans. At
the banquet, after listening to former Governor Thomas McKean
assure the audience that there was nothing in Monroe's conduct to
cause an American to blush, the ex-Minister replied that his sole
concern had been to preserve friendly relations between the two republics—a task at once close to his heart and fully in accord with his
instructions.[5] The toasts were remarkably restrained, avoiding direct
condemnation of the administration or excessive praise of France. This
cautious approach was dictated by the presence of the Vice-President
and by the current public resentment of the Directory's recent policy.

Several days later, as Monroe was packing to go to New York to visit
his wife's family, he received a letter from Alexander Hamilton demanding an explicit declaration in writing that the ex-Minister had
been fully satisfied in 1792 with Hamilton's explanations of his relations with Mr. and Mrs. Reynolds.[6] This request (similar letters had
gone to Venable and Muhlenberg) was prompted by James Thomson
Callender's recent publication of the records made by Monroe and his
confrères of the 1792 investigation.[7] Monroe, unaware that John Beckley was responsible for these revelations, put off answering until he
could confer with Venable and Muhlenberg. However, no sooner had

he arrived in New York than a "very much agitated" Hamilton appeared at his lodgings, indignant at Monroe's failure to reply and blaming him for releasing the documents to Callender. Hamilton was not in the least mollified by Monroe's explanation for his delay in replying nor by his assertion that he had no part in the publication, since he had left his copy of the documents with a trusted "friend in Virginia." At Hamilton's angry comment that this was "totally false," Monroe's temper flared and a tense scene (as reported by David Gelston) followed: "Colo. Monroe rising first and saying do you say I represented falsely, you are a scoundrel. Colo. H. said I will meet you like a gentleman[.] Colo. M. said I am ready get your pistols, both said we shall for it will not be settled in any other way." At this point Gelston and Hamilton's brother-in-law, John Barker Church, intervened to calm the two men. Hamilton was prevailed upon to wait until Monroe conferred with his friends and both promised to forget any remarks made during the meeting.[8] Considerably more agreeable to the returned Minister was the "elegant" public dinner presided over by General Horatio Gates. With such ardent Republicans as Burr and Edward Livingston present, the speeches and toasts were considerably more hostile to the administration than had been the case in Philadelphia. When Monroe gave the toast "Perpetual union between the two Republics of America and France," Burr topped it with "Success to the efforts of Republicanism throughout the world." The celebration ended appropriately with "Ca ira" played on the Irish harp.[9]

Back in Philadelphia Monroe found only Muhlenberg in town. Together they drafted a joint letter affirming confidence in Hamilton's explanation of his association with Reynolds and denying that the original investigation had been undertaken out of party spirit.[10] Still dissatisfied, Hamilton insisted that Monroe repudiate a memorandum written on January 1, 1793, several days after the interview between Hamilton and the three congressmen. This memorandum was a record of a conversation with Jacob Clingman, one of Hamilton's accusers, who asserted (citing Mrs. Reynolds) that all the letters had been prepared by her husband at Hamilton's request to support the Secretary's story. Had the Reynolds affair been exposed four years earlier, before party rivalries had become so bitter, it is likely that Monroe would have readily repudiated Clingman's preposterous accusations, but in view of all the personal attacks made by Hamilton on Jefferson and other Republicans, generosity and fair play were no longer possible between political opponents. Consequently, Monroe evasively stated that his memorandum was not intended as a judgment on the facts.[11] In the furious exchange of letters which followed, he stubbornly refused to affirm Hamilton's innocence of speculation. Whether these imputations were correct or not, he told his adversary on July 21, "depends upon the facts and circumstances which appear against you upon your defense." Hamilton, recognizing this as an attempt to give the affair greater notoriety by forcing him to make a public vindication, accused Monroe of acting from "malignant" and "dishonorable" motives.[12] The interchange ended on a rather pompous note, which might be considered comic if it had not been for the real danger of a duel. In a final exchange of letters each demanded whether the other intended to make the disagreement a personal affair; each took the view that the other was the party injured and hence, as required by the code of honor, waited for the challenge to arrive. Seconds were appointed, but neither challenged the other.[13] Monroe's behavior in this affair did not seem in the least improper to his Republican friends. Madison, on reading the letters after Hamilton published them, felt Monroe had indeed bested his opponent.[14] Hamilton's action in publishing the correspondence struck Madison as a "curious specimen of the ingenious folly of its author. Next to the error of publishing it at all is that of forgetting that simplicity and candor are the only dress which prudence would put on innocence." [15] It was impossible for the Republicans to shake off the fixed idea that Hamilton had engaged in speculation, even though proof was wanting.

II

Monroe lingered in Philadelphia during July unsuccessfully pressing Pickering, as a "matter of right," for a formal statement of the reasons for his recall.[16] After a wait of ten days, the Secretary of State sent a chilly response:

The request contained in your letter of the 6th was unexpected. It is easy to conceive that the President ... may be possessed of facts and information which would not only justify but require the recall of a foreign minister ... altho' they should not furnish the ground of a legal investigation. When the tenure of public offices (that of the Judges excepted) was *deliberately* and *confidentially* placed in the pleasure of the President ... it certainly was not contemplated to test the propriety or expediency of particular acts of that pleasure, or discretion, by a formal trial or a public discussion. These remarks, I trust, exhibit satisfactory reasons why I cannot undertake to comply with your request.[17]

Restraining his temper at this insolent reply, Monroe answered stiffly:

If you supposed that I would submit in silence to the injurious imputations that were raised against me by the administration you were mistaken. I put too high a value upon the blessing of an honest fame, and have too long enjoyed that blessing, in the estimation of my countrymen, to suffer myself to be robbed of it by any description of persons, and under any pretence whatever.

Readily admitting the right of the Executive to remove public officials, he questioned the premise that this power authorized the President to "dispense with the principles of justice or the inalienable rights of freemen in favor of Executive pleasure." With vigor he asserted the right not only to be informed of the charges but also of the name of the informants. Indignation gave unusual power to his words:

I have been injured by the administration and I have a right to redress. Imputations of misconduct have been by it raised against me, and I have a right to vindicate myself against them. . . .

You suggest that you have facts & information which warrant this procedure. Let me know them, as likewise your *informers,* that I may be able to place this act of the Executive, and my own conduct in the light which they respectively merit to stand. . . . Why then do you evade the inquiry? Is it because you know the imputation was unjust & you wish to avoid the demonstration of a truth you are unwilling to acknowledge? Or that you fear a discussion which may throw light upon a topic heretofore too little understood? [18]

The Secretary of State persistently declined to provide information about either the charges or the informants: they might be "communications from sources . . . entitled to credit, but under restrictions which would not permit a disclosure. . . ." If the names were revealed, then the door would be closed to all future revelations about governmental officers. On the pretence of stating a hypothetical situation, the Secretary continued insultingly:

It is not true that removal from office necessarily implies actual misconduct. It may merely imply a want of ability. Or in respect to a minister, it may imply only a change in political affairs which demands, or renders expedient for the public good, the substitution of a different character.[19]

On the same day on which Monroe received this letter, a second note of a private character arrived from the Secretary, offering, "as an individual citizen, to communicate the considerations" which led to the Minister's recall.[20] From this it was apparent that Pickering wished to let the public suspect the worst by leaving the whole issue in the shadows, for a written explanation would reveal that the charges rested on nothing but unsubstantiated gossip and Monroe's known enthusiasm for the French Revolution.

Monroe closed the correspondence on July 31 with two letters.[21] In the first he curtly rejected the proffered private interview as improper when official business was involved. In the second letter, intended as much for the public as for the Secretary of State, he acknowledged, in terms nearly as offensive as those used by Pickering, that he had not been surprised at the refusal of his request: in view of the Secretary's politics, he had never expected anything like a "candid answer." "On the contrary," Monroe continued, "I expected an evasive one, dealing in hints and innuendoes, thrown out to divert the mind from the true object of the inquiry. Nor have I been disappointed in my expectation, for I am persuaded no impartial person can read your several letters upon this subject without entertaining the same opinion of them." He had only contempt for a government which had implicit faith in *"spies and informers."* He scarcely expected to find these customs of the "despotic governments of Europe" entrenched in a republic. The letter ended with some very pertinent questions: Why, if there had been sufficient confidence to appoint him in 1794, had this been withdrawn? Were his political views different? Was there any object then desired from his mission but now no longer important? After releasing this correspondence to the press, he left for home, trusting to Jefferson and John Dawson to settle his financial accounts with the State Department.[22] In demanding information about the charges against him Monroe hoped to silence Federalist rumors such as those disseminated by John Adams in a letter to Elbridge Gerry:

But I have heard such reports of his own language in France at his own table, and the language of those he entertained and of his correspondence with Bache, Beckley, etc., and his communications through the Aurora that I wonder not at his recall—his speech at his audience of recall was a base, false, and servile thing. . . .[23]

Gerry, still politically neutral but personally well disposed to Monroe, asked the former Minister for the facts in the matter without revealing the identity of his source.[24] On this occasion Monroe was able to defend himself, but for the most part he was helpless to curb the rumors.[25]

III

Late in August the Monroes returned to Charlottesville, passing through Alexandria, but, as the ex-President tartly noted, without calling at Mount Vernon.[26] Settling in their old home, the Monroes were greeted by friends at Monticello and Montpelier. But not all friendships survived the vicissitudes of party passions. Thus when Monroe was welcomed by a throng of citizens at the courthouse in Charlottesville, one friend stood aside. John Nicholas, Clerk of the Albemarle County Court and a Federalist, whom Jefferson considered an administration spy, did not come forward. Although, as Nicholas later told Monroe, he still had a high personal regard for the returned Minister, he had not extended his hand lest a public greeting be taken as an expression of approval of Monroe's conduct and thereby imply a condemnation of administration policy.[27] In his old house on the edge of Charlottesville, the Monroes were so cramped that the best accommodations that he could offer Madison and his wife (married in the fall of 1794) was a room in a building formerly used as an office.[28] The tie between the Monroes and the Madisons was unusually close at this time, the two families supplying one another with superfluities from their own stores. Monroe, who was engaged in building activities, was able to offer Madison nails and other materials and Mrs. Madison thoughtfully sent the Monroes preserves, bottled gooseberries and pickles, since their late return had deprived them of the season's fruits. In the spring Madison forwarded seed potatoes, then rather scarce since the 1797 crop had failed, in order to enable Monroe to put in a garden.[29] Friends did not think residence abroad had changed the Monroes: he had retained his simplicity and frankness of manner. His wife, as William Wirt noted, was still the "very model of a perfect matron," but in her reserved and formal manner he still detected a "little too much of New York." [30]

Monroe had been impatient to return to Albemarle to start farming operations and to construct a home on the 3500-acre plantation adjacent to Monticello, which he purchased just before leaving for France. On this new estate, then merely called the "lower plantation," but later referred to as the "Highlands" or "Highland" (now known by the later name of Ashlawn), he built a one-story frame structure of about six rooms into which he moved in December 1799. Although intended as a temporary dwelling, it remained his home for the next twenty years. Long absences abroad and continued financial difficulties made it impossible for him to carry out his plan of erecting a grander house.[31] During the first winter he was home, he managed to clear enough land to increase the tobacco crop—the mainstay of his farm—by 20,000 pounds.[32] He was deeply in debt at this time, for his salary of $9,000 a year, plus an allowance for his passage, had been inadequate to meet the payments on this property. Nor had his salary, which was large by American standards, been sufficient to permit him (and other ministers complained of this problem) to live in the style then the rule for foreign emissaries in European capitals. To meet his most pressing obligations, including absurdly high freight charges on furniture shipped from France, he mortgaged his Albemarle lands at unfavorable interest rates. To prevent foreclosure, he sold his first tobacco crop as soon as it was harvested for a price lower than he would have received if he had been able to hold it until later in the year.[33] All efforts to lighten his burden by selling other property proved unavailing: for his old farm near Charlottesville he received no offers proportionate to its value and Kentucky lands could not be sold. A year after his return, when he learned that he must reimburse the government to the extent of $350 to settle his accounts, he was so short of funds that he had to borrow money from some relatives of his wife in Philadelphia. In 1801, still finding his situation difficult, he offered to sell three large tapestries purchased in France, which he had been unable to hang in his small house.[34] It was at this time that he acquired the first portion of the debt, which, as he continued in public service, grew larger year by year, until on his retirement from the Presidency he was on the verge of ruin. The rewards of public office were by no means commensurate with the cost. Monroe and other Virginians of this era, accustomed as young men to a relatively stable standard of living, were quite unprepared for the steady shrinkage of their agricultural income during the first quarter of the nineteenth century. Moreover, the declining productivity of Virginia plantations reduced property values to such an extent that it was impossible to pay off indebtedness by selling land.

Once again Monroe turned to the law—a profession still no more to his liking than in the past—as the best means of enlarging his income. Since John Marshall and Bushrod Washington now held federal posts, the opportunities seemed better in Richmond than before, but—as Edmund Randolph warned—Monroe was of the wrong political persuasion: only Federalist lawyers could hope to prosper. Jefferson, knowing his friend's dislike of the law, wisely urged him to hold off moving to Richmond until he was certain no other career was open to him. From his past experience Monroe knew that it was impossible to combine office-holding and an extensive law practice; he therefore decided to confine his practice to the county courts. In any case, until it was certain that he was not returning to politics, clients would be reluctant to entrust cases to him.[35]

In spite of these pressing private concerns, Monroe was deeply involved in public affairs. Always hypersensitive to criticism, he chafed under the steady stream of innuendoes in the press about his involvement in speculation in France. These attacks reached a peak in the spring when a congressional committee was appointed to investigate the theft of official funds from Skipwith's residence in Paris.[36] Indignant at the imputation that these funds (intended for Dutch bankers) had been used for speculative purposes, he was only restrained from involving himself in the dispute by the combined advice of Jefferson, Madison and John Dawson, who reminded him that this would merely distract the public from the fundamental issues which centered around his official conduct as Minister.[37] With this counsel in mind Monroe decided not to publish the documents collected for his defense, although they were privately circulated. In December 1799, when he was nominated for the governorship, Madison took copies to Richmond to allay any doubts among the Republican leaders about Monroe's private character.[38]

Although his friends united in advising him to refrain from responding to attacks touching on his private conduct, all agreed that it was vital that he refute the critics of his public career. As Robert R. Livingston commented, only a complete account of his ministry would reveal the perfidy of the administration in making "improper sacrifices to Britain . . . under the pretence of Neutrality" and in ignoring the nation's obligations to France. Livingston, responding to Monroe's request for advice, counseled him to present the unadorned facts rather than a defense of his conduct. Without an official statement of the charges against him, an effort to refute supposed accusations would be pointless, for the Federalists would simply shift the attack to new grounds. Above all Livingston cautioned him to "repress every harsh and acrimonious" comment about Washington in view of the reverence for the ex-President felt throughout the nation.[39] Monroe's vindication, which bore the lengthy title *A View of the Conduct of the Executive in the Foreign Affairs of the United States Connected with the Mission to the French Republic During the Years 1794, 5 & 6,* followed Livingston's suggestion.[40] Anxious to have his work in print before the end of the year, Monroe, conferring frequently with Jefferson and Madison, was able to send the manuscript to Benjamin Franklin Bache in Philadelphia early in November 1797.[41]

The *View*, a formidable volume of 407 pages preceded by a sixty-page introduction, included every official paper of any consequence (except those never disclosed to the President) with the key passages in italics. At least the Federalists could not accuse him of concealment or evasion. In the introduction he indicted the administration for pursuing a policy contrary to the best interests of the United States by not cultivating the friendship of France. It was his contention that if the administration had been wise enough to secure French aid in behalf of American claims against England, then it would never have been necessary to sign a humiliating treaty with the ancient enemy of the nation. This foolish policy had now resulted in a rupture with France. In the final sentences of the preface he summed up his case:

Our navigation is destroyed, commerce laid waste and a general bankruptcy threatening those engaged in it; the friendship of a nation lost, the most powerful on earth, who had deserved better things from us, and had offered to place us, our vessels, and commodities on the footing of its native citizens in all its dominions; war hanging over us, and that not on the side of liberty and the just affections of our people, but of monarchy and our late most deadly foe; and we are made fast, by treaty and by the spirit of those at the helm, to a nation bankrupt in its resources, and rapidly verging to anarchy or despotism. Nor is this all. Our national honor is in the dust; we have been kicked, cuffed, and plundered all over the ocean; our reputation for faith scouted; our government and people branded as cowards, incapable of being provoked to resist. . . . Long will it be before we shall be able to forget what we are, nor will centuries suffice to raise us to the high ground from which we have fallen.[42]

The *View* was compounded of the same elements running through Republican polemics since 1793. There was no question of advocating American entry into the war on the side of France, but only that America should demonstrate a friendly disposition toward her ally. Monroe was quite sincere in his belief that the Federalists were seeking an alliance with England not just in the interests of trade but, like the aristocrats of Europe, in the hope of checking the onrushing tide of republicanism. From this point of view any means of exposing the machinations of antidemocratic elements was justified, even the questionable expedient of publishing official diplomatic correspondence without the consent of the Executive. The conclusions drawn by the readers of the *View,* which presented no concrete evidence of a pro-British policy on the part of the Washington administration, depended entirely upon political affiliation.

It is difficult to assess the effect of the *View.* Its bulk and cost ($1.50) inevitably restricted the circle of readers.[43] Monroe himself was disappointed when only a few copies reached Virginia before the legislature adjourned, thus depriving him of a most influential audience.[44] His friends were warm in their praises, but such opinions were scarcely the result of a critical study, for, as John Taylor of Caroline honestly confessed, the *View* only confirmed what he had anticipated.[45] Jefferson's reaction was enthusiastic. It was, he told Madison, considered "masterly" by all those not opposed to Monroe in principle. He assured the author that the book "works irresistably [*sic*]," winning "unqualified eulogies" from all who read it.[46]

The Federalists, of course, saw no merit in the *View.* It is scarcely surprising that all Pickering's friends (as he reported) considered the *View* Monroe's "own condemnation . . . his death warrant." To Oliver Wolcott it was but a "wicked misrepresentation of fact." [47] Writers in the Federalist press assailed Monroe for exhibiting to the world both his servility to France and his betrayal of American interests. Of all the anonymous publications only one cut Monroe to the quick—the essays of "Scipio." The author of these sharply penned letters, whom the Republicans believed to be Charles Lee, was in fact Uriah Tracy of Connecticut, gifted with a shrewd and sarcastic wit.[48] Although Monroe considered Scipio to be "quite in the admn. style, much low spleen and malice and otherwise without force," Tracy's barbs struck home.[49] The opening number, characteristic of the style of the whole, was introduced by the striking heading: "The Felo de Se, Or Munroe *convicted* of inconsistency, infidelity, *and* ingratitude; *from his own* DOCUMENTS." [50] Scipio cleverly struck at the weakest points in Monroe's conduct, stressing his partisan behavior, his overly obsequious letters to the French government, his thoughtless promise to provide the text of Jay's Treaty prior to ratification, his rash encouragement of France's attempt to borrow money in the United States, and his failure to take up the subject of Jay's Treaty promptly with France. Monroe planned a reply, but finally gave up the project, since a rebuttal would suggest that he doubted the efficacy of letting the record speak for itself.[51] He was especially annoyed over President Adams' comment in a reply to an address from the citizens of Lancaster County, Pennsylvania, that Monroe was

a "disgraced minister, recalled in displeasure for misconduct." In view
of the silence maintained by Washington about the recall, Monroe's
rage at the "dishonorable & unmanly attack of our insane President"
is understandable.[52] Once again he was tempted to make a public reply,
but was restrained by the temperate advice of his friends.

Monroe never saw the comments made by Washington, which would
have interested him far more than any others. The former President
read Monroe's book carefully, jotting comments in the margin of his
copy. These extensive notations, occupying more than forty pages in
his printed correspondence, constituted a running argument with the
opinions of the former Minister.[53] Washington felt, and in this he was
correct, that Monroe had been less than just in his refusal to acknowledge the strict neutrality adopted by the administration. Somewhat less
correctly Washington believed that Monroe's subservience to France
led him to sacrifice the interests of the United States. Thus, to Washington, Monroe emerged as the dupe of the French, who misled him
into thinking he could obtain satisfaction for American grievances.
There was no merit to be seen in a Minister who "was promoting the
views of a party . . . that were obstructing every measure of the Administration and by their attachment to France were bringing it (if not with
design, at least in its consequences) into a war with Great Britain in
order to favor France." It is clear that Washington either did not grasp,
or else could not admit, that the passages in Monroe's instructions relating to the Jay mission were at best ambiguous. Having been convinced by Pickering that the Minister had exaggerated the seriousness
of French resentment over Jay's Treaty he could not give Monroe credit
for any positive achievements.

The marginal jottings of Washington, now in retirement at Mount
Vernon, constitute a dialogue with Monroe and a few examples will
serve to illustrate the chasm separating their interpretation of America's
interest:

MONROE: My wish was to conciliate the French government towards the
treaty which was not ratified, and most anxiously had I looked to the
administration for the means of doing it.

WASHINGTON: What means is it he wanted? Did he expect to be authorized
to declare that the Government was in error in having made a treaty without first obtaining the consent of France; and to ask pardon for not having
submitted Mr. Jay's instructions and the terms of it to the rulers of that
Country before it was ratified?

MONROE: With respect to the Declaration [in a letter from Pickering], that we were an independent people and had a right to decide for ourselves, etc. . . . I did not perceive how it applied at this time: There had been no question on that point. . . .

WASHINGTON: None are more dull than those who will not perceive. If there was no question of this sort, whence proceeded the discontents before the Treaty was promulgated, and after repeated assurances had been given that nothing contained in it infracted our engagements with that Country?

MONROE: France had attempted to impose on us no conditions; had asked of us no favours; on the contrary had shewn a disposition to render us many; under which circumstances we had made a treaty with Britain.

WASHINGTON: There the shoe pinches. This Treaty defeated all hope of embarking this country in the war on the part of France. . . . She was liberal in promises but what has she done? Promising and performing are two distinct things.

MONROE: Much too was said in . . . the President's address to Congress in 1795 of the advantage of our accomodations [sic] with Britain, as likewise of the favorable disposition of that power towards us without the slightest attention being shown to the French Republic.

WASHINGTON: To state facts for the information of Congress, and not write eulogiums on the French Nation, or conduct was the object of the then President. If Mr. Monroe should ever fill the Chair of Government he may (and it is presumed he would be well enough disposed) let the French Minister frame his Speeches.

MONROE: I should not notice my recall . . . if it were not for the state in which our affairs were in my hands, when my recall, being decided . . . at a period, when it appeared I had succeeded in quieting the French government for the time, and was likely to do it effectually.

WASHINGTON: For this there is no better proof, than his own opinion; whilst there is abundant evidence of his being a mere tool in the hands of the French government, cajoled and led away always by unmeaning assurances. . . .

MONROE: To stand well with France through the whole European war was the true interest of America; since great advantage was to be derived from it in many views, and no injury in any.

WASHINGTON: But to stand well with Fr. was, in other words to quit neutral grd; and disregard every other consideration relying wholly on that nation; and this is what Monroe was aiming at.[54]

IV

During the first two years after his return Monroe worked closely with Jefferson and Madison managing the inner affairs of the Republican Party. The moves of the three Virginia leaders are not easy to follow, since, with good reason, they hesitated to trust confidential matters to letters, which might fall into hostile hands. With Monroe but three miles from Monticello and Madison not far distant in Orange County, party business was easily handled at casual meetings arranged by sending a servant with a verbal message. Monroe had been back in the United States but two weeks when Jefferson sought his advice about the recent publication in garbled form of a letter he had written to Mazzei some years earlier. In this letter Jefferson had not only commented harshly upon administration policy, but he had made critical allusions to Washington. The newly returned Minister, full of his own wrongs and burning with plans to publish a justification, urged Jefferson to acknowledge the authenticity of the letter, which could be used to reiterate his conviction that the "principles of our revolution and of Republican government have been substantially swerved from of late. . . ." This advice was too strong for Jefferson, who always shied away from newspaper quarrels; in the end he preferred to remain silent, a course recommended by Madison.[55]

Again, in September 1797, Jefferson summoned Monroe and Madison to Monticello to discuss a grand jury presentment against Samuel J. Cabell, Republican representative from the district, which included Albemarle County. A Federalist-dominated grand jury in Richmond had condemned one of Cabell's printed circular letters to his constituents as a calumny against the administration and as tending to increase foreign influence in America. Viewing this presentment as an infringement upon freedom of speech and a direct attempt to stifle opposition to the administration, Jefferson prepared a petition to be submitted by the citizens of Albemarle to the Virginia legislature requesting that the jurors be impeached for violating the constitutional rights of citizens of the state. When Monroe read this petition, he at once raised the pertinent question whether "a state legislature can interfere in a question between a citizen of the United States and his representative in Congress." If this were true, then it would mean that federal officials could be held liable for their actions before state tribunals. Consequently, Monroe suggested that the petition should rightfully be addressed to Congress.[56] Jefferson admitted that he shared Monroe's doubts on this point, but he saw no other means of proceeding. An appeal to a Federalist Congress would not produce effective action. It was Jefferson's firm opinion that it was of "immense consequence, that the states retain as complete authority as possible over their own citizens" to combat the tendency of the central government to seize powers not specifically excluded from its sphere.[57] When Monroe visited Madison some weeks later, he found that Madison also shared his view of the constitutional question. Yielding to the combined opinion of his friends, Jefferson agreed to a modification of the petition, entrusting the work of revision to Monroe.[58] Monroe's temperately worded revision condemned the presentment as an usurpation of power and an infringement upon freedom of speech, but omitted all references to impeachment. Although the Virginia House of Delegates approved a resolution in harmony with the petition, the Senate failed to act. Again in the next session the petition was brought forward only to be pushed aside by the greater interest in the Virginia resolves.[59]

Monroe, who had been ill (as was his wife) in the fall of 1798, did not participate in the drafting of the Kentucky and Virginia resolutions directed against the Alien and Sedition Acts. However, he was privy to the arrangements and used his influence to promote legislative action in Virginia. In the following year he helped plan the second stage of the protest. At a meeting at Monticello in August 1799 Monroe, Madison and Jefferson agreed that the Virginia legislature should adopt a formal answer to the many state replies to the resolutions of 1798. The labor of preparing the reply was entrusted to Madison, whose work, the Report of 1800, was approved by the legislature.[60] A second meeting was held at Monroe's farm to avoid the surveillance of local spies and minimize Jefferson's connection with the protest.[61]

In the early years after his return Monroe was very cautious in commenting upon politics in his letters; he avoided writing old friends in Europe lest it be suspected that he was engaged in treasonable activities. This concern was prompted by a real anxiety that his letters might be used as the basis for impeachment proceedings. His apprehensions on this score mounted after Adams' condemnation in the reply to the Lancaster address.[62] This anxiety was not as fanciful as it seems today, for at this time there was much excitement over efforts in the House of Representatives to impeach ex-Senator William Blount on charges dating back to 1796, when he had been territorial governor of Tennessee. It was only to his most intimate associates that Monroe ventured to comment upon politics. In these letters he expressed considerable distress that after a three-year absence the Federalists were entrenched in all branches of the government. The political situation had so altered while he was away that he almost doubted that it was the same country "we inhabited 12 or 15 years ago: whether we have not by some accident been thrown into another region of the globe ... for every thing we see or hear of the political kind seems strange and quite unlike what we used to see." [63] Wherever he looked the "royalists" seemed to be on the way to ultimate victory. As every turn of foreign affairs operated to the benefit of the Federalists he became more discouraged: by the end of 1798 he fully expected the nation to be at war with France as an ally of Great Britain.[64] There was very little consolation in the thought that war at least would save the Republicans "infinite trouble" by exposing the machinations of the Federalists.[65] As the year drew to a close and the probability of war receded, he began to feel more optimistic about the future of his party.[66]

Sitting idly on the sidelines was by no means to his taste. It was important to him and to the party that he again hold high office, if only to demonstrate Republican confidence in his integrity and ability. The difficulty lay in finding a suitable post. His own preference was for the governorship of his native state, but this office was not immediately available. His friends had considered putting him forward in 1797, but the failure of the *View* to appear before the beginning of the legislative session led them to give up the project.[67] In the following year, although some of the Republicans were dissatisfied with Governor James Wood for failing to call the legislature into special session to deliberate on the Alien and Sedition Acts, they did not propose Monroe's name, since it was customary to re-elect governors for the three successive terms permitted under the Constitution. The feeling against Wood was not strong enough to justify removal.[68]

Jefferson and Madison both pressed Monroe to enter the House of Representatives in order to have a forum from which he could answer his critics and publicize his principles to the nation. Disagreeing with his friends, Monroe contended that membership in the House would expose him to personal attacks which would obscure the vital issues relating to his mission to France. Moreover, as he pointed out, much would be expected from him, but in a body in which the Republicans were a minority, he could accomplish nothing. The net result would diminish rather than enhance his reputation. The subject was dropped when Jefferson discovered that the incumbent from the Albemarle district did not intend to resign. A little later Jefferson thought the problem of Monroe's future had been solved when Henry Tazewell's death in January 1799 created a vacancy in the United States Senate. He at once wrote John Taylor of Caroline (then in the state legislature) urging that Monroe be chosen as Tazewell's replacement, but the letter did not arrive until after the end of the session. In the spring Monroe planned on running for the state legislature to join the Republicans in combating the Alien and Sedition Acts, but he withdrew his name from the Albemarle poll when he learned that he was to be the Republican gubernatorial candidate.[69]

Electing Monroe governor of Virginia was the most convenient way in which the Republicans could reaffirm their confidence in him. It could also be carried out with a minimum of difficulty, for the governors were elected by the legislature. Since the planter domination of state politics had been perpetuated from the colonial period, the choice was actually controlled by a handful of legislators. In view of the overwhelming strength of the Republicans, once the state leaders decided on a candidate, election was automatic. Intraparty contests were rare, and there was no preliminary discussion in the press. Although there was no serious objection to Monroe, some state leaders felt that he should offer a fuller explanation of his conduct in France. As anxious as he was to return to public life, Monroe flatly refused to go to Richmond during the session to answer questions about his mission. Instead he gave Madison letters and documents, which he considered adequate to refute the major charges raised about his conduct in France. When Madison nominated Monroe, the Federalists, led by George K. Taylor and Richard Bland Lee, demanded an investigation of his mission. Madison and John Taylor of Caroline defended Monroe, insisting that all the relevant facts had been stated in his *View*. Once the move to investigate his mission had been defeated, he was elected by a strict party vote of 116 to 66 over James Breckenridge, the Federalist candidate.[70]

CHAPTER 10

GOVERNOR OF
VIRGINIA

THE GOVERNORSHIP of Virginia was an office of great honor but little power, for the framers of the Virginia constitution of 1776, laboring under an excessive fear of executive authority, had reduced the governor, as Thomas Ritchie commented some three decades later, to a "mere shadow" by denying him both the veto and the power to make significant appointments.[1] Chosen annually by the legislature, the governor was restricted to three consecutive terms. The financial rewards were indeed modest—a salary of $3,333 per year and the use of a house in Richmond which was too dilapidated to be inhabitable at the time of Monroe's election.[2] The governor had only two effective powers: he could summon the council, and he was commander-in-chief of the militia when it was embodied.[3] His other responsibilities were shared with an eight-member council, referred to as the Council of State or the Privy Council, whose members served for indefinite terms, although the legislature was required to replace two members every three years. Those removed were then ineligible for a further three years. This power was frequently used by the Republicans to discipline those who had displeased the party leadership.[4] The governor could not undertake any executive action without the approval of a majority of his council (four constituting a quorum); indeed, the term "executive" as used in Virginia meant the governor acting with his council. Although the governor summoned the council, presided over it and expressed his opinions, he was technically not a member, and therefore did not have the right to vote even in the case of a tie. Of this absurd situation, Jefferson recalled that Governor Benjamin Harrison had once remarked "in his dry way" that the executive branch was composed of "eight governors and one councillor." [5] It was true that during the Revolution the governors had acted when the council was divided, but this had not established a firm precedent. [6] Shortly after Monroe became governor, he wrote Edmund Pendleton for his opinion on this point. Pendleton's verdict apparently did not favor executive authority, for Monroe accepted ties as a negative on executive action. [7] Yet in spite of these restrictions the governorship was a prestigious office awarded only to outstanding state leaders.

Characteristically, Monroe brought to the governorship not only great abilities, but a determination to use the power of office within the limits of the state constitution to inaugurate basic reforms. He gave to this lesser office the same dedication and steady application to detail that he gave to other posts. He did not regard it as just an award for meritorious service to the state and to the party, but he sought to press the legislature to act on a variety of issues. By and large his recommendations, conceived in terms of the liberal views of an eighteenth-century *philosophe,* were coolly received by conservative planter-legislators more interested in governmental economy than progressive reforms. Moreover, in a state where local issues remained secondary to national concerns in determining party affiliation and attitudes, Virginians were far too involved in federal concerns to give much heed to Monroe's liberal proposals for improving state conditions. For Monroe the principal gain of his service as governor was that he had an opportunity to demonstrate his abilities in an administrative office and thus obtain further recognition. His performance as governor was so outstanding that Thomas Ritchie, editor of the powerful semiofficial Republican organ, the Richmond *Enquirer,* praised him unreservedly:

It is perhaps one of the greatest compliments that has ever been paid to the political qualifications of Mr. Monroe, that he erected the negative functions of a governor into the instruments of a most respectable influence. If there was any of the public money to be disbursed, Mr. Monroe would enquire into the exigency and extent of the occasion and lay his researches before the executive council. If there was an officer to be appointed, Mr. Monroe would take care to sift out the official qualifications and political opinion of the candidates, and present them under this light to the view of the council. [8]

Monroe was also responsible for another innovation overlooked by Ritchie—the presentation of an annual address to the legislature com-

parable to the President's annual message to Congress. His predecessors
had submitted occasional communications to the legislature, but these
were brief statements which did not attempt to present a comprehensive view of the affairs of the state. Monroe's messages were lengthy
examinations of pressing needs to which solutions were often indicated.
Since the legislature still relied on the cumbersome method of initiat-
ing legislation on petition (some two hundred being received at each
session), these messages provided a much-needed guide. This new concept of the function of the state executive was outlined in his first annual address in December 1800:

> It belongs to me to give you an account of these [executive] transactions
> for the information of the General Assembly. Such an account fully and
> fairly rendered, submits to its inspection the conduct of the Executive: over
> which one branch is the constitutional inquest. It likewise submits such a
> view of the laws and measures of Government, in their operation, as may
> assist the Legislature to form a sound judgment how far they severally
> answer the ends of their institution, and to apply a suitable remedy where
> they are defective. Under this impression of the duty of the trust reposed in
> me, I make to you the following communication.[9]

The main portion of each message was taken up with reports on the
state projects involving the disbursement of funds amounting to nearly
$400,000. Thus, in his first message of December 1800, Monroe dis-
cussed at length the progress made on the construction of the new
penitentiary, which was ready to receive prisoners in March. He requested additional appropriations to provide for the cost of transport-
ing prisoners from the county jails and for medical care, so that these
expenses would not have to be met from the contingent fund. Monroe
also requested an appropriation for the construction of a wall around
the prison for greater security.[10] The first message included an extensive report on the progress made since 1798 in establishing an armory
and a manufactory of arms.

Not all his messages were quite so restricted in scope as the first. In
subsequent addresses he revealed a sensitivity both to broad public
needs and to the liberal aspirations of the day. He went beyond the
popular view, that the primary function of government was to maintain public order, to recommend utilization of the state's resources to
enrich and improve the life of the people. Highly characteristic of this
breadth of view was his moving plea in 1801 for the establishment of
an effective state-supported educational system:

In a government founded on the sovereignty of the people the education of youth is an object of the first importance. In such a government knowledge should be diffused throughout the whole society, and for that purpose the mean, of acquiring it made not only practicable but easy to every citizen. To preserve the sovereignty in the hands of the people it is not necessary, however desirable, that every person should be qualified to fill every office in the State. It is sufficient that the mass of the people possess a correct knowledge of the principles of the government. . . . It is only when the people become ignorant and corrupt that their representatives forget their duty and aspire to the sovereignty. In such a government education should not be left to the care of individuals only. . . . A people well informed on the subject of their rights, their interests, and their duties would never fall into the excesses which proved the ruin of the ancient republicks.[11]

This appeal was made to persuade the legislature to revise a law of 1796 authorizing the counties to provide for public education. This law had proven quite ineffective, since each county court had been granted discretionary power. Needless to say, a legislature composed of justices of the peace, who were not only the principal taxpayers but also cherished the aristocrat's contempt for mass education, was not interested in altering an act carefully framed to satisfy the liberal demand for education, but at the same time designed to be inoperative.

In this same message Monroe touched upon a subject in which he had long taken a particular interest—that of national defense. In one sense this was not the concern of the state, but in an era in which national security was founded on the militia, it was essential that state units be well trained. Virginia, like most of her sister states, had been most lax: muster days saw little drilling, but much roistering; units were ill-equipped, and the officers were without the experience needed to train their companies. The governor now urged that the officers be given special training at state expense, and that the militia regulations be thoroughly revised to shape an effective fighting force. This proposal, like most of his constructive suggestions, was received with little enthusiasm, since it required a notoriously parsimonious legislature to spend money. Thus his vigorous endorsement of a state-supported road program was ignored, although none would have denied his assertion that the state's roads "are at no time good . . . and in the winter when the produce of labors of the year is carried to market, almost impassible; in addition to which . . . the routes are not always the most direct, or through the country the most favorable." Blaming these shortcomings on the law placing responsibility for road construction on the county courts, which placed local interests first, he sensibly suggested that the General Assembly assume the cost for roads utilized by all the citizens of the state.

One characteristic of his messages, later equally noteworthy in his Presidential addresses, were the self-congratulatory sections in which he indulged in flattering and platitudinous comments about the benefits enjoyed by the people under a republican form of government. Rather typical is this example from his 1801 message:

The good people of these States (and of this State as a portion of that great society) have many advantages for free government, which no other nation ever enjoyed. Called to act in an enlightened age, having never recognized hereditary orders, all the citizens born with equal rights and expectations, their title to that sovereignty is supported by every consideration that can give stability or permanence to the possession of it. It is equally sanctioned by nature, by early habits, and political institutions. With such advantages we have it in our power, and it is our duty, to transmit this blessing to our latest posterity. Should that be the case America will remain an instructive, an illustrious example to nations.[12]

Under Monroe there was a notable improvement in the administration of state affairs. Always a dedicated public servant, he gave his full attention to the most tedious aspects of his office. The executive letter books, which are much fuller than those of his predecessors, reflect this concern. The council now met less frequently (usually twice a week), but the sessions were longer and the attendance better than in the past. As was customary in Virginia, the councilors were chosen from both the older generation of state leaders and rising young men, most of whom were to play important roles in the Republican Party during the next three decades. Among the older leaders, the most important were Alexander Stuart from Staunton, who had been helpful in fostering the pro-French resolutions of 1793, and William Foushee, a Richmonder who later became postmaster of the city. John Clopton, a former congressman defeated by Marshall in 1798, served briefly on the council until he was re-elected to Congress in 1801. Clopton and two younger members of the council, John Guerrant and Alexander McRae, became Monroe's devoted partisans. The only councilor with whom he was not on good terms was former Governor James Wood, characterized by John Dawson as "crusty and somewhat disagreeable." Wood, who resented some of Monroe's administrative decisions, which seemed to reflect upon Woods' conduct while in office, constantly opposed the

Governor in the council, entering his protest regularly in the journals of that body.[13] When Monroe's tenure ended, Wood was the only councilor refusing to join his colleagues in presenting a commendatory address to the retiring Governor, on the grounds that it might be deemed self-praise since the governor could not act independently of the council.[14] Immediately after Monroe's last term, Wood and another councilor were removed, when the legislature purged that body of the last vestiges of "aristocracy." The vacant seats were then filled with two of Monroe's admirers, John Brockenbrough and George Hay, later his son-in-law.[15]

The city of Richmond, where the Monroes resided during his three terms, had grown rapidly since he had last served in the legislature more than a decade earlier. The town, now numbering nearly five thousand inhabitants, sprawled along the banks of the James and onto the hill on which the capitol was located. From a distance this massive classical structure designed by Jefferson gave an imposing aspect to the town, but on closer inspection the city emerged as a nearly untamed wilderness cut across by dusty, unpaved streets and riddled by gullies, which increased in size with every rain. The capitol hill itself was just as undisciplined—the open, unfenced area in front of the building was bare of any plantings.[16] The governor's residence, somewhat hopefully labeled the "palace," was to the right and slightly to the rear of the capitol. Although the "palace" was by no means old, it was in such a state of disrepair that it could not be occupied until the crumbling plaster and collapsing walls had been renovated. Not until the fall of 1800, when these repairs had been completed, did the Monroes settle into the official residence.[17]

The major responsibility facing Monroe after his inauguration was the completion of the armory and arms manufactory, which had been authorized in January 1798. The legislature had then given the executive full discretionary power without even fixing a specific appropriation.[18] By the end of 1801 construction of the armory on the banks of the James was well under way and extensive contracts had been let for the purchase of arms. Energetically setting about his duties, Monroe carefully scrutinized all existing commitments. One of his first acts was the appointment of Captain James Clarke as supervisor of construction and director of the manufactory of arms at a salary of $2,000. Although many considered this salary excessive, Clarke proved himself so capable that his authority was extended to all state construction projects.[19] In 1801 the Governor sent him to recruit workers in the North, but, aware of local sensitivities, Monroe cautioned him to engage only those possessing skills not to be found in Virginia. In a departure from previous usage, which had prevented governors from making disbursements until contracts had been fulfilled, Clarke was allowed to advance funds for the transportation of workers and to promise that public funds would be available for constructing homes near the armory. This action was typical of Monroe's conviction that executive officers must be prepared to assume responsibilities not spelled out in detail by law.[20] As a result of these efforts, the armory was nearly completed by the end of his last term, and the manufactory was producing sufficient pistols, rifles and sabres for the use of the state militia. The cannon foundry, however, was still inoperative, for it had been impossible to engage a founder.[21] Until the arms manufactory was operative the state still had to rely on private sources. The Governor, aware of the shortcomings of previous suppliers, now insisted that all arms be carefully inspected. He had not been in office long when he refused a shipment from James Swan and Company, in spite of the fact that an arbitrator appointed by Governor Wood had approved them in an examination Monroe considered too superficial. A year of negotiation was required to persuade Swan and Company that the state need accept only those arms which could be fired without damaging them.[22]

The completion of the penitentiary, a handsome building of monumental proportions designed by Benjamin Latrobe, involved fewer responsibilities than the supervision of the nearby armory. The prison had been under construction since 1797, when the legislature had appropriated $30,000 for a building large enough for two hundred prisoners.[23] Here, in accordance with the latest concepts of penology, the inmates worked and lived in solitary confinement in six-by-eight cells. It was, the Governor observed, a "benevolent system" based on the "doctrine that in punishing crime, the society or rather the government ought not to indulge in the passion of revenge. . . ." [24] To complement the work of reform a milder penal code had been enacted to become effective with the opening of the penitentiary. Since the system was as yet untried in Virginia, Monroe wrote for information from the governors of New York and Pennsylvania, where similar prisons were operating.[25] In March 1801, the Governor ordered the first prisoners to be transferred to the new building and appointed Martin Mims keeper with a salary of $1,200 and an allowance of sixteen cents per diem for the maintenance of each prisoner. Councilor Wood, as was his habit, protested both sums as extravagant. Since the original appropriation had been inadequate to construct a wall around the penitentiary, it proved insecure. When the legislature refused additional funds, the building was surrounded with an ugly wooden palisade, marring the effects of Latrobe's design.[26] In his last message the Governor reported the experiment a success. Not only had there been no increase in the prison population following the enactment of milder punishments, but none of the prisoners released had been rearrested. The Governor, however, did not mention the reservations of keeper Mims, who had informed him that not all the prisoners responded to benevolent treatment: nearly ten per cent were so recalcitrant that rigid discipline was required.[27]

During his governorship Monroe labored to restore executive powers (originally authorized by the state constitution) which had been either lost or restricted, as a result of usages originating in the colonial era. In appointing justices of the county court and militia officers, he departed from established precedents, although careful not to overstep constitutional limitations on his authority. Legally, militia appointments were made by the governor with the advice of the council upon recommendations from the county courts, but it had become the custom to select the first person named on the list of nominees.[28] Seeing no reason why these appointments should be controlled by "little cabals, the ties of consanguinity or of family interest," he refused to appoint inexperienced men. After receiving numerous complaints, he entered into the journals of the council a firm statement of the constitutional basis of his power. The constitution, he declared, had vested the appointive power in the executive and not in the county courts, whose nominations were merely informative in character and not binding on the executive. He did concede, however, that considerable weight was ordinarily given these recommendations from those most familiar with local conditions.[29]

In selecting justices of the county courts, the Governor did not enjoy such great latitude, since he was legally confined to the list of candidates submitted by the county courts. However, on occasion he ignored the long-standing custom that the first-named candidate be appointed. The need to improve the efficiency of the courts and to strengthen the Republican party seemed adequate justification for this innovation. Since these self-perpetuating bodies not only acted as courts but also recorded deeds, collected taxes and supervised elections, the justices were in an advantageous position to control the politics of the county. On one occasion, when he received recommendations for the appointment of a sheriff (they were always chosen from the justices), Monroe appointed the second candidate on the list simply because he had a better record of attendance at court sessions than any other nominee. Again, when an incumbent sheriff was not renominated for a second term, as was the general rule, he wrote the court to inquire why the name had been omitted.[30] During his second term he sent a circular letter to all courts reminding the justices that the executive bore the responsibility for making appointments and had the right to reject nominations which were improper. The justices were also urged to pay strict attention to the composition of the courts, choosing only well-qualified men and distributing the justiceships evenly throughout the county. The courts were ordered to make annual returns of both the number of sitting justices and the frequency of their attendance at court sessions. It was, he reminded the justices, particularly important that nominations for vacancies not be made when only a few justices were present.[31]

Monroe was equally zealous, if not quite as successful, in asserting the dignity of the governorship in its relations with the federal government. When he entered office he had assumed that all correspondence between the states and the federal government would be between the President and the governors, but he discovered to his surprise that governors corresponded directly with federal department heads. This seemed an improper procedure implying that the governors, like department heads, were subordinate to the President, whereas the President in relation to the governors was but the first among equals.[32] However, his plan to challenge this system under President Adams was not approved by Jefferson, who did not think that questions of ceremony should impede government business. Without raising the issue specifically, Monroe addressed his letters to Adams, but accepted without protest replies from Cabinet officers. After Jefferson became President, Monroe again raised the question, recommending a formal announcement from the President that correspondence from the states be sent directly to him. When he did not hear from the President, Monroe, assuming that Jefferson did not agree with him, wrote his old friend to indicate that he would continue to address his official letters to the President, but would not object to replies from the Secretaries.[33] In his reply to the original query, which crossed Monroe's second letter, Jefferson reiterated his earlier opinion that convenience was a better guide than rules of etiquette; questions of detail should be taken up with department heads, and only those letters on general subjects should be sent to the President. Jefferson disagreed with Monroe's contention that the President and the governors, as heads of sovereign political units, were equals. He took the position that the governors were subordinate to the federal executive in all matters relating to powers granted to the federal government; only when the reserved rights of the states were in question could the governor as the head of a state government be regarded as on the same footing as the President.[34]

II

In electing Monroe governor in 1799, the Republicans had been as much concerned with the political aspects of that office as with either his vindication or his ability as an executive. The critical nature of the approaching presidential election made it essential that the governor be a national figure dedicated to the Republican cause. Not only must he promote victory within the state, but also coordinate state policy with party activities in other parts of the Union. As far as the victory of the party within the state was concerned, the governor's most important duty was to execute the new election law, replacing the district system of choosing presidential electors with the general ticket, and thereby guaranteeing the victor control of all the electors. Under the terms of this act, the governor appointed three election commissioners in every county to qualify voters and to determine whether the polls might be kept open an extra day in the event of bad weather. Obviously, it was vital that these commissioners be Republicans, and hence the added importance of the gubernatorial office. One other duty linked the official functions of the governor with partisan activities. The legislature had ordered that copies of Madison's Report of 1800 reaffirming Virginia's stand on the Alien and Sedition Acts be distributed throughout the state. Usually, in circulating official documents, the governor utilized the county courts, but in this case, suspecting that Federalist courts would destroy this politically oriented report, Monroe sent the packets of the report to known Republicans in the various counties. To guarantee the widest possible circulation, he also dispatched a copy to Congressman Dawson, so that it could be printed in Philadelphia for distribution in the Northern states.[35]

The prestige which Monroe enjoyed among the Virginia Republicans was of enormous value to Jefferson's campaign since it rendered the state leaders fully amenable to the direction of the national party heads. Thus, in the spring of 1800, Monroe canceled a visit to Madison in order to return to Richmond to forestall public demonstrations which local Republicans were contemplating to prevent John Thomson Callender, the notorious Republican publicist, from being tried for violation of the Sedition Act. With the election so close, it seemed unwise to defy federal authority. At Jefferson's suggestion Monroe arranged for Callender's defense through private subscription, rather than through official action as he had at first considered. The three outstanding Republican lawyers engaged for the defense—William Wirt, George Hay and Philip Norborne Nicholas—walked out of the trial in protest against Justice Samuel Chase's prejudiced behavior. Callender was fined two hundred dollars and sentenced to nine months in jail, where he rendered his greatest service to the party, not as a political hack but as a martyr to liberty.[36]

Shortly after the Callender trial began, Jefferson paid a quiet visit to Richmond. Although he stayed with the Governor, there were no official receptions or public demonstrations in his honor. In general, Jefferson disapproved of the "system of pomp and fulsome attention by citizens to their functionaries," but on this occasion he had been prepared to accept some public demonstration, since it might benefit the Republican cause in this Federalist stronghold. However, when the Federalists refused to participate, plans for a public ceremony were abandoned. The more ardent Republicans wished to carry on alone, but on Monroe's advice Jefferson rejected their proposal. The Governor opposed a purely Republican demonstration, because he wished to prevent the "Tories" from organizing a partisan reception for the newly appointed Secretary of State, John Marshall, who was expected on a visit. If Jefferson were to take part in a partisan affair, he would, Monroe felt, be placing himself in an undignified competition with Marshall.[37]

The spring elections of 1800, in which twenty-five Federalists were eliminated from the roster of delegates, were highly gratifying to Monroe. Although Richmond remained Federalist, Henrico County, which surrounded the city, had been captured by the Republicans. With unconcealed amusement the Governor regaled Jefferson with the story of the desperate efforts of two Federalists—one of them James McClurg, mayor of Richmond and a member of the Philadelphia Convention—to stem the tide of Republicanism in John Marshall's old congressional district. These gentlemen "after voting in the city and county of Henrico, pushed up to Hanover, as I am told, to throw their mite into the federal scale (as it is called). . . ." [38] Their journey proved unavailing, for Republican Littleton Waller Tazewell was chosen Marshall's successor. Monroe scrutinized the elections in other states closely, but none was of such concern as that in New York State, which was believed to be pivotal. Congressman Dawson, knowing the Governor's interest, jubilantly conveyed the first news of the results: "The Republic is safe—our ticket has succeeded in the city of New York. . . . Burr is in charge—to his exertions we owe much—he attended the [polling] places within the city for 24 hours without sleeping or resting. . . ." [39]

During the summer lull in political activity, Monroe escaped from the heat of the city to Albemarle, a move he deemed absolutely necessary, since his infant son had whooping cough and it was hoped that the country air would prove beneficial.[40] The health of his son, who had been born in May 1799, was causing Monroe and his wife grave concern. Although the symptoms of whooping cough had vanished by the middle of August, the child was still feverish and much debilitated. After a surgeon had lanced his gums, for some of his difficulties were attributed to teething, the outlook seemed more hopeful.[41] During this critical time Monroe was able to remain only briefly with his family, for he was summoned to Richmond on several occasions by reports that yellow fever had broken out in Norfolk. In the course of one week, in the excessive August heat, he made two trips over the seventy miles between his farm and Richmond; these hurried journeys left him so exhausted that he was unable to relieve his wife from her sickroom duties. When he was again summoned to Richmond on August 20, he had the satisfaction of leaving his son in better health. Before departing, he sent his family to visit his sister, Elizabeth Buckner, in Caroline County, hoping that the change in air would help the boy regain his strength.[42]

On August 23 Monroe issued a proclamation closing all the ports in Virginia to ships coming from Norfolk and requiring them to remain in quarantine until Norfolk should be free of fever. At the suggestion of George Hay, Monroe ordered that huts be constructed on isolated lots at the quarantine stations to house the healthy members of the crews, who were to have no contact with local inhabitants. It was hoped that this would prove more beneficial to the crews than shipboard confinement.[43]

III

It was fortunate for the residents of Richmond and the neighboring counties that the Governor had been summoned to the capital by the quarantine emergency, for the state was on the verge of a major slave insurrection. Had the Governor been at his farm, the time required to reach the city might have rendered it impossible to prepare adequate defenses before the rebellion was under way.

At two in the afternoon on Saturday, August 30, 1800, Mosby Shephard of Henrico County called on Monroe with the alarming news that two of his slaves had just informed him of a revolt planned for that very evening. According to Shephard's informants, the slaves in Henrico planned to kill their masters during the night, then move on to Richmond and set fire to the city, utilizing the subsequent confusion to seize the arms stored in the penitentiary.[44] Reports earlier in the month of an uprising had been too vague to justify action, but now with more tangible evidence the Governor at once called out the militia of the town, stationing detachments at the penitentiary, at the city magazine and at the capitol.[45] The Governor's decisions constituted a break with precedent, for the Virginia constitution had been interpreted as authorizing the embodiment of the militia only if insurrection were under way. The Governor rightly took the position that, if he had to wait for the insurrection to break out, then the intent of the constitution would be frustrated—an interpretation subsequently endorsed by the legislature.[46] Patrols were sent out at once in the county, and a warning message dispatched to the mayor of Petersburg. Late in the day, just about sunset, "a most terrible thunderstorm, accompanied by an enormous rain" swept over Richmond and Henrico County. The area between the city and the suspected center of the rebellion (a plantation owned by Thomas Prosser about six miles from town) was flooded, rendering the approaches to the city impassable. The sudden storm disrupted the plans of the rebels, forcing them to disperse. The investigations of the commanders of the patrols left no doubt that an uprising had been intended. Quantities of crudely made weapons were discovered, and by the time the council met on Monday, September 2, twenty slaves had been arrested. Additional troops were ordered into service, and the council instructed the Governor to warn county authorities throughout the state, urging them to maintain regular patrols. Investigation revealed that the plot originated on the plantation of Thomas Prosser, who reportedly treated his slaves with great "barbarity." One of Prosser's slaves named Gabriel, "a fellow of courage and intellect above his rank in life," had planned the insurrection, which included slaves in Henrico, Chesterfield, Louisa, Caroline and Hanover Counties, as well as the city of Richmond.[47]

As commander-in-chief of the militia, the Governor exercised extraordinary powers, with the whole burden of defending the state resting upon him. For several weeks his days were occupied in assigning troops, arranging for the relief of patrols, and utilizing the opportunity provided to see that the militia units were given some badly needed training. He ordered all arms and powder in public stores to be removed to the penitentiary and placed under heavy guard. Acting on the Governor's orders, Captain Clarke rushed the completion of the palisade around the prison. Richmond bore the air of a beleaguered city, while the citizens of both the city and the neighboring counties were enveloped in an atmosphere of apprehension, which increased as the trials began. From the confused and contradictory evidence collected from the terrified slaves, it was difficult either to assess the extent of the uprising or to be certain that it had been completely repressed. As long as Gabriel remained at large, no one could be certain that the danger was over. Moreover, since there was considerable, though unjustified, fear that whites had been involved in the plot, further precautions seemed necessary.[48] As Monroe later informed the legislature, it seemed incredible that the slaves alone could have embarked upon such a complex plot. "It was natural to suspect that they were prompted to it by others who were invisible, but whose agency might be powerful." [49]

The Governor never doubted for a moment the necessity of the strong measures he had adopted. "It is," he told Jefferson in mid-September, "unquestionably the most serious and formidable conspiracy we have ever known of the kind: tho' indeed to call it so is to give no idea of the thing itself." [50] The recent horrors of the slave uprising in Santo Domingo were too well known to push the matter lightly to one side. Consequently, on September 9 he called up two additional militia regiments to be stationed in the city and the outlying counties. However, during the following week as the first executions took place without any retaliation by the slaves, Monroe considered the danger to be less pressing and dismissed all except a detachment of 225 men who were kept to guard the city, the federal arsenal (across the river in Manchester), and to provide a small unit to patrol near Prosser's plantation. During the next few weeks the guard was gradually reduced until by the eighteenth of October only twenty militiamen were still in service.[51]

In the midst of his worry over the insurrection, Monroe experienced a tragic personal loss. On September 20 his son's illness took a critical turn. During the week which followed, as the boy's condition worsened, he was unable to attend council meetings. On Sunday, September

28, at 10 P.M. his son died. Monroe felt the loss deeply. His wife, according to Monroe, was so prostrated by the death of her son that she did not recover her health for many months.[52] But public business could not be entirely pushed aside by private grief. Late on the afternoon of the twenty-seventh, when his son lay on his deathbed, a large crowd congregated before the Governor's residence as Gabriel, who had been apprehended in Norfolk, was brought before the Governor.[53] Unable to meet with his councilors, he requested that they make arrangements for a strong guard to be mounted over the prisoner, who was taken to the penitentiary. In the hope that Gabriel would confess and thus expose the full extent of the conspiracy, a special committee of the council (James Wood, Alexander McRae and William Foushee) went to the prison to question him, but unless they agreed to mitigate his punishment, he refused to make any statement. The Governor subsequently went to see Gabriel, finding him to "have made up his mind to die, and to have resolved to say but little on the subject of the conspiracy." [54] After Gabriel was convicted and condemned to death, a stay of execution was granted in the hope that he would confess.[55]

Although many Virginians were demanding harsh punishments, Monroe condemned this passion for vengeance, for he realized that much of the testimony extracted from the intimidated slaves was of doubtful value. As early as September 15, he had raised this question privately to Jefferson: "When to avert the hand of the Executioner, is a question of great importance. It is hardly to be presumed, [that] a rebel who avows it was his intention to assassinate his master, etc., if pardoned will ever become a useful servant. And we have no power to transport them abroad, nor is it less difficult to say whether mercy or severity is the better policy in this case, tho' when there is cause for doubt it is best to incline to the former policy." [56] His council proved far less sympathetic to this lenient course than Jefferson. The council, after approving his first request for six pardons, was divided in October when the Governor proposed to reprieve all who were less deeply involved until the legislature should meet. Without the right to vote to break the tie, Monroe had no alternative but to let the executions take place. In all, about thirty-five slaves were executed for their complicity.[57]

To guard the community more effectively in the future, Monroe recommended preventive measures to both the Richmond city government and the state legislature. He also suggested that the mayor establish special patrols within the city at Christmas time, since many Negroes were in town from the nearby coalpits and plantations. All Negroes should be required to have passes and none be allowed to remain in town after sunset without special orders signed by the owner. As another means of protecting the city he proposed that a permanent force of eight full-time constables be created.[58] When the legislature convened, the Governor appealed for a thorough study of the problem:

It belongs to the Legislature to weigh with profound attention, this unpleasant incident in our history. What has happened may occur again at any time, with more fatal consequences, unless suitable measures be taken to prevent it. Unhappily while this class of people exists among us we can never count with certainty on its tranquil submission. The fortunate issue of the late attempt should not lull us into repose. It ought rather to stimulate us to the adoption of a system, which if it does not prevent the like in the future, may secure the country from any calamitous consequences.[59]

These phrases were not as moving as Jefferson's privately uttered cry— "We are truly to be pitied" [60]—but they reflect the same liberal orientation. Monroe shared Jefferson's conviction that slavery was an evil which must be eliminated, but at the same time he felt that the danger of outright abolition was so great that the institution must be maintained until another solution could be found. Ultimately, like most Southern liberals, Monroe became an ardent advocate of the colonization of freed slaves in Africa as the best means of resolving the problem. The legislators of Virginia, who did not share the Governor's misgivings about the rectitude of slavery, ignored his pleas. Instead they preferred to occupy themselves with the exciting presidential campaign then reaching its climax.

CHAPTER 11

REPUBLICANISM TRIUMPHANT

THE PRESIDENTIAL election, which took place two months after Gabriel's uprising, was a sweeping triumph for the Republican ticket. Although a Central Corresponding Committee with branches in all the counties had been set up to conduct the campaign, Monroe was also directly involved in the management of party affairs. One of his most important functions was to serve as a point of contact with Southern Republicans. He corresponded with Charles Pinckney, who was engineering the Republican victory in South Carolina, and conferred with Pierce Butler and Wade Hampton, when they passed through Richmond in October.[1] Important but lesser contributions were the distribution of pamphlets sent him by John Beckley and answering requests for information to refute the allegation that Jefferson was antireligious.[2] Throughout the autumn he was in close touch with Jefferson and Madison, although he entrusted little to the post.[3] Monroe's contact with Northern leaders was ordinarily not as close as with those in the South, but in November, George W. Erving, a New Yorker and a personal friend of Monroe, arrived in Richmond to discuss whether anything could be done to frustrate what he believed to be Burr's plan of becoming President by arranging a tie vote.[4] When Erving suggested that the Virginians throw several electoral votes away from Burr, Monroe sent him to Madison at Montpelier, leaving it to Madison to decide whether any action should be taken. Madison, having already exchanged a reciprocal pledge with one of Burr's spokesmen, that all the electoral votes of New York and Virginia would be cast for Jefferson and Burr, preferred to let the matter rest.[5] Even if there were a tie, an event considered unlikely in view of Burr's assur-

ances that some of the Maryland and Rhode Island electors voting for
Jefferson would not vote for the New Yorker, the election could be
readily settled in the House of Representatives by a word from Burr.
Madison, who served as an elector, saw to it that the Republican pledge
was kept.[6]

When the electors assembled in Richmond early in December the
city seethed with rumors, most of which, according to Elector John
Preston, were Federalist inventions to demoralize the Republicans. A
report that the Federalists had carried South Carolina, a state considered essential for Republican success, momentarily reduced Jefferson's supporters to despair. The Federalists, claiming victory, were overbearing in their behavior, as every "petty British merchant, Scotch factor, speculator in the fund" paraded about "disputing with and insulting the good citizens to a degree hardly to be borne with." Preston
considered this a mild sample of the fate in store for the Republicans
if this in fact had been true; then "chains, dungeons, transportation
and perhaps the gibbet" would have been offered them. However, when
it was learned that South Carolina had gone Republican, "joy and
pleasantry pervaded every Republican face without insolence. . . ." [7]
The rejoicings of the victors were tempered by the disturbing news that
Jefferson and Burr were tied, which gave the Federalists an unexpected advantage. Suspicions were immediately voiced that Burr had
deliberately arranged this in order to secure the first place for himself,
a conclusion which his conduct during the next two months did little
to modify.

Monroe, however, was at first quite optimistic. Although it was "mor-
tifying [that] the election should be attended with any circumstances,
which checks or delays the public will . . . ," he predicted that the opposition would ultimately ratify the public choice after indulging its
irritation. As long as the Republicans were united, there could be no
real threat to Jefferson's final triumph.[8] Even as more precise reports
reached him, that the Federalists planned to deadlock the election
until after March 4 and then elect Marshall or some other Federalist,
he still remained hopeful. He simply could not believe the Federalists
capable of such a "degree of boldness as well as wickedness. . . ." [9]

In January, as tension mounted and the outcome became more uncertain, Monroe resisted the demands that the state act to bring pressure on Congress in Jefferson's behalf. He was levelheaded enough to
understand that the worst thing the Republicans could do would be to

provoke the Federalists by a rash move. When efforts were made to keep
the legislature in session until after the election, Monroe urged moderation, finally persuading the legislators to adjourn by giving his personal pledge to summon the Assembly if there should be a Federalist
usurpation of power. In spite of these apprehensions, the Virginia Republicans organized a victory celebration, slighting Federalist Richmond in favor of Petersburg, where the Governor, the councilors, legislators, congressmen and citizens—some two hundred in all—assembled
for a public dinner late in January.[10]

When Monroe saw the first returns of the House balloting, in which
Jefferson received eight states to six for Burr with two casting blank
votes, he realized that he had underestimated the determination of the
opposition. On February 14 he received an alarming letter from Congressman Dawson written at midnight on the twelfth after the nineteenth ballot. "In this state I hold it my duty to give information to
the Executive of my state—it behoves [sic] them to guard against a
situation truly awful as I am persuaded there will not be a change of
a single vote." Fearing the Federalists might hold back the mails, the
Governor at once set up a special express between Richmond and Washington to have prompt information so that he could summon the legislature should it prove necessary.[11] The anxiety felt in Richmond was
not relieved until February 19, when expresses brought the news of
Jefferson's election; at long last the "reign of witches" (to use Jefferson's phrase) was ended.[12]

What would Monroe and the Republicans have done if the Federalists had indeed attempted to usurp power? What weight is to be given
to the rumors about the possibilities of armed resistance? If the highly
inventive recollection of John Randolph can be relied upon, it would
seem that in establishing an armory in 1797 the leaders of the Old
Dominion had this very eventuality in mind. When Randolph made
this revelation in a speech in the House in 1817, it was promptly contradicted by two other members of the Virginia delegation, Samuel
Pleasants and James G. Jackson, both of whom had been in the state
legislature when the armory bill had been enacted. Although Pleasants
recalled that during the debates over the bill, Federalist Henry Lee had
accused John Taylor of Caroline of sponsoring the measure in order
to enable Virginia to resist federal authority, it seems unlikely that
many in 1797 thought in such definite terms.[13] At that time many other
states were also establishing armories in order to meet the needs of the

militia. In 1799 John Nicholas, Federalist clerk of Albemarle County, asserted in a Richmond paper that the legislature had appropriated additional funds for arms in order to be ready for an armed insurrection. A year later the editor of the Fredericksburg *Virginia Herald* repeated the accusation, adding that the Republicans were not only planning to oust the administration but to destroy the government itself.[14]

Yet the expectation that force might be used to control the elections was not restricted to Federalists: Republicans suspected that federal troops might be employed against them. Shortly after Monroe entered office, his old friend Henry St. George Tucker warned him of the steady increase of federal troops within the state. Tucker could see no reason for this augmentation other than a plan to use them at polling places to intimidate the voters.[15] In May 1800, the Governor, puzzled by an encampment of four hundred regulars not far from Richmond, expressed skepticism at the official explanation that they had been assigned to guard Harpers Ferry.[16] Every slight move of the War Department caused a further ripple of alarm. When the election was pending before the House, Thomas Mann Randolph (Jefferson's son-in-law) nervously wrote Monroe that supplies were about to be moved from the federal arsenal at New London. Interpreting this as a measure to reduce the effectiveness of resistance to the approaching Federalist usurpation, Randolph arranged with local Republicans to block any attempt to transport these supplies.[17]

What was Monroe prepared to do? In agreeing to call the Assembly into special session, he was certainly aware that measures of resistance might be undertaken. He could scarcely have been startled by Congressman John Tyler's letter of February 11 from Washington, reporting the arrival of a courier from Pennsylvania with news that 22,000 men in that state were ready to take up arms. Tyler urgently recommended that the legislature be convened, if there were no change in the balloting during the next week, so that Virginia could join hands with Pennsylvania and New York to prevent a Federalist coup.[18] Monroe's correspondence does not reveal any explicit commitment on his part to use force, but, in the draft of a letter to an unknown correspondent expressing his hope that the Federalists would not seek to override the wish of the people, he added this significant phrase: "But if anything requires decision on our part, be assured it will not be wanting." [19] The Governor was evidently prepared for drastic measures should they prove necessary.

II

Not until Monroe heard the joyous news of Jefferson's election did he leave the capital for a brief respite in Albemarle. He returned to Richmond to be on hand for the city celebration on March 4, which featured as its most notable attraction the illumination of the capitol by his orders.[20] Monroe regarded the election not only as a victory for a close personal friend, but also as a major step in the ultimate triumph of republicanism over the principles of monarchy. Although the issues dividing the two parties were many—ranging from the Hamiltonian fiscal program through Jay's Treaty to the Alien and Sedition Acts— Monroe and his contemporaries always phrased the conflict in terms of a great struggle involving basic principles. While he gloried in the victory of his party, Monroe was well aware that the margin of success had been narrow. He knew that the election returns did not demonstrate that the Federalists had been turned out of office by an angry electorate. They had been defeated, but not destroyed. As he reflected on the status of the Republican party, he felt that the most important problems facing its leaders were how to consolidate the victory, how to prevent a resurgence of Federalism, and most importantly, for it was obvious that this factor had played a central role in Jefferson's election, how to retain the recent converts from Federalism without alienating loyal Republicans.

It was with these conclusions in mind that Monroe offered his advice to the President-elect when he heard some disturbing reports about Jefferson's plans. Late in February Congressman John Dawson reported to the Governor that he had heard Wilson Cary Nicholas and Philip Norborne Nicholas, who lived in the same house in Washington with Jefferson, declare that the President-elect intended to adopt a "system of accomodation" towards the opposition, thus drawing over former opponents by extending them favors. Expressing his regret that Monroe and Madison were not in the capital to advise Jefferson, Dawson sarcastically observed of the Nicholases: ". . . you know them and I believe entertain the same opinion of their *wisdom* and *firmness* which I do." [21] Dawson's concern was excessive, for it seems likely that the Nicholases were only suggesting that Jefferson could hasten the destruction of the opposition by refraining from persecution of its members.[22] Complying with Dawson's request that the President be warned of these reports, Monroe at once wrote Jefferson:

There is no political error more to be avoided, than a step wch. gives cause to suspect an accomodation with that party. . . . Such a step wod. shake the republican ranks, and prove the foundation of a growing interest to its antagonist. The royalist faction has lost deservedly the publick confidence. It will sink under its own weight if we leave it to itself.[23]

Thanking his friend for this letter, which arrived after the inauguration, Jefferson told Monroe that he considered these views so sound that he had communicated them to his "coadjutors as one of our important evidences of the public sentiment, according to which we must plot our course." Aware that "incorrect" notions of his views were current (he had received a letter from John Taylor on the same subject), Jefferson assured Monroe he had no intention of appointing Federalists, although he did hope to avoid actions offensive to moderates in that party. Some removals must be made, but as yet it was impossible to say where the line should be drawn. He confidently trusted that his inaugural address would be sufficient to clear up all doubts.[24]

When Monroe read Jefferson's inaugural, he hastened to compliment the author on a statement "strong and sound in principle," which would not only be "grateful to the opposite party," but also please the Virginia Republicans. He considered this a suitable occasion to expand more fully on his views on the policy to be pursued towards the Federalists. Although it was desirable to cherish recent converts by showing them some attention, it had to be done in a way that would not alienate Republicans of long standing. Certainly former Federalists could not be given high political office, nor did he think such marked honors were essential. It seemed unlikely that recent converts, who had broken from their leaders in disgust, would ever return to their former loyalties. "A union broken in such circumstances, and with so much violence, is not easily repaired. It usually leaves a coolness, often a hatred between the parties." Admittedly the question of removals was a difficult one, for which he could not offer a ready formula. His only practical suggestion was a congressional investigation of the Treasury, which would undoubtedly reveal much evidence of misconduct and thus provide a basis for removals. In view of his own recent experience in connection with the ministry to France, the weight to be given to political affiliations in making removals was more than an abstract issue. He proposed this rule: "The principle is sound that no man ought to be turned out for mere difference of political sentiment, since that is a right in which

he ought to be protected." This he qualified only to the extent of
recommending the dismissal of those who had gained office by violent
partisanship.[25]

Monroe did not find it easy to adhere to this program of moderation, which was not shared by most Republicans, who (according to
Giles) anticipated a complete "purgation" of Federalist office holders.[26]
Republican clamors for removal soon centered on one particular officer
—Rufus King, Minister to England. Monroe, responding to pressure
from John Taylor and others, began a letter to Jefferson late in April,
arguing that the sensitivity of this post made the retention of a Federalist most impolitic. As long as King remained, the British would
conclude that the Republicans felt insecure in office, and treat the nation accordingly. However, as he read over his letter, Monroe realized
that he was not only contradicting views expressed a month earlier, but
that he was recommending for King much the same kind of treatment
he had received from the Washington administration. Consequently,
he discarded his first letter and drafted a new one, which he posted.
The second letter reported Republican uneasiness over King without
endorsing the demands for removal, since for him to do so in view of
his own experience before a "packed jury" would make it appear that
he was seeking revenge for past wrongs.[27] Resisting all pressure, Jefferson left King in London, a decision resented by the more extreme
Republicans.

Monroe's position in the party and his intimacy with the President
naturally meant that he was deluged with requests for aid from office
seekers. This scramble for office, so distressing to purists like John Randolph, who saw the "mania for office" as "another melancholy proof of
the truth of the old established maxim that prosperity often subverts
what adversity cannot destroy," was not disturbing to the more realistic
Governor.[28] In proposing candidates, he was by no means presuming
on his friendship, for he did not offer any suggestions until assured that
his recommendations would be welcomed. In many cases his advice
was solicited on specific appointments.[29] Many of the requests came
from young men he had known in Paris—John Purviance, John H.
Forbes, Joel Barlow, John B. Prevost and William Lee. He made a
special effort to assist George W. Erving, whose loyalist parentage and
long residence in England had deprived him of American contacts.
Feeling a special debt of gratitude towards Erving, who had arranged
for the publication of the *View* in England, Monroe urged that he be

given a diplomatic appointment in recognition of his efforts on Jefferson's behalf in New York. It was difficult to refuse those who sought his assistance, but in cases where he was not familiar with the candidate, although acquainted with the sponsors, he carefully qualified his recommendations.[30]

Only one measure of the administration failed to receive Monroe's approval. Although he agreed with the move to restrict the power of the Supreme Court, he did not think it wise to postpone the sessions of the Court for one year, since this might create the impression that the Republicans were avoiding a direct confrontation. Moreover, it seemed improper to deprive the Court of the means of defending itself. The issue, he felt, would be resolved without difficulty: "The people will have a simple, tho' important question before them. They will have to decide whether they will support the court, or in other words embark again under the authority of the Federal party, or cling to an administration in two of the departments of the government which lessens their burdens and cherishes their liberty." [31]

Not long after Jefferson's inaugural Monroe proved himself most useful to the President in the delicate negotiations to pacify James T. Callender, who was enraged over the delay in refunding the fine levied at his sedition trial. The federal marshal of Richmond (an Adams appointee) had refused to honor Jefferson's order to refund the fine, and Callender was now accusing his former patron of leaving him in the "ditch." When Callender, who was alcoholic and paranoid, went to see Monroe, he was in such a state of agitation that Monroe asked him to return another day. At first Monroe was tempted to advance Callender the money but, sensing his disturbed state, held back lest the disgruntled propagandist use this against the Governor.[32] He warned Jefferson and Madison that they must be most circumspect in dealing with Callender, who was on his way to Washington to apply for an office. Above all it was most important that Jefferson get his letters back, for Callender might well publish them if he failed to receive an appointment. When he failed to obtain an office, Callender returned to Richmond angrier than ever, but Monroe quieted him temporarily, arranging a private subscription to enable the editor to study law.[33] The peace was temporary. By the end of the year Callender turned his venom against Jefferson in the columns of the Federalist *Recorder*. To defend the President, Monroe obtained a list of all the sums paid Callender, although declining to describe them as charity (as the President had suggested), since this would only draw further abuse. In the course of the year, Callender revived all the scandals with which the Federalists had once plagued Jefferson, dwelling at length on the stories about Mrs. Walker and Sally. His voice was only stilled by death in 1803.[34]

III

Of much greater moment than the Callender affair during his last year in office were the problems created by the recurrent apprehension in Virginia over slave insurrections. As a partial means of protection, the legislature established a regular guard to protect the capitol, the armory and the penitentiary. Monroe, appreciating the long-standing antagonism of the public towards permanent military garrisons, issued detailed instructions to the commander to prevent any unnecessary offense to the citizens. He instructed the commander to exercise great care in recruiting, so that only sober and reliable men were to be enlisted. To prevent incidents which might arise from soldiers idling about the town, all unmarried recruits were to be kept in quarters at night under the charge of a noncommissioned officer. Since the citizens of the town might resent the constant sight of a military body, the Governor ordered that all drilling be conducted behind the walls of the penitentiary rather than on the plaza before the capitol and that the men not be marched through the town without his express orders.[35]

The executions following Gabriel's rebellion had stirred the humane feelings of many Virginians. To terminate this drastic form of punishment the legislature authorized the Governor to sell outside the boundaries of the United States all slaves convicted of conspiracy or other crimes.[36] To facilitate this arrangement, the legislature also requested the Governor to investigate the possibility of purchasing territory in the West to which persons dangerous to the peace might be removed. The law had been vaguely worded, failing to specify that it was restricted to Negroes involved in insurrections; consequently, when Monroe turned to Jefferson for assistance, he carefully explained that the measure was intended as an alternative to the death penalty. Although it was true that the legislature had had in mind nothing more than the purchase of territory in the western regions, Monroe felt that other possibilities should be explored, and urged Jefferson to take as broad a view of the whole subject as possible, ruling out only a proposal for general emancipation, for the simple reason that he regarded the expense as rendering it impracticable as far as the legislature was concerned. Jefferson was not able to provide any easy solution to the problem. It was true that land could be purchased in the West, but he thought it unwise to establish a colony of rebellious slaves on the borders of the United States, nor was it a measure likely to be viewed with approval by either Spain or Great Britain, whose interests would also be involved. Should territory be acquired in the West Indies, it would locate a dangerous element close to the shores of the United States. If the legislature so desired, Jefferson offered to investigate the possibility of a refuge in Africa.[37]

When the Governor submitted Jefferson's letter, the General Assembly at once modified its resolution indicating a preference either for Africa or South America. Jefferson now suggested that slaves might be sent to Sierra Leone, a colony in Africa established by British philanthropists as a refuge for slaves removed from America during the Revolution.[38] Monroe agreed that this seemed the most readily available haven, but pointed out one major obstacle—all Negroes received in Sierra Leone must be sent there as free persons, whereas the legislature in selecting transportation as a substitute for the death penalty certainly had no intention of freeing convicted slaves. To free them would seem to reward rebelliousness, and thus encourage rather than deter insurrections. However, he agreed that the Minister to England should sound out the Sierra Leone Company. If the response was favorable, then the legislature might be induced to free those condemned to transportation. The project never advanced beyond this point, since the directors of the English company were not responsive to the suggestion that such disturbing elements be introduced into their colony.[39] In the future all slaves convicted of crimes were kept in prison until purchased by traders agreeing to remove them from the United States.

In 1801 and 1802 the state was again convulsed by alarms over slave uprisings, which, for the most part, were based on rumor rather than on fact. Monroe did not succumb to the general panic, continuing instead to examine all reports critically and refusing to take any action unless positive evidence could be presented. In January 1802 he called out the militia when a conspiracy was uncovered in Nottaway County. Since the legislature was in session at the time, Monroe seized the opportunity to recommend that laws providing for regular patrols in the counties be revised to make them truly effective. Further unrest, he told the legislature, was to be expected—the slaves were not only experiencing a growing sentiment of liberty, but they could not help but contrast their condition with that of the increasing numbers of free Negroes.[40]

The Nottaway trials sparked a panic throughout the state, starting in Norfolk, where the citizens became alarmed at the obvious excitement among the slaves as they heard reports of the rebellion in Santo Domingo. City authorities appealed to the Governor to intervene, but he declined to act without more specific evidence. He reminded the local officials that the county courts had full power to order the removal of all Negroes considered undesirable.[41] As the alarm spread arrests took place in Pennsylvania, Campbell, Charlotte, and Halifax Counties, but the trials produced no evidence of a conspiracy. Indeed, it was noted that as soon as the slaves learned that the whites were alarmed, their conduct became exemplary. In May 1802, when the mayor of Norfolk, exceeding his authority, called out the city militia, Monroe upheld the action, taking the position that it was impossible to preserve peace and order unless the militia were embodied prior to the outbreak of an insurrection.[42] However, Monroe declined to go beyond this, refusing other requests to summon the militia. He felt, as he told Jefferson, that the whole business bore an "equivocal" air, although he admitted it could not be denied that the "spirit of revolt has taken deep hold in the minds of the slaves. . . ." [43] Still, without direct evidence he could not see the need to call on the militia. As a measure of reassurance, he urged the county courts to maintain regular patrols until the end of the year. Since the Richmonders continued to be highly nervous, a special militia unit of one hundred men was ordered to guard key points during fire alarms until the end of the summer.[44]

His own reservations about the reality of a conspiracy and his humane inclinations led him to commute many of the death sentences imposed by county courts to transportation. His leniency brought him into conflict with the influential Councilor Alexander Stuart, who maintained that gentleness would only encourage future conspiracies; as far as Stuart was concerned, the issue was not guilt or innocence, but the preservation of public order. In only one case—that of two slaves condemned to death in Norfolk—did Monroe yield to Stuart, since there was no evidence casting doubt on their guilt.[45] Slaves awaiting transportation were lodged in the Richmond penitentiary, where they constituted a burden on the resources of the prison. Monroe disapproved of the keeper's suggestion that they be put to work on the walls, since this activity would bring them into direct contact with other Negroes. Until a purchaser willing to remove them from the United States was found in 1802 they were employed in their cells.[46]

In December 1801, shortly after Monroe had been re-elected for a third term, he was subjected to an exasperating Federalist-sponsored legislative inquiry into executive expenditures. The inquiry was sparked by troublesome Councilor Wood, who had constantly protested executive expenditures, including such trifling amounts as $25.78 for the illumination of the capitol to celebrate Jefferson's inauguration. The Federalists, who were an impotent minority in the legislature, commented so much on the Governor's free use of the contingent fund that the Republicans set up an investigating committee under the chairmanship of Creed Taylor, a Republican well disposed to Monroe. The council also chose a committee (from which Wood was excluded) to confer with the legislative committee. Taylor reported to the legislature that the investigation had shown no misapplication of funds, but he did not present an itemized account, thus leaving the impression that perhaps the Governor had been careless in his expenditures. Monroe considered this generalized statement an implicit criticism of his conduct. His annoyance was all the greater, since it had long been the habit of the legislature to authorize expenditures without making any specific appropriation, and, consequently, the Governor had to make disbursements from the contingent fund. After discussing the matter with the council, Monroe (with Wood objecting) sent a letter to the legislature pointing out that unless itemized expenditures were examined, the use of the contingent fund could not be understood. The legislature promptly complied with Monroe's hint, and requested that he submit an itemized account.

Most gratifying to the Governor was a joint resolution of both houses affirming that all Monroe's disbursements had been made in full conformity with the law. The General Assembly also expressed its "high sense of the distinguished ability, attention to duty and integrity, with which James Monroe . . . has heretofore discharged every duty of his office." [47] This endorsement was not only pleasing to one so sensitive to criticism as Monroe, but it was absolutely indispensable if he was to continue his career in national politics. Monroe fully merited the praise: not only had he been a capable administrator acting with decision in the most serious crisis to threaten the state since the Revolution, but he had succeeded in elevating the office to a new dignity and importance.

CHAPTER 12

THE LOUISIANA
PURCHASE

AT THE END of his third term Monroe, having decided to practice law in Richmond, leased a house in the city.[1] For the moment his heavy load of debt made it advisable for him not to continue in public office. Consequently, he ruled out a nomination to one of the newly created state chancery courts and declined to replace Stevens Thomson Mason, who wished to retire from the United States Senate. Instead he joined with Jefferson in successfully pressing Mason to remain in office.[2] Before settling down to the law, he projected a western tour to look into his land holdings, to be followed by a trip to New York so that his wife could visit her relatives for the first time in six years.

In January 1803, when these plans had been barely formulated, Monroe received a hasty note from Jefferson informing him that he had been nominated Envoy Extraordinary to France to join the resident Minister, Robert Livingston, in an effort to purchase a site at the mouth of the Mississippi to be used as a port of deposit. Jefferson had made the appointment without waiting for Monroe's consent, as the surest means of quieting the "fever" stirred up in the West after the suspension of the right of deposit at New Orleans in October by the Spanish authorities. Serious as this action was in itself, it was doubly alarming when viewed in conjunction with the reports reaching the President during the past year that Spain had retroceded Louisiana to France. Deeply concerned over the prospect of the establishment of a major power on the western frontier in place of the impotent Spanish government, Jefferson and Madison had long since instructed Livingston either to secure from France a recognition of America's claim to the free navigation of the Mississippi or to purchase territory near New Orleans. Livingston, however, in spite of persistent efforts had not even obtained a clear admission that the retrocession had taken place. The recent suspension of the right of deposit now made the matter critically important to the very preservation of the Union.

In view of all these circumstances Jefferson called on Monroe for "a temporary sacrifice to prevent the greatest of all evils in the present prosperous tide of our affairs." [3] The Senate, responding to the urgency of the President's appeal, confirmed Monroe on January 11 (the same day on which his name was submitted) by a strict party vote of fifteen to twelve. The Federalists, unable to prevent the nomination, vented their spleen by recalling the circumstances of his mission to France and by questioning the wisdom of sending a former admirer of the Jacobins to negotiate with a ruler known to regard them as his bitterest enemies. [4]

As soon as Monroe had been confirmed, the President wrote a second time enlarging on his reasons for sending a special envoy and explaining why the ex-Governor was the only suitable choice. In reaching this decision, the President wrote, he had been influenced by the pressing need to neutralize the Federalists, who were hoping to regain power by allying themselves with the outraged Westerners. Since the nation was unaware of the efforts made to protect Western interests through diplomatic channels, only a dramatic gesture such as the appointment of a special envoy would serve to quiet the public mind. Once this course had been chosen Jefferson and his advisers had at once concluded that there could not be "two opinions among the Republicans as to the person." Aware that personal finances made him reluctant to return to public office, Jefferson marshaled those arguments which he knew would sway his friend:

You possess the unlimited confidence of the administration and of the western people and generally of the republicans everywhere; and were you to refuse to go, no other man can be found who does this. . . . All eyes, all hopes, are now fixed on you; and were you to decline the chagrin would be universal and would shake under your feet the high ground on which you stand with the public. Indeed I know nothing which would produce such a shock, for on the event of this mission depends the future destinies of this republic. . . . I am sensible after the measures you have taken for getting into a different line of business, that it will be a great sacrifice on your part, and presents from the season and other circumstances serious difficulties. But some men are born for the public. Nature by fitting them for the

service of the human race on a broad scale, has stamped with the evidences
of her destination and their duty.[5]

The President well knew that Monroe could not refuse an appeal to
his sense of duty coupled with the plea that he was the only person
who could ease a crisis threatening the future of both the party and
the nation. Certainly few men were better fitted for the task. His prominent role during the Jay-Gardoqui negotiations had identified him
more closely than any other national leader of his generation with the
interests of the West. In addition to this his previous service in France
gave him a unique advantage, since he knew many of those now in
power.

The appointment did not offer any financial advantages, for special
missions were not allowed outfits, which then amounted to one year's
salary, on the grounds that a temporary envoy did not need to establish a permanent residence. Hence, Monroe would receive only his
traveling expenses, a salary of $9,000 a year and a quarter's salary to
defray the cost of his return.[6] His additional appointment as special
envoy to Spain, where it was thought some of the negotiations might
have to be carried out, added nothing in the way of remuneration
above his expenses. From a purely personal standpoint the mission he
began in 1803 was costly and left him still further in debt. As in the
past he entrusted his affairs to his friends. His uncle was too old, however, and both Jefferson and Madison were too busily engaged in public
affairs to supervise his Albemarle holdings. He was unfortunate in his
selection of a manager, for Colonel John Lewis, who looked after his
plantation, was inefficient. Madison and Jones agreed to meet the payments on his debts, for which Monroe allocated his first year's salary.[7]
To meet his immediate needs Monroe sold all his plate and much of
his china and furniture to Madison, since he hoped to order replacements in Europe.[8] All these arrangements were hastily made, for Jefferson was anxious that he depart at once.

Possessing the full confidence of the administration, Monroe was
understandably much better prepared for this mission than he had
been in 1794. He was able to spend several weeks in Washington conferring at length with the President and the Secretary of State and
studying the correspondence in the State Department relating to France
and Spain. From reading Livingston's dispatches he knew that the Minister to France was discouraged over his inability to secure any precise
statement from Talleyrand about Louisiana. This pessimistic view was

somewhat tempered by private letters written to Jefferson by Pierre Samuel DuPont de Nemours. When DuPont de Nemours had gone to France a few years earlier, Jefferson had given him an unofficial diplomatic status and had asked him to ascertain whether it might not be possible to purchase the desired port of deposit. In a letter which arrived shortly before Monroe's departure, DuPont had reported that he did not think France would negotiate until the transfer had actually taken place, but he did not anticipate that there would then be any difficulty in securing an arrangement favorable to the United States.[9] When Monroe reached France his observations led him to feel that such unofficial representations were apt to be harmful, and he then wrote the President urging him to avoid political topics in letters to his European friends.[10]

Among the topics discussed with the new envoy was the possibility that failure to obtain any concessions in France might require him to go to England, and there seek an arrangement which would advance American interests. The groundwork for this alternate course had already been established by Jefferson and Madison, who, during the winter, had been openly friendly with the British chargé, Edward Thornton. When Monroe departed for France he carried with him a letter from Thornton to Lord Whitworth, the British Ambassador.[11] The overtures to Thornton had a double purpose, for Jefferson and Madison wished to impress the French chargé, Louis Pichon, with America's determination to seek a *rapprochement* with England if it proved necessary. These gestures were not lost on Pichon, whose dispatches expressed a steadily mounting alarm. He meticulously reported Monroe's remark that if his mission to France failed, then the United States was prepared to receive the "overtures which England did not cease to make." Pichon warned Talleyrand that Monroe had *"carte blanche* and that he goes to London if badly received in Paris."[12] The envoy, according to Pichon, spoke with the full authority of the administration, for the Republicans had just honored him at a public dinner to which the foreign ministers had been invited. Before the envoy, the assembled congressmen and members of the administration, Senator Samuel Smith had offered the bold toast: "Peace if peace is honorable, war if war is necessary."[13]

Monroe's departure was temporarily delayed because Madison could not complete his instructions until Congress had passed the legislation required to implement the mission, including an appropriation of $2 million to be applied to the purchase of territory. Before his instructions were ready, Monroe went on to arrange passage in New York, where he arrived so exhausted by the severities of a winter journey that he was confined to his room for a week.[14] He was still further detained, for it was not until March 2 that Madison was able to forward the instructions authorizing an offer of 50 million francs ($9,375,000), including the $2 million already appropriated, for New Orleans and the Floridas or "as much thereof" as France would sell.[15] This price was to include the claims of American citizens against France. While lingering in New York Monroe made last-minute arrangements concerning his private affairs. Among the items he had been unable to attend to had been the erection of a headstone over his son's grave. This he asked John Clarke to do, directing that it bear only the initials "J.S.M." [16]

II

On March 8 Monroe, his wife and two daughters put to sea on the *Richmond*. Also on board were Colonel James Mercer, son of General Hugh Mercer of Fredericksburg, and Mrs. Paul Benthalou, who was joining her husband in France where he had been pressing spoliation claims. During the Louisiana negotiations Mercer was to serve as Monroe's secretary without pay (special envoys were not granted clerical assistance).[17] Although the *Richmond* departed in a snow storm the passage proved calm, without any unpleasant incidents apart from the seasickness of his family. After a passage of twenty-nine days, they reached Le Havre on April 8, where the new envoy received a welcome decidedly in contrast to that accorded him nine years earlier. As the *Richmond* entered the harbor it was saluted from the battery, and when Monroe arrived at his hotel he found a guard of fifty men, of whom he dismissed all but two. Later the town officials called to inform him that the news of his arrival had been sent to Paris by the semaphore telegraph recently installed by Napoleon. After a day's rest the Monroes set out for Paris on the tenth, arriving in the city on the twelfth. En route they paused briefly at St. Germain to see "one of their oldest and most esteemed" friends in France, Mme. Campan. Eliza was again enrolled in what was now the most fashionable school in France. The younger daughter, Maria Hester, just old enough to run about, remained with her parents.[18]

Once in Paris the special envoy was surprised at his colleague's indifferent greeting.[19] From reading Livingston's dispatches, he had expected an enthusiastic reception from the discouraged Minister, who might be expected to regard Monroe's arrival as offering renewed hope for his negotiations. His anticipation of a warm welcome had been heightened by a letter Livingston had written on April 10 as soon as he had heard of Monroe's landing. This had reached the envoy while on the road to Paris:

I congratulate you on your safe arrival. We have long and anxiously waited for you. God grant that your mission may answer yours and the public expectation. War may do something for us, nothing else would. I have paved the way for you, and if you could add to my memoirs an assurance that we are now in possession of New Orleans, we should do well. . . .[20]

Monroe had the first intimation that his appearance on the scene was not entirely pleasing to the resident Minister from Fulwar Skipwith, the Consul General in Paris. Skipwith, who had arranged lodgings for Monroe, took time from pressing personal affairs—his first child was born the day Monroe arrived—to greet his friend and patron. Although Livingston was fundamentally gregarious and affable, he had the unfortunate habit of treating those whom he regarded as his inferiors in the lordly manner of a patroon dealing with a tenant. Skipwith, having been offended by the Minister's haughty manner, was only too happy to comment unfavorably on his behavior. When Monroe met Livingston later in the day, he was astonished by Livingston's complete lack of interest in learning the latest views of the administration or in examining the instructions which Monroe had brought with him.[21] It was not that Livingston was overtly hostile; on the contrary, he showed his colleague every courtesy that the envoy could expect as a public official and as an old friend. They had, after all, shared a passionate Francophile enthusiasm for many years.[22] As Monroe listened to Livingston he quickly realized that his colleague's indifference sprang from something far more momentous than annoyance over the appointment of a special emissary: on April 11, the day after his despairing letter to Monroe, Livingston had suddenly discovered that the long-sought object of his mission was seemingly within his grasp.

As Monroe hastened to Paris, the resident Minister was scrambling about in a frantic effort to conclude an agreement before his colleague appeared. On the eleventh of April Livingston had been invited to Talleyrand's office, where to his astonished disbelief (he was, after all, extremely deaf) he heard the Foreign Minister casually ask if the United States would like to purchase all of Louisiana. Startled by this overture after so many rebuffs, he could only repeat that the United States was interested solely in New Orleans and the Floridas. Talleyrand, observing that Louisiana was valueless to France without New Orleans, pressed Livingston to make an offer. The American Minister's proposal of 20 million livres, if France assumed all claims, was dismissed as inadequate by Talleyrand, who suggested that Livingston think it over and let him know the next day. It was only after he had left the Foreign Minister's office that Livingston realized the full significance of the proposal. Not only was the offer genuine, but, according to Daniel Parker, an American claimant with important official contacts, it emanated directly from Napoleon.[23] With this reassurance Livingston determined to press for an immediate agreement before his colleague appeared on the scene.

Unfortunately Livingston had missed his opportunity (if there had really been one), for the Foreign Minister now reverted to his usual evasive manner, and, as so often in the past, refused to admit that France possessed Louisiana. Undaunted by this repulse—for experience had taught him the value of persistence in dealing with Talleyrand—Livingston on the same day wrote the Foreign Minister asking him to state in writing that France had decided to sell Louisiana in response to Livingston's representations and proposing that they begin work on a treaty without waiting for Monroe's presentation. To this communication, which ended with the plea, "Please, Sir, regard this as confidential," Talleyrand made no reply. Needless to say, Livingston never supplied a copy of this letter to his superiors in Washington nor to his colleague in Paris.[24]

Livingston's efforts to complete the cession of Louisiana before Monroe's arrival were probably wasted, since Talleyrand had never been empowered to make such an offer. It is true that the First Consul had decided to sell Louisiana, but he had not entrusted the negotiations to the Foreign Minister. Instead he placed them in the hands of François de Barbé-Marbois, Minister of Finances, who learned of Napoleon's intention to sell Louisiana at St. Cloud on April 10.[25] Why, then, did Talleyrand, who had no part in the decision and no control over negotiations, make an offer to Livingston? Although conclusive evidence is lacking, it seems that he was acting as a marplot to confuse or delay negotiations long enough to convince Napoleon to retain Louisiana. At this time Talleyrand and Napoleon's brothers, Lucien and Joseph, were being tempted by the British Ambassador with an enormous bribe (perhaps as much as £2 million) if they could persuade Napoleon to abandon his claims to Malta. He had been promised this island in the

Peace of Amiens, but the British had not yet withdrawn. The British government now wished to retain an island vital to the protection of the nation's imperial interests. As one of the original promoters of the scheme to revive France's American empire, Talleyrand hoped, if Napoleon were persuaded to retain Louisiana, that he might then drop his claim to Malta and avoid a conflict with England. Thus the celebrated scene—so brilliantly depicted by Henry Adams—when Napoleon angrily splashed bath water on his brothers, as they protested the sale of Louisiana, had its roots in greed and not in patriotism.[26] It may very well have been Talleyrand's close association with the Louisiana project which led to the appointment of Marbois. The Minister of Finances also had other qualifications notably absent in the Foreign Minister. Marbois was on excellent personal terms with Livingston; he liked Americans (his wife was a Philadelphian); and he was not tainted with imputations of bribery.

From the behavior of his colleague, Monroe concluded that Livingston, who informed him of Talleyrand's offer, was attempting to exclude him from active participation in the negotiations. The day after his arrival, when he went to look over the resident Minister's recent correspondence, Livingston still made no effort to examine their joint instructions. Monroe's suspicions led him to decline the suggestion that he be presented informally to Talleyrand at an evening party; instead, he asked Livingston to obtain an appointment at the Foreign Office for that purpose. If it had been Livingston's intent to delay the accreditation of his colleague by an informal introduction, he made no objection to this alternative. Monroe's presentation took place at the Foreign Office on April 14.[27] On the evening of the thirteenth Livingston invited his colleague to dinner, including Skipwith and Mercer among the guests. While they were still at dinner, Marbois called, and in a private conversation with Livingston informed him of the decision at St. Cloud. Livingston's unhesitating acceptance of Marbois' invitation to call on him that very evening to discuss the proposal led to a blunt discussion between the two envoys, the sharpness of which was concealed behind the formal courtesy each maintained. The emotions aroused by this scene were still vividly felt when Monroe recounted it to Madison some months later:

I hesitated on the idea of his going alone; before I was presented; before we had read our instructions together or adopted any plan: intimated delicately that too much zeal might do harm, that a little reserve might have a better effect. He could not see the weight of these objections . . . declared it altogether impossible for me to go with him, as I was not presented; of the rigorous etiquette observed by the govt. on that point. . . . I observed that I had no idea of going myself and ceased to oppose his going, tho' I most earnestly pressed on him the propriety of his being reserved in the conference—to tell him [Marbois] that he had not read his instructions; in short to hear and not to speak.[28]

Marbois informed Livingston at their eleven o'clock conference that the First Consul was willing to sell Louisiana for 100 million francs (Napoleon had in fact specified 50 million as the price), if the United States would assume all claims against France. This sum, as well as Marbois' second figure of 60 million, struck the American Minister as excessive. Returning home shortly after midnight, and without waiting to inform Monroe, Livingston sat up until three drafting a jubilant dispatch imparting the news of his success. It was a victory, as he pointedly reminded the Secretary of State, achieved before the special emissary had been formally received.[29]

At this point the American negotiators were on the verge of a rupture, which was averted only by their high sense of public responsibility, for both realized that they must act at once before the First Consul changed his mind. After several frank discussions Livingston agreed to include his colleague in the negotiations, although the reception at Talleyrand's office did not constitute a formal recognition of Monroe's powers. This could only be granted by Napoleon at the monthly reception for official presentations. While they were still at odds, Monroe drafted a letter of complaint to Madison, but withheld it once the conflict was resolved.[30] Not until a month later, when it became apparent that Livingston was misrepresenting his role in the cession, did Monroe inform the Secretary of State of the difficulties he had encountered in Paris. Yet in spite of considerable resentment, he was sufficiently fair to admit: "It is a justice however which I owe to my colleague to observe that he has manifested an invariable zeal to promote the object of the cession, and to extend our rights on the Mississippi. . . ."[31]

III

Once these personal differences were resolved, they had no difficulty in agreeing to ignore their instructions and accept the offer of all Louisiana. As they later explained, they took this step simply because it was a choice of all or none. Fixing on a top price of 50 million francs, with an additional 20 million to cover the claims, they opened the bargaining by offering Marbois 40 million above the claims. Again Marbois repeated that the price was 100 million francs, but he indicated that he could persuade the First Consul to take 60 million if the Americans would assume the claims. At this point a back injury made it impossible for Monroe to participate in the discussions for several days. In the meantime, Livingston, much to the alarm of Skipwith, Joel Barlow and Mercer, who did not trust the resident Minister, continued the discussions alone.[32] On April 24 Monroe was able to receive Marbois and Livingston to continue the bargaining as he reclined on a sofa. Within a few days, since Marbois remained inflexible, the American negotiators agreed to pay 60 million francs and to allocate 20 million francs for the payment of the claims.

Throughout the conferences Livingston made what Monroe (and later Madison and Jefferson) considered an improper attempt to settle the claims in a separate agreement to be drawn up before the treaty of cession. Livingston, whose family possessed substantial interest in claims, was apprehensive that they might never be paid if included in a treaty of cession which should not be ratified. He nearly exhausted his colleague's patience on one occasion by insisting on reading a long paper establishing France's full liability for the claims. Monroe took particular exception to Livingston's contention that failure to validate the claims might lead to a Republican defeat at home. It was an absurd argument, but Monroe had apparently forgotten he had used a similar approach a decade earlier. Nonetheless, he signed the paper thinking that it could do no harm, whereas a refusal would simply give his colleague grounds for asserting that Monroe had been indifferent to the claims. In the end Livingston lost the contest to divorce the claims from the treaty of cession.[33]

Complete agreement was reached on the terms of the sale by April 29: France promised to cede Louisiana for 60 million francs ($11,250,-000); an additional 20 million francs ($3,750,000) would be set aside to liquidate the claims. Such a sum was too large for the United States to pay at once, and to accommodate the French, who wished for immediate payment, a special agreement was drawn up providing for the issuance of stock bearing six per cent interest, which the French government could sell in the open market.[34]

Having reached this point Marbois suggested that Monroe, now recovered from his injury, ask Talleyrand to fix a day for his official presentation to the First Consul. When Livingston volunteered to make the arrangement, Monroe's distrust of his colleague revived. Consequently, the next morning he sent a note to Livingston asking him to stop on his way to see the Foreign Minister in order "to guard against accidents." [35] His suspicions proved unfounded, for Livingston had already seen Talleyrand before he received the reminder. After the official reception at the Louvre on May 1, the two American diplomats dined with the First Consul. The reception and dinner, like all official ceremonies of the Napoleonic era, were stiff and solemn affairs, during which the First Consul interrogated his guests with such abruptness that there was little occasion for more than the briefest replies. To Monroe Napoleon addressed such queries as: "Do you speak French?" "You had a good voyage?" "Well, Mr. Jefferson, how old is he?" "Is he married or single?" [36] After dinner the final phrasing of the treaty of cession and of the two conventions relating to the payment was worked out.

The only portion of the treaty presenting a serious difficulty was that defining the boundaries of Louisiana. Since the American envoys were convinced that West Florida was part of Louisiana, they were anxious to include a specific statement to that effect in the treaty. They quickly discovered, however, that there was no hope of obtaining either a description or a guarantee of the boundaries of the purchase—no one in fact seemed at all certain of the exact limits of France's ancient colony. They had to be content with Marbois' vague verbal assurance that France would support the United States in negotiations with Spain for Florida. In lieu of a more specific statement they were gratified by France's willingness to permit the transfer from the treaty of retrocession (whose text they had only recently seen) of the sole provision relating to the boundaries of Louisiana; thus incorporating into the treaty a phrase of monumental imprecision:

... The Colony or Province of Louisiana, with the same extent it now has in the hands of Spain, and that it had when France possessed it; and such as it should be after the treaties subsequently entered into between Spain and other states.

The treaty of cession and its companion agreement providing for the stock issue were signed on May 2, but dated April 30. A convention setting up machinery to process the claims was signed a week later, although also dated April 30. The execution of the two lesser agreements was made dependent upon the ratification of the treaty of cession.[37] The vague wording of the passage relating to the limits of Louisiana did not shake the conviction of the negotiators that the territory included West Florida. Livingston was eager to inform Madison of this view, but Monroe demurred, considering it essential to probe the matter thoroughly. Nonetheless, Livingston promptly wrote the Secretary of State on his own advising that West Florida be seized. Not until mid-May did the envoys complete their investigation into the history of Louisiana. Then, with Monroe supplying important links in the argument, the emissaries presented evidence which struck Jefferson and Madison as conclusive, although never accepted by Spain. The arguments developed in Paris became the basis of American negotiations with Spain during the next few years, and ultimately served as justification for the occupation of West Florida in 1810.[38] In spite of all prodding, French officials declined to elucidate the vexed problem of the extent of Louisiana beyond Talleyrand's enigmatic remark to Livingston: ". . . you have made a noble bargain for yourselves and I suppose you will make the most of it." [39]

The spontaneous burst of enthusiasm with which the news of the purchase was greeted in the United States completely removed whatever misgivings the envoys had felt in overstepping the limits of their instructions. The first sensation of the nation was one of relief at the removal of a serious threat; only gradually did an awareness of the magnitude of the achievement capture the public imagination. The vision of the future, which many now beheld, was most effectively expressed by Jefferson—it was "an empire for liberty." [40] Madison promptly wrote the envoys extending the "entire approbation" of the President, who would have authorized the purchase of all Louisiana had it been known that France was willing to dispose of the territory in its full extent.[41]

During his four months in France, Monroe renewed some of his old friendships. Not long after he arrived he received a welcoming note from Lafayette, who was confined with a broken hip. He at once visited his Revolutionary comrade, whom he had not seen in twenty years. It gave him particular pleasure to be able to deliver the act of Congress ceding western lands to Lafayette in recognition of his past services. When Lafayette, who was experiencing severe financial difficulties, was unable to borrow money on this grant from Continental bankers, the envoy acted as an intermediary in securing a loan from Baring Brothers in London.[42] Monroe also called on another hero of the American Revolution—Kosciusko, who was living on the edge of Paris absorbed in the unwarlike task of gardening.[43] Mme. Campan's nieces (one of whom had married Marshal Ney) showed the Monroes every courtesy, as they sought to repay him for the aid he had rendered them in 1794. The Consuls Cambacérès and Lebrun, whom Monroe had known well ten years before, greeted him warmly and received him before he had been presented to the First Consul. This was contrary to usage, but, as Cambacérès told Monroe, they could not regard him as a stranger. Not all of his former friendships could be resumed. Regretfully, Monroe had to avoid those who were in disfavor with the present regime lest he damage the prospects of success for his missions in France and Spain. Consequently, it was not until he returned from Spain in 1805, when he no longer had any official standing in France, that he felt free to call on Reubell, the former Director.[44]

IV

The apparent harmony between the envoys during the negotiations concealed a deep undercurrent of mutual irritation. As Monroe told Madison in a private letter accompanying the treaty, the "most difficult vexations and embarrassing part of my labors has been with my associate." [45] The friction between them mounted as Monroe sought to diminish the effect of Livingston's campaign to prove that he alone was responsible for the acquisition of Louisiana. The public was never fully aware of the rift between the envoys, for both had too strong a sense of decorum and national pride to permit European statesmen to amuse themselves over the spectacle of two American diplomats squabbling for personal glory. Moreover, neither wished to elevate a personal difference into a party feud. Thus they preserved the outward appearances of personal amity. Seeing them together touring the monuments of London in the spring of 1804, none would have guessed that they were privately expressing the most unflattering opinions of each other.[46] Their former friendship was never restored. In the future the Livingston family cherished a lasting resentment, which erupted during Monroe's Presidency when John Armstrong (Livingston's brother-in-law) reasserted Livingston's claims in the press.[47] In this unseemly contest for glory Livingston bears a large share of the blame, for he sought to attribute the victory to his efforts, whereas Monroe merely asserted that the treaty was a joint work in which administration policy had played a decisive role. Monroe's sole failing towards his colleague was that he did not allow Livingston sufficient credit for propagating in French official circles the notion that the United States might buy all Louisiana.[48]

Monroe might have been more generous had he not been exasperated by efforts to tamper with the evidence. In order for Livingston to prove that the decision to cede Louisiana stemmed from his representations, it was imperative to demonstrate that Napoleon had made up his mind to sell Louisiana before it was known that the special envoy had landed at Le Havre. Since the news of Monroe's arrival had been sent by semaphore telegraph and thus had been known to the First Consul on April 9, Livingston set about proving that Napoleon had decided to rid himself of Louisiana prior to that date.

Forgetting that the correct sequence of events was recorded in his letters to Madison, Livingston first undertook to revise his version in a series of letters written during April and May to Rufus King, who was preparing to return home after serving as Minister to Great Britain. Correctly gauging that King would be delighted to spread reports unfavorable to Monroe, Livingston began by informing King that the sale of Louisiana had been proposed before the arrival of the special envoy, but that he had insisted on postponing negotiations until his colleague was present. Only after several rather general letters did Livingston date the offer as ten days prior to Monroe's arrival.[49] A somewhat more modest adjustment of dates was attempted in a letter to Madison on May 12 in which he asserted that Talleyrand's offer had been made on April 9. If this version were accepted, then it would shift Napoleon's decision to the eighth, the day Monroe disembarked. The saddest episode in the whole affair was Livingston's clumsy effort to alter the record in his own letter book by changing the date of his note to Talleyrand from April 12 to April 10 by writing a "0" over the "2." He does not seem to have been in the least troubled by the fact that his own letters on file in the State Department would readily expose his deception.

Monroe very quickly had positive proof of the accuracy of the rumors about Livingston's activities, when he discovered his colleague inserting April 8 as the date of Napoleon's decision in the draft of a joint letter informing the American Minister in Spain of the recent purchase. Monroe avoided directly challenging Livingston's veracity by suggesting that a more general letter be sent.[50]

By the end of May Monroe decided he could not ignore Livingston's systematic campaign to take credit for the purchase. Although he had

never seen a copy of Livingston's letter to Madison of April 13, in
which events were correctly stated, he possessed means of refuting his
colleague from information received from Marbois and from his colleague's pessimistic letter of April 10. He presented his case in the
form of a statement of the facts in a letter to the Virginia senators intended to be circulated among the members of Congress.[51] Although
he ascribed the success of the mission to the firmness of administration
policy, he stressed the fact that the decision to sell had not been made
until he reached France. To support his contention that the negotiations had reached a stalemate prior to his arrival, he enclosed a copy
of Livingston's letter of April 10. Avoiding all criticism of his colleague,
Monroe concluded: "Personally I pretend to nothing but zeal and
industry after I got there, a merit which was equally due to my colleague." [52]

Later in the year Livingston gave wider publicity to his claims by
releasing a version of a memoir which he had presented to French officials in printed form in 1802. This document was an attempt to prove
that Louisiana would be an economic liability to France, whose best
interests would be served by disposing of the colony. The publication
of the memoir was accompanied by a letter purportedly written by an
American in Paris, who was producing the memoir to prove Livingston's instrumentality in the purchase. Although both Monroe and
Madison thought that they detected in this letter the hand of James
Swan, who was currying favor with Livingston to advance dubious
spoliation claims, they were convinced that the resident Minister had
inspired the publication. The release of the memoir was considered
particularly indiscreet, since it contained comments hostile to England.
When asked to explain its appearance in the press, Livingston at first
attributed it to the zeal of his friends, but later shifted the blame to the
French government. This episode substantially weakened Jefferson's
confidence in the judgment of the Minister.[53]

As provoking as Livingston's activities were, Monroe counseled
against any reprisals or public replies: "With respect to this old friend,"
he told Madison, "I have but one opinion and wish since my association
with him; it has been to put it out of his power and those about him
to give an improper character to a particular transaction . . . and that
being done he should be treated with the utmost kindness possible."
He did, however, make one suggestion. It was then (November 1803)
rumored that Livingston wished to return to the United States early
in 1804 in order to capitalize on his diplomatic fame by seeking the vice-

presidential nomination. To forestall this possibility, Monroe recommended that Livingston be urged to stay on, which he would undoubtedly agree to do, since the request would flatter him.[54] This advice was
rather belated, for George Clinton had already been nominated for
the vice-presidency in February 1804 before the letter arrived.

V

Which of the envoys was correct in interpreting French policy? Was
Napoleon influenced by Livingston's arguments? Or had Monroe's
special mission with its implications of a drastic reversal of American
policy been the catalytic agent? Monroe and Livingston agreed on two
points: namely, that the prospect of a renewal of the war with England
and the failure of General Leclerc's expedition to Santo Domingo had
influenced the decision of the First Consul. But beyond this they were
completely at odds.

Livingston was convinced that Napoleon had been induced to sell
because of the effect of the contention advanced in Livingston's memoir
of 1802 that Louisiana would be a liability to France since the mother
country lacked the capital needed to develop such a vast wilderness.
This memoir, bearing the title, "Whether it will be Advantageous to
France to Take Possession of Louisiana," had been distributed in 1802
in printed form to twenty high-ranking officials (including Joseph
Bonaparte) in the hope that it would reach the eyes of the First Consul.
Primarily intending to dissuade Napoleon from taking possession of
Louisiana, Livingston had presented the view that in the event France
should occupy Louisiana, then the only way in which she could ensure
the prosperity of the colony was by selling New Orleans to the United
States and by permitting Americans to trade freely in Louisiana.[55] If
the First Consul ever read this memorial, which Monroe somewhat
unjustly condemned as "long-winded and empty," then it is conceivable
that it might have led him to question the value of Louisiana for
France.[56] As the second item in support of his case Livingston adduced
the proposal which he made in January 1803 that France cede New
Orleans, West Florida and Louisiana north of the Arkansas River. It
is quite probable that this offer, though it was rejected at the time,
may have given currency to the idea that the United States might be
willing to take all Louisiana.

Monroe judged both of these representations as completely ineffectual, since they had not led to an offer to sell prior to his arrival in

France. It was not that he considered himself an important factor, but that his arrival forced Napoleon to make a decision about his course towards an envoy representing a government which had taken an increasingly unfriendly tone towards France after the retrocession of Louisiana. In Monroe's view the firm policy of the administration was the decisive factor in reversing French policy.[57]

Attempts to assess these contending interpretations immediately encounter an insuperable difficulty in that the principal agent never explained his motives apart from an inadequate official explanation designed to make the sale of Louisiana less offensive to the French public. Napoleon's assertion that he had ceded Louisiana in order to rid France of a liability now that war was about to begin was popularized by Henry Adams, who was only too happy to minimize the effect of Jeffersonian foreign policy. However, the most recent student of the Louisiana Purchase, E. Wilson Lyon, has demonstrated that several important elements have been ignored. As Lyon pointed out, the renewal of the war should not have altered French policy toward Louisiana: Napoleon expected to win the war and could regain the colony in the peace treaty, if it should be seized by England. In fact there seems little doubt that some months before Monroe's arrival Napoleon had turned his attention away from the vision of an American empire and back to his earlier dream of French domination in the Middle East. From his own experience in Egypt Napoleon realized that he must possess Malta in order to carry out his Mediterranean ambitions; yet to secure the island, war with England was necessary. Therefore Louisiana had long faded to insignificance in the plans of the First Consul. It was of no moment that England might seize it during the war—he simply had no further interest in the project.

Why then did Napoleon decide to sell rather than return Louisiana to Spain, as he had promised in the treaty of retrocession? The last was a solution which might have amused him as a means of confounding the world, since France had never publicly admitted the retrocession. His decision seems to have been influenced by the only new factor affecting the diplomatic scene early in 1803—the assumption of a more forceful policy by the Jefferson administration, which greatly increased the likelihood that the United States might seize New Orleans and enter into a close understanding with Great Britain. For six months the letters of the French chargé in Washington had been filled with reports of the belligerent tone of the administration. These reports gained substance from the publication in the spring of 1803 of Senator James

Ross's warlike resolves, a copy of which Livingston sent Talleyrand shortly before Monroe landed. The French government was not then aware that the Republicans had replaced Ross's resolutions with milder substitutes. Under these circumstances the First Consul, by selling Louisiana (a property on which he placed no value), was offered an opportunity to assure the friendship of a nation seemingly on the verge of forming an alliance with his principal enemy. It was too much for him to resist such a stroke, which was accompanied by substantial financial advantages. The pledge to restore Louisiana to Spain, if France did not occupy the colony, was easily ignored in view of the complete subservience of the Spanish crown to the will of the First Consul. Napoleon realized that American friendship could have been obtained by a lesser cession, but in yielding the whole, he may have envisaged the creation of a maritime power in America as a counterweight to Great Britain.[58]

Although the ramifications of the Consular mind remain ultimately impenetrable, Monroe was not far wrong in his conclusion "that a desire to place us at repose with respect to France, to establish a solid peace between the two nations, and prevent our connection with Engld., by a liberal policy, were among the strong motives which had induc'd the cession of Louisiana. . . ."[59] Somewhat less valid was his conviction that a secondary element inducing the sale had been Napoleon's desire to appease the republican elements in France by pursuing a mild course toward a nation with which they felt a deep bond.

VI

The friction generated between the envoys continued after Monroe went to England in July 1803 to take up his post as Minister. In transmitting the treaty they had urged immediate ratification in a special session of Congress in order to prevent Napoleon from using any delay as an excuse to evade his commitments. Their anxiety on this score seemed to be verified when they were informed that the First Consul considered his ratification void unless the first payment was made within the three-month period stipulated for American ratification. Somewhat puzzled by this declaration, which in no way altered the treaty, Livingston and Monroe were further perplexed when Talleyrand told them that until ratifications were exchanged the First Consul considered the treaty under his control and hence might impose further conditions. Refusing to accept this unusual doctrine, the American diplomats only conceded that failure to ratify within the stated time would justify France in reconsidering her commitments. Talleyrand's mystifying comments were at once relayed to Madison with a renewed plea for immediate ratification.[60] Jefferson found this information most useful in persuading reluctant Republicans to overcome their scruples about the constitutionality of the purchase when Congress met in special session in October.[61]

Monroe suspected that these remarks about the treaty screened a move to obtain an advance payment, which he and Livingston had proposed during the negotiations, although the offer had not been accepted. Since a down payment would make it difficult for France to withdraw prior to the ratification of the treaty, Monroe was quite willing to use the special appropriation of $2 million for this purpose. Consequently, on June 7, Monroe, conferring alone with Talleyrand (Livingston had not heard the invitation), renewed the offer, which was again declined. Upon learning of this interview Livingston expressed relief that the offer had not been accepted, but he made no objection to the idea of an advance payment.[62]

Nothing more was said about the matter until late August when Livingston notified Monroe, who was then in London, that Marbois had asked for an advance. Promptly forwarding an order on the British banking firm of Hope and Co. for $2 million, Monroe was astonished when Livingston refused to approve the advance, because it exceeded their powers and would expose them to serious difficulties if the treaty were rejected.[63] In referring the request to his colleague Livingston had suggested that Monroe assume the full responsibility for the payment. Monroe was not unwilling to do this, but, as he reminded Livingston, their authority was a joint one and thus he could not validly dispose of the sum placed at their discretion. The Minister to France finally signed only because he feared that he might bear the full blame if Napoleon should use their refusal as a justification for withdrawing the cession.[64] Livingston, however, did manage to withhold his signature until news from America made it certain that the treaty would not encounter any difficulties in the Senate. Monroe's willingness to make the advance was rather risky, for the envoys had not been specifically authorized to make such a payment, but the importance of the purchase for the future of the nation seemed ample justification for an act calculated to bind the First Consul. Fortunately for the envoys the news of the advance did not leak out prior to the ratification of the treaty. It would have provided effective ammunition for the opponents of the treaty.[65]

The confidence of the Republican leaders in Livingston's judgment was completely undermined during the next year by his quarrel with the commissioners, which he and Monroe had chosen to pass on claims arising under the convention. By the terms of this agreement the claims were first approved by a three-member commission, and then authenticated in turn by the French government and the American Minister, who issued the orders for payment. This clumsy arrangement was imperiled from the outset by the fact that an insufficient sum had been allocated for the claims. Moreover, the ambiguously worded convention seemed to reinstate claims invalidated in 1801. Monroe had followed Livingston's lead in providing for the claims on the assumption that his colleague, who had been discussing the claims for two years, was better informed than he. Livingston, surrounded by a court of flattering claimants playing on his vanity, was soon in open conflict with the commission, which refused to honor claims for which he sought priority.[66] The commissioners, contrary to Livingston's wishes, would not pass any claims before the ratification of the treaty, and they insisted that disbursements should not be made until all the claims had been examined. The commissioners indignantly repudiated Livingston's assertion that they were under his authority. Rather unjustly, Livingston attributed the stubbornness of the commissioners to Monroe's influence over the "Virginia faction" (two of the commissioners were Virginians).[67] By December 1803 the dispute had reached such embittered proportions that the commissioners and Skipwith, the commercial agent for the committee, refused to attend a dinner organized by the Americans in Paris to celebrate the ratification of the treaty, since Livingston would be present.[68]

When the disputants appealed to Monroe, he expressed the opinion that the commissioners were the sole judges of their powers and in no way under the jurisdiction of the Minister to France.[69] In relaying the details of the controversy to Madison, who also received reports from the other parties, Monroe affirmed his confidence in the integrity of the commissioners. The quarrel raged on into the next year as the commission resisted Livingston's pressure in behalf of favored claimants. Livingston again appealed to Monroe in 1804 but rejected the suggestion that both parties state their views in writing so that he could arbitrate the dispute. Nothing damaged Livingston's reputation as much as this unseemly and well-publicized squabble.[70]

After the conclusion of the purchase treaty, Monroe had intended to leave for Spain and there settle the boundaries of Louisiana. Since it was assumed that success would depend on the support of France, he first wrote Talleyrand to remind him of Marbois' verbal promise that France would use her influence to assist the United States. The fact that he did not receive an immediate reply did not seem significant until Second Consul Cambacérès pointedly remarked at a dinner party that Monroe should not go to Spain at present. When Monroe pressed for an explanation he was referred to Marbois. Unable to see the Minister of Finances, he turned for enlightenment to the Spanish Ambassador, Azara, who told him that a messenger had just been sent to Madrid at Livingston's request to propose that the negotiations for the Floridas be transferred to Paris. Monroe was truly exasperated the next day by his colleague's urbane queries about his plans for going to Madrid. To Monroe's questions about the conversation with Azara, Livingston would admit nothing more than that the Spanish Ambassador had apparently misunderstood a casual remark expressing the hope that he would urge his government to cede the Floridas. At Monroe's insistence Livingston called on Azara to request that his comments be ignored, since Monroe was about to leave for Spain. Monroe was quite correct in suspecting that Livingston had deliberately attempted to transfer the negotiations to Paris.[71] Livingston, with his enormous capacity for self-deception, now felt that his colleague, by interfering at this point, had deprived him of the opportunity to secure the Floridas.[72] As he told his brother some months later, he had commenced negotiations with Spain with "flattering hopes of success" but his colleague had taken his "interference amiss . . . and I having no power I was obliged at his request . . . to revoke what I had done." [73]

Cambacérès' hint to Monroe, however, was in no way related to Livingston's conversation with Azara, but directly expressed the views of the First Consul, who preferred not to antagonize his only ally by pressing for the cession of the Floridas in the face of Spain's outraged protests over the sale of Louisiana. Once it was evident that France would not endorse American claims to Florida, Monroe concluded that a trip to Spain was pointless, but he hesitated to alter his plans, since he did not want the French government to assume that its attitude was the determining factor. His dilemma was resolved when Madison notified him that he had been appointed Rufus King's successor in London. Since Rufus King had departed without appointing a chargé, the renewal of the war made it imperative that the United States be represented in Great Britain.[74] Late in June Monroe called on Talleyrand, who had never replied to his letter soliciting French aid in Spain, in order to take his leave. On the assumption that Talleyrand expected him to press for an answer, Monroe took particular delight in opening the conference with a reminder of the promise made by Marbois, but before the Foreign Minister could reply he announced his departure for London. This, he hoped, would create the impression that his decision was not related to French policy but resulted exclusively from his recent instructions.[75]

On the twenty-fourth of June Talleyrand escorted Monroe to St. Cloud for his audience of leave. It was on this occasion that Napoleon, in the midst of the platitudes usual on ceremonial occasions, declared that in selling Louisiana his motive had not been financial gain but a desire to win the friendship of the United States—a remark seeming to substantiate Monroe's conclusions about the impact of Jefferson's firm measures on France's policy. Napoleon, who obviously expected further rewards for his generosity, now expressed the hope that the United States would not permit its flag to be used as a screen for British commerce. To this Monroe firmly countered that there would be no difficulty on this score, if the First Consul would adhere to the doctrine that free ships make free goods. Such a policy was far removed from the intent of the First Consul, who noncommittally replied that he would give the subject his serious consideration. Although Napoleon repeated Cambacérès' advice that this was not the proper time for Monroe to go to Spain, he left Monroe with the vague impression that France would be willing to back America's claims when Spain's sense of grievance was less acute.[76] After making farewell calls on Marbois and the other consuls, Monroe set out for London by way of Calais on July 12.[77]

CHAPTER 13

ENGLAND AND SPAIN

ONROE ARRIVED in London on July 18, 1803, slightly anxious about the reception awaiting him. Since the beginning of the French Revolution a powerful wave of conservative reaction had engulfed the English ruling classes, who now condemned even the mildest reform measures as Jacobinical innovations. Consequently he anticipated a rather cool reception in view of his Republican background and his well-advertised sympathy for the Revolution as Minister to France in 1795. His misgivings were unwarranted, for he was greeted, at least on the official level, with every manifestation of good will by the Addington ministry, which had already demonstrated a friendly attitude towards the United States during Rufus King's tenure as Minister to Great Britain. Monroe naturally looked forward with curiosity to his presentation to the King—a rebel encountering his former sovereign. His long-cherished animosity towards George III was modified by the courtesy of the King's reception. When the American Minister voiced the desire of the President to maintain friendly relations between the two nations, the King, expressing reciprocal sentiments, spoke of the great interest he had taken in the welfare of the United States since the Revolution. After these formal remarks George III inquired about conditions in Virginia, and revealed, to Monroe's surprise, a considerable knowledge of the early history of the College of William and Mary. The only embarrassing moment during the interview occurred when the King queried about the French: "They have no religion, have they?" After a momentary hesitation Monroe cautiously ventured the opinion that he believed there were many in France, who, indeed, had none. Since this seemed

225

to accord with the King's opinion, the reception ended on an amicable note. The new Minister felt that the King, at the request of the Foreign Secretary, Lord Hawkesbury, had made a sincere effort to create a friendly atmosphere.[1]

In numerous conferences with Hawkesbury, Addington, and other Cabinet members during the next few months, Monroe was much encouraged by their apparent friendliness towards the United States. Most pleasing was the general approval of the recent acquisition of Louisiana. Pitt, he was told, had spoken with high praise of Jefferson's skillful policy, which had resulted in such a glorious achievement. Yet, in spite of these verbal demonstrations of good will, it was soon evident that the government was unwilling to discuss specific issues; thus little more could be expected than general assurance that everything possible would be done to satisfy the legitimate grievances of the United States.[2] His inability to induce Hawkesbury to come to grips with the main problems was not entirely the result of the slothful habits for which the Foreign Secretary was known, but sprang in large measure from the weakness of the ministry. Although Henry Addington, Viscount Sidmouth, was much respected, his contemporaries felt that he lacked the energetic qualities needed to push the war to victory, and hence, his government, which was slowly losing strength in the Commons, was not in a position to embark upon new policies.[3] But, as Monroe soon understood, the caution of the Addington ministry was not just a matter of instability; at this time British policy was limited by the deeply rooted prejudices of the British ruling classes, whose members not only cherished a distaste for the government and institutions of the United States, but also for the seeming pro-French policy which America had pursued in the past. Many Englishmen, as Monroe observed, still held to the illusion that a close alliance with the United States was possible if the Federalists regained power, an impression fostered by Anthony Merry's dispatches from Washington. Monroe noted too the jealousy of the merchants, who resented the prosperity American shippers were enjoying as a result of the war. For this reason the mercantile element wished to preserve the old restrictive commercial system in its own interest. Since the ministry had to draw its support from the Commons, where these groups had a decisive influence, radical ventures in policy could not be undertaken as long as absolute unity was deemed essential for victory over France. He quickly perceived that the members of the government were distinctly more liberal in their views on

America than the members of the Commons, for the ministers saw the advantages accruing to Britain from friendly relations with the United States.[4]

At a very early stage of his residence in England Monroe reached a conclusion destined to affect his conduct during his tenure as Minister: namely, that American objectives, which would never be granted in treaty form, could be achieved through administrative orders. "There is," he wrote Madison in July 1804, "a great difference between obtaining a treaty which trenches on their ancient usages and pretensions, or what they call maritime rights, and an accommodation precisely the same in effect, by their own orders to the admiralty." [5] Monroe was one of the very few Americans of his generation to comprehend that Great Britain would never formally yield a principle considered vital to her own interests—a fundamental fact never clearly understood in Washington until the end of the War of 1812.

With this interpretation of British policy, it was logical that he should advise his superiors not to press for a treaty with Great Britain until the international situation should be such as to incline her to make a favorable settlement. At this juncture it seemed far more advantageous to him for the United States to avoid treaty commitments, which might prove inhibiting, in order to be free to take advantage of opportunities offered by the European war to secure more satisfactory terms. Indeed, he felt that American trade was currently enjoying far more extensive privileges than would ever be granted in a treaty.[6]

At this time Monroe considered impressment the only issue on which some concessions might be obtained. He was able to take this view because he did not attach the same importance to impressment as did his superiors in Washington.[7] Not only did he consider incidents of impressment to be much less frequent than in the past, but he was struck by the absence of any sign that the American people regarded it as a vital issue. What Monroe failed to realize was that Jefferson and Madison, who were still faced by frequent incidents on the American side of the Atlantic, placed major emphasis upon the elimination of this violation of American rights. In replying to Monroe's first dispatches, which had stressed the infrequency of impressment in European waters, Madison was careful to note that the situation in "American seas . . . is very different, and . . . is growing worse and worse. Impressments and other outrages are multiplying . . . [and the] public mind is rising in a state of high sensibility." [8] As proof of the current popular feeling,

Madison cited a measure before Congress to exclude from the ports of the United States British warships which had impressed crew members from American vessels. When this bill, widely believed to have Jefferson's approval, was ultimately withdrawn in the face of violent Federalist opposition, Monroe concluded that the "publick mind is not altogether ripe for a rupture on that ground, since the quarter of the Union [New England] most injured" by impressment had not complained.[9] From the outset of his mission his attitude towards impressment was quite different from that of Madison and Jefferson. He also urged that punitive measures against England be avoided, for such action would merely force the British government to abandon recent modifications of maritime usages introduced through administrative channels.[10]

The first issue taken up by Monroe with the Addington ministry was impressment, which he approached from the point of view of obtaining specific modifications through Admiralty orders rather than in the form of a public agreement. When he began these discussions, he was not aware that Rufus King had failed to secure a convention banning impressment because of the British insistence that the waters around the British Isles (the so-called "narrow seas") be excluded from the operation of the agreement. Moreover, since King had neglected to leave any papers when he sailed home in May 1803, the new Minister was also unfamiliar with the terms of another convention settling the Maine boundary dispute, which King had taken with him for ratification.[11] Monroe entered these discussions with Hawkesbury in a rather hopeful frame of mind, since Anthony Merry, the newly appointed Minister to the United States, who seemed a "worthy candid man," had indicated that the Foreign Secretary would do everything in his power to accommodate the wishes of the American government.[12] In the light of this assurance, Monroe instructed George W. Erving (the agent for American seamen in London) to draw up a report on the current practices and enumerating the cases pending before the Admiralty. In submitting this report to Hawkesbury, Monroe deliberately omitted any discussion of the American position on impressment in the hope that this would facilitate the voluntary modification of British practices. To test the good will of the Cabinet, he altered his habit of meeting informally with Hawkesbury, a practice King had found useful. Monroe, however, believed that these casual interviews tended to leave everything in a vague and undecided state.[13] Aware of the deep preoccupation of the ministry with plans for fending off Napoleon's anticipated invasion, Monroe did not press for an immediate action. In deciding to allow Hawkesbury ample time to consider the issue, Monroe had Madison's full approval.[14]

In contrast to the friendliness of his reception by the members of the government, the Minister's treatment in London society—and this extended to official social affairs—was not only cool but at times verged on rudeness. Although this hostility was expressed more openly after reports reached England of Merry's difficulties with Jefferson on matters of etiquette, from the outset Monroe was conscious that he was not accorded "the respect due to the office I held, [or] to the govt. and country I represented. . . ." [15] It galled him to be compelled to listen to criticisms and condescending remarks about the United States. Of one of his most unpleasant experiences, which took place at a dinner party given by Lord Hawkesbury, he sent a bitter account to Jefferson:

At Ld. H's table when speaking with his Lady, who appears to me to be an amiable woman on the subject of our climate, of its variety, etc. I mentioned that while the northern parts were perhaps in snow, the southern enjoyed the bloom of Spring; that in Feby at Charlestown [sic], I remembered they had the *course,* and from the want of other topicks of conversation, I added that on such occasions there was always a great concourse of people with gay equipages, etc. Ld. Castleray [sic] asked me what kind of equipages had they? I cod. not but be surprised at the enquiry, nevertheless replied, such as I saw here. Sir Wm. Scott then remarked he had lately read an acct. of a grand fête at the cape of good hope, which concluded with that all "the beauty taste & fashion of Africa were assembled there." This occasion'd some mirth as you will suppose at our expense, in which I cod. not well partake, & in justice to Ld. H. it is proper to say that by his reserve he did not appear to think that the remark was made on a suitable occasion. I was really embarrassed what part to take on the occasion. It was disagreeable to me to let it pass unnoticed, but I cod. not well notice it, without appearing to be hurt at it, nor without throwing the company into some confusion. I was therefore silent. Shortly afterward, in conversing with Ld. Castleray and some other gentlemen on the rapid growth of the U States, I observed that I was astonished to find persons of distinction by their offices and talents so extremely uninformed on that subject, as they were generally in this country: that in truth they knew as little of us as they did of the cape of good hope.[16]

He was equally annoyed by the precedence given the most "subaltern" powers, which did not have "one hundredth part of the political weight in the affairs of the world that we enjoy, even at this court." On one occasion, when he was seated at the foot of the table between the representatives of two principalities no bigger than his farm (as he put it), his irritation led to a momentary awkwardness from which he was rescued by the Russian Ambassador. After the first toast had been drunk Monroe inadvertently put his wineglass in the finger bowl, but the Russian Ambassador, who had observed Monroe's discomfiture over the seating arrangement, courteously proposed a toast welcoming the new Minister and honoring the President. Gratefully the American Minister returned the compliment, toasting the Tsar as a friend of America.[17] Hypersensitivity led him to suspect slights where none were intended. Thus he took amiss the failure of the English Cabinet ministers to acknowledge his calls, until he later realized that it was not the custom for them to return calls. He found little comfort in the knowledge that the excuses made by Hawkesbury and other officials for not accepting his dinner invitations were deliberate reprisals for the ill-treatment which Merry claimed to have received from Jefferson.[18] In spite of these rebuffs Monroe conducted himself with dignity, and did not emulate Merry by elevating these social slights into a public scandal. He also believed that the status of American ministers might be greater if the President and other public officials in America were more discriminating in receiving foreigners. The "facility with which subalterns" from England were received by "those in the highest places among us, does harm instead of good here." [19]

The first winter the Monroes spent in London was far from agreeable. Not only were social relations unpleasant, but they found it difficult to adjust to the damp and smoky London climate which resulted in constant colds in his family. Moreover, the fantastically high cost of living in London, where ordinary household items were five times as expensive as at home, made it necessary for him to borrow large sums of money in America, since the income from his estates had to be applied to the payments on the Loudoun property.[20] Colonel Lewis, in charge of his holdings in Albemarle, was so heavily pressed by Monroe's creditors that he sold the property near Charlottesville for £1500—a price Monroe considered far below its real value. Unfortunately neither Jefferson nor Joseph Jones had been able to advance sufficient funds to prevent the sale, nor could Jones, whose health was failing, do anything to check the deterioration of Monroe's lands under Lewis' poor management. Jones' death in 1805 was a deeply felt loss, for it meant not only the severance of a tie with a close relative, but also the loss of a beloved patron and confidant.[21]

II

The discomforts of London life made the prospect of going to Madrid in the late spring of 1804 most inviting. However, just as he was planning to leave in May a new ministry, headed by William Pitt, was organized. Although Monroe did not expect any change in policy, it seemed advisable for him to remain until he had ascertained its disposition. He was disappointed that Charles Fox, as had been rumored, was not included in the Cabinet, for Fox in contrast to Pitt was considered well-disposed to the United States.[22] Pitt's Cabinet was essentially a regrouping of the same elements composing the Addington ministry, and it was dedicated to the same objective—unremitting prosecution of the war, to which all other programs were subordinated. Pitt had replaced Addington largely because it was felt that the latter lacked the energy and stature to conduct the war with vigor. Although Hawkesbury remained in the Cabinet, his post in the Foreign Office was assumed by Lord Harrowby, who had little knowledge of foreign affairs. In coping with his duties Harrowby seems to have been guided by the advice of a friend, who counseled him that all he needed to do was to avoid saying anything definite to diplomatic callers, since their visits were usually made for the purposes of filling a dispatch.[23]

When Pitt entered office, Monroe was anxious to take up a treaty project submitted to Hawkesbury in April, although he had not pressed for action previously, since the ministry was expected to fall. This treaty, which had been drawn up by Madison in January, called for an absolute ban on impressment, a definition of contraband restricted to materials of war, the recognition of the neutral carrying trade, and the acceptance of the principle that a blockade to be legal must be maintained at the port under blockade. Madison, in lengthy instructions on January 5, which remained in effect during Monroe's mission, extensively reviewed the American position, pointedly concluding:

The essential objects for the United States are the suppression of impressment and the definition of blockades. Next to these in importance, are the reduction of the list of contraband, and the enlargement of our neutral trade with hostile colonies. Whilst you keep in view therefore those objects, the two last as highly important, and the two first as absolutely indispensable, your discretion, in which the President places great confidence, must guide you in all that relates to the inferior ones.

In submitting the treaty project, Monroe omitted the provision that contraband be restricted to war materials. He did this not only because he considered it impossible to obtain such a concession, but also because he believed France would be angered by any provision short of the doctrine that free ships make free goods. He also left out a number of minor points relating to the return of deserters from British ships in order to have some basis for bargaining during the negotiations. Madison raised no objections to these alterations.[24]

The Minister's first encounter with Lord Harrowby late in May was not pleasant. The Foreign Secretary, studiously refraining from the vague sentiments of friendship customary on such occasions, spoke in a deliberately irritating manner as he took his caller sharply to task for what he deemed the bad American habit of striking out specific sections of treaties prior to ratification. He had in mind the recent Senate action excluding a provision from the boundary convention signed by Rufus King. This section, relating to the northwestern boundary, had been eliminated to avoid conflict with the Louisiana cession, whose exact extent was not yet defined. Ignoring the explanation that this deletion was fully justified, since Rufus King had not been aware of the Louisiana Purchase, Harrowby harshly rejected American ratification. In spite of the Foreign Secretary's unsympathetic attitude, Monroe did not believe it reflected a change in British policy.[25]

Before Monroe had time to digest the implications of this conference, he was briefly distracted by the unexpected arrival in London of Robert R. Livingston, whose visit was most unwelcome, for the publication of the *Mémoire* of 1802 had rendered him *persona non grata* with Pitt. Livingston's visit was doubly embarrassing in view of the rumors then current that the Minister to France was in fact an unofficial peace emissary from Napoleon. This was not true, but Livingston did nothing to discourage a report so flattering to his self-esteem. Most annoying was Livingston's open association with Fox and other members of the opposition, with whom Monroe had little social contact in order to avoid the suspicion that he might be involved in political intrigue. Fox's friends, delighted in goading Pitt by consorting with a reputed French emissary, made much of Livingston. Sorely tried though he was by Livingston's indiscreet conduct, Monroe treated his former colleague with great courtesy, accompanying him on sightseeing expeditions to Westminster Abbey, St. Paul's, and the House of Commons. Only the illness of the King prevented him from gratifying Livingston's wish to be presented at Court. His visitor had to be content with a glimpse of George III driving with the royal family in Hyde Park.[26]

Although Harrowby was much friendlier in subsequent interviews, he steadily evaded the major issues, pleading that the demands of more pressing affairs made it impossible for him to study the pertinent documents. This behavior, as Monroe realized, simply screened the Cabinet's unwillingness to change its policy. The only positive overture came in August, when Harrowby suggested renewal of the commercial provisions of Jay's Treaty, which were about to expire. Agreeing to forward this proposal to his government, Monroe expressed doubt that it would be favorably received in view of the greatly changed conditions since 1795. Not only did the United States now have a better understanding of its interests, but the nation had also grown in importance as a power. He pointed out to Harrowby that there seemed little reason for renewing a treaty which neither power had liked, when it would be far more advantageous to start on a fresh basis. After six months of delay Monroe saw no point in continuing these aimless discussions with a Foreign Secretary who now professed to be unable to find a copy of the treaty project in his predecessor's files.[27] After supplying Harrowby with a copy of the treaty, Monroe set out on his long-postponed mission to Madrid, leaving his private secretary, John H. Purviance, to function as chargé.[28]

It was disappointing not to have made any progress with the British government, but Monroe was not deeply concerned by his failure, for he was still of the opinion that the Cabinet, although anxious to avoid a quarrel with the United States, was not yet willing to conclude an agreement settling all disputes. Again he reported to Madison that one of the major obstacles to an understanding was the prevailing conviction that Britain would benefit by postponing a settlement until the Federalists returned to power. The only way to disabuse the British of this error was for the United States to adhere to its policy of neutrality and prove that the nation was capable of pursuing a policy calculated to advance its own interests.[29]

III

Monroe, who had put off going to Madrid in 1803 on the assumption that France would redeem Marbois' verbal pledge to assist the United States in obtaining West Florida after Spain's wrath had cooled, now journeyed to Paris to remind Talleyrand of this promise.[30] Here he discovered, as Livingston's recent letters had asserted, that Talleyrand was now endorsing the Spanish claim that West Florida had never been part of Louisiana.[31] Monroe blamed this reversal on Livingston's suggestion to Talleyrand that the United States might be willing to lend Spain a substantial sum (perhaps as much as 70 million francs) if she would cede the Floridas. This proposal was of considerable interest to Talleyrand, since it would enable Spain to pay the arrears in her military subsidy to France. Consequently, Monroe believed that France was now seeking to obstruct a settlement between the United States and Spain until it was certain that Spain would profit. Monroe not only resented Livingston's meddling, but he considered it highly unlikely that Spain would ever repay a loan.[32]

In view of these recent developments, Monroe, in drafting a letter to Talleyrand to remind him of Marbois' promise, did not restrict himself to a simple request for assistance. Instead he reviewed the American claim that West Florida belonged to the nation by right, since it had been part of Louisiana. Moreover, he made it quite clear that American claims, which included seizures by French privateers using Spanish ports, would absorb any money payment likely to be offered to Spain for East Florida. Livingston was so angered by this indirect repudiation of his own proposal that he flatly refused to serve as an intermediary in transmitting the note to Talleyrand. Without formal diplomatic standing in France, a direct appeal by Monroe to the Minister of Foreign Affairs would afford a convenient excuse for a refusal. Nonetheless, since France's aid seemed so important for his mission, Monroe decided to risk a direct approach.[33] He made a further effort to secure Livingston's cooperation by enlisting the support of John Armstrong, Livingston's brother-in-law and recently arrived successor. When Armstrong failed, Monroe went to the Foreign Office, but finding Talleyrand occupied, he could not present his letter. After further reflection upon the inadvisability of this course, he again talked to Livingston, who, in his impulsive way, withdrew his objections and drafted a satisfactory covering letter.[34]

After waiting nearly a month for the reply promised as soon as Napoleon could be consulted, Monroe learned from unofficial sources that France would neither endorse the American claim to West Florida nor permit Spain to assume liability for depredations committed by French privateers operating from Spanish ports. He had no doubt that this decision was undertaken to compel him to agree to Livingston's scheme, for Marbois told him frankly that the affair was entirely a question of money. There was nothing to be gained by lingering in Paris, but Monroe put off his departure for several weeks to attend Napoleon's coronation as Emperor on December 2, in order to avoid giving offense by departing just before the ceremony. He was seated in Notre Dame, not, as he noted, with ministers of his rank but with lesser officials. This seemed to him to be a deliberate slight to emphasize Talleyrand's displeasure over his refusal to endorse a loan to Spain.[35]

In spite of France's refusal to pledge her support, Monroe decided to continue his journey to Madrid. He was aware that this was a departure from the spirit of his instructions of April 15, 1804, in which he had been told that the success of his mission would depend on the "active cooperation or favorable dispositions of France."[36] Since the final decision had been left to his discretion, Monroe felt that circumstances justified his move, even though the outlook was unfavorable. His primary motive, as he explained to Madison in a letter written en route to Spain, was to make it clear to France that she could not extract money from the United States in order to fulfill a freely given pledge. Moreover, he considered it important to prevent the transfer of the negotiations to Paris, where they would be under French control.[37]

Monroe later elaborated more fully upon these themes in a daily journal kept during the negotiations and subsequently transmitted to the Secretary of State. He admitted that France had the power to determine the outcome of the negotiations; yet, as long as the nation clung to the "negative and sordid" policy of submitting to French pressures, the other European states would consider the United States in a "species of dependence" on France. Only by "stepping forward and taking our own independent ground" could the nation hope to "become an object, commanding the respect of every power, and of political calculation of each."[38] Realistically he concluded: "Justice, favor, or fear, or to use a more civil phrase, respect, forms the basis of every negotiation with these powers." Since justice carried little weight, and favor rarely applied except under unusual conditions, such as those existing between France and the United States during the early phases of the French Revolution, it was essential for the nation to win the "respect" of the European powers if its diplomatic objectives were to be realized. The "respect," he continued, "which one power has for another is in the exact proportion of the means which they respectively have of injuring each other with the least detriment to themselves." Every negotiation must be viewed as an "affair of calculation, dependent upon the physical forces which each has at its command, the relative exposure of their possessions and the probability of the interference in the case of war of other powers." [39] The application of this rule to Spain was obvious: a weak nation with exposed frontiers in America must inevitably yield to the terms offered by the United States. Moreover, the conflict raging in Europe made the intervention of any other power in Spain's behalf quite unlikely.

This formula (which he was eventually to apply to Spain during his own Presidency) was far too belligerent for the Republican leadership in Washington. Yet, in urging this course on his superiors, Monroe thought he had evidence that such recommendations were in accord with administration policy. Early in 1804 Jefferson, acting under congressional authorization, established a revenue district in West Florida, a move which seemed to indicate an intention of occupying this region. The Spanish Minister in Washington, the Marquis de Casa Yrujo, had protested this action with such vehemence and rudeness that Madison had asked him to leave the capital and had instructed Monroe to request his recall. From these events Monroe concluded that a rupture between the two nations might be in the making. This interpretation was not correct, for these measures were merely intended as threatening gestures. Indeed, they alarmed Spain not at all, for Yrujo had reported their true intent to his government.

It was not until he reached Madrid that new instructions made the limitations of Jefferson's policy clear to Monroe. Although willing to take drastic steps to obtain Louisiana, Jefferson was not prepared to go quite so far in regard to Florida, which did not involve the vital interests of the nation. Jefferson's instinctive isolationism, his distaste for war as an instrument of national policy, and his scruples over the constitutionality of executive actions which might precipitate a conflict, led him to prefer a moderate and temporizing policy. Monroe, less doctrinaire, and also in a position of lesser responsibility, was more willing to take risks in order to exploit the unusual opportunities offered by the European war.

The threatening stance assumed by the administration was augmented with positive inducements to Spain. Early in 1804 Jefferson persuaded the Senate to ratify the convention providing for the payment of spoliation claims concluded by Charles Pinckney in 1802, but rejected at that time because it omitted claims arising from the depredations of French privateers operating from Spanish ports. Although

Spain had never approved the agreement, it was now hoped that Monroe and Pinckney could use it in their negotiations. The envoys were also authorized to offer 2 million dollars with the stipulation that it must be applied to pay the claims of American citizens. To make the American offer more attractive, Madison, in October 1804, instructed Monroe and Pinckney to offer the Colorado River as the western boundary of Louisiana with an unsettled buffer zone extending to the Rio Bravo.[40] Neither these inducements nor Monroe's earnest negotiations in Madrid had the slightest chance of success, for France's opposition precluded any settlement. It is difficult to say to what extent Jefferson and Madison grasped the degree of France's control over Spanish policy. Not only was France the dominant power on the Continent, but Charles IV, the Bourbon ruler of Spain, entertained a curious admiration for the Corsican upstart. No threat, no pressure, no bribe was sufficient to induce him to sign an agreement which did not have Napoleon's approval. Even Monroe does not seem to have fully understood the complete subservience of the Spanish crown to French influence.

IV

When Monroe departed for Madrid early in December, he left his family behind, to spare them the discomforts of travel in Spain for such a brief sojourn in Madrid. Eliza was happily ensconced with Mme. Campan, while Mrs. Monroe and Maria Hester stayed with the Skipwiths at St. Germain. Engaging relays of mules, Monroe reached Madrid on New Year's Day 1805 after a three-week journey through a desolate and barren country where inns were infrequent. The threat of bands of brigands added hazards not encountered in France or England. Once in Madrid he settled in comfortable lodgings with a "good chimney, which is a rare thing in Madrid, and very good rooms and fare." His accommodations, which had been chosen by resident Minister Charles Pinckney, were on the best street in Madrid (the Calle de Alcala en frente de la Aduana) close to the public walks and gardens.[41] Monroe, like so many other visitors to Spain, was impressed by the contrast between that country and the rest of Europe. The plight of the poverty-stricken people seemed but proof of the evils of a "government which is perfectly despotic, in which the people count for nothing." In other governments it was possible to see the great passions which motivated the individual, but in Spain all was different. As he shrewdly noted: "Of man, you have an inanimate painting before you. His passions are hidden and the human character is lost." [42]

Monroe was enthusiastically greeted by Pinckney, whose recent relations with Spanish officials had been far from pleasant. Anticipating that his difficulties might handicap joint negotiations, Pinckney had already requested his passports. Although empowered to negotiate alone, Monroe, declining Pinckney's offer to withdraw, persuaded him to participate in the negotiations. [43] Monroe admitted that "defects of a personal character" limited Pickney's effectiveness as a diplomat, but there could be no doubt of either his integrity or "independence of foreign influences. . . ." [44] These were traits which Monroe particularly prized after his recent experience with Livingston. He did not elaborate on Pinckney's shortcomings, which largely stemmed from his vanity and an exaggerated confidence in his own ability. Monroe usually had no difficulty in establishing excellent working relations with his colleagues, and Pinckney proved no exception. Throughout the negotiations he followed Monroe's lead, making no particular contributions of his own. The genial South Carolinian, who had found Madrid socially barren, was delighted with Monroe's company. When his colleague departed, Pinckney, as he candidly admitted, felt "like a fish out of water . . . lonesome and melancholy." [45]

Negotiations were delayed until the end of January pending the relocation of the Court at Aranjuez, where the American envoys also had to move. In the meantime, although there was little hope of French assistance, Monroe called on Pierre S. de Beurnonville, the French Ambassador, whom he had known during the Directory. Apparently de Beurnonville inadvertently aroused Monroe's hopes that he intended to use his good offices in behalf of American negotiations. Only later did Monroe realize that he had taken the Ambassador's personal expression of opinion as indicating an official position. [46] Only a few days after the negotiations started, Talleyrand's long-delayed reply to Monroe's request for French support finally arrived. In this letter, which had been addressed to Armstrong, Talleyrand denied that West Florida had ever been part of Louisiana. In grand and rather insulting terms, he expressed his distress over recent American menaces toward Spain. [47]

The emissaries opened their campaign on January 28, 1805, with a note to the Foreign Minister, Pedro de Cevallos, restating the arguments for the American contention that West Florida lay within the limits of the Louisiana Purchase. They also reviewed the American claims for damages arising from seizures and from losses following the suspension of the right of deposit at New Orleans. Appended to this note was a copy of a treaty project drafted by Madison proposing the cession of Florida and the assumption of all claims by Spain. If any payment were made the sum must be used to discharge the claims.[48] A few days later, Monroe called on the former Prime Minister, Manuel Godoy, the Prince of Peace, who, as the Queen's favorite, still exercised a decisive influence on Spanish policy. In this, the first of several interviews with Godoy, Monroe was told that America's claims were quite unreasonable. Denying the responsibility of Spain for seizures by French privateers, Godoy was equally firm in rejecting any liability for damages arising from the suspension of the right of deposit, which he described as an action properly within the power of the King. To the suggestion that the Louisiana boundary be arranged with the French, from whom the United States had purchased the territory, Monroe sensibly replied that the United States had acquired only the title from France; the boundaries must be settled with powers having lands adjacent to Louisiana. In the midst of the verbal fencing during this and subsequent interviews, Godoy, who was at all times courteous to Monroe, constantly made vague observations about his desire to see the matter settled, which gave Monroe more hope of a successful outcome than the circumstances justified.[49]

With a promptness not again encountered during the negotiations Cevallos replied to the first note of the American envoys within three days, proposing that all questions in dispute be discussed point by point until each had been disposed of. He specifically repudiated liability on Spain's part for the damages resulting from either the suspension of the right of deposit or the depredations of Spanish-based French privateers. In regard to the recently ratified convention of 1802, he took the position that it must be re-evaluated by his government prior to its acceptance.[50] From this reply Monroe concluded that Cevallos probably intended to protract the negotiations, while raising points to use as a justification for breaking off the discussions at his pleasure.[51] Monroe, however, preferred not to terminate the negotiations until he was absolutely certain that Spain would not yield to American pressure.[52] Therefore, in a temperately worded reply the envoys briefly summarized the American case for the claims. They considered this quite adequate, since these questions had been before the Spanish government so long that they did "not doubt that its mind is made up on the course the business is to take." [53] Their request for immediate consideration of the treaty project was ignored by Cevallos, who sent two sharply worded notes outlining alterations needed to make the convention of 1802 acceptable and repudiating all responsibility for seizures by French privateers.[54] Taking exception to the rudeness of Cevallos' remarks, the envoys sought an interview to ascertain whether Cevallos "intended to put a prompt end to the negotiation, and that not in an amicable manner. . . ." [55] During the conference, the Foreign Minister expressed his regrets; he had, he assured them, not meant to be disrespectful. For four hours they sought to extract from him some positive statement concerning the terms on which Spain would settle, only to encounter steady evasion. As far as Monroe was concerned, the interview had only one advantage—it gave them an opportunity to show that they were in earnest in their efforts to settle, and that they would not hesitate to break off negotiations as soon as it was evident that no settlement could be reached.[56]

Monroe now sought to use the tension generated by Cevallos to exert pressure on France to reverse her position. On the very day on which he and Pinckney received Cevallos' notes, they had been on the verge of sending Armstrong an account of their progress. They now held the messenger back ten days, as they drafted a reply to Cevallos intended to impress Talleyrand with the seriousness of the crisis in Madrid rather than to win concessions from Spain.[57] In firm tones the envoys justified American claims for compensation for French spoliations, and informed Cevallos that no agreement was possible unless these claims were included. They ended with a pointed warning: "Many years have elapsed since these injuries were received; during which time the sufferers have looked to their government for relief without effect. Their last hope is founded on this negotiation and great would their astonishment and disappointment be, if they were told that more than one-half of them were to be abandoned." [58]

As they waited to hear from Armstrong, who was to put this letter and other correspondence with Cevallos before Talleyrand and warn him of the likelihood of a rupture, the negotiations moved at a slower pace. Feeling that they had fully stated their position, they made no reply to two notes from Cevallos reiterating his views on the claims. Thus, during March, Monroe and Pinckney restricted themselves to replying to a note on the eastern limits of Louisiana.[59] Monroe's gambit in Paris proved ineffectual. Talleyrand, either because he questioned the alarmist reports from Madrid or because he doubted Jefferson's determination to take decisive action, bluntly told Armstrong that France must take the side of Spain in any breach. In view of this affirmation Armstrong did not submit the other documents lest they afford France an occasion to make a public declaration in Spain's behalf.[60] Armstrong believed that Napoleon opposed the payment of American claims to prevent a drain on the Spanish treasury, which would deprive France of funds to be used during the war.[61] Undoubtedly Spain's impotence in America led Monroe and others to underestimate the importance Napoleon attached to Spain, which, even in her decline, was still a European power and France's only ally.

Spurred by the unfavorable news from Armstrong, the American negotiators assumed a more aggressive tone; now it seemed all the more essential to prove that the United States would not subordinate its rightful claims to the arbitrary disposition of France. Moreover, if a rupture should take place, Monroe considered it unlikely that France, blockaded in every port, could render effective support to Spain in the event of American action against the Floridas.

On March 30 the envoys sent a sharp note to Cevallos, asking why there had been no reply to their note of March 15 on the boundary of Louisiana. Were they to take this as an indication that he wished to terminate the negotiations? If so, then they were ready to depart.[62] Ten days later, as they still waited for Cevallos to reply, they penned a still-stronger note: "The undersigned . . . consider the negotiations as essentially terminated by what has already occurred; and, if they pursue it, it will be only on the proof of such disposition . . . as shall convince them, that there is just cause that it will terminate to the satisfaction of the United States." [63] In return they received a short note, which included an extract from a letter from Talleyrand upholding the Spanish view that West Florida had never been part of Louisiana. Refusing to discuss this point any further, the envoys insisted that definite proposals be submitted as a basis for negotiations. To increase the pressure by making a rupture between the two nations seem imminent, Monroe and Pinckney now requested Yrujo's recall, which they had been authorized to do in a dispatch received from Madison some weeks earlier.[64]

With one exception the envoys held firm to their determination not to engage in further debate about the issues between the two nations: they replied to a note concerning the western boundaries of Louisiana. Since this had not previously been explored, they preferred to answer the note rather than give Spain a convenient excuse for breaking off the negotiations.[65]

Three weeks later on May 12 (they still had never received any counterproposals from Cevallos), Monroe and Pinckney decided to bring the matter to a head by presenting a final offer. In this note, which incorporated concessions authorized by Madison in October, they offered to assume the spoliation claims, to establish the western boundary at the Colorado with a neutral buffer zone to extend to the Rio Bravo, and to relinquish demands for compensation for the losses resulting from the suspension of the right of deposit and the depredations of French privateers, if Spain would cede Florida. As a solace to Spanish pride, they were prepared to accept Florida without the express stipulation that West Florida had been part of Louisiana.[66] As they expected, the offer was rejected. Spain, Cevallos told the envoys, could not accede to proposals depriving her of territory without "receiving anything in return but the renunciation of a right which she does not acknowledge in the United States, which is to reclaim the damages arising from the suspension of the right of deposit, and for those occasioned by the French privateers. . . ."[67] In the face of the finality of this statement, the envoys promptly terminated the negotiations.

This completely inconclusive end to the negotiations was not quite what the administration had envisaged. In July 1804, Madison had instructed Monroe, in the event that it proved impossible to obtain Florida, to propose as a working agreement that the United States would guarantee to observe the existing boundaries if Spain would promise not to obstruct American access to the sea through the rivers in West Florida. The envoys apparently never received this dispatch until just before Monroe left Madrid. Curiously, Madison, who at the very time the envoys were breaking off in Madrid was drafting a new set of instructions restating this proposal, never queried them about their failure to bring this suggestion forward.[68] In any case there was little chance of its approval by Spain.

V

After arranging for Pinckney to remain until the new Minister, James Bowdoin, arrived, Monroe left for England. Pausing for several weeks in Paris, he learned through unofficial sources that Napoleon was still convinced that the United States would ultimately pay a substantial price for the Floridas. Again blaming Livingston for the persistence of this notion, Monroe suggested that Jefferson not show Livingston any signal honor when he returned to America. If the Minister were treated to any particular mark of distinction, the French would conclude that Jefferson approved his proposals.[69] Monroe's own views on policy towards Spain had been expressed in a "private and confidential" letter, which he and Pinckney had sent to Madison several days after the conclusion of the negotiations. Absolutely convinced that Spain "would never cede one foot of territory otherwise than by compulsion," they recommended that the President seize the Floridas and occupy the region between the Colorado and the Rio Grande as preliminaries to a settlement. Faced by this aggressive move, they did not doubt that France would then intervene to force a settlement. From Paris Armstrong proposed similar action. American diplomats in Europe seemed united in their conviction that France must be shown that the United States was willing to risk a conflict with Spain in order to secure its just demands.[70]

This vigorous policy was not in harmony with current administration views. At the same time that the envoys in Madrid were formulating their suggestions, Madison had just completed a new set of instructions making it clear that the administration would not pursue a course which might lead to war with Spain, since only Congress possessed the power to declare war.[71] However, when the news of the collapse of negotiations in Madrid reached Jefferson, he had been momentarily inclined to adopt measures "which would engage France to compromise our differences . . . and to correct the dangerous error that we are a people whom no injury can provoke to war." If such a drastic course were followed, then serious consideration must be given to an alliance with England.[72]

In October, when he reviewed these questions with his Cabinet, both Madison and Gallatin opposed a harsher policy toward Spain. Moreover, in view of the recent *Essex* decision reversing Britain's moderate policy towards the neutral carrying trade, a *rapprochement* with England seemed out of the question. Thus economy, caution in the face of threatening international developments, and doubts about the power of the executive to undertake measures tending toward war, resulted in a rejection of the suggestions made by the American envoys in preference for an attempt to renew the negotiations in Paris. The wisdom of this decision seemed verified a few days later, when a dis-

patch from Armstrong brought the news that France was willing
to arrange for the cession of Florida, if the United States would pay
Spain $7 million. This, Armstrong estimated, would leave a surplus
of $4 million after the claims had been paid. Although willing to go
only as high as $5 million, Jefferson saw no objection to this arrange-
ment.[73] After all, as he cynically commented to Madison about the
payment: "We need not care who gets that. . . ." [74]

In order to maintain a belligerent appearance, the President in his
annual message of December 1805 spoke in hostile terms of Spain's
behavior. However, he revealed his true policy in a secret message
requesting an appropriation of $2 million for diplomatic purposes.
This duplicity produced an outraged cry from one of Jefferson's hitherto most loyal supporters—Virginia Congressman John Randolph of
Roanoke. Randolph, who also nursed other grievances against the President, vehemently opposed an appropriation smacking of bribery to
France. He accused Jefferson of concealing from Congress dispatches
sent by the envoys in Spain, which, if known, would have prevented
approval of the President's request. Randolph was not quite correct
in making this charge, for Jefferson had held back only one of Monroe's
official letters simply because it dealt with Anglo-American problems
and had touched on Spain only in passing. Yet Randolph struck closer
to home than he realized, for the President had withheld the "private
and confidential" letter in which the envoys in Madrid had recommended direct action against Spain. Randolph now emerged as an
outspoken administration critic, and as an implacable, if erratic, enemy
of Madison, whom he considered the evil genius behind Republican
foreign policy. The Virginia congressman fixed his loyalties on Monroe,
not so much because he approved of the course advocated by the Minister to England, but rather because Monroe held opinions contrary
to those adopted by Jefferson.

Although Randolph and Monroe had not been intimate prior to
Monroe's departure for France in 1803, they had recently been drawn
together by Randolph's gratitude for the kindness the Minister had
shown his nephew, St. George Randolph, a deaf-mute, who had been
sent to school in England. Randolph, one of the most brilliant Virginians of the post-Revolutionary generation, had made a mark for
himself as Jefferson's floor leader in the House, where he reigned
supreme, routing his opponents with barbed speeches delivered in an
unmistakable shrill voice. During the 1790s he had been so infected

with the revolutionary spirit that he had signed his letters "Citizen Randolph" and had used the dating of the French revolutionary calendar, but after Jefferson's election his radicalism gave way to a narrow State Rights position. His remarkable talents were never fully realized, for his personality was warped by flaws which undermined his judgment and involved him in senseless squabbles and long-standing feuds. His embittered railings against erstwhile friends, such as Jefferson, as well as his erratic behavior, alienated like-minded men and prevented him from assuming the leadership of the numerous discontented Republicans (mostly Virginians) who were critical of the so-called "federalising" tendencies of Jefferson's administration.

Among the most notable of these critics was John Taylor of Caroline, who had been disappointed by Jefferson's failure to support constitutional amendments reducing the power of the federal government. Moreover, Taylor regarded Gallatin's fiscal policies as a continuation of the hated Hamiltonian system. Taylor and Randolph, and those who had similar views, thought of themselves as the guardians of the true principles of Republicanism, and hence, happily assumed the label "Old Republicans." With the exception of Randolph, they remained personally loyal to Jefferson, blaming Madison for the corruption of Republican ideals. In search of a nationally prominent leader (Taylor had no desire for the role and Randolph's aberrations disqualified him) they turned to Monroe.[75]

From these malcontents Monroe now received letters condemning administration foreign policy, which, the writers asserted, did not have public approval. Moreover, they strongly suggested that his advice had been ignored in order to reduce his popularity and to advance Madison as Jefferson's successor.[76] Monroe might not have heeded these letters had he received a full explanation of the course Jefferson was following towards Spain. Unfortunately, it was not until he had been back in London for a year that Madison commented on American policy towards Spain and then only to describe the measures adopted.[77] Madison, however, cannot be blamed for this failure to write Monroe. Not only was the winter of 1805 an exceptionally busy one for the Secretary of State, but there seemed no reason to write an envoy who had announced his intention of returning home shortly after he left Madrid. Indeed it was in anticipation of the Minister's early return that Jefferson had offered him the governorship of Louisiana in January 1804, which he had declined because of pressing private affairs.[78]

Without direct information from the administration, Monroe was entirely dependent on the press, which provided only a partial view of American policy since the secret message had not been released. Thus it was natural for Monroe to welcome Jefferson's annual message, which by combining "moderation with firmness" proved to the world that "our government understands its rights and interests and will vindicate them. . . ." It was exactly what he wished it to be. He was particularly gratified by Jefferson's declaration that force must be met by force if the outrages of England and Spain could not be checked by peaceful means. The President's invitation to Congress to consider the strengthening of the navy struck Monroe as another meaningful indication of the new spirit animating the government.[79] He had no idea, of course, that this message was largely a propaganda instrument. Had he been aware of Jefferson's secret message recommending an appropriation, he would have tempered his enthusiasm.

As he gradually realized the direction of administration policy, he was keenly disappointed. He felt that the contrast between the President's belligerent language and his suppliant attitude towards France was lessening the chances for a satisfactory Anglo-American settlement. How, he frankly asked Jefferson, could the British be expected to regard as serious the threats of reprisals against them, when similar threats directed against a power as feeble as Spain obviously meant nothing? [80] Instead of clarifying his policy, Jefferson was far more concerned with the effect of the letters from Randolph and other dissidents. Consequently, when the President wrote in the spring of 1806, he confined himself to warning the Minister that Randolph was not to be trusted. Whatever the Virginia congressman might say to the contrary, the President assured Monroe, administration policies had the full approval of the nation.[81]

Unfortunately, neither Jefferson nor Madison comprehended the reaction of their old friend to the disregard of his advice. They seem to have taken it for granted that Monroe, both as a close associate and as a Minister charged with carrying out administration decisions, would accept without question policy formulated in Washington. On the other hand, Monroe, who had long held an equal rank in the formulation of the Republican party program, assumed that advice based on his observation of the European scene would serve as the principal guide for the administration. As far as he was concerned, the correctness of his advice was confirmed late in 1806 by the fiasco in Paris, when

Napoleon inexplicably refused to supervise a settlement of Spanish-American issues, even though Spain had agreed to his intervention.[82] All in all, Monroe could but reflect that the President's failure to follow his advice had not only indefinitely postponed a settlement with Spain, but had substantially impaired American prestige.

CHAPTER 14

THE REJECTED TREATY

MONROE RETURNED to London on July 23, 1805, the very day on which a British Admiralty court (in the *Essex* case) condemned the neutral carrying trade between enemy colonies and the mother country. This trade, permitted since Jay's Treaty under the fiction of a broken voyage, was now declared illegal; in the future cargoes of enemy colonial products carried in American ships would be seized unless it could be proven that a bona fide import duty had been paid in the United States. This decision, striking at a major segment of American commerce, created such a serious crisis that Monroe postponed his plans for immediately returning home.[1] He at once lodged a strong formal protest, which he pressed in a series of interviews with Lord Mulgrave, who had recently preplaced Harrowby in the Foreign Office. Mulgrave received Monroe much more coolly than any of his predecessors. In place of the former protestations of friendship, the American Minister encountered a blunt defense of British policy. Informing Monroe that neutrals had no right to expect to trade with enemy colonies during a time of war, Mulgrave made it clear that the *Essex* decision would be rigidly enforced. In spite of his stout defense of the British position, Mulgrave was no more anxious to quarrel with the United States than previous Secretaries had been. Consequently, to avoid a sharp clash he promised to submit Monroe's protest to the Cabinet, which had the practical effect of indefinitely postponing a formal reply.[2]

After waiting for an answer for two months (during which more than fifty vessels were seized), Monroe submitted a second protest restating the American arguments against the British interpretation of neutral rights. It was, he told Mulgrave, high time to resolve the long-standing conflicts between the two nations—indeed the rights of the United States had so long been trampled upon by the British that the "astonished world may begin to doubt, whether the patience with which those injuries have been borne ought to be attributed to generous or unworthy motives. . . ." [3] This note again elicited assurances of an early reply, but none was forthcoming.

The dilatory behavior of the ministry obliged Monroe further to defer his return home. Not only did he consider it unwise for the United States to be represented during the current crisis by a diplomat with a rank lower than that of Minister, but he was concerned that an abrupt departure, which might be interpreted as a prelude to a rupture, would precipitate harsher measures.[4] As he waited for the Cabinet to answer his protests, he drafted a careful analysis of the new English policy for the benefit of his superiors in Washington. Although his general conclusions were much the same as those expressed two years earlier, he now had a better grasp of the complex forces involved. For one thing he saw more distinctly the opportunistic character of British policy, which altered according to the circumstances of the war. Thus, in 1804 Britain had adopted a liberal policy in order to avoid conflict with the United States, since she was fighting alone and hence in a weak position. However, after the organization of the Third Coalition early in 1805 Britain's situation had changed: secure in the support of her allies, she had not hesitated to impose stiffer restrictions on the neutrals. Moreover, it was apparent that the British government was deeply influenced by the resentment of British merchants over the profits which American shippers were reaping from the colonial trade. As proof Monroe cited the enormous success of James Stephen's pamphlet, *War in Disguise,* published in October 1805. Stephen, acting as the spokesman of the mercantile element, had advocated stringent control of neutral shipping. In return for short-term discomforts resulting from the exclusion of neutrals from the carrying trade, Stephen promised that British merchants would ultimately reap handsome profits when their ships took over this commerce. Although Monroe considered this publication a statement of ministerial views, for it was obvious that Stephen had seen some of the notes he had submitted, technically the pamphlet was not official. It had been shown to Pitt in advance of publication, and he had not expressed disapproval. The real importance of *War in Disguise* stemmed from the fact that it ex-

pressed the views of a powerful segment of parliamentary opinion, to
which concessions had to be made to ensure continued support for
Pitt's war measures.[5]

The recommendations which Monroe now made to Madison were
in line with his unwavering conviction that the United States must
show a real determination to be prepared to defend its own interests.
He felt that the British Cabinet had not hesitated to enforce the *Essex*
decision because of a prevailing belief that the Jefferson administration
was incapable of forceful action. In this light the recent seizures must
be viewed as a test of American strength; and, if nothing were done to
resist them, then further restraints must be expected.[6] He made the
same point in a letter to Jefferson on November 1:

> But without an attitude of menace and an evident ability, which will be
> judged of by the apparent measures, and determination to execute it if
> necessary, nothing will be gained of them [the European powers], not
> even of Spain, the most feeble and vulnerable of all powers.... All will
> insult us, encroach on our rights, and plunder us if they can do it with
> impunity. Should they conclude that they have nothing to fear from us or
> to hope, be their conduct respectively what it may; that we are not ready
> to resent injuries and to hazard much in defense of our rights honor
> and interests, it is fairly to be presumed that they will pursue that system
> of policy towards us, which each may find its advantage in.[7]

Specifically, he proposed the adoption of a restrictive duty of fifteen
to twenty-five per cent *ad valorem* on imports from Great Britain and
that an embargo be levied against West Indian trade. Since he believed
these measures would be sufficient to force concessions from the
ministry, he urged that no step be taken which might lead to an immediate break.[8]

In January 1806, Monroe felt that the impact made by the President's annual message, and the collapse of the Third Coalition after
Austerlitz, provided the right moment to renew pressure on Mulgrave
for a reply to the notes on the *Essex* decision. For this purpose he
journeyed to London from Cheltenham, where he had taken his ailing
family. An unusually friendly reception at the King's levee aroused his
hopes, but Pitt's death late in January 1806 precluded any negotiations
pending the formation of a new Cabinet. Now, for the first time since
he had been in England, Monroe had reason to be truly optimistic

when he learned that Charles Fox, after twenty years in opposition, was at last to be included in a Cabinet as Foreign Secretary. Fox was widely regarded as sympathetic to American interests, if for no other reason than his long-standing hostility to Pitt. Although Fox was the dominant influence in the new "Ministry of All the Talents," William Grenville as First Lord of the Treasury was the technical head of the government. In many ways Grenville, whose thinking on colonial matters was influenced by the liberal views of Lord Auckland, was more overtly pro-American than Fox, who had never expressed a clear-cut point of view on the American question.[9]

For the first time in twenty years a reform administration was in power, and Monroe was but one of many anticipating a drastic reversal in policy—perhaps even peace with France. As soon as he learned of the composition of the ministry, he canceled the homeward passage arranged for April. With some real hope of an agreement, it seemed essential to press on before the war ended.[10] There was, of course, a personal element in his decision to linger in England—if he could return home as the author of the long-sought treaty with Britain, then his position as a major party leader and as a candidate for the presidential succession could not be challenged. Monroe now wrote Madison asking to be continued in London and at the same time specifically requesting to be allowed to negotiate alone, for he had heard reports that an envoy extraordinary was to be appointed. His reasons for this request were explicitly stated:

It had been my fortune to stand the storm, under circumstances of great personal responsibility, the ill effects of which I thought, perhaps improperly, I had contributed in some degree to mitigate; it will be that of a successor to take the ground at a moment of calm, under auspices more favorable, when it is not probable that he will be called on to take any measure of tone, involving high responsibility, or other measure than that of concluding a bargain after the opinion of both parties has in some measure been made up. Be this however as it may it will produce no effect on my conduct.[11]

This plea arrived too late, for William Pinkney, a successful Baltimore lawyer of moderate Republican views, had already been chosen, and now Monroe found himself in the same position in which he had placed Livingston in 1803. Although he kept his word not to let the appointment of a colleague impair his efforts to reach a settlement, he felt some resentment. He would have been less displeased if Madison or Jefferson had explained that they had appointed a special envoy in deference to congressional pressure. Not until two years later, when Monroe was alienated from Madison, did Jefferson fully explain this decision.[12]

The first interview with Fox left Monroe in a state of euphoria. He was, as he told Madison, received "with great kindness and attention, and in fact [Fox] put me more at ease in that short time than I have ever felt with any person in office since I have been in England." Although previous ministers had promised to give American problems prompt attention, he believed Fox's pledge sincere. There was every prospect of "arranging our affairs with this government, especially that one which respects [our] trade with the colonies of its enemies, on satisfactory terms. . . ." [13] With each succeeding conference his optimism mounted. In March, when he learned that Fox had read all the communications submitted since 1803, Monroe inquired: "Cannot we agree?" To which Fox responded that he saw "no reason to suppose the contrary." In the same interview the Foreign Secretary assured Monroe that the recent modifications of neutral rights accorded to Russia would not be denied to other powers. Since Britain had granted the Russians a limited trade with the colonies of her enemies, this comment seemed a hopeful augury.[14]

In reporting these conversations to Madison, Monroe failed to make it clear that Fox's comments on trade with enemy colonies were posited on the assumption that the rules governing the broken voyage before the *Essex* decision would be restored.[15] Moreover, the fact that Monroe said little about impressment was apparently overlooked by an administration which interpreted his optimistic reports of an impending settlement to mean an agreement in terms of the American interpretation of neutral rights. Jefferson's sweeping conclusion early in June that every "communication from Mr. Monroe strengthens our expectation that the new pretence of the British to control our commerce with belligerent colonies will be properly restricted, and the outrage on our seamen brought to an end" was not entirely justified by a careful reading of Monroe's dispatches.[16] That Monroe said little about impressment but much about problems of trade was easily overlooked by an administration contemplating an Anglo-American agreement in terms of neutral rights.

In spite of Fox's friendly demeanor toward the United States, he did not move at once in the direction of a settlement, a hesitation which Monroe ascribed to his need to win over those elements in the Cabinet hostile to an agreement impinging on British maritime interests. Monroe correctly understood that the Order in Council of May 1806 (known as Fox's blockade) was intended to modify the harshness of the *Essex* decision without specifically repudiating it. This order placed the Continental ports from Brest to the Elbe under blockade, but declared it to be absolute only between the Seine and Ostend. Beyond this limit neutral ships would not be seized unless caught attempting to enter or leave enemy ports. This new order, restoring somewhat indirectly the old rule governing a broken voyage, left (according to Monroe) impressment as the only major point of conflict.[17]

Fox had issued this order in the hope of preventing the United States from passing a threatened nonimportation act, but the news arrived too late to have any effect. In any event, knowledge of Fox's order would not have deterred Jefferson, who interpreted it as another violation of neutral rights in the form of a paper blockade. Although Monroe had originally recommended such a bill during Pitt's ministry, he had written Madison after Fox came to power urging postponement, since it would be embarrassing to a government so well disposed to the United States. When Monroe's letter arrived, Congress had not yet approved the nonimportation measure, which imposed a selective ban on British imports, but the administration considered the bill too far advanced to withdraw it without inviting disagreeable criticism from dissident Republicans and Federalists.[18] Since the effective date of the act was postponed until November 15, Monroe was able to respond to Fox's protests by presenting it as a moderate measure framed to allow time for negotiations.[19] Fox's blockade had the most unfortunate consequences, for it served as the pretext for the Berlin Decree, and thus set the stage for the British retaliatory measures which completely obstructed an Anglo-American accord.

Monroe also attributed the slowness of the ministry in beginning negotiations to its doubts about the strength and unity of the Republican administration. He felt that American policy toward Spain was not calculated to inspire confidence in a government which first uttered threats and then quietly indicated a willingness to pay a substantial price for the Floridas, knowing that the larger part of this amount would be extracted from Spain by Napoleon; and, hence, was little more than an indirect bribe to France. The administration, as Monroe put it in an unsent letter to Jefferson, seemed to be letting itself be "swindled" by France. In view of these circumstances, how could British statesmen be expected to take American threats against Britain seriously? [20] The renewed effort to negotiate for Florida through France seemed so seriously damaging to American prestige that, in May 1806, he drafted a letter for the British press in which he sought to prove that France was only intervening to prevent a rupture and not because she expected to profit from the transaction. With such a feeble argument to support his case Monroe decided against publication.[21]

The well-advertised breach between John Randolph and the administration in February 1806 served to lower the standing of the nation abroad. To many Englishmen (and Merry's dispatches played upon this theme) this party rupture presaged a return of the Federalists to power. The internal strife among the Republicans was further highlighted in the spring of 1806 shortly after Monroe distributed to members of Parliament Madison's anonymous pamphlet outlining the American position on neutral rights. Although completed before the publication of *War in Disguise,* Madison's essay was an effective reply to Stephen's arguments. Unfortunately much of the impact of Madison's case was dissipated when Randolph's criticisms of Madison's essay and his praise of *War in Disguise* were featured in the British press.[22] All these developments made it more and more difficult for Fox to persuade vested interests in Parliament that England stood to gain rather than lose by an accord with the United States.

In June, just as it seemed that negotiations were about to start, Monroe encountered an unexpected obstacle when Fox, who had seen reports that a special envoy was to join Monroe, suggested that discussions be suspended until the envoy arrived. This delay not only gave Fox more time to study the relevant documents before formulating his position, but it also gave him an opportunity to win over his more reluctant followers.[23] Although Monroe preferred to press on with the negotiations, he had no choice but to accede to Fox's evident wish that nothing be done for the moment. He merely asked for an assurance that discussions would be resumed as soon as his colleague arrived.[24]

II

When Monroe first learned in April of the probable appointment of a special envoy, he had not been resentful. Indeed, he had assured Madison that he would not regard the action as arising from a "want of friendship," for he understood that political considerations might make it necessary.[25] But he shortly came to view Pinkney's appointment as a deliberate effort to reduce his importance in the party. The explanation of this drastic shift is quite simple: in the months after the selection of the special envoy Monroe received letters from John Taylor and John Randolph of Roanoke, and from two congressmen closely associated with Randolph—Joseph H. Nicholson of Maryland and James M. Garnett of Virginia. These letters had two common themes. First, they asserted that Madison had induced the President to abandon Republican principles in order to follow a course akin to that of the Federalists. Secondly, they maintained that Monroe was being sacrificed in order to enhance Madison's waning prestige in the party and thus advance the presidential candidacy of the Secretary of State. "There is no doubt," Randolph assured Monroe, "that the principles of the administration have changed. . . ." Nicholson (brother-in-law to Albert Gallatin) was quite specific in declaring that Pinkney had been sent to "take from you, the credit for settling our differences with England." Grimly the Marylander concluded: "The canker of Federalism I fear is eating the heart, I almost said the head, of the body politick." All these correspondents assured him that the "Old Republicans" (as these dissidents liked to call themselves) would never support Madison for the Presidency. They pledged themselves to Monroe, urging him to return as soon as possible to safeguard both his own interests and those of the party.[26]

The impact of these letters was all the greater, since they were followed closely by others from loyal Republicans warning Monroe not to place any trust in the rages of an embittered minority. Among the first to write in this vein was Jefferson, who cautioned Monroe not to commit himself to such a "soi disant friend" as Randolph; his true friends, the President affirmed, were those who supported the administration. William Wirt and John Beckley, obviously prompted by Jefferson, also begged Monroe to remain aloof from attempts to prevent the nomination of Madison as Jefferson's successor. According to Wirt and Beckley the Republicans were united in behalf of the Secretary of State. Beckley, however, in concluding his letter with the observation that he considered Monroe better qualified for the Presidency than Madison, who was "too timid and indecisive as a statesman, and too liable to a conduct of forbearance to the federal party," voiced the reservations many loyal Republicans felt towards Madison.[27] Although Jefferson was aware that Randolph and the dissident Republicans were promoting Monroe as a presidential candidate, he was not aware of their charge that Monroe was being deliberately sacrificed for Madison's political advantage. Had Jefferson been familiar with the character of the letters the Old Republicans were sending across the Atlantic, it seems likely that he would have explained his policies in greater detail and also clarified the considerations which led to the appointment of Pinkney. In the silence of these old friends Monroe detected further proof that he no longer enjoyed their full confidence.

Jefferson remained unaware of the true state of Monroe's feelings, simply because the aggrieved Minister could not bring himself to express his bitterness. On several occasions Monroe began letters exposing the roots of his dissatisfaction, but none was ever posted. In these discarded drafts he complained that the appointment of a special envoy not only indicated a lack of confidence in the resident Minister, but that it also created an impression in England of confusion within the councils of the administration. He also voiced his objections to recent Spanish policy, reasserting his conviction that only by continued pressure on Spain could American aims be achieved. His personal reaction was summed up in the remark that after Pinkney's appointment he considered himself "nothing." [28] In the letter he finally sent to Jefferson, he eliminated all reference to the area of greatest sensitivity, confining himself to the evasive observation (this in reference to the President's comment upon his friendship with Randolph) that the danger of sending letters at such a distance rendered it inadvisable to discuss the "delicate topics" which Jefferson had raised. Once again he rejected the recently renewed offer of the governorship of Louisiana, citing the demands of his personal affairs. This was by no means the true reason for his refusal. Conveniently ignoring the fact that the governorship had originally been offered at his own suggestion, Monroe now considered it a means of disposing of him in a secondary post.[29]

In replying to John Randolph, Monroe was more direct than in his letter to Jefferson, although his native caution led him to be somewhat reserved. He admitted that as an advocate of stern measures towards Spain he had been distressed by aspects of the recent session of Congress. Thanking Randolph for wishing to put him forward for the Presidency, he urged that the move be checked, since there were older party members whose claims must be considered first. Moreover, he did not think it wise to risk a Federalist revival by fostering a split within the Republican ranks.[30] Later in the year, as his discontent mounted, Monroe expressed himself much more openly to Randolph:

... when I frankly own to you (what I withhold from others) that circumstances have occur'd during my service abroad which were calculated to hurt my feelings and actually did hurt them, which may produce a change in the future relation between some of them and myself, unless satisfactorily explained. . . .

Nonetheless, in spite of his strong resentment, he still urged Randolph not to attack the administration, whose faults did not arise from erroneous principles but from mistakes made under the pressure of a crisis.[31]

III

As displeasing as Pinkney's appointment had been, Monroe greeted his colleague warmly on his arrival in mid-June, for he was eager to press the negotiations forward while Great Britain was still enmeshed in the war with France. Throughout their joint mission the two envoys worked together harmoniously. Pinkney, one of the most brilliant and successful lawyers of his day, possessed considerable talents, although some Americans were put off by his cultivated "air of a man of fashion" and by his hauteur and egotism. He was well-fitted for his assignment, since he had served for eight years in London as a member of the commission set up under the Jay Treaty to examine the claims of American merchants. This experience, along with his knowledge of the Baltimore mercantile community, gave him an unusual familiarity with the problems of Anglo-American trade.[32]

Much to Monroe's disappointment it proved impossible to begin the negotiations at once. On the day on which Pinkney reached London, Fox became ill and never recovered sufficiently, prior to his death on September 13, to assume supervision of American affairs. It was not until August 20, when all hope for Fox's recovery had vanished, that two commissioners were appointed to treat with the American emissaries.[33] They were Lord Henry Holland, Fox's favorite nephew, who at thirty-three had little political experience but was ranked with the most liberal Whig element, and William Eden, Baron Auckland, president of the Board of Trade and an intimate adviser of Grenville. Auckland, now over seventy, had had a distinguished diplomatic and political career. It was false to assume, as Jefferson did, that his position on the Board of Trade made him a guardian of entrenched commercial interests; on the contrary, he was convinced of the need to cultivate American trade.[34]

From a personal and political point of view the British choice was excellent as far as the American commissioners were concerned. The Monroes were already on friendly terms with the Hollands and soon established a warm relationship with Lord and Lady Auckland. The negotiations were conducted in an agreeable atmosphere punctuated by pleasant dinners and evenings at the opera. So casual were the proceedings that at one point Pinkney, who was inclined to adhere to formalities, complained that Lord Holland was "pushing his *informality* rather too far." [35] Of the two American negotiators, Lord Holland had a much higher opinion of Monroe, whom he characterized as a "sincere Republican," who had in the past "imbibed a strong predilection for France" and an "aversion" to England, but had been sufficiently open-minded to overcome his initial dislike of England upon a closer view of that country. Although Monroe was "plain in his manner and somewhat slow in his apprehension," Holland considered him a "diligent, earnest, sensible and even profound man." Pinkney, with "more of the forms and readiness of business, and greater knowledge and cultivation of mind," did not measure up to Monroe in Holland's estimate, for Pinkney's "opinions were neither so firmly rooted nor so deeply considered as those of Mr. Monroe." Holland's liberal views led to considerable freedom in the political discussions between negotiators. Monroe felt no hesitation in commenting to Holland that he considered the British "monarchy more republican than monarchical, and the French republic infinitely more monarchical than your monarchy." There were few Englishmen to whom Monroe would have been willing to make such an admission.[36]

Monroe and Lord Holland also found themselves in complete agreement on the subject of European intervention in South America, a question which came into prominence early in 1806, when the British government had to decide whether to reinforce Sir Home Popham, who had seized Buenos Aires on his own authority. Both Holland and Monroe opposed any European intervention which was not undertaken to liberate the South American nations and to open their ports to the nations of the world. In discussing the matter with Lord Holland, while it was still pending before the Cabinet, Monroe stressed his wish that "nothing be attempted without a concert with the United States. . . ." [37] Although the British forces in Buenos Aires were augmented, the expedition ended in failure.[38]

During the negotiations Monroe and Pinkney were governed by

Madison's instructions of May 17, 1806, which amplified earlier instructions sent to Monroe, but did not fundamentally alter the American position except for a proposal that the British recognize the Gulf
Stream as marking the limits of American territorial waters. The long-
vexed questions of contraband, blockades, compensations for illegal
seizures and trade were all reviewed at length. On the matter of trade
Madison adhered to the well-established American policy of seeking
the adoption of the most-favored-nation clause. The instructions specifically set down two conditions essential for the conclusion of a treaty:
first, there must be limitation on impressment, in return for which the
American negotiators were to agree to a stipulation that the United
States would undertake to return all deserters; and second, there must
be a complete restoration of the re-export trade as a necessary condition
for the repeal of the Nonimportation Act. Madison's explicit statement that an agreement on impressment was "indispensable" to a restoration of friendly relations reflected the importance which he and
Jefferson attached to this issue.[39] It was not just a matter of abstract
rights, which both took seriously, but of their deep resentment of the
overbearing conduct of British naval officers in American waters.

At the very time Madison was phrasing his instructions, the public
was still in a state of excitement over an incident involving H.M.S.
Leander. The *Leander,* operating within American territorial waters,
had killed an American crew member in firing a warning shot at a
merchant ship. In New York, when the body of the dead sailor had
been displayed, mobs had roamed the streets, burning the British flag
and menacing the residence of the consul.[40]

Neither Monroe nor Pinkney, who had just come from America,
comprehended the extent of Jefferson's determination to end impressment. To Monroe the question lacked the immediacy it possessed in
America, for incidents in British waters had been infrequent now that
the victory at Trafalgar had given England undisputed control of the
seas.

From the very first meeting of the commissioners on August 23, it
was evident that as long as the two nations adhered to their existing
positions, impressment constituted the primary obstacle to a settlement.
Auckland and Holland, aware of the intensity of American feeling
and themselves sympathetic to concessions, were handicapped by the
fact that Fox, prior to his illness, had never outlined a precise policy
on any of the points in dispute between the two nations. All they could

offer the American negotiators was the vague promise that some arrangement could be reached. As a preliminary move to reduce opposition to granting favorable terms to the Americans, Holland and Auckland asked that the Nonimportation Act be suspended to prove the
good intentions of the United States. Acting on the basis of this hopeful, if indefinite pledge, Monroe and Pinkney at once wrote Madison
asking that the British request be honored. Although Madison and
Jefferson followed this recommendation, the news did not reach England soon enough to influence the outcome of the negotiations.[41]

Fox's death in September greatly reduced the possibilities of extensive concessions to the United States. Grenville was well-disposed to
the Americans, but he lacked the personal influence needed to persuade
supporters of the ministry to accept an unpopular course of action.
Fox's successor in the Foreign Office was Lord Howick (later Earl
Grey), whose experience as First Lord of the Admiralty, as well as his
conviction that the Jeffersonians were pro-French, made him unwilling
to yield on such a vital point as impressment.[42] Consequently, when
the negotiations were resumed several weeks after Fox's death, Auckland and Holland were unable to persuade the Cabinet to authorize
concessions on impressment. Howick and others lacked confidence in
the sincerity of the American promise to restore deserters from the
royal navy. Thus, early in November the British commissioners had the
unpleasant task of informing their American colleagues that impressment could not be included in the treaty. The American emissaries
reacted so strongly to this news that there seemed little point in continuing the discussions.

In an effort to keep the negotiations open, Auckland and Holland
proposed, as a substitute, a formal note defining impressment in such
a way as to drastically curtail its effect. This plan had the advantage,
as they pointed out, that neither power would be obliged to abandon
its principles. Having complete confidence in the sincere intent of the
British commissioners to grant every concession acceptable to the Cabinet, Monroe and Pinkney agreed to examine the note before terminating negotiations.[43] The promised note (dated November 8)
opened with an affirmation of the right of impressment, but, in order
to "remove every cause of dissatisfaction," Auckland and Holland
promised that "instructions have been given, and shall be repeated
and enforced for the observance of the greatest caution in the impressing of British seamen; and that the strictest care shall be taken

to preserve the citizens of the United States from any molestation or injury. . . ." This, in effect, meant the preservation of the status quo, but it was an arrangement which the British commissioners felt should be acceptable, since there were then so few causes of complaint.[44]

Monroe and Pinkney were now confronted with one of the constantly recurring dilemmas which then faced all American diplomats in Europe. With transatlantic communications so very slow, it was not possible for them, as it was for representatives of European powers, to refer such crucial questions to their superiors. American diplomats had to decide whether to break off a negotiation which offered some hope of success because one objective could not be secured, or to abandon a hopeless demand to secure other important concessions. Either way their actions might be subject to condemnation at home. Monroe and Pinkney reflected for two days on the issue confronting them, before they decided to accept the note as a temporary arrangement in order to continue the negotiations.

Once the decision had been made, the emissaries drafted an explanatory letter to Madison stressing two elements: first, the evident impossibility of obtaining a superior provision in a treaty, and, secondly, that the note was as binding as a treaty provision. They pointed out that it had the advantage of leaving the United States in full possession of its rights, whereas a treaty provision might have required some modification of the American position on impressment. Only by acceding to this proposal could they continue discussions offering every prospect of a favorable settlement. They had made it clear to the British commissioners, they assured Madison, that the treaty might well be rejected, since they were acting contrary to their instructions. However, it seems that the emissaries thought this unlikely; they had assumed this responsibility "in full confidence that our conduct and the motives of it will be approved." [45]

Unfortunately, the envoys failed to include an explanation of the British note, which Holland had privately described to Howick as "indefinite but conciliating." [46] In a dispatch to Madison on November 11 Monroe and Pinkney had merely observed that "we think it fair to infer that this government intends to conform its conduct in the future to the just claims of the United States on this great interest," although "it deems it improper to relinquish a claim, especially at this time, which had been long sustained and acted on by it, and which has been heretofore strongly supported by the national feeling, or more properly speaking prejudice. . . ." Not until January 3, when they forwarded the text of the treaty, were the negotiators more explicit in describing the note as providing that impressment would be "essentially, if not completely abandoned. . . ." [47]

Although this additional clarification did not arrive until after Jefferson had rejected the treaty, it would not have altered his opinion, for he had long since been determined that impressment must be prohibited in the treaty itself. Indeed, as soon as he knew that the envoys had agreed to accept the British note, Jefferson ordered Madison to remind them that their instructions required them to break off unless impressment was included in the treaty. Obviously Monroe had never won over his superiors to the view that the British would yield in practice what they refused to abandon in principle. Madison's letter, which did not reach the emissaries until after the treaty had been signed, again rejected Monroe's frequently reiterated contention that incidents of impressment had substantially declined; on the contrary, the Secretary of State asserted, they were multiplying as the conduct of British officers in American waters became more and more overbearing.[48] While Jefferson and Madison continued to regard the prohibition of impressment as the central objective of American policy, Pinkney and Monroe had moved to a quite different position. The envoys in England accorded primacy to the American re-export trade, which had been barred after the *Essex* decision. In their eyes commercial concerns had emerged as the proper vital interest of the United States.

In accepting the British note on impressment, Monroe and Pinkney expected this concession to open the way for more generous commercial arrangements. As the negotiations proceeded, however, they were unable to advance beyond the provisions for trade and neutral rights which had been incorporated in Jay's Treaty—indeed, the powerful East India Company insisted that trade with India must be more severely restricted than it had been in the past. So unyielding were British commercial interests that Monroe and Pinkney were unable to obtain any stipulations concerning the West Indian trade. On only one point did the Americans make an important gain: the British commissioners agreed to allow the re-export trade subject to the condition that the goods be landed in America and that a bona fide duty be paid, although it was agreed that this might be partially refunded upon reshipment. While this fell short of the desired revocation of all restrictions on broken voyages, it permitted the re-establishment of a highly profitable trade under clear and precise terms. One other concession—a slight one—was obtained, when the British agreed to extend the territorial limits of the United States to a line five miles off shore. Its significance was reduced by the qualification that it would not be binding if any third party not accepting this line should attempt to seek shelter from the royal navy within this limit. The British gained a point in the provision that the United States would not impose any restrictions on British trade for ten years, a limitation particularly displeasing to Jefferson and Madison since it seemed to deprive the United States of its most effective retaliatory weapon against British depredations. Although the treaty did not provide for the settlement of outstanding claims, it was understood that these would be taken up in future negotiations. In postponing these issues Monroe and Pinkney had been influenced by the argument of the British commissioners that provisions requiring payments for seizures which the British public considered legal would render the approval of the treaty doubtful by making it unpopular with the mercantile community.[49]

Just before the commissioners concluded their work, the news of the Berlin Decree, imposing a blockade on the British Isles and excluding British goods from the Continent, nearly led to a termination of the negotiations in the face of the Cabinet's insistence that the United States pledge itself to resist the enforcement of the French decree. Monroe and Pinkney, however, succeeded in convincing Auckland and Holland that the United States could be relied upon to maintain its rights against French encroachment. The British commissioners had to admit the force of the American contention that acceptance of this condition was tantamount to a public declaration of hostility towards France. Monroe and Pinkney also pointed out that the position of the United States in dealing with France would be strengthened by an Anglo-American treaty. Although the Cabinet finally agreed to forego a specific treaty provision on this point, the deep-rooted suspicions about America's pro-French inclinations led the ministry to insist on attaching a note declaring that British acceptance of American ratification was contingent on effective action against the Berlin Decree. Monroe and Pinkey were not pleased with this arrangement, but they concurred since there was no other way to secure a treaty. In an effort to make the note less offensive to American sentiment, Monroe and Pinkney accepted the invitation to revise its phrasing.[50]

In spite of its omissions, Monroe considered the treaty satisfactory when measured against the reality of British power. It contained, as he explained privately to Jefferson, the best provisions the nation could hope to obtain, for on "all points on which we have had to press this govt., interests of the most vital character were involved. . . . At a time too when the very existence of the country depended on an adherence to its maritime pretentions." There was still another factor which played a large role in his thinking at this time. "It is," he told Jefferson, "important for us to stand well with some power. I think the U. States have sustained the attitude they took with dignity, and that by this arrangement they will terminate a controversy, not in favor of themselves alone, but of neutral rights with some degree of credit. The mov'ment has drawn the attention of Europe, and will make us better known and more respected as a power." [51] The treaty, in Monroe's estimation, was not only a major step in restoring American prestige, which had declined in the face of recent diplomatic reverses, but it was also the start of a new era in which the two nations would gradually draw together—the first step in a general *rapprochement*. Monroe certainly saw no reason to question the validity of Auckland's comment: "The notions of my countrymen on colonial policy are not quite groundless, tho' pressed to extreme absurdity. But give us time, and we always grow reasonable a little sooner or a little later." [52] In accepting this agreement Monroe may well have been influenced by the same view of the European scene which led Jefferson to remark to him in May 1806 that the United States would remain neutral even though it was Jefferson's opinion "that an English ascendancy on the ocean is safer for us than that of France." According to General James Wilkinson, who talked to Monroe shortly after his return, the former Minister had declared that he considered "the power and ambition of Bonaparte dangerous to the civilized world." [53] From this point of view an accord with England did not seem incompatible with national interests.

IV

On January 3, 1807, Monroe and Pinkney dispatched the treaty to Madison by a special messenger, who also bore a lengthy explanatory letter reviewing every article of the treaty. This painstaking justification was wasted effort, for Jefferson and Madison had decided to reject any agreement not banning impressment. Indeed, the formal rejection of the treaty took place prior to the arrival of the official copy and its accompanying letter. On the last day of the congressional session David Erskine, the British Minister, brought Madison a copy of the treaty, which he had just received, so that the session of Congress might be extended to permit ratification. Hastily examining the text of the treaty to confirm the news that impressment was omitted, Jefferson informed a senatorial delegation that he did not intend to submit a treaty which fell so short of American demands. Madison at once wrote the envoys to suspend negotiations pending further instructions. In the meantime the Nonimportation Act would continue suspended.[54] During the next month, as Jefferson and Madison studied the treaty, its faults seemed even greater, and nothing the envoys said minimized these defects. Not until May 20 did Madison forward new instructions, insisting that the treaty must be revised to include the prohibition of impressment, recognition of the re-export trade, a reopening of the West Indian trade, and the payment of indemnities for ships seized. So intransigent were these demands, that the door was closed on further discussion.

Although Monroe and Pinkney had warned the British commissioners that the omission of impressment might jeopardize the treaty, they had been certain that Jefferson would approve their work. Thus the news that the President would not submit the treaty to the Senate came as a shock to both men, who, in anticipation of its approval, had opened negotiations to settle two major issues not included in the recent discussions—the northeastern boundary and the regulation of Canadian-American trade. By mid-April they had reached an agreement with Holland and Auckland to draw the boundary along the line established in Rufus King's convention of 1803. They were unable to persuade the British to depart from the provisions in Jay's Treaty by which Canadian nationals were allowed to cross freely into American territory while traveling from one part of Canada to another. Although this arrangement had been extended reciprocally to citizens of the United States, it had been highly advantageous to Canadian merchants, who abused the privilege in order to trade with Indians residing under American jurisdiction. However, to make their refusal more palatable, the British commissioners consented to open Hudson's Bay to American traders. The news of the rejection of the treaty terminated these discussions. Had a Canadian trade convention been signed on this basis, it would never have been approved in Washington, for instructions making the exclusion of British traders a *sine qua non* were then on their way across the Atlantic.[55]

Monroe's incredulity and shock over Jefferson's decision were not reduced by the news that his work had been repudiated before the President had received the official text of the treaty or had read the explanatory letter, which he and Pinkney had drafted. This lack of faith in his judgment on the part of such close friends and political associates wounded Monroe deeply. Apparently the first word he received of the administration action came in a letter from William Branch Giles, who enjoyed Jefferson's confidence. From the Virginia congressman, Monroe learned that the failure to include impressment and the addition of the British condition about the Berlin Decree had rendered the treaty unacceptable to the people and the government. Although Giles had not seen the treaty, which had not been released to the public, he fully concurred in the decision. It was scarcely pleasant for Monroe to read that the opinions which he and Pinkney had entertained in London were vastly different from those of the nation, or to be told how many Republicans now feared that Monroe had mistaken the "wild effusions" of the Old Republicans and Federalists for "indications of public sentiment." The imputation that he had been disloyal to the administration was galling.[56] He certainly doubted that Giles' views were any more representative of public opinion than his own, for he was assured by other friends that the public was ready to approve of any treaty supported by the President, for there had never been any clear expression of the public will on the issues involved.[57]

A letter which Monroe received from Jefferson several weeks after that of Giles offered little comfort. After warning Monroe not to pay any heed to the Federalist press, which was attempting to "produce mischief between myself, personally and our negotiators . . . by putting a thousand speeches into my mouth," Jefferson declared that he had never said anything about the treaty other than to state that the omission of impressment had made it unacceptable. The President made his dislike of the treaty perfectly clear: "But depend on it, my dear Sir, that it will be considered a hard treaty when it is known. The British commissioners appear to have screwed every article as far as it would bear, to have taken everything, and yielded nothing." [58] Entirely absent from this letter, as well as from those written by Madison, was any consideration of the arguments which Monroe had previously advanced to justify his conduct—it was apparently assumed that his error would be obvious to him. Jefferson was, in fact, far more disturbed about the credence Monroe might give to reports circulating in the Federalist press that the rejection of the treaty had been influenced by a desire to elevate Madison at Monroe's expense. Consequently, when he wrote Monroe again in May it was not to clarify administration policy but to reassure his old friend:

I had intended to have written to you to counteract the wicked efforts which the federal papers are making to sow tares between you and me, as if I were lending a hand to measures unfriendly to any views which our country might entertain respecting you. But I have not done it because I have before assured you that a sense of duty, as well as of delicacy would prevent me from ever expressing a sentiment on the subject; and that I think you know me well enough to be assured I shall conscientiously observe the line of conduct I profess.[59]

Although Monroe accepted Jefferson's explanation, it was not sufficient to absolve Madison. Once again Monroe seemed unable to state his grievances frankly to the President. Although he made an attempt early in June to explain to Jefferson why it was that "at no period of my life was I ever subjected to more inquietude than I have suffered since my return from Spain," he never forwarded the letter.[60] It was not until March 1808 that Monroe, who was at home in Albemarle, fully unburdened himself to Jefferson. Using the unsent draft of June 1807 as an outline, Monroe further elaborated upon what he deemed Madison's failure, not only to keep him properly informed when he was in England, but also Madison's neglect after his return from Spain to indicate whether the President wished him to continue in London or to return home. Although he professed himself "perfectly satisfied" that Jefferson had never intended to injure him, still the "circumstances of my having signed a treaty, which was disapproved for imputed great defects; of having exceeded our powers in signing it, which I should not have done but in a firm belief that I promoted thereby the best interests of my country and of the administration, while I exposed myself to great responsibility by the measure, have given a handle to those who have wielded it with great effect against me." [61] There is, of course, no evidence to support (nor any reason to believe) the charge that Madison was seeking to eliminate Monroe as a rival. All indications are that the decision to reject the treaty was entirely Jefferson's, and that he expected Monroe to accept this judgment.

Although Monroe's character was in so many ways admirable, his one most conspicuous failing was an excessive *amour-propre,* which did not emerge as vanity, but rather in the form of an undue sensitivity to criticism. Operating as he did with such an elevated sense of his own integrity, he could not easily adjust when old friends failed to approve his conduct. His extreme self-consciousness about the purity of the motives upon which his actions had been based led him to regard the rejection of the treaty as a direct reflection upon his character and ability. It was also quite characteristic that Monroe, instead of immediately voicing his protests, should have brooded upon the matter and let each small item take on an ever-growing significance. Thus, in condemning Madison for not writing him frequently after his return from Spain, he forgot that the Secretary had seen no reason to write at length since Monroe had constantly declared his intention of sailing for home as soon as he had returned to England. It is not entirely possible to select with any assurance the motives for this reticence towards these intimate friends, while at the same time writing rather freely to John Randolph. Was it the instinctive dislike that all Virginians had of introducing disagreeable matters into normally pleasant personal relationships? Fortunately, his lack of malice as well as his own hard-headed sense of political realities restrained him from violent polemics in the style of John Randolph.

When the news of the rejection of the treaty reached London, the discussions with the British commissioners had already been suspended for some weeks following the collapse of the "Ministry of All the Talents" in the face of the stubborn refusal of George III to agree to Catholic emancipation. Nor were they resumed by the new ministry headed by the Duke of Portland, which brought the Pittite element to power once again. Portland was little more than the nominal head of a government composed of strong personalities, each of whom exerted an independent influence. The dominant member was Spencer Perceval, Chancellor of the Exchequer, who, in his determination to achieve victory in the war, saw no reason to tolerate a neutral trade calculated to benefit England's enemies. He was one of the principal authors of the Orders in Council of November 1807 which so enraged American opinion. In view of what seemed to be America's preference for the arch-enemy of liberty, Perceval regarded a harsher policy toward the

United States as eminently just. The Foreign Secretary was thirty-five-year-old George Canning, whose brilliant talents and vibrant personality had advanced him to the first rank of parliamentary leadership, in spite of the fact that by birth he was not a gentleman. Canning did not cherish any strong antagonism toward the United States, but he still had a career to make, and it was not to be expected that he would support policies at once unpopular with the nation and in conflict with the views of his ministerial colleagues. Although he was courteous and patient in personal interviews, the ironical and satirical barbs in his letters had a way of sharply irritating American opinion.[62]

Not until July, when new instructions arrived from Madison, were Monroe and Pinkney able to request a resumption of negotiations in order to revise the treaty. At Canning's suggestion they submitted a formal note indicating the proposed alterations, which were never discussed, for the treaty question was pushed aside by the news that the United States frigate *Chesapeake* had been disabled by H.M.S. *Leopard,* whose captain had demanded the surrender of three British deserters believed to be on the American vessel.[63] Monroe first learned of the incident from Canning, who assured him that reparations would be promptly made if the British officer were culpable. On Canning's invitation, Monroe, who had as yet no official report from Washington, submitted a brief protest. In spite of the fact that Canning had invited Monroe's note, he replied with one of his characteristically haughty and acid letters, chiding the Minister for failing to produce evidence of an outrage. To Monroe's subsequent embarrassment Canning took up a proposal, which Monroe had offered in passing, that the *Chesapeake* affair be considered separately from all other pending disputes. This might have led to a satisfactory settlement, but late in August Monroe received precise instructions that an apology and reparations must also be accompanied by a pledge to abandon impressment.[64] The linking of these issues made an agreement impossible. Canning rejected Madison's ultimatum, but like his predecessors he still sought to avoid a quarrel with the United States. When Canning decided in September to send a special emissary to Washington to settle the *Chesapeake* dispute, there was nothing to detain Monroe in England.[65] Turning over the affairs of the legation to Pinkney, Monroe sailed for home in November.

CHAPTER 15

A QUARREL AND
A RECONCILIATION

A FTER AN absence of more than four years Monroe and his family arrived in Norfolk on December 13, 1807, exhausted and ill after a stormy crossing.[1] His return, awaited so eagerly by the Old Republicans, was regarded uneasily by the regular Republicans, who dreaded a split in the party if the popular Minister openly sided with the opponents of the administration. For the moment all factions joined to welcome him home. In the House of Delegates only a handful of the members refused to approve a welcoming address; however, in the Governor's Council party tensions were fleetingly exposed, when Governor William Cabell refused to sign an address prepared by the council, most of whose members favored Monroe as Jefferson's successor. According to Councilor Alexander McRae, one of Monroe's more ardent backers, Cabell would not sign because he was afraid that the address would promote Monroe's candidacy.[2]

Monroe lingered only ten days in Virginia before setting out for Washington, where he met with a disappointing reception. It was not that Jefferson and Madison neglected the usual tokens of friendship, but they carefully avoided discussing political matters and made no attempt to seek his advice on policy towards England. Since not a word was said about his future preferment, he returned to Virginia quite convinced that he was being shelved to ensure Madison's election. For the first time he was ready to give a favorable hearing to those seeking to persuade him to run against Madison.[3]

Monroe could not postpone the decision about his candidacy, since the state and congressional caucuses were expected to meet in January.

Although he refused to countenance the organization of a new party and declined to identify himself formally with the Old Republicans, he agreed to let his friends promote him as a candidate for the regular party nomination. In the now-familiar language of politicians, he declared that he was not an active candidate, he would do nothing to obtain the nomination, but if chosen he would run. With this oblique permission the Old Republicans and those party regulars who were personally attached to him launched a drive for his nomination.[4]

The struggle in his behalf was waged in two theaters—Washington and Richmond. The drive in Washington failed almost at once, for none of the congressmen friendly to him was willing to push his candidacy in the face of an overwhelming preference for Madison.[5] The pro-Madison congressional phalanx had been shaped by Representative Wilson Cary Nicholas and Senator William Branch Giles, two masters of political manipulation in the gentlemanly Virginia style. Their original plan, which miscarried to some extent, was to hold the Washington caucus prior to that in Virginia (contrary to the usual custom) in order to permit the decision reached in Congress to influence the Virginia Republicans. The problem faced by Madison's managers was not limited to excluding Monroe; it was equally important that the supporters of George Clinton of New York, who also cherished presidential aspirations, be prevented from embarrassing the party by putting forward a third candidate. When the congressional caucus assembled on January 23 with Giles in the chair, a prearranged motion was promptly approved providing that the balloting for candidates take place without prior nominations. This motion enabled Madison's backers to avoid unpleasant comparisons between the candidates. Of the eighty-nine votes cast, eighty-three were for Madison, while Clinton and Monroe each received three. The result of the caucus seemed to indicate party harmony, but seventy-nine Republican members of Congress had not attended. The absentees were mostly Clintonians who abstained in order to keep Clinton on the ticket as the vice-presidential candidate, while leaving themselves free to run him independently for the Presidency. John Randolph and the Old Republicans were also absent. Before the caucus adjourned a corresponding committee was appointed with one member for each state—Giles, significantly, was the Virginia representative.[6]

On the state level, however, the Republicans were not so easily controlled. Until mid-January the forces of the rival candidates were evenly balanced in the legislature, while a majority of the Governor's

Council continued to favor Monroe.[7] His support came primarily from Old Republicans and personal admirers among the regulars. Since the latter were willing to back him only as long as this could be done within the ranks of the party, a number of his friends, such as the rising young lawyer William Wirt, withdrew their support when it was apparent that he could not win the regular nomination.[8] Giles and Nicholas, who were managing the campaign from Washington, concentrated on this vulnerable point. Their principal tactic was to create an unshakable impression that Madison's support was so powerful throughout the nation that continued opposition would injure Monroe's prestige and at the same time place Virginia in the unenviable position of being the only state to resist the will of the party. Letters to this effect flowed in a steady stream from the national Capital. Rumors were circulated that Monroe's backers in Washington had arranged to yield Clinton the first place on the ticket. To stir up the feelings of those loyal to the President, it was alleged that Monroe was allied to Jefferson's bitter enemy, John Randolph of Roanoke.[9]

Although these reports caused many of his Virginia supporters to withdraw, a loyal core still planned to contest the nomination in the caucus. Instead of waiting for news of the decision in Washington, Madison's organizers in Virginia decided to advance the date of the state caucus from January 28 to January 21 and also to exclude Monroe's followers. Apparently they considered it preferable to avoid an open conflict which would publicize the disagreement within the party. Therefore, the party regulars circulated private invitations to a caucus to be held on January 21 at the Bell Tavern. When Monroe's friends heard of this, they introduced a resolution in the House of Delegates to summon a general caucus on the same day, but they were blocked by a motion to adjourn. Consequently, two caucuses met on January 21: one, at the Bell Tavern, attended by 124 regular Republicans, who unanimously nominated Madison and appointed a central corresponding committee to direct the campaign; the other, at the capitol (the usual meeting place), where Monroe was nominated by a vote of fifty-seven to ten.[10] Since they had been surprised by this sudden maneuver, Monroe's managers did not have time to select members of the county committees nor to draw up a slate of electors. For this purpose they held a second caucus several days later. The Monroe central corresponding committee, which was responsible for the over-all conduct of the state campaign, was composed of George Hay (who was to become his son-in-law in the fall), John Clarke, Edward C. Stanard,

William T. Robinson and John Brockenbrough. Significantly, only Stanard can be identified as an Old Republican. The others were regular Republicans with considerable influence in the state, and two—George Hay and Brockenbrough—had been members of the controlling group in the state party (usually known as the Richmond Junto). The roster of electors included two prominent Old Republicans and close personal friends of the candidate—John Taylor of Caroline and Littleton Waller Tazewell, a prominent lawyer in Norfolk.[11]

Once nominated, Monroe continued to adhere to the formula developed early in January. Resisting all efforts to persuade him to withdraw, he adopted the position that the voters had a right to choose between two Republican candidates. He would do nothing to promote his election, but he would not decline to serve if elected. This was substantially the answer he gave Jefferson, when the latter sadly commented: "I see with infinite regret a contest between yourself and another, who have been very dear to each other, and equally so to me." [12] Although Monroe did not actively direct the policy of his central committee, he gave frequent advice to the members and was undoubtedly responsible for preventing personal attacks on Madison or blanket condemnation of administration foreign policy.[13] In allowing his name to be entered in the race, Monroe does not seem to have cherished the illusion that he could defeat Madison. His object, as he frequently repeated, was to show by attracting a sufficiently large following that he commanded the loyalty and confidence of the people of his native state. Had he seriously sought victory, he would have taken Tazewell's advice to attempt to unite with George Clinton, who was being offered as a presidential candidate in New York.[14]

II

It was not until Monroe allowed his friends to run him against Madison that Jefferson grasped the extent of his friend's discontent. On February 18 the President wrote expressing his concern that Monroe's political involvement might cause a rupture with Madison. "I have ever," he declared, "viewed Mr. Madison and yourself as two principal pillars of my happiness. Were either to be withdrawn, I should consider it as among the greatest calamities which could assail my future peace of mind." [15] It was this plea which finally induced Monroe to unburden the grievances of the past two years. Responding to this opportunity, Jefferson explained at some length the basis of administration decisions, making clear that he had never doubted either Monroe's ability or integrity. It gratified Monroe to be told that a special envoy had been appointed solely because the administration had not expected him to stay in Europe after leaving Madrid. Equally comforting was Jefferson's assertion: "But as to myself, I can solemnly protest, as the most sacred truths, that I never, one instant, lost sight of your reputation and favorable standing with your country, and never omitted to justify your failure to attain our wish, as one which was probably unattainable." He blamed the misunderstanding on mischief-makers influenced by the rancor of party spirit.[16] With these explanations Monroe professed himself "perfectly satisfied." [17]

Jefferson's overtures preserved his friendship with Monroe, but they did not lead to the restoration of close relations between Madison and the former Minister, nor, as Jefferson undoubtedly hoped, culminate in Monroe's withdrawal from the campaign. At the time that Monroe was expressing his gratitude to Jefferson, he quietly broke off all social and political contact with the Secretary of State. Why he should have done this is by no means clear. It was the President, after all, who made the policies which were carried out by the Cabinet members. Madison and Monroe had corresponded until mid-April, exchanging the usual family greetings, which suggested the preservation of at least the appearance of amity.[18] The occasion for their rupture seems to have been a misunderstanding over a minor question. Largely to gratify the returned Minister, Jefferson and Madison were transmitting to the Senate the official text of the rejected treaty together with the relevant dispatches from the envoys. In an effort to assuage Monroe's resentment, they even included a long justificatory letter he had written to Madison on February 8, 1808. This letter, submitted after the end of his mission, was not properly part of the official report, but it was included in deference to Monroe's wishes. Unfortunately, Madison failed to send in two dispatches specifically selected by Monroe for publication. Presumably the ex-Minister was so irritated by the omission (Madison had considered them unrelated to the central issue) that he did not reply to the Secretary's letter of April 18 explaining the deletion.[19] More than two years elapsed before they again corresponded or saw one another.

The campaign, which began immediately after the caucuses, was most unusual. Perhaps its most remarkable feature was the generosity of Thomas Ritchie, the editor of the most important Republican newspaper in the state, in opening the columns of the Richmond *Enquirer* to Monroe's advocates, although he supported Madison. In an age of intense partisan journalism such conduct was nearly unprecedented. Had it not been for this gesture, which stemmed from issues quite unrelated to the presidential campaign, the minority element would have lacked a public forum, for the other Republican newspapers did not allocate space to Monroe's supporters. Not until late in the summer did the Old Republicans establish a paper in Richmond—the *Spirit of '76*, edited by Edward Stanard.[20]

During the first phase of the campaign, which lasted until September, both sides placed primary emphasis upon peripheral issues. The publication of the dispatches from Monroe and Pinkney did not precipitate, as might have been expected, a flood of polemics. Indeed Monroe regarded the documents as an ample vindication of his conduct. Moreover, a frontal attack on administration policy would only invite a split in the party, a development Monroe was anxious to prevent, since it might open the way to a Federalist resurgence.[21] The Madisonians were equally willing to avoid the subject of foreign policy.

Since the main issues were only lightly touched upon, the early phases of the campaign were curiously unreal. The innumerable pro-Monroe pseudonymous writers concentrated their rhetoric on the alleged rigging of the caucuses by a handful of politicians in order to deprive the people of a voice in the nomination. The first address of Monroe's central committee in March was almost entirely confined to this topic. Naturally, the rebuttals were even lengthier.[22]

During the summer, when many Virginians retired to the springs, there was a relaxation in the campaign. Apart from endless letters defending the Embargo, only one important political item appeared late in June. Wilson Cary Nicholas released a circular letter to his constituents, which is particularly interesting because it was the first open denunciation of the rejected treaty and a direct attack on Monroe's diplomatic ability. Nicholas accused Monroe not only of violating his instructions but of accepting conditions humiliating to the nation. This harshly worded attack, all the more significant because it was published without the disguise of a pseudonym, galled Monroe. If Nicholas hoped to provoke Monroe's committee into a rash answer, for he published his letter when Monroe was in Kentucky, he was disappointed. The committee held back until Monroe's return, and then on his advice made no response. Later in the year Monroe's anger was intensified when Nicholas asked for the repayment of a loan in such a way that Monroe felt it had been done to inconvenience him. The ensuing rupture was never healed in spite of Jefferson's efforts as a peacemaker. Less violent, but equally long enduring, was the antagonism which developed between Giles and Monroe. Although Giles did not publish any attacks, he wrote many critical private letters. Every event now became infected with party bitterness. In June regular Republicans, members of the minority, and Federalists organized a meeting in Richmond to encourage domestic manufactures—a program then popular to reduce American dependence on British imports. Although Monroe was chairman of the committee selected to draw up a report, only regular Republicans were named to the committee appointed to implement the recommendations of the meeting.[23]

In September, shortly after Monroe returned from the trip to Kentucky, his central committee issued its first circular letter since March. After reviewing the caucus issue, the address broke new ground when it asserted that the major objection to Madison was the state of foreign affairs resulting from his policies. The committee, however, did not present a bill of particulars. Monroe was praised as the candidate whose diplomatic experience qualified him to solve the nation's problems. The committee pointed out that Monroe was neither committed to war nor to the Embargo and, consequently, would be free to introduce new policies. This statement implied, without putting it in categorical terms, that Monroe was opposed to both the Embargo and war, and left the impression that he was the advocate of a new, if unspecified policy.[24] As numerous critics immediately pointed out, these were topics on which his views were quite unknown, for, as the editor of the Richmond *Argus* acidly noted, Monroe had been "indignantly mute" since his return.[25] The address failed to provoke a general debate on foreign policy. In the weeks before the election the newspapers abounded with letters urging Monroe to withdraw in the interests of party unity. To answer these appeals the committee issued a final address in October. Once again the members of the committee denied the existence of a split in the party, insisting that they were merely exercising their right as citizens to support a Republican candidate whom they preferred. Affirming their loyalty to the party and denying any affiliation with the Federalists, the committee members promised their support to the victorious candidate.[26] With this pronouncement the committee ceased its activities, leaving the final word to the candidate. Just two weeks before the election Monroe broke his silence by publishing—with Jefferson's reluctant consent—the letters they had exchanged earlier in the year.[27] His purpose was to affirm his friendship with the President and establish clearly that he was not the member of a factional opposition.

The Madison ticket was overwhelmingly victorious in Virginia with 14,665 votes to 3,408 for Monroe's electoral slate. The Federalists apparently voted for the Republican candidates, for Charles Cotesworth Pinckney trailed far behind with only 760 votes.[28] Once Madison's election was assured, the Richmond Junto thirsted for revenge. It required the combined influence of Giles and Nicholas to prevent the Republican electors from refusing to ballot for Clinton as Vice-President. Two of Monroe's principal supporters were deprived of their seats on the Governor's Council. Although pressure was put on Jefferson to remove George Hay as federal attorney for Virginia, the President declined to act. Since Hay had not been associated with the Old Republican movement, he was restored to good standing in the party within a few years. The Junto, however, pursued John Taylor of Caroline and John Randolph of Roanoke vindictively for almost a decade. Monroe, of course, was distinctly unpopular with the Junto, but his friendship with Jefferson spared him from drastic reprisals, although for the moment he was excluded from state party councils.[29] The resentment which many members of the Junto felt towards Monroe was still evident a decade later when he became President.

III

Since he had consistently maintained that he had entered the presidential race as a Republican and not as a member of the opposition, Monroe did not expect his conduct to affect his standing as a party leader. Consequently, in January 1809, he did not hesitate to suggest to the President that he be sent back to England as a special envoy in a last effort to prevent a rupture. It was, he thought, a task for which his diplomatic career uniquely fitted him. "I am willing," he wrote Jefferson, "to undertake this trust and set out in discharge of it without a moment's delay, leaving my family behind." The last, in view of his close attachment to his wife, was a true mark of earnestness. Even if this mission failed, he continued, it would at least rally all the Republicans to the administration.[30] Jefferson responded to this startling proposal with a kind but firm rejection, frankly observing that it would be degrading to the nation to send a special mission after so much ill-treat-

ment from Britain. In any case the imminent repeal of the Embargo
rendered further negotiations unnecessary: it was now up to the European powers to make overtures to the United States.[31]

In spite of this rebuff Monroe anticipated some major appointment—
perhaps even the Secretaryship of State—in the new administration.
This optimism was not entirely fanciful. Madison apparently did consider offering him the State Department after congressional opposition forced the withdrawal of Gallatin's name. Madison, however,
quickly discovered that Monroe was equally unacceptable to the powerful cabal of Senators William Branch Giles, Samuel Smith, and
Michael Leib—the so-called "invisibles," who sought to exercise a
controlling influence on administration policy. To appease this faction
Robert Smith (the brother of the Senator), who had been Secretary of
the Navy in Jefferson's Cabinet, was shifted to the State Department.[32]
As much as Madison may have desired the support of Monroe and
his followers, he could not secure it without alienating a powerful
senatorial faction. In view of the continued silence of the administration, Monroe concluded by October that his withdrawal from public
life might well be permanent.[33]

His exile from politics had one advantage—for the first time in a
decade Monroe was able to concentrate on his private affairs. Although
he rented a house in Richmond shortly after his return with the idea
of practicing law, he soon gave up the lease to devote himself to his
Albemarle plantation and the property in Loudoun County. At first
he planned to sell the Loudoun property, which had been neglected,
but ultimately he retained it, for farm prices were depressed in the
wake of the Embargo. To meet his most pressing needs he borrowed
$10,000,[34] and set about improving his Albemarle plantation, which
consisted of 2,800 acres of land worked by thirty hands. Like most
planters in the Piedmont he turned to grain crops to replace tobacco,
from which returns had long been declining. Local farmers, he reported, were at first amused when he planted clover and spread the
ground with plaster of Paris, but when they saw his improved grain
yields they acknowledged the worth of his experiments. Monroe was
also interested in viniculture and imported vines from Bordeaux. Unfortunately, his re-entry into public life in 1811 made it impossible
for him to pursue this interest further.[35]

Settling into the simple house at the "Highlands," the Monroes were
again surrounded by old friends. From this familiar circle the Madisons
were conspicuously missing. Although the President and his wife fre-

quently visited Monticello, they never paused at the Highlands nor did Monroe call on Jefferson during Presidential visits. When Eliza married George Hay in September 1808, the Madisons were not present, although they had recently visited Monticello.[36] George Hay, some twenty years older than Eliza Monroe, was a distinguished lawyer, who had been long active in Virginia politics. Considered one of the most capable Republican publicists, he wrote frequently for the press under the pseudonym Hortensius. After his marriage Hay became an intimate adviser to his father-in-law, and after Monroe's election as President he and his wife lived much of the time at the White House. After the wedding, since Hay was still active at the bar in Richmond, Eliza and her husband settled near Richmond at "Ashfield," a small estate presented to them by Monroe.[37] A year later the Monroes were delighted by the birth of Hortensia Hay, their first grandchild.[38] This enthusiasm was shared by six-year-old Maria Hester, who according to the fond father and grandfather was constantly "contriving many ways of amusing Hortensia, who always forms one of her society, even in her absence, in her play with her babies." [39]

The Monroes were always admired for their elegance and taste, but this time it was Maria Hester, clad in the latest children's fashion, who attracted the most attention when they landed in Norfolk. St. George Tucker was so impressed by the novelty of her dress, which he thought ideal for his granddaughter, that he described it in detail for his daughter:

Your mama has refer'd you to me for an account of little Maria Monroe. . . . She was dress'd in a short frock, that reach'd half way between her knees and ancles [sic]—under which she display'd a pair of loose pantaloons, wide enough for the foot to pass through with ease, frill'd round with the same stuff as her frock and pantaloons. . . . The little monkey did not fail to evince the advantages of her dress. She had a small Spaniel dog with whom she was constantly engaged in a trial of skill—and the general opinion seemed to be that she turned and twisted about more than the Spaniel. . . .[40]

In his enforced retirement Monroe was not forgotten by Jefferson, who anxiously sought to restore the old bond between his two most cherished friends and at the same time reunite the party. After dining with Monroe late in March 1809, Jefferson happily informed the President of Monroe's decision to give up his house in Richmond, which would lessen his association with those individuals who, to Jefferson's way of thinking, had recently exerted too much influence on the ex-

Minister.[41] Jefferson was quite correct in reporting that Monroe was "sincerely cordial to the administration," for in the months after the election he had written to all his associates to join him in uniting behind the President. Although Taylor and Tazewell, his closest advisers, agreed that this was the proper course for him, they preferred to remain outside the active Republican circle.[42] In October 1809, Jefferson's friendship and patronage was sufficient to ensure Monroe's presence at a public banquet in Richmond in honor of the former President. Here in the presence of such party stalwarts as Spencer Roane and Thomas Ritchie, Monroe delivered a volunteer toast: "National honor is national property—its protection among the first duties of Freemen." [43]

Encouraged by Jefferson's reports, Madison, who had heard from a seemingly reliable source that Monroe was willing to accept the governship of Louisiana, asked Jefferson to sound out his neighbor without directly making an offer. Hastening to Monroe's farm the day after he received this letter, Jefferson found Monroe preparing to leave for an extended trip to Loudoun County. With more eagerness than discretion, Jefferson informed him of Madison's offer, only to meet with a blunt refusal. "The sum of his answers," Jefferson sadly informed the President, "was that to accept of that office was incompatible with the respect he owed himself; that he would never act in any office where he should be subordinate to any but the President himself. . . ." Monroe's response to the suggestion that he consider a military post under Major General Wilkinson was even more curt: he would "sooner be shot" than serve under such a commander. It was abundantly clear that he would only accept an appointment in the Cabinet or the diplomatic service. "Everything from him," Jefferson concluded, "breathed the truest patriotism, involving, however, a close attention to his honor and grade." [44] Monroe was indeed offended and his bitter comments gave rise to rumors that he had quarreled with Jefferson.[45] During the next few weeks new developments brought these old friends to the verge of a rupture.

Monroe had been away from home only a few days, when he was dumbfounded by the news that a special election had been called for mid-December to replace Wilson Cary Nicholas, congressman from the Albemarle district, who had just resigned. The additional news that Jefferson's son-in-law, Thomas Mann Randolph, was to be put forward as a candidate convinced him that the announcement had been timed to coincide with his absence in order to prevent him from entering the race. Although he found it difficult to believe that Jefferson had been unaware of Nicholas' intention at the time of his visit to Highlands, it is possible that he had not been informed. If Jefferson had known, it seems likely, in view of his interest in promoting party harmony, that he would have wished to sponsor Monroe. Monroe's friends entered his name, but they were unable to organize an effective campaign since they were uncertain about his willingness to run. Monroe was understandably irritated on his return by queries about his failure to announce his candidacy. Although Jefferson and Monroe were in Charlottesville on election day, they did not meet. In fact two months elapsed before they saw one another. Again it was Jefferson who made the advances late in February by calling on Monroe, who was ill. On this occasion neither referred to the recent election. Monroe was pleased by Jefferson's gesture, and friendly, if somewhat restrained relations were restored.[46]

While still irritated over these events, Monroe began working on a defense of his mission to England, but the manuscript never advanced beyond preliminary sketches, for his prospects of political advancement improved markedly in the spring of 1810.[47] Although it cannot be determined exactly when he was given to understand that he might anticipate a high-level appointment, the events of the spring of 1810 indicate that some hint already had been given to him.[48] At that time the friction between Madison and the "invisibles," who had been harassing the administration, as well as Madison's exasperation over Robert Smith's incompetence, had reached such a point that rumors were current that Smith might be removed from the State Department.[49] Smith stayed in the Cabinet for another year, but there is little doubt that Madison intended to dispose of him as soon as suitable opportunity arose. Every consideration made Monroe his logical successor—his former friendship with Madison, which Jefferson had helped restore; the general recognition that Monroe possessed the experience and ability required for the post; and Monroe's unswerving loyalty to the President since 1808. Not the least among these factors was the strength Monroe could bring to the administration, which was beset with criticism from Federalists and Republicans alike over the conduct of foreign affairs.

In the spring of 1810 Madison's prestige was damaged following the British repudiation of the Erskine Agreement, which had been negotiated in April 1809, shortly after the Embargo had been replaced by the Nonintercourse Act. Under the terms of the Nonintercourse Act commerce was to be restored with the first power lifting its trade restrictions. On this basis, David Erskine, the British plenipotentiary, negotiated an agreement settling the *Chesapeake* affair and providing for the repeal of the Orders in Council. Without waiting for British ratification Madison at once reopened trade with Great Britain. The news of the repudiation (Erskine had exceeded his powers) had a devastating effect, raising doubts about the President's judgment. So great was the criticism that the administration-sponsored substitute for the Nonintercourse Act, which was due to expire in the spring of 1811, failed. Macon's Bill No. 2—a measure pleasing neither Macon nor the President—was pushed through in its place. Macon's Bill No. 2 restored trade with all European states and authorized the President, if either France or Great Britain suspended its trade restrictions and the other power did not follow suit, to restore nonintercourse with the recalcitrant nation.[50] In the face of the continued hostility from the "invisibles" and the mounting criticism from all sides, the administration badly needed reinforcement.

IV

Before Monroe could be elevated to a major post, it was necessary for him to demonstrate that he could win the confidence of party regulars and also effect a reconciliation with the dissident Republicans. The first step in the realization of this objective—election to the House of Delegates—presented no difficulties. On election day in April 1810, Monroe delivered a speech in Charlottesville, which—and this was most unusual in the case of a county election—was reported in the *Enquirer:*

I have been asked to lay open my political mind! This demand astonishes me not a little, for I had supposed that my politics were well known to all my countrymen. I have always been a Republican. I have fought and bled for the cause of Republicanism. I have supported it for thirty years, with my most strenuous exertions. When persecuted and hunted down by the federal party, I returned to you firm and unmoved. Is it to be supposed, that I will, in the noon of life, abandon those principles, which have ever actuated me, and join that party, by whom I was once persecuted? If I was a Republican, when the Republicans were the minority, and had to struggle with the over bearing force of the opposition, is it probable that I will cease to be one, when, by your exertions, we have acquired command, and when a Republican sits at the helm of State? I shall ever be ready to support the administration whilst I think it acts with propriety. I am confident that you would not wish me to support it when it acts improperly. Mr. Madison is a Republican and so am I. As long as he acts in consistence with the interests of his country, I will go along with him. When otherwise, you cannot wish me to countenance him.[51]

This profession of loyalty was carefully framed to impress the Richmond Junto rather than the voters of Albemarle.

The next step in his rehabilitation—a public reconciliation with the President—took place in May 1810, when Monroe visited Washington for the first time in two years. Ostensibly he made the journey to settle his diplomatic accounts, about which there had recently been some unfavorable comment in the New England press.[52] His reception by Madison and other members of the administration was, as Monroe reported to John Taylor of Caroline, of a "kind and friendly" nature, and, in short, everything that he could wish. Relations were further improved by Madison's explanation of the misunderstanding which had led him to renew the offer of the governorship of Louisiana.[53] No one was more pleased than Jefferson, who assured the President after Monroe's return that his neighbor would "rejoin us with zeal. The only embarrassment," however, "will be from his late friends. But I think he has firmness of mind to act independently of them. The next session of our legislature will show." [54]

The coming session was indeed crucial, for Monroe had to prove his ability to win the endorsement of both party regulars and his backers in the election of 1808. He carefully prepared the ground in advance with the cooperation of John Taylor of Caroline, who had long favored the entry of his friend into the administration in the hope that it would lead to a modification of foreign policy. On September 10, 1810, Monroe drafted a long letter (it fills twenty-nine pages in his *Writings*) to Taylor.[55] This was not a private communication, but a document to be circulated among the party leaders during the December session of the General Assembly. Since Taylor was much admired by the Old Republicans, the fact that he was willing to let the letter be seen would do much to win them over. In this letter Monroe justified his decision to let his name be entered against Madison in 1808 as the only means then at his disposal of giving the voters a chance to indicate their confidence in his judgment and integrity. He stressed the fact that he had run as a Republican and not as a member of the minority. He reiterated his conviction that a direct attack at that time would not only have hindered the President in future negotiations with England, but it would have split the party and invited a Federalist resurgence. A direct concession to the Richmond Junto was his declaration: "With the political course of the republican minority I never had any connexion."

The Old Republicans, he told Taylor, should seek their goals within the ranks of the party; otherwise, as a permanent minority, they would never be able to influence policy. His letter was a skillful affirmation of loyalty to the party, yet he did not retract his belief that his treaty had been sound. He also managed to detach himself from the Old Republicans without specifically condemning their principles.

Although Taylor and Tazewell agreed that the Old Republicans could exert greater influence by remaining in the party, Randolph's passionate temperament made it unlikely that he would accede to Monroe's persuasion. Realizing that Randolph required careful handling, Monroe never suggested in his letters the possibility of a reconciliation with the administration, nor did he repeat the comments made to Taylor about the warmth of his reception in Washington. Since a personal interview seemed advisable, Monroe invited Randolph to stop in Albemarle on his way home from the springs in the summer of 1810.[56] Although he arrived at Monroe's farm a few days after a visit from the "royal family" (as Randolph referred to the Madisons), he was so wedded to his obsessions that he did not envisage a renewal of the old bonds between his host and the President. Randolph, however, did sense a certain sadness in his friend, which he attributed to Monroe's awareness that he would never again hold a prominent position.[57] Monroe left no account of this visit, but it is possible to guess what took place from Randolph's letters. Undoubtedly Monroe's visible preoccupation arose from the difficulty in approaching his temperamental guest on the subject of restoring party harmony. One can imagine many uneasy attempts to broach the matter, followed by hasty retreats as Randolph unleashed his fury against the President. In the end Randolph departed quite unaware of the recent reconciliation.[58]

When the legislature convened, Monroe was assigned important committee posts, receiving among other appointments the chairmanship of the Committee on Privileges and Elections, an honor accorded ranking party leaders. On his advice the Republicans did not introduce the usual resolutions approving measures of the national administration, for Monroe felt such declarations would aggravate existing tensions within the party.[59] Monroe's advancement to some important elective office, to give proof (as Jefferson remarked) of the "fidelity of his Republican principles," presented difficulties.[60] The governorship was not immediately available, for there was no valid reason for failing to re-elect John Tyler for the customary third term. Plans to send Monroe to the Senate collapsed when Giles failed to resign, as had been rumored. It seemed too risky to run Monroe against Giles, even though the Senator's association with the "invisibles" had lessened his popularity with the Junto. A defeat might irreparably damage Monroe's career.[61] The problem was solved early in January when Governor Tyler resigned to accept a federal judgeship. Undoubtedly Madison's promptness in appointing Tyler, as soon as he learned of the death of the incumbent judge, had more to do with Monroe's advancement than a concern over judicial efficiency.[62]

Before Monroe was elected governor further negotiations took place to win over those Junto leaders who felt that James Barbour, the Speaker of the House of Delegates, should be given preference over a former dissident. In making these arrangements Chapman Johnson, a young delegate from Louisa County, friendly to Monroe, was the intermediary. In response to a query from Johnson asking if he would carry into the governorship a disposition to cooperate with the administration, Monroe drafted a letter to be shown to party leaders. In this letter Monroe admitted that he had differed with the administration in the past, but he assured Johnson that he had no "disposition to oppose or counteract any measure of the government, or to impeach its claims to the respect and confidence of the people." Nonetheless, he felt that not even his critics would subscribe to the principle that every administration policy must be "approved without examination." [63] While the election was pending the letter to Taylor was also circulated among the delegates. Although some Junto members wanted a stronger statement of party loyalty, Monroe refused to accede to their demands.[64]

In the midst of these sensitive negotiations Congressman John Randolph appeared in Richmond. Somehow he obtained a copy of Monroe's letter to Taylor, which was certainly never intended for his eyes. His reaction was characteristic: "Richmond, James Monroe, Traitor" was the sole entry in his diary for that day.[65] His explanation for Monroe's conduct was simple—an insatiable thirst for office. As soon as Monroe learned of Randolph's arrival, he sent George Hay to persuade the visiting congressman to join the other Old Republicans in supporting the Madison administration. Angry that an emissary had been sent, Randolph demanded a personal conference, which Monroe refused, since he could not afford to appear to be bargaining with the most detested leader of the minority and thus give substance to the reports that he had been under Randolph's influence.[66] After his election to the governorship on January 16, Monroe again appealed to Randolph through John Taylor, but he was decisively rebuffed.[67] Randolph never forgave Monroe for this seeming desertion, although formal relations were restored during Monroe's Presidency. Taylor and Tazewell, on the other hand, fully approved of Monroe's return to public life and used their influence to reconcile other Old Republicans to the Madison administration.[68]

V

Monroe served only three months as governor. On March 14, 1811, when he returned to Richmond from a visit to Albemarle, he found a letter from Senator Richard Brent asking whether he would accept an appointment as Secretary of State. Madison had finally decided to free himself from Smith, who resigned under pressure. It seems unlikely that Monroe was greatly astonished by the contents of this letter, which Brent had written at the President's request. In a carefully phrased reply Monroe indicated his willingness, but pointed out two obstacles: first, he felt he could not casually resign the governorship; second, he raised questions about the extent to which the administration was wedded to its current foreign policy. Was any change possible?[69] Monroe also wrote at once to Taylor and Tazewell, who urged him to accept.[70] When a reply from Monroe failed to arrive as soon as expected, Madison, fearful that he might have been offended by an indirect approach, wrote personally to tender the post. In his answer Monroe reiterated the objections raised in his letter to Brent. Was Madison, he asked, willing to have as Secretary of State a person known to hold views on foreign policy differing from those held by the administration? "It would not become me," he continued, "to accept a station, or act a part in it, which my judgment and conscience did not approve. . . . I could not do this nor would you wish me to do it."[71] The President wrote at once assuring him that past opinions did not constitute an impediment. To make it easier for Monroe to resign the governorship, Madison, following a suggestion made by Monroe, rested the appointment on a need for the Governor's services on the national scene during the current crisis. By far the most satisfying portions of Madison's letter related to the treaty of 1806:

These differences however lie fairly within the compass of free consultation and mutual concession, as subordinate to the necessary unity belonging to the Executive Department. I will add that I perceive not any commitments even in the case of the abortive [1806] adjustment with that power, that could necessarily embarrass deliberations on a renewal of negotiations; inasmuch as the variance of opinion turned not a little on different understanding of certain facts and constructive intentions rather that [sic] on the merits of the questions decided, and as the questions more immediately interesting to the harmony of the two countries, namely as to the *Chesapeake,* the Orders in Council and blockades, are either of a subsequent date or left without any positive decision.[72]

Gratified by the admission that he had not violated his instructions in 1806, Monroe had no hesitation in accepting.[73]

Although the principals in this transaction had no difficulty in understanding the terms on which Monroe entered the Cabinet, historians have differently interpreted the interchange. Henry Adams, who disliked both parties, described the President's letter as a total capitulation to Monroe's demand that policy be changed. Irving Brant, in his monumental biography of Madison, interpreted the President's letter as a basic affirmation of policy without a hint that change might be feasible. Brant accepted John Randolph's judgment that Monroe was ready to take office on "virtually any terms." [74] These contradictory views can only be sustained by citing specific passages in the letters without reference to the complete texts. What is really most remarkable about Monroe's letter of March 20 and Madison's response is the vagueness of both writers—each deliberately and delicately blurred the issues to eliminate bitterness, but at the same time to avoid an admission of error. The interchange can best be summarized in this fashion: to Monroe's inquiry whether the President was willing to work with a person whose policy views had recently differed from those of the administration, Madison gave his assurance that this did not constitute an obstacle; the situation was still fluid and a change might be possible if circumstances altered. Monroe had not demanded a pledge about the future course of the administration. He had received what he had most wanted, an acknowledgment of the rectitude of his conduct in 1806.

The relief over Smith's resignation was so great that not even party regulars expressed much resentment over Monroe's appointment. It is true that Ritchie thought Monroe's conduct in England had rendered him unsuitable, but he did not raise any further objections. The chief opposition came from the allies of the "invisibles," whose chief spokesman was William Duane, the editor of the Philadelphia *Aurora*.[75] The Smith faction, discredited by the adverse reaction to Robert Smith's anonymous pamphlet criticizing Madison's policies, was unable to block the appointment, which Giles called the "wickedest of all . . . [Madison's] contrivances." Giles was only able to delay the confirmation by raising awkward questions about Monroe's unsettled accounts dating from his missions to France and England. Yet even Giles finally joined in the unanimous approval of Monroe as a courtesy to a former member of the Senate.[76] Monroe, deeply gratified by the "liberal and manly" terms of the President's offer, did not cherish any lingering resentment toward Madison. The old bond of friendship was renewed and the two worked together in complete harmony.[77] Jefferson, of course, was especially pleased by these events, not only for personal reasons, but because he felt that Monroe would bring strength to the administration at a critical time.[78]

CHAPTER 16

SECRETARY OF STATE

A T THE TIME of Monroe's entry into the Cabinet, Washington had been the seat of government for a decade, yet it was still lacking in urban amenities. Unpaved streets, unfinished buildings, vast swamps stretching along the Potomac, garbage dumped in the streets for roving pigs to scavenge—the city of magnificent distances (as the Portuguese Minister tactfully described it) was more like a frontier community than a major population center on the Eastern coast. The more fortunate officials lived in Georgetown, but most congressmen came without their families and put up in the numerous boarding houses (sometimes referred to as messes) primarily composed of members from the same state and party. The public buildings, many of which were still under construction, did not offer an impressive spectacle. Thomas Law, the great speculator in Washington real estate, who had every reason to look for the best, saw little to approve in 1811:

When I walk over this city and see a bridge with a wall on one side. When I view the Patent Office with plank to its frameless windows. When I perceive the President's circumvalliattor [sic] unfinished, his garden in gullies & the rooms of his house unplastered; when the rain drips on my head through the roof of the Capitol; when I survey the neglected spot alloted to a garden which cost 30 Ds. p. acre—I ask, can these disgusting scenes to strangers be pleasing to Citizens.[1]

Not only was the roof of the capitol leaky, but the two wings stood isolated, for the domed connecting gallery had not as yet been built.

Life in the Capital was a strange and, to Europeans, a baffling mixture of formality and republican simplicity. It was not at all unusual for

Monroe to dine casually at a congressional mess, or, as he did on a hot
July evening in 1813, to take a drive during which he collected Vice-
President Elbridge Gerry for a call on Henry Clay. At Clay's boarding
house the Vice-President and Secretary of State sat on the verandah
long into the evening talking with the Kentucky congressman and other
lodgers.[2] Informal visits of this kind were not without pitfalls, for the
Secretary's comments on these occasions were often given a wider currency as official pronouncements. Thus a remark made by Monroe
late in 1811, while dining at William Lowndes' mess, about the probable effect of war in raising grain prices, was published in the Baltimore
press, much to the Secretary's embarrassment.[3]

There were, of course, much grander social gatherings, attended by
the wives of Washington officials in finery so advanced in style that
the more conservative guests were shocked. Mrs. Sarah Seaton, daughter
of Joseph Gales and wife of William Seaton (coeditors of the Washington *National Intelligencer*), was an interested if not entirely approving
spectator at the Gallatins' New Year's Ball in 1813. She was startled to
see ladies of fifty "decked with lace and ribbons, wreaths of jasmine
across their bosoms, and not kerchiefs!" Critically she noted that it was
the "fashion for ladies a little advanced in age to rouge and *pearl,* which
is spoke of with as much *sang froid* as putting on their bonnets." Mrs.
Monroe, she continued, "paints very much, and has besides an appearance of youth which would induce a stranger to suppose her age to be
thirty: in lieu of which she introduces them . . . to her daughter Mrs.
Hay of Richmond." [4] Monroe's straitened circumstances did not permit
him to live on such a lavish scale as the wealthy Secretary of the Treasury. The British Minister was astonished at the plain way in which
the Monroes lived, "entertaining very sparingly, which does not fail
to be commented on in a place where good dinners produce as much
effect as in any part of the world." Perhaps the British Minister's standards were too exalted, for Congressman Lowndes reported that Monroe's
dinners were among the best in Washington.[5] The wife of Benjamin
Crowninshield, the Secretary of the Navy, after a dinner at the Monroes', which she considered "the most stylish dinner I have been at,"
was sufficiently impressed to provide a detailed account for her
mother:

The table wider than we have, and in the middle a larger, perhaps silver,
waiter, with images . . . and vases filled with flowers, which made a very
showy appearance as the candles were lighted when we went to table. The
dishes were silver and set round this waiter. The plates were handsome

china, the forks silver, and so heavy I could hardly lift them to my mouth, dessert knives silver, and spoons very heavy. . . . Mrs. Monroe is a very elegant woman. She was dressed in a very fine muslin worked in front and lined with pink, and a black velvet turban close and spangled. Her daughter Mrs. Hay, a red silk sprigged in colors, white lace sleeves and a dozen strings of coral round her neck. Her little girl, six years old, dressed in plaid. The drawing-room lighted—transparent lamps I call them;—three windows, crimson damask curtains, tables, chairs and all the furniture French. . . .[6]

The Secretary and his wife regularly appeared at official occasions, such as receptions and dinners at the President's residence (not as yet called the White House), and at public celebrations. On July 4, 1812, Monroe and Secretary of War William Eustis were escorted to the President's house by a company of dragoons, and thence accompanied the President to the capitol, where the party was greeted by an eighteen-gun salute. After listening to Attorney General Rush read an oration to the assembled crowd, Monroe and Eustis returned with the President to his residence for a militia review. The day ended, as was customary, with a public dinner attended by Washington officialdom.[7]

During his tenure as Secretary of State the pressure of business made extended visits to Albemarle impractical. Monroe now began to spend more time on his Loudoun County property, which he owned outright after 1808, having inherited the balance from Joseph Jones, Jr. Since this estate, which he named "Oak Hill," was within thirty miles of the Capital, he and his family could easily get away for brief visits. At this time, when at Oak Hill the Monroes occupied a simple, six-room frame cottage.[8] Monroe's last long sojourn in Albemarle until the end of the war took place in 1811. During the following year, however, he was able to spend only a week at Highlands to attend urgent family matters, having been called home by a bitter quarrel between Eliza Hay and his brother Joseph. Joseph, who had never managed to set himself up independently, still constituted a drain on Monroe's limited resources. Since 1798 Monroe had disbursed more than £1600 to pay his brother's debts. The disagreement had been precipitated by Joseph's refusal to accept Mrs. Hay as mistress of the house when she was in Albemarle during her mother's absences. Undoubtedly the proud Mrs. Hay resented this ne'er-do-well, who had disgraced the family with a misalliance. When Monroe sided with Eliza, Joseph (now a widower) angrily departed leaving his daughters behind. By this time relations were so strained that Monroe did not feel he could take Joseph's children into his own family. In a letter, which obviously caused him much distress to write, he explained his dilemma to one of his nieces:

Situated as I am in public life with a painful recollection of many distressing circumstances to me and my affairs, which have attended my connection with your father through life, I cannot undertake to invite you into my family, but will always be your friend.

He offered to pay for their support either with his brother Andrew, who lived near Milton in Albemarle County, or with his sister Elizabeth Buckner in Caroline County.[9] These concerns kept him so occupied that he could not spare time to visit Monticello before hastening back to the Capital.[10]

II

It was only natural that many interpreted Monroe's appointment as indicating that the President was about to adopt a policy more favorable to British interests.[11] To draw this conclusion, however, was to overlook the fact that the new Secretary was neither pro-British nor at odds with the administration over the nature of America's fundamental interests. His alienation from the administration was not the result of a basic disagreement over the aims of American foreign policy, but arose from his dissatisfaction with measures which not only failed to achieve administration objectives but also lowered the prestige of the nation. In a letter to John Taylor of Caroline shortly after the outbreak of the war, he explained that he had long considered a "fair and reasonable arrangement with the great maritime power . . . [in] the true interest of this country," but if it could not be realized on honorable terms then the nation had to make an end of "dealing in the small way of embargoes, non-intercourse, and non-importation with menaces of war. . . ."[12] Monroe's entry into the Cabinet made a resolution of the long Anglo-American controversy inevitable; if a settlement could not be arranged, then the nation must protect its rights with force.

Although the new Secretary was moderately hopeful that his appointment might stimulate the British government to open the way to an agreement by some "generous act," no such gesture was forthcoming. Not only were his Whig friends out of power, but recent administration measures had stiffened the determination of the Perceval ministry to adhere to the restrictive policies in effect since the adoption of the Orders in Council in 1807. In November 1810 (six months before Monroe became Secretary of State), Madison had issued

a proclamation announcing the restoration of nonintercourse with
Great Britain under the provisions of Macon's Bill No. 2. The President had taken this step on the basis of a letter from Napoleon's Foreign Minister, the Duke of Cadore, to the American Minister in Paris,
in which Cadore left the impression that the Berlin and Milan Decrees
were no longer applicable to American shipping in Continental ports.
As events soon proved, this was not the case. In issuing his proclamation Madison had ignored Cadore's ambiguously phrased qualifications
that the suspension of the French decrees depended upon similar action
by Great Britain.[13] In the hope that the Cadore letter would provide
the British Cabinet with adequate justification to relax the Orders in
Council, Madison had chosen to disregard the conditional character of
Cadore's statement. Since it could not be denied that the French were
still seizing American ships and issuing licenses for the Continental
trade, the British demanded positive evidence of repeal before revoking
the Orders in Council. While many thought Madison acted precipi-
tously, his position was not without justification. The great importance
of American trade to the British war effort made it seem reasonable
that English statesmen might welcome the Cadore letter as a convenient
pretext for modifying the restrictive orders. Madison's expectation was
not realized, largely because the British ministry did not believe that
the President would long persist in a nonintercourse policy known to
be widely unpopular. Once Madison had issued the proclamation retreat became impossible: to admit he had erred in interpreting Napoleon's action would merely increase the humiliation of the nation.
The real value of the Cadore letter, therefore, lay in its use as a weapon
to persuade Britain to alter her maritime policy. Neither Monroe nor
the President had any illusions about the status of the French decrees,
but Monroe, unlike his predecessor, never voiced his doubts to the
British Minister.[14] He never departed from the official view that the
Cadore letter was sufficient proof of the repeal of the French decrees.

One of Monroe's first responsibilities was to obtain a clarification
of the Cadore letter before the arrival of the new British Minister in
order to place the administration on a stronger ground. Since Jonathan
Russell, the American charge in Paris, had been unable to secure an
explanation, Monroe summoned the French Minister, Louis Sérurier,
late in June to ask why American trade was still subject to restriction
in spite of the revocation of the decrees. Sérurier, accustomed to pleasant interviews with Robert Smith befitting the emissary of a friendly
power, was astonished by the new Secretary's coldness. Of this, the first

of many disagreeable conferences, Sérurier sent a vivid report to the Foreign Minister:

Mr. Monroe's countenance was absolutely distorted. I could not conceive how an object, apparently so unimportant could affect him so keenly. He continued thus: "You are a witness, sir, to the candor of our motives, to the loyalty of our principles, to our immovable fidelity to our engagements. In spite of party clamor and the extreme difficulty of the circumstances, we persevere in our system; but your government abandons us to the attacks of its enemies and ours, by not fulfilling on its side the conditions set forth in the President's proclamation. We are daily accused of a culpable partiality for France. These cries were at first feeble, and we flattered ourselves every day to be able to silence them by announcing the Emperor's arrangements in conformity with ours; but they become louder by our silence. The Administration finds itself in the most extreme embarrassment; it knows neither what to expect from you, nor what to say to its own constituents. Ah Sir!" cried Mr. Monroe, "if your sovereign had deigned to imitate the promptness which our President showed in publishing his proclamation; if he had reopened, with the necessary precautions, concerted with us, his ports and his vessels,—all the commerce of America was won for France. . . ." [15]

Although the French Minister's discomfiture mounted as he listened to Monroe enumerate America's grievances, he could not refute the charges, for his latest instructions had confirmed the fact that the Continental system was still applicable to American ships. In these circumstances he temporized, pleading a lack of authority to order the consuls to cease issuing licenses.

Several days after this interview the new British Minister, Augustus J. Foster, disembarked at Annapolis. His arrival was followed a few hours later by the *Essex* bearing William Pinkney, who had left London after giving up all hope of reaching an agreement. Also on board the *Essex* were dispatches from Jonathan Russell, which it was hoped would resolve the doubts about the decrees. The President and Secretary of State spent the next day (a Sunday) poring over Russell's letters without finding anything to confirm the effective repeal of the French decrees. When Sérurier called on Monday (he described his reception as icy), Monroe asked whether he had had any pleasing news from his government. The French Minister, who had received dispatches ordering him not to make any pledges about the status of the Berlin and Milan Decrees, lamely fell back on the excuse that the President's seven-months-old proclamation was too recent for France to have had time to act. To shift the ground of discussion, he complained of the long delay in sending an American Minister to France, which might be interpreted as an unfriendly act. Joel Barlow had been named to the French post in February, but he had been held back awaiting news from Russell. After casually expressing his regrets, Monroe resumed his complaints about France's conduct. On the assumption that Madison was more sympathetic to France than the Secretary of State, Sérurier privately conveyed his protest about Barlow to the President. Only when the vague reply came back through Monroe that Barlow would leave shortly did Sérurier abandon the notion that Monroe and Madison held conflicting views about American policy.[16]

Sérurier was unnecessarily alarmed that the conversations begun between Monroe and Foster in July might radically alter American policy towards France, for the British Minister's instructions did not allow him to make any concessions other than settling the ancient *Chesapeake* affair.[17] Indeed, everything he had been ordered to do was calculated to irritate rather than to appease. Nonetheless, Foster, who was presented to Madison on July 2, began his mission in a hopeful mood, encouraged by the friendliness of his reception. He was impressed, as Monroe intended, to see the Secretary of State "rather more dressed" than had been the rule on ceremonial occasions during Foster's service on Merry's staff in the Jefferson administration.[18] Handsome and self-assured, Foster was well liked in Washington, for in spite of his aristocratic attitudes, he managed to conceal his contempt for Americans. In his dispatches, which usually stated the American position fairly, he steadily recommended the revocation of the Orders in Council, for he grasped that this was considered an essential preliminary to a general settlement. Unfortunately his defective understanding of American politics frequently led him astray. He could not comprehend how an administration subject to such widespread criticism could still enjoy the support of the nation as a whole. Like other European diplomats accustomed to the intrigues of royal courts, he ascribed undue significance to small events. Thus he concluded at first that Monroe's friendliness reflected a disagreement with the President over policy.[19] The weight he attached to the opinions of the Federalists who frequented his house led him to underestimate the President's determination to resort to war if American demands were not met. All too frequently his dispatches presented a confused picture, as he simultaneously stressed the necessity of repealing the Orders and minimized the danger of war.

Monroe and Foster began their discussions at once, but before tak-

ing up the central issues the British Minister insisted on an explanation
of the attack made by the United States frigate *President* on the British
sloop *Little Belt* in May 1811. This engagement had taken place when
Commodore John Rodgers hailed the *Little Belt,* which he mistook
for the ship-of-the-line *Guerriere,* to demand the release of a sailor recently impressed. The *Little Belt* responded with a shot, leading to an
engagement in which the British sloop was disabled. In a conciliatory
tone Monroe admitted that Rodgers had not been authorized to use
force to recover impressed seamen, but he deemed it improper for
Britain to demand satisfaction for an injury occurring years after the
still-unsettled *Chesapeake* affair.[20]

In the same interview, when Foster protested the seizure of West
Florida in 1810, Monroe defended the action of the United States on
the basis of its claim to this territory as part of the Louisiana Purchase. It was with considerable "astonishment" that Foster listened to
Monroe's "extraordinary" argument that occupation had been an act
of humanity to save the Spanish garrison from annihilation by the
insurgents. The Secretary's next statement caused the Minister "real
pain": Monroe blandly contended that Spain should be so grateful to
the United States for not aiding her rebellious colonies as to readily
accept the occupation of West Florida. Foster then taxed the administration with complicity in fomenting the rebellion in West Florida,
citing the secret act of January 1811, authorizing the President to occupy East Florida if there were danger of the province falling into the
hands of a third power. On this matter Monroe maintained with "some
gravity" that he knew nothing of the law. As Foster belabored the point,
the Secretary of State, unable to "command his countenance" at last
"betrayed by his laughter his consciousness" of its authenticity. Monroe
could afford to be amused, for British protests on this subject, which
was no concern of the British government, did not disturb the administration. Moreover, as he rightly guessed, they were of little moment
to the British Cabinet, which ignored Foster's suggestion that he be
allowed to threaten reprisals if the United States intervened in East
Florida.[21] After he received a reply to his formal note of protest, Foster
never revived the question.

The central issue between the two nations was reached on July 3,
when Foster presented a note protesting the application of nonintercourse to Great Britain, since the French decrees had not been repealed
in fact. In his verbal response Monroe introduced the nice distinction

that the French regulations then in effect were derived from municipal law and were not international regulations of trade. The decrees, the Secretary insisted, had been repealed in their international aspects, which was all that the United States or any other nation could reasonably expect. The present restrictions, which were based on customs regulations within the power of every government, could not be questioned by a third power. Foster was not convinced by these "shadows of arguments," as he termed them, but he could not extract anything further from the Secretary. This line of defense was far from satisfactory to Monroe himself, who delayed a formal reply to Foster until July 23 in the hope of extracting a more acceptable statement from Sérurier.

In an interview with the French Minister on July 9, the Secretary of State, using sharper language than ever before, asked Sérurier to explain why the President was still waiting for adequate assurances that the decrees had been repealed, although the nonintercourse proclamation was eight months old. Was this not sufficient proof of American intentions? As long as the question remained unresolved, Monroe told Sérurier, Barlow's departure would be postponed. If he were allowed to depart under the existing circumstances, the administration would be generally condemned. As it was, Monroe could not walk from his home to his office without twenty citizens asking him why a minister should be sent to France in view of the contempt that nation was showing towards the United States. The interview concluded with some pointed remarks, which Sérurier considered sufficiently noteworthy to report verbatim:

Believe me [Monroe declared] the American government will not be inconsequent; but its patience is exhausted and . . . it is determined to make itself respected. People in Europe suppose us to be merchants, occupied exclusively with pepper and ginger. They are much deceived, and I hope we shall prove it. The immense majority of our citizens do not belong to this class, and are, as much as your Europeans, controlled by principles of honor and dignity. I never knew what trade was. The President is as much a stranger to it as I; and we accord to commerce only the protection that we owe it, as . . . to an interesting class of citizens.[22]

Sérurier warned his government that a rupture seemed likely unless French ports were opened freely to American ships. As distressed as he was to see France's affairs deteriorating, he was powerless to alter the course of events.

Shortly after this conference, Monroe received unofficial reports that ships sequestered in France since November 1, 1810 (the date of Madison's proclamation), had been released, although those seized before that date were still impounded. When Sérurier was summoned to confirm this report, so that Barlow could sail, he was so alarmed by Monroe's attitude that, in spite of strict orders not to make any binding pledges, he submitted a note affirming that the release of the ships was an indication of the revocation of the decrees. Monroe and Madison, however, considered this statement too unsatisfactory to present to Foster in confirmation of the American position. In his formal reply to Foster's note the Secretary of State simply cited the release of the ships as full proof of the repeal of the decrees. Although Barlow departed, Sérurier was quite mistaken in thinking that the pendulum was swinging back in favor of the French. During the next month the President and Monroe continued to voice their displeasure with France.[23]

Monroe was much more courteous to Foster than he had been to the French Minister, but the policy outlined was just as firm. A few days after the news of the release of the sequestered ships, Monroe informed Foster that the United States had decided not to conduct a formal inquiry into the *Little Belt* affair, since there was no point in settling this or any other minor difference as long as Foster was unable to satisfy American demands about the Orders in Council. Moreover, it did not strike the President as suitable to settle this incident while the *Chesapeake* outrage was still unresolved. From these comments the British Minister concluded that the President intended to leave every minor issue open as a source of irritation.[24] Having reached this point in the discussions with the two Ministers, Monroe and Madison were free to go to Virginia for their customary summer vacations. Until further instructions arrived for Foster and Sérurier, nothing could be accomplished in Washington. Before setting out Monroe drew up instructions for Barlow in harmony with the representations to Foster. The Minister to France was instructed not to request a formal declaration about the decrees, but, assuming that they were no longer operative, he was to demand indemnities for vessels sequestered since November 2, 1810. He was also to press for a modification of the regulations affecting American ships in French ports and a cessation of the licensing system. If these conditions were met then there could be no doubt about the repeal of the decrees. So extensive were the grievances outlined by

Monroe that under other circumstances these instructions might have been the prelude to a rupture.[25]

III

On arriving at Highlands in August, Monroe was cheered to find his wife and Maria Hester in good health. He had little chance, however, to look after his plantation, for he had been home only a few days when he was knocked from his horse by a tree limb, suffering a bruised shoulder and a deep cut on his leg which confined him for nearly a month. Not until late in August could he ride to Montpelier to confer with the President about Foster's recent notes alleging that French privateers were violating American neutrality. The evidence on which these charges rested was so flimsy that not even the British Minister took them seriously, and he was easily satisfied with the promise of an investigation. It seems likely that Monroe and Madison at this time reached an agreement to move toward war if Britain did not respond to American demands by the end of the year. At least this is the inference to be drawn not only from the decisive action undertaken in the late fall but also from Monroe's plea that Madison omit his regular visit to Jefferson to avoid the imputation that administration policy was being directed from Monticello. Madison, who did not consider the consequences of a visit quite so serious, preferred to risk criticism rather than neglect an old friend.[26]

When Madison and Monroe arrived in the Capital late in October for the opening of Congress (summoned a month early by the President), Foster, refreshed by a sojourn in Philadelphia, was already on hand. He immediately revived an old issue by pressing for an answer to his two-month-old note about American activities in East Florida.[27] He received scant satisfaction for his efforts. In an interview on October 30 the Secretary of State asserted in "very plain language that he had been of the opinion that the United States should have seized on that country long ago and held it as a pledge for the payment of the debt due by Spain . . . for illegal captures."

If the United States had refrained from occupying East Florida, Monroe went on, it had been out of tenderness for Spain's position, but Britain's attitude, suggesting an ambition to possess this region, was rapidly eroding American patience with Spain. On the basis of these strong comments Foster concluded that the administration intended

to take East Florida whatever the consequences. He also thought, from
Monroe's account of Barlow's instructions, that relations between
France and the United States were nearing the breaking point.[28] In
an effort to exploit this situation, Foster now proposed to settle the
Chesapeake affair along the lines of the rejected Erskine agreement of
1809. This offer was accepted with indifference, for, as Madison noted
privately, the disposition of this "rusty and corrosive" controversy removed but "one splinter from our wound." To Foster's disappointment
the President did not refer to the settlement in his annual message,
and when he submitted it to Congress he did so without comment.[29]

Foster's action was much too late, for the President, as Monroe was
telling his friends at that time, had decided to "act offensively" if a
general settlement proved impossible.[30] Among the President's advisers
only Gallatin, who preferred to continue commercial warfare, expressed
misgivings about war with Britain.[31] The new spirit was evident in
the President's annual message, in which he proclaimed that "time had
arrived" which "claims from the legislative guardians of the national
rights a system of more ample provision for maintaining them . . ." by
"putting the United States into an armor and an attitude demanded
by the crisis. . . ." To implement this program he suggested that Congress consider raising an auxiliary military force and increasing the
size of the navy.[32] The President did not invite a declaration of war, but
requested only that the nation be readied for that eventuality. Although
the day of threats and economic pressure was over, the administration
still had to convince both the American people and the British ministry
that Madison meant what he said.

In making these recommendations to Congress the President was not
yielding to popular pressure nor deferring to the collective force of the
new congressional leaders, who have become celebrated as the War
Hawks. When the President drafted his message the temper of the new
Congress was an unknown quantity. It was true that Clay's selection
as Speaker had placed a known advocate of aggressive measures in a
position to give important committee assignments to like-minded congressmen. By ignoring seniority Clay deprived John Randolph and
other opponents of administration policy of the key posts they had once
held. At the beginning of the session, while the War Hawks dominated the machinery of the House, but they did not control the Republican majority. Most Republicans were still deeply committed to
the antimilitaristic principles of the party and feared the political consequences to themselves of the increased taxation which war would re-

quire. Even though the Republicans were momentarily jolted out of their apathy at the beginning of the session by the news of the battle of Tippecanoe, it is doubtful that the War Hawks could ever have induced the House to adopt warlike measures without the steady backing of the administration.

At the start of the session, the President, working largely through Monroe, turned to the War Hawks to implement his program. Had he not been determined on war in the event that an agreement could not be reached, he would have cooperated with the main body of the Republicans, who much preferred to continue the policy in effect.[33] The burden of piloting administration measures through Congress was assumed by Monroe, who proved his worth by providing the President with an effective liaison with congressional leaders. Not only was Monroe on friendly terms with many congressmen, including Clay, Calhoun, and William Lowndes, but he commanded wide respect among the Republicans. He also had the great advantage of not being identified with the ineffectual measures of the past. Since it was not Madison's habit to outline details in his messages, Monroe supplied a channel of communication with Congress hitherto lacking in the Madison administration.

The administration program was worked out in late November in a series of conferences, some of which ran far into the night, between Monroe and the House Committee on Foreign Affairs—then far more important than its Senate counterpart.[34] This committee, which had been carefully chosen by Clay to ensure War Hawk control, numbered among its members such prominent War Hawks as Calhoun, Philip M. Key, Joseph Desha, Felix Grundy, and Peter B. Porter as chairman.[35] It was to this body that Monroe delivered the President's pledge to support a declaration of war in the spring if Britain still refused to relent. Porter's report of November 29 was everything the administration desired. Accepting the repeal of the French decrees as an accomplished fact, Porter recommended that 10,000 regulars be enlisted for three years and that the President be authorized to summon an additional 50,000 volunteers if necessary. Porter's resolves also advocated a naval expansion program and the arming of merchant vessels. His report went beyond the President's message in singling out impressment as one of the outrages justifying military preparedness. Madison had omitted this grievance, not because he considered it less vital than in the past, but because he wanted to concentrate attention on the revocation of the Orders in Council as an essential preliminary for an Anglo-

American *rapprochement*. Porter's resolutions were approved by an overwhelming majority, which included many moderate Republicans who did not regard an affirmative vote for the resolves as committing them to support the specific legislation needed to carry them out.[36]

In the Senate, where Monroe lacked a personal following, Madison's bitterest opponents—Giles, Samuel Smith, and Michael Leib—obstructed the administration program. Knowing full well that the President did not want a force larger than 10,000, to avoid a heavy tax increase, Giles (with Federalist support) put through a bill providing for 25,000 regulars. Senatorial persistence frustrated House efforts to modify the bill in accordance with executive wishes. Even Clay and the War Hawks had to accept this higher figure lest by opposing they seem to contradict their demands for belligerent measures.[37] It was in this unsatisfactory form that the President signed the bill. Appalled by the tax program which Gallatin outlined, party regulars objected to additional military and naval expansion. To stir the lagging spirit of Congress the President transmitted a month-old note from Foster with Monroe's reply. In this note Foster had attempted to refute the allegation that Britain was refusing to accept the evidence that the Berlin and Milan Decrees had been repealed in order to use the United States as a means of forcing France to admit British goods to Continental ports. In his skillfully worded reply Monroe managed to leave the impression that this was precisely what Great Britain was trying to do, providing Congress with another proof of the British contempt for American rights. Although the Republicans finally accepted the bill authorizing 50,000 additional volunteers, they refused to enlarge the navy.[38]

If the administration hoped to force the British to revoke the Orders in Council and ban impressment, then Madison and Monroe had to convince the ministry that a new spirit was animating the American government. Knowing that there would be much scepticism on this point, Monroe spelled out the intention of the United States in a letter to an English Whig leader written shortly after the commencement of the session. "War," he told his correspondent, "dreadful as the alternative is, could not do us more injury than the present state of things, and would certainly be more honorable to the nation and gratifying to the publick feelings." [39] In this letter and in almost every public and private statement made by Monroe, by the President, and by congressional orators, the theme of national honor was reiterated again and again as the most compelling motive for a declaration of war. Yet after so many years devoted to economic reprisals, many were not easily convinced that war was imminent. Foster, for one, reported himself in a "sea of uncertainty." [40] While he understood that nonintercourse would remain in effect as long as the Orders were operative, he was by no means convinced that war was likely. With his limited knowledge of American politics, he was at a loss to interpret speeches hostile to war measures which were delivered by congressmen regarded as Republicans. His confusion stemmed in part from his habit of listening to Federalists, who assured him that the President did not want a conflict with England, but was promoting war talk to ensure a Republican victory in 1812. He saw nothing odd in the behavior of Federalist congressmen who claimed that they had voted for war measures to expose Madison's duplicity, by putting through bills which he did not want adopted, although he had given them his approval. Guided by this advice, Foster, in a secret cipher dispatch, suggested to Wellesley in February that the overthrow of the Republicans in the next election would be facilitated if the Orders in Council were kept in effect.[41] Such reports simply confirmed existing prejudices in England.

In order to revitalize the Republicans in Congress, who were showing resistance to the administration tax program, Madison submitted the John Henry letters on March 9, 1812.[42] These documents, which had been in the hands of the Cabinet for a month, had been held back in accordance with a promise not to release them until Henry had left the country. John Henry, an Irishman who had briefly held a commission in the United States Army in 1798, had been sent to New England in 1809 by the Governor General of Canada to offer secessionist leaders British cooperation in the event of an Anglo-American conflict. Although prominent Federalists, unaware of Henry's mission, had freely expressed their distaste for the Republican regime, his reports to the Governor General contained little not to be found in the Federalist press. Considering the Governor General's recompense inadequate, Henry (after failing to obtain a larger payment in England) came to the United States to sell his letters. Henry had arrived in America in 1811 accompanied by a French adventurer posing as the Count de Crillon, who acted as the intermediary in arranging for the sale of the letters for $50,000. This amount, comprising the entire contingent fund for the State Department, was a fantastic price in view of the limited departmental budgets of the day. Yet Monroe and Madison unhesitatingly made this disbursement for letters of which they had read only portions. The Henry letters, although genuine, made disappointing reading. Their most important revelation was that the British had employed an agent to foment subversion in New England. Nonetheless, the purchasers considered them damaging. As Monroe told Jefferson, they proved that the British government had attempted "to promote division and discussion" by appealing to Northern Federalists.[43] Not until the documents had been published did the Republicans realize that the lack of specific information (Henry had deleted all names) greatly weakened the case. Later Monroe unsuccessfully tried to extract additional details from Henry, who had gone to France.

The Henry revelations failed to salvage Madison's tax program, but they provided essential momentum to the War Hawks in laying the groundwork for a declaration of war by inflaming anti-British sentiment. Within a week after the letters had been submitted, Clay and Monroe reached an understanding that the President would recommend a thirty-day embargo as a preliminary to a declaration of war.[44] This arrangement, however, was temporarily postponed while the President re-evaluated his policy in the light of recent news from the Continent. On March 21 Foster received dispatches reaffirming the British refusal to repeal the Orders unless the United States produced a copy of the French decree revoking the restrictive system. Politely Monroe told Foster that it was quite useless to discuss the subject any further, since the President had long since proclaimed the decrees repealed.[45]

Much more disturbing to the administration was the news that French frigates had burned two American merchant ships bound for Spain with grain for Wellington's army. This action, so flatly contradictory to the American position on the decrees, dampened the ardor of the war party and gave greater force to the argument that France should be subjected to the same treatment as Great Britain. As soon as Monroe heard this news he summoned Sérurier. The Secretary's opening words were not calculated to put the Minister at ease: "Well, Sir, it is then decided that we are going to receive nothing but outrages from France! And at what a moment too! At this very instant when we are going to war with her enemies." Ignoring Sérurier's expostulations Monroe went on: "Remember where we were two days ago. You know that warlike measures have been taken for three months past. . . . We have made use of Henry's documents as a last means of exciting the nation and Congress. . . . Within a week we are going to propose an embargo, and the declaration of war . . . to be the immediate consequences of it. . . ." But now France had placed the administration in the "falsest and most terrible position in which a government can find itself. . . ." Powerless to do anything, Sérurier feebly argued that the ships had, after all, been engaged in a trade forbidden by American laws, a contention which Monroe considered quite irrelevant, since they were neutral vessels carrying noncontraband. How, he queried, could the President justify French policy to Congress at the very time when he was preparing to go to war with England over her infringements of American maritime rights? [46] During the next few weeks the French Minister dreaded his interviews with the President and Secretary of State as they relentlessly pressed him for an explanation.

In spite of this development the President continued to move toward war with England. On the last day of March Monroe again met with the Committee on Foreign Affairs to report that the President was still of the same opinion—"that without an accommodation with Great Britain Congress ought to declare war before adjourning." It was, he added in phrases which found a response in the hearts of all the committee members except John Randolph, who recorded the Secretary's remarks, a move necessary to preserve the nation's "character" in the eyes of the world. Monroe then proposed the enactment of a sixty-day embargo, which would allow time for news of recent decisions of the British Cabinet to reach America. On the following day the President requested a sixty-day embargo in a one-sentence message to Congress.[47]

Madison's laconic communication, a characteristic reflection of his concept of the role of the executive, did not provide the nation with any clue as to the purpose of the embargo. Nor did the people receive any clarification from the debates which were conducted behind closed doors. As soon as the embargo was approved, Joseph Gales, the editor of the *National Intelligencer,* asked the Secretary of State for elucidation. This request was not unusual, since the *Intelligencer* functioned as a semiofficial administration organ. Moreover, Gales had an understanding with Monroe not to print anything which might be interpreted as emanating from the State Department without the prior approval of the Secretary.

In response to Gales' inquiry Monroe did not, as might have been expected, propose that the embargo be described as a prelude to war, but he preferred that it be presented as a measure to "prove that the spirit of the nation is up, resolved no longer to submit to the oppression and degradation which have heretofore been inflicted on us almost with impunity by foreign powers." In line with Monroe's suggestions, Gales carefully pointed out that the embargo applied to both Great Britain and France.[48] This editorial, which appeared on April 7, was ambiguous, because the administration was considering whether France should be included in a declaration of war. Not until the President had decided against going to war with France did Monroe draft an explicit statement for the April 14 issue of the *Intelligencer*. In this unsigned editorial, which was so belligerent in tone that it was promptly attributed to Henry Clay, Monroe put his main point bluntly, if inelegantly: "Let war therefore be proclaimed forthwith with England," for only by an "open and manly" war could the nation redeem its honor. France, however, was not to be placed on the same footing, since there was every reason to expect a favorable settlement of recent difficulties. Monroe felt that France's repeal of the Berlin and Milan Decrees, an action acknowledged in the President's proclamation of November 1810, entitled her to special consideration.

Obviously Monroe, like most Americans, believed England to be so deeply involved in the Continental war that she would not be able to launch large-scale operations against the United States. With this comforting thought, Monroe assured the people that there was little danger of an invasion, but if it did occur, then the militia would be able to repulse the landing parties.[49] During the next month he wrote three more editorials pillorying the Federalists for pretending that the war measures were the work of a Republican faction, when the Federalists themselves had voted for most of the bills. Monroe had no qualms about quoting those passages in Washington's farewell address touching on the duty of the people to obey federal laws and condemning factional opposition to administration policies.[50] From this point there was no wavering. Early in May (a month before the declaration of war) Monroe instructed Russell, who had been transferred to England as chargé, to warn Americans there of the imminence of a rupture with England.[51]

Although maritime issues were uppermost in American diplomacy in 1812, in April Monroe had to resolve a minor problem arising from long-range American expansionist aims in Florida. In January 1811, Congress, at the request of the President, had authorized the executive to occupy East Florida, if requested to do so by local authorities or if a foreign power attempted to seize the province. Under the terms of the act (supposedly secret though in reality widely known) former Governor George Mathews of Georgia had been appointed special agent to negotiate with local authorities should the occasion arise. Small naval and military detachments were also sent to the St. Mary's River on the east coast of Florida to be ready in case of need. In June and again in August 1811, Mathews had reported to Monroe that the inhabitants were ready to revolt providing they were promised American support. Monroe made no written reply to Mathews' communications, and it is uncertain whether he sent a verbal answer through Senator William H. Crawford of Georgia, who was acting as an intermediary. Undoubtedly it was assumed in Washington that Mathews would follow the course adopted in West Florida, where dissatisfied elements had been encouraged to revolt without directly involving American officials. Mathews, however, had raised a revolutionary force among local adventurers, which he had already used to seize Amelia Island in the mouth of the St. Mary's. After the "insurgents" requested him to intervene, Mathews employed a detachment of United States riflemen to lay siege to St. Augustine. This imprudent conduct was highly embarrassing to an administration reveling in its own virtue after the John Henry exposé. Mathews, as the President noted. by converting the affair into a "tragicomedy in the face of common sense" had presented him with a "distressing dilemma." The dilemma was resolved on April 4 in a letter from Monroe to Mathews depriving him of his commission on the grounds that he had exceeded his instructions. Mathews' death, as he hastened to Washington to vindicate himself, relieved the administration of further unpleasantness.

Monroe now empowered Governor David B. Mitchell of Georgia to negotiate with Spanish authorities about the return of the island to Spain. Mitchell's instructions contained a significant qualification: he was instructed to see to it that the insurgents, who had placed their trust in the United States, did not come to any harm. This clause provided the Governor with an excuse to continue the occupation of the island and a portion of the Spanish mainland. Most conveniently there was no Spanish Minister in Washington to challenge the occupation, for Madison had never recognized Don Luis de Onís, the appointee of the Spanish regency. Foster's repeated protests also went unanswered.[52] Not long after the declaration of war with England an attempt was made to legalize the occupation by congressional action, but the bill was defeated in the Senate by a combination of Federalists and Northern Republicans unsympathetic to Southern expansionist aims. The administration approached Congress again in January 1813, when

Monroe submitted a report advocating the occupation of all Florida as a war measure. In the absence of proof that there was a British threat to the province, Congress declined to approve continued American action. Consequently, the remaining troops were withdrawn from Spanish territory.[53]

IV

By the middle of May the nation was well on the road to war. The President had started work on a war message and Secretary Monroe was assisting the House Committee on Foreign Affairs in drawing up a manifesto in response to the expected Presidential communication. Late dispatches arriving from Europe on May 23 offered no basis for reversing this course. Russell reported that he did not expect Viscount Castlereagh, who had succeeded Wellesley in the Foreign Office, to alter British policy. This conclusion was confirmed a few days later, when Foster showed Monroe his latest instructions. Castlereagh, like his predecessor, insisted that there could be no relaxation of the Orders since recent events confirmed that the Berlin and Milan Decrees were still applicable to American shipping. Although these instructions were not hostile in tone, Castlereagh gave particular offense when he asserted that Britain admitted no obligation to repeal her Orders even if it were proven that France had revoked the decrees. These instructions, which seemed to close the door on any hope of repeal, gave no hint of the pressures mounting in Britain in favor of modifying the restrictive system. Not until Monroe categorically refused to discuss the status of the French decrees did Foster present the conciliatory proposal authorized by Castlereagh. In return for a suspension of nonintercourse Great Britain promised to cease requiring licenses from American ships engaged in the Continental trade. This offer, which might have paved the way to negotiations had it been made six months earlier, was rejected. Castlereagh's instructions seemed to provide such an excellent justification for war that Monroe pressed the British Minister for a copy. Foster stubbornly declined to provide a complete text, but the correspondence between him and the Secretary of State about the contents of the instructions proved sufficiently damaging when it was submitted to Congress several weeks later.[54]

Dispatches from Barlow, which arrived late in May, were also most disappointing, for the Minister to France had been unable to obtain an explanation for the continued restrictions on American commerce. The widespread public sentiment in favor of war with France caused Sérurier some anxious days until administration policy was clarified in an editorial in the *Intelligencer* on May 30. Adhering to the position that the decrees had been repealed, the writer in the *Intelligencer* admitted that France had evaded American demands for reparations for the vessels destroyed at sea. Future policy toward France, he declared, would depend on the resolution of these grievances.[55]

In his war message on June 1 Madison reviewed the long history of conflict over neutral rights—impressment, illegal blockades, and the harassment of shipping under the Orders in Council all received attention. Following his usual oblique approach, he asked the legislature to decide whether the nation should "continue passive under these progressive usurpations" or whether it should "oppose force to force in defense of . . . national rights." At the end of the message Madison expressed his disapproval of France's recent conduct, but he recommended that action be postponed until further information was available.[56] Two days later, Calhoun, the acting chairman of the House Committee on Foreign Affairs, submitted a war bill and a lengthy manifesto.[57] This manifesto, drafted under Monroe's guidance, summoned the "free-born sons of America" to resist this new threat to independence. In words echoing Monroe's past statements, the committee asserted that the "period has now arrived, when the United States must support their character and station among the nations of the earth, or submit to the most shameful degradation." Both the war message and the manifesto laid stress on neutral rights, which were equated to natural rights, thus making a declaration of war more acceptable to traditionally minded Republicans.

The House quickly approved the declaration of war by a vote of seventy-nine to forty-nine. Except for fifteen Republicans, the opposing votes came from the Federalists, who had been so generous in voting for war preparations.[58] In the Senate, where, as Monroe bitterly commented, "every pestilential scheme has been contrived and managed since the commencement of the session," [59] the war bill was obstructed by the usual antiadministration cabal of Giles, Smith, and Leib, abetted by the Federalists; they brought forth an amendment to limit the war to naval operations, and, when that failed, they tried to further modify the war bill by requiring belligerent measures against France unless proof of the repeal of the decrees was received in a short time.[60]

Although the proceedings of Congress were held behind closed doors, the city was alive with rumors that the war bill was in jeopardy in the Senate. At one point, when obstructionist amendments failed because of a tie, Foster hit on the idea of having a member of his staff see to it that Senator Richard Brent of Virginia, a devoted Madisonian famed for his affection for the bottle, be kept sufficiently intoxicated to be unable to appear in the Senate. This ruse failed: drunk or sober, Brent never missed a roll call.[61]

As long as the war bill remained in the Senate, Foster clutched desperately at every sign indicating that war would also be declared against France. Thus on June 9 he informed Castlereagh that Monroe favored war with both nations. His source? A newspaper report of a public meeting in Richmond at which Monroe's son-in-law, George Hay, dissented from resolutions advocating war with Great Britain. He had offered as a substitute a resolve condemning both nations for violating American rights and leaving it to the wisdom of Congress to decide the proper course. Foster failed to realize that these resolutions were in harmony with the administration policy of continued pressure on France.[62] In the Senate, Crawford, George W. Campbell of Tennessee, and George Bibb of Kentucky were able to fend off the antiadministration forces. Indeed, it seems that Giles and his associates were much more interested in harassing the President than in preventing a declaration of war, for Giles, Leib, and Smith all voted for the war bill, which was approved on June 17 by a vote of nineteen to thirteen.[63]

When Monroe notified the British Minister of the declaration of war, Foster, with a determination more creditable to his persistence than his judgment, suggested that hostilities be suspended until the news reached England. Since he could not guarantee that the ministry would accept an armistice, Madison rejected the offer. A few days after the arrival of the first unconfirmed press reports that the Orders had been repealed, Foster renewed his offer and was again turned down. As Monroe explained, the repeal of the Orders was not sufficient for the restoration of peace—impressment must also cease. Foster's final interviews with Monroe were on the same easy footing which had prevailed during his mission. In spite of the rupture between the two nations Foster willingly accepted Monroe's invitation to tea after their final conference.[64]

Sérurier found but scant comfort in the declaration of war against England, for it was obvious that anti-French sentiment was mounting. In June he had been relieved to see little of Madison and Monroe, who, he thought, were avoiding him to prevent the impression that they were under French influence. Monroe did nothing to put Sérurier at ease during their first conference after the declaration of war. The French Minister was bluntly informed that only administration pressure had prevented Congress from including France in the declaration of war. Sérurier found his position so uncomfortable that he took an extended vacation to be freed from the constant reproaches of Monroe and the President.[65]

When he returned in the fall the atmosphere was much friendlier, for Napoleon had finally provided a formal statement of the repeal of the old decrees in the form of a new decree dated at St. Cloud, April 28, 1811. When Barlow was presented with this document, the French Foreign Minister professed his incredulity that the United States was apparently unaware of this document, since a copy had been given to Russell and another sent to Sérurier. All this was patently absurd and fooled no one. The Decree of St. Cloud was obviously predated. In no position to quibble about fine points, Barlow accepted it without comment. The Decree of St. Cloud provided the justification needed for the British Cabinet to revoke the Orders in Council. On June 23 the British Cabinet, which had been reorganized after the assassination of Spencer Perceval (a leading proponent of the Orders) formally repealed them. The members of the Cabinet questioned the authenticity of the French decree, but found it convenient to accept it as valid.[66] Following the revelation of the Decree of St. Cloud, there was not the slightest change in French policy—seizures and sequestrations continued and nothing was done to compensate the United States for previous violations of neutral rights.

As soon as he received the French decree, but before he knew that the Orders in Council had been revoked, the President ordered Monroe to revise Russell's instructions. Previously Russell had been authorized to agree to a truce if England would give a written pledge to end impressment. Now, since it was assumed the Orders would be repealed after the publication of the Decree of St. Cloud, Russell was given authority to accept an informal understanding on impressment as a basis for an armistice. This proposal was rejected by Castlereagh, who refused to abandon a right considered essential to maintain Britain's naval strength.[67] Impressment proved as much an obstacle to Anglo-American understanding in 1812 as it had in 1806. The President also rejected a second armistice proposal submitted by Foster from Halifax as soon as he learned of the repeal of the Orders.[68] There seemed no point in accepting Foster's offer, since it did not contain a guarantee that impressment would cease. Although in the months before the war the dispute over the Orders in Council had occupied a more prominent place than impressment in administration statements, it was by no means forgotten. Once the war began, Madison was determined that it should not end until England had put an end to this detested practice which had been a source of Anglo-American irritation for a decade.

CHAPTER 17

THE NATION
IN PERIL

ONCE THE WAR began, Monroe chafed at continuing in the State Department, now a post of secondary importance. A military command seemed a much more satisfactory way of serving the nation. The fact that he was fifty-four was not considered a bar, for most of the field commanders were considerably older. Although the President was willing to gratify his friend, the obstacles seemed insurmountable. At first Madison thought of entrusting him with the command of the invasion of Canada, a project much favored by Monroe as the best way to wring concessions from the British. The President was deterred, however, by the resentment he could expect if he placed Monroe over officers who had achieved much higher rank during the Revolution than the colonelcy held by the Secretary of State. Monroe also considered raising a volunteer regiment in Virginia officered by friends. He gave this up reluctantly when all whom he consulted reminded him that he could perform much more valuable service to the country by remaining in Washington than in such a minor military capacity. Moreover, as Monroe remarked, if he entered the army in a low rank, many would conclude that he had such an insatiable thirst for military glory that he was willing to sacrifice the interests of the nation.[1] When it was learned that General William Hull had surrendered at Detroit in August 1812 without firing a shot, Madison was on the verge of replacing him with Monroe, who had always been popular in the West. Although this arrangement was approved by the Western congressmen still in Washington, it was abandoned in the face of the widespread expectation in the West that

William Henry Harrison, the victor of Tippecanoe, would be the new commander.[2] A month later, when another disaster seemed imminent on the Niagara frontier, Monroe's name was proposed as a replacement for General Henry Dearborn, who seemed incapable of either organizing his forces or controlling his subordinates. To circumvent the problem of placing Monroe, if he were made a major general, over senior officers of the same grade, Madison planned to give him the rank of lieutenant general. Once again new developments induced the President to rule out the appointment.[3]

In early September, when the possibility of placing Monroe in command of the northern army was under consideration, public criticism of Secretary of War William Eustis had risen to such a pitch that his removal was unavoidable. Eustis, a well-to-do New Englander who had served as a surgeon during the Revolution, had been given this normally undemanding post as a reward for his services to the party. Unfortunately, he lacked the ability to cope with the larger problems with which his department was confronted after the outbreak of the war. The case against him was bluntly put by Senator Crawford in a letter to Monroe: "A Sec. of War, who instead of forming general and comprehensive arrangements for the organization of his troops, and for the successful prosecution of the campaign, consuming his time in reading advertisements of petty merchants, to find out where he may purchase a 100 shoes, or 200 hats. . . ." ought not to be retained in such a demanding post.[4]

All looked to Monroe, who was considered the only member of the Cabinet with any knowledge of military affairs, as the ideal replacement. From the beginning of the war Monroe had been the recipient of a steady stream of letters from young officers who criticized military arrangements and recommended reforms. When General George Izard sent Monroe plans for consolidating the engineers with the artillery corps, the Secretary of State turned them over to the President. Izard also reported to Monroe about the inadequacy of the fortifications of New York, for he, like the other officers, deemed it pointless to inform Eustis. General Dearborn went so far as to send copies of his letters to Eustis to the Secretary of State to ensure that his requests received proper attention.[5] Although Eustis' withdrawal was postponed until after the presidential election, Madison had already decided in September to place Monroe in the War Department.[6]

Out of consideration for his friend, Madison was also anxious not to damage Monroe's candidacy for the presidential succession by placing a potential rival in the State Department. Jefferson was considered for the slot, but the plan was dropped before the former President was consulted—to bring him into the Cabinet would reinforce the cries of those denouncing the excessive "Virginia influence" in the government. The simplest solution would have been to permit Eustis and Monroe to exchange posts, but, as Gallatin sensibly pointed out, this would improve the efficiency of the War Department but do nothing to strengthen the administration.[7] As soon as Eustis resigned in December, Monroe was transferred to the War Department on an acting basis, while the Comptroller of the Treasury, Richard Rush, disharged the now-routine duties of the State Department.

Much to Monroe's dismay, his appointment as permanent Secretary was thwarted by a senatorial opposition which had nothing against him except that he was a Virginian. The temper of some political leaders can be judged from Josiah Quincy's comments in a speech in the House on January 5, 1813. Although Quincy was a Federalist, there were many Republicans who agreed with him when he declared that it was "a curious fact . . . that for these twelve years past the whole affairs of this country have been managed, and its fortunes reversed, under the influence of a cabinet little less than despotic, composed to all efficient purposes, of two Virginians and a foreigner." And now, he continued, the President intended to make a Virginian his successor.[8] Monroe learned of the resistance to his nomination from Senator Crawford, who told him that a Senate confirmation was by no means assured.[9] Rather than risk a rebuff after the recent military reverses, Madison continued the quest for a Secretary of War. Monroe readily acquiesced in this decision, since he was promised a military command after a permanent occupant for the War Department had been chosen.[10]

As soon as Monroe became Acting Secretary of War, the House and Senate military committees, which had been dozing over the President's request in his annual message for additional forces, sprang into action. Both chairmen called on Monroe for a report on manpower requirements. With an energy impressive to the most hardened congressmen, Monroe drew up a comprehensive statement of the forces needed for coastal defense and for the offensive operations planned for the summer of 1813.

His report called for the expansion of the army beyond the current strength of 35,000, which he considered inadequate for war operations. This force, as he pointed out, had not been significantly enlarged by last session's bill allowing the President to summon 50,000 volunteers.

Under the volunteer bill, which had permitted the men to form the units themselves, very few regiments had been established. Most men preferred to remain in the state militia rather than join volunteer units, since volunteers might be summoned for a year's duty at any time within a three-year period. He proposed that this measure be replaced with a bill to recruit 20,000 additional regulars for one year. The anticipated manpower requirements for the coming year were carefully analyzed. According to Monroe's estimate 17,000 men would be needed to garrison the key coastal cities, with the largest concentration (a total of 4,500) to be divided between Savannah and Mobile in order to prevent a British seizure of Florida. The remainder would be employed in the invasion of Canada. The latter operation, upon which Monroe believed victory to depend, would require an active force of 20,000 with 10,000 men kept in reserve. He also recommended that the President be allowed to appoint all officers below the rank of field grade, rather than let the men choose them as had been the case in the old volunteer act.

Impressed by the cogency of Monroe's reasoning and the critical situation of the country, Congress approved his recommendations with only one serious alteration. The economy-minded legislators reduced the bounty for enlistments from the forty dollars recommended by the Acting Secretary to sixteen dollars, a sum insufficient to offset the attractions of state militia service.[11] Consequently, recruiting under this law was not notably successful. Although the Republicans were suitably cooperative about military expansion, they balked at Gallatin's tax program, refusing to approve anything but a bill authorizing a loan. Indeed, throughout the war Congress's failure to adopt adequate tax measures forced the administration to rely on loans, which were extremely difficult to float in view of the hostility of the commercial community to the war.

During his ten weeks of service as Acting Secretary of War, Monroe drew up plans for the Canadian invasion, which he expected to command. He envisaged the first strike at Niagara, for he believed it would be easy to overcome the small garrison at Fort George, which he correctly estimated at less than 2,000 men. After capturing the fort, the army was to move overland to Kingston, a move making it unnecessary to secure control of Lake Ontario before commencing the campaign. Once these objectives had been achieved, then the operation against Montreal and Quebec could be conducted either through the St. Lawrence River or Lake Champlain. In his preliminary sketches for the

invasion he was insistent that it not be launched before adequate supplies had been collected as close as possible to the enemy positions.[12]
Monroe was one of the few military leaders during the war who placed
proper emphasis upon this factor in large-scale operations. By the time
John Armstrong, the new Secretary of War, entered office on February
13, 1813, the arrangements for the northern campaign were well under
way.

II

Although the selection of Armstrong, one of Madison's unhappiest
appointments, had largely been determined by the need to strengthen
the administration, it was only after General Henry Dearborn and
William H. Crawford had declined that Madison turned his attention
to two New Yorkers—Governor Daniel D. Tompkins and John Armstrong, both of whom had earned his gratitude by their loyal support
during the election of 1812, when they defeated De Witt Clinton's
antiwar faction.[13] In view of the fact that much of the burden of fighting would fall on the New York militia, it was obviously advantageous
to bring an important New York leader into the administration. From
a personal point of view Tompkins was much preferable, but if he
vacated the governorship the Clintonians might regain control of the
state and be in a position to impede the war effort. Moreover Tompkins
was completely lacking in military experience. Although Gallatin was
willing to take over the War Department and yield the Treasury to
Tompkins, Madison chose Armstrong, who was then in command of
New York City's defenses with the rank of brigadier general.

This choice was made with considerable misgiving on the part of
the Cabinet members and prominent Republicans, for Armstrong's
shortcomings were well known. Gallatin, who admitted that the appointment would substantially strengthen the administration, feared
that Armstrong might not bring to the Cabinet that "entire unity of
feeling, that disinterested zeal, that personal attachment which are so
useful in producing hearty cooperation and unity of action." [14] Jefferson some years earlier had singled out two other faults: the New Yorker's
cynicism and his implacable hatreds.[15] Armstrong's abrasive personality
and his acid tongue had always made him difficult to work with. His
reputation for duplicity was a subject of commonplace gossip. Nearly
the same age as Monroe, Armstrong had risen to the rank of major during the Revolution, when he had served as an aide-de-camp to General

Horatio Gates. Still in service when the war ended, he had achieved considerable notoriety as the author of the Newburgh letters, earning a reputation for intrigue, which his subsequent career had done nothing to lessen.[16] After his marriage to a sister of Robert Livingston, he became a power in New York State politics, first as a Federalist and later moving with the Livingstons into the Republican camp in the early 1790s. After serving briefly in the United States Senate he replaced his brother-in-law in the unrewarding post of Minister to Napoleonic France, where he remained until 1811. If he had never demonstrated singular ability, he had always been competent. Once in the Cabinet another fault became evident—he tended to shirk routine departmental work.

A more fortunate appointment on Madison's part was that of William Jones, who replaced Paul Hamilton, another victim of public criticism, as Secretary of the Navy. The removal of this agreeable South Carolinian was not quite as justified as the forced retirement of Eustis, for the navy was proving its worth in contrast to the incompetence manifested by the army. However, Hamilton's constant inebriation— he was regularly reported drunk by noon—was scandalizing his colleagues and the members of Congress. When efforts to control his drinking failed, Madison took him to task, chiding him for appearing in a drunken condition at a public ceremony on board the *Constitution.* Deeply hurt by the President's reproaches, Hamilton abruptly resigned.[17] William Jones, who had declined the post in 1801, was a former sea captain with substantial mercantile interests in Philadelphia. Not a distinguished figure, he was nevertheless an efficient administrator with little interest in political matters.[18]

Armstrong, who anticipated that he would be "assailed by personal and party malevolence," went to the Capital girded for battle on both the military and political fronts.[19] From the outset there was friction between him and Monroe. Throughout his career Monroe had been able to work harmoniously with difficult and even hostile colleagues; however, toward Armstrong he displayed none of his usual tolerance. In the first place, the Secretary of War, who nurtured the Livingston family grudge against Monroe, did not disguise his animosity. Moreover, now that he was in high office Armstrong set his sights on the Presidency. To accomplish this ambition it was essential that the principal contender for the succession be denied whatever glory might accrue from the war. Consequently, Armstrong blocked his colleague's appointment as lieutenant general in command of the northern army.

This he managed, not by frontal opposition, but by convincing the President that Monroe should be appointed a brigadier general to avoid the criticism which would arise if an entirely new rank were created. When Monroe was informed of this arrangement, he refused to accept. To leave the Cabinet for a junior military rank, he told Madison, would create the false impression that he had a "passion for the military life." Nor did he see how he could render any effective service under Dearborn, who had given "no proof of activity or military talent" during the past year. His presence with the northern army would merely augment the squabbles among the junior officers.[20] Monroe's resentment reached a peak when he discovered that Armstrong intended to direct the invasion of Canada in person. In a long letter to Madison he protested this fusion of the office of commander of the army and that of Secretary of War, which would inevitably diminish the President's role as Commander in Chief. Nor would Madison be in a position to supervise a Secretary of War functioning as a field commander 600 miles away. The proper place for the Secretary of War, according to Monroe, was close to the President, so that he could serve as a channel for communicating with the generals in the field. Gallatin also disapproved of this plan, which would deprive the War Department of badly needed supervision, but, nonetheless, Madison deferred to Armstrong's determination.[21]

III

This blow to Monroe's ambitions was softened by the prospect that the diplomatic theater was about to resume its former importance. Shortly after Armstrong was appointed, Monroe received a dispatch from John Quincy Adams, the Minister to Russia, presenting a proposal from the Czar to mediate between Great Britain and the United States. This timely offer, which Madison promptly accepted, was sufficient to persuade reluctant Americans to subscribe to the fifteen-million-dollar loan offered by the Treasury. With the administration's financial problems somewhat eased, Gallatin, weary of his post after twelve years, felt free to request an appointment as one of the peace commissioners to be sent to St. Petersburg. He welcomed this appointment not only from a personal inclination for diplomacy, but because it would give him a respite from Armstrong, who, with a total disregard for his colleague's political position, had named as adjutant general Gallatin's most relentless enemy, William Duane, editor of the

Philadelphia *Aurora*. Duane's sole qualification for this post was his power to advance Armstrong's presidential ambitions through the columns of the *Aurora*.[22] Monroe would have preferred adding a Westerner (he had Henry Clay in mind) to the three-man peace commission, which also included James A. Bayard, a Delaware Federalist, and John Quincy Adams. Although Monroe anticipated difficulty in securing Gallatin's confirmation in the Senate, he acquiesced.[23] The instructions to the commissioners, which Monroe drew up in April, restated the long-standing complaints against Great Britain, singling out the abandonment of impressment as a *sine qua non* for ending the war. Although the commissioners were to attempt to obtain a recognition of the doctrine "free ships make free goods," it was left to their discretion to accept terms short of this principle. In a confidential paragraph Monroe ordered them not to renew those provisions of Jay's Treaty enabling Canadians to trade with Indians living within the jurisdiction of the United States. With slight modification these instructions remained in force for the next year.[24]

Before the commissioners sailed in May they raised additional questions about American policy, which the Secretary of State answered in private letters. Gallatin, perturbed that the absence of a clear statement about East Florida might hamper negotiations, if Britain and Russia supported Spain's interest, was assured that orders had been issued for the withdrawal of all federal troops from Florida. When Bayard appealed for some latitude on impressment, since he felt Britain would never yield on a point so vital to her survival, Monroe consulted the President, who insisted that it was an essential condition for peace. Monroe told the commissioners that the President considered it better to have no treaty than leave this issue unresolved.[25] The Secretary also prepared a description of an official uniform to give the commissioners a dignity suitable for European ceremonial occasions. It was to consist of a single-breasted blue coat lined with buff or white silk; the collar to be a standing one, and the cuffs, buttonholes and pocket flaps embroidered with gold or silver thread. Monroe felt that this coat worn over white or buff breeches would be "handsome . . . , national and economical." [26] His suggestions were adopted, but the commissioners did not report whether the uniform had the effect promised by the Secretary.[27]

The Senate, as Monroe had anticipated, balked at confirming Gallatin. The Secretary of the Treasury had never been popular with the

Southern Republicans, who contemptuously referred to him as the foreigner responsible for perpetuating Hamiltonian fiscal policies. Unfortunately, the recent appointment of Crawford as Minister to France had deprived the President of the services of the one Senator then capable of checking Giles, who demanded Gallatin's resignation from the Treasury as the price for confirmation. When Madison refused to agree, the Senate rejected Gallatin by a one-vote margin in August—nearly three months after the commissioners had sailed.[28] The anti-Gallatin forces then raised difficulties about the proposal to appoint Jonathan Russell Minister to Sweden, a move recommended by the President, since peace negotiations were expected to take place in that country. The opposition to Russell was not personal, as it had been with Gallatin, but it concealed a maneuver to force the administration to expose France's duplicity in connection with the predated Decree of St. Cloud. The Senators, who had heard reports of Russell's denial that he had received the decree while chargé, wanted to bring his statement out into the open. The Senate committee appointed to call on the President was denied an interview; not only was Madison seriously ill, but this direct approach to the executive was considered an infringement on his constitutional position. When the Senator stubbornly refused to confer with Monroe, he became so distrustful of this opposition group that he believed them capable of planning for the day when Giles, the President pro tem of the Senate, would succeed to the Presidency, since at that time Madison and Vice-President Gerry were both thought to be fatally ill. The Senate took its revenge for the President's rebuff in a resolution declaring the Swedish mission inexpedient.[29]

The House took up where the Senate failed. In June, Daniel Webster, a fledgling Federalist representative from New Hampshire, introduced a resolution calling on the executive for information as to whether or not Russell had received the decree. After the resolve was modified to allow the President to omit whatever portions of Russell's dispatches he considered harmful to the public interest, it was passed with Republican support.[30] Monroe's report of July 12, made in answer to this request, was like all administration statements relating to the Berlin and Milan Decrees—a carefully woven fabric of equivocation and evasion, which neither commented on the authenticity of the Decree of St. Cloud nor clearly answered the question whether it had been known in Washington before Barlow had transmitted it. Since Russell's letter denying knowledge of the decree had been marked private, it was not included in Monroe's report. In view of the administration's insistence that the French restrictions had been repealed by the Cadore letter in 1810, anything casting doubt on the validity of the date of the Decree of St. Cloud was not welcome. Fortunately Monroe's report was secret, which deprived the Federalist editors of the pleasure of poking fun at the Secretary's obvious evasions.[31]

IV

During the late summer of 1813 the gloomy news of the failure of the operations in the Niagara theater trickled into Washington. Although Fort George had been captured in May, the British commander had escape with his force intact. General Dearborn, who lacked confidence as well as the capacity for bold action, had then decided that his army was too weak to invade Upper Canada. Consequently, he lost the opportunity to take Kingston and win control of Lake Ontario.[32] As a result of this mismanagement and for his failure to prevent the senseless burning of York (now Toronto), the capital of Upper Canada, Dearborn was removed. Technically, operations were now in charge of General James Wilkinson, recently shifted from New Orleans because of doubts about his ability to defend that city, but in fact Armstrong took over command in August from his headquarters in Sackett's Harbor. Wilkinson's appointment to the northern command produced a crisis of a kind not uncommon during the war. His second-in-command, General Wade Hampton, who had expected an independent command, resented his subordination to an officer about whose name so many unsavory stories of intrigue and double-dealing had gathered. Hampton, like most officers, considered Wilkinson a disgrace to the army and regarded his continuation in the service as political favoritism. When Hampton, who commanded the forces at Lake Champlain, refused to receive orders from Wilkinson, Armstrong resolved the conflict by the unusual arrangement of allowing all orders from Wilkinson to Hampton to be transmitted through his office, which, as Monroe sarcastically commented, left Hampton under Wilkinson's command only in a "metaphysical sense which nobody understood." The movement against Montreal, not begun until October and fatally hampered by the bickering between Wilkinson and Hampton, foundered in November without ever coming close to its objective.

Since forces in the Niagara region were weakened to reinforce the army attacking Montreal, it was necessary to evacuate Fort George in December. When General George McClure gave up the fort, he permitted the burning of Newark, an act he mistakenly believed authorized by Armstrong, and thus set off a chain of reprisals which devastated the American settlements along the Niagara.[33]

The collapse of the northern campaign brought to the fore Monroe's resentment against Armstrong, which now assumed the proportions, to quote John Randolph, of a "deadly feud." [34] The tension between them had already been apparent early in the summer when they clashed over the ultimate objective of the large British fleet which had appeared in the Chesapeake in the spring. Regarding this force as a prelude to an invasion directed against Washington, Monroe urged that immediate steps be taken to strengthen the defenses of the Capital. Armstrong, on the other hand, mocked these apprehensions and insisted that the expedition was only intended to harass the Bay area. In his opinion the state militia was adequate to defend the region. Madison, accepting the conclusion of the Secretary of War, left defense arrangements to the governors of the states, who were by no means happy to have this responsibility shifted to their ill-trained and poorly equipped militia units.

Monroe was especially concerned about the need for an intelligence service to provide advance warning of enemy movements. Consequently, he suggested to Madison that a communications system based on a chain of expresses under a central command be set up along the Chesapeake. In view of Armstrong's persistent refusal to admit the possibility of a thrust at the Capital, this proposal was not implemented, and when the invasion took place in 1814 there was still no means of obtaining reliable information about enemy movements.[35]

Although Armstrong was supremely confident about the accuracy of his opinion, he experienced a moment of doubt when a British squadron appeared at the mouth of the Potomac in July 1813. While the Secretary of War hastened to Fort Washington with 600 regulars, Monroe rode down the river with a handful of "gentlemen volunteers." After locating the British detachment digging wells on Blackstone's Island, he requested 350 regulars to capture the British force. His offer to "take charge of this little expedition" was promptly vetoed by the Secretary of War, who refused to part with half the regular troops available to defend Washington for an operation which, he reminded Monroe, was properly the job of the militia.[36] The alarm subsided after the British withdrew from the Potomac, but raids continued along the shores of the Chesapeake Bay.

The open hostility between the Secretaries had embarrassed their colleagues. It seemed, as Secretary Jones commented, that they were "really running for the presidential purse intent only on each other" rather than concentrating on their official duties.[37] Monroe was aware of these comments and realized that this rivalry could hamper the war effort; consequently, in the fall he talked to a number of Virginia congressmen, suggesting that they should withdraw his name as a presidential candidate. The congressmen understood his motives, but they dissuaded him, arguing that a public declaration of this kind might be taken as a confession that he despaired of victory.[38]

The rivalry between the Secretaries was in abeyance after Armstrong's departure for Sackett's Harbor in August, but it erupted in full force when he returned to Washington in December after a leisurely six-weeks journey through New York State. The Secretary of War had been back in the Capital only a few days when Monroe wrote the President urging Armstrong's immediate removal as the only way to prevent the ruin of the administration and of the "whole republican party and cause." He made this demand on the grounds of the mismanagement of the northern invasions and on the basis of undeniable evidence of Armstrong's disloyalty to the President. On the day on which Monroe wrote this letter, he had learned from Jones that Armstrong was actively lobbying for the enactment of a conscription bill. Without consulting the President, the Secretary of War was informing his friends in Congress that the only way to raise an army large enough to bring victory was to divide the able-bodied men into small groups and make each group responsible for maintaining one man in the army for the duration of the war. Such a proposal, terrifying to orthodox Republicans, would undermine congressional support for the administration. Monroe also informed the President that General Hampton had informed him that Armstrong was "engaged in the seduction of the officers of the army" by promising them promotions and encouraging them to look to him rather than to Madison for advancement.[39]

Monroe's facts were quite correct, but Madison, reluctant to advertise the disharmony within the Cabinet, preferred to retain Armstrong. However, he took the precaution of ordering the Secretary of War to remain in Washington, and he also began to scrutinize military plans more carefully. The President might not have been quite so tolerant had he been aware that Armstrong was complaining about the Virginia influence in the Cabinet and threatening to resign unless he was given his rightful place in the administration.[40] Moreover, Armstrong's bitterness led him to express his views freely about the President's incompetence during the war emergency.[41] The plans for operations in 1814, which were drawn up in June, reveal Monroe's influence.[42] Once again Kingston was to be approached from the Niagara, with a strong concentration to be stationed on Burlington Heights to prevent a flanking movement. Echoing Monroe's plan of the year before, provisions were made for a large enough force in order to provide an adequate garrison for the Niagara frontier during the advance on Montreal.

The President's decision to retain Armstrong had probably been made easier by the hope that peace might not be far distant. On December 30, 1813, Madison had received Castlereagh's offer of direct negotiations in place of Russian mediation. The President had hesitated briefly before agreeing, since he thought it might be improper to accept without first ascertaining Russia's reaction. He was won over by Monroe, who argued that Russia could scarcely object to direct negotiations, if she sincerely wished to see Great Britain and the United States at peace. Monroe also felt that the British offer had been prompted by a desire to exclude the Czar, who was known to favor a liberal definition of neutral rights.[43] The President added Clay and Jonathan Russell to the peace commissioners, and Gallatin was now confirmed when his resignation from the Treasury was announced. The Treasury Department was first offered to Alexander J. Dallas, a distinguished Philadelphia attorney with excellent financial connections, but he refused to work in a Cabinet which included Armstrong. Madison then turned to Senator George W. Campbell of Tennessee, a stalwart administration supporter. Apart from two years as chairman of the Ways and Means Committee, Campbell had little knowledge of finances. His rapport with the financial community was so slight that Monroe had to negotiate with the Philadelphia bankers in the spring of 1813 to take up part of a ten-million-dollar loan. Much more successful was the appointment of thirty-four-year-old Richard Rush of Pennsylvania to replace Attorney General William Pinkney.[44]

The new instructions drafted by Monroe for the peace commissioners differed but little from those drawn up the year before. The most important addition was the proposal that the United States would agree to exclude all British seamen from American vessels, if the British would prohibit impressment. In a confidential paragraph the commissioners were instructed to urge the advisability of cession of Canada to the United States as a means of preventing future Anglo-American conflicts.[45] As the months passed without word from the commissioners, hopes for an early peace faded. The collapse of Napoleon in February 1814 not only made it unlikely that the United States would obtain concessions from England, but placed the nation in a much more critical position. Great Britain could now, if she wished, launch a massive invasion of the North American continent.

In June 1814, Madison reviewed American policy with his Cabinet in the light of the new developments. Although the prospect of giving up the American demand that impressment cease was a painful one, it was agreed that the commissioners be allowed to defer this issue to subsequent negotiations, if no agreement were possible at the peace conference. Before Monroe could incorporate this decision in a dispatch, a month-old letter arrived from Bayard and Gallatin, who spelled out in unequivocal terms that peace was impossible on the basis of existing instructions in view of the bitterness of the British people against the United States. Once again Madison conferred with his Secretaries, who agreed with him that the commissioners must be empowered to omit impressment entirely.[46] If Monroe felt any satisfaction in seeing the administration back at the point which had been reached in 1806, he refrained from comment.

Prior to the modification of the American peace terms, the administration had already revised its commercial policy to adjust to changing conditions on the Continent. In December 1813, Congress had placed an embargo on all shipments to Europe in an effort to increase the pressure on Great Britain by cutting off trade with those portions of the Continent under her control. By March 1814, this measure was obsolete, for it had the effect of excluding Americans from those Continental states which had re-established their independence. On the last day of March, Republican congressmen were astounded by the President's request that the embargo be repealed except for those portions relating to trade with the enemy. Since Madison characteristically had not explained his reasons, Calhoun, on behalf of the House Committee on Foreign Affairs, turned to Monroe for enlightenment. Together they drew up a report endorsing repeal, which was presented as necessary to prevent American merchants from losing the benefits of trade with independent Continental powers.[47] There was still resistance in Congress, for many believed that the repeal had been requested because the British naval commander at Halifax had insisted upon it as a preliminary to an armistice. It was true that a truce had been offered which Madison had rejected, since it did not provide for a cessation of naval hostilities. Not until Monroe personally explained this matter to John Wayles Eppes, the chairman of the Ways and Means Committee, did Congress revise the embargo along administration lines.[48] Having reached this point, the administration could only continue to prosecute the war while awaiting the outcome of the negotiations at Ghent.

CHAPTER 18

THE CAPITAL INVADED

IN MIDSUMMER 1814, just as the northern campaign was commencing, the conflict over Armstrong flared up again. Although the
Secretary had confined himself to the affairs of his office since the
beginning of the year, he had not run his department in a manner
calculated to advance the war effort. From his desk in Washington
there was a steady flow of orders to the officers in the field concerning
matters of detail, which the commanders felt could only be resolved
by the officer on the spot. Major General George Izard, one of the
most capable young commanders, resented these directives which
seemed to emanate from a "pedagogue." The irritated officers not only
protested to the Secretary of War, but, suspecting that their complaints
would not reach the President, they also informed Monroe of their
grievances.[1] Monroe and Armstrong were also at odds once more over
the defense of the Bay area. Monroe was convinced that both the increased British naval activity in the West Indies and the reports of
the large concentrations of troops in European ports intended for
America indicated an approaching attack on Washington. All this
Armstrong grandly dismissed as a fable, never ceasing to affirm his
confidence in the adequacy of the militia. Even if it were true that a
force of 4,000 regulars had been collected in the West Indies, he did
not believe this force large enough to make "any serious impression
on any important points of our bays or sea-coast."[2]

Yielding to Monroe's pressure, Madison on July 2 established a new
military district (the tenth) to include the Potomac and Chesapeake
Bay. Ignoring Armstrong's recommendations, the President placed the
new district under the command of William Winder, a successful
Maryland lawyer. From the outset Winder was hampered by the hos-

tility of the Secretary of War, who refused to allow him to call out the militia prior to a direct invasion threat in order to train the men and inspect the equipment of the state units. Armstrong also neglected to expedite Winder's requisitions for supplies. Madison, who had gone to Virginia, was not aware of this obstructionism until late in July when Monroe went to the White House as soon as he learned of the President's return. Routing Madison from bed, the Secretary of State informed him of Armstrong's conduct. The next day the President ordered the Secretary of War to permit Winder to call out the Pennsylvania and Maryland militia. These orders, sent by ordinary post, did not catch up with Winder for three weeks. In fact, he did not get them until two weeks before the battle of Bladensburg.[3]

Following the discovery that Armstrong had disregarded his orders, Madison drafted a severe letter of reprimand on August 13, in which he also took the Secretary to task for infringing on the authority of the executive.[4] Before the issues relating to Armstrong's conduct could be resolved, the news of the appearance on August 16 of a large British squadron at the mouth of the Potomac pushed aside every consideration not relevant to the defense of the Capital. In the face of this new crisis, the President preferred not to force Armstrong's resignation.

Although the Secretary of War continued in the Cabinet for another month, his role in organizing the defenses of the city was insignificant. The President assumed direction of military affairs, closely assisted by Monroe and Winder. It was quite natural in this crisis that Madison should rely more and more on the Secretary of State, who not only inspired general confidence, but whose predictions about British operations had been proven correct.

Even though the President in July had belatedly recognized that the Capital was a prime military target, he does not seem to have been entirely convinced. At that time he declined to allow Monroe to publish an editorial in the *Intelligencer* to alert the people to the danger of an invasion. The Secretary of State felt that unless the nation was warned, the sudden appearance of a large enemy force might have a disastrous effect—an impact that would be all the greater, since even the "government shakes to its foundation." He also considered it important to give the inhabitants of the seaboard towns some proof of the government's concern for their welfare.

This editorial was withheld largely because Secretary of the Treasury Campbell feared that such a portentous warning might jeopardize the success of his new six-million-dollar loan. Monroe was skeptical about the chances of the loan in view of the general apathy of the business community toward the war. Indeed, as he then counseled the President, the only practical solution for the nation's fiscal problems was to call Congress into special session to provide needed taxes, to prohibit the export of specie, and to charter a national bank.[5] Monroe's pessimism about the loan was justified. By the end of July, only a third had been subscribed. Early in August the President, agreeing with Monroe's advice, instructed him to summon Congress to meet on September 19.

Madison's worries over finances, the status of the peace negotiations, and the quarrels within his Cabinet were all superseded by the disaster which overwhelmed Washington at the end of August. On the sixteenth of that month, Sir Alexander Cochrane, commanding a flotilla of fifty ships with an expeditionary force of nearly 5,000 regulars under General Robert Ross, appeared at the mouth of the Potomac, where he joined Admiral Cockburn's raiding squadron. After a brief war council the British commanders agreed to attack Washington by moving overland from Benedict on the Patuxent River, while a diversionary force ascended the Potomac to capture Alexandria.[6] The burden of organizing the Capital's defenses fell largely on Winder, who was later severely criticized for his shortcomings. While he lacked experience, it must be said in his defense that he received no cooperation from Armstrong, who insisted that the British objective was Baltimore, which could be defended by the local militia. Far too much fell on Winder, who recklessly expended his energy during the next week, so that he was on the verge of collapse on the day his army faced the enemy at Bladensburg. His task was further complicated by the resignation of General John P. Van Ness, commander of the District of Columbia militia, who refused to accept Winder as his superior.[7]

Since there was no intelligence service, the only information available in Washington was that a large squadron had appeared in the Potomac. Nothing was known of its size or movements. To obtain information, Monroe, with Armstrong's reluctant consent, led a troop of cavalry out of the city on the eighteenth.[8] So great was the alarm and so desperate the need for intelligence that none thought it odd for a Cabinet officer to lead a scouting party. For Monroe, it was not only a release from the mounting anxiety in the city, which he could do nothing to ameliorate, but, at the moment, it was the only kind of service he could render the nation. It took him two days to trace the enemy to Benedict, located some fifty miles from the city on the Patuxent River, where the British had occupied the deserted town. Although he was informed that another squadron was ascending the Potomac, Monroe concluded that the twenty-three ships in the Patuxent were the main force and hence should be kept under observation. For twenty-four hours he watched the landing from the pine-covered heights about three miles from Benedict, too distant to estimate accurately the size of the forces.

When the British began their march on the twenty-first, he preceded them to Nottingham, where, with the aid of the Maryland militia, Monroe and his cavalry guarded the approach to the town to permit the inhabitants to remove their possessions. This was an unnecessary precaution, for Ross had given strict orders forbidding either looting or the destruction of private property. Monroe then hastened to Winder's headquarters at Wood Yard halfway between Benedict and the Capital. As soon as he reported to the commanding general, Monroe sent a special messenger to the President with an accurate count of the enemy forces, which he estimated at nearly 5,000 infantry without cavalry. There was no doubt, he informed Madison, that the expedition was bound for Washington. Although he suspected that the British move up the Potomac was diversionary, he approved Winder's decision not to withdraw troops from the Potomac area until the character of the British operation was clearer. Monroe's diligence in ferreting out information on the Patuxent had failed to promote a similar response in the War Department, for Madison, in his reply to Monroe's letter from Wood Yard (which reached him shortly before dawn on the twenty-second) had to admit that nothing was known about the fleet on the Potomac.[9]

As the British marched slowly toward Upper Marlboro, Monroe continued his reconnaissance and attempted to establish contact between Winder, who had shifted his camp to Long Old Fields (now Forrestville, Md.), and General Tobias E. Stansbury, who had reached Bladensburg (six miles north of the Capital) late on August 22 with 3,500 Maryland militia. Winder had chosen Long Old Fields because it was located at the junction of the two principal roads from Washington—one by way of Bladensburg, the other by way of the Navy Yard Bridge across the Eastern Branch of the Potomac. Since the latter was protected by massive batteries, it was not expected that the British would use that route. Consequently, Monroe and Stansbury waited at Bladensburg for Winder. As the twenty-third wore on without news from him anxiety mounted at Stansbury's camp, a concern deepened by reports that Winder had been captured by the British. Winder, on the contrary, was at liberty, but in the city of Washington, where he had taken his army on the night of the twenty-third. Unfortunately, he had interpreted a British feint as indicating a move toward the Navy Yard Bridge. He had neglected to observe the main British force, which turned down the road to Bladensburg. Winder's appearance in the city, which coincided with the arrival of the news that the British were at Upper Marlboro less than twenty miles from the Capital, added to the panic, as the citizens clogged the roads to Virginia with carriages and wagons loaded with belongings. In the government offices the clerks were hastily packing records, a precaution Monroe had recommended to the President the day before. Not until two-thirty in the morning of the twenty-fourth did Stansbury learn of Winder's move to Washington. Considering his force too small to challenge the enemy, he planned to evacuate Bladensburg, although Winder had promised to join him there. Only the discovery that the Bennings Bridge had been destroyed prevented Stansbury from retreating toward the Capital.

To bring some order out of this chaos Monroe hastened to Washington early on the twenty-fourth. When he reached the city he located the President and the Cabinet at the Navy Yard, where they had assembled at dawn in response to Winder's earnest plea for counsel. Monroe did not stay for the conference, but hastened to Bladensburg to aid Stansbury in preparing to face the British. Winder promptly put his exhausted army (the men had had little rest for four days) on the march in the hot August sun. For the first time since the invasion, Armstrong assumed an active role, accompanying the President's party in the wake of Winder's forces. This momentary reconciliation was effected when Madison expressed the hope that the Secretary of War would not let the recent reprimand deter him from exercising his proper function. Deeming this sufficient apology, Armstrong resumed the duties of his office, although it was far too late for his services to be of value.

By the time Monroe returned to Bladensburg shortly after eleven, Stansbury had withdrawn from the town and had stationed his army on a gently rising hill facing the bridge across the Eastern Branch, which the British would have to cross. With an energy justified by the emergency, for it was evident the battle would begin within an hour, Monroe assisted Stansbury in distributing his army in a wide arc on the side of the hill. This participation of a civilian Cabinet member in

a military operation was not considered extraordinary. Monroe had
had as much military experience as the other commanders, for none
of them was a professional. When Winder appeared at noon, he stationed his army about a mile up the hill to Stansbury's rear—much
too far back to support the advance lines. The President arrived shortly
after Winder, and rode so far down the hill that he nearly crossed into
the enemy lines before he was stopped. As Madison rode back, he
paused to talk to Monroe, who then resumed placement of the troops.
It was apparently at this time that Monroe made some rearrangements
in Stansbury's line, which the commander only noticed after the battle began, for the general was at that time engrossed in a debate with
Brigadier General Walter Smith of the Georgetown militia over which
one was second-in-command under Winder. Monroe shifted the Fifth
Baltimore Regiment to a position a quarter of a mile to the rear of its
original post to prevent it from being flanked by the British. It is
doubtful that this order (later dubbed by Armstrong as the interference of a "busy and blundering tactician") had any effect on the outcome of the battle; Monroe's redeployment saved the unit, for the
British attempted a flanking movement after fording the river.

The engagement at Bladensburg, which nominally lasted from one
until four in the afternoon, was really over almost as soon as it began.
The militia units in the front line broke and ran after the first shots
were fired. Much of the panic was generated by the unfamiliar Con-
greve rocket, a relatively harmless but disconcerting weapon. The collapse of the front line set up a chain reaction affecting all the other
units. Within a half-hour after the battle began, as Stansbury's men
poured into the rear, Winder ordered a general retreat in the hope that
he could reorganize the army outside Washington. The British were
held back two hours by Commodore Joshua Barney and a detachment
of marines and sailors, whose telling artillery fire delayed the advance.
Winder's plan proved unworkable as the retreat turned into a chaotic
rout—the "Bladensburg races" were under way. It seemed incredible
that an army of 7,000 occupying a defensive position had retreated
before a force of 4,000 men without artillery or cavalry. The American
humiliation was all the greater, for the flight had begun before Ross's
main force had been brought into action.[10]

Monroe was not a witness to the debacle, for shortly after the firing
began, the President (who may have heard Stansbury's irritated comment about Monroe's redeployment) suggested that the Secretaries
retire with him and leave the field operations to the military. The news

of the defeat reached the presidential party when the fleeing militia overtook the President on the Bladensburg road. In the city, now largely abandoned except for servants, groups of soldiers wandered aimlessly about. As soon as Winder arrived, Madison accepted his opinion (endorsed by Monroe) that it was impossible to execute Armstrong's suggestion of garrisoning the capitol for a siege. After agreeing that Winder should continue to Montgomery Courthouse in Maryland for reorganization, Madison hastened to Virginia, where his wife had fled some hours before with a wagonload of White House valuables. The Cabinet members also departed: Rush and Jones accompanying the President; Armstrong and Campbell (who had been too ill to go to Bladensburg) heading for Frederick. Monroe, who stayed to help Winder evacuate the troops, did not leave for Virginia until eight in the evening just as the British entered the city. Fortunately, he was spared anxiety about his family, for Mrs. Monroe was in Albemarle. Monroe spent the night at "Rokeby," near Little Falls, where Mrs. Madison, much concerned about her husband's whereabouts, had taken refuge. From Rokeby on this hot August night, the refugees saw the sky turn red from the fires set by the British as they systematically destroyed the public buildings—the White House, the State Department, the capitol, and other structures all went up in flames. Monroe was himself near collapse after a week of ceaseless activity during which he had not changed his clothes nor had slept more than a few hours at any one time. In spite of his weariness he still had sufficient spirit to reassure the nervous Mrs. Richard Love, the mistress of Rokeby. In response to her query about their safety, he asserted with more confidence than he probably felt: "Madam, as safe as if you were in the Allegheny Mountains." [11] The next day, Monroe left to join Winder at Montgomery Courthouse. However inadequate Winder may have been in the field, he undoubtedly possessed considerable organizational talents, for by August 26 he had reformed his army and was moving toward Baltimore.

It was not until the late afternoon of August 27 that the President, Monroe, and Rush reached the devastated city from which the British had retired on the twenty-fifth. During the twenty-four hours of his occupation, General Ross had destroyed every public building except the Patent Office. This structure had been saved by Dr. William Thornton, apparently the only federal official to remain in the city— he was a clerk in the State Department in charge of patents. Thornton had managed to convince the British that models in the Patent Office were private property and, in conformity with Ross's directives, could not be destroyed. Few private houses were molested, although Admiral Cockburn, who had resented editor Gales' acid comments about his raiding activities, had personally supervised the destruction of the presses of the *Intelligencer*. Most of the looting in the city was not done by the soldiers but by the servants left behind by the inhabitants. The Capital had suffered both from the destruction of the occupying forces and from a devastating windstorm on the twenty-fifth which caused extensive damage to private houses. Fortunately, nearly all the public records except those in the capitol had been removed to Virginia by departmental clerks.[12]

Only a few hours after he reached the city, Monroe heard the sound of distant cannonading followed by a tremendous explosion. It was not until the next morning that he learned that Fort Washington had been bombarded by a British squadron moving up the river. The explosion had resulted from the destruction of the fort by the commander, who had not fired a shot in its defense. The British fleet then moved to Alexandria, which capitulated without resistance. In view of the continued absence of the Secretary of War, and the desperate need for effective leadership, Madison asked Monroe to assume command of the defenses of the city. The citizens, returning to the ravaged Capital which Winder had stripped of troops for the protection of Baltimore, were so demoralized by the destruction of Fort Washington and the occupation of Alexandria that many considered surrender the only means of saving the Capital. On the morning of the twenty-eighth, as Madison, Monroe, and Rush were inspecting the defense arrangements, they met Dr. Thornton, who requested permission to send a deputation of citizens to surrender the city to the commander of the British squadron. Thornton carried considerable weight with the people of the city, for, as the sole federal official to remain in the city, he had been effective in checking the looting. When Madison refused to agree, Thornton persisted in his argument that the impossibility of preparing adequate defenses in such a short time made the situation hopeless. The discussion ended when Monroe broke in angrily, declaring that if "any deputation moved towards the enemy it would be repelled by the bayonet." After this there was no more talk of capitulation. Heartened by Monroe's determination, the citizens of Washington supported his defense measures, which were never put to a test, since the British did not advance beyond Alexandria.[13]

By the time Armstrong appeared in Washington on the afternoon of the twenty-ninth resentment against him was so great that many officers, who blamed the fiasco at Bladensburg on the Secretary's refusal to take steps to defend the Bay area, were angrily threatening to refuse to take orders from him. Although the President was still unwilling to remove the Secretary, he suggested that Armstrong go to New York on a visit to his family. Sending the Secretary of War on a vacation in the midst of a major invasion was a curious and unsatisfactory arrangement, but Madison apparently felt that removing Armstrong would damage the prestige of the administration. A week later, however, Armstrong submitted his resignation from Baltimore. In a letter to the press he justified his conduct and bitterly assailed Monroe for interfering in the War Department and undermining his influence in the Cabinet. While Monroe had spoken critically of his colleague to the President, there seems no basis for Henry Adams' conclusion that the intrigues of the Secretary of State had driven Armstrong from the Cabinet. At all times Monroe had addressed his complaints directly to the President and had never attempted to form a cabal among congressmen or his colleagues in the Cabinet. Certainly Armstrong did little during his tenure in office to win Monroe's confidence in his judgment. There were few Americans in 1814 who did not blame the Secretary of War for both the disaster in Washington and the failure of the northern campaign. Once a powerful figure in New York, Armstrong could not even muster token support in his attempt to win election to the Senate of the United States immediately after his resignation. His friends refused to endorse the discredited Cabinet officer. After this rebuff Armstrong withdrew from public life, but until his death in 1843 he continued to publish pamphlets and essays attempting to discredit Monroe in connection with both the Louisiana Purchase and the defeat at Bladensburg.[14]

II

With Armstrong out of the Cabinet, Monroe once more became acting Secretary of War, but much to his surprise Madison hesitated to make the position permanent. The recent military reverses and the rising hostility to the war made Madison fearful of the repercussions if he placed a Virginian in the War Department. Determined to retain the post until victory had been won—he never doubted his qualifications for achieving this goal—Monroe again considered announcing that he would not be a presidential candidate, if this would lessen the resistance to his nomination.[15] He finally forced Madison's hand in a letter in which he told the President that failure to appoint him would have an unfavorable effect upon his own career as well as on the administration. As far as Monroe himself was concerned, should he not be appointed, then many would conclude that he shrank from the responsibility lest failure jeopardize his political career. If Madison did not act at once to fill the War Department, public confidence in the administration would be seriously shaken. Moreover, Monroe added, if he did not become permanent Secretary, he would once again be in the unhappy position of planning a campaign which he would not execute.[16] The letter had the effect intended—the next day Madison submitted his name to the Senate, which promptly approved.

In order to broaden the base of the administration, Madison considered bringing a Federalist into the State Department (he had Rufus King in mind), but Monroe objected, since such a move seemed tantamount to bringing into power a party repudiated by the electorate.[17] Ultimately, when Governor Tompkins declined, Monroe was named acting Secretary of State.[18] Two new members joined the Cabinet before the year was out. Campbell, discouraged by the difficulty of floating new loans, resigned on the grounds of poor health. His place was taken by Alexander J. Dallas, who was quite happy to serve now that Armstrong had departed. Secretary of the Navy Jones, plagued by private financial worries, also resigned to be replaced by a New England Republican, Benjamin W. Crowninshield.[19]

Once he was in the War Department Monroe directed all his energies toward preparing for the defense of Baltimore, where the British were moving after evacuating Washington and Alexandria. Wisely leaving the fighting to the commanders in Baltimore, Monroe concentrated on raising troops, summoning the militia, assembling supplies, and setting up an intelligence system. Until the British were repulsed at Baltimore Monroe slept on a camp bed in his office to be on hand to receive reports, which arrived at all hours. He brought to the Department what it had so long needed—a competent and dedicated administrator. In view of Winder's deficiencies as a field commander, Monroe placed General Samuel Smith, the former "invisible" Senator but a devoted patriot after the outbreak of the war, in charge of the defense of Baltimore, although he was nominally subordinate to Winder. With ample time to deploy his superior forces in well-prepared defensive positions, Smith easily repulsed the British, who suffered an irreplaceable loss in the death of General Ross. The defeat at Baltimore on September 14 ended the British invasion of the Bay area, but until the fleet vanished into the Atlantic, Monroe kept a close surveillance on Cockburn's movements.[20]

When Congress assembled on September 19, using the ramshackle Patent Office as temporary quarters, Madison was at least able to counteract the disaster at Washington with news of the success in Baltimore and of the naval victories which had given the United States command of Lake Champlain and the Great Lakes. This optimism was tempered by his sober reminder that the nation must be prepared for a further extension of the war now that England was freed from her Continental commitment. Victory could be achieved only if Congress provided a dependable source of revenue and placed the army on a sound footing. The President did not offer specific recommendations on either point, but all were aware of the critical condition of both the nation's financial resources and its military strength. None needed to be reminded of the spectacular failure of recent loans, and it was well known that Secretary of War Monroe had been reduced to the expedient of borrowing on a personal basis from state banks to meet the day-to-day needs of his department.[21] Recruiting in the past year had not been successful, for only 10,000 of the additional 25,000 regulars authorized by Congress had been enlisted. Consequently, in the fall of 1814, two years after the beginning of the war, the army was nearly 30,000 short of its full strength of 60,000.[22]

Although it was never Madison's custom to make detailed proposals in his messages, he had every reason to avoid specifics in his September message, for the administration was still debating solutions to the most pressing problems. So great was the crisis that the President and his advisers had concluded to recommend two measures, long anathema to orthodox Republicans—the establishment of a federally chartered bank and the formation of a conscript army.

On October 17 Monroe outlined the administration's military needs in a report submitted at the request of Senator Giles, chairman of the Senate Committee on Military Affairs. The Republicans were stunned to learn that the Secretary was abandoning the cherished Republican dogma that the militia constituted the best defense of a free people in order to propose the creation of a conscript army of 100,000 men. To spare state and local pride Monroe refrained from commenting on the most obvious defect of the militia—the inability of untrained units to stand up under fire. Nor did he allude to the recent refusal of the governors of the New England states to permit the militia to serve under federal commanders. Instead he rested the argument—and it was one he hoped would appeal to the Republicans—on the less offensive ground that experience had proven the militia to be three times as costly as regular troops. Anticipating objections to conscription on constitutional grounds, Monroe, following the example set by Alexander Hamilton in his report on the bank, relied on loose construction: the power to raise armies was sufficiently broad to embrace conscription.

The Secretary outlined several systems, but he expressed a preference for an arrangement classifying all males between eighteen and forty-five into groups of one hundred and making each group responsible for keeping four men in service at all times. As an alternate he proposed dividing the militia into three classes according to age. Each class would be subject to call for two years of service. With less enthusiasm he outlined a plan exempting every five men from militia service if they would provide one man for the regular army. In the event that none of these proposals was acceptable, he requested an increase in the bounty for enlistment.[23] It was, of course, an indication of the magnitude of the crisis facing the government that Madison and Monroe were willing to endorse a program highly offensive to the Republicans, and one which they had not been willing to let Armstrong advance in 1813.

Senator Giles, who momentarily came to the support of the administration, put through a series of bills which were as close to the administration plan as he believed the Republicans would accept. First, in accordance with the Secretary's recommendations, the Senate approved a bill lowering the recruiting age to eighteen and doubling the bounty paid volunteers. This bill also contained a provision that every five militiamen who provided one man for the regular army would be exempted from militia service. Giles' second bill permitted the President to draft 80,000 militiamen for two years' service by calling on the states to provide quotas in proportion to the population of the state. It was hoped that this plan would be more acceptable than other conscription proposals since it left the method of raising the quotas to the state governments.

Although the first Senate measure was passed by the House, Giles' modified conscription bill was bitterly opposed. Unfortunately, the administration had lost some of its most effective supporters in the house—Clay was in Ghent; Calhoun, who had been ill, was late in returning to Congress; others were in military service or had retired. Some of the most influential Republicans, including John Wayles Eppes (Jefferson's son-in-law and chairman of the Ways and Means

Committee), joined with the Federalists under the leadership of Daniel Webster to drastically modify a bill which, in effect, took the militia out of the control of state authorities. When the Senate refused to agree to modifications, the measure was dropped.[24] Not even the appearance of British marauding parties off the coast of New England was sufficient to convince Congress of the necessity of a measure so contrary to American convictions. Late in January Congress enacted a substitute measure allowing the President to accept into the regular army up to 40,000 men recruited by the states. This bill, which was quite contrary to the wishes of the administration, was a recognition of the fact that the states had begun to recruit armed forces apart from the militia. In practical terms the new law meant that future recruiting would be done by the states at federal expense. Moreover, it implicitly granted priority to state needs and tended to weaken the concept of the Union. The effectiveness of the measure was never tested, for the war ended a few weeks after its passage.[25]

The financial program of the administration, equally as offensive to the Republicans as the conscription proposal, also encountered considerable opposition. Additional taxes were approved at once, although they would not alleviate the immediate needs of the government. Between September 4 and October 13, when Dallas arrived to take over the Treasury Department, Monroe borrowed on his own signature (a proceeding of doubtful legality) over $5 million in paper currency from banks and municipal corporations—the city of New York advancing over $1 million.[26] In view of the immediate fiscal crisis Madison concluded that the sole hope of reorganizing the government's finances lay in chartering a federal bank. The war had amply demonstrated the necessity of a bank, and, as Dallas pointed out, it was the only measure which would persuade the financial community to advance money needed for government loans.

Jefferson and many other Republicans, however, were scandalized at the revival of an institution they had been so vigorously condemning as unconstitutional for two decades. Since his retirement Jefferson had rarely sought to influence administration policy, but he considered this departure from Republican principles so serious that he actively promoted as a substitute a plan to issue treasury notes redeemable over a period of twenty years. Monroe was not unsympathetic to this scheme in the abstract, and he transmitted it to Dallas without committing himself one way or the other.[27]

Although Jefferson's proposal was based on Republican financial theory, Monroe felt that the situation of the country was so desperate that the government had no choice but to accept the bank, since this was the only arrangement acceptable to businessmen. Moreover, as he wrote to Madison somewhat later, he saw another advantage in a federal bank: it would, he believed, "attach the commercial part of the community in a much greater degree to the Government; interest them in its operations. . . . This is the great desideratum of our system. . . ." [28] Monroe had indeed traveled a long way since the 1790s. He was the first national figure in the Republican party to understand how drastically the character of the party had altered since 1800 and to realize that it was no longer primarily agrarian in its composition. Concessions must be made to the mercantile element, which was forming an increasingly important segment of Republicanism in the Northern and Middle states. Consequently, Monroe posed no objections to the plan for a federal bank outlined by Dallas to Congress in October, nor did he support Eppes' efforts to introduce a bill calling for an issue of treasury notes. The Senate passed the bank bill quickly, but in the House alterations introduced by anti-bank Republicans and Federalists made the bill unacceptable to the administration. Since the bill omitted the provision requiring the bank to make loans to the government—the most important reason for chartering the bank—Madison vetoed the measure. Once again Congress left the administration with no recourse but to borrow money in the open market.[29]

There seemed to be no end to the difficulties besetting the administration. In December it appeared that the New England states meeting in convention at Hartford, Connecticut, might secede. Rumors about the assembly were so disturbing that Monroe sent Colonel Thomas S. Jesup to Hartford as a confidential agent in the guise of a recruiting officer. Unable to secure any information about the proceedings, since the convention met behind closed doors, Jesup's first report was not very reassuring.[30] Monroe considered the situation sufficiently threatening to authorize Governor Tompkins of New York and General Robert Swartwout to take prompt action in the event of an uprising in New England.[31] In order to win moderate Federalist support for the administration, Madison considered bringing into the State Department Samuel Dexter, a Federalist who had been supported by Republicans as a gubernatorial candidate in Massachusetts in 1814. The proposal was not carried out, for the news that the moderates had prevailed in Hartford relieved the anxiety of the administration about the secessionist danger in New England.[32] Since the outcome of the

Hartford Convention seemed to indicate that most Federalists except for a few extremists were loyal to the Union, the President and Secretary of War considered it safe (and also advisable) to permit Federalists to hold commands in the new volunteer forces.[33]

III

When Monroe became Secretary of War, the nation was threatened by two major invasions other than the attack on Washington and Baltimore. First, a large army was poised in Canada ready to enter northern New York; and, second, according to all information then available, the British were massing a large expedition directed against New Orleans. The first threat ended with McDonough's victory on Lake Champlain on September 11, which blocked British invasion plans for the remainder of the year. Concerned about New Orleans, Monroe, as early as September 5, had written General Andrew Jackson, the commander of the American forces in the Southeast, warning him of the threat and urging him to go at once to New Orleans. At that time Jackson, who had established his headquarters at Mobile, was more interested in evicting a British force established at Pensacola in Spanish Florida.[34] Aware of Jackson's preoccupation with this secondary object, the President and Monroe were fearful that he might linger in Mobile to the neglect of New Orleans. Consequently, when letters arrived from Jackson indicating his intention of attacking Pensacola, Monroe wrote warning him against taking steps which "would involve this government in a contest with Spain." The Secretary of War reminded Jackson of the greater importance of New Orleans and informed him that 10,000 additional men had been ordered to his command.[35] Six weeks later, since nothing had been heard from the general, Monroe became more urgent. However, by that time, Jackson had reached New Orleans, although it was not known in Washington. He had left Mobile, not because of the prodding from the Secretary of War, but because he had succeeded in driving the British from Pensacola.[36]

The 10,000 men promised by Monroe were on hand when the general arrived in New Orleans on December 1, but to his dismay they lacked regulation arms and accoutrements, although most of the men had rifles. Since Jackson customarily paid little attention to detail, he had not requisitioned additional arms until October 31. When Monroe became aware of this deficiency (long before Jackson's requisition arrived), he promptly ordered the Ordnance Department to send 5,000 stands of arms with accoutrements and bayonets to New Orleans.[37] This shipment was dispatched from Pittsburgh and Franklinton, Ohio, between November 11 and 15 and should have reached Jackson within three weeks. Unfortunately, the shipper lingered along the river engaging in private trade, and the arms did not reach New Orleans until after the battle. The matter would have been quite forgotten, if Jackson, who was always willing to magnify his own achievements, had not complained after the British retreat that his position had been rendered difficult by the failure of the administration to send him supplies.[38] Monroe did not wish to deprive the general of the credit for his truly magnificent victory, but neither did he wish the administration to appear remiss in its duties. Consequently, he printed the correspondence relating to the shipment in the *Intelligencer* in February 1815.[39]

In spite of Jackson's victory, so gratifying to national pride, the success at New Orleans on January 8, 1815, had no effect on the outcome of the war, for peace had been concluded two weeks before the engagement. The Treaty of Ghent, which reached Washington in mid-February (ten days after the news of the British defeat in New Orleans), was not a very pleasing document, since it touched on none of the controversies behind the conflict. Yet there was no great protest, as had been the case in the past over treaties failing to achieve American objectives, for no one had really hoped for substantial concessions. In concluding a treaty establishing the *status quo ante bellum* the commissioners had been guided by instructions prepared by Monroe in October 1814, permitting them to drop the American demands on impressment and neutral rights.[40] Only one fault was found with the conduct of the envoys: they had signed their names below rather than on the same line as the British plenipotentiaries, an oversight which might be interpreted as indicating an inferior status. Monroe at once wrote John Quincy Adams, the Minister to Great Britain, to inform him that this fact had been specifically noted in the American act of ratification to prevent it from establishing a precedent.[41]

Although the war was at best an ignoble stalemate in which the nation had only been saved from disaster by the decision of Britain not to prosecute the war on a massive scale, the conflict was at once portrayed in popular mythology as a victory, which had again proven the effectiveness of the valor of a free people in a contest against the world's mightiest power. To many it seemed a second war of independence. Monroe may not have been willing to go quite this far in assessing the significance of the war, but he did think that it had been a most important test of strength for the nation. As he told the Senate Committee on Military Affairs in February 1815:

The late war formed an epoch of a peculiar character, highly interesting to the United States. It made trial of the strength and efficiency of our government for such a crisis. It had been said that our Union, and system of government, would not bear such a trial. The result has proved the imputation to be entirely destitute of foundation. The experiment was made under circumstances the most unfavorable to the United States, and the most favorable to the very powerful nation with whom we were engaged. The demonstration is satisfactory that our Union has gained strength, our troops honor, and the nation character, by the contest.[42]

CHAPTER 19

PEACE AND
POLITICS

SINCE MOST Americans viewed the end of the war as a final settlement and anticipated no other threats to American security, they were by no means inclined to share Monroe's conclusion that the war had unequivocally demonstrated the need for a larger and more effective national defense system. As far as the President and the Secretary of War were concerned there was one great lesson to be learned from the war—that the safety of the country should never again be exposed to such risks as a result of the traditional Republican antipathy to military and naval expenditures. One of Monroe's last duties as Secretary of War was the drafting of a report for the Senate Committee on Military Affairs on a peacetime military establishment. In this report, which was submitted to Senator Giles on February 22, 1815, Monroe urged that the army be maintained at 20,000 (twice its prewar level). He presented two considerations which he felt made this increased force imperative: the presence of 35,000 regulars in Canada and the unsettled state of American relations with Spain over Florida and the Louisiana boundary. In the same report he also proposed an extensive program for improving coastal fortifications, whose inadequacy had been apparent during the war. If the United States neglected its defenses, then other countries would take advantage of the nation's weakness. As an additional argument, and one which he considered most compelling, he told the committee: "By the war we have acquired a character and rank among other nations which we did not enjoy before. We stand pledged to support this rank and character by the adoption of such measures as may evince on the part of the United States a firm resolution to do it. We cannot go back. The spirit of the nation forbids it." [1] Privately Monroe admitted that he considered an army of 20,000 insufficient, but he did not think that the Republicans in Congress would approve of a larger number.[2] He was far too hopeful, for parsimonious congressmen happily whittled the army to its former strength of 10,000. The proposal for fortifications, however, struck a more sympathetic cord and an appropriation of $400,000 was made to start a long-range construction program at key points along the coast.[3]

On March 15 Monroe gave up his post in the War Department. Not only was the State Department making greater calls on his time, but the strain of the preceding six months had seriously impaired his health. He had lost so much weight and become so haggard that his old friend John Minor was shocked when he saw him in the spring of 1815—he had never seen anyone so altered except by disease.[4] It was to be six months before Monroe fully regained his health. The day-to-day operation of the War Department was temporarily assumed by Dallas, since William H. Crawford, the new Secretary, had not yet returned from France, where he had been serving as Minister since 1813. After a brief rest in Albemarle, Monroe came back to Washington in April to share with Dallas the unpleasant task of selecting the officers to be retained in the army. To avoid bitterness every effort was made to find civil posts for those wishing to remain in the service, but many were not easily satisfied. Wilkinson, who was eliminated when it was decided to keep only Jackson and Jacob Brown as major generals, proved particularly troublesome. The Republicans felt an obligation toward him for his past services, but his unpopularity in the West made it impossible to grant his request for the post of Superintendent of Indian Affairs. Nor did the President dare place him in any post involving financial responsibility. When Wilkinson failed to obtain a satisfactory appointment, he departed angrily denouncing the administration.[5] Since most cases were not so troublesome, Dallas and Monroe were able to complete their task by the end of April.

Their joint work on the army list had just been finished when news of Napoleon's return from Elba reached Washington. Perhaps because he was so exhausted, Monroe's assessment of the significance of Napoleon's reappearance lacked his usual good judgment. He became so alarmed that he urged Madison to delay the army reduction and to call Congress into special session. Madison considered such drastic action premature, since it was by no means certain that Napoleon would return to power, nor, if he were successful, was there any reason to think he would re-establish the Continental system. Crowninshield and

Dallas, who were still in Washington, agreed with the President that nothing should be done until more was known about Napoleon's activities.[6]

Once this decision was made, Monroe left the Capital, hastening to Ashfield, his son-in-law's estate near Richmond. His journey was prompted by his anxiety over his daughter's health. Eliza, who had always been very close to her father, had become depressed during her illness over their prolonged separation. As George Hay wrote Monroe in March, "she actually moans over your absence. Ten times a day she repeats, if I could but see my father and dear mother *here*. Sometimes I try to comfort her; but I do not often succeed. . . ." [7] Mrs. Monroe had gone to Ashfield early in the spring to look after her daughter. Eliza's illness had been so serious that her husband had consulted (by mail) the celebrated Dr. Wistar of Philadelphia, whose course of treatment brought an improvement late in the spring.[8] By the middle of June she was well enough to go to Albemarle, where her father hoped that the cooler climate of the uplands would benefit her health.

Monroe, who was eager to have the Hays nearer, suggested that they sell Ashfield and purchase land adjacent to his estate in Albemarle.[9] This plan had to be kept in abeyance, for his inability to sell the Loudoun property made it seem likely that he would have to dispose of the Albemarle plantation. The farm at Highlands was in a deplorable state, for he had not been able to supervise the planting since he entered the Cabinet in 1811, and his managers had lacked experience in cultivating grains, the only crop planted there. The potentially more productive Loudoun estate was not in much better condition. Although his brother Andrew "had been an honest, industrious and attentive" estate manager, he had been deficient in "skill, arrangement and method." [10] It was at this time that he began to think of moving permanently to the Loudoun County plantation, which had the advantage of being close to the Capital.

Freed at last from official responsibilities for the first time in four years, Monroe slowly regained his health during the summer of 1815, although, as he confessed, the improvement was not discernible in his appearance. In August, at the insistence of his family physician and neighbor, Dr. Charles Everett, Monroe and his wife spent a month at the springs—visiting in turn Sweet Springs, White Sulphur and Warm Springs. The prolonged rest proved beneficial: his strength came back and he gained weight. His mind was also relieved late in the summer by the news of Napoleon's defeat, which he had not expected to be so easily accomplished.[11] Late in September he set out for the Capital with his wife and the Hays, who now began to spend most of the year with Eliza's parents. Also in the party were Hortensia Hay and Maria Hester. Monroe, whose younger daughter was twelve, fondly told a friend that she was a "most excellent child without fault that we discover, and with the best qualities. She is apt at school, and getting forward in reading, writing and drawing." [12] Allowing for fatherly exaggeration, these qualities accord with the gentle and modest character of Maria Hester in her later years. Overshadowed by her forceful elder sister, Maria Hester did not emerge as a distinct personality until after her marriage. On their journey north they stopped to visit the Madisons before going to Oak Hill, where Monroe left his family. He went to Washington alone, arriving on October 7 after a three-months absence.[13]

II

Peace brought renewed activity to the State Department, but in contrast to the prewar years the problems which occupied Monroe were relatively insignificant. One of his first duties after the war ended had been to draft instructions for the peace commissioners sent to Algiers. In March, Congress had authorized hostilities against Algiers in retaliation for continued depredations against American commerce, although the Algerian treaty of 1796 had presumably guaranteed American ships immunity in return for an annual tribute payment. Monroe instructed the commissioners to obtain complete security for American ships without the payment of tribute. The expedition, which was commanded by Commodore Stephen Decatur, proved successful and secured a treaty in full accordance with administration wishes.[14]

In spite of the fact that the Treaty of Ghent provided for almost nothing of any consequence, it presented several difficulties in its interpretation. Perhaps the sharpest disagreement arose over the provision requiring the restoration of property removed by British forces in America. Since more than 3,500 slaves (400 of whom were reputedly employed on Admiral Cochrane's Jamaica estate) had been seized by the British, there was considerable pressure on Monroe to obtain either their return or the payment of an indemnity. Monroe and Anthony Baker, the British chargé, clashed on this issue in March 1815, when the Secretary of State refused to accept Baker's contention that this provision applied only to that property still in the place where it had been originally captured. In the face of this sharp rebuff Baker transferred

James Monroe, age twenty-eight. Artist unknown. *Courtesy James Monroe Law Office and Memorial Library, Fredericksburg, Va.*

James Monroe, by John Vanderlyn. Painted about 1820. The President is shown standing in the White House. The carpet and one of the chairs ordered from France in 1817 can also be seen. *Courtesy New York City Art Commission.*

James Monroe, by Samuel F. B. Morse. Painted in 1819. *Courtesy White House Historical Association.*

James Monroe, by Gilbert Stuart. *Courtesy Metropolitan Museum of Art.*

John Quincy Adams, by Gilbert Stuart and Thomas Sully. Painted about 1830. *Courtesy Harvard University.*

Smith Thompson, by Charles B. King. *Courtesy Mrs. Donald E. Dent, Kansas City, Mo.*

William H. Crawford, by John Wesley Jarvis. Painted about 1820. *Courtesy Pennsylvania Academy of the Fine Arts.*

William Wirt, by George Inman. *Courtesy Museum of Fine Arts, Boston.*

John C. Calhoun, by John Wesley Jarvis. Painted about 1819. *Courtesy Yale University.*

North Front of the White House about 1810. The familiar portico designed by Latrobe was not completed until 1829. The front undoubtedly looked much like this during Monroe's administration with an unpaved yard set off by wooden palings. *Courtesy White House Historical Association.*

South Portico of the White House from an English engraving published in 1831. *Courtesy White House Historical Association.*

Oak Hill (Loudoun County), front entrance. *Courtesy Virginia State Library.*

Oak Hill (Loudoun County), portico. This shows
Oak Hill as constructed by Monroe before the wings were extended
and enlarged in the twentieth century.
Courtesy Virginia State Library.

Mrs. James Monroe, by Benjamin West. Collection of Mrs. Gouverneur Hoes. *Frick Art Reference Library.*

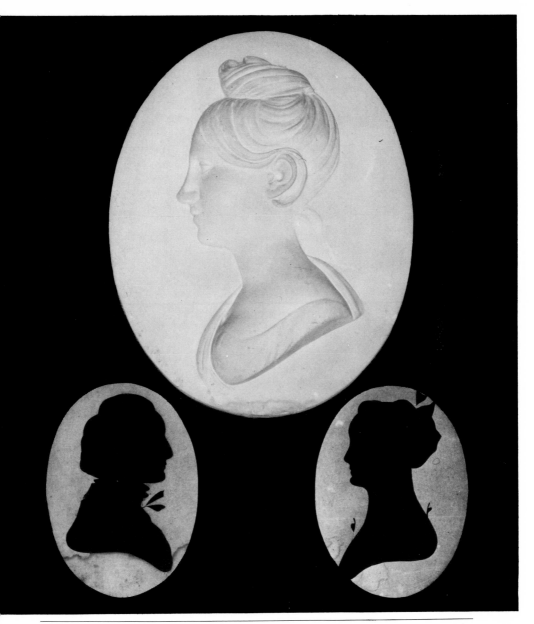

(Top) Mrs. Samuel Lawrence Gouverneur (Maria Hester Monroe). Plaque by P. Cardelli, 1820. *James Monroe Memorial Foundation, Fredericksburg, Va.* (Bottom left) Samuel Lawrence Gouverneur (Monroe's son-in-law). Silhouette cut by C. W. Peale about 1820. *James Monroe Memorial Foundation, Fredericksburg, Va.* (Bottom right) Mrs. James Monroe. Silhouette cut by C. W. Peale about 1820. *James Monroe Memorial Foundation, Fredericksburg, Va.*

Mrs. George Hay (Eliza Monroe), by Caruson.
Painted about 1810.
Courtesy Frick Art Reference Library.

George Hay, by Cephas Thompson. Collection of Miss Margaret N. Robins. *Courtesy Frick Art Reference Library.*

(Top) Judge Joseph Jones (Monroe's uncle). Miniature by an unknown artist. *James Monroe Memorial Foundation, Fredericksburg, Va.* (Bottom) James Monroe. Engraving by Charles B. Saint-Mémin about 1798. *James Monroe Memorial Foundation, Fredericksburg, Va.*

Daniel D. Tompkins, by John Wesley Jarvis. Painted in 1824. *New-York Historical Society.*

the negotiations to London. To assist Adams in presenting the American case, Monroe collected detailed information by querying ship captains and sending agents to the West Indies and Nova Scotia to gather data. Discussions on this minor but complex issue dragged on intermittently until 1823, when the controversy was submitted to the Czar for arbitration. Although the fisheries had not been included in the Treaty of Ghent, this also proved a subject of postwar irritation between the two nations, not to be resolved until the Convention of 1818.[15]

In spite of these trivial disputes, relations between the two recent belligerents were surprisingly amicable after the war. Much of this improvement was the result of a deliberate cultivation of American friendship by Lord Castlereagh, who tried to settle outstanding disputes on a basis of parity. This limited good will marked a recognition of the new standing of the United States in the eyes of the European powers. Although they were fully aware of the poor military showing of the United States in the war, the fact that America had abandoned its negative attitude by entering the conflict meant that in the future calculations of the European states some attention had to be given to American concerns. In view of Britain's commercial interests and the vulnerability of Canada, there were powerful practical reasons for British statesmen to welcome an Anglo-American *rapprochement*. Much of the credit for giving substance to the new spirit of amity must be given to Sir Charles Bagot, the first postwar Minister, who reached Washington in March 1816. John Quincy Adams considered his talents mediocre, but he admitted that Bagot was by far the most tactful, considerate and courteous British diplomat ever sent to the United States. Although Bagot liked America no better than his predecessors, he at least acknowledged that Washington was a much better city than he had expected. During his three years as Minister he built up a remarkable reservoir of good will.[16]

The most satisfactory and lasting fruit of this *rapprochement* was the Rush-Bagot Agreement limiting naval armaments on the Great Lakes to vessels for customs purposes.[17] Although Richard Rush's name has been attached to this understanding, his connection with it was quite nominal; he happened to be acting Secretary of State in the spring of 1817, when the formal notes were exchanged between the two governments. The negotiations leading to the demilitarization of the Lakes took place in June and July 1816 when Monroe was still in the State Department. In November 1815, Monroe, at Madison's request, instructed Adams to propose to Castlereagh that the two powers agree either to abolish or strictly limit naval armaments on the Great Lakes as a means of reducing the friction between the two nations. This suggestion was prompted by the action of Congress in terminating all naval construction under way on the Lakes. Since it was unlikely that Congress, which had proved impervious to Monroe's pleas for enlarging the peacetime army, would be moved to expand the navy to counteract British power, the only way to ensure American security was by naval limitation. Although the British response to this offer was slow, Castlereagh welcomed it as a means of sparing Britain the expense of striving for naval superiority on the Lakes. When Bagot opened the subject to Monroe in July 1816, they quickly agreed to limit naval strength to four ships to enforce revenue laws. These terms were embodied in provisional notes exchanged between Monroe and Bagot in August subject to the approval of the British government. In the meantime both powers suspended further construction, except that Monroe, for the sake of the record, obtained permission for the United States to equal existing British armaments on the Lakes. Actually, no construction was planned. He merely wanted to shield the administration from the charge that it was ceding naval superiority to Great Britain. When the British Cabinet approved the agreement the formal notes were drafted in April 1817, but the accord was not formally proclaimed until April 28, 1818, after Senate ratification. Although the two nations disarmed on the Great Lakes, they continued to maintain forts and garrisons along the border. This agreement, which saved the United States a considerable sum, was not regarded as remarkably significant in 1818—it merely spelled out a policy in effect since the Revolution.

In the summer of 1816 Monroe was plagued by a host of minor diplomatic problems, which scarcely deserved the effort required to cope with them. The first, and most trivial, grew out of the arrest in Philadelphia of the Russian Consul General, Nicholas Kosloff, for raping a twelve-year-old servant girl. When Madison, who had no authority over state officials, refused to intervene, the Russian Minister, André de Dashkoff (who, according to Dallas, shared Kosloff's tastes), presented the affair to the Czar as a breach of diplomatic immunity.[18] In retaliation the Czar banned the American chargé in St. Petersburg from the Court. As soon as they learned of this development, Madison and Monroe sent a special messenger to Russia with documents fully explaining the case. When the Czar learned the facts, he lifted his ban on the chargé and recalled both Kosloff and Dashkoff.[19]

Equally trying to Monroe's patience was the conduct of the newly arrived Minister of the restored Bourbons, Baron Jean Guillaume Hyde de Neuville, who behaved in such a blustering and overbearing manner that he seemed determined to create a rift between France and the United States. His behavior was all the more unexpected, since he had lived contentedly in the United States for five years as an exile. However, his uncontrollable temper led him into serious indiscretions whenever he sensed any criticism, direct or implied, of the royalist tradition. He was particularly offended by the toasts delivered in the presence of exiled Napoleonic generals at a public dinner in Baltimore on July 4, 1816. The Baron had originally planned to attend the celebration, until Monroe tactfully pointed out that he might not find the toasts to his liking. De Neuville was especially enraged by Postmaster John S. Skinner's reference to Louis XVIII as an "imbecile tyrant." In a rude note he demanded Skinner's removal as a redress for the insult to the French crown. As an afterthought he also requested the recall of William Lee, who for many years had been the consul at Bordeaux, on the grounds that Lee had been engaged in antimonarchical activities. Refusing to comply with the request for Skinner's removal, Monroe reminded the French Minister that Skinner was fully protected by the constitutional guarantee of freedom of speech. Moreover, it also seemed to Monroe that Skinner, who was only postmaster of Baltimore, was much too low-ranking an official to be considered as involving the government when he spoke as a private citizen. Since Lee was returning home, Monroe was able to push this matter to one side.[20]

The Baron was still besieging the State Department with complaints when Monroe left in July for a badly needed rest—his health was still none too good. He took along Attorney General Rush, who was overjoyed at visiting Montpelier, where he was much impressed by the French cooking and the fine Madeira laid down by Madison in 1796. From there the impressionable Attorney General accompanied Monroe to Albemarle, where his visit was climaxed with a dinner at Monticello.[21] Monroe was pursued to Virginia by De Neuville's recriminations. Shortly after Monroe left Montpelier, a special messenger arrived with a note from De Neuville to the Secretary of State. In order to spare his ailing friend, Madison accepted the letter. Grateful for this consideration, Monroe told the President: "If I could be free from this kind of persecution, from these little men, who make great affairs out of trifles and be at liberty to busy myself in my private affairs only, and take the exercise incident thereto, I think I should soon be well." [22]

The Baron was finally calmed in the fall, when the *Intelligencer* pub-

lished a vague article drafted by Monroe stating that the French Minister had received explanations concerning a delicate (but unspecified)
matter. The French Minister was also pleased by Madison's personal
courtesy toward him and by seeing at his official reception portraits of
Washington and Louis XVIII hanging side by side.[23] In spite of this
unfortunate beginning, De Neuville, who had many excellent qualities,
including, according to Adams, an admiration for the practical effects
of republican government, became generally well-liked.[24]

III

After the war was over, it was inevitable that Monroe, as a leading contender for the Presidency in 1816, should become deeply engrossed in
politics. During the war his presidential ambitions had been forced
into the background, although not entirely forgotten. In 1813, he had
asked George Hay to contradict a disturbing report current in Virginia
that Jefferson did not favor Monroe as Madison's successor. This rumor
had its origins in the outspoken hostility of Peter Carr, Jefferson's
nephew, toward Monroe. Monroe did not expect the former President
to endorse him publicly, but he did not welcome publicity suggesting
a rift with Jefferson.[25] In 1815 Monroe's brother Joseph, who never
seems to have taken much interest in politics, suddenly announced
that he was publishing a pamphlet exposing the hostility of Carr and
other members of the Jefferson circle toward Monroe. Joseph, who
had been reconciled to his brother after their rupture in 1812 and had
continued to live in Albemarle, had private resentments of his own
against Jefferson and his family. Only by direct pressure on his brother
was Monroe able to prevent the publication of the pamphlet. In the
hope of relieving Monroe's anxiety about his brother's continued inability to become financially independent, Madison offered to give
Joseph a post in the Mississippi Territory. Although Monroe had
scrupulously avoided seeking patronage for his relatives, he consented
if other recommendations could be obtained. He thought his brother
had the ability, but frankly doubted that he had a sufficient sense of
responsibility even for a minor post. Either Joseph declined the suggestion or the additional references were not forthcoming, for he was
not appointed.[26]

While Monroe never enjoyed Jefferson's great popularity in the
nation, he was, nonetheless, a widely respected figure. If most of his
contemporaries did not judge him to have talents comparable to those

of the first two Republican Presidents, all acknowledged that his sound judgment, his administrative abilities and his long service to the nation for four decades gave him a just claim to the succession.[27] In spite of the general recognition of his claims, his nomination in the congressional caucus was by no means assured. The principal opposition came from two directions. First, the New York Republican leaders wished to terminate the long control exercised over national politics by the Virginians. Unfortunately, their only candidate was Daniel D. Tompkins, a capable wartime governor who was not widely known outside the state. A far more significant rival was the jovial and handsome William H. Crawford, enormously popular with the congressmen who would decide the nomination. His most important support came from the South and the West, and from the more conservative Republicans, who had not relished Monroe's conscription scheme nor his support of a federal bank. Since Crawford had been in Europe during the last years of the war, he had not had to commit himself on these issues.

Although Monroe wanted to avoid the stigma of being the Virginia candidate, the backing of his own state was essential. There was some uncertainty, however, whether the members of the Junto, some of whom had never forgiven him for his conduct in 1808, would endorse him. Fortunately, he enjoyed the unquestioned support of a substantial block of influential Virginians—Senators James Barbour and Armistead T. Mason, Governor Hugh Nelson and a trio of important congressmen —James Pleasants, Thomas Newton and William H. Roane. Former Old Republican sympathizers John Taylor of Caroline, Littleton Waller Tazewell and Alexander McRae lent their weight to his candidacy. Among his former supporters in 1808 only John Randolph, now quite without a following in his native state, was overtly hostile. During 1815 Monroe and George Hay, who acted as his father-in-law's campaign manager in Virginia, devoted considerable effort to wooing reluctant state leaders. Special attention was given to Thomas Ritchie and Spencer Roane, both of whom were rather cool to Monroe. They were again shown the letters which Monroe had written in 1808 asserting his attachment to the Republican cause and his hostility to the formation of a third party.[28] After examining these letters Roane endorsed Monroe, who, as he wrote James Barbour, merited the nomination "on the ground of having chimed in with the present administration, and rendered great and meritorious services." [29] Monroe was especially worried about Giles and Nicholas, two of his severest critics in the past. Indeed, Monroe believed that they were conspiring with the New

Yorkers to form an anti-Monroe coalition. The only basis he had for this suspicion was a trip Giles made to New York in 1815. Nicholas ultimately gave his support to Monroe, and apparently Giles raised no objections.[30] The Virginia caucus, meeting in advance of the congressional caucus, chose electors favorable to Monroe but did not name him as the candidate. This was in accordance with his wishes, for it reduced his identification as the Virginia candidate.[31]

The sharpest conflict over the nomination was waged in the halls of Congress during the session 1815–1816, as the supporters of the rival candidates sought to assure victory in the caucus. The forces were so evenly matched and the outcome so uncertain that Monroe's backers, capably led by James Barbour, seriously contemplated not attending the caucus and permitting him to be nominated by state legislatures.[32] In the contest over the nomination, which was essentially between Crawford and Monroe, for Tompkins had no following outside his own state, the Secretary of State had a distinct advantage. His long public career had made him much better known than Crawford to state leaders. Consequently, he had the endorsement of state party organizations, although in many cases the congressmen from those states preferred the Georgian. Following the example set by Jefferson, Madison was outwardly neutral, but it was accepted that Monroe had his support. In practical terms this meant that the columns of the *National Intelligencer,* whose contents were copied widely by other papers, were full of pro-Monroe articles. Moreover, as a member of Madison's Cabinet, Crawford hesitated to contest the nomination with a senior colleague known to be favored by the President and having wide national support. If Monroe were nominated in a contest with Crawford, then the Georgian could hardly expect further preferment in office or look forward to Monroe's endorsement in 1824. At forty-four, Crawford felt he could afford to wait eight years. Although he did not withdraw, as Monroe's managers wished, he never publicly admitted his candidacy. This ambiguity, which placed his supporters in an awkward position, substantially lessened his chances. Undoubtedly Crawford would have pursued a more aggressive course if he had been more certain of victory in the caucus.

In the years after the election, Crawford saw himself as deserving Monroe's lasting gratitude for having stood aside in favor of his senior colleague. Consequently, when Monroe remained neutral during the election of 1824, Crawford was understandably bitter, for he felt entitled to the President's endorsement. That Monroe never accepted the view that Crawford had smoothed the way for him in 1816 was partly the fault of Crawford's managers. In the event that he was not nominated by the caucus, Crawford had instructed them to issue a statement that his name had been put forward without his consent. Their failure to issue this declaration and Crawford's silence left the impression that he had organized an extensive campaign for the nomination.[33]

The choice of Monroe was facilitated not only by Crawford's uncertain course but also by the complexities of New York State politics. Although the New Yorkers felt that it was high time that a native of their state, now the most populous in the Union, should be advanced to the Presidency, they realized that neither Tompkins nor any other state leader was sufficiently well-known to command a majority in the caucus. The best they could hope for was the second place on the ticket. Under these circumstances the logical course for the New Yorkers, if they wished to curb the "Virginia influence," was to turn to Crawford, but internecine rivalries made this an impossibility. At this time Ambrose Spencer (a devoted Clintonian) was battling with Martin Van Buren for control of the state party. From the moment that Spencer announced his preference for Crawford, Van Buren was unwillingly committed to opposing the candidacy of the Secretary of the Treasury, since Crawford's nomination would be a victory for the Clintonians. Yet the hostility to another Virginia President was so great in New York that Van Buren had no choice but to insist that the state's congressional delegation, which he controlled, remain pledged to Tompkins until the caucus assembled. He was also successful in preventing the state legislature from nominating Crawford. Had it been known in advance of the caucus that fourteen of the eighteen members of the New York delegation would vote for Crawford, Monroe's chances would have been substantially reduced. Van Buren with the help of three members pledged to Monroe, Peter B. Porter, John W. Taylor and Enos Throop, was able to prevent the alignment of the delegation from being generally known.[34] Although many Pennsylvanians, among them Albert Gallatin (absent in France), were inclined to Crawford, the delegation was kept in the Monroe camp by Senators Jonathan Roberts and Abner Lacock. At one point Lacock called on Crawford to plead with him to withdraw so that Monroe, the last of the Revolutionary generation to offer for the Presidency, would be nominated.[35]

As the session wore on it seemed likely that the caucus might not assemble, for the managers of both candidates did not feel confident of victory. In mid-March, long after the usual date for the caucus, the Crawfordites posted an anonymous notice summoning the Republicans to a meeting to nominate candidates for the Presidency and vice-presidency. At this meeting on March 21, only fifty-seven members—less than half the Republicans in Congress—were present. Since a nomination by a minority was out of the question, the assembled congressmen issued a formal call for a caucus to be held on March 16. The second caucus drew 118 members, for only twenty-four regular Republicans (nine of whom were out of town) failed to attend. Although Monroe's backers realized after the rump caucus that they could probably muster a small majority for the Secretary of State, the margin was insufficient since a victory won by a handful of votes would be more damaging than congressional inactivity. Consequently, Barbour enlisted the support of Henry Clay and John W. Taylor to prevent a caucus nomination. However, both Clay's resolve declaring it inexpedient to nominate candidates and Taylor's resolution condemning the caucus system were voted down. Unable to control the meeting, Monroe's managers were obliged to place his name in competition with Crawford. The outcome was close: sixty-five for Monroe to fifty-four for Crawford. A number of last-minute defections from the Crawford camp brought Monroe his safe, if not overwhelming majority.[36] Monroe owed his victory to his popularity among state party leaders. Congressmen, no matter what their personal preference may have been, could not afford to ignore endorsements of Monroe such as that of the Pennsylvania legislature and of the Republican conventions held in Rhode Island and Massachusetts.[37] The vice-presidential nomination presented no difficulties, Tompkins winning easily over Simon Snyder of Pennsylvania.

In a very real sense the election began and ended in the caucus, for the only contest was between Monroe and Crawford. The Federalists nominated Rufus King, but the party was so shattered that they offered only token opposition. Consequently, there was none of the bitter party animosity which had been characteristic of previous elections and which had served to stimulate public interest. Of campaigning there was none. Prior to the election of 1840, the candidates assumed a detached stance: they undertook no tours, made no speeches, and issued no statements. If propaganda was thought necessary, it was left to local leaders, who might call public meetings, but who usually allowed the anonymous writers in the press to carry the burden.

In 1816, each side had little to attack and less to defend. The Federalists could think of nothing to say other than to revive stories about Monroe's conduct as Minister to France during the Washington administration. Some New York Republican editors complained unhappily about the "Virginia influence" in the party, but even they fell into line with other party newspapers and dutifully published laudatory sketches reviewing Monroe's career and praising his patriotic devotion. For the first time the Presidency seemed to be offered as a reward for meritorious service or as an honor bestowed on a respected public servant, rather than as a prize to be carried off by the strongest party in a bitterly fought contest. It was not that Monroe was unpopular nor that his claim to the succession was in doubt, but without opposition there was no need for strenuous exertions. In many states factional conflicts were far more interesting than the Presidential election. The results of the electoral balloting were scarcely surprising: 183 votes cast for Monroe, 34 for Rufus King. Although Tompkins received the same number of electoral votes as Monroe, the Federalists scattered their second ballots among a number of candidates.[38]

IV

Once the election was over there was considerable speculation about the composition of the Cabinet, for the President-elect, although he consulted many, was noncommittal about his intentions. It was not until mid-February 1817 that his choice was generally known.[39] In shaping his Cabinet he took as his guideline a frequently repeated phrase: ". . . the Chief Magistrate of the Country ought not be the head of a party, but of the nation itself." [40] This did not mean, as some orthodox Republicans feared, that Monroe intended to give a practical application of Jefferson's maxim that we are all federalists, all republicans, by including Federalists in the Cabinet.[41] While Monroe regarded political parties as an anomaly in a democratic state and hoped to facilitate the amalgamation of all parties into one, he was not prepared to go quite so far as to act on Andrew Jackson's suggestion that Federalist William Drayton of North Carolina be made Secretary of War. Nor was he prepared to endorse George Sullivan's recommendation of Daniel Webster as Attorney General.[42] He did not think the time was right for such an advanced step, although he agreed with Jackson that many Federalists who had rallied to the government during the war merited recognition. However, many others still cherished "principles unfriendly to our system of government," of which the Hartford Convention had furnished adequate proof. If he appointed a member of the opposition, might he not risk the renewal of a seemingly defunct party? Moreover, might not such an action discourage loyal Republicans? Ought he not, he asked Jackson, seek to preserve "free government" by depending on its "decided friends, who stood firm in the day of trial? . . ." [43]

Insofar as his Cabinet appointments were concerned, Monroe interpreted his maxim that he was the head of the nation to involve only more effective representation to the sections than had been the case in the past. He was particularly interested in placing a prominent Westerner in the War Department, although he was not able to execute this intention. At the same time, he was also anxious to lessen Southern influence, about which there had been so much complaint, and to disassociate the State Department from the popular notion that this was the post assigned to the President's chosen successor. In his own case he believed his tenure in the State Department had been far less important in winning him public esteem than his services either as diplomat or in the War Department. [44] From a practical point of view, it was impossible to appoint either Crawford or Clay—the chief contenders for the succession—to the State Department, for the disappointed aspirant would inevitably organize an opposition to the administration. With these considerations in mind Monroe constructed his ideal Cabinet: John Quincy Adams, Secretary of State; William H. Crawford, Secretary of the Treasury; and (here he was not successful) Henry Clay, Secretary of War. Honoring the usages of his predecessors, Monroe proposed to retain those members of Madison's Cabinet still in office—Crowninshield as Secretary of the Navy and Richard Rush as Attorney General. Since Rush preferred a diplomatic assignment, this post was shortly vacated. Technically, Crawford was a holdover, but his retention was more than a courteous gesture. As a leading Republican Presidential aspirant and responsible (in his own estimation at least) for assuring Monroe's nomination in 1816, Crawford expected the Secretaryship of State. Early in January, however, Monroe called on him to explain why political considerations made this impossible. Reluctantly Crawford agreed to remain in the Treasury, since he did not want to lose either the backing of a popular President or the extensive patronage under the control of his department. [45] This was an important victory for Monroe, for Crawford, if not in the Cabinet, could easily become the focal point of a formidable opposition. Monroe certainly considered the Georgian, of whose abilities Gallatin had a high opinion, eminently qualified for the Treasury.

Monroe was less successful with Clay, who declined to enter the War Department, which he regarded as inferior to the post allotted Crawford. Instead, he preferred to be free to oppose or support the administration in Congress. Finding another prominent Westerner proved impossible. Jackson was considered, but he was not offered the appointment, when Monroe learned that he was not interested in entering the Cabinet. Monroe next wrote former Governor Isaac Shelby of Kentucky, whose popularity in the West as well as his administrative ability made him an excellent choice. Shelby, however, who was sixty-seven years old, declined because of his age. The other names suggested to Monroe—William H. Harrison, Richard M. Johnson, Lewis M. Cass—were ruled out either because they lacked stature or were considered unsuitable for other reasons.[46] Not until October did Monroe give up the quest for a Westerner, offering the appointment to John C. Calhoun, who promptly accepted. Although Calhoun had no military experience, he had one important qualification—as a member of Congress during and after the war he had supported the administration's military program. At least Monroe could count on his full cooperation in carrying out the improvements in the nation's defenses which he planned.

Calhoun, who joined the Cabinet in December, was at thirty-five the youngest member. He was a far different person from the gloomy States' Rightist and frustrated politician of the 1840s—the sombre countenance and the sunken and burning eyes were still in the future. In 1817 he was tall and angular, his handsome face surmounted by a shock of brown hair. Between Adams and Calhoun a strong and lasting bond was immediately established, for they shared many intellectual interests, a love of order and logic, and a common enthusiasm for a nationalist program. Both were ambitious, but neither placed ambition before the demands of conscience. It was rather remarkable that these two men of such disparate background both possessed a puritan conviction of righteousness—for Adams and Calhoun political judgments tended to be moral rather than pragmatic. When Adams described Calhoun as a man with a fair and candid mind, quick understanding, and enlarged philosophic views, which enabled him to move above sectional and factional prejudices, he was in a sense projecting his own image—or at least what he liked to think of himself at his best. Calhoun was a superior Secretary of War, bringing to the department an administrative energy and efficiency it had never previously enjoyed.[47]

Had a poll been taken in the Capital in the fall of 1817, most Washingtonians would have selected Crawford as the outstanding figure in the administration. The tall, good-looking Georgian with a rather heavy build exuded a self-confidence derived from his past successes, his unquestioned personal popularity, and the assurance that he would be the next President. A facile raconteur fond of society, he was, in contrast to Secretary Adams, at home in the most varied circles. Behind the bluff and hearty manner, which had won him many followers, he concealed a masterly sense of political manipulation. On all the great questions of the day his stand was temperate, or more accurately tentative, for he had never directly endorsed nor firmly repudiated any of the major national issues. In a Cabinet composed of lesser men, such as Wirt and Crowninshield, he would easily have been the dominant figure. It was his misfortune to be pitted against two men of equally great ambition, but who possessed more subtle minds; and to serve under a President who, for all his apparent simplicity of manner, preferred the more scholarly and intellectual qualities of Crawford's chief rivals. It was also Crawford's misfortune that he did not grasp Monroe's idealistic approach to public service. The willingness of the President to sacrifice his popularity to carry out policies essential for the nation was alien to Craford's pragmatic approach to public life. Crawford also failed to realize that the President, reared in the old Virginia school of manners, attached particular value to outward harmony. Not that Crawford's manners were bad, but having been trained in the rougher school of Georgia politics, he tended to bluster when opposed; and in contrast to his colleagues, he often appeared to be tactless and rude. As Crawford witnessed Adams' growing ascendancy in policy making and realized that Monroe was not going to endorse his candidacy, the Secretary of the Treasury not only tended to be openly impatient with the President but secretly condoned opposition to administration policies. In the belief that the stature of both Adams and Calhoun would be reduced, Crawford after 1821 encouraged his supporters (dubbed the Radicals) to attack the President's program. In the long run Clay's open hostility to the administration did his reputation less harm than Crawford's secret antagonism.[48]

To long-time residents of Washington, the least familiar Cabinet appointee was Secretary of State John Quincy Adams, who had been absent from the United States for almost nine years on diplomatic missions in St. Petersburg, Ghent and London. Although he was not formally invited to join the administration until March 6, Monroe had decided early in January to place him in the State Department.[49] From every point of view, this appointment, which astonished many, was unexceptionable. It assigned a major post to a prominent New Englander of undoubted talents (previous Cabinet members from this section had been mediocrities), who possessed unusual diplomatic experience. The son of a Federalist President and himself an ex-Federalist (his authorship of *Publicola* was by no means forgotten), Adams represented that moderate wing of Federalism which had made its peace with the Republicans in the Jefferson era. In giving Adams this post, Monroe was also recognizing the growing importance of the commercial element in the Republican party. No one, including the new Secretary, had any suspicion that a New Englander, so long absent in Europe, would, within a year after his return, attract such a significant following that he would be regarded as a prime contender for the succession. Had Monroe anticipated this development, he might not have appointed Adams, since he wanted to disassociate this office from the presidential succession. The only opposition to Adams' nomination came from Clay, whose close friend Jonathan Russell cherished a personal grudge against Adams.[50]

Unlike his colleagues, Adams was not physically impressive. Short, fat, bald and plagued with a constantly running eye, he seemed like a pigmy among a race of handsome and vigorous giants. As harsh in judging himself as he was in condemning others, Adams pictured himself as a "man of reserved, cold, austere and forbidding manners; my political adversaries say a gloomy misanthropist, and my personal enemies an unsocial savage." [51] Ill at ease in large gatherings, the Secretary of State was quite a different person in small groups, where he could be a voluble, if at times pedantic conversationalist. While his personal coldness was somewhat of a handicap in a politically sensitive post, he more than compensated for this shortcoming by his ability to present his views with remarkable clarity and persuasiveness. In the confines of the Cabinet his arguments more often than not succeeded in removing the doubts of hesitant colleagues. Not the least of his virtues was a true sensitivity to the moods and feelings of others.

As Secretary of State, he worked closely under Monroe's direction, seeing the President more frequently than the other department heads. In the course of their long association, Adams came to have a sincere admiration for the President, although at first he was irritated by Monroe's slowness in reaching decisions, which he then interpreted as indecisive-ness and procrastination, but eventually he realized that this was simply the President's reflective habit. Moreover, Adams came to understand that the President often delayed reaching a decision simply to gain time to achieve unanimity in the Cabinet. One trait he admired in the President, perhaps because he lacked this to some degree, was Monroe's ability to listen to and to evaluate advice, which Adams felt was a quality "which in so high a place is an infallible test of a great mind." [52] Since Adams saw the President nearly every day when Monroe was in the Capital, it is a tribute to the degree of understanding between them that only once in nearly eight years of close association did they verge on a quarrel, and then not on an issue relating to basic policy. Even this was a momentary episode without the slightest effect on their sub-sequent relations.

In view of the detailed account of his activities which he provided in his diary, and the general conviction that he was much more capable than his chief, there has been a tendency to depict Adams as the guiding force in foreign policy. This conclusion is far from correct. If Adams' diary is read with attention to his conferences with the President rather than with an eye to his discussions with the European Ministers in Washington, then it becomes quite clear that Monroe, like his prede-cessors, controlled foreign policy, which was the largest independent authority vested in the executive. He not only read and revised all Adams' dispatches, but he indicated the direction which he wished Adams to follow during discussions with the Ministers. This does not mean that Monroe was impervious to advice—he always listened to Adams with attention and frequently revised his own thinking as a result of the Secretary's arguments. On those occasions when the Presi-dent adhered to his own conclusions, Adams fully accepted the finality of Monroe's decision, for the Secretary believed in the concept of the unity of the executive—the Secretaries, in Adams' view, were but agents in carrying out presidential policy. Monroe certainly gave Adams a much greater area of independent action than previous Secretaries had enjoyed, for he insisted that resident diplomats take up all public business with the Secretary of State. Consequently, the Secretary of State was a much more important figure (indeed much like a European Foreign Minister) than he had been under Jefferson and Madison, who freely discussed official business with the diplomats in Washington. Adams regularly reported to the President about his conferences and was given specific guidelines for all continuing discussions. Their association was such a happy and successful one largely because they shared a common view of the basic objectives and interests of the United States. Perhaps the fairest assessment of their relationship was Bradford Perkins' comment that Monroe determined broad outlines of policy, leaving tactical considerations to Adams.[53]

Since Attorney General Rush (filling in as acting Secretary of State until Adams arrived in October) was slated for the London ministry, Monroe hoped to replace him with a Westerner; but again the search was fruitless, for none of the candidates seemed to be properly qualified.[54] In the end Monroe turned to an old friend, William Wirt, now a successful Baltimore attorney. The forty-five-year-old Wirt was perhaps the most personable member of the Cabinet—tall and heroically proportioned, he moved with the ease of a famous and successful man. According to John P. Kennedy, Wirt's first biographer, the Attorney General with "his clear, kind blue eyes, the light hair falling crisp and numerous curls on a broad forehead, the high arching eyebrow, the large nose and ample chin, might recall a resemblance to the portrait of Goethe." This comparison was undoubtedly relished by Wirt, who had won considerable contemporary fame for his life of Patrick Henry published in 1817 and his earlier light satire on American manners, *The Letters of a British Spy.* Inclined to be indolent and fond of good company, Wirt much preferred the life of a man of letters, but his limited means and the demands of ten children forced him to devote his talents to the law. By 1816 he was a ranking figure at the bar, admired for his eloquence rather than for his learning. He had no trace of political ambition and interested himself but little in party affairs. He accepted the appointment only on the understanding that he could continue to practice law. Although the office was looked upon as a part-time post, he was punctilious in his duties and established the first systematic records kept in his department.[55]

All of Monroe's department heads remained with him during his eight years in office except the Secretary of the Navy, Benjamin W. Crowninshield, who resigned in September 1818. Crowninshield, who had been appointed by Madison in 1814, was a member of a prominent merchant family of Salem whose members had rendered useful services to the Republican cause. He had little involvement in national politics, and was usually only to be seen in Washington during the sessions of Congress. As Adams noted of both Crowninshield and his successor, Smith Thompson, this was an office which sat lightly on the shoulders of its occupants.[56] Crowninshield seems to have been a competent administrator, but he made little contribution to the formulation of policy. He left the Cabinet in 1818, nominally because his wife declined to live in Washington, but this was not the real reason. Monroe, who rarely lost his temper, had spoken harshly to Crowninshield about a mistake in the arrangements for the President's inspection tour of the forts in the Bay area in the summer of 1818, for which he blamed the Secretary of the Navy. It was after this incident that Crowninshield, who was hurt by the President's tone, resigned.[57]

Monroe happened to be in Albemarle when he received Crowninshield's resignation, and on his way back to the Capital he discussed the matter of a replacement with Madison, who rather astonishingly recommended that the post be abolished and the duties of the Secretary turned over to the Board of Navy Commissioners. Monroe, however, did not apply this advice, which disagreed with his own view that the responsibility of the Navy Department was sufficient to justify a Cabinet rank.[58] Although the President wished to use this vacancy to appoint a Westerner, none of those proposed was acceptable to him. When Adams suggested former Governor Thomas Worthington of Ohio, the President eliminated him because he had been told that Worthington was "a man of indirect ways, upon whose steadiness no reliance was to be placed." [59] The President then turned to the Middle states, a region not represented in the Cabinet, and approached Commodore John Rodgers, who declined since he did not want to give up his naval rank. Monroe then appointed Smith Thompson, the chief justice of the New York Supreme Court and a close ally of Martin Van Buren. Thompson had been reluctant to accept, because he considered the salary inadequate, but he yielded to pressure from Martin Van Buren, who wanted to strengthen the position of New York Republicans in the national administration.[60] In the Cabinet Thompson tended to judge issues primarily in relation to their effect on his own political fortunes or those of the New York Republicans. It was only gradually realized that Thompson had presidential ambitions. In 1823, he very unwillingly, and again under pressure from Van Buren, who did not regard him as a serious presidential prospect, accepted an appointment to the United States Supreme Court. He was replaced by thirty-six-year-old Samuel L. Southard, the first citizen from New Jersey to hold a Cabinet appointment. An active Republican (as was his father, Representative Henry Southard), Samuel Southard had served in the Senate and been a Republican elector in 1820. He apparently owed his appointment to Calhoun's recommendation and the President's desire to continue to have representation in his Cabinet from the Middle states. Southard was an energetic Secretary, spending more time in Washington than his predecessors and recommending a number of important reforms, only one of which—the construction of naval hospitals—was carried out during his tenure in office. Personally agreeable, he was a close friend of Monroe's son-in-law, Samuel L. Gouverneur, with whom he shared a warm admiration for Calhoun. Both Wirt and Southard continued in the Cabinet during the Adams administration.[61]

Not unexpectedly, the least important figure in the Monroe administration was Vice-President Daniel Tompkins. A self-made man who had been enormously popular in New York, he had been placed on the ticket to gratify the New York Republicans and to reward him for his loyalty to the administration during the war. Any opportunities which he may have had to exert influence in an office whose powers had been strictly circumscribed by the Constitution, and by tradition, were negated by his personal misfortunes. As war governor and as commander of the Third Military District, he had borrowed large sums of money (often on his own signature) and made extensive disbursements without getting proper receipts. When the war ended his accounts were found to be short, although none doubted his integrity, and his personal fortune was seized to satisfy creditors. Under the strain of these disclosures, he had begun to drink heavily. On the rare occasions when he presided over the Senate he was often drunk. Ordinarily he was not present, either confined to his boarding house or at his home in New York. His accounts were finally balanced by the state in 1820, but the shortages had been so highly publicized that he was defeated by Clinton for the governorship in 1820, although the regular Republicans, who had supported Tompkins, won control of the legislature. In 1824 Congress reimbursed him to the extent of $95,000, which was considered a fair commission on the money he had borrowed during the war. Broken completely in health long before Monroe's second term ended, he died in June 1825.[62]

CHAPTER 20

THE ERA OF
GOOD FEELINGS:
IDEAL

ALTHOUGH the phrase "Era of Good Feelings," so inextricably associated with the Monroe administration, was coined by a Federalist newspaper in Boston in 1817, no term more aptly describes the objectives of President Monroe.[1] In its most general aspect the phrase reflected the new awareness of the community of interest and purpose binding the people of the United States together—a unity all the more prized since it had so nearly been destroyed during the war by internal divisions and external threats. The President, who was aware of this vague and unspecific aspiration, sought to harness it to broad national aims. He hoped that this new sense of "oneness" would operate as a useful force in leading the nation to a full utilization of its resources and that it would also serve as a means of reconciling party animosities. The two goals were thought of as complementary, for the elimination of party rivalry would enable the people to inaugurate policies on the basis of national, not party interests. That Monroe identified these interests with the goals and objectives of the Republican party goes without saying. His view of the Republican party, however, was different from that which he had entertained in the 1790s. He now viewed the party as embracing all elements of American society, and therefore he accepted the fact that it must also adopt measures meeting the needs of the widest possible spectrum of American opinion. In one sense Monroe's policies were founded upon the acceptance of compromise, or, to use a more modern phrase, upon the politics of consensus. An agreement had to be forged among the differing interests within the community to achieve a program which would be generally accepted without requiring one group to suffer unduly in order to provide an advantage for another element. To the translation of these generalities into a specific program Monroe devoted his energies during his two terms in office.

Monroe was not alone in thinking that the time had come to put an end to party warfare. He had, after all, inherited a party which had made considerable advances toward the absorption of Federalism, having reconciled itself just before the end of the Madison administration to a national bank and a protective tariff. As Nicholas Biddle commented shortly after the election: "The nation has become tired of the follies of faction and the ruling party has outgrown many of the childish notions with which they began their career 20 years since...." [2] With this conclusion many of the younger Republicans were in full accord. Even Madison, who did not share Monroe's enthusiasm for the amalgamation of parties admitted to William Eustis some years later that the Republicans "had been reconciled to certain measures and arrangements which may be as proper now as they were premature and suspicious when urged by the champions of Federalism." [3]

II

On the morning of March 4, 1817, the city of Washington was in the grip of an unaccustomed excitement as thousands of citizens made their way over the rutted and dusty streets toward Capitol Hill to witness the inauguration of President Monroe. The weather itself was sufficient to bring out the citizenry—warm and sunny, an unusually mild day for the season. By noon nearly 8,000 persons—the largest crowd ever to gather in the Capital up to this time—had assembled before the temporary structure where Congress sat pending the restoration of the burned-out capitol. In front of this frame building, located some two hundred yards east of the capitol, a platform had been erected upon which the President was to take the oath of office.

This open-air ceremony had been made necessary by the inability of the Senate and House to agree on the inaugural arrangements. The dispute had begun when the House flatly refused to permit the Senators to introduce their elegant red velvet armchairs into the quarters of the Representatives, where the inaugural ceremony usually took place. Unable to reach an accord, at the last minute they had agreed on an outdoor ceremony. The stubbornness manifested by the House was attributed to Speaker Clay's resentment at not being made Secretary of State. If this interpretation was correct, it was a singularly petty action for a man whose conduct was generally marked by much generosity. The fact that Clay was conspicuously absent from the inaugural seemed to confirm the report.[4]

This was not the only quarrel brought forth by the occasion. The members of the diplomatic corps, as so often happened in Washington where no rigid protocol had been established, were enmeshed in an unpleasant wrangle over precedence. The impasse was resolved by a decision not to attend—a conclusion facilitated by the failure of the diplomats to receive an official invitation.[5]

At noon the President-elect and Vice-President Tompkins arrived, having been escorted by citizens on horseback. At the capitol, Monroe was greeted with military honors by the Marine Corps and several militia regiments. Then, accompanied by Madison and the justices of the Supreme Court, they entered the House chamber, where Tompkins took the oath of office. After the Vice-President, who was not expected to play a conspicuous role, delivered a five-minute speech, the official party moved to the outdoor platform where Monroe, flanked by the members of the Madison administration, the justices and members of Congress, stepped forward to deliver his inaugural address.

To the residents of Washington the President-elect was a familiar figure. They had long been accustomed to see him go about the city clad in the small clothes of an earlier age—usually a black coat, black knee breeches and black silk hose. On ceremonial occasions he sometimes wore a blue coat and buff knee breeches, an outfit reminiscent of the military uniform of the Revolutionary era. Now in his fifty-ninth year, the President was still erect in bearing, robust and vigorous in manner, although his hair had grayed and his face had become deeply lined during the war years. In the hearts and minds of his auditors Monroe did not arouse a sense of passionate devotion, but rather a sentiment of respect and esteem and a feeling of gratitude for his unselfish service to the nation. Insofar as emotions were touched, it was at the sight of one of the last remaining veterans of the Revolution still in high office.

His abilities as a practical leader were universally acknowledged, although none thought of him as possessing remarkable intellectual qualities. Perhaps no one better stated the contemporary opinion of Monroe than William Wirt in his *Letters of a British Spy* published in 1803. In his widely quoted portrait of Monroe, Wirt observed: "Nature has given him a mind neither rapid nor rich, and therefore he cannot shine on a subject which is entirely new to him. But to compensate him for this he is endued with a spirit of restless emulation, a judgment strong and clear, and a habit of application which no difficulties can shake, no labours can tire." [6] In private, Wirt was somewhat more direct, expressing the opinion that the original dullness of the President's mind had been overcome by application and intensive study, which had given him a depth of knowledge and understanding usually considered an attribute of natural and superior talent.[7] Monroe's ability to apply himself was a virtue much admired by Wirt, whose mind was indeed agile, but whose indolence prevented him from making the most of his capacities.

Calhoun, whose intellectual attainments were considerably greater than Wirt's, made a rather similar evaluation of his former chief. Shortly after Monroe's death in 1831, Calhoun commented to Monroe's son-in-law: "Tho' not brilliant, few men were his equals in wisdom, firmness and devotion to the country. He had a wonderful intellectual patience; and could above all men, that I ever knew, when called on to decide an important point, hold the subject immovably fixed under his attention, until he had mastered it in all of its relations. It was mainly to this admirable quality that he owed his highly accurate judgment. I have known many much more rapid in reaching a conclusion, but few with a certainty so unerring." [8] Of the accuracy of Calhoun's assessment the diary of John Quincy Adams offers more than ample proof. Monroe, who rather resented Wirt's imputation that his mind was slow in its operations, considered his ability to reply extemporaneously to the addresses presented to him during his tour of New England, in 1817, as refuting Wirt's charges.[9] These formal and rather stereotyped responses, however, were not what Wirt had in mind when he commented on the intellectual powers of the President.

Although Monroe's natural dignity made his public bearing impressive, he was never at his best on such occasions as the inaugural. Never a distinguished speaker and without any facility for a well-turned phrase, his address, badly read in an almost inaudible voice, was not calculated to stir his audience. As one of those present commented, it was written in a plain style with a "homespun character," which made it pleasing to the average person.[10]

In accordance with established custom, Monroe used the address to formulate in simple and direct phrases the principles upon which his administration would be based. In broad terms he formulated a program of moderate nationalism, speaking of the need to encourage industry, trade and commerce, and to construct a system of roads and canals with "constitutional sanction." His comment upon the deeply controversial subject of internal improvements left his audience in considerable doubt about his views on the legality of such projects. He also touched on the need to foster manufacturing to free the nation from its dependence on foreign imports and at the same time provide a market for American raw materials. The longest and most detailed portion of his address was concerned with the improvement of the nation's defenses, a subject in which he took a particular interest, and also one which revealed that his concept of the limits of nationalism was somewhat different from that of his fellow citizens. Although he admitted that the distance of the United States from Europe provided a considerable security for the country, he did not believe that the restoration of peace had eliminated all danger. As long as American citizens were engaged in commerce on the high seas and active in the fisheries, the nation must be ready to protect its maritime interests. A country which failed to jealously guard its rights "scarcely can be said to hold a place among independent nations. National honor is national property of the highest value." Security could only be permanently ensured by maintaining an army large enough to repel the first attack while other forces were being mobilized. He urged the complete reorganization of the militia in order to provide more adequate training. Such fundamental changes, he pointed out, could only be undertaken in the leisure provided by peace. Although he did not make the point in his address, he also considered a stronger defense establishment essential to implement American foreign policy—a diplomacy based on strength had a far better chance of realizing its objectives than a policy derived from weakness.

These opinions, which were so contrary to Republican doctrine, did not receive a warm response. The public was far more interested in his views on the relationship between the two parties, for there had been much speculation that the Federalists, having largely ceased their opposition since the war, would be welcomed into the administration and thus end the party conflicts of the past. Monroe, indeed, had turned over the whole question for several months, consulting his friends and listening to comments from major political leaders. Except from Andrew Jackson and the Federalists themselves he met with no encouragement to take such a positive step. Even the younger generation of party workers, who were for the most part deeply attached to Monroe, and

whose hostility toward the Federalists was much less than that of their
elders, had cautioned him against advancing Federalists lest he divide
his own party.[11] Therefore, in his inaugural Monroe did not go beyond
a vague statement praising the harmony prevailing among the people,
who now constituted one family with a common interest. As one observer commented, this approach tended to bury the members of the
opposition in oblivion rather than reconcile them with the Republicans. If they were disappointed by the President's attitude, the Federalists made no complaint, but joined the Republicans in lavishing praise
on his address.

Since Congress was not in session and since there were no pressing
foreign or domestic problems, there was no need for the President to
remain close to the Capital. Instead of following the example of Jefferson and Madison, who retired to Virginia for most of the summer,
Monroe announced shortly after his inauguration that he intended to
make a tour of the Northern and Eastern states. His declared purpose,
and this was logical in view of his recent emphasis upon national defense, was to inspect coastal and frontier fortifications.[12] A more important but unstated motive was to create an occasion for the Federalists
to demonstrate their loyalty to the national government in a public way
and thereby hasten the process of party amalgamation.

Thoroughly convinced that the "existence of parties is not necessary
to free government," the President had set as a primary goal of his
administration the elimination of all parties. Although this could be
most easily accomplished by honoring the Federalists with offices, Monroe felt there were many reasons rendering such appointments out of
the question. He explained his reluctance to elevate Federalists to high
office at some length to Andrew Jackson in December 1816, when the
general had suggested that William Drayton, a North Carolina Federalist who had served with distinction during the war, be made Secretary of War.[13] In the first place, Monroe cited what might be termed
the Republican myth—the belief entertained by the Republicans that
the ultimate goal of the Federalists had been to convert the government
into a monarchy. This objective had never been realized, according to
Monroe, because the Federalists had never found the right opportunity
to carry it out and because of Washington's hostility to the plan during
the formative years of the new government. In view of the past history
of the opposition party, how could he trust its former leaders? Had not
the Hartford Convention shown that this spirit was not yet dead? If
he conferred appointments on Federalists, he might encourage the re-

vival of this expiring but not entirely defunct party. Secondly, he pointed out to Jackson that showering honors on the Federalists would automatically arouse hostility in his own party, whose members expected him to place his trust in those who had stood by the government in its hour of trial. Even though he believed that the perpetuation of republican institutions depended on the elimination of parties, he was not prepared to elevate the Federalists to office.

This carefully phrased letter was designed to place his views on record early in the administration and enable him to refute charges that he was federalizing the Republican party. The letter served its purpose, for Monroe kept it on his desk, reading it to those who voiced such complaints. In 1824 Jackson also found his letter to the President useful in winning support of Tennessee Federalists for his presidential candidacy. Early in 1824, much to Monroe's embarrassment, his retained copy was removed from his files and published along with Jackson's letter. The President was distressed not only because of his harsh comments about the Federalists, which seemed to negate the concept of an Era of Good Feelings, but also because it involved him in the presidential electioneering at a time when he was observing strict neutrality. Rufus King, for one, was so offended by Monroe's remarks that he terminated the friendship which had developed between him and the President.[14]

Although Monroe did not announce his plans for a tour until the spring of 1817, the decision had been made some months earlier. He never elaborated on the reasons which led him to undertake the journey, but there was an obvious analogy with Washington's tour begun in New England in 1789 and completed two years later by a visit to the Southern states. Just as Washington's tour was intended to give meaning to the newly formed Union in the form of a personal symbol, so Monroe sought to provide an occasion for the people to demonstrate the new spirit of unity animating the nation. The sight of Republicans and Federalists joining hands to welcome the Chief Executive would provide indisputable testimony that the political passions of an earlier age had at last subsided. Perhaps in reaching his decision Monroe may have recalled a letter he had received in the spring of 1816 from Christopher Hughes, a talented young Boston Republican, who reported that Harrison Gray Otis had expressed a strong wish to see the leading men at Washington travel throughout the country. Such a journey, Otis had told Hughes, would have a highly beneficial effect in New England.[15] Otis, one of the most important moderate Federalists, had already announced his intention of supporting the new administration. He, like so many others, saw no point in further opposing a party which had absorbed so many of the basic policies of the Federalists.[16]

Following the example of Washington, Monroe divided his tour into two sections, leaving the Southern and Western states until 1819.[17] However, he did not emulate the first President in all particulars. Anticipating that critics would liken his tour to a royal progress, he traveled as a private citizen, paying his own expenses and doing without an official escort. Nor did he stand on ceremony, as Washington had done in Boston, when he refused to dine with Governor John Hancock because the latter had not called on him first. On the contrary, Monroe made himself completely accessible to all parties and went out of his way to show respect to former Federalist leaders. Monroe was the ideal person to undertake this reconciliation. Most men immediately liked him, although he never aroused the same kind of enthusiasm which Jefferson could among his associates. In spite of his rather formal manners, Monroe had a rare ability of putting men at ease by his courtesy, his lack of condescension, his frankness and by what his contemporaries looked upon as his essential goodness and kindness of heart. These traits seem not only vague, but rather unexciting, yet they were the ones most commonly stressed by the people who knew him. Abigail Adams was struck by the same characteristics, when she met him during the tour. All who met him, she declared, were captivated by his "agreeable affability . . . unassuming manners . . . [and] his polite attentions to all orders and ranks." [18] However difficult it is to describe Monroe's charm, there can be no doubt that it was real. The Federalists, of course, could have resisted the blandishments of the most dazzling personality had they not wanted to be charmed. By his tact and courtesy Monroe built up a valuable reservoir of good will toward the administration.

Monroe began his journey on Sunday, June 1, setting out in his carriage for Baltimore accompanied by General Joseph Swift, chief engineer of the army and Superintendent of West Point, and his private secretary. Richard Rush and a few other officials accompanied him for several miles along the Bladensburg road. If Monroe had seriously hoped to be able to travel as a private person, he had to give up that notion in Baltimore. As he approached the city he was welcomed by hastily assembled cavalry units, which escorted him to the Fountain Inn, where Samuel Smith, William Winder and other local notables greeted him. The two days he spent in the city were a foretaste of what lay before him. Delegations of citizens presented addresses, to each of which he replied—often to as many as five a day—public dinners, parades, militia reviews and a tour of public monuments. In the midst of these activities he still found time to inspect the city's fortifications.[19] Wherever he went he was followed by a huge crowd, which surrounded him like "an agitated sea." [20] Although he declined all private invitations in Baltimore, he found this impossible as he traveled northward, for refusals might be taken as a rejection of Federalist overtures and thus defeat his purpose of effecting "a union of parties in support of our republican govt." [21]

Leaving his carriage in Baltimore, Monroe continued his journey by steamboat and in carriages leased from mail contractors, whose exorbitant charges he later paid out of his own pocket. Except for the first day's trip to Baltimore, he never again traveled on Sunday, for there had been some unfavorable newspaper comment on his failure to observe the Sabbath.[22] As he moved northward the claims on his time increased in each city, since the inhabitants had ample time to make elaborate arrangements. On his way from Philadelphia to New York the President stopped in Trenton, where, stirred by the memories evoked by the town, he delivered one of the most felicitous responses to the innumerable addresses, in which he referred to Trenton as the site where the hopes of the nation had revived at the ebb tide of the Revolution. Of his wound he said nothing, but the local press adequately reminded the citizens of his heroism. Here, as in every place, the people flocked not merely to behold the Chief Executive but to view one of the last of the patriots of 1776 who would hold high office.

After lingering in New York for a week broken by a steamer trip to West Point, Monroe moved to New England, where his tour reached a climax in a love feast of unparalleled enthusiasm. Few presidential visits before or since have aroused such an outpouring of emotion. Everywhere the leaders of both parties joined to welcome the President —the roar of cannon, streaming banners, ringing bells and cheering throngs betokened a degree of adulation for a Republican leader never thought possible a few years earlier. Only in Boston, where party animosity was still intense, did the two parties fail to cooperate. Here a species of rivalry developed as each tried to outdo the other in honoring the President. The Federalists stole a march on their Republican adversaries by sending a delegation headed by Otis to meet the President at Providence. This contention was embarrassing to Monroe, who had to exercise his tact to appease the Boston Republicans.[23] It was appropriate that his tour should reach its culminating point in the Citadel of Federalism, where he arrived on July 2 and remained to participate in the ceremonies of the Fourth of July.

The linking of the President's visit with the usual patriotic observances of the Fourth led to the most elaborate reception of the tour. The official functions commenced when he was met at Dedham by an aide of Governor John Brooks and a military escort. As he advanced to the city the procession was augmented by the carriages of public officials and private citizens. His progress toward the Boston Common, where the official welcoming party was waiting, was marked by cannon shot. A vast crowd, estimated at 40,000, lined the streets and filled every window along the route. As the President neared the Common mounted on a horse lent by West's Circus, he beheld an imposing spectacle—4,000 boys and girls from schools in Boston and nearby towns lined the approach to the official welcoming party. The boys were clad in buff trousers and blue coats, the girls in white; each bore a red or a white rose, an unmistakable allusion to the reconciliation of warring parties. Bowing to the ladies, who fluttered their handkerchiefs from the windows and porches of the buildings around the Common, Monroe rode on to the Exchange House. After the official welcome he sat down to a public dinner attended by the Governor, ex-President Adams, General Dearborn, Captains Hull and Perry, and, *mirabile dictu,* his old antagonist Timothy Pickering.[24] The Federalists had indeed come a long way.

During his five days in Boston, Monroe was incessantly on the move from early morning until late in the evening as he inspected naval and military installations and attended the entertainments arranged by the Federalists. Indeed, the eagerness of his former enemies to honor him was so great that Abigail Adams likened their attentions to an "expiation."[25] Bostonians who had not spoken to one another in years appeared side by side at private and public gatherings as though united in bonds of life-long friendship. In New England, at least, a new era was dawning.

On the third of July Monroe rose at six to breakfast with General James Miller, and then at eight he boarded a barge from the *Independence* for a tour of the forts in the harbor. After dinner at two with Governor Brooks, the President enjoyed a brief respite at a performance of West's Circus, famed for its equestrian display.[26]

The next day (the Fourth) another early breakfast, this time with Commodore Bainbridge, followed by an inspection of the Watertown arsenal and a cotton factory at Waltham, where he managed to find time to eat a "strawberry" with the ailing Christopher Gore, who was appalled at the President's taxing schedule. On his return to Boston he was greeted by delegations from the Society of the Cincinnati and from local Republicans, who had been rather lost sight of in the Federalist-sponsored activities. To each he extended the usual complimentary reply before proceeding to Faneuil Hall to hear Edward Channing's oration. True to the spirit of the occasion, Channing stressed the spirit of conciliation prevailing over the country, which promised to open the way to a rapid growth of the nation. The day ended with a banquet tendered to the President by the Cincinnati.[27]

Again on the fifth he rose early for breakfast with Commodore Hull and the personnel of the Navy Yard. During his inspection of the ships he was much impressed to see "Old Ironsides," which he hoped could be preserved as a national monument. Accompanied by a large entourage, he rode to Bunker Hill to preside at a militia review. Later he dined with Governor Brooks at Medford, returning to the city in time for a concert of the Haydn and Handel Oratorio Society. The evening was rounded off by a splendid party at the Otises, which was enlivened by a band of music in the garden and a display of fireworks.

Sunday, the sixth, was a bit less strenuous. The President, perhaps in deference to local emphasis upon the observance of the Sabbath, attended two church services; the first at Christ Episcopal Church and the second at the Federal Street Church of William Ellery Channing, whose Unitarianism was arousing much controversy. In the evening he was the guest of honor at a large party given by General Humphrey and his wife.

On his last day (the seventh of July) Monroe paid homage to the Brahmins, starting with a visit to the Boston Athenaeum. After viewing the collection, he drove to Harvard, where with great pomp and ceremony he was awarded an honorary Doctor of Laws degree. In the afternoon he reviewed the militia on the Cambridge Common and then went on to Braintree to dine with former President Adams, who had invited forty guests to dinner. As Monroe returned to town in the evening he managed to squeeze in visits to Benjamin Hichborn, a friend from his French mission in 1794, and George Sullivan, the son of General John Sullivan, whom Monroe had known during the Revolution.[28] Although George Sullivan, as a Federalist congressman, had vehemently opposed the Madison administration, he was now in the vanguard of those advocating reconciliation. Gratified by Monroe's friendliness, he wrote the President a few days later urging him not to select appointees from either the New England Republicans or Federalists of the older generation, for both were ambitious and power-hungry. Instead he suggested that the President look to younger men among the Federalists, who were not identified with the errors of the past; in particular, he recommended that Monroe consider Daniel Webster for the Attorney Generalship.[29]

The rest of Monroe's tour was far less tempestuous, although there was no lessening of public enthusiasm nor any decline in ceremonial receptions. Only one jarring note was heard during the last stages of his tour, when Governor William Plumer of New Hampshire declined to call out the militia to escort the President. Plumer, a Federalist of decided and independent views (he was the only elector not to vote for Monroe in 1820), insisted, in spite of pressure from the Federalists in the state, that the governor could not summon the militia for purely ceremonial purposes. Plumer's refusal was not so much motivated by die-hard Federalism, as by a distinctly lukewarm feeling on his part about Monroe. When Monroe arrived in the state, Plumer was ill with typhoid, but Monroe characteristically ignored the slight and wrote a kindly letter to the ailing Governor.[30] Rarely in the published accounts of the tour was a personal note injected. In Vermont, however, the President recognized, in the widow of President John Wheelock, the former Maria Suhn, who had dressed his wound after the battle of Trenton.[31]

Not until late in July, when he was in Plattsburg, did the President have time to reflect on the implications of his enthusiastic reception. It had been quite unprecedented, and he was not immune to a sense of personal gratification. Nonetheless, he did not consider the popular demonstrations along his route to be the result of personal popularity. As he explained to Madison, they had originated in a "desire in the body of the people to show their attachment to our union, and to republican govt., of which they seem'd to be aware, there was just cause to certain doubts, from the events of the late war...." By treating members of both parties without discrimination, he felt that he had given the Federalists a chance to "get back in the great family of the union" and at the same time to eradicate unfavorable impressions left by the past.[32]

The people had hailed him not as a hero, but as a symbol of national unity. He was naturally annoyed when the editor of the Richmond *Enquirer,* who condemned such excessive public adulation as contrary to republican principles, intimated that personsal vanity had led Monroe to encourage these demonstrations.[33] It was, of course, easy for Crawford to make fun of the scramble to honor the President in the "land of shady habits," or to join Clay in attributing the "pomp and ostentatious parade" of the tour to the sycophantic attempt of Federalists to regain power by currying favor, but Monroe's own conclusion that the behavior of the Federalists had been "evidently from the heart" was much closer to the truth.[34]

The Federalists, who naturally hoped that reconciliation might open the way to federal appointments, had listened closely to everything Monroe had said for a hint about his intentions. The President, knowing that his own party would not approve if Federalists were rapidly advanced in office, had been extremely cautious. The more realistic New Englanders agreed with Jeremiah Mason's conclusion that Monroe would welcome their support but not at the expense of alienating his followers.[35] Although the Federalists were disappointed at Monroe's failure to make appointments from their ranks, they continued to support the administration in Congress throughout his two terms.[36] As the editor of the Baltimore *Federal Republican* commented in 1819: "The nearer the Democratic administration and party come up to the old federal principles and measures, the better they act and the more we prosper—that is the reason that every body is contented with President Monroe's administration, which is in system and effect strictly federal." [37]

In the years following his tour the President had every reason to consider the policy of conciliation successful. Every sign indicated that party warfare on the national scene had ceased—by 1819 every New England state except Massachusetts was controlled by the Republicans, and in Congress there was only a handful of Federalists, who ordinarily supported the administration with more fidelity than many Republicans.[38] The presidential election of 1820 with its lone dissident elector seemed to be the final proof, as Monroe commented in his second inaugural address, that powerful forces had drawn the people together in a lasting unity of sentiment.[39] At this point, since de-federalization had advanced at such a rapid rate, the next logical step would have been the appointment of a few Federalists to office. Monroe, however, made the discovery that the opposition to such a step was even more powerful than it had been in 1817. As a result of several minor appointments, he was charged with showing too much favor to former opponents. Although no one really took this accusation seriously—it was all part and parcel of the electioneering over the presidential succession

—Monroe dared not single out prominent Federalists for appointments, lest this produce an organized opposition to the administration. Moreover, the controversy over the admission of Missouri, in which former Federalists were among the leading advocates of the restriction of slavery, had persuaded many Republicans, including the President, that the Federalists were trying to organize a new party with the help of discontented Northern Republicans. This alone was sufficient to make Monroe shy away from advancing Federalists in office. Some notable appointments would have been a splendid way of epitomizing the Era of Good Feelings, but political developments had rendered this impossible. In any case, the Federalists had journeyed too far along the road of conciliation to turn back.

CHAPTER 21

THE ERA OF
GOOD FEELINGS:
REALITY

THE PARTY reconciliation, which Monroe so ardently envisaged as an essential development to ensure the stability of republican institutions, complicated the problem of executive leadership, since the President could no longer appeal to party solidarity as a means of putting his program through Congress. From the moment that Monroe adopted as his guiding principle the maxim that he was the head of a nation, not the leader of a party, he repudiated for all practical purposes party unity as a means of realizing presidential policies.[1] Historically the Republican party had been bound together as much by a shared fear of Federalism as by a common set of principles. During the Jefferson and Madison administrations nothing had been more effective in bringing reluctant Republicans into line than the cry that refusal to support administration policy would invite a resurgence of Federalism. It was this sense of solidarity against a common enemy which had enabled Jefferson to sustain unpopular measures such as the Embargo. With the elimination of the Federalists, the internal divisions in the Republican party between rival leaders, factions, and sections now emerged.

This loosening of party ties, which went on apace during Monroe's administration, had already been detected by William H. Crawford, as the Federalists moved to support Madison during his last two years in office.[2] Another equally important result of the weakening of party ties was the disappearance of those restraints which had prevented ambitious politicians from seeking popularity by opposing presidential programs. Although this phenomenon, which became the rule during Monroe's second term, was not immediately in evidence, Rufus King noted during Monroe's first year in office that the apparent harmony in Congress was deceptive, for beneath the surface "strong passions" were "concealed waiting only for an occasion to show themselves." Although the President had no enemies, he also lacked ardent friends.[3] Early in the administration Adams was also struck by the conviction that seemed to be current among members of Congress that Monroe's administration would terminate by bringing into power that element which most opposed his policies. Consequently, many congressional leaders felt obliged to oppose administration measures whether they disapproved of them or not.[4] The warfare which eventually developed between the supporters of rival candidates for the presidential succession was particularly deadly in those cases in which the measure under attack was associated with one of the aspirants to the Presidency. Less evident in 1817 was the divisive force of sectionalism, which by the end of Monroe's second term was exerting a powerful influence on political alignments.

After a lifetime dedicated to public service, Monroe had some definite measures which he hoped to carry out in the Presidency. Since he could not depend on organized party support, he had to explore other avenues in his quest for congressional approval. It was typical of his complete acceptance of the principles and practices established by Jefferson and Madison that he sought to exercise executive power within the limits established by his Republican predecessors. Consequently, he did not attempt either to exploit the personsal popularity exhibited during his tour nor to utilize the patronage to discipline recalcitrant congressmen. It is true that Monroe, like his predecessors, made many appointments from congressional ranks, but these were never coordinated with the realization of administration programs in Congress. Monroe, in fact, disapproved of this practice, but he considered it too well entrenched to be abandoned without offending congressmen, who had come to expect this form of recognition.[5]

When Monroe entered office, he inherited a loose conglomeration of precedents and a vague body of Republican attitudes about the nature of the presidential office and the exercise of executive leadership. The Republicans, having come to power in 1801 on a wave of protest against executive domination in the government, adopted a rather simplistic view of the role of the President within the federal structure.

He was regarded merely as the agent for carrying out the will of the people as expressed in Congress. The legislature was assigned a central position as the proper agency for guiding the destiny of the nation. Only in foreign affairs was the President accorded independent authority, which was subject to strict constitutional limitation. This was the theory, but, as has often been pointed out, Jefferson exerted far greater influence over Congress than the Federalist Presidents had deemed possible. In deploying his congressional forces, Jefferson enjoyed the inestimable advantage of a highly unified party, although it was not organized in a modern sense. He actively directed legislation with the assistance of members of Congress who functioned as recognized, if unofficial administration spokesmen. Jefferson also utilized his own personal contacts and those of his Secretaries among the members of Congress.[6]

Madison was less successful in following the route established by Jefferson. Internal divisions within the party and the Federalist revival before the War of 1812 reduced his margin of support as critics became more outspoken. He never enjoyed the same degree of popularity as Jefferson with the rank and file of the party, many of whom could not persuade themselves that the author of the *Federalist* could be trusted to uphold pure Republican doctrines. In 1811, when his administration seemed on the verge of collapse, only the slender thread of the fear of a Federalist return to power held the Republicans together. At this point Madison was able to strengthen his leadership by bringing Monroe into the Cabinet. Monroe's ability to establish effective liaison with Congress through the War Hawks fully compensated for the alienation of the "invisibles." [7]

It was in the light of his knowledge of Republican attitudes toward the Presidency and his own experience in the Madison administration that Monroe guided his conduct as President. He never doubted that it was a basic function of the Chief Executive to supply leadership on crucial domestic issues as well as in foreign relations, where his authority was more generally conceded.[8] He considered it a great handicap that the Presidents, unlike the British prime ministers, were not allowed official spokesmen in Congress to defend policies and answer questions. Since he could not always count on friendly congressmen to undertake this burden, Monroe regularly used his annual messages as an important opportunity to defend his measures and to anticipate objections.[9] It was for this reason, for example, that he regularly included passages commenting favorably on the Latin American independence movement.

Secretary Adams was never happy over these pronouncements, but he had to admit that they were effective in fending off Clay's attempts to force congressional action in behalf of recognizing the new states before the administration was ready to act.[10] Since the President obviously was not hostile to these states, Congress was all the more willing to accept his decision that the time was not yet ripe for recognition.

Monroe was also well aware that failure to provide leadership could jeopardize executive programs. Although he was uncertain about the course to recommend to Congress in 1819, when Spain failed to ratify the treaty negotiated earlier in the year, he rejected the suggestion that he simply state the facts without making a specific recommendation. If he did this, he told Adams, then nothing would be done. In his opinion Madison's failure to recommend precise action to Congress in his messages had been one of the reasons for the difficulties which his predecessor had encountered.[11] There can be no doubt that pressure from the administration was vitally important in putting measures through Congress in the form desired by the President. When Henry Clay was raising objections to the execution of the treaty with Spain, he bemoaned the fact that executive influence was so overpowering in its support that it would be approved as it stood in spite of major shortcomings.[12] A particular case in which executive pressure proved all-important was in connection with Jackson's conduct in Florida in 1818. Crawford believed that only the President's influence had prevented the House from voting to censure Jackson.[13]

Monroe also relied heavily upon personal contact with congressmen, not so much by seeking them out but by making himself readily accessible. Every day there was a constant stream of callers at his office in the executive mansion, where he received all visitors with unfailing courtesy. At the frequent dinner parties and at the regular evening receptions, his warmth and natural courtesy won many friends. In dealing with Congress the executive also enjoyed the considerable advantage of possessing detailed information about issues, which made it necessary for congressional committees to rely upon the administration for guidance. Although standing committees assumed a new importance in the postwar years, they still did not possess continuity in either membership or in the form of permanent staff members, which would give them full independence. It was the established practice for committee chairmen to consult with the appropriate department heads and even enlist their assistance in drafting legislation.[14]

Although Monroe never enjoyed Jefferson's advantage of having

regular semiofficial spokesmen, from time to time individual congressmen (most frequently committee chairmen) undertook to defend his
measures. Unfortunately, such support was not dependable. In a body
which took the theory of legislative supremacy seriously, congressmen
were hypersensitive to the charge that they were tools of the administration. Consequently, congressmen ordinarily friendly to the President
would suddenly oppose measures for no other reason than to establish
their independence from executive influence. Such was the behavior of
Representative John Forsyth of Georgia, chairman of the House
Committee on Foreign Affairs, who had effectively checked Clay
in his attempt to defeat an administration-sponsored neutrality act.
Yet within a matter of weeks Forsyth was reported ready to sponsor a
resolution to seize Florida—a measure known to be contrary to the
President's wishes. According to Adams, Forsyth had taken this position
in order to prove his independence from the executive and thus refute
Clay's charge that he had supported the administration in order to
obtain a diplomatic appointment. At the President's request, Crawford,
who was on intimate terms with Forsyth, went to see the congressman.
Although he was unable to persuade his fellow Georgian to drop the
resolution, he brought back the agreeable news that it would not be
endorsed by the committee.[15]

In exercising executive leadership Monroe placed the greatest reliance on the utilization of the contacts of the members of his Cabinet
with senators and representatives, having learned from his own experience in the Madison administration the value of this approach. He
was particularly fortunate in that three of his Secretaries—Crawford,
Adams and Calhoun—had important congressional followings, which
to a considerable extent were amenable to direction. Throughout his
two terms the implementation of administration policies depended
entirely on the support of these three figures, all of whom were aspirants
to the succession. Of these, Crawford possessed the largest and most
cohesive congressional party.

Far more than any of his predecessors Monroe operated on the basis
of "consensus" within his own administration. The innumerable
Cabinet meetings about which we know so much from Adams' extensive
diary make this very clear. Monroe did not meet with his Cabinet
primarily for advice (his mind was usually already made up on most
issues) but to hammer out an agreement and to secure a commitment
to his program. Some of the lengthiest sessions were those devoted to
harmonizing conflicting opinions. Once he had achieved a basic agree-

ment, then the likelihood of congressional obstruction was greatly reduced. As Monroe explained to Adams on one occasion, he sought unanimity among his Cabinet members, because any suggestion that the
Secretaries were not in agreement was seized upon by the enemies of
the administration in their efforts to defeat executive measures.[16] As a
rule the President never brought up issues on which he knew there were
irreconcilable differences among the department heads. For example,
he never sought the advice of the Cabinet about internal improvements
nor about the proposal to exclude slavery from Missouri until after the
compromise bill had been passed. Conversely, any measure on which
he could not obtain full Cabinet approval was apt to be in danger.
Thus the slave-trade agreement negotiated in 1823 was drastically
modified by the Senate in the following year, because Crawford did
not consider himself bound to support the original provisions, which
had been approved by the Cabinet. Under these circumstances his
supporters felt free to attack the treaty.

The fact that Monroe was highly successful in obtaining congressional
approval for his policies has been generally overlooked in the emphasis
placed upon the rivalry between the contestants for the succession and
the attention given to Clay's opposition. Although Clay was highly
articulate, he never succeeded in defeating a single administration
measure. Clay did not dominate the House, for he never used his power
as Speaker to build up a personal following. In making appointments,
Clay played no favorites—all sections and all factions were given assignments on the committees. Indeed, if he had attempted to use his
position to control the House, he would never have been re-elected.
His success as Speaker lay in not excluding supporters of rival candidates for the Presidency from key positions.[17]

II

The strength of the administration was tested during the first session
of the Fifteenth Congress, which met in December 1818. Although
Monroe had returned to the Capital in September, he did not begin
preparing for the session until late October. Since he was tired from
his journey and could not as yet occupy the executive residence, he
lingered in the city only long enough to greet John Quincy Adams,
who arrived to take up the duties of the State Department on September 20. After discussing with Adams the instructions to be drawn up
for Richard Rush, who was replacing Adams as Minister to Great

Britain, the President took his family to Virginia, where he rested for a month, visiting Madison and Jefferson and looking after his plantations.[18] On his return to Washington in late October, he began discussing the contents of his first annual message with the Cabinet. In preparing his message, Monroe used a procedure which he followed throughout his two terms. First he roughed out each topic on separate sheets of paper, using only the left side of each page and making revisions on the blank half. These "Sibylline leaves," as Adams jokingly called them, were then read to the assembled Secretaries.[19] After listening to their comments and suggestions, the President made such alterations as he thought advisable. In his messages he recurred to Washington's practice, which had been followed in a limited way by Madison, of indicating specific areas in which congressional action was needed—a method quite unlike that used by Jefferson. Monroe's messages all had a strong family resemblance, whose lineaments were etched by Adams in 1820:

[The messages] . . . begin with general remarks on condition of the country, noticing recent occurrences of material importance, passing encomiums upon our form of government, paying due homage to the sovereign power of the people, and turning to account every topic which can afford a paragraph of public gratulation; then pass in review our relations with the principal powers of Europe; then, looking inwards, adverting to the state of the finances, the revenues, public expenditures, debts, and land sales, the progress of fortifications and naval armaments, with a few about the Indians, and a few about the slave-trade.[20]

The President listened readily to criticism and did not hesitate to make changes. For some sections, such as those relating to finances, he relied almost entirely on the head of the particular department involved, and he frequently called on Adams to draft relevant passages on foreign affairs. So free were the discussions of these documents that jokes at maladroit expressions used by the President were not considered amiss. The President laughed as heartily as his department heads when Adams observed, in connection with his fourth annual message, that he did not like to see the President end his message with the phrase "disgraceful traffic," which he had used in connection with the slave trade.[21]

The first annual message fell into the pattern outlined by Adams: a paragraph of felicitation on the growing strength of free government in the United States; a report on foreign affairs, which included an announcement of the Rush-Bagot Agreement; a summary of the work

of the commissioners under the Treaty of Ghent; the status of negotiations with Spain over spoliations and the use of Amelia Island by
pirates; a cautiously friendly account of the advance of the independence movement in South America; and a favorable report on America's
finances. His positive recommendations were rather limited. He proposed that Congress take steps to facilitate the introduction of the
"arts of civilized life" to the Indians, that the Constitution be amended
to authorize federally sponsored internal improvements and to permit
the establishment of "seminaries of learning," and that pensions be
provided for veterans of the Revolution. His final suggestion was the
most welcome of all to the people and politicians alike—the repeal of
the internal taxes levied during the war.[22]

The House and Senate at once appointed committees to report on
the various sections of the message. Within a month the House approved bills for repealing the internal taxes and establishing pensions
for veterans.[23] In response to the President's comments on internal
improvements, Senator James Barbour promptly introduced an amendment granting Congress the necessary power.[24] On the surface everything seemed to be harmonious, but a note of warning was sounded
in the report of a House Committee on Internal Improvements. This
report, presented by George Tucker of Virginia, not only affirmed the
power of Congress "to construct roads and canals . . . with the assent
of the States . . . leaving the jurisdictional rights in the States, respectively," but it also accused the President of invading the privileges of
the legislature. It was the opinion of the committee that in any conflict
between the President and Congress, the executive should yield to the
legislative majority. By expressing an opinion before Congress had
enacted a specific measure, the President might prevent the consideration of a measure, when, in fact, there might be a two-thirds majority
in its favor. The committee also pointed out with some asperity that the
President seemed rather inconsistent in his interpretation of the constitutionality of internal improvements, since he had authorized army
units to construct a road from Plattsburg to Sackett's Harbor in the
fall of 1817.[25]

As soon as Monroe read the report he wrote Madison for clarification
on the constitutional issues, with which he expected Madison to be
familiar as one of the framers of the Constitution and as a member of
Jefferson's Cabinet, when the first bill providing for the construction of
the Cumberland Road had been signed.[26] Although Madison did not
think Congress had the power to construct a general system of internal

improvements, and he had vetoed a bill to that effect just before leaving office, he admitted that he could not recall having discussed the issue with President Jefferson. He could only assume that Jefferson had signed the bill "doubtingly or hastily," and subsequent bills relating to the Cumberland Road had been accepted with less investigation than was "perhaps due to the case." The best he could offer was the suggestion that the Cumberland Road might possibly be justified on the grounds that it was located in a territory over which Congress had a general power, which it did not possess over the states.[27]

The committee's criticism by no means prepared Monroe for Clay's violent onslaught in March. Apparently the President was not aware of the rumor current in Washington that Clay, who resented his exclusion from the State Department, entertained no kindly feelings toward the administration.[28] After the usual series of dull speeches replete with abstract legal arguments, which the internal-improvements issue always brought forth, Clay arose on March 13. Ignoring the question of congressional power, he denounced the President for his "irregular and unconstitutional" behavior in expressing his opinions before any specific legislation had been adopted. He went on to expound a view of the relationship of the executive and legislative branches contradicting that presented by the President:

The Constitutional order of legislation supposes that every bill originating in one house shall there be deliberately investigated, without influence from any other branch of the legislature, and then remitted to the other House for a free and unbiassed consideration. Having passed both Houses, it is to be laid before the President—signed if approved, if disapproved to be returned, with his objections to the originating House. In this manner, entire freedom of thought and action is secured, and the President finally sees the proposition in the most matured form which Congress can give to it. The practical effect, to say no more, of forestalling the legislative opinion, and telling us what we may or may not do, will be to deprive the President himself of the opportunity of considering a proposition so matured and us the benefit of his reasoning, applied specifically to such a proposition; for the Constitution further enjoins upon him to state his objections upon returning the bill.[29]

Any other procedure, he declared, deprived Congress of its rights to record its views upon a matter of great public concern. The Speaker also ridiculed in his best manner Monroe's failure to present substantial arguments to support his conclusion that Congress could not construct roads and canals. The President, he proclaimed, "has furnished us with no reasoning, with no argument in support of his opinions—nothing addressed to the understanding. He gives indeed an historical account of the operations of his own mind, and he asserts that he has made a laborious effort to conquer his early impressions, but the result is a settled conviction against the power without a single reason." [30] To these disparaging remarks, he added some gibes about the President's tour, which he compared to a royal progress with loyal subjects performing sycophantic homage. He waxed equally witty over Monroe's inconsistency in ordering the construction of a road in upstate New York by military fatigue parties while denying the same power to Congress. Clay's views on internal improvements did not come as a surprise, but no one had anticipated such a bitter personal assault on the President. During the next few sessions Clay's querulous opposition and advocacy of impractical proposals did nothing to enhance his reputation as a statesman.[31]

Tucker's resolution in behalf of internal improvements was never voted on; instead the House considered a series of substitutes. Of these, all were voted down but one affirming that Congress had the power to appropriate money for the construction of canals and roads. This was by no means a clear resolution of the issue, for it left unanswered the question whether Congress could actually construct such improvements. Shortly after these debates ended the House approved a resolution calling on the Secretaries of War and the Treasury to prepare reports on a general plan of internal improvements.[32] The resolution directed toward the Secretary of War also requested him to advise Congress as to the extent of its authority. This was undoubtedly an effort to promote disagreement within the administration, for Calhoun had endorsed congressional power over internal improvements in the past. The Secretary of War drew up a general plan, but before it was submitted, he removed at the President's request all passages intimating that Congress had the power to construct internal improvements.[33]

Although Monroe was convinced of the necessity of constructing a general system of roads and canals in order to develop the full resources of the nation, his loyalty to his Republican predecessors and his own convictions had led him to express his views on the constitutional aspect of this subject. It had seemed to him only fair that at the beginning of a new administration Congress should be informed about his convictions on this issue. The topic was rather fresh in the public mind, since Madison a few days before the end of his second term had vetoed the Bonus Bill, which had allocated both the bonus paid by the Bank of the United States for its charter and future dividends on government-owned stock for internal improvements. Most congressmen, however, had been dumbfounded by Madison's veto. It was true that he had on several previous occasions expressed the opinion that Congress lacked this power, but never in such precise terms as those later employed by Monroe. It had been assumed that Madison, who had signed bills extending the Cumberland Road, would have no objection to such a modest measure as the Bonus Bill. Monroe had hoped that his explicit statement following so closely on Madison's veto would lead to a modification of the Constitution to expressly authorize internal improvements, which he considered essential for the development of the nation's resources. In this he was disappointed, for Barbour's amendment disappeared from view after the House debates. The discussions in the House had shown that the majority favoring improvements would never approve an amendment granting a power which they insisted was already within the authority of Congress.

The President took Clay's gibes about his failure to offer sound reasons for his opinions very much to heart. In the course of the next year he drafted a lengthy essay analyzing the basis for his interpretation of the Constitution. Although his argumentation was tortuous, his conclusion was simple: Congress could appropriate money for internal improvements, but it lacked the power to construct such works. His essay was a baffling production, in which he resorted to a loose interpretation of the power to appropriate money but turned to a strict-construction view when it came to enumerating the purposes for which the money could be spent. He was unable to find any justification for internal improvements, as the proponents of such measures did, in the commerce clause, the grant of power to establish post roads, or in the clauses relating to the military powers. The major obstacle he saw to a federal program lay in the fact that Congress did not have the power to establish jurisdiction over any roads or canals which might be built. Only the states had this authority, and it was a power which they could not cede to the federal government. From this point of view, projects built by federal authority could not be policed by officials of the United States.

Monroe had been led to make a distinction between the power to appropriate and the power to construct roads and canals in an effort to justify the bills for the Cumberland Road, which had been signed by Jefferson and Madison, and which Monroe, in the light of this precedent, continued to approve. He did not, however, find Madison's suggestion that the project might be justified on the grounds that the United States had greater authority over territories than over states at all helpful, for up to this time the only portions of the Cumberland Road to be completed lay entirely within the boundaries of states outside the Northwest Territory. To get around this difficulty he argued that these appropriations had not violated the Constitution since the land used for the highway had been obtained by the states, which had cleared the right of way. Tolls had never been collected nor had federal patrols been used to police the road. Congress, he wrote, had merely appropriated money and "caused to be constructed" the Cumberland Road. However unsatisfactory this hair-splitting may seem, it was a genuine effort to compromise the issue and leave a narrow route open for additional appropriations. If a general system was contemplated, obviously the only solution was a constitutional amendment. In the meantime the Cumberland Road could be extended and improved on a limited basis, but once a section was constructed it passed into the jurisdiction of the states.[34]

Determined not to give ground on this matter, Monroe wanted to present his essay to Congress with his third annual message. This seemed a suitable time, since a new Congress was assembling, which could be assumed, at least technically, to be unfamiliar with his views. The Cabinet was distinctly unenthusiastic. Adams reminded the President that he would only stir up a discussion, which was bound to be disrespectful toward the executive. Nor did he see any reason to think that the new Congress would be any more inclined to approve the President's remarks than its predecessor. Indeed, Adams regarded it as morally certain that Congress would not respond favorably to a request for a constitutional amendment. Adams realized how deeply the President felt about this issue, for, as he commented, it was unusual for Monroe, "a man of strong judgment and great discretion," to persist in such an "injudicious" policy. Reluctantly Monroe filed away his essay to be used on a more suitable occasion.[35] The opportune moment did not arrive until the spring of 1822, when Congress enacted a bill providing for the collection of tolls to maintain the Cumberland Road. The President promptly vetoed the measure without consulting the Cabinet, and transmitted his lengthy essay with the veto message. His veto was upheld without any discussion of the constitutional issues, since it was late in the session.[36]

Monroe's pronouncement did nothing to stimulate the amending process, but at least it established clear guidelines for future measures relating to internal improvements. In the next year Monroe approved a bill appropriating $25,000 for repairing the Cumberland Road and another measure providing funds for a survey of a general system of internal improvements.[37] Monroe's essay, which at best can be described as an ungracious work on an ungrateful subject, was a notable, if unsuccessful, attempt to provide executive leadership in resolving one of the bitterest issues of the day. One of the peculiarities of this controversy was the probability that Congress would never have adopted a system of general internal improvements, even if Monroe had been willing to approve such legislation.[38] After 1819 sentiment in favor of internal improvements declined rapidly in areas where it had once been favored. The New Yorkers, for example, lost interest in federal projects as the Erie Canal neared completion. Moreover, the Panic of 1819, which caused a rapid curtailment in government revenues, checked enthusiasm for costly government projects.

III

Monroe's difficulties with the first session of the Fifteenth Congress were not limited to internal improvements. Just a few days after Clay's criticism of the President for his infringement on the prerogatives of the legislature, the Speaker assailed the administration for pursuing policies hostile to the revolutionary governments of South America. Clay, who had cast himself in the role of principal advocate for the recognition of these states, opened his attack by condemning the administration-sponsored neutrality bill introduced by John Forsyth, chairman of the House Committee on Foreign Affairs, as a measure intended for "the benefit of His Majesty the King of Spain." [39] Clay based this conclusion on a passage in the bill, which was actually largely a consolidation of existing legislation, forbidding the sale of armed vessels either to Spain or to the insurgents. The President had requested this revision to satisfy the complaints of European nations about American traffic with the insurgents and to make it easier to curb pirates, who posed as privateers on the authority of irregular commissions from insurgent groups.[40] Thanks to Forsyth's skillful management, Clay was unable to amend the bill.

Forsyth again upheld the administration cause when Clay sought to prevent an appropriation of $30,000 to defray the expenses of commissioners Monroe had decided to send to South America to report on the insurgent regimes. Normally, Clay was ready to support such projects, but on this occasion he found it convenient to accuse the administration of using the commission to conceal its hostility to the insurgent cause. Why, he asked, was a commission necessary, when all the facts needed for recognition were available in the public prints? With a fine awareness of the President's more sensitive spots, Clay questioned his constitutional power to dispatch a commission whose members had not been confirmed by the Senate. As a countermeasure the Speaker proposed that Congress appropriate $18,000 to send a Minister to the United Provinces of the Rio de La Plata, which Clay glowingly, if inaccurately, proclaimed the only other republic in the Western Hemisphere apart from the United States. In a highly effective speech Forsyth defended the President's power to make interim appointments, and presented a detailed picture of affairs at La Plata, which left no doubt that whatever claim this state had to recognition it could not be grounded on the republican character of its government, since it was an out-and-out dictatorship. When Clay alluded to the willingness of the administration to send ministers to lesser European courts, such as Sweden, while ignoring the free states in the Western Hemisphere, Forsyth was ready with a retort. He silenced Clay with the comment that it was as well known to the Speaker as to any member of the House, why there was still a Minister in Sweden. He did not need to go further, for it was common knowledge that Monroe, who preferred a diplomat of a lower grade than a Minister in Sweden, had reluctantly allowed Jonathan Russell to stay on as Minister only because of pressure from Clay.[41] The Speaker's resolution was overwhelmingly defeated and the administration received an appropriation to pay the expenses of the commissioners sent to South America.

The President, according to Adams, was so distressed over Clay's attacks that he could scarcely think of anything else. Undoubtedly the President, exhausted from a severe bout of influenza, was somewhat more sensitive than usual.[42] Since the President was, if anything, overly scrupulous about his constitutional authority, he was shocked by the imputation that he had exceeded his powers. It also pained him to be portrayed as an enemy of liberty, when he was sympathetic to the insurgent cause, although he insisted that the new regimes must give evidence of stability before the United States would extend recognition. These debates were still uppermost in his mind when he wrote Madison in April shortly after Congress had adjourned: "The late session, considering the flourishing and happy condition of the country, has been unusually oppressive on the Executive Department. There have been more calls for information, than I can recollect to have been made at any former session, and in some instances, a very querulous spirit has been manifested." [43] It was disappointing to the President that the harmony evident in national politics had failed to produce a corresponding tranquility in the halls of Congress.

Although some of the "querulous" character of the session can be attributed to Clay's determination to set himself up as an independent leader, the numerous calls for information were the outgrowth of the reorganization of the House after the War of 1812. In March 1816 six new standing committees on public expenditures were created in addition to those already in existence. These new committees, as well as the old ones, undertook to scrutinize the operations and expenditures of the federal government much more closely than had been the case in the past. Since these committees operated without any permanent staff, they inevitably had to rely on the executive for detailed information. Since the 1790s the Republicans had clamored to increase congressional control over federal expenditures, but until the postwar era nothing had been done to carry out this program. Monroe, as the first President to be exposed to the congressional control long advocated by the Republicans, apparently did not recognize this application of ancient party doctrine.

Monroe's irritation over some aspects of the session led him to judge the Congress too harshly. The editor of the *National Intelligencer,* on the contrary, felt that it had been a productive session in which only a few important measures had been neglected. Although Congress had been unwilling to accept executive leadership in the area of internal improvements, other administration proposals had fared much better. No difficulties had been raised about passing three measures recommended by the President in his annual message—pensions for Revolutionary veterans, a moderate increase in the protective tariff, and a measure imposing restrictions on British shipping to retaliate against the British exclusion of American trade from the West Indies. On both

Latin America and Amelia Island, Congress had accepted Presidential guidance. Moreover, Congress had made adequate provisions for the army and navy and for continuing the work on fortifications, measures particularly important to the President. It was, all in all, an excellent record for the administration. The *Intelligencer* considered the most serious shortcomings of the session were the failure to enact bills revising the militia system, establishing new circuit judgeships, and providing for a uniform system of bankruptcy.[44] None of these were administration measures, but proposals held over from previous sessions. The administration had done well, but Monroe's sensitivity to criticism led him to underestimate his successes.

CHAPTER 22

THE WHITE HOUSE

W HEN President Monroe was inaugurated in March 1817, the President's residence, like so many public structures, was still in the process of renovation. Even when he moved in, after the plasterers and painters had finished in October, the house was not entirely completed. The front portico was not built until 1824 and the East Room remained unfinished until the Jackson administration. Although the official residence was most frequently referred to as the President's House, or on occasion as the President's Palace, the term "White House" first came into use during the postwar era when the scars on the stone facing left by the fire were covered by a gleaming coat of white paint.[1] The Monroes' occupancy not only left a mark on the interior of the White House—for the task of selecting furniture and ornaments fell upon the President and his wife—but during his era lasting social changes were instituted. These innovations struck contemporaries as a more radical departure from the past than was actually the case. Monroe, in fact, only continued the trend begun by Madison of returning to the greater formality of the Washington era. The new rules of etiquette, however, produced much ill-natured comment about the aristocratic tendencies of the President and his family.

The first important change, which only affected the diplomatic corps, did not arouse widespread resentment. At the beginning of his first term Monroe decided that all diplomats in Washington should be placed on the same social footing as that followed in European courts. From now on they would be received by the President only on official occasions. No longer would they be allowed, as during the Jefferson and Madison administrations, to make informal calls to take tea and converse with the President as with a friend. In making this rule

Monroe was influenced by the knowledge gained from his European experience that Jefferson's and Madison's casual behavior, while in harmony with the ideals of republican simplicity, had done nothing to elevate the prestige of the nation in the eyes of foreign diplomats. Far more important, however, was his belief that these informal associations tended to create an impression that one nation was being accorded favored treatment. He also felt that it was unwise for the President to discuss public affairs with the ministers, lest in a casual conversation he leave an impression contrary to that created by the Secretary of State in official conferences.[2] The diplomats welcomed this new policy, which was more in conformity with European practice. Only one diplomat, the Abbé Corrêa da Serra, the Minister from Portugal, who had been on intimate terms with Madison, was offended by Monroe's seeming coldness.[3]

At official receptions Monroe conducted himself, according to Adams, in much the same manner as the Prince Regent. The ministers in full court dress were presented by the Secretary of State to the President, who stood in the middle of the drawing room. When the ministers handed the President their letters of credence, he turned them over to the Secretary of State without reading them. To the ministers' remarks, Monroe had a set reply, expressing the interest of the people of the United States in the welfare of the minister's sovereign. The President made no other conversation, and none of the diplomats except the Portuguese Minister ever attempted anything beyond a formal exchange.[4] The whole ceremony was usually over in ten minutes. As part of the new formality Monroe considered the creation of a dress uniform for department heads, but this project was never carried out.[5]

Monroe encountered much greater difficulty, however, in trying to solve the problem of precedence at diplomatic dinners, not from the ministers, who accepted the rule that the diplomat with the longest residence in Washington ranked first at official affairs, but from the members of the Cabinet. At first when Monroe only invited the Secretary of State to such functions, the other Secretaries felt slighted; but when they were invited, the ministers resented sitting at the foot of the table below Cabinet officers. The alternative of inviting other officials and private citizens, who would be seated below the diplomats, proved equally unsatisfactory, since the ministers objected to associating with persons of inferior status. The problem was finally solved by Adams, who suggested that the President invite only one department head at a time.[6] These dinners were solemn affairs, starting at four or five in the afternoon, when the members of the diplomatic corps were greeted in the Oval Room by the President. After conversing with them formally until all were present, he led the way into the dining room.[7] Monroe, following the custom of his predecessors, accepted no invitations to the many dinners and evening parties of the diplomats. He also declined attending ceremonies which might have political overtones, such as the memorial service commemorating the death of Louis XVI arranged by the French Minister.[8]

This new formality, so much appreciated by the diplomatic corps, was vehemently reprobated when applied to congressmen and permanent residents of the Capital. By the end of 1817 the drawing rooms of the city and the halls of Congress were buzzing with angry comments about the Monroes' application of European rules of etiquette. The greatest resentment was aroused by the announcement that Mrs. Monroe would neither make nor return calls, but that she would be at home in the morning to receive visitors.[9] In practice she saw but few of them, delegating the responsibility to her daughter, Mrs. Eliza Hay, who lived at the White House during Monroe's Presidency.[10] This was a radical departure from the custom of Dolley Madison, who had valiantly called on the wives of all the members of Congress (fortunately most did not bring their wives) and returned all visits. Secretary Adams regarded this practice as a veritable "torture" in a city without paved streets and where the residents were scattered miles apart.[11] Mrs. Monroe's decision was an extension of the rule she had followed when her husband had been Secretary of State. At that time she paid no visits except to acquaintances, although she returned calls. These rules, much as they were disliked, were made necessary by the changing character of Washington, which was no longer a wilderness capital. In the postwar era there was a considerable increase in the number of congressmen, corresponding to the increase in the population in the nation, and also in the number of permanent residents. There was much more entertaining than in the past, as social life became more elaborate and also more formal. In addition to this the introduction of the steamboat, offering cheap and rapid travel, brought a steadily rising flow of visitors, many of whom were relatives or friends of congressmen, and thus, under the old rules of etiquette, were entitled to receive the first call. Since Mrs. Monroe was not in the best of health, such a routine was an impossibility. The Secretary of State and his wife Louisa fully approved Mrs. Monroe's decision. Mrs. Adams, a successful hostess whose weekly parties were among the most agreeable in the city, governed her conduct by the same rules used by Mrs. Monroe when her husband had been in the Cabinet. Louisa Adams, as she told the President's wife, could see no reason why she should be "doomed to run after every stranger." Consequently, she limited her visits to calls for the purpose of acquaintance or to return visits.[12] Until Washington ladies accepted the finality of these decisions, neither Mrs. Adams nor the President's wife met with much approval.

Since Mrs. Monroe was sheltered by her position, the most vociferous complaints were directed at Louisa Adams. Most of the wives of the senators refused to call and boycotted her evening parties.[13] At the beginning of the social season of 1819, Monroe met with the Cabinet to work out common rules of etiquette, which he hoped would reduce the criticism leveled against the administration on this trivial matter. No agreement could be reached, for Crawford preferred to keep the old usages rather than invite resentment by adopting the policy approved by the President and the Secretary of State. In the end, each Cabinet member went his own way.[14] To pacify wounded sensibilities, Adams wrote Vice-President Tompkins, explaining that he had not altered his conduct on matters of etiquette since he had been in the Senate in the Jefferson administration. At that time, he had never expected members of the administration to make the first call. In 1822, when Adams' political opponents began to make much of his so-called aristocratic rules of etiquette, he published the letter to counteract these reports.[15]

The wives might disregard Mrs. Adams, but curiosity was too great, and the occasion too important, to allow them to ignore Mrs. Monroe's "drawing rooms," as the fortnightly evening receptions given at the White House were called—the old phrase "levee" in use during Washington's day being considered "vulgar." [16] The presidential evening parties introduced by Washington, abandoned by Jefferson, and restored by the Madisons, were the major social occasion for Washington officialdom. Open to all who were suitably dressed, they provided an opportunity for diplomats, members of Congress, public officials of all degrees, and private citizens to be presented to the President and his wife and behold the great men of the day.

With memories of Dolley Madison's personal warmth and social adroitness, which had made these crowded affairs much less solemn, it is not surprising that Washingtonians found Mrs. Monroe's reserved and formal manner little to their liking when they attended the first drawing room on New Year's Day 1818. The affair began at eleven-thirty in the morning (regular drawing rooms were at eight in the evening) when Louisa Adams and the other Cabinet wives were ushered into the Oval Room, where Mrs. Monroe sat with her niece, Miss Gouverneur, and with Mrs. Hay. As soon as the President greeted the ladies and presented them to his wife, the members of the diplomatic corps (all in court dress) and their wives were admitted from the adjoining drawing room. When they had made their bows to Mrs. Monroe, the doors of the lobby were opened at noon and a huge crowd pressed in, jamming the rooms until three. On New Year's Day the crowd was more varied than usual, since many informally dressed citizens with spurs and muddy boots made their way into the President's House. On occasion Indian delegations appeared, adding a savage note to the melange of official uniforms, sober congressional dress, and the mixed attire of the citizens.

These receptions, as Harrison Gray Otis rather grimly remarked, were the most "amusing, fatiguing, squeezing" ceremonies to be imagined. Servants circulated through the throng with trays of wine, tea, and ices. Although a band of music usually played, Washingtonians were deprived of the two most popular staples of city parties—dancing and cards. The President greeted the guests in the Oval Room, or in one of the adjacent rooms, flanked by Cabinet members and the more prominent men present. Conversation was restricted to the most general comments. The guests, after greeting the President and Mrs. Monroe, customarily made a tour of the rooms, stopping to speak to friends and visiting dignitaries.

At this first reception, and indeed at most of the drawing rooms in the next few years, attention was focused as much on the furnishings as on the hosts. During the first few years in the White House the Monroes used their own furniture, including the magnificent Louis XVI pieces with brass inlays purchased many years before in Paris. Louisa Adams was amazed that in only three months they had managed not only to get the house in good order but that they had been able to train servants. On this occasion she noted that six servants in livery were stationed in the hall, while two out of livery announced the guests in the drawing rooms. Since there was no White House staff—not even a watchman to look after the grounds when the President was absent—the servants were probably from either the Albemarle or the Loudoun plantations. During the course of the next few years, as furniture, carpets, and other decorations arrived from France, the White House was even more widely admired, although the heavy Empire gilt chairs covered in crimson satin and decorated with gold eagles did not have quite the elegant character sought by the Monroes for the Oval Room. Had mahogany been used, as the President wished, the effect would have been much finer. Still, the handsome French mantelpieces with caryatids and the ormolu clocks (ordered without nudities lest the public be offended) made a splendid appearance. Even foreign observers, usually inclined to be critical of republican ways, admitted that the house was furnished in superb taste, if not as richly as seemed appropriate for a person of the President's rank.

Prior to the New Year's reception of 1818 it had been rumored that Mrs. Monroe had spent more than $1,500 for dresses ordered from Paris. Whether this figure was accurate or not, the ladies were not disappointed. Mrs. Monroe's dress of white figured silk trimmed with a profusion of white point lace and her hat with white plumes—all in the height of style—were the envy of all the ladies. In spite of her poor health, Mrs. Monroe still looked much younger than her years and her beauty was much admired. Although Washington ladies considered her rather haughty and cold, Louisa Adams did not think they were being fair. She did not feel that the First Lady's reserve was at all unsuitable to her station, and she was impressed with the ease with which Mrs. Monroe discharged her duties as a hostess. As she rather sadly concluded after the New Year's reception, "tastes differ and Dear Dolly [sic] was much more popular." Although Mrs. Adams never became intimate with the President's wife, who seems to have had no close friends outside her family, she much admired her poise, regarding the First Lady's manners as much superior to those of the other ladies present. After seeing the President's wife at a drawing room in January 1818, Louisa Adams enthusiastically wrote her father-in-law: "She was dressed in white and gold made in the highest style of fashion and moved not like a Queen (for that is an unpardonable word in this country) but like a goddess." Queens and goddesses are remote figures to be admired and not loved, and this was Mrs. Monroe's fate. Perhaps too, she failed to conceal completely her dislike for these ceremonial occasions, and this diffidence was sensed by her guests. Nonetheless, through the eight years of Monroe's Presidency the drawing rooms were regularly thronged except when it was rumored that his wife would not be present.[17] Only the appearance of such cele-

brated figures as General Jackson had the power to distract the ladies
from Mrs. Monroe's gowns, and those of Mrs. Hay, who dressed with
equal splendor and style.[18]

The growing size of the city and the constant stream of visitors to
the Capital created problems which were not easily solved in view
of the general conviction that the President should not set himself
apart from ordinary citizens. Since no restrictions, other than being
decently dressed, were placed on admission to the drawing rooms, unpleasant incidents became increasingly common. Late in 1819, when
a minor clerk mistreated one of the servants, Monroe consulted Adams
about the desirability of establishing specific regulations about the
admission of guests. Adams, who felt this would cause unpleasant comment, advised him not to, but suggested instead that unarmed soldiers
be placed at the gates and the door. At least this had the advantage
of expediting traffic. No longer did the wife of the Secretary of State
have to sit marooned in her carriage for a half-hour listening to hackney
coachmen abusively disputing the right of way.[19]

Presidential dinners, of which there were several each week, were
somewhat more relaxed except for those given to the diplomatic corps
or involving large batches of congressmen and strangers. All visitors
with any pretension to social or political standing were presented by
their congressmen to the President, who received such callers between
one and two every day. Since visitors expected (and often obtained)
an invitation to dinner, there were frequently many guests quite unknown to one another and to the President, a situation not making for
easy conversation. At most White House dinners ladies were not present, a not unusual circumstance in Washington, for many congressmen did not bring their wives to the Capital. When there were ladies
among the guests, Mrs. Monroe or her daughter presided. The guests
assembled shortly before dinner (usually at four or five) in the Oval
Room, where they were welcomed by the President. As soon as the
last guest arived the party moved into the dining room, with the President escorting the lady nearest him. Mrs. Monroe would be led in either
by the Vice-President, the Secretary of State or a Cabinet member. Except at diplomatic dinners no rigid rules of seating were followed,
although the senators did expect places at the head of the table. The
number of guests was always a matter of uncertainty, since many visitors and residents had the annoying habit of not informing the President of their intentions. At times it seemed as if the White House were

regarded as little more than a tavern at the disposal of all who wished to use its facilities.[20]

The dining room, like the rest of the house, was admired for the taste of the furnishings, which were much simpler and less crowded together than was then the rule. The large table, covered with a fine cloth, was set off by the magnificent gilt plateau purchased in France, which still graces White House banquets. The decoration on the French porcelain dinnerware, depicting an eagle bearing an olive branch, was considered highly appropriate by the President's compatriots. To American visitors the plate was sumptuous, but to Europeans it seemed no more than that ordinarily found in the houses of private citizens without official rank. Dinners were served in the French manner with servants handing the dishes to the guests. On great occasions, Louisa Adams reported, the guests were served with an abundance of "good viands," but at other times the dinners seem to have been somewhat indifferent in character—for her husband usually returned hungry after dining at the White House.[21] After dessert, when Mrs. Monroe and the ladies withdrew, the President and his guests sat drinking a few glasses of wine before joining the ladies for coffee. The guests usually departed well before nine.

At smaller parties both the President and his wife appeared at their best. Relaxed and conversing freely with an innate warmth and courtesy, Monroe readily made his guests feel at ease, avoiding, in the characteristic Virginia way, subjects which might cause irritation or awkwardness. Thus, when Harrison Gray Otis at a dinner attended by Republican luminaries sought to obscure himself at the foot of the table, he was deeply touched by the gesture of the "Old Sachem," who "in a few minutes looked at me with a great significance and kindness and called to me aloud to know if I were warm. He then drank a glass of wine with me to make friends." To a gentleman of the old school like Otis, this was worth as much as an appointment to office as a token of esteem. On another occasion, Otis (himself a polished host) told his wife: "I dined at the palace, and at the right hand of the Queen who was most exceedingly gracious and conversible, and I believe has no colour but what is natural, at least her colour very much increased during dinner time in the glow of occupation and attention to her guests. . . . A very superb dinner and much less funereal ceremony than common." Another New Englander, Congressman Elijah H. Mills, was equally pleased with Monroe, whom he found much less reserved than

Madison.[22] The presence of lively wits and raconteurs like Henry Clay gave color to the smaller parties. The President, in spite of his grave demeanor, had an excellent sense of humor. On one occasion, when the President served a wine sent him by a South American, which all agreed to be bad, Clay's comment that it should have been sent to the House with the recent documents on South America delighted Monroe as much as the guests.[23] The President, although he imported wine from France for use in the White House, had a fondness for serving native wines, particularly scuppernong in place of madeira.[24]

The cost of maintaining the White House (there was no expense allowance at that time) far exceeded Monroe's salary of $25,000. By 1822 he was in debt to the extent of $35,000. When efforts to alleviate his financial distress by selling the Albemarle lands fell through, he seriously considered eliminating all dinner parties and canceling the drawing rooms. Although Jefferson approved a policy designed to put an end to the use of the White House as a general tavern, others were not in agreement. Adams felt that a curtailment in entertaining would be attributed to meanness and stir up unnecessary antagonism among the members of Congress. Only homespun Republican purists like Abner Lacock of Pennsylvania urged that the "Drawing Rooms," a form of "miserable pageantry," be abandoned. In the end the President continued his mode of entertainment, but on a restricted scale. Since his wife and daughter were both ill during his last two years in office, he gave few large dinner parties.[25]

The Monroes did not enter into the official social life of the city. Following the precedent established by Washington, they did not accept invitations to dinner or to evening parties at the homes of Cabinet officials or diplomats. Only on rare occasions did the President accept private invitations without political implications. In the spring of 1820 he attended a dinner given for the members of the Prince George County Agricultural Society by Thomas Law at his country residence. This was a lively affair with the guests joining in songs over the punch bowl as the President beat time with his fork.[26] Monroe and his wife attended affairs of a ceremonial nature, such as the annual balls on Washington's birthday, a function at one time bitterly condemned by the Republicans as a monarchical institution.[27] On Sundays the President and his family might be seen at St. John's Episcopal Church across from the White House.[28] When the pressure of public business permitted, Monroe attended public lectures given in the hall of the House of Representatives by visiting celebrities, such as Joseph Lancaster, the educational reformer.[29] On the whole, the early Presidents were involved in relatively few ceremonial functions. Perhaps the most common, apart from the Fourth of July celebrations and the Washington birthday balls, were the receptions accorded visiting Indian delegations, who flocked to Washington to render homage to their "Great Father." When the Pawnee chieftains were in the Capital in 1822 they staged an elaborate farewell ceremony in front of the White House which was watched by a crowd of 3,000. During the course of the dance, each chieftain approached the President and recited at length his tribal achievements in war. At the end of the function the President shared a pipe of peace with the Indians and then distributed a suit of clothing to each chieftain, perhaps a tactful suggestion that loincloths were not entirely appropriate in the Capital of a civilized nation.[30]

II

To a remarkable degree the Monroes lived a completely private life in the White House, enjoying a domestic seclusion respected by their contemporaries, who did not consider the family life of public figures a subject for public curiosity. Although Adams left a voluminous record of the political activities of the Monroe administration, he had almost nothing to say about the personal aspects. Throughout his two terms, a number of relatives of both the President and his wife made prolonged visits to the White House. These included the President's brother, Joseph Jones Monroe, who served as a private secretary until he moved to Missouri in 1820, and Joseph's son, James Monroe. Another resident was Samuel L. Gouverneur, Mrs. Monroe's nephew, who filled in as a private secretary until he married Monroe's younger daughter in 1820 and returned to New York. Samuel Gouverneur's mother and sister were also frequent visitors.

Apart from the President and his wife, the only member of the family circle to make a deep impression on Washington society was the President's elder daughter, Mrs. George Hay, who lived at the White House and frequently replaced her mother as hostess. Mrs. Hay, like her mother a stylish and beautiful woman, acquired the reputation of being at once a difficult and formidable person and yet at the same time rather flighty. Her years at Mme. Campan's school seem to have left her with exaggerated notions of her own importance—she could never let anyone forget that she had been a classmate of Hortense de Beauharnais; indeed, it was once unkindly, but not unaptly, said of her that she could have been truly happy only if she had married a marshal of the Empire.[31] She always seems to have felt displaced in America, and after the deaths of her husband and her father, she returned to Paris, where she became a Catholic convert, lodging in a convent until her death.[32] In the White House she assuaged her nostalgia for France by reminiscing about her schooldays and by seeing to it that the White House cooks were provided with that basic manual—Beauvillier's *L'art du Cuisinier*.[33]

Early in her father's first term she was embroiled in a pointless conflict with the wives of the foreign ministers, who she insisted must pay the first call, which they refused to do, considering her to be a private person. Consequently, Mrs. Hay would not attend any parties given by the members of the diplomatic corps, a decision which, as Louisa Adams tartly commented, amounted to an insulting rejection of all social contact with the diplomats and their wives. Mrs. Hay's position was rendered all the more absurd by her insistence that when she did go out in society she not be accorded any special mark of attention as the President's daughter, although she seemed to expect it as the wife of Mr. Hay. Since her husband was but a private citizen, there was no resolution of this dilemma unless she expected a recognition of her husband's claim that his father (who had owned the Raleigh Tavern in Williamsburg) was a younger son of the Earl of Erroll. On the one occasion on which she attended a party given by the French Minister, she laid down so many conditions about her treatment that she made all the guests uncomfortable.[34] Washington ladies came to dread the visits of this stylish lady, who, to quote Louisa Adams, was so "full of agreeables and disagreeables, so accomplished and ill bred, so proud and so mean," and who had such a "love for scandal that no reputation is safe in her hands."[35]

Perhaps no story so fully characterizes Mrs. Hay as the anecdote told by John Quincy Adams. One evening, while his wife was in Quincy, Adams called on the Calhouns, where Mrs. Hay was also present. The callers constantly queried Adams about his wife, and, as he recounted:

Mrs. Hay after hearing me answer the same question four or five times . . . at last broke out Lord! said she, how tiresome such questions are! Last winter one evening at the drawing room after Mr. Hay went to Richmond a hundred and fifty people came up to me one after the other asking when did you hear from Mr. Hay and how is Mr. Hay? At last I said to one of them—He's *dead!*—I have just got the news.—He's *dead!* and buried! and the subject is *so distressing* that I will thank my friends to say no more to me about him.

When Louisa Adams heard the story, she considered it so like Mrs. Hay that it was impossible to doubt its veracity.[36] Vain, proud and sharp-tongued though she was, Mrs. Hay was not unkind. Devoted to her parents, she cared for her mother during her many illnesses. In 1820, when the Calhouns' five-month-old daughter was fatally ill, Mrs. Hay sat up with the child for three nights and proved herself a capable nurse. This generous act was performed at some sacrifice, for Mrs. Hay was then supervising the preparations of her sister's wedding.[37]

A much less distinct figure in the Monroe family circle was Maria Hester, the President's younger daughter. Only fifteen at the time of the inauguration, she remained in school at Philadelphia until 1819. She seems to have been a much gentler person than Mrs. Hay, and it is not surprising that the two sisters did not get on together.[38] After her marriage Maria Hester preferred to remain in New York, rarely visiting either the White House or Oak Hill—more usually her mother went to New York for long visits. Maria Hester was married to her cousin Samuel L. Gouverneur at the White House in 1820 at a private ceremony with only close friends and members of the family present. Even the most curious gossips of the city could report little more about the wedding than that the ceremony had been conducted in the New York style with seven bridesmaids and seven groomsmen. The wedding occasioned much unkind comment among the envious who were not included among the forty-two guests at the wedding dinner. Louisa Adams, however, felt that the President had a perfect right to keep it a family affair. Since he could not hope to please everyone in private matters, it was her opinion that he should simply please himself. The wedding was marred by a tempest over etiquette stirred up by Mrs. Hay, who did not think it proper for the wives of the diplomatic corps, who had declined to call on her, to pay their respects to the newlyweds. It was necessary for the President to intervene and instruct Adams to inform the ministers that their calls would be welcomed. After a brief wedding trip to Virginia the bride and groom returned to Washington, where a series of balls and receptions had been planned for them. The first of these at the Decaturs was also the last, for the death of Commodore Stephen Decatur two days later from wounds received in

a duel led to a cancellation of the other festivities.[39] The joy felt by
the Gouverneurs at the birth of their son (named after the President)
in 1822 soon turned to sorrow, when it was discovered that the child
was a deaf-mute.[40]

Like his predecessors Monroe spent much of the summer away from
Washington, either at Oak Hill or in Albemarle. Oak Hill was not in
any sense a summer White House, for the President was not accompanied by an official staff. In case of need he returned to the Capital
at the summons of the members of his Cabinet. During his absences
one or more of the Secretaries remained in Washington to examine
correspondence and forward important items to the President. Ordinarily Monroe communicated with his Secretaries through the regular post office service. Although he began to spend more time at Oak
Hill after his first term began, it was not until 1819 that he finally
decided to build a larger house at Oak Hill. Up until then he continued to make improvements at Highlands and talked of retiring
there after the end of his second term. The decisive factor in his move
to Loudoun County was not only its proximity to Washington but his
inability to sell Oak Hill for anything like the price he thought it would
bring. The value of Virginia property, depressed for more than a decade, sank even lower in the wake of the Panic of 1819.[41] Monroe made
this decision with regret, for it involved separating himself in his old
age from Jefferson and other close friends in Albemarle.[42]

CHAPTER 23

SPAIN AND
HER COLONIES:
THE PROBLEM

THE RESTORATION of peace in Europe liberated American foreign policy from the inhibiting factors which had been dominant since the Washington administration.[1] The central issues of the preservation of neutrality and the protection of neutral rights, which had been the preoccupation of American diplomacy, faded into the background. Monroe was not hesitant in exploiting the opportunity offered him to go beyond the negative policies forced upon his predecessors by circumstances. The most important over-all object of his foreign policy was to ensure the recognition of the United States, not only as the strongest power in the Americas, but also as the only republic of any consequence in either hemisphere: respect and honor were key words in his thinking. It was not that he neglected the pragmatic aspects, but he wished to achieve these goals in a manner which would command the respect of the European powers. No longer should the United States depend on the patronage of other states, such as France, to secure its diplomatic aims. Monroe, whose own diplomatic career had exposed him to many rebuffs and humiliations, was much more concerned about this question of the status of the United States in relationship to European powers than was Adams. Thus when the British offered to mediate between the United States and Spain during the crisis over Florida, Monroe at once rejected this proposal which Adams was willing to accept.[2]

The all-absorbing problem in foreign affairs during Monroe's Presidency was that created by Spain's crumbling American empire. Nearly all his major decisions either centered on this issue or had to be closely correlated with the questions it raised. The Spanish problem had three primary aspects: firstly, how to secure Florida without war and without making concessions to Spain which would ignore the obligations of the United States to the Latin American revolutionaries; secondly, how to prevent European intervention to restore Spain's authority in her colonies; and, thirdly—and this was a corollary of the first two—how to demonstrate friendship toward the new states in South America in a manner which would neither invite European interference nor jeopardize the quest for Florida. The successful accomplishment of these three objectives, which was the most notable achievement of the Monroe administration, was the result of careful planning by the President and the Secretary of State, and did not depend, as had been so often the case in the past, on fortuitous alterations in the European balance of power. Constantly subjecting his policy to re-evaluation, Monroe never permitted it to be confined by rigid dogmatism. His achievement was all the more noteworthy in that it took place in the face of powerful domestic opposition, which was not aimed at the policies themselves but at exploiting the President's program for the benefit of rival presidential candidates. Nearly all Americans approved of Monroe's policies, but some found it politically advantageous to expose them to a running fire of criticism. Under these circumstances, when Monroe often seemed hesitant or indecisive, he was simply maneuvering for time to let passions cool and to solidify his support.

Monroe's policy toward the Latin American revolutionary movements was a logical extension of that formulated by Jefferson and Madison.[3] In 1808, after Napoleon occupied Spain, a number of colonies had set up autonomous regimes, but did not declare themselves independent. At that time Jefferson had taken the position that the United States not only had a common interest with those colonies seeking independence, but also that the nation should seek to prevent the European powers from influencing events in the Western Hemisphere. More pressing international problems, however, prevented the practical implementation of this policy. It was not until 1810 that Madison sent the first special agents to South America—the most important being Joel R. Poinsett, who was sent to Chile, Peru, and Buenos Aires (also known as the United Provinces of the Rio de La Plata). He was instructed to give unofficial encouragement to the insurgents by affirming the good will of the United States. South American agents, who were permitted to reside in the United States and purchase supplies, established an indirect and unofficial contact with the government through John Jacob Astor, Stephen Girard, Nicholas Biddle and other private citizens with influential contacts.

Monroe first became directly involved with the problem in 1811 shortly after he entered the State Department, when a congressional committee came to him for information about the recent Venezuelan declaration of independence. The committee report, framed in accordance with executive wishes, was confined to a declaration of friendly interest in the independence movement and a promise to establish diplomatic relations as soon as stable regimes were set up. This cautious restatement of Jeffersonian policy was prompted by the fear that bolder action might precipitate European intervention. Since the Venezuelan government proved short-lived, the question ceased to be important. Not until after the War of 1812, when there was a rapid increase in the number of insurgent states, did the problem of American policy toward the new regimes assume a new significance. Moreover, the rapid expansion of American trade with both the insurgents and the loyal colonies during the postwar years created a much greater interest in Latin American affairs than had been the case in the past. Public attention was also stimulated by the propaganda produced by insurgent agents resident in the United States and by Americans sympathetic to the revolutionaries.

As the revolutionary movements gained in intensity, European statesmen observed American reactions attentively. Monroe had been President only a few weeks when the French Minister questioned acting Secretary of State Rush about the intentions of the administration in relation to the rebellious colonies, since he presumed that the United States was as unwilling as France to let Britain reap the benefits of South American independence. Hinting that European intervention might well take place without advance notice to the United States, De Neuville suggested that France and America join in promoting a reconciliation between Spain and her colonies. The reward for each would be in the form of commercial advantages from which England would be excluded. Monroe rejected this proposal, observing that the inevitability of independence in the colonial area made it to the interest of the United States to be among the first to acknowledge the new nations. To his query whether De Neuville would not prefer the United States rather than Britain to stand first in the esteem of the new states he received no reply.[4] Although hostile to European action to re-establish Spain's authority in her colonies, the President was not willing to support the insurgent movement in an official way. When

Manuel de Aguirre, the agent for Buenos Aires, arrived in Washington in the summer of 1817 he was not accorded official recognition, because the President feared precipitate action might invite European intervention—an opinion confirmed by Adams' dispatches from London.[5] From the beginning of his administration, it was a cardinal principle of Monroe's Latin American policy to avoid steps which might provoke interference by the allied powers. This policy, which he considered the greatest service the nation could render the insurgents, was explicitly defined in a letter to Gallatin in May 1820:

With respect to the Colonies, the object has been to throw into their scale, in a moral sense, the weight of the United States, without so deep a compromitment as to make us a party to the contest. All Europe must expect that the citizens of the United States wish success to the Colonies, and all that they can claim, even Spain herself, is that we will maintain an impartial neutrality between the parties. By taking this ground openly and frankly, we acquit ourselves to our own consciences; we accommodate with the feelings of our constituents; we render to the Colonies all the aid that we can render them, for I am satisfied that had we even joined them in the war, we should have done them more harm than good, as we might have drawn all Europe on them, not to speak of the injury we should have done to ourselves.[6]

In Monroe's interpretation, support in a "moral sense" meant issuing benevolent statements favoring the revolutionary movement and the enactment of neutrality laws which would operate in favor of the rebels.

II

Early in Monroe's first term the activities of insurgent groups presented immediate problems. The internecine conflicts within the revolutionary forces in South America and the careless practices of the insurgents in appointing agents provided an excellent opportunity for adventurers to engage in various illicit activities ranging from piracy to slave trading and smuggling, all supposedly in behalf of the cause of liberty. The most conspicuous of these adventurers was the Scots trader Gregor McGregor, who seized Amelia Island in the mouth of the St. Mary's River on the pretext of using it as a base for Venezuelan revolutionaries. Under McGregor's control Amelia Island, which lay on the American frontier but within the boundary of Spanish Florida, rapidly became a haven for pirates, slave traders and smugglers. A similar so-called insurgent group was also operating at Galveston within the limits of the territory claimed by the United States under the Louisiana cession. Since Spanish authorities seemed incapable of ejecting these interlopers, Monroe late in 1817 was faced with the choice of condoning these unsavory elements as a gesture of sympathy for the Latin American revolutionary movement or expelling them in the interests of American shipping.[7]

When Monroe met with his Cabinet on October 17, 1817, to discuss the draft of his annual message, the problem of the Amelia Island pirates required immediate solution; but, as with all matters concerning Latin America, it had to be examined in relation to the total picture of America's interests in the Western Hemisphere. Consequently, Monroe propounded a series of questions for discussion which revealed the interconnection between his expansionist aims in Florida and the obligation of the United States to foster the insurgent movement. The first question he put to the Secretaries was whether the executive had the power to recognize former colonies whose independence had not been acknowledged by the mother country? Was it, if this were within his power, expedient to extend recognition to Buenos Aires? What position should the United States adopt toward Spain in view of her constant evasion of American claims for reparations for injuries? Was it expedient to break up the piratical groups on Amelia Island? Should he adhere to the decision he had made in the spring to send a special commission to South America to report on the character of the states claiming independence? These questions clearly established the framework within which Monroe's Latin American policy operated. After the October discussions, during which only Adams offered any significant commentary, the President decided to send expeditions to both Amelia Island and Galveston and to let the commissioners depart, as originally planned. The President fully agreed with Adams' strongly worded objection to extending recognition to Buenos Aires.[8]

In his annual message on December 2 the President defined his position on recognition, from which he made no significant variation during the next few years. The United States, he announced, would continue its policy of neutrality, keeping its ports open to both parties on an equal basis. As an oblique warning to the British, who were generally believed to be seeking special commercial privileges from the new states, he declared that the United States would not seek any concessions other than those granted to all other nations. Briefly reviewing the history of the Amelia Island adventurers, he announced that an expedition had been sent to restore order. He had little to say about

Spain other than the general comment that the most recent proposals from that country did not offer any hope for an early settlement.[9]

The message was not very encouraging to the friends of recognition. Clay privately condemned the President for his refusal to recognize Buenos Aires and for the decision to expel the insurgent agents (as he called them) from Amelia Island, but for the moment he held his fire in Congress.[10] Monroe felt that his message had placed American policy upon a sound footing, and extended to the colonies, as he explained to Charles J. Ingersoll, "all the countenance we can, without too great a compromitment with the allied powers who may possibly be disposed to take the other side. The pulse of the allied powers will be felt, while we are left at liberty, to act, hereafter, as the interest of the United States may require." [11] The interest which Monroe had in mind was the acquisition of Florida and the favorable definition of the western boundary of Louisiana. The Amelia Island expedition was but one phase in the drive to exert pressure on Spain to cede Florida, for Monroe had been convinced since 1805 that nothing but a show of force would compel her to yield this territory. While the Amelia Island expedition was en route, the President and his Cabinet examined other measures calculated to put additional pressure on Spain by publicizing her inability to maintain order in Florida. For the past year the southern frontier had been subjected to incessant forays by the Indians, who took refuge in Spanish territory. Under the clause in Pinckney's Treaty requiring Spain to restrain the Indians living in her jurisdiction, Monroe felt amply justified in sending a punitive expedition against the Indians involved in the frontier raids. On December 26, the President ordered General Gaines, who had previously been given command of the Amelia Island expedition, to start operations against the Indians with authority to pursue them into Spanish territory. He was specifically ordered, however, not to attack them if they took refuge in a Spanish post. In the latter event he was to notify the War Department.[12]

When it was learned shortly after these orders had been sent that Gaines had departed for Amelia Island and could not supervise the Florida campaign, Monroe entrusted the command to Andrew Jackson and sent him a copy of Gaines' orders. The appointment was amply justified by Jackson's record in the War of 1812 and by his familiarity with the Southwest. Since the end of the war, Monroe, who not only felt a debt of gratitude to Jackson for his services but also welcomed the support of a popular hero, had maintained a confidential correspondence with the general. The President knew that Jackson's *amour-propre*, excessive sensitivity to criticism, and violent temper did not make him an easy person to deal with in a subordinate capacity. Only recently Monroe had been obliged to use all his tact to abate the general's rage over a minor episode, in which, as was so often the case, Jackson was in the wrong.

In 1817, acting Secretary of War Crawford had transferred an engineer serving under Jackson without informing the general. Without pausing to reflect that this action was fully within the President's power as Commander in Chief, Jackson promptly issued a general order forbidding compliance with commands which did not bear his signature. After he returned from his tour, Monroe had assumed the burden of explaining that Crawford's order was not an infringement on the general's authority. In the face of Jackson's stubborn determination to be vindicated for what was at worst an oversight on Crawford's part, the President patiently sought to conciliate the general. The conflict was resolved when Monroe proposed that Calhoun (who had now taken over his duties as Secretary of War) issue a regulation requiring that orders from the War Department to individual commanders be transmitted through the commanding generals. To avoid the imputation that this was a reprimand, Monroe agreed that Jackson need not rescind his earlier general order nor formally publish Calhoun's regulation in his district. In accepting this solution, which was virtually an unofficial apology, Jackson, whose gratitude on occasion could be as overwhelming as his wrath, praised Monroe for exhibiting that "magnanimity of conduct only to be met with in great and good minds. . . ." [13] If Jackson cherished any lingering resentment against the President, it was eradicated by his appointment as commander of the Seminole expedition.

Long before he was notified of his new command, Jackson's thoughts had already turned to the possibility of using the Indian raids as a means of seizing Florida. On January 6, 1818—just a few days before he received news of his appointment—Jackson wrote to share his reflections on Spanish-American policy with the President. The United States, he suggested, should not only occupy Amelia Island, but should also seize East Florida as an indemnity for Spain's past outrages. "This can be done," he cheerfully confided, "without implicating the government. Let it be signified to me through any channel, (say Mr. J. Rhea) that the possession of the Floridas would be desirable to the United States, and in sixty days it will be accomplished." [14] In view of the decision to place Jackson in command of the Seminole expedition, this was indeed a letter deserving a cautionary reply, but amazingly it did not elicit a response. When it reached the Capital the President was seriously ill. On the assumption that it dealt with military concerns, the ailing President showed it to Calhoun, who returned it remarking that it required Monroe's attention. Crawford also read the letter but made no comment. Apparently neither department head examined it carefully, and the President, who did not have a private secretary at the time, put it aside with other papers. Not until almost a year later, when Crawford reminded him of it during the congressional investigation of Jackson's conduct in Florida, did the President read the letter.[15]

More than a decade later, during the Jackson-Calhoun imbroglio of 1830, the disposition of this letter became a matter of prime concern. At that time, Crawford, citing his "tenacious and accurate" memory, claimed that Monroe had read it to the Cabinet in the course of the deliberations about Jackson's seizure of the posts.[16] These recollections were completely at odds with those of the President and the other Secretaries, who could not recall the incident.[17] By insisting in 1830 that the Cabinet had been familiar with Jackson's letter, Crawford was attempting to make it seem all the more reprehensible that Calhoun had advocated censuring the general in 1818, since he knew that Jackson had asked for permission to seize Florida. Although this letter would seem to constitute an important item in Jackson's defense of his conduct during the Seminole War, it was never mentioned in all the appeals and protests which he directed to the President in 1818. His silence remains quite inexplicable, for he does not seem to have forgotten about it. On December 15, 1818, William B. Lewis, a Jackson intimate, published a letter in the Philadelphia *Aurora* over the signature "B.B." in which he asserted that the failure of the administration to answer Jackson's request for express authorization to seize Florida was tantamount to approval.[18] When Monroe saw this item (Crawford pointed it out to him), his first thought was to explain to Jackson that illness had prevented him from answering the letter of January 6. As he reflected further, it seemed much wiser not to refer to a communication never mentioned by the general.[19]

In 1830 Jackson, whose memory was far more acute than it had been twelve years earlier, advanced another explanation of his conduct. Directly impugning Monroe's integrity, he alleged that the President had empowered him to seize Florida by sending instructions through John Rhea, a representative from Tennessee. Regrettably, Jackson re-

called, he had destroyed Rhea's letter at the President's request. Only
with much prompting from Jackson could the aged Rhea (he was
seventy-seven), who honestly admitted the decay of his faculties, be
brought to recall dimly his role in this transaction. At the insistence
of the general, Rhea wrote Monroe to verify the facts as stated by
Jackson. When this request reached New York, the President was fatally
ill at the residence of his son-in-law, who turned to William Wirt for
advice. Although Wirt shrewdly guessed that the reply would not
silence Jackson, he agreed that the charges were so serious that they
must be brought to the attention of the former President in spite of
the gravity of his condition. On June 19, 1831, two weeks before his
death, Monroe made a deposition positively denying Rhea's statements.[20] As Wirt predicted, this did not satisfy Jackson's passion to
shift the blame for his conduct on Monroe—two years later the story
was revived in the *National Intelligencer*. When Samuel L. Gouverneur rushed to defend the memory of his father-in-law, Jackson pun-
ished him by summarily dismissing him from the postmastership of
New York City.[21]

The story of the Rhea letter seems to have been nothing more than
a fabrication on Jackson's part, for Monroe certainly never authorized
the general to seize Florida. Nothing was further from his intention in
1818, for he believed that it required only moderate pressure to bring
Spain to the point of ceding Florida. The possibility that Jackson might
perform some unwelcome exploit had occurred to the President shortly
after Jackson had been appointed. On January 30, 1818, the President
wrote Calhoun to send instructions to Jackson "not to attack any post
occupied by Spanish troops, from the possibility it might bring the
allied powers on us." [22] Monroe was not the only administration official
to be inattentive to his correspondence, for Calhoun never issued orders
containing this explicit restriction.

III

Early in January 1818, following the arrival of the news that Amelia
Island had been occupied on December 23 without opposition, the
President conferred with his Cabinet about the disposition of the island. This discussion, as did most of those relating to Florida and Spain,
produced considerable disagreement. When the President produced a
draft message to Congress expressing his intention of withdrawing
American forces from the island, Adams and Calhoun vigorously

pressed him to retain the territory as a useful bargaining point in negotiating with Spain, while Crawford, Wirt and Crowninshield favored withdrawal. Adams did not consider the views of either the Attorney General or the Secretary of the Navy significant, for he felt they would always be inclined to agree with the President, but he placed an interpretation on Crawford's stand which, whether justified or not, revealed Adams' ambitions. "Crawford's point d'honneur," he noted in his diary after the meeting, "is to differ from me and to find no weight in any reason assigned by me." [23] This judgment was unfair, for Crawford was seriously concerned that continued occupation might lead to war with Spain.[24] Only after Monroe assured the Secretary of the Treasury that such an event was improbable did he withdraw his objections. In his message on January 13, the President announced the occupation of Amelia Island under the provisions of the secret act of 1811 (only recently published), which authorized the executive to occupy Florida if necessary to prevent its seizure by powers hostile to the United States. Although some congressmen entertained misgivings about the exercise of executive power involved in sending military expeditions to occupy foreign territory, most accepted his conclusion that Spain's jurisdiction "necessarily ceases" in a region over which she "fails to maintain her authority, and which she permits to be converted to the annoyance of her neighbors. . . ." He trusted that the problems presented by Spain's weakness could be solved by negotiation.[25]

As Monroe had expected, the expedition to Amelia Island seemed to provide the impetus needed to break the deadlock in the negotiations with Spain in which George W. Erving, the Minister to Spain, had been engaged since 1815. As soon as the President announced the occupation of the island, the Spanish Minister, Don Diego de Onís, called on Adams to protest. In subsequent conferences Onís outlined the terms of a settlement recently received from the newly appointed Foreign Minister, José García de Leon y Pizarro. Although Pizarro faced up to the realities of Spain's position in North America better than his predecessors, he still cherished the belief that Florida could be bartered for a settlement of the Louisiana boundary favorable to Spain. Consequently, the terms offered by Onís, which did not go beyond those rejected by Erving, were disappointing. Pizarro had proposed that in exchange for Florida and for the payment of the spoliation claims the United States agree to fix the Louisiana boundary at the Mississippi. Flatly refusing these terms, the President and Adams coun-

tered with the long-established American claim to the Colorado River
and also suggested that a line be drawn northward from the source of
the river to the Rocky Mountains. Since Onís had no power to accept
a boundary so unfavorable to Spain, he proposed that they agree on the
line of 1763.[26] In resuscitating this ancient and never precisely determined boundary, which would involve a review of the whole controversy, Onís was taking refuge in delay and evasion. "It is impossible,"
Monroe commented to Adams, "to read the note of the Spanish Minister without sensations, which it might not purport with the character
of the government to express. Dignity and policy equally forbid, the
use of expressions which indicate passion or resentment. . . ." [27]

In no haste to reply to a diplomat who clearly lacked power to make
a settlement along lines satisfactory to the United States, the President and the Secretary of State restudied in some detail the American
position on the disputes between the two nations. While they were
engrossed in this investigation, the British Minister tendered Castlereagh's offer to mediate if the United States requested Britain's intervention. Although Adams was willing to accept, the President was
firmly opposed. In turning down the offer, Monroe wished to take the
position that the mediation of a third party was unnecessary, since
the dispute was not likely to result in war. Adams persuaded him,
however, to rest the refusal on the grounds that American opinion
would not tolerate outside interference. The British, having reluctantly
made the offer at Spain's request, were relieved at the American rejection. Castlereagh feared that Anglo-American relations might be irreparably damaged if the results of an arbitration proved unfavorable to
the United States.[28]

The most important new concept to emerge in the course of the
re-evaluation of administration policy toward Spain was a compromise
proposal on the Louisiana boundary. The President summed up their
conclusions in a note to Adams: "We may agree to fix the boundary
by the Trinity, from its mouth to its source, then to the Arkansas at
its nearest point, and thence due West to the Pacific." [29] The new line
was a concession to Spain in that it shifted the boundary eastward from
the Colorado, but, far more significantly, it ensured the protection of
the American claim to the Columbia River by extending the northern
boundary to the Pacific. Although this suggestion, which was developed
by Adams, became the cornerstone of the American position on the
Louisiana boundary, it was not included in Adams' reply to Onís. There

was nothing to be gained by offering a major concession to a diplomat who lacked the power to locate the boundary west of the Mississippi. Instead Adams merely restated the evidence supporting the American claim to the Colorado. Faced by the unyielding stand of the administration, Onís shifted the negotiations to Madrid, where Erving met with no greater success than he had in the past.[30]

When Congress adjourned on April 20, Monroe, who had decided to postpone his western tour for a year in view of his poor health, went to Virginia for a rest. Returning briefly to the Capital in mid-May he again discussed basic policy in the light of Jackson's success in Florida. At this time it was known that the general had moved into Florida and had occupied St. Marks, which the Spanish had evacuated at his approach. Once more Monroe propounded a series of questions: Should Florida be evacuated at the end of Jackson's campaign? Should an armed force be sent along the Atlantic and Pacific coasts of South America to protect American commerce? Should American ministers in Europe be instructed that the United States would not join any project to intervene between Spain and her colonies unless it be to insure their independence? Should an effort be made to ascertain whether Britain also shared this attitude toward intervention, and if so, should an effort be made to coordinate the policies of the two nations?

Not all these issues were resolved, but in the lengthy meeting on May 13, 1818, several basic decisions were made. In the first place, all the Secretaries agreed that American forces be kept in Florida until Spain provided adequate garrisons. The President and the Cabinet also concluded to instruct American ministers to declare on their own responsibility that the United States would regard with hostility any interference in Latin America. The question of sounding out Great Britain about her attitude toward the insurgents was left unsettled. This was a matter of particular interest to Monroe and Adams, who realized that the action of the Continental powers in regard to the rebellious colonies ultimately hinged on British naval power. Although Britain was publicly committed to the principles of legitimacy governing the operations of the Holy Alliance, still it was known that the importance of the trade between Britain and the insurgent states had created a strong sentiment hostile to a restoration of Spain's power. Since no immediate American action was planned, however, there was no urgency in seeking British cooperation in South America. At the same meeting the Cabinet agreed to set up naval patrols to protect American shipping from pirates posing as privateers and to open negotiations with England to renew the commercial convention expiring on July 3, 1819.[31]

A few days later the President, accompanied by Calhoun, Crowninshield, and Monroe's brother Joseph, who was acting as his secretary, set out for the Chesapeake to inspect the fortifications. Although the strategic importance of the Bay area made his journey much more of an official occasion than the tour of 1817, public demonstrations were arranged in Williamsburg, Annapolis, Yorktown and other towns along his route. Monroe traveled as far south as Elizabeth City, North Carolina, which he reached via the incomplete Dismal Swamp Canal. Here Calhoun and Crowninshield parted from the President—the former heading for South Carolina, the latter traveling northward to Salem. The President abruptly terminated his tour in mid-June after reading alarming press accounts of Jackson's conduct in Florida. According to the newspapers, many of which were bitterly critical of the general and the administration, Jackson on April 29 had summarily executed two British subjects, Robert Ambrister and Alexander Arbuthnot, who allegedly had incited the Indians against the United States. Then the general, who in truth had not found many Indians during his campaign, had attacked Pensacola on May 24, forcing the Spanish governor and his soldiers to depart for Havana.

The President had every reason to be disturbed, for the general had not only transgressed his orders in attacking the Spanish garrison at Pensacola and thus committing an act of war against Spain, but by his arbitrary execution of two British subjects had risked involving the United States in hostilities with Great Britain. When he reached the Capital on June 19 he learned that nothing had been received from Jackson since he left St. Marks. After waiting a week, the President went to his farm in Loudoun County. Adams was not at all pleased by the President's departure, for he felt that Monroe was procrastinating in the face of the "rapidly thickening" storm.[32] Yet there was nothing that could be done until official accounts arrived from Florida. Monroe's absence made it easier for Adams to fend off Onís, who had hastened to Washington from his summer residence in Bristol. When Onís and the French Minister, who sought to act as a moderator, called on Adams to protest, the Secretary informed them that no reply could be made until the President had seen the official documents. As soon as these reached him on July 9, Monroe hastened to the Capital.[33]

When Monroe met with the Cabinet on July 15, he found the

members sharply divided, with the majority urging that Jackson be publicly disavowed for exceeding his authority. Calhoun was outspoken in his condemnation and demanded an official investigation. Although somewhat less vehement than the Secretary of War, Crawford concurred with this view. Wirt, who said much less than the other department heads, was inclined to support Crawford and Calhoun. Only Adams spoke out boldly in Jackson's defense, urging the President to retain both St. Marks and Pensacola. The motives of Calhoun and Crawford in this controversy have often been questioned, but Adams' conclusion that they condemned Jackson solely to eliminate a potential rival for the Presidency seems extreme. As Secretary of War, Calhoun had a natural concern in insisting that orders be obeyed and that military commanders be properly subordinate to civil officers. Moreover, Jackson's conduct was indeed shocking to those reared in a tradition of strict constructionism, for his seizure of the posts seemed to be a clear invasion of the power of Congress to declare war. Was the nation about to be subjected to the tyranny of a backwoods Napoleon?

In spite of all that has been written about these July Cabinet meetings, Monroe's role has never been fully understood. The widely accepted view, that he at first wished to disavow Jackson but was won over to a different policy by the Secretary of State, rests on Adams' diary.[34] This all-important record for the Monroe era is essentially correct in its facts, but it must always be remembered that Adams wrote with his own particular commitment on the issues uppermost in his mind. Thus during all the Cabinet meetings relating to events in Florida, he assessed the comments made by his colleagues entirely in relation to his unshakable conviction that Jackson had been fully justified in his actions and that his conduct should be unequivocally endorsed by the administration. From this point of view, anyone not in agreement was automatically classified as opposing his stand. It is clear from the details presented by Adams that both Crawford and Calhoun vehemently argued that Jackson should be publicly repudiated for transgressing his orders, which had not permitted him to seize the posts. This particular act, they maintained, was an act of war and hence a violation of the Constitution, for only Congress could declare war.

During the discussions on July 15 and 16, of which Adams gave a briefer account than he wished because of a tremor in his right hand, the President said very little, but listened closely as the Secretaries debated. On the seventeenth, he gave Adams the draft of a note to Onís, which the Secretary reworked and presented to the Cabinet the following day. At that meeting, according to Adams, his letter to Onís was modified "to be conformable to the President's original draft." This meant, in effect, the elimination of everything "which imported a justification of Jackson's proceedings." There seems no doubt from Adams' narrative that the draft note Monroe had given him neither justified the general nor repudiated him. On the contrary, it expressed the President's conclusion that Jackson had exceeded his instructions in seizing the posts, but accepted the view that he had been guided by information discovered during the campaign which made the occupation of the posts seem necessary. This was as far as the President was willing to go, since he felt that the seizure of the posts had been an infringement of the power of Congress to declare war.

At the last Cabinet discussion of the subject on July 20, after both the editorial Wirt had drafted for the *Intelligencer* and the President's explanatory letter to Jackson had been read, Adams commented: "The President heard with candor and good humor all that I said, but without any variation from his original opinion, and my draft of a note to Onís, with all its amendments was finally fixed on the grounds of the President's original sketch." This cannot be taken to mean that the President still wished to repudiate Jackson, but only that he still disagreed with Adams' contention that Jackson should be unequivocally approved by the administration. The President, obviously, had long before made up his mind to take a stand short of full endorsement, and had used the Cabinet discussions to reach a consensus midway between the extremes advocated by the Secretaries. With their agreement he could hope to check any movement in Congress to condemn Jackson and thereby cast doubt on his decision to invade Florida. By adopting this position the President also retained the diplomatic advantages gained by the seizure of the posts and avoided the domestic repercussions which might ensue if he repudiated a popular national hero. Moreover, in declining to officially endorse Jackson and by insisting that he had transgressed his orders, the President sidestepped the constitutional issue.[35]

In a lengthy letter on July 19, the President undertook the disagreeable task of persuading Jackson that the administration position was not a reflection on the general's honor, integrity, or wisdom. In somewhat more direct terms than was his habit in dealing with Jackson, Monroe stated the central problem: "In transcending the limits prescribed by . . . [your] orders you acted on your own responsibility, on facts and circumstances which were unknown to the Government when the orders were given, many of which, indeed, occurred afterward, and which you thought imposed on you the measures, as an act of patriotism, essential to the honor and interests of your country." To make this hard truth more palatable, Monroe pointed out that there were cases (and this was one) in which a general could exceed his authority with "essential advantage to his country," and thereby garner merit for his action. Although Jackson had felt that circumstances had justified his action, the posts must be surrendered to Spain. In the first place, Monroe continued, the limitations of the Constitution must be observed: to retain the posts would be tantamount to a declaration of war, a power exclusively vested in Congress. In the second place, the restoration of the posts would facilitate the cession of Florida by avoiding further humiliation of Spain. As a special gesture of friendship, Monroe suggested that Jackson, who had written his dispatches hastily, might wish to modify them to eliminate passages leaving the impression that he had taken the posts as a matter of expediency. If Jackson agreed, Monroe was willing to delete the passages which would provide potent ammunition for the general's enemies. What Monroe did not add was that he desired to remove these portions of the dispatches because they tended to weaken the ground taken by the administration.[36]

Up to this point all the discussion had been conducted in private letters. When Calhoun refused to write Jackson until the general communicated his views directly to the War Department, Monroe advised Jackson to explain his position to the Secretary of War, promising a friendly reply setting forth administration policy. Such a course, he reminded the general, would enable him to place his interpretation of his orders in the official record.[37] Indignantly Jackson turned down the President's suggestion. He could not see any ground on which a letter to Calhoun could be "bottomed," for he had no reason to think that there was any difference of opinion between himself and the administration except from Monroe's private letters and comments in the press. The President, he maintained, would have been fully aware of the way in which Jackson understood his orders if he had read the general's dispatch of May 5, which according to Jackson the departmental clerks had tossed aside on a pile of old pension claims.[38] Faced by this massive intractability, Monroe ended the debate in December (six months after his first letter) with a friendly note acceding to Jackson's refusal to write Calhoun. At this time Monroe stressed the unanimity existing in the Cabinet, for Jackson had recently singled out Crawford as the instigator of the criticism of his conduct.[39] Throughout the correspondence Jackson never referred to any authorization received through John Rhea, although he recalled it vividly when the issue was revived in 1830 at the time of his break with Calhoun.

CHAPTER 24

SPAIN AND HER COLONIES: THE SOLUTION

IN SPITE OF the difficulties created for the administration by Jackson's conduct, the incident afforded a golden opportunity to force Spain to cede Florida and to accept a satisfactory western boundary for the Louisiana territory. Well aware of the Spanish habit of procrastination in the face of critical decisions, Monroe and Adams exerted considerable pressure on Onís to hasten a settlement. No concessions were made to the Minister's protests about events in Florida, for Adams rigidly insisted that Spain was responsible for the Indian disturbances which had made the invasion necessary. Although Adams agreed that Pensacola would be restored at once, St. Marks, which had been abandoned before Jackson occupied it, would not be returned until Spain established a garrison at the post strong enough to control the Indians. Even before answering the Minister's formal protests, Adams pressed Onís to outline terms for a settlement, but he made no progress, since Onís' power was still limited. During these conferences in July 1818, Adams continued to advance the Colorado as the western boundary, but he added the proposal that a line be drawn to the Pacific from the source of the Missouri to establish the northern limit of Louisiana. Neither this offer nor the alternative that Spain cede Florida and pay the claims, while leaving the Louisiana question to future negotiations, came within the scope of Onís' instructions, which were based on the assumption that Spain could obtain a definition of the Louisiana boundary in her favor in return for Florida. After listening to the Secretary of State assert that Congress might well authorize the occupation of Florida if an agreement were not in sight, Onís agitatedly wrote the Foreign Minister that there should be no delay in "making the best settlement possible, seeing that things certainly won't be better for a long time." [1]

Since nothing could be accomplished until new instructions arrived from Spain, Onís retired to Bristol. The President, as usual, vacationed in Virginia, while Adams went to Braintree late in August for six weeks. When they returned to Washington in October, there was a month of intense activity as the President and the Cabinet discussed the annual message and policy questions relating to Spain and also to England, where Rush and Gallatin were engaged in negotiations involving the Canadian-American boundary. Every aspect of the question was thoroughly examined in daily conferences with Adams and in the frequent Cabinet meetings—one of which lasted from one until nine with an interruption for dinner with the President.[2] Monroe was especially anxious to include in his message some comment indicating that an agreement with Spain was likely, in order to still the congressional criticism anticipated over Jackson's conduct. Since Onís' formal reply to the offer made by Adams some months earlier had been unsatisfactory, the President, in the hope of extracting some hopeful sign from Onís, ordered Adams to bring the Spanish Minister to the point or to break off negotiations. Consequently, on October 31, Adams sent Onís a virtual ultimatum proposing the cession of Florida and the fixing of the Louisiana boundary at the Sabine River, then due north to the Red River, and finally along a line running west to the Pacific along the 41st parallel. Although the Spanish Minister's most recent instructions permitted him to retreat to the Sabine, they did not allow him to accept either the Red River or to draw a line to the Pacific. Therefore, his reply was so far removed from Adams' proposal that the President did not feel justified in venturing optimistic comments.[3]

Monroe prepared his message of November 16, 1819, with great care for he had to answer questions raised at home and abroad about the Florida affair and Spanish-American relations. Moreover, he wanted to state American policy in a way which would not give the European powers any justification for coming to Spain's assistance, and yet at the same time his statement must be forceful enough to make Spain realize that she could no longer evade a settlement with the United States.[4] On the many occasions when he discussed the message with the Cabinet, the only objection to its contents was raised by Calhoun, who felt that the President overemphasized the Amelia Island expedition and that he devoted too much space to defending Jackson. Monroe, however, did not consider these criticisms sufficiently significant to alter his text.[5]

He began his message by explaining the reasons for the expedition sent to Florida. The most important consideration, he told Congress, had been Spain's inability to restrain the adventurers, smugglers, and Indians within her borders from committing outrages against the United States. Assuming full responsibility for ordering the invasion under the terms of the Treaty of 1795, he made it clear that Jackson had acted on his own authority in seizing the posts. The general, acting on information received during the campaign, had considered this step necessary to achieve the objectives of his expedition. Without commenting on the accuracy or value of Jackson's interpretation of the facts on which he had based his actions, Monroe announced that the posts would not be retained, since the executive did not have the power to hold them. Pensacola had already been restored, and St. Marks would be handed back as soon as an adequate garrison was sent to the fort. Before moving to other topics, the President promised to submit the relevant documents, including the proceedings against Arbuthnot and Ambrister—his only allusion to this episode in the message. He was able to dismiss it so casually, since it seemed unlikely that Britain would demand satisfaction. Bagot had already informed Adams that neither Arbuthnot nor Ambrister had government sanction for their activities, a point of view later endorsed by Castlereagh.

After this long discussion of the Florida expedition, Monroe briefly touched on the status of the South American republics. Avoiding his customary benevolent comments about the progress of liberty, he simply listed the states recently declaring themselves independent. These remarks disappointed many, for the fact-finding mission dispatched in 1817 had been back nearly six months, and specific recommendations had been expected. Monroe had dispatched three commissioners to South America late in 1817 to collect information about the character and stability of the new regimes. Since the mission had been established to gratify Clay and other proponents of recognition, it is not surprising that two of its members were strongly sympathetic to the revolutionaries. They were Caesar A. Rodney of Delaware and Theodorick Bland, who was closely connected with the Baltimore privateering interests. The third member, and the only one who could speak Spanish, was John Graham, who had been chargé in Madrid and Chief Clerk of the State Department since 1807. He alone had no commitment to the insurgent cause. They returned in such disagreement over their findings that they were unable to prepare a joint report, and their separate reports were useless as guides for administration policy. About the only point on which they agreed was that Buenos Aires seemed to be secure in its independence, although they saw little to praise in the dictatorship under which the state was governed. The indecisive character of the reports did much to diminish congressional enthusiasm for recognition.[6]

The passage in the message relating to South America had been drafted by Adams, who successfully resisted the efforts of Calhoun and Crawford to persuade the President to announce that he intended recognizing Buenos Aires in the near future. In opposing recognition, Adams had taken the stand that the United States should avoid obstructing current plans of the allied powers to mediate between Spain and her rebellious colonies, even though he thought the mediation would not succeed. The President had been quite willing to omit all reference to recognizing Buenos Aires, since such an announcement might prevent a settlement with Spain.[7] As always, he hesitated to move too rapidly toward recognition, since this might encourage the European powers to intervene, although, as he informed Congress in the message, they had agreed in 1818 at the Congress of Aix-la-Chapelle to confine their efforts solely to mediation.[8]

The President's message, which had been dispatched to the major cities by special expresses set up by the newspapers, met with general approval. Even Jackson's friends were not displeased with the President's comments on the general's conduct. Congress considered his explanation of the invasion so satisfactory that resolutions condemning it were rejected in the House by a large majority. Since the remarks in the message about Jackson were too general to provide an explanation sufficient to answer the anticipated objections, Adams had been at work on an explicit justification in the form of a reply to the Spanish protest, which was incorporated in a long dispatch sent to Erving on November 28 and made public a month later. This dispatch was a scathing exposure of Spain's incompetence, which had left the United States no alternative but to send an expedition into Florida to protect American citizens living in the Southwest. Inexorably Adams concluded that Spain must either fulfill her treaty obligations or yield a province only nominally under her control, for the United States could "as little compound with impotence as perfidy." Adams' dispatch was an affirmation of independence—a declaration that the United States was assuming its rank as an equal among the nations of the world—and it was so judged by contemporaries.[9]

II

Although the administration experienced no difficulty in fending off criticism of the decision to invade Florida, the anti-Jackson forces could not be so easily contained. A massive campaign to discredit the hero of New Orleans was mounted by the States' Rightists and the supporters of rival candidates for the succession. Both Clay and Crawford (who worked behind the scenes) labored to damage Jackson's reputation and thus eliminate a potential presidential rival. The States' Rightists, not all of whom approved of either Clay or Crawford as presidential candidates, were determined that such an outrageous disregard of the constitutional limitations on the executive should not go unpunished. The Richmond *Enquirer* had been a major influence in stirring up anti-Jackson sentiment. Although Monroe blamed Ritchie for this assault, some of the most telling attacks on Jackson were written by Spencer Roane under the pseudonym "Algernon Sidney." The extreme character of the hostility in Virginia reflected not only an antipathy to Jackson, but also an antagonism toward the prevailing spirit of nationalism in the Monroe administration.[10]

In January the House Committee on Military Affairs presented a report condemning Jackson's execution of Arbuthnot and Ambrister, the most questionable episode in the campaign. When the measure reached the floor, Thomas Cobb, one of Crawford's closest associates, amended the report to add resolutions disapproving the seizure of the posts and recommending the passage of a bill forbidding the invasion of foreign territory without the consent of Congress except in direct pursuit of a defeated enemy. The debates on these resolves, which lasted nearly a month—the longest up to this time devoted to a single issue—kept the city in an uproar, as the leading orators performed as much for the benefit of the ladies who filled the galleries as for their colleagues.[11] Clay, the star of the occasion, was devastating in his commentary on Jackson, but surprisingly gentle in his references to administration policy in relation to Florida. The final vote, which came a few days after it was known that Spain had ceded Florida, was a decisive defeat for the anti-Jackson forces. An important factor in the administration victory, according to Crawford, had been the fact that Monroe

threw the whole weight of his influence against the resolutions. Crawford sought to exploit the anti-Jackson sentiment and also strike a blow
at Calhoun, whom he regarded as his chief rival for the presidency, by
promoting a resolution advocating the reduction of the army. It failed
by such a slight margin that Crawford felt confident that in the coming
session he would be able to compensate for the anticipated deficit (government revenues were down as a result of the depression) by cutting
War Department expenditures.[12] The attack on Jackson only made the
general more popular than ever. Indeed, Rufus King uncharitably spec-
ulated that perhaps Jackson had encouraged the investigation to promote his presidential ambitions.[13]

The edge of the attack on Jackson had been blunted from the outset
by the knowledge that the administration had begun negotiations with
Onís from which there was every probability of a successful outcome.
Early in January the Spanish Minister received instructions (written
after the news reached Spain that the administration would not repudiate Jackson) empowering him to establish the northern boundary of
Louisiana to the Pacific. At the outset of the discussions Onís made a
last attempt to establish the Mississippi as the boundary by showing
Adams some articles recently published in the Washington *City Gazette*
which asserted that the negotiators of the purchase had never advanced
such extreme claims for Louisiana as those now presented. These essays
(Armstrong was believed to be the author) were crude efforts to prove
that Monroe was behaving inconsistently in claiming that Louisiana extended west of the Mississippi. Since these articles did not cite specific
documents, Adams easily brushed them aside.[14] With help from De
Neuville, who acted as a mediator throughout the negotiations, Adams
and Onís rapidly reached an understanding on the most significant
issues except for the location of the northern line to the Pacific and the
question of whether the western boundary of Louisiana should be in
the middle of the rivers in accordance with international usage or, as
Adams insisted, along the western banks.

The bitterest disagreement arose over the line to the Pacific, which
Onís wanted to draw in such a way that Spain would control the coast
as far as the Columbia River. He was determined not to accept Adams'
proposal of the 41st parallel, which would exclude Spain, as the United
States intended, from this region.[15] Monroe and the other Secretaries
were willing to make some concession in such a remote and unsettled
territory, but, persuaded by Adams' conviction that he could bring
Onís to agree, the President allowed him to persist. Ultimately, Adams

and the Spanish Minister compromised on the 42nd parallel, which kept Spain comfortably distant from the Columbia. The dispute over the river bank boundaries was the last to be resolved, for Adams was adamant on this point. The Spanish Minister, frantic to obtain some favorable concession, directly appealed to the President. On February 17, as Onís approached Monroe at the regular evening reception, the President, who was delighted over the progress of the negotiations, greeted the Spanish Minister with unusual warmth. Considering this a propitious occasion, Onís raised the river boundary question and understood the President to say that he would do anything the Spanish Minister wished on this point. The next day Onís triumphantly faced Adams with the news, producing a treaty draft incorporating a provision establishing the boundaries in the middle of the rivers. Adams, quite furious at both Onís' presumption and what seemed to be an arbitrary decision by the President, made no comment, but took the project to Monroe. At the Cabinet meeting on the following day, Adams, without referring to Onís' conversation with the President, informed his colleagues that the Spanish Minister still insisted on boundaries in the middle of the rivers. When Adams replied affirmatively to an inquiry whether Onís could be brought to accept the American proposal, Thompson, who rarely said anything, declared that the United States should "insist on it." Although the President felt that this scarcely seemed a sufficiently important point on which to risk jeopardizing the negotiations, he agreed that Adams should continue to press Onís.[16]

Immediately after this meeting Adams summoned De Neuville and read him a lecture about the impropriety of Onís' behavior in directly speaking to the President about a pending negotiation. Onís, Adams informed De Neuville, had misunderstood Monroe's general comment, that small matters should not be allowed to endanger a negotiation, to mean that the United States was yielding on this point. The President, Adams continued, "would be much and justly displeased if he had reason to think that a complimentary expression of politeness . . . was to be construed into an abandonment of an important principle in a pending negotiation." In view of Monroe's consistent refusal to discuss public affairs with resident ministers, Adams' account undoubtedly correctly depicted the exchange between Onís and the President. The Spanish Minister took his defeat in good grace. After commenting that Adams was much harder to deal with than the President, he agreed that the boundaries should be along the western banks of the rivers.[17] In addition to ceding Florida and settling the boundary of Louisiana, the treaty invalidated the claims convention of 1802 (only recently ratified by Spain) in favor of a provision obligating the United States to assume claims against Spain up to $5 million. It also provided for a renewal of those clauses of the treaty of 1795 not in conflict with the new agreement. The rather carelessly worded article providing that the only Spanish land grants to be validated were those "ratified and confirmed" before January 24, 1818, later proved most embarrassing to the otherwise meticulous Secretary of State. The agreement, which ultimately became known as the Transcontinental Treaty, was ratified unanimously by the Senate and signed by the President on February 24, 1819.

Three weeks after the signing of the treaty, Speaker Clay informed the President that the King of Spain had disposed of nearly all the remaining land in Florida in a series of grants issued shortly before the terminal date established for the invalidation of land grants. Clay's information, to Adams' distress, was quite accurate, as he discovered on rereading Erving's dispatches. In a rare moment of inattentiveness, Adams had failed to set the date back far enough to cancel recent land grants. To repair the oversight John Forsyth, the new Minister to Spain, was instructed to obtain a specific declaration invalidating the grants before Spain ratified. If Spain refused, however, he was authorized to approve the treaty without this stipulation. The President was willing to make this sacrifice because he "considered the treaty of such transcendent importance . . . that if we should not get an inch of land in Florida, the bargain would still be inexpressibly advantageous to us." [18]

Although the treaty ran into considerable obstacles in Spain, which held up ratification for two years, the land grant question was an insignificant factor in the delay. King Ferdinand VII was quite willing to abrogate the grants, but the Council of State raised so many objections to the other provisions that he agreed to suspend ratification, while an attempt was made to alter the treaty in Spain's favor. The path to ratification was not made smoother by the conduct of John Forsyth, who had replaced Erving in Madrid. The choice of the new Minister had not pleased Adams. Not only was Forsyth an ally of Crawford, but Adams felt that he lacked both the "weight of character" and the "force of genius" needed for a diplomatic assignment; or as the Secretary's wife put it more pithily, he was much too "flighty" for the responsibility involved. Although Adams had considered Forsyth a "mild and amiable" person, reports from Madrid indicated that he had an unsuspectedly quarrelsome disposition. From the moment that he landed at Cadiz, where Spanish officials raised difficulties about his baggage, he disliked the country. He found the ways of the Spanish government—its intrigue, procrastination and obscurantism—incomprehensible. Since he could speak neither French nor Spanish, he was completely isolated from Spanish officials and from the diplomatic community. Unfortunately, relations were already strained when he arrived, and his raging and storming did nothing to alleviate the tension. Although recognized as an unsatisfactory diplomat, he was enabled, through the protection of his important political connections, to stay on until 1823.[19]

III

Although the President had been noncommittal in his message about the possibility of recognizing the insurgent regimes, the problem was constantly in his thoughts in December 1818.[20] At that time David de Forest, the agent from Buenos Aires, applied to Adams for acceptance as consul and for formal recognition of his government. De Forest's request was rejected, for Monroe was not willing to extend recognition until he was certain that American action would not precipitate European intervention.[21] Since he knew that English policy would be the determining factor in Continental decisions about Spain's colonies, Monroe decided to sound out the British government. Consequently, at the President's direction Adams instructed Rush to inform Castlereagh that the United States intended to recognize Buenos Aires (and perhaps Chile and Venezuela), if nothing occurred to justify postponement. Rush was authorized to invite Great Britain to join in extending recognition. The American suggestion met a cool reception, for Castlereagh was not willing to abandon the principles uniting the Continental powers, even though he was firmly opposed to European action to restore the colonies to Spanish rule.[22]

The conclusion of the Transcontinental Treaty led the President to postpone recognition pending Spain's ratification. Consequently, there was no hint of immediate plans for recognition in the draft instructions for American agents in South America, which Monroe prepared for Adams' guidance in March 1819. Monroe wished the agents to stress the benefits accruing to the insurgents from the freedom allowed them in using American ports and also to remind the revolutionary leaders that premature recognition could easily precipitate European intervention. Monroe's comment that the best service the United States could render the revolutionary cause was by observing a strict neutrality did not indicate any change of policy on his part. In these same instructions he also touched on the constant depredations of privateers on neutral shipping, resulting from the careless practices of the new states in issuing commissions. These privateers, many of whom were nothing more than pirates bearing a commission of doubtful legality, were molesting the shipping of all nations, including the United States. The agents were instructed to protest and secure the revocation of irregular licenses. Monroe also urged the agents to point out that the continuation of these "piracies" would have the worst possible effect on the European powers and give them still another motive for intervening.[23]

The activities of insurgent privateers had already been a matter of concern during the last year of the Madison administration. Under existing American neutrality legislation, it was possible for agents of insurgent groups to purchase and outfit armed ships in American ports. As a result of protest from the European nations, whose ships were being seized, American neutrality laws were modified in the spring of 1817 to ban insurgents from purchasing armed vessels or from arming them in the United States. Again at administration request in 1818, the existing legislation was codified in a new act designed to eliminate inconsistencies in the former laws. Under the terms of the act of 1818, the revolutionaries gained substantial advantage, when the earlier prohibition on arming vesssels purchased in America outside the limits of the United States was eliminated. As a result of the laxity in the enforcement of this law, however, privateers multiplied and American shippers began to suffer much more than in the past. To afford greater protection to American ships, Congress in 1819 authorized the navy to convoy merchant ships and to recapture American vessels seized illegally on the high seas. Regular naval patrols were established in the West Indies, the South Atlantic and the Pacific to eradicate piracy. The rash conduct of the naval commanders occasionally proved embarrassing to the administration. Commodore David Porter's use of landing parties in Puerto Rico to hunt out pirates raised a great furor in the United States and created a serious international incident in 1824. These patrols, which gave American shippers considerable protection, were by no means popular with the insurgents, who considered any restriction on privateering as beneficial to the royalists. Because of the constant menace of pirates, Monroe in 1818 permitted naval commanders to transport bullion and specie for private individuals—an executive act regularized by Congress in 1819.[24]

Although the act of 1819 did much to reduce piracy it was not entirely effective, for it proved almost impossible to obtain convictions. American sympathies with the insurgent cause made juries sympathetic in cases when the accused held any kind of a commission. A good many Americans were involved in this illegal trade—it flourished especially in Baltimore—resorting to all kinds of subterfuges, including false ownership papers and assigning Spanish names to crew members. Monroe himself contributed to the difficulty of enforcement, when he appointed Theodorick Bland to the Federal District Court in Baltimore, in spite of Adams' objection that Bland's well-known connection with privateering and insurgent groups made him completely unsuitable. Although Bland's direct involvement was never proven, his son-in-law Joseph Skinner (also postmaster of Baltimore) was deeply involved. Bland owed his appointment to the intercession of William Winder and William Pinkney, who were active in defending shipowners prosecuted under the neutrality laws.[25]

A by-product of American permissiveness toward privateers was the rift which took place after 1819 between Monroe and the Abbé Corrêa da Serra, the Portuguese Minister to Washington and an intimate of Jefferson and Madison, who enjoyed the society of this learned and respected *philosophe*. Indeed, according to Adams, Corrêa's greatest feat as a Minister was to appear to be anything but a diplomat. "He introduces himself," Adams reported in his diary, "as a familiar acquaintance, to talk literature and philosophy, as a domestic inmate to gossip over a cup of tea." This familiarity had been welcomed by Madison, but Monroe, "having no taste for literature and philosophy, and no time to listen and laugh at jokes," had kept the Abbé at "arm's length," treating him with the same formality as the other resident ministers. Although Corrêa had been displeased by Monroe's coldness, he did not become seriously offended until 1817, when the President refused to condemn officially the sale of arms to insurgents in northern Brazil. Prior to this incident the Abbé had protested frequently about the activities of privateers with American connections, for Portuguese trade probably suffered more than that of any other nation. When he failed to obtain satisfaction for his complaints about the sale of arms, he issued a public statement proclaiming that the rebel ports were under a strict blockade. Considering this a breach of his diplomatic status, Monroe took Corrêa to task for his pronouncement. Corrêa was so angry that Monroe had acting Secretary of State Rush explain the facts at length to Madison, so that there would not be a misunderstanding if

Corrêa should give a false impression of the incident during his annual summer visit to Virginia.[26] During the next two years the Abbé became increasingly bitter, making in private conversation "little sarcasms at the expense of the nation and its government." [27] On one occasion he reportedly refused to drink to the President's health, following toasts to the kings of France and Portugal, because he did not want to introduce bad company.[28]

In 1820 Corrêa became indignant over the President's refusal to pay damages for Portuguese ships seized by American-owned privateers. When told that his sole recourse was through American courts, he bitterly complained that Portuguese subjects never obtained justice from the federal judiciary. During a visit to Monticello in the summer of 1820, when he sought Jefferson's assistance in pressing his claims, the Abbé met with the same response. At that time he drew up a counterproposal, which had Jefferson's endorsement. The Abbé revived in slightly different form a plan presented by Portugal at the Congress of Aix-la-Chapelle in 1818, when the Portuguese representative suggested that the powers condemn privateering as piracy and establish a joint patrol for its suppression. Corrêa now proposed that the United States and Portugal unite in an "American system" to extirpate piracy in the Western Hemisphere and request the European nations to undertake the same obligation in the Mediterranean. When Jefferson spoke approvingly of the plan to Monroe, the President agreed that it had "something imposing" about it, but he considered the Abbé's "American system" unacceptable, because it would link the United States with a European monarchy in a common front against the insurgents. He also rejected Corrêa's request that a commission be appointed to investigate Portuguese losses as a result of privateering. When the Abbé returned home later in 1820, he felt considerable bitterness toward the nation he had once so much admired.[29]

The President could not have picked a better time to complete his tour of the nation by visiting the South and the West than the spring and summer of 1819, for in no section of the Union were the achievements of his Spanish policy more enthusiastically admired. The scenes of the New England tour were again repeated—banquets, parades, addresses and private parties—but the emotional impact was not as great. The vast distances to be covered in the West, where the roads were wretched and the accommodations inadequate, induced the President to eliminate St. Louis from his itinerary. In Nashville he was handsomely entertained by Andrew Jackson, who seemed to bear no resentment over the failure of the administration to fully support his activities in Florida. Jackson's decision to accompany the President to Lexington produced the only unpleasant episode of the western journey. Apparently because of Jackson's presence, Clay absented himself from Lexington during the President's visit. It is true that Clay claimed pressing private business and managed to spend the day with Monroe in Harrodsburg, but, nonetheless, the President felt the slight, and there was some unpleasant comment in the press. When Monroe learned that Crawford was unable to meet him in Wheeling as originally planned, he decided not to return by the Cumberland Road, but to take the more direct route from Lexington to his home in Albemarle. After four months of travel—covering 5,000 miles—the President reached Highlands fatigued but in good health. Indeed, he seemed to have withstood the rigors of the trip better than Samuel L. Gouverneur (his wife's nephew) and his brother Joseph's son, Lieutenant James Monroe, both young men in their twenties, who had accompanied him.[30]

IV

In August, Monroe went to Washington to discuss with Adams, Crawford, and Calhoun American response to Spain's failure to ratify the treaty before the dates fixed for ratification had expired. Crawford, who usually favored temperate measures, astonished his colleagues by proposing that Forsyth be instructed to depart unless Spain ratified at once. Monroe thought this step too drastic, for it would imply that the United States was about to declare war. After considerable discussion the Cabinet approved the President's suggestion to request authorization to occupy Florida, if ratification were not received by the beginning of the session. All shared his opinion that Spain was absolutely bound to ratify a treaty negotiated within the limits of Onís' powers. To exert pressure on Spain, instructions were drafted for Forsyth and the other American ministers in Europe, announcing that Florida would be occupied if Spain rejected the treaty. The ministers were to make it clear that this move was made necessary by Spain's breach of faith. Forsyth was also notified that ratification would still be accepted even though the stipulated date had passed. The President carefully went over the dispatch to Forsyth, making some changes, but, as Adams smugly noted, he deleted only those passages which the Secretary had deliberately introduced for this purpose. Adams believed that it was necessary for him to introduce some such "alloy" to be cast off in order to prevent the excision of the "pure metal itself." The Cabinet also scrutinized the dispatch, a process Adams found unpleasant but had to accept gracefully, since the President submitted his messages to the same criticism.[31]

In November 1819, when the President began working on his message, the outlook for ratification prior to the opening of the session was dim, although it was hoped that the U.S. sloop-of-war *Hornet,* which had taken dispatches to Forsyth, might still bring favorable news. The stages in the drafting of this message, as recounted by Adams in his diary, provide an excellent insight into the President's working habits.[32] On November 10, Monroe read Adams the preliminary sketches for the paragraphs relating to Spain and Latin America. At this point he was ready to request congressional authorization to permit him to occupy Florida. He also intended to announce that the United States had proposed joint action with Great Britain in recognizing Buenos Aires, which he thought would serve to demonstrate American intentions, although the proposal had been rejected. A week later, when he met with the Cabinet (Calhoun was ill at home in South Carolina) he presented two additional paragraphs to obtain the reaction of the Secretaries as to which should be incorporated in his text. The first dealt in a general way with possible American action if Spain refused to ratify the treaty; the other specifically proposed, in the event of Spanish rejection, that the United States occupy the region between the Sabine and the Rio Bravo.

Crawford expressed a preference for the more general paragraph, which he thought would be more dignified in European opinion. To explain his meaning he cited William Lowndes, who had told the Secretary of the Treasury shortly after returning from Europe that in France and England the Americans were considered an "ambitious and encroaching people." Adams, sharply disagreeing with his colleague, did not consider such comments of any importance. Great Britain, he told the Cabinet, after "vilifying us for twenty years as a mean, low-minded, peddling nation, having no generous ambitions and no God but gold, had now changed her tone, and was endeavoring to alarm the world at the gigantic grasp of our ambition. Nothing," he continued, "would remove this impression until the world shall be familiarized with the idea of considering our proper dominion to be the continent of North America." That the United States would inevitably incorporate

Canada and Texas seemed to him "as much the law of nature as that the Mississippi should flow to the sea." The President, as was his habit, listened patiently but did not announce his decision.

Some ten days later, when the Cabinet reassembled, news received by the *Hornet* produced a changed outlook. Forsyth did not report ratification but only that a special emissary had been appointed to secure explanations about sections of the treaty prior to ratification. Much more meaningful was a dispatch from Gallatin, who informed the President that both the French Foreign Minister and the Russian Ambassador had spoken to him earnestly, deprecating any violent reaction on the part of the United States over Spain's delay. Since these strong statements by spokesmen of two of the major powers indicated that they would press Spain to accept the treaty, Monroe, after conferring with Adams, concluded that it would not be necessary to request authority to occupy Florida. Instead, he proposed to announce that the United States, in deference to the wishes of friendly powers, would wait to receive the explanations of the Spanish emissary, although Spain's conduct fully justified reprisals.

The next day (November 26), when he discussed this solution with Adams and Crawford, he was astounded to discover that the Secretary of the Treasury had reversed his earlier stand. Adams, who never put a favorable interpretation on anything the Secretary of the Treasury did, believed that Crawford, as soon as he learned that Adams was advocating moderation, had taken the opposite view and was now urging immediate action in Florida. In the face of this sharp disagreement, Monroe merely observed that "it was an exceedingly difficult question, and he would think profoundly upon it before coming to his final determination." Sensing the President's unhappiness and perplexity over this change in the point of view of his advisers, Adams privately explained that he had been led to withdraw his own preference for the occupation of Florida, when he realized that the President's opinion had changed after reading Gallatin's dispatch. At this conference Adams suggested that the best course might be for the President to request a contingent authority to occupy Florida. The President promptly adopted Adams' proposal, incorporating it in the final version of the message. This solution apparently satisfied Crawford, for he raised no objections when the President read it to the Cabinet.

Not until an agreement had been reached on this point did the President take up American policy on Latin American recognition. When this question was considered on December 3, Adams strongly recommended the deletion of those passages in the message relating to the recognition of Buenos Aires, for De Neuville had told him that a major factor impeding Spanish ratification was the conviction that recognition of Spain's former colonies was imminent. Although Monroe modified the wording of this section considerably to meet Adams' objections, he retained the references to the administration proposal of a joint Anglo-American recognition, since their retention was essential to appease the pro-recognition forces in Congress. After reading the revised passages about Latin America, the President asked the Secretary of State for his opinion. Adams' frank but witty response broke the tension so often generated at Cabinet discussions:

Sir, to be quite candid with you, I have brought my mind to the conclusion that the less there is said in *this* message upon South America the better it will be. Whatever, therefore, you consent to strike out will, in my judgment, be an improvement, and whatever you conclude to retain I must put up with and make the best of it that I can.[33]

Although most of the message dealt with Spain and Latin America, the President also commented upon the failure of the administration's efforts to persuade Britain to open the West Indies to American shipping. In view of the continued refusal of the British to modify their maritime practices, he recommended further restrictions on British shipping in American ports. In place of the usual platitudes about the blessings of liberty, Monroe presented a rather somber view of the economic distress observed throughout the country during the past year. He attributed the decline, as did most of his contemporaries, to the difficulty experienced by the banks in re-establishing specie payments, which had led to a retraction of the currency, and to the fact that European products were being sold in America at prices lower than those in the country where they were manufactured. The President had intended to reassert his views on internal improvements, but the Cabinet persuaded him to omit them.[34]

V

In spite of the care lavished on the message, it aroused little response among the members of Congress, who were totally preoccupied by the Northern drive to prevent the admission of Missouri as a slave state. Although the Missouri question shifted attention from international affairs, and thus eased the pressure for retaliation against Spain, it also had the unexpected effect of reducing the popularity of the treaty. Many Northerners felt little enthusiasm for an agreement substantially extending the slave area. At the same time many Southerners, angered by the Northern attack on slavery, began to comment unfavorably on a treaty which had failed to include Texas. Clay, in particular, was outspoken on this subject.[35]

Not until the Missouri question had been laid to rest in March did Chairman Lowndes of the House Foreign Affairs Committee take up the President's request for contingent authorization to seize Florida. Lowndes recommended the occupation of Florida, but contrary to administration wishes his report did not grant the President discretionary authority. According to Adams, Lowndes, who did not expect Congress to take any action on the issue, had advocated this particular measure to show his independence from the administration influence.[36] The President was relieved of the dilemma presented by Lowndes by the arrival of dispatches from Madrid, which indicated that Forsyth, who had recently stated his intention to depart, had yielded to the persuasion of the Russian Ambassador to continue in Madrid. Moreover, letters from George W. Campbell, the Minister to Russia, brought an account of an interview with the Russian Foreign Minister, who had expressed the hope that the Spanish-American crisis would be amicably resolved. This, together with a similar report from France, gave the President sufficient grounds for a special message proposing that the United States defer action until the arrival of the Spanish emissary as an act of courtesy to the powers taking a friendly interest in American affairs.[37]

Lowndes' report vanished, but Clay introduced a resolution questioning the power of the President to alienate territory (he had Texas in mind) without the consent of Congress. Another Clay resolve asserted that Florida was an insufficient equivalent for the sacrifice of the region west of the Sabine. In his supporting speech Clay made much of what he called foreign intermeddling in American affairs and denounced the President's subservience to the European powers. Lowndes, who declined to discuss the constitutional issues raised by Clay, defended the President's decision to postpone action in Florida, since there seemed to be every reason to expect a resolution of the problem in favor of the United States. These resolves, which were only intended to provide a platform for Clay's oratory, were never brought to a vote.[38]

A few days after Clay's resolutions were put aside, the Spanish emissary, Francisco Vives, arrived after a leisurely journey by way of Paris and London. Although it was assumed he did not have power to exchange ratifications, he was treated with the utmost courtesy. Several days after his formal reception on April 12, the President honored him at a dinner for the department heads and the members of the diplomatic corps.[39] Politeness was all that he received, for the President refused to reply to Vives' demands for explanations. Spain, Monroe felt, had no reasonable ground for objecting to a treaty drawn up within the limits of the instructions sent to Onís. When Vives presented as the conditions for Spanish ratification the demand that American neutrality laws be revised to exclude the insurgents from their application and also required a pledge that the United States would not recognize the independence of the new states, he was bluntly refused. The only concession, if it can be called such, was Adams' comment that the United States would not act precipitately in extending recognition. This pledge probably seemed meaningless to Vives, since Clay had just put through a resolve (by the slender majority of eighty to seventy-five) that it was expedient to provide funds for outfits for any ministers the President might send to South America.[40]

Since Congress was still in session when Vives arrived, the President had the unpleasant duty of announcing the new delay. Although he still preferred a discretionary power to occupy Florida, he knew there was no likelihood of obtaining it. Again European developments provided a solution. News had just arrived that revolutionary forces in Spain had compelled Ferdinand VII to restore parliamentary institutions. In view of this turn of events, Spain, it was argued, could make a dignified retreat from her refusal to approve the treaty. Consequently, the President, while informing Congress that ratification was no closer than before the arrival of Vives, recommended that American action be postponed until the new regime had time to reconsider the treaty.[41]

Adams and the other Secretaries assumed that the matter would rest at this point until further news arrived from Spain. However, to the amazement of Adams and his colleagues, Monroe summoned a Cabinet meeting ten days later to discuss additional demands to be made on Spain prior to ratification. Utterly at a loss to understand this development, Adams reminded Monroe that Vives had already dispatched a special messenger recommending that the treaty be ratified in spite of the American refusal to make any explanations. When other Cabinet members supported Adams in his contention that new demands would

needlessly complicate the issue, Monroe dropped the subject, and
Adams was instructed to inform Forsyth that the United States would
accept ratification, although he was not to press for it.

While Monroe probably spoke more freely to Adams than to any
other Cabinet member, he did not take the Secretary into his confidence
on this occasion. It was not until several days later that Adams discovered the reason behind the recent Cabinet discussion, when Calhoun
told him that Monroe had received a letter from Jefferson advising that
ratification be suspended until Texas was included in the treaty. Of
this advice, Adams wryly commented that it was like an old sea captain,
who never liked to see his mate make a better voyage than himself.[42]

Monroe took up the matter with the Cabinet, not just out of deference to the former President, but because Jefferson had voiced an
opinion shared by many Southerners. As usual, Monroe wanted unanimity among his advisers, if the demand for Texas should continue
to mount. Monroe's reply to Jefferson is particularly interesting, since
he rested his decision not to press for Texas on domestic considerations
rather than on the basis of the questionable validity of American claims
to this region. If he were to demand that Texas be included in Louisiana, he told the former President, then he would simply arouse the
same forces which had raged during the recent Missouri crisis. It was
not just a question of slavery, but an attempt by Northern leaders to
impede the development of the West, an objective sought by the
Northerners ever since the Jay-Gardoqui negotiations. "From this point
of view," he concluded, "it is evident, that the further acquisition of
territory, to the West and South, involves difficulties of an internal
nature which menace the Union itself. We ought therefore to be cautious in making the attempt. Having secured the Mississippi, and all
its waters, with a slight exception only, and erected States there, ought
we not to be satisfied, so far at least as to take no step in that direction,
which is not approved, by all the members, or at least a majority of those
who accomplished our revolution." [43]

The President's cautious policy in relation to Spain was amply
justified. The new regime in Madrid, which could not expect any
support from the European powers in view of its liberal principles,
approved the treaty in September 1820 and annulled the land grants.
Monroe submitted the treaty to the Senate again, although Adams considered this unnecessary since the Senate had already approved it unanimously. The President, however, thought it wise to consult the
Senate whenever there was "any plausible constitutional reason for so

doing." This time four senators voted in the negative. Adams singled them out as two Clay supporters, one enemy of Jackson and a fourth who acted from "some maggot in the brain" of unknown cause.[44] Although Monroe did not record his emotions at seeing the treaty finally approved, he undoubtedly shared Adams' feeling that it was the "most important event" of his life.[45] For the President the Transcontinental Treaty was an achievement of special personal significance, for it rounded out the Louisiana Purchase in which he had participated and it secured Florida by the very means he had advocated as far back as 1805.

The ratification of the Transcontinental Treaty in February 1821 removed a major obstacle to the recognition of the independent states of Latin America. Although there had been much interest in the United States in the progress of the South American revolutions, it cannot be said that there had been an overwhelming pressure for recognition, for the administration had been able to restrain the pro-recognition forces in Congress during the two years which elapsed between the negotiation and the ratification of the treaty. It is true that in the spring of 1820 Clay had exploited the resentment generated by Spain's delay to put through a resolution declaring that it was expedient to provide an outfit for a Minister to South America. In the following session his effort to implement this resolve by a specific appropriation was rejected, when it became known that Spain had ratified the treaty. As a substitute Clay secured the adoption of relatively innocuous resolutions expressing sympathy for the people of South America in their struggle for independence and promising to support the President whenever he deemed it expedient to recognize the new states.[46] Even Clay realized that most congressmen were content to let the administration set the pace.

Clay condemned the President's Latin American policy much more harshly in a speech which he delivered in May 1821 in Lexington. John Quincy Adams considered Clay's views, which many interpreted as a plea for active support of the insurgents, so dangerous that he undertook to refute them in an elaborate Fourth of July oration in Washington. Unfortunately for Adams' purpose, contemporaries were so impressed by his denunciation of Great Britain that the other portions of his speech were virtually ignored. Everyone expected Britain to be damned in Fourth of July orations, but when the Secretary of State indulged in such vituperation, it was of more than passing interest. Although his oration attracted little attention, it was in this address that Adams expressed the view that the proper policy for the United States (and also for the European powers) was one of nonintervention in the affairs of other nations. In many ways Adams' oration seemed like a defense of isolationism.[47]

Monroe did not comment on these public utterances, which did not correspond with his own position, which was midway between these two extremes. Monroe felt that the United States had an obligation to do something more than make a parade of its libertarian principles and democratic institutions, which seemed to be the only role Adams assigned the nation in relation to Latin America. On the other hand, he saw the dangers of a position as extreme as Clay's. During the French Revolution, Monroe had criticized the Washington administration for its rigid neutrality toward France, which at best spelled out indifference, at its worst suggested hostility. Yet he had not at that time been an advocate of intervention in the war on France's behalf. Finding himself in a position similar to Washington's, he was neither an interventionist nor an advocate of a rigid neutrality. The policy of the United States, as he saw it, must be neutral, but it should be a neutrality which benefited rather than harmed the insurgent cause. This had been the course he had followed since the beginning of his administration.

While ratification of the treaty removed the major impediment, it did not eliminate all the obstacles to recognition. As Adams told Clay during a conversation in the spring of 1821, there was still considerable uncertainty about the stability of the new governments. In the course of the year, however, the military victories won by the insurgents seemed to assure the success of most of the new states. The carelessness of the Latin American states in commissioning privateers had always been a potent argument against recognition, but this objection lost considerable force when Buenos Aires (one of the worst offenders) revoked all privateering licenses in 1821. Since there seemed to be no real threat of European intervention, Monroe sent a special message to Congress on March 8, 1822, recommending that Congress cooperate with the executive in extending recognition to five states— Buenos Aires, Chile, Peru, Mexico and Colombia.[48] In response the House approved an appropriation of $100,000 to defray the costs of the missions to be sent out by the President.

Rather surprisingly, Monroe took it very much to heart that Robert M. Garnett of Virginia cast the only negative vote against the appropriation. Monroe wrote Garnett asking him to reverse his position on the next measure relating to recognition, and to make a public statement that he considered recognition hazardous, but that he was willing to join his countrymen in supporting the movement to recognize the new states. Garnett declined to alter his voting habit, but he did publish a declaration explaining that his opposition was not based on hostility to the insurgents, but on a conviction that recognition was dangerous to the United States, since it might provoke European intervention.[49] Although the European powers had failed to support Spain in the past, Monroe felt there was still some element of risk in extending recognition; yet, as he told Jefferson and Madison, there was as much danger in standing still as moving forward. If the United States failed to recognize the new states, then the nation might alienate them and turn them towards Europe.[50]

In spite of the House action there was considerable delay in sending emissaries. In the first place it proved difficult to find suitable appointees. Monroe had been anxious to send prominent figures on these missions to demonstrate the importance the United States attached to the Latin American countries.[51] One name which came immediately to mind was that of Henry Clay, whose private concerns had compelled him to give up his seat in 1821, and hence deprived him of the pleasure of participation in recognition proceedings. Although Adams had sounded out Clay on this possibility in 1821, Monroe declined offering him a mission, since he felt that conferring such a signal honor on Clay would prove that the highest rewards were given to the enemies of the administration. Jackson was another obvious possibility, but the recent unpleasantness during his governorship of Florida was too fresh in the President's mind to make this a welcome selection.[52]

The problem was not made any easier by the disagreement in the Cabinet, whether to send ministers or diplomats of a lower grade. Adams, never very enthusiastic about the character of the new governments, felt that the United States should wait to receive representatives and then send emissaries of the same rank. Adams, as was so often the case, was supported by Calhoun. Crawford, however, wished ministers to be sent immediately. The most meaningful commentary was made by the usually silent Thompson, who recommended that appointments be postponed until Congress reconvened, because many senators questioned the power of the President to make interim appointments of this character. In this he was quite correct, for, as Rufus King warned Adams, it was quite probable that the Senate would refuse to confirm any ministers appointed during the recess on the grounds that the President could not create new diplomatic posts by using the appointive power.[53] Monroe considered this interpretation incorrect, as did Madison, whom he consulted. Madison agreed with Monroe that diplomatic posts only came into existence when the President made an appointment, and expired when the incumbent died, resigned, or was recalled. In view of a recent bitter conflict over military appointments, in which the Senate had stubbornly refused to confirm two of his nominees, Monroe felt it was wiser to postpone action rather than invite further disagreement with the Senate. Not unnaturally, Adams suspected that Crawford was deliberately encouraging the President to make appointments in order to damage the administration by provoking a dispute with the upper house.[54]

As a result of the delay over appointments, the first formal recognition was extended to Colombia, when Manuel Torres was received as chargé.[55] Torres, who was the only accredited agent from Latin America in the United States at that time, was received in a memorable interview on June 19, 1822. This interview, like all Monroe's official receptions, was short, but it moved the participants deeply. Adams was especially touched at the sight of the fatally ill Colombian, who had come from Philadelphia, although he had "scarcely life in him to walk alone." When the President seated Torres and spoke to him kindly, the Colombian chargé, who had devoted his life to the insurgent cause, was so overcome with emotion that he could scarcely speak.[56]

When Congress met, Monroe named his first three ministers—Caesar A. Rodney, Buenos Aires; Richard C. Anderson, Colombia; and Heman Allen, Chile. The instructions (particularly those for Anderson) which Adams framed under Monroe's direction, defined American objectives in Latin America as the encouragement of political, commercial, civil, and religious liberty—for Adams had singled out the establishment of the Roman Catholic Church in Colombia for specific disapproval. The instructions also revealed an awareness of the ties binding the new states to Europe and of the need to counter this influence. No positive guides were offered, however, other than to urge the ministers to encourage the development of republican institutions and the granting of commercial equality to all nations. The policy outlined was essentially a continuation of past attitudes—the United States would continue its neutrality and seek only to exert a moral influence in South America.[57]

CHAPTER 25

THE POLITICS
OF SLAVERY

IDWAY IN Monroe's first term an issue was raised which, to the dismay of the people and politicians alike, reached such an intensity that the Union seemed on the verge of destruction. Certainly no one guessed in February 1819 the extent to which passions would be stirred by the introduction of a bill to permit Missouri to organize a state government. The bill itself was harmless, but not the amendment of Representative James Tallmadge, Jr., of New York, who proposed to alter the Missouri bill to require the emancipation of all slaves at the age of twenty-one and to forbid the further introduction of slavery. This measure, reflecting the antislavery sentiments of Northern Republicans, was unacceptable to the Missourians, who were deeply committed to a slave economy, as well as to Southerners, who saw their fundamental interests subject to direct attack. When the session ended, the issue, which had only been discussed briefly, was left unsettled. The House had approved the Tallmadge amendment by a slight majority, but the Senate had refused to accept any measure imposing conditions on the admission of Missouri.[1]

The central concern in the debates, in which the public had taken little interest, had been over the balance of power, for the Southern congressmen had concentrated their objections upon the fact that the admission of Missouri would forever destroy the equal balance then existing between slave and free states. Even the Virginia state leaders, ever hypersensitive to measures either impairing Southern interests or infringing on the rights of the states, gave little heed to the subject, for they were much too deeply absorbed in a rabid denunciation

449

of Chief Justice Marshall's opinion in McCulloch *vs.* Maryland. As late as December 1819, Spencer Roane, the most powerful Virginia defender of States' Rights, still gave priority to the bank issue, which was a matter of "principle," whereas the Missouri question was but a "particular measure." [2] He rapidly revised this opinion, however, as soon as the Missouri debates got under way in January 1820.

"Who would have thought," Senator James Barbour commented in the midst of the Missouri debates, "that the little *speck* we . . . saw [last session] was to be swelled into the importance that it has now assumed, and that upon its decision depended the duration of the Union." [3] What, indeed, had elevated this "speck" to the most fearful issue in the last two decades? By the end of 1819 the Tallmadge amendment had taken on a much more threatening aspect in the wake of the massive propaganda campaign and the innumerable public meetings organized in the Northern states by antislavery groups. The Southerners, naturally, replied in kind. Thus when Congress met in December, it was apparent that the deadlock of the previous session still existed but in a far more dangerous form. The nation had split into two sectional blocs, each fulminating that the Union would be disrupted unless its demands were met. In the House the restrictionists had a ten-vote edge, whereas in the Senate the pro-slavery forces were securely in command. The resolution of the impasse required nearly three months, during which the senators and representatives tediously recapitulated the arguments on both sides, ranging over abstruse interpretations of the Constitution, the meaning of the Louisiana Purchase Treaty, and the inequity of the three-fifths clause, which allowed Southern states to count slaves for purposes of representation.

II

Historians have usually portrayed Monroe as an ineffective and indecisive figure during the Missouri crisis, in which he shrank from assuming the leadership needed to save the nation from impending disaster.[4] If Monroe is to be judged by the standards of executive conduct established by Lincoln and twentieth-century Presidents, then this conclusion may not be unwarranted. However, within the limitations imposed upon the executive in the early nineteenth century both by tradition and Republican theory, there was little that he could do. Indeed, open pressure on his part would have set up a cry of executive interference and driven many moderates to adopt extreme positions in order to prove their independence. In order to exert an effective influence the President had to remain behind the scenes, allowing others to function as his spokesmen and permitting them to affirm his support, whenever such endorsement could serve a useful purpose. As deeply concerned as he was during the Missouri debates, Monroe kept his activities on behalf of a compromise discreetly veiled. After a lifetime devoted to the cause of the Union, he could not be indifferent to a conflict which threatened the destruction of the nation. Monroe also had a personal reason for seeking to settle the controversy as quickly as possible, for he realized that the passions stirred up by the dispute could jeopardize his re-election in 1820.

The fact that John Quincy Adams, the most important informant of the Monroe administration, said virtually nothing about the President's course during the crisis has lent color to the view that Monroe remained inactive. It is true that the President never discussed the Missouri question with his Cabinet until March 1820, when the compromise was about to be approved in Congress and then only in a *pro forma* meeting to secure unanimous approval of the bill, which he had long since decided to sign. Monroe deliberately avoided the subject with his advisers, for a premature discussion would have invited an unpleasant confrontation between Adams, who had strong antislavery views, and his Southern colleagues, who were outraged by the restrictionist proposal. Although Monroe never raised the issue with Adams, he apparently discussed the Missouri question with Crawford and Calhoun, who lent their support to the congressional leaders seeking an acceptable middle ground.

From the beginning of the session Monroe's mind was made up on one point—he was absolutely determined to veto any measure which imposed restrictions on Missouri as a condition for admission to the Union. In December he assisted George Hay in gathering material for antirestrictionist essays published in the Richmond *Enquirer*.[5] It was probably at this time that Monroe made a rough draft of a veto message to be delivered if Congress approved the Tallmadge amendment. He based his main argument on the constitutional requirement that new states must be admitted on an equal footing with the other states. If a condition were imposed on Missouri not applicable to the older states, then both Missouri's constitutional rights and her sovereignty would be violated. In this draft he also voiced several other arguments of a distinctly Southern character. It seemed to him that if slavery were confined to the states where it existed, then the whites would eventually desert these regions. What would become of these states? Would they be accepted as black republics with representation in Congress? He also expressed the common Southern view that the best way to ameliorate the lot of the slave, and perhaps achieve emancipation, was by distributing slavery throughout the Union.[6]

The session had been under way but a few weeks when Monroe told Adams early in January that he fully expected a compromise would be found. Although Adams thought this opinion overly optimistic, the President had good reason for his conclusion.[7] Monroe was somewhat more specific a few days later, when he wrote George Hay that it seemed probable that an agreement would be worked out to use a western extension of the northern boundary of Missouri as a line to divide the remainder of the Louisiana Purchase into free and slave areas.[8] This statement, which was made a month before the compromise was introduced in the Senate, indicates the close contact between the President and congressional leaders, for no hint of such a solution had appeared in the press.

At this time Monroe was regularly in touch with Senator James Barbour of Virginia, who was one of the most active figures in promoting a compromise. Barbour's importance in working out the final agreement has been obscured by the greater emphasis placed upon Clay's brilliant maneuvering in the House. Barbour's first plan had been to circumvent the restrictionists by combining the bill to admit Maine with that authorizing Missouri to draft a constitution. The application of Maine, previously a district of Massachusetts, had not been received until the beginning of the session of 1819. Since Maine had been part of another state, it could be admitted directly into the Union without securing the consent of Congress to draft a constitution. Barbour hoped to achieve two purposes by linking Maine and Missouri. First, by preserving the balance between free and slave states, he hoped Northerners would be willing to admit Missouri without restrictions. Secondly, he believed this arrangement would expedite action, since the enabling act of Massachusetts had provided that Maine would return to her previous status unless statehood were granted by March 4, 1820.

Barbour ultimately decided to modify this plan, since he was not certain he had a safe majority for it in the Senate. While it was still pending, Barbour conferred with the President on February 2 about his strategy. After thinking the matter over, Monroe wrote the Senator the next day to recommend that Maine and Missouri be separated. Monroe felt that prompt Senate action on Maine, which would please the Northerners, might prompt them to reciprocate by accepting Missouri as a slave state. He also suggested that Barbour obtain the approval of other Southern members for this arrangement.[9] Although Barbour did not withdraw his bill linking Maine and Missouri, he kept it before the Senate only as part of a more complex strategy. On the same day on which Monroe wrote Barbour, Senator Jesse B. Thomas of Illinois, an antirestrictionist, submitted an amendment to the Missouri bill to exclude slavery from the Louisiana Purchase north of 36′ 30″. This proposal, however, was withdrawn three days later, ostensibly to permit Thomas to modify it, but actually to allow time to organize support among Southern congressmen.[10] Barbour simply kept the Maine-Missouri bill before the Senate as a holding action until the forces had been mobilized behind a compromise.

As soon as the Thomas amendment was introduced, Monroe let it be known that he approved the measure in order to assist Barbour in rounding up Southern support.[11] There is no record of the conferences held by congressional leaders, but there seems little doubt that members of the administration actively participated in the implementation of the compromise proposal. Thomas, who introduced the compromise, was one of Crawford's most devoted followers, and the influential William Lowndes, Calhoun's close friend, gave the proposal his full support in the House. Monroe was also in contact with the handful of Northern Republicans seeking to arrange a compromise. On February 9 he met with a number of congressmen including Mark L. Hill, a representative from Maine, who was among the few Northerners voting for the final compromise bill. After talking with the President, Hill rather enigmatically reported that he and his colleagues had "induced the President to *think,* and advise his Southern friends to be cautious." [12]

Apparently Monroe saw no reason to inform Hill of his relations with Barbour, nor that he was then engaged in exerting pressure on the state party leaders in Virginia to accept a compromise. This was by no means an easy task, for the members of the Richmond Junto, proud of their adherence to principle, were not likely to approve an accommodation in the interest of national unity without protest. The President rarely intervened in state affairs—he knew that the members of the Junto were not overly fond of him personally and that they had never liked his program of moderate nationalism. But he could not afford to remain aloof in February 1820, for the stakes were much too high. The Virginia legislature, which usually adjourned in February, was about to hold a caucus to nominate presidential electors. It was quite conceivable that the Junto, in its rage, might either attempt secession, for the Virginia press had been full of such rumblings, or refuse to endorse Monroe for a second term.

The President was especially anxious to restrain the Junto from rash action in relation to the Presidency, because he and other Republicans were convinced that behind the attempt to exclude slavery from Missouri was a carefully concealed plot to revive the party divisions of the past either openly as Federalism or in some new disguise.[13] He drew this conclusion from several circumstances. Not only had he been struck by the emergence of former Federalist Rufus King as the outstanding congressional spokesman of the restrictionists, but the anti-slavery campaign in the North had been largely dominated by ex-Federalists. It was widely, if erroneously, believed that Rufus King was in league with De Witt Clinton, who was at odds with the regular Republicans in New York State and whose perennial presidential ambitions could not be realized through the regular party organization. King had been returned to the Senate in 1819 by a Republican legislature so divided between Clintonians and Bucktails (the supporters of Van Buren) that they could only agree on a Federalist. In fact King owed his election much more to Van Buren's influence than to Clinton's. Monroe, who had a long memory, also recalled King's activities in the Confederation Congress during the Jay-Gardoqui negotiations, when King and other Northern delegates sought to impede the growth of the West, a movement which he then believed concealed a desire to dominate the Union. Might not the nation be witnessing a revival of the same quest for power in the guise of a restriction on slavery? It seemed to Monroe that restricting slavery would place the control of the nation permanently in the hands of the Northern states. Since, to his way of thinking, the real objective of these leaders was power, he believed that they were willing to accept disunion, if their plans could not be achieved in any other fashion.[14] These conclusions about the character of the restrictionist movement seemed to gain added weight when it was recalled that Tallmadge was one of Clinton's close associates. Monroe was not just concerned about his re-election, but about the future of the Union, which he did not think could survive the formation of parties based on a North-South sectional alignment.

These alarms may seem excessive, but they were taken seriously. Even Clay, who closely observed political trends in Congress, suspected that the restrictionist campaign masked an attempt to form a new party.[15] Although there is nothing to suggest that the political aspirations of the Federalists were responsible for the move to restrict slavery in Missouri, once the controversy erupted the Federalists were not unwilling to consider the possibility of a new political alignment. They did not think in terms of a revival of Federalism, but rather of establishing a liaison with discontented Republicans, which would offer them an opportunity to re-engage in political activity in some other form than as a permanent minority.[16]

III

The Virginia Republicans were indeed incredulous, when a letter arrived in Richmond from Senator Barbour on February 8 (the day before the presidential nominating caucus was scheduled to meet) informing them of the probability of a compromise which would admit Missouri without restriction but exclude slavery north of 36'30" in the Louisiana Purchase. The intimation that Monroe had approved this arrangement led to the postponement of the caucus for a week, among angry threats to repudiate him as candidate if the report was true. The Virginians deluged Barbour and Monroe with letters reminding them of their duty as States' Rightists, as Virginians, and as statesmen.[17] None were more astonished by this development than George Hay and Charles Everett, who had been acting as Monroe's campaign managers in Richmond, for Hay had apparently not taken seriously Monroe's earlier hint of a probable compromise. Left momentarily without guidance, they could only reiterate their own conviction that the President would never consent to such an agreement. Alarmed by the outcry in Virginia, Monroe sent Everett a letter intended for public circulation, in which he argued for the necessity of a compromise to save the Union, but without committing himself unequivocally on the measure.[18] Monroe also sent a letter to Hay to give to Judge Spencer Roane, indicating that he had not fully made up his mind on the question. Hay, however, never delivered the letter, since he felt its ambiguous character would create an unfavorable effect just before the caucus.[19] There was, indeed, no point in appealing to Roane, who had just written the President that he would rather take the South out of the Union than be "damned up in a land of slaves by the Eastern people." Roane took it for granted that the President would not approve a settlement depriving the South of its rights.[20]

In answering the questions of the Republicans in Richmond, Hay was careful not to commit himself about his father-in-law's stand, but

simply replied that the President would do his duty. Although Hay
declared that they went into the caucus expecting Monroe to put his
"veto on the infamous cabal and intrigues in all its forms and shapes,"
it seems unlikely that this conviction was deeply rooted.[21] All of those
present must have noted the prominently featured item in the *Enquirer*
on the morning of the caucus, appearing under the heading of a letter
from a gentleman in Washington to a friend in Richmond. This communication, prepared by Barbour and Monroe, informed the Virginians
that it was necessary to accept the compromise not only to preserve the
Union but to prevent Rufus King and De Witt Clinton from carrying
out their plans of reorganizing the parties on a sectional basis. If the
Virginians allowed their pride, which "revolts at the idea of a compromise," to prevent them from accepting the proposal before Congress,
then they would render themselves "the instrument of the views of
Mr. King and his friends. . . ." [22] This warning and the influence of
moderate leaders were sufficient to ensure an electoral slate favorable
to Monroe—admittedly with little enthusiasm on the part of the Junto.
There was some resentment against the compromise, but the legislature adjourned without taking action. Monroe had not won the support of Virginia, but only her neutrality. Although the *Enquirer* spoke
bitterly about the betrayal of the principles of Republicanism, not all
Virginians disapproved of Monroe's conduct. Chapman Johnson at
least managed to see some humor in the melodrama enacted in Richmond:

> We have been exceedingly wroth of late on the Missouri subject. Gov-
> ernor Barbour rang the alarm-bell, and we were forthwith in great com-
> motion. . . . You would have been quite amused to have seen how the news
> of a compromise . . . and of Mr. Monroe's concurrence therein excited us.
> The news immediately preceded the meeting of our caucus to recommend
> electors. We met in high session, scolded threatened and adjourned for
> further information. The further information we have received by no means
> exculpates Mr. Monroe from the guilt of concurrence (if guilt it be)! Yet
> we shall meet again tonight, perfectly calm, and proceed with our nomina-
> tions as if nothing had disturbed us. I am very glad of this result, for I am
> of the opinion that the territorial expansion is a fair subject of compromise.[23]

IV

On the same day that the caucus met in Richmond, the Senate passed
the bill to admit Maine and Missouri with the Thomas amendment
attached. In the House, Clay took charge of the complicated maneuver-

ing required to secure the admission of Missouri without restriction on slavery. It was a considerable triumph for him when the House voted to delete the clause forbidding slavery, by a vote of 90 to 87 on March 2, for in the past there had always been a ten-vote margin on the other side. This victory was made possible by the votes of fourteen members from the free states. The compromise line in the Louisiana Purchase was approved by a vote of 134 to 42. Of those in the negative thirty-seven were Southerners, and of these nineteen were from Virginia.[24] The support of the administration was undoubtedly a major factor in the final result. Even Adams, who wished to see slavery destroyed, used his influence to persuade his friends in Congress to accept the compromise.[25]

As soon as the Missouri bill cleared the House, Monroe summoned the Cabinet. At this, the only meeting held on the Missouri question, he departed from his usual habit of prolonged discussion and asked for opinions in writing on two points: first, whether Congress could prohibit slavery in the territories; and second, whether such a prohibition if adopted was binding on future states created north of 36′30″. The Secretaries were unanimous on the first point, although Adams detected some embarrassment on the part of his Southern colleagues at not finding the power specifically stated in the Constitution. They had to fall back on the clause empowering Congress to make needful regulations for the territories and other property of the United States. When Adams expressed the opinion that the word "forever" in the passage prohibiting slavery north of the compromise line was binding on all future states organized in this region, a sharp exchange took place between him and Crawford, who thought his colleague sounded like Rufus King —a comparison not in the least offensive to the Secretary of State. The President and the Southern members of the Cabinet felt that the term was not applicable to future states, since it would be a limitation on their sovereignty. In view of the President's obvious desire for unanimity, Calhoun suggested a rewording of the second question so that all could give an affirmative reply. In accordance with his proposal the Cabinet members were now asked whether the section containing the word "forever" was in conflict with the Constitution. All agreed that it was not, but each interpreted the application as he saw fit.[26]

Madison, who was consulted by the President, upheld the Southerners in their interpretation of the passage. Although the former President entertained some doubts about the power of Congress to forbid slavery in the territories, he recommended that Monroe accept the measure, since there was nothing in it directly in conflict with the Constitution.[27] In approving the compromise, Monroe did so convinced that this was the only way in which the Union could be preserved. The plot to dismember the Union, he wrote Jefferson, had only been prevented "by the patriotic devotion of several members in the non slave-owning states, who preferred the sacrifice of themselves at home, to a violation of the obvious principles of the Constitution...." [28] In placing this emphasis upon the political implications of the conflict over Missouri, Monroe and other Southerners obscured the very real weight of anti-slavery sentiment involved in the restrictionist movement.

V

In spite of the bitterness stirred up by the Missouri debates and the rumors about the formation of a new party, there was no substantial opposition to Monroe's renomination for a second term. Admittedly, there was no great enthusiasm on his behalf, but this indifference did not reflect any general dissatisfaction with his policies, but rather resulted from the disappearance of the two-party system, which had served to generate rivalry between opposing candidates. Since he was the only nominee there was no challenge in the quest for victory. The process of renomination had begun in 1819, when the state legislatures started to choose electors pledged to Monroe. After the extensive criticism of the caucus nomination during the election of 1816, there was considerable opposition to a congressional caucus. Although few objected to Monroe as the party candidate, there was considerable hostility to running Vice-President Tompkins for a second term.[29] De Witt Clinton's followers were more than willing to engineer his replacement, for he was now closely associated with Clinton's arch-rival, Martin Van Buren. Tompkins had allowed Van Buren's Bucktail faction to run him against Clinton in the 1820 New York gubernatorial race. Since he considered his chances slim in view of all the publicity about the shortages in his accounts during the war, Tompkins intended to protect his career by remaining on the national ticket as Vice-President. The effort to block his nomination failed, when only forty members attended a caucus summoned by Samuel Smith on April 8. They adjourned after approving Richard M. Johnson's resolution that it was inexpedient to make a nomination.[30]

Never in the history of the United States have the people been so completely apathetic during a presidential election as in 1820. Indeed, there was currently much more comment about the next election, still four years distant, when it was expected that the rivalry between Calhoun, Crawford, Jackson, Adams, and Clay would transform the contest into a veritable "war of the giants." [31] The disappearance of the Federalist party had created a void in American politics, for it was the intense rivalry between the two parties which had been responsible for arousing voter enthusiasm. Without opposition within his own party, there was nothing to make the election more than a routine formality. Whether a citizen voted or not, Monroe would be elected. It is not surprising, therefore, that voters turned out in small numbers. In Virginia, out of a population of 600,000 whites only 4,321 bothered to go to the polls. Everywhere the voting followed the same pattern.[32]

Although Monroe was unopposed, he did not, as had been expected, receive the unanimous ballot of the electors. One elector, Governor William Plumer of New Hampshire, triumphantly cast his vote for John Quincy Adams, much to the Secretary's embarrassment. Plumer was one of the few Federalists not reconciled to the new dispensation of the Era of Good Feelings. Apparently, his hostility to Monroe had not been known and he had been placed at the head of the ticket as a mark of respect to a distinguished citizen of the state. John Adams had headed the Massachusetts electors, but he had not hesitated to vote for the former Minister to France whom he had once condemned so bitterly.[33] Tompkins, who lost the gubernatorial race in New York, did not fare quite as well as Monroe, for he received only 218 votes to Monroe's total of 231. With characteristic independence, Plumer cast his second ballot for Richard Rush.

If the public was unruffled, the congressmen were not quite so calm, for a violent conflict erupted over the counting of the ballots of Missouri, which had not as yet been formally admitted to the Union. Indeed, at the time the ballots were counted, it seemed possible that Missouri might not be admitted, since antislavery congressmen considered several provisions of her constitution unacceptable. In order to avoid an indefinite postponement of the electoral count, for no one expected the problem presented by Missouri would be easily resolved, Clay and Barbour worked out a compromise, by which it was agreed the electoral votes of Missouri would be counted unless an objection was raised. In that event the Vice-President would announce the two different sets of figures, letting the public take its preference. Unfortunately, things did not go as planned. When Arthur Livermore of

New Hampshire protested counting the Missouri returns, John Floyd and John Randolph of Virginia launched a violent attack on the restrictionists. The indignant senators walked out, returning to complete the count only when order had been restored.[34]

As much as Monroe and other political leaders had hoped that the compromise of 1820 would end the discussion over slavery, the issue was revived again in the session of 1820–1821 in a new form. The resulting debates, although less bitter than those of the previous session, were more prolonged. Not until nearly the end of the session was the issue resolved. The second crisis was precipitated by the provisions in the constitution of Missouri banning migration of free Negroes into the state and prohibiting the legislature from emancipating slaves without the consent of the owners. Both clauses exasperated the restrictionists, but the first was particularly offensive since it seemed to contradict the provision of the federal Constitution guaranteeing the citizens of a state the privileges and immunities of citizens of the United States. It would have been possible to permit the Supreme Court to rule on the offensive passages, but the antislavery forces rallied to demand that these clauses be expunged before Missouri was admitted to the Union.[35]

The first skirmish in the battle over the Missouri constitution was fought before the House was formally organized, when John W. Taylor, a New Yorker (and a restrictionist), was chosen Speaker in a field of four candidates. Although the Missouri question was not the only issue, it was probably the most important factor in securing his victory.[36] As soon as the Speakership had been settled, the condition of the previous year was repeated—the two houses completely deadlocked. Monroe had hoped for an early compromise, for the Southerners had been much less outspoken than the year before, but when Clay took his seat in mid-January the House and Senate were still at odds. Once again Clay worked to promote a compromise. The first effort based on a resolution requiring Missouri not to pass any law excluding citizens of the United States from settling in the state was rejected on February 12 by a vote of 83 to 81.[37] While Clay worked on another formula, Monroe summoned Nicholas Biddle to the Capital from Philadelphia. Biddle, an old friend of the President's, who had just been made one of the government directors of the Bank of the United States, carried considerable weight with the Pennsylvania delegation, most of whom had voted against the compromise. He used his influence to persuade three Pennsylvania representatives to change their votes.[38] In the meantime

Clay engineered the selection of a special committee (elected by the House from a list he circulated, and not appointed by the Speaker) of twenty-three members to confer with a Senate committee. The joint committee produced a vaguely worded resolution asserting that nothing in the Missouri constitution was to be construed as depriving citizens of the United States of any privileges and immunities which they enjoyed under the federal Constitution. On February 26 the House approved the committee's resolve (frequently called the Second Missouri Compromise) by a vote of 87 to 81.[39] At last the Missouri controversy was terminated, although it left a lasting bitterness. Clay engineered the agreement, but Monroe, with Biddle's help, was instrumental in rounding up sufficient votes to assure its adoption.

CHAPTER 26

POLITICS OF
RETRENCHMENT

THE PRESIDENT had been in office only two years when the nation was overtaken by a major economic crisis. The Panic of 1819, the first peacetime depression to confront the nation, was compounded of many factors—overexpansion of credit during the postwar years, the collapse of the export market after the bumper crop of 1817 in Europe, low prices of imports from Europe which forced American manufacturers to close, financial instability resulting from both the excessive expansion of state banking after 1811 and unsound policies of the Second Bank of the United States, and widespread unemployment. Since there was nothing in the national past or in the simple republican faith in the doctrine of progress to prepare Americans for a disaster of this magnitude, both public leaders and businessmen were at a loss for either explanations or remedies. On the whole, there was a widespread tendency to minimize its effects, and in some cases, to refuse to admit that a depression existed. In an age in which the primary function of government was collecting taxes and providing an adequate defense, there was little thought that either the President or Congress should do more than insure monetary stability. In any case, since the causes of the depression were but dimly understood, there were no comprehensive remedies involving extensive governmental action. The most popular formulas for curing the economic ills of the country were those in harmony with the republican ideal of a state composed of frugal and industrious husbandmen, a point of view usually summed up in the words *industry* and *economy*. From all sides Americans were urged to work harder and spend less—a rule considered applicable to federal agencies as well as private citizens. The Panic of 1819, which lasted only three years, had repercussions far beyond the purely economic issues involved. The problems presented by the depression gave an opportunity to the older, more conservative Republicans to reassert themselves by attributing the economic dislocation to a departure from the principles of the Jeffersonian era. It also gave the adherents of rival candidates (most notably the supporters of Crawford) a means of attacking the administration indirectly without committing themselves to a wholesale condemnation. The issues arising from the Panic of 1819 led to the creation of an opposition to the Monroe administration in the form of a loosely defined alliance of conservative Republicans, partisans of rival candidates for the succession and advocates of governmental economy.[1]

II

The President, who had seen evidence of the distress caused by the economic dislocation during his tour in 1819, was not indifferent to the problem, but within the limits of his office and the prevailing concept of the role of the federal government he could do little but repeat the commonplaces of businessmen, economists and public leaders. The depression had a direct impact on the government in that it produced a drastic decline in revenues, which were largely derived from the customs duties. There was also a marked decrease in the income from the sale of public lands, for many purchasers now defaulted. It was in connection with the falling governmental receipts that Monroe referred to the general economic distress in his annual message of 1819. After commenting on the great number of bankruptcies (which he attributed to the rapid contraction of credit and to the scarcity of money, as well as to a lack of confidence on the part of the business community), he turned to the specific problem created by the numerous failures among manufacturers. Accepting the view that they were largely the result of the sale of European products in the American market at prices below cost, he suggested that Congress consider how it might "give encouragement to our domestic industries." [2] In response to this oblique recommendation of a higher protective tariff, Representative Henry Baldwin of Pennsylvania in April 1820 introduced a bill increasing duties on cottons and a few items of lesser importance. The opposition from the South was intense—only nine Southern representatives voted for the bill. Their chief objection was the old cry that agriculture was being taxed for the benefit of the manufacturers. They also argued that higher duties would reduce revenues still further and make internal taxation necessary. Apparently this mild protectionist measure, which the President had not discussed with his secretaries, did not have the united backing of the Cabinet, for the *National Intelligencer* condemned it strongly. The position of the *Intelligencer,* whose editors were close to Crawford, undoubtedly reflected the views of the Secretary of the Treasury, who had become hostile to protectionism. Adams and Calhoun, however, both accepted the desirability of higher duties to encourage domestic manufacturing. Among the chief objectors in the House was William Lowndes, who had actively supported the Tariff of 1816. His shift marks the retreat of most Southerners from the moderate nationalism, once approved by them after the war and still a cornerstone of Monroe's program. Baldwin's tariff was passed by the House, but in the Senate, where all but three Southerners were in the negative, it failed by one vote.[3]

In his fourth annual message in November 1820 the President sounded a more optimistic note than the year before, as he encouraged the people not to regard the depression as either permanent or as undermining the fabric of national life. Although he confessed that there was not an "unvaried prosperity" in "every interest in this community," he still found "much cause to rejoice in the felicity of our situation." He did not think it possible that all sections of the community would ever be equally flourishing in a country as large and complex as the United States. His conclusion that the depression was not to be blamed on domestic conditions reflected the growing understanding of the scope of the problem. He attributed the economic difficulties of the nation to the "peculiar character of the epoch in which we live, and to the extraordinary occurrences which have signalized it. The convulsions with which several of the powers of Europe have been shaken and the long and destructive wars in which all were engaged, with their sudden transition to a state of peace presenting in the first instance unusual encouragement to our commerce and withdrawing it in the second even within its wonted limit, could not fail to be sensibly felt here." In spite of the economic pressures, however, he urged the people not to lose sight of the "great circumstances which constitute the felicity of a nation—every individual in the full enjoyment of his rights, the Union blessed with plenty and rapidly rising to greatness under a National Government which operates with complete effect in every part without being felt in any except by the ample protection which it affords...." The citizens of the country should regard the current difficulties as "mild and instructive admonitions, warning us of the dangers to be shunned in the future, teaching us lessons of economy and corresponding with the simplicity of our institutions...." [4] In short, frugality, economy and industry were Monroe's remedies.

In all previous eras of general economic distress Americans had always accepted governmental intervention to provide debtor relief. Although most debtor problems lay within the province of the state governments, the administration was confronted with large-scale indebtedness on the part of purchasers of public lands. Under federal law, land purchasers had been required to pay one-fourth of the price within forty days after the sale and the balance in three annual installments. Unless full payment were completed within five years the land was forfeited. By 1819, as a result of the postwar boom, the debt on lands totaled $23,000,000, but much of the payments were in arrears. To alleviate the pressure caused by the severe curtailment of credit and state note issues Congress had granted one-year extensions of the forfeiture clause since 1818. Monroe, in his annual message of 1820, proposed as a permanent solution to this problem that the debtors, who had acquired land when prices were high, be given a "reasonable indulgence," so that they would not be penalized by having to pay the balance during a depression, when prices were lower and money scarce. A few weeks later Crawford outlined a specific plan in his annual report to Congress, in which he recommended that debtors unable to pay the balance due on land purchases be allowed to surrender the unpaid portion and then be granted a clear title to the remainder. Those wishing to keep the full amount of land were to be allowed a longer period of time in which to pay—or, if they paid the full sum at once, they would receive a substantial discount. In February 1821 Congress approved a bill drafted along the lines suggested by the Secretary of the Treasury. Payments could now be extended over eight years and those relinquishing unpaid portions of the land would be given a title to the remainder. A special discount of 37½ per cent was allowed debtors who paid promptly. [5]

It was during the Panic of 1819 that the Second Bank of the United States (chartered in 1816) built up so much of the public animosity instrumental to its ultimate destruction, for many were convinced that the Bank precipitated the Panic by its drastic curtailment of loans in 1818 and 1819. However, at the worst, this rapid reduction of credit had only aggravated the economic pressures already operating. The first President of the Bank, William Jones (formerly Secretary of the Navy), had not only adopted a much-too-generous policy in granting private loans but he had also failed to supervise closely the operations of the branches. Consequently, by early 1818 the Bank had overextended its loans to the point that its existence was endangered. Not all the problems of the Bank were due to mismanagement, but resulted in part from an agreement President Jones had made with the state banks to begin specie resumption on February 17, 1817—a date fixed by Congress. Even under the terms of this arrangement, which had been worked out under the supervision of Secretary of the Treasury Crawford, specie resumption was more apparent than real, for it depended on a deliberate restraint on the part of the Bank and of the Treasury in not pressing state banks for redemption of their notes. This agreement had not only placed a heavy burden on the Bank for the validation of state bank notes, but it had also promoted a further expansion of credit.[6] When the directors realized the danger confronting the Bank early in 1818, they inaugurated a rapid curtailment of loans, which had a sharp impact on the economy. At the same time the Bank refused to accept notes from state banks in which government funds were deposited. From now on the Treasury had to make its own arrangements with state banks. In practical terms this meant that the decision about pressing for redemption was shifted to Crawford, who attempted to avoid pressures which would cause banks to fail and increase the economic difficulties of the nation. Therefore he accepted state notes which were not redeemable in specie, paying them out whenever possible in those states where they circulated at par. During 1819 and 1820 the Secretary of the Treasury also shifted federal deposits to state banks experiencing difficulties.[7] Although these activities were scrutinized by the House in 1823 in a politically motivated investigation, the inquiry revealed only that he had been guilty of generosity in his dealings with the state banks; there had been no loss of federal funds.

Monroe, like his predecessors, left the Secretary of the Treasury a large area of independent action. He discussed broad policy with Crawford—such as the method to be used in redeeming the Louisiana Purchase bonds in 1818—but the day-to-day fiscal operations were very much the affair of the Secretary. In all matters which did not involve his political interests Crawford, who was admired by Gallatin with whom he corresponded regularly, seems to have been a competent financier.[8] His report on the currency of February 24, 1820, presented a plan for a paper circulating media which revealed a sound understanding of the problems of public finance. This report, submitted in response to a congressional request, outlined a plan for paper money based on Treasury notes exchangeable on demand for specie or government bonds paying low interest. This system overcame the problem of specie redemption by requiring banks to redeem their notes in Treasury certificates. Under this arrangement, when there was a demand for money, banks would exchange federal bonds for Treasury notes and thus expand credit, since the profit to be made from loans would be greater than that from the bonds. When the economy was moving at a slower rate, the process would be reversed. In short, Crawford's plan looked forward to a flexible currency and avoided the insoluble problem of specie redemption in an economy perennially deficient in specie. However (and this is characteristic of his political involvement), he rejected his own carefully outlined plan on the grounds that past experience had proved that governments could not be trusted with paper money, since they invariably issued too much and thus created inflationary trends. This conclusion, so much at odds with his reasoning, placed him in the camp of the conservative Republicans while providing them with ample material for criticizing all paper issues.[9] During the Monroe administration Crawford worked closely with all three presidents of the Bank, and it is noteworthy that none—including Nicholas Biddle, Monroe's close friend—ever commented unfavorably on his ability.

Crawford's political enemies always hoped (in vain) that he would be implicated in the mismanagement of the Bank, although he had no direct role in its operations. In 1818, a House investigation of the Bank revealed nothing more than carelessness in the policies established by President Jones and his board of directors. Much to the relief of the administration, the report of the House committee, while it discovered some rather dubious practices in the operations of the Bank, did not recommend the revocation of the charter. Luckily for the Bank, the worst defalcations—those of the Baltimore branch—were not exposed until after Congress adjourned. The Bank's legal status, if not its solvency, was reinforced early in 1819, when Chief Justice John Marshall upheld the constitutionality of the Bank in McCulloch v. Maryland. Monroe was especially relieved that the Bank survived these attacks, for, as he told Adams early in 1820, experience had amply demonstrated the necessity of the Bank. Without its services Monroe believed it would be impossible to provide adequate credit facilities throughout the nation or to maintain specie payments. As to the constitutionality of the Bank, that seemed to him to have been settled by "twenty years of practice and acquiescence under the first bank." [10]

Although the administration never involved itself in the daily operations of the Bank or attempted to direct its role in the private sector of the economy, the President had a constant concern for the welfare of the Bank, since it not only functioned as the major depository for federal funds but also provided the only means of stabilizing the currency. Moreover, in emergencies such as arose in connection with the deficit of 1820 the Bank was an invaluable source of loans. Consequently, it was important that the Bank be well run and not subject to public criticism. After the investigation of 1818 both the President and the Secretary of the Treasury brought pressure to bear on the directors (the five members of the twenty-five-man board appointed by the government were not sufficient for federal control) to replace Jones with Langdon Cheves. Under the latter the Bank was restored to a sound basis, although Cheves' loan policies were somewhat more stringent than Crawford thought entirely necessary. In 1823, when Cheves resigned, the directors, after securing the approval of Monroe and Crawford, elected Nicholas Biddle to the presidency of the Bank. This choice was highly pleasing to Monroe, for Biddle frankly accepted the view that the Bank must work closely with the Treasury. Not only did he have a more statesmanlike concept of the role of the institution than his predecessor but he also returned a handsome profit to the stockholders.[11]

III

Among the many subjects covered in the President's annual messages, public finances occupied a secondary position. The fiscal material was general and confined to a summary statement of the receipts, expenditures and payments made on the national debt. These paragraphs were usually prepared by the Secretary of the Treasury, who then presented a fuller analysis in a separate annual report, submitted directly to Congress without being shown to the President. This practice, which originated in the Washington administration, had not created any difficulties, for the Secretaries' reports merely illustrated the general statements made by the Presidents.[12] In 1819, however, the account of the state of the public finances appearing in the President's message was at odds with that presented in the annual report of the Secretary of the Treasury. The material Crawford provided for the message indicated that the revenues for 1820 would be adequate to cover the current expenses of the government, whereas the Secretary's report announced a probable deficit of five million dollars by the end of 1820.[13] Monroe was embarrassed by this discrepancy, which Adams believed intentional in order to injure the administration as a means of strengthening Crawford's position as a Presidential candidate.[14] The omission was certainly deliberate, for Crawford had anticipated a deficit as early as July.[15] Apparently he held the information back to prevent the President from proposing internal taxes, an unpopular measure for which most congressmen would blame the Secretary of the Treasury, who was traditionally regarded as the responsible agent for such recommendations. In his own report, Crawford made no suggestions other than to indicate that it was up to Congress to decide whether to impose internal taxes to augment the revenue or to reduce expenditures to the level of governmental income. Pending the enactment of these measures, he proposed that a loan be authorized. To meet immediate needs Congress promptly approved a three-million-dollar loan.

At the end of 1820 the discrepancy between the account of the public finances given by the President and that of the Secretary of the Treasury was even more glaring, especially in the light of the President's comments in his message minimizing the depression. The President had not given the slightest indication in his message of November 14 that the deficit for 1820 was greater than had been anticipated. Not until Crawford's report two weeks later was Congress informed that the expenses for 1820 would exceed revenues by seven million dollars—a figure reduced to five million in a supplementary report.[16] To alleviate the deficiency Crawford recommended that the importation of foreign spirits be prohibited and that an excise be placed on domestic spirits. In the meantime a loan would be "indispensable." As a result of this second experience the President carefully scrutinized Crawford's report for 1821 to make certain that it did not contradict the remarks in his message. In both the message and the Treasury report in 1821 the public was assured that the improved condition of the economy, which had yielded an increase in the customs receipts for the third quarter of the year, made a deficit unlikely. Only after carefully analyzing Crawford's figures did Monroe decide not to request internal taxes, a possibility he had indicated in his second inaugural. However, he did warn that in the event of a recurrence of a deficiency "the course presented to a virtuous and enlightened people appeared to be a plain one." [17]

The coolness between Monroe and Crawford which became evident in 1822 undoubtedly had its roots in this episode. Monroe was not only angered by Crawford's failure to give him an accurate statement of public finances, he was also deeply offended because the revenue deficiency was used to justify extensive budget cuts in areas the President considered vital to national welfare. He naturally felt that Crawford was encouraging the drive for retrenchment in order to escape the odium of advocating new taxation. Most of the cuts were at the expense of the War Department, a branch of the government never popular with old-fashioned Republicans, who looked with horror at the War Department's expenditure of nine million out of a total federal budget of $25.5 million in 1818. That the War Department should suffer was not displeasing to Crawford, for Calhoun was one of his major rivals for the Presidential succession. The retrenchment drive marks the beginning of the alliance between conservative Republicans (often called the Old Republicans) and Crawford's partisans—an alliance which virtually wrecked the administration defense program. The association between these two groups was still loose, for the Old Republicans, who found Crawford's record on the Bank and the tariff unpalatable (although he had now lost his enthusiasm for protectionism), did not move completely into his camp until 1822.[18] Clay's supporters also joined the attack on the War Department.

Although the War Department had been efficiently operated by Calhoun, who had reduced the cost of maintaining enlisted men from $451 to $299 per year, it was particularly vulnerable to criticism. For some years private fur trading interests, notably John Jacob Astor's American Fur Company, had kept up a running fire against the system of government-operated trading posts, which had been expanded during the Monroe administration as a means of civilizing the Indians and of preventing their ruthless exploitation by private traders. In connection with this program Calhoun and Monroe were establishing military posts throughout the Louisiana Purchase. The most ambitious of their undertakings was the post planned on the Yellowstone River, to be set up by an expedition going up the Missouri. Unfortunately James Johnson (brother of influential Congressman Richard M. Johnson), who held most of the contracts for supplying the Missouri expedition, had used federal advances for private obligations. Consequently the expedition (which was also costing much more than anticipated) was under considerable criticism in the press. This, together with irregularities discovered in a contract for stone to be used in the construction of Fort Calhoun came under discussion during the session of 1819–1820. In spite of the interest in retrenchment, the Missouri debates prevented Congress from making much headway other than to bombard Calhoun for reports to be used in planning reductions. The President's favorite project—the construction of fortifications—received the substantial sum of $800,000. The President, however, was given an intimation of what was to come when the House requested the Secretary of War to submit at the next session a plan for reducing the Army from 10,000 to 5,000 men.[19]

The news at the beginning of the session of 1820–21 that the deficit was larger than had been anticipated spurred the economizers to reject Calhoun's proposal that the officer corps be maintained at its existing strength, while the number of enlisted men be reduced by half. Congress insisted that there be an absolute reduction in all ranks. The funds for fortifications were cut to $220,000 (plus $100,000 not expended the year before), while the appropriations for Indian affairs were halved.[20] The cut in the budget for fortifications especially concerned Monroe—who, as Adams commented, "had set his heart upon its accomplishment, and looks to it as one of the great objects by which his administration may be signalized in the view of posterity." [21] In an effort to halt the economy drive Monroe released to the *Intelligencer* his report to William Branch Giles of February 22, 1815, in which he had cogently put the case for retaining a large army and for the necessity of a network of coastal defenses. Although the editor denied that there was any intention of exerting executive influence on Congress, the objective of the publication was obvious. A few days later the *Intelligencer* featured an editorial stressing the serious loss to the Army in releasing large numbers of experienced officers.[22] Some of the cuts, such as the elimination of appropriations for the fort on Dauphin Island, on which construction was under way, were quite arbitrary. At Calhoun's request a special Cabinet meeting was called to consider whether it would be possible to use unexpended funds to pay for contracts already let, since it was likely that the contractor might be ruined. Although Adams was sympathetic to Calhoun's plight, he felt that the use of these funds would be illegal, since Congress had specifically deleted this project. Crawford remained noncommittal, although it was undoubtedly hoped that he might exert his influence

with Samuel Smith, the chairman of the Ways and Means Committee
and a Crawford supporter, to restore the cut. The President agreed
with Adams and decided that he could do nothing but recommend
that Congress pay for work already under contract.[23] Although Adams
shared Monroe's views about the undesirability of these extensive
reductions of the military budget, he felt that nothing effective could
be done to check a program which had such wide public support.[24]
Indeed, as Rufus King noted early in the debates, the President, although nearly unanimously re-elected, had no friends in Congress
willing to "explain or support those measures which are supposed to
have the recommendations" of the executive.[25] Or, as Clay put it more
bluntly in a conversation with Adams: "Mr. Monroe has just been
re-elected with apparent unanimity, but he has not the slightest influence
in Congress. His career was considered as closed. There was nothing
further to be expected by him or from him." [26]

Since the army-reduction bill did not take effect until June 1, 1820,
War Department expenses still remained high—nearly $8,000,000 for
the year. Not until 1821, as a result of these and other economies,
did the departmental budget fall below $5,000,000, where it remained
during the remainder of Monroe's second term. Although other
services were cut, the reductions were not as drastic. The Navy, for
example, was only cut from $3,800,000 in 1819 to $3,300,000 in 1821.
During the same period the total expenditures of the government
declined from twenty-five million to nineteen million dollars. The
Navy, although no more popular with Old Republicans than the
Army, never became a storm center for economizers. For one thing the
Navy was performing useful services in protecting American commerce
from pirates. Moreover, it cannot have been a disadvantage to the
Navy Department that Secretary Thompson was on excellent terms with
Crawford and that he also possessed considerable influence on the
New York delegation through Martin Van Buren.[27]

IV

On March 5, just three days after the passage of the army-reduction
bill and a week after the second Missouri Compromise, President Monroe mounted the dais in the hall of the House of Representatives to
take the oath of office for his second term. This unusual date had been
chosen after consultation with the justices of the Supreme Court
because it was considered inappropriate to hold the inauguration on

a Sunday. Until a few days before the ceremony the President had been somewhat uncertain about delivering an address. Apparently some of the Virginia Republicans had objected that such speeches were not only unrepublican in character but that they were also not authorized by the Constitution. The President took up the question with the department heads, all of whom except Smith Thompson favored the continuation of the custom. At the same meeting Monroe also discussed the contents of his address. At Adams' suggestion he deleted a comment unfavorable to the practice of resorting to loans to finance governmental expenditures, for, as Adams pointed out, the remark might be used against him in the event that another loan was necessary to cover a deficit. In accordance with Calhoun's wishes the President toned-down his comments approving the protective tariff as a means of encouraging domestic manufacturing.[28]

The scene of the second inaugural was the newly decorated chamber of the House of Representatives, which had been completed in 1819. Most Americans considered the semicircular room with its red damask settees for the foreign ministers, the Brussels carpet, the gold curtains in the gallery and the silk canopy over the speaker's chair (which in turn was surmounted by a gilt eagle) appropriate for a legislative hall. Stratford Canning, however, thought this lavish decor in the French fashion rather "tasteless." The new chamber had one advantage over its predecessor in that the public galleries were larger and much better located. Its most serious defect was a wretched echo (partially remedied by draperies), which made most speakers unintelligible.[29] It was fortunate that the ceremony took place indoors, for the day was rainy and cold. An enormous crowd attended—it was estimated that some three thousand persons managed to squeeze inside the House, while another throng equally large clogged the entrances. As usual, no arrangements were made for controlling the crowd, so that the British Minister had to push his way through a horde of "sturdy and ragged citizens"; he was able to derive some small pleasure from seeing that the "Prezzy" was accorded no greater courtesy.[30] Monroe arrived shortly after noon, having driven from the President's residence in a plain carriage with four horses and a single colored footman. His sole escort was the secretaries, who followed him each in a carriage and pair. Monroe was clad in a "full suit of black broadcloth of somewhat antiquated fashion, with shoe- and knee-buckles. . . ." In the House chamber he was seated on a dais in front of the Speaker's chair with the justices of the Supreme Court and the heads of the departments on either side. The only notable public figure absent was Vice-President Tompkins—who was still in New York, where he took the oath privately. Throughout the ceremony there was considerable noise in the galleries, which did not subside while the President read his address in a very low voice. After the ceremony the hall resounded with a "cheering shout from the people in the galleries" as the President departed to the accompaniment of "Yankee Doodle" played by the Marine Band. The rest of the day fell into the usual pattern—congratulatory calls at the White House from public officials and legislators and in the evening an inaugural ball at Brown's Hotel, attended by the President and his family.[31]

The President's inaugural address reviewed the achievements of his first term and indicated the course he intended to follow during the next four years.[32] After expressing his gratitude to the people for the confidence shown him in the election, he renewed his plea for the completion of the coastal defense program, stressing past accomplishments and indicating further needs. In foreign affairs he cited the success of the administration in negotiating treaties with Spain and England and the effectiveness of American neutrality during the revolutionary conflict in Latin America. For the future he promised continued neutrality and a renewal of efforts to obtain more favorable trade concessions from Great Britain and France. With understandable pride he recalled his success since the end of the war in liquidating nearly $67,000,000 of the national debt without imposing new taxes. He alluded to the depression only in passing, when he commented that he had resorted to loans to meet the deficit on the assumption that the economic difficulties were only temporary. He admitted, however, that it would be necessary to request internal taxes if the deficit continued. The protectionists were disappointed by the vagueness of his endorsement of higher tariffs to protect manufactures. Prompted by recent attacks on the government system of Indian trading posts, Monroe gave special emphasis to Indian affairs. In terms reminiscent of his youthful liberal orientation, he asserted:

The care of the Indian tribes within our limits has long been an essential part of our system, but, unfortunately, it has not been executed in a manner to accomplish all the objects intended by it. We have treated them as independent nations, without their having any substantial pretensions to that rank. The distinction has flattered their pride, retarded their improvement, and in many instances paved the way to their destruction. The progress of our settlements westward ... has constantly driven them back, with almost the total sacrifice of the lands which they have been compelled to abandon. They have claims on the magnanimity and, I may add, the justice of this nation which we must all feel. We should become their real benefactors; we should perform the office of their Great Father, the endearing title which they emphatically give to the Chief Magistrate.... Their sovereignty over vast territories should cease, in lieu of which the right of soil should be secured to each individual... and for the territory thus ceded some reasonable equivalent should be granted, to be vested in permanent funds for the support of civil government over them and for the education of their children, for their instruction in the arts of husbandry....

This rather innocuous scheme of "civilizing" the Indians and ending their tribal organization was not approved by Congress or by the public, for it meant positive guarantees of Indian land titles. Americans much preferred to maintain the fiction that Indian tribes were independent nations, because as such they could be assumed to have the power to cede *all* their lands.

Most Presidents do not consider inaugural addresses suitable for reviewing disagreeable events; consequently the only reference to the Missouri controversy was so oblique as to be almost unnoticeable. Monroe merely said that while it was too much to expect "perfection" in all governmental institutions, still there had not been a serious conflict in America which had not "been managed by argument and fair appeal to the good sense of the people...." With the optimism so typical of his generation the President concluded that by "steadily pursuing this course in this spirit there is every reason to believe that our system will soon attain the highest degree of perfection of which human institutions are capable...." To Monroe this was something more than rhetorical hyperbole suitable to the occasion.

CHAPTER 27

AN AMERICAN SYSTEM

T HE RECOGNITION extended the Latin American states in Monroe's message of March 1822 marked the culmination of only one phase of the administration's Latin American policy. A major problem still remained: how to safeguard the Western Hemisphere from European intervention aimed at restoring former colonies to Spain. Since the beginning of his first term, he had been concerned about the possibility that the European concert of powers, which had been established primarily to repress liberal uprisings in Europe against the "legitimate" rulers, might extend its operations to the New World. This danger had subsided after the Congress of Aix-la-Chapelle in 1818, when Great Britain, unwilling to forego the profits from the South American trade, declined to approve Russian and French interventionist proposals; in 1819, Monroe had attempted to strengthen the position of the South American states by appealing to Great Britain to join the United States in recognizing Buenos Aires. Although the British Cabinet was unwilling to support intervention, it was not ready to confirm the independence of the insurgent states. Monroe's offer had consequently been rejected. On several occasions the President considered the possibility of issuing a public statement of principles to assert American support of liberal political institutions and to condemn European interference in the affairs of other nations.[1] Early in 1821 he discussed with Adams the advisability of expressing his hostility to the invasion of the Kingdom of the Two Sicilies undertaken to suppress a revolution. Since it was not easy to overcome traditional American reluctance to involvement in European controversies, nothing was done.[2] Much as the idea attracted the President, there had been no suitable occasion for a pronouncement.

The opportunity for the United States to publicize its opposition to European interference in Latin America came in 1823 from a most unexpected source. In October 1823, when Secretary Adams returned from his annual sojourn in New England, the President showed him two recently arrived dispatches from Richard Rush containing a proposal made by British Foreign Minister George Canning that Rush join him in a public statement condemning any attempt on the part of the European powers to restore Spain's authority in her former Empire. The British Foreign Minister maintained that this pronouncement was essential to restrain France after her successful operation early in 1823 that restored Ferdinand VII to the Spanish throne. This suggestion, first made orally, was repeated on August 20 in a private and confidential note to Rush, in which Canning proposed that they jointly announce:

1. We conceive the recovery of the Colonies by Spain to be hopeless.
2. We conceive the question of recognition of them, as independent States, to be one of time and circumstances.
3. We are, however, by no means disposed to throw any impediment in the way of an arrangement between them and the mother country by amicable negotiation.
4. We aim not at the possession of any portion of them ourselves.
5. We could not see any portion of them transferred to any other power with indifference.[3]

In the face of Canning's offer and entirely without guiding instructions, Rush was prepared to enter into a joint declaration on his own responsibility, providing Canning agreed to recognize the Latin American states. On this point, however, Canning could not make any promises, for he knew that his colleagues in the Cabinet, who were unaware of his approach to Rush, would not consent. It was not that the other Cabinet members wished to see Spain's authority re-established, but they felt so deeply committed to the concert of Europe and the principle of legitimacy that they were unwilling to contemplate such a drastic change in British policy. When Canning refused to indicate an intention to extend recognition in the future, Rush referred the matter to Washington.[4]

Rush, like most Americans who had unpleasant recollections of Canning's previous tenure in the Foreign Office between 1807 and 1809, was inclined to question the motives behind this offer. Adams, for example, was convinced that Canning was using the prospect of joint action against European intervention as bait to secure from the United States a disavowal of any intention to take Cuba. Since Adams felt that Cuba would fall into the hands of the United States by a kind of continental law of gravitation, he was naturally unwilling to subscribe to the fourth point of Canning's statement. While Canning considered the fourth proposal important, he was also sincerely concerned about the rumors circulating in Europe that France would crown her successful operation in Spain by mounting an expedition to subdue her colonies. Although Canning had already warned France through the British Ambassador against annexing Spain's colonies, he was disturbed by the persistence of these reports. The British government did not need the support of the United States to check this action, but Canning felt that it would be helpful in advancing what was essentially a propaganda war against those circles in France which were advocating a Latin American expedition. Moreover, it was hoped that the offer would facilitate the Anglo-American rapprochement begun after the war and now considered a basic objective of British policy.[5]

Monroe, who had been waiting for Adams' return before going to Oak Hill, left the Capital the next day without discussing Rush's dispatch with the Secretary of State.[6] Since the American Minister in London had not presented it as an urgent matter, the President naturally preferred to reflect carefully on this momentous and flattering proposal, which seemed to acknowledge the United States as one of the handful of powers governing the affairs of the world since Napoleon's downfall. He saw this offer, which was so gratifying to national pride, as a magnificent opportunity to forge an absolute guarantee of the security and future independence of the Latin American states. This was a goal, he knew, which could only be achieved with the support of the greatest naval power in the world. Yet, tempting as he found Canning's proposal, it involved a major departure from the long-established tradition of noninvolvement in European affairs, a tradition instituted by Washington and sanctified by the Republicans as a cornerstone of American foreign policy. Was not, he wondered, an exception to this rule justified by the distinctly American character of the central problem? Should he relinquish this opportunity to strike a decisive blow for the cause of republicanism throughout the world? Was it not possible that Britain had arrived at the point at which she realized that she "must take her stand either on the side of the monarchs or of the United States, and in consequence, either in favor of Despotisms or of liberty . . . ?" In the light of these considerations his first reaction had been that the administration "ought to meet the proposal" advanced in London and "make it known, that we would view an interference on the part of the European powers and especially an attack on the colonies . . . as an attack on ourselves, presuming that if they succeeded . . . they would extend it to us." From these comments made in a letter to Jefferson shortly after he reached Oak Hill, it is evident that Monroe was impressed with the importance of utilizing this opportunity to declare that the United States regarded intervention in South America as a threat to its own security.[7]

From Jefferson and Madison, to whom he turned for advice, Monroe received enthusiastic support for cooperation with Great Britain. This offer, Jefferson told him, was the most "momentous" question offered for his "contemplation since independence." "Our first and fundamental maxim," Jefferson continued, "should be never to entangle ourselves in the broils of Europe, and our second never to suffer Europe to intermeddle with Cis-Atlantic affairs. America, North and South has a state set of interests distinct from those of Europe, and peculiarly her own. She should therefore have a system of her own, separate and apart from that of Europe." [8] This concept of two spheres was by no means new, for Jefferson and Monroe had discussed the idea some years before in connection with Corrêa's proposal that the United States and Brazil create a common policy for the Americas. Indeed, during the last decade such notions had been frequently articulated on both sides of the Atlantic.[9] So delighted was Jefferson at the prospect of detaching England from the despots that he felt it was worth renouncing future American territorial expansion. Madison, if somewhat more skeptical that Britain was moving in a prorepublican direction, was equally enthusiastic about American participation in a joint declaration. "There ought not to be," he wrote, "any backwardness . . . in meeting her the way she has proposed; keeping in view of course the spirit and forms of the Constitution in every step in the road to war which must be the last step, if those short of war be made without avail." Shrewdly he concluded that Canning's offer "tho' made with an air of *consultation* as well as concert, was founded on a predetermination to take the course marked out whatever might be the reception given here to his invitation." [10]

In spite of this endorsement from the party's elder statesmen, Monroe's reflections during the next month led him to question the wisdom of a joint policy statement. A major objection was the effect on public opinion in the nation and in Latin America of an action seeming to place the United States in a subordinate capacity to Great Britain. The good relations which had existed between the two governments since the war were by no means reflected in public attitudes. Americans continued to resent the critical comments about the United States made by Englishmen in Parliament and in the British press. Not only would participation with the British government injure national self-esteem, but (and this was far more serious) the Latin American governments, well aware that Britain had initiated the undertaking and that its success depended on the British navy, might be drawn more closely into the British orbit. Would not Great Britain emerge as the real protector of South American liberty? If (and dispatches from Rush confirmed this) British policy were based exclusively on self-interest and not on second thoughts about supporting republican governments, the United States would be compromising its principles by entering in a declaration primarily for the economic benefit of its recent enemy.[11] The degree to which Monroe had withdrawn from his first response of accepting Canning's offer can be measured by the fact that he never mentioned the letters from Madison and Jefferson to the Cabinet. Only Adams was shown them privately on November 19, after the decision had been made to turn down the British proposal.[12] As Monroe reflected on American policy, it became apparent that a joint declaration could be justified only if there were no other way to prevent European action on Spain's behalf.

II

The President thoroughly explored the implications of Canning's proposal starting November 7 in a series of Cabinet meetings attended by all the secretaries except Crawford, who was ill. From the outset the department heads were agreed about the necessity for an American declaration of principles, but they were uncertain about the best means of framing the statement. At the first meeting, after expressing his reluctance to act in a secondary role to Great Britain, the President tentatively advanced the possibility of sending a special envoy to register American protests against intervention with the allied powers, but this was promptly ruled out since it implied a willingness to attend the conferences held by the European powers, a policy rejected in the past. The President listened attentively as his secretaries discussed broad aspects of American policy. Adams was outspokenly opposed to joint action, which seemed to reduce the nation to a "cock-boat in the wake of the British man-of-war." Canning's offer he thought no more than a screen to exact a pledge from the United States not to annex Cuba. Calhoun was equally positive in urging acceptance, for he took the threat of interference much more seriously than Adams did. Southard, who said little, endorsed Calhoun's views. The only practical suggestion to emerge from the discussion was that the American Ministers in Europe should be instructed to state to the various governments American principles, which would constitute "parts of a combined system of policy." [13] This plan was suggested by observations contained in a note delivered on October 16 by Baron de Tuyll, the Russian Minister, informing the United States that the Czar, in conformity with the principles of the allied powers, would not receive diplomatic representatives from the South American states. Although this mild and innocent-sounding note had been embellished with fulsome compliments to the Monroe administration for its neutrality during the revolts, it left the distinct implication that Russia might support the cause of Spain unless this neutrality were continued.[14] Adams' reply, delivered on November 15 after revision by the President, informed Tuyll that the United States, acting on principles which were far different from those of Russia, had recognized the new states as irrevocably independent from the mother country.[15] This cautious statement was far removed from the final formulation of American policy which emerged in the President's message.

After the meeting of the seventh, a week elapsed before the department heads were again assembled. In the interim the President began working on his message, which was due on December 2. On several occasions he discussed Canning's offer with individual secretaries, but no decisions were reached. On the thirteenth Adams gave Monroe the paragraphs on foreign relations for use in the message. These drafts, which were included almost verbatim, discussed recent developments on the Pacific coast, where Russian expansion had been a matter of prime concern since 1821 when the Czar announced that the coast north of the fifty-first parallel was closed to all foreigners. The Russians had suspended this order after Great Britain and the United States protested, but there was still much anxiety over Russian ambitions in the Northwest.

The most important passage in Adams' draft was the declaration that "the American continents by the free and independent condition which they have assumed, and maintain, are henceforth not to be considered as subject for future colonization by any European power." [16] It was in this manner that the first principle of Monroe's December policy statement was formulated. It was exclusively Adams' contribution and represented a point of view conspicuously expressed in his Fourth of July oration in 1821. When Adams took his suggestions for the message to the President he had found him still "unsettled in his own mind as to the answer to be given to Mr. Canning's proposals, and alarmed, far beyond anything I could have conceived possible, with the fear that the Holy Alliance are about to restore immediately all South America to Spain." [17] In attributing Monroe's apprehension to Calhoun's influence, Adams was somewhat less than just to the President. Monroe was in a most difficult position. If American failure to underwrite Canning's proposals opened the way to armed intervention, he would bear the responsibility. Although Adams, secure in his own conviction that the threat of intervention was an illusion, minimized the danger, there were signs to the contrary. Canning had certainly presented the dangers as substantial in his conversations with Rush. Moreover, the news of the recent surrender of Cadiz to French troops had been accompanied by reports that an expedition was being gathered there for an invasion of South America. Without any intelligence service or access to European cabinet deliberations, there could be no absolute certainty that British pressure would be sufficient to check the interventionists. After all, British opposition at the Congress of Verona had not prevented the other powers from intervening in Spain.[18] In evaluating the European situation Monroe was probably more influenced by Adams' views than by those of the other secretaries. The President, however, had to be certain in his own mind that there was no reason to alter the conclusion reached in 1818 after the Congress of Aix-la-Chapelle that the powers would never be able to agree to restore Spain's colonies. Two days later, when the Cabinet met, Adams still reported Monroe "moon-struck" as he listened to Calhoun elaborate on the probability of armed intervention.[19]

The President's dilemma was resolved shortly after the meeting on November 15, when additional dispatches from Rush reported that Canning had apparently lost all interest in promoting a joint declaration. From this news Monroe surmised that some important change had taken place reducing the likelihood of French intervention. The President was quite correct. Although Rush had known nothing about it, Canning, impatient over American delay, had extracted a pledge from France that she deemed it impossible to restore the colonies to

Spain and that she did not intend to annex any of Spain's possessions in America. This agreement, usually known as the Polignac Memorandum, effectively quashed French interventionism. After receiving these dispatches from Rush the President gave no further thought to accepting Canning's offer. As Adams realized several days later, the President's worried air was largely due to anxiety over his wife's illness.[20]

At the President's direction Adams began work on a dispatch to Rush rejecting the British proposals but expressing general agreement with their principles. In these instructions, which Rush was to read to Canning, Adams announced the willingness of the United States to cooperate, short of a joint declaration, if Great Britain would recognize the independence of the Latin American states. In the event an emergency seemed to make joint action advisable, Rush was to refer the question to Washington so that the administration could participate within the limits of the Constitution in "any act by which we may contribute to support the cause of human freedom, and the independence of the South American Nations." This dispatch was completed on November 29 after considerable revision by the President. The most important change made in the final stages of Adams' draft was the elimination of a statement disclaiming any intention of acquiring Cuba or Puerto Rico. This disclaimer seemed redundant, since the United States was endorsing all of Canning's proposals, including the fourth point. Moreover, there was nothing to be gained by a specific unilateral renunciation of territorial expansion.[21]

Monroe's only regret in choosing this method of reply was that it deprived the nation of the credit to be gained in Latin America from a public avowal of principles. For the past year Monroe had felt that the time had arrived for the nation to "take a bolder attitude . . . in favor of liberty" than had been possible in the past. If it were admitted that the United States had erred in not making such a declaration of policy during the French Revolution, might not the error be compounded by keeping silent? Was it not proper for the United States to encourage nations seeking their freedom while condemning those seeking to deprive others of their liberty? When Monroe raised these questions in a letter to Jefferson in June 1823, the latter had expressed cautious approval. He agreed that European efforts to dictate "to an independent nation the form of its government" were "so arrogant, so atrocious" that they merited execration, but this was as much as any nation had the right to expect in the way of American support. "I have ever," he reminded Monroe, "deemed it fundamental for the United States, never to take an active part in the quarrels of Europe. Their political interests are entirely distinct from ours." [22]

Since Canning's communication to Rush had been confidential, the President could not refer directly to it in his annual message without a breach of confidence. Consequently, he cast about for some means of making a general declaration of policy without citing the British proposal. His first thoughts along this line were presented to the Cabinet on November 21, when, after outlining the details of the projected instructions to Rush, he read some new portions of his message. According to Adams, Monroe began in a tone of alarm over the "imminent and formidable dangers" facing the country, which would call for vigorous measures and a high degree of unity. He then read the paragraphs taken from Adams' draft. At this point Adams was startled to hear the President speak of the principles underlying the French invasion of Spain in "terms of the most pointed reprobation." Equally startling to the Secretary was Monroe's "broad acknowledgement of the Greeks as an independent nation" coupled with a recommendation that Congress appropriate funds for sending a Minister to Greece.[23] Adams, who never relished Monroe's benevolent generalities about the cause of liberty, immediately objected to these specific references. Not only did he think the somber note of the message unduly alarming to the people, who were not aware of any immediate danger, but he regarded the comments on Greece and France as suggesting a call to arms against the European powers. Might not such intemperate remarks impel France and Russia to sever relations with the United States? He also emphasized the contradictions involved in commenting unfavorably upon the conduct of the European powers and yet challenging their right to interest themselves in the affairs of the New World. After listening to Calhoun, who approved the President's text, Monroe, as he often did, proposed to draft for further consideration two paragraphs incorporating the disparate views of his counselors. The next day Adams pressed his case privately with arguments he deemed inappropriate in the Cabinet. With more flattery than was his wont, he told Monroe that his administration "would hereafter . . . be looked back to as the golden age of this republic," and hence Adams wished it to end as it began—delivered to the President's successor at peace with the world. The United States should not risk provoking European aggression in South America, but only be prepared to meet an invasion if necessary. "The ground I wish to take," Adams concluded, "is that of earnest remonstrance against the interference of the European powers by force with South America, but to disclaim all interference on our part with Europe; to make an American cause and adhere inflexibly to that." [24] In short, Adams wished the President to go no further in his message than he had in the instructions to Rush. Monroe was not deeply attached to the proposal for Greek recognition—apparently suggested by Gallatin, who had recently returned from Paris. There was no certainty that recent Greek military successes were sufficient to eliminate Turkish control. He dropped his plea for recognition, although retaining a warm endorsement for the Greek revolution, which was an enormously popular cause with the public.[25] On November 25 Monroe read the revised portions of his message to the Cabinet. Not only had the reference to Greek recognition vanished, but the comments on France's intervention in Spain were also much milder. It was at this meeting that Monroe first read the passages relating to South America, which constituted the Monroe Doctrine (as his policy statement was called after the 1850s), along with the noncolonization principle.[26] Monroe had discovered a suitable justification for a general declaration of principles in the contents of a note delivered by Baron de Tuyll to Adams on November 17. Just as the Secretary was beginning to draft Rush's instructions, the Baron had presented him extracts from a recent circular from the Russian Foreign Minister expressing the Czar's pleasure in the recent success of the allied powers in liberating European states from the perils of revolution. It was, the Czar announced, his policy to ensure tranquility in all civilized states. When Adams inquired whether this meant restoration of Spain's authority in America, the Baron replied affirmatively.[27] Although Tuyll's note suggested no specific move on Russia's part, it provided—as Monroe later told Rush—a suitable basis for an American declaration. Should Congress press for details, Tuyll's note and Adams' reply could be submitted.[28] From a practical point of view this solution allowed the United States to reap whatever credit it could from appearing in public as a protector of Latin American independence without the positive commitment involved in Canning's proposal.

When the President finished reading his draft, not a voice was raised against the principles enunciated, but Wirt, who had said almost nothing at previous meetings, questioned the wisdom of expressing an "attitude of menace without meaning to strike," even if the allied powers interfered in America.[29] It was not that Wirt looked upon the President's statement as binding the nation to a precise course of action (for he and the other secretaries agreed that only Congress could take steps leading to war), but he argued that failure to resist interference in Latin America would diminish the prestige of the nation. Moreover, Wirt also felt that neither Congress nor the public was sufficiently concerned about the republican cause in Latin America to approve military action. Wirt's comments led to considerable discussion, with Calhoun and Adams defending the President but from different points of view. Adams, who deemed armed intervention an impossibility, considered the declaration necessary to prevent Britain from emerging as the sole protector of South America; Calhoun, who thought an allied invasion inevitable, believed a public statement was necessary to insure Britain's future cooperation in protecting the new nations. It was his contention that Britain would be compelled to accept the allied program unless assured of American backing. Indeed, Calhoun thought the United States was much more apt to become involved in a war to protect the Latin American states if the administration remained silent.[30] Monroe said nothing during this interchange. As far as congressional reaction was concerned, he was not worried, for he had already secured Senator Barbour's promise to introduce a resolution urging cooperation with Great Britain if the administration considered it useful.[31]

Although Calhoun had been enthusiastic about the principles included in the President's message, he objected to replying to Tuyll's note of November 16. He thought that the statement in the message was an adequate answer. His colleagues, however, reminded him that it had always been contrary to American practice to permit foreign governments to notice remarks made in Presidential messages. The only correct way to answer Tuyll was through diplomatic channels. When Adams read his reply to Tuyll, the President and the other secretaries were unanimous in disapproving the second paragraph, in which he asserted:

The principles of this form of Polity [republican government] are; 1 that the institution of government to be lawful, must be pacific, that is founded upon the consent and by the agreement of those who are governed; and 2 that each Nation is exclusively the judge of the Government best suited to itself, and that no other Nation can justly interfere by force to impose a different Government upon it. The first of these principles may be designated, as the principle of *Liberty*—the second as the principle of National *Independence*—They are both Principles of *Peace* and of Good Will to Men.

In the face of Adams' insistence that this paragraph constituted the heart of his argument, Monroe, who was unhappy over the tone of the note as well as the didactic character of this portion, reluctantly allowed Adams to retain it. At the last moment, however, just before the Russian Minister arrived in his office, Adams, experiencing some second thoughts, struck out the offensive paragraph.[32] In its final form the note to Tuyll adhered closely to the policy formulated in the President's message. The most important departure was the inclusion of the No-Transfer principle, which announced that the United States could not "see with indifference" the transfer of any Spanish colony to another European power. This corollary to Monroe's statement was also included in the instructions to Rush, although it was not part of the message of December 2.[33]

The President's message, as usual, touched on a multiplicity of subjects, including brief reports on fortifications, finances, naval operations and negotiations with France and England on minor issues. On domestic affairs his most important recommendations were to increase the tariff for the protection of American industry and to turn over the Cumberland Road to the states so that tolls might be collected for its maintenance. The principles which constituted the American system (or as it was called after 1850, the Monroe Doctrine) were stated in two widely separated portions of the message. The first, which appeared relatively early, was enunciated in connection with the President's account of the effort to clarify American rights in the Northwest by direct negotiations with Russia. On this subject he observed:

In the discussions to which this interest has given rise ... the occasion has been judged proper for asserting, as a principle in which the rights and interest of the United States are involved, that the American continents, by the free and independent condition which they have assumed and maintain, are henceforth not to be considered as the subjects for future colonization by any European powers.

The second and third principles of the new system were presented after a long section on domestic affairs, when the President turned to the subject of the activities of the allied powers. Beginning with a reaffirmation of America's traditional policy of noninterference with European affairs, he announced that the United States took a very different view of affairs in the Western Hemisphere, because "the political system of the allied powers is very different from that of America." On the basis of this premise he asserted:

We owe it, therefore, to candor and to the amicable relations existing between the United States and those powers to declare that we should consider any attempt on their part to extend their system to any portion of this hemisphere as dangerous to our peace and safety. With the existing colonies or dependencies of any European power we have not interfered and shall not interfere. But with those Governments who have declared their independence and maintained it, and whose independence we have, on great consideration . . . acknowledged, we could not view any interposition . . . by any European power in any other light than as the manifestation of an unfriendly disposition toward the United States. . . .

It is impossible that the allied powers should extend their political system to any portion of either continent without endangering our peace and happiness; nor can anyone believe that our southern brethren, if left to themselves, would adopt it of their own accord. It is equally impossible, therefore, that we should behold such interposition in any form with indifference.[34]

III

The day after the President's message was read to Congress, news from Europe seemed to verify the apprehensions Wirt had voiced in the Cabinet. On December 3, the editors of the *Intelligencer* informed Monroe that a London newspaper of October 30 had carried a detailed account of an expedition of 12,000 men being readied in Cadiz to suppress the insurgent government of Colombia.[35] Understandably perturbed by this news, the President dashed off a note to Adams suggesting revisions in supplemental instructions the Secretary was preparing for Rush, in order to permit the Minister in London to "state [to Canning], that we will unite with the British government in measures to prevent the interference of the allied powers, in the affrs. of So. Am., and particularly in sending troops there." Samuel Flagg Bemis, who read the phrase *we will unite* as *he will unite*, interpreted this letter to mean that Monroe was willing to give Rush blanket authority to cooperate with Canning. Monroe's tortuous syntax created an additional misunderstanding, for Bemis took the reference to sending troops as indicating that the President was prepared to resort to armed resistance and was authorizing Rush to extend this pledge. A careful reading of the letter makes it clear that the phrase *sending troops* refers to the activities of the allied powers in sending an army to South America. In view of Monroe's scruples about the power of the executive to commit the nation to war, it is unthinkable that he would have either made the promise to use force himself or have permitted a subordinate to do so. At the most, Monroe contemplated a willingness to enter into a joint declaration with Great Britain without requiring a prior commitment from Canning about Latin American recognition.[36] Adams' opinion that the story of the expedition at Cadiz was an absurdity obviously prevailed, for on December 6 the *Intelligencer* condemned the report as a fabrication of stock speculators in London.[37] Adams unfortunately did not record the proceedings of the Cabinet meeting held on the fifth to work out the details of the additional instructions to Rush. In the supplemental dispatch Adams informed him:

Since the surrender of Cadiz, rumours have been prevalent, that . . . an army of twelve thousand men, was to be dispatched immediately to accomplish the reconquest. There are obvious impediments of execution to such a project . . . which require time for their removal. And that time may yet be employed, if necessary, by Great Britain and the United States, in a further concert of operations to counteract that design, if really entertained. You will communicate freely and cautiously with the British Government with regard to *their* ulterior views. And while adverting to the frank and explicit manner in which *we* have spoken to the world . . . you will . . . lead the mind of Mr. Canning to the necessary inference, that to the end of concert and cooperation, the *intentions* of Great Britain . . . should be unequivocally known to us.[38]

Although Rush was permitted to indicate the willingness of the United States to consider joint action under certain circumstances, the final decision was to be made in Washington. In a private letter to Rush on December 17 Monroe was explicit in stating that the declaration in his message did not bind the United States "to engage in war." [39] To keep the administration informed Monroe sent Alexander McRae, a Richmond friend, who was serving as a special courier to take Rush the new instructions, to observe the operations of the powers and report on the proceedings of the Congress, which was expected to meet during the winter. The Congress, however, never met, and McRae was recalled in the spring of 1824.[40]

With very few exceptions, the message, as the British Minister in Washington wrote Canning, was "received with acclamation throughout the United States," where "the explicit and manly tone . . . with which the President has treated the subject of European interference in the affairs of this hemisphere . . . has evidently found in every bosom a chord which vibrates in strict unison with the sentiments conveyed." [41] The nation welcomed this positive assertion of American principles as a sign of maturity and strength. Here and there a few newspapers expressed concern that the President's doctrines might have to be backed up by force, but they were a distinct minority. The attitude prevailing among the people was aptly expressed by John J. Crittenden of Kentucky, who told the President: "It [the message] has given us a more dignified and heroic attitude. It has made us the protector of the free governments of South America and arrayed us boldly against any attempts on the part of the Holy Alliance to extend to this hemisphere that despotism and slavery which it has fastened on Europe." [42] The message aroused little comment in South America, although the reaction was favorable whenever it was noticed. However, most of the patriot leaders were well aware that the British navy was the only meaningful deterrent to the European powers. That it was not entirely overlooked was evident in 1824, when Colombia sought an alliance with the United States, citing the President's message as the basis of its request. Monroe declined the offer, for he saw no need to commit the nation to a military alliance when the danger of intervention had passed. Consequently, Adams was instructed to inform Colombia that American policy was fully embodied in Monroe's message.[43]

The British press generally praised Monroe's message, but Canning, annoyed at being outmaneuvered, greeted the President's American system coldly. He particularly disliked the noncolonization principle, although he protested only verbally to Rush. To ensure that his government received credit for its opposition to intervention, Canning released the Polignac Memorandum in March 1824 and at the same time announced that Britain would not participate in the conference on South American affairs sought by Ferdinand VII. Canning's decision in August to recognize Buenos Aires ended all uncertainty about Britain's role in Latin America.[44]

The relative silence in Congress on the contents of the message cannot be interpreted as indicative of either hostility or indifference. There is no reason to suppose that congressmen reacted any differently than the people as a whole. In matters such as this Congress did not usually act unless specifically requested to do so by the administration. Senator Barbour had been willing to introduce a resolution urging the President to cooperate with Great Britain, but this was never presented, since it would have required publishing Canning's confidential letter to Rush.[45] It was for this reason that Monroe turned down in January a House request asking whether he had any information that a European government had opposed intervention in South America.[46] Late in January Clay introduced a resolution declaring that the people would not regard "without serious inquietude, any forcible intervention of the Allied Powers in behalf of Spain. . . ." [47] This resolve was never discussed, for it was submerged by the debates over Webster's proposal for an appropriation to send a mission to Greece—a measure not approved by the administration. Ultimately both Clay's and Webster's resolutions were postponed.[48]

The Monroe Doctrine has had a long and varied history as the keystone of American policy toward Latin America. Only in recent times has it faded into the background, as a result of the imperialistic connotations attached to it. Most of these subsequent developments were not contemplated by Monroe; if he had guessed at them, he would indeed have been alarmed. To Monroe (and his contemporaries) the declaration had only a moral character; it was not an assertion of imperial mission. The notion of two alien political systems—one in the New World, the other in Europe—was not original, but it was essentially the application of the utopian vision of the Revolution to conditions in Monroe's administration. If the peoples of the Old World could not be liberated, at least the citizens of Latin America should be free. The really important thing about the Monroe Doctrine lay not in its principles but in the way in which they were enunciated. The fact that Monroe chose not to cooperate with Britain, although advised to do so by such a strong Anglophobe as Jefferson, made his policy statement a diplomatic declaration of independence.

During his career as a diplomat, Monroe had again and again been humiliated and frustrated by the contempt and indifference manifested by European governments toward the United States. He had once been critical of Jefferson and Madison because their foreign policy seemed to debase the nation by its dependence upon France. In his days as a diplomat the nation had not been respected nor were the views of its government taken seriously. For Monroe to have accepted the British offer would have perpetuated the view that the United States was a secondary power echoing the opinions of the great powers. Moreover, the principles involved were specifically those identified with the United States and not with European monarchical governments.

The only way to establish an American system was for the United States to act independently. By including the policy statement in his annual message Monroe gave his declaration a character reminiscent of Washington's well-remembered Farewell Address. He focused attention upon his utterances as a declaration of national policy and achieved an impact which was far greater than if the same principles had been embodied in a series of diplomatic notes. Monroe, of course, was responding to the feeling of national awareness which had emerged since the war. It seemed as if the nation had finally reached the point seen so distantly in 1776: it had achieved an American identity. In what better way could this be articulated than in the principles enunciated by Monroe in his message of December 1823?

CHAPTER 28

THE WAR
OF THE GIANTS

"**T**HE WAR OF THE GIANTS," to use the phrase coined by a writer in the Richmond *Enquirer* in 1820 to characterize the Presidential election still four years distant, began for all practical purposes during the congressional session of 1821–1822.[1] There had been some preliminary skirmishes between Crawford, Clay, Calhoun, Adams and Jackson (not a major contender until 1822), but the conflict did not become deadly until December 1821, when Calhoun announced his candidacy. During the five-sided rivalry (reduced to four in 1824 when Calhoun set his sights on the Vice-Presidency) the administration was exposed to constant criticism from the supporters of Jackson, Crawford and Clay, who found it convenient to discredit Presidential policies in order to damage the popularity of Adams and Calhoun, who steadfastly supported Monroe's policies whether they agreed with them or not.

The impact of Presidential rivalries upon administration programs was first sharply exposed in December 1821, when the economy drive of the previous session was renewed, now directed exclusively against the War Department. What had formerly been primarily a genuine move to reduce federal expenditures to correspond with shrinking revenues now degenerated into a frank campaign to expose Calhoun as an ineffective and extravagant administrator. Although Crawford's supporters were most prominent in the attack on Calhoun, it is difficult to measure the extent to which the Secretary of the Treasury was involved in the drive to discredit his colleague. Adams, of course, pictured Crawford as the evil genius behind antiadministration forces in Congress, but Monroe may have been closer to the truth when he complained some years later about the failure of the Secretary of the Treasury to curb the excesses of his partisans. If not directly instrumental in organizing an antiadministration opposition, Crawford certainly did nothing to restrain his followers. It was impossible for a politician as aggressiyely ambitious as Crawford to remain indifferent while one rival after another emerged to challenge his claim to the Presidency—an office to which he felt entitled by virtue of his sacrifice to Monroe in 1816. If the destruction of his opponents involved the obstruction of Presidential policies, he had no qualms about granting his backers free reign. After 1822, when it became evident that Monroe would not endorse him, he openly refused to use his influence to defend administration policies in Congress. The bluff and jovial manner of the Secretary of the Treasury not only concealed a shrewd intelligence, it also masked a surprisingly vindictive character. In view of his latter involvement with antiadministration forces, he has perhaps been undeservedly blamed for promoting measures calculated to advance his Presidential aims as early as 1821, when the fault lay with congressmen not identified with his candidacy until a later date. Not all congressmen who ultimately endorsed him had joined his ranks as early as 1820, or even by 1822.[2]

The Tenure of Office Act of 1820, which established a four-year term for every federal official whose duties involved financial responsibility, seems to have been one of the earliest manifestations of antiadministration maneuvering for partisan purposes. Under the provisions of this act, the terms of these officeholders (most were in the Treasury Department) automatically lapsed after four years unless they were reappointed.[3] About this law, which was enacted on May 15, 1820, without debate, roll calls or any contemporary comment in the press or private correspondence, there has always been some degree of mystery. In the first place, Monroe signed the bill without knowing its contents—it was among the many measures passed during the final hours of the session, which he customarily signed at the capitol. On this particular evening, when he signed this bill and thirty-three other laws, all the secretaries were with him examining the bills to see if they were properly engrossed, but none commented on the Tenure of Office Act.[4] The evidence linking the measure, which historian James Schouler labeled "Crawford's Act," to the Secretary of the Treasury rests almost exclusively on the testimony of John Quincy Adams. In 1828 Adams informed a New York congressman that the bill had been drawn up

by "Mr. Crawford, as he himself told me." The purpose of the measure, Adams continued, had been to promote the election of the Secretary of the Treasury by opening up a large segment of federal
patronage to his followers.[5] As supplementary proof Adams cited the
fact that it had been introduced by Senator Mahlon Dickerson of New
Jersey, one of Crawford's devoted partisans. He might also have added
that it had been strongly supported by another Crawford admirer,
Senator Nathan Sanford of New York. The Secretary of the Treasury,
however, explained the bill in quite another light. A month after its
passage he assured Monroe that it had not been designed to initiate
a wholesale replacement of officeholders, but only to enable the President to eliminate unsatisfactory or dishonest employees by the simple
expedient of not renewing their commissions. According to Crawford,
the bill had been aimed at one particular official—David Gelston, the
eighty-year-old Collector of the Port of New York, now grown peevish
and crabby.[6] In view of the character of New York state politics and
the importance of the collectorship (it was one of the more lucrative
federal posts, since the salary was based on a percentage of fees collected)
this was not an improbable explanation. It still remains a mystery why
a law aimed at a limited target but with such sweeping provisions went
through Congress so easily and quite unnoticed. If the politically ambitious hoped that the Tenure of Office Act would enlarge the patronage, they were soon disillusioned, for Monroe (and later Adams) automatically reappointed all officeholders upon the expiration of their
commissions unless they were charged with misconduct. Monroe regarded the measure as unconstitutional (an opinion shared by Madison
and Jefferson), but he saw no alternative other than conforming with
its provisions, for he knew that it would be useless to seek repeal.[7]

The enactment of the Tenure of Office Act may also have been connected with the congressional drive to exert greater influence over
executive appointments, a tendency noted by Adams at this time.[8] Not
only was Congress scrutinizing expenditures and other executive activities more closely than in the past, but there was also an obvious effort
on the part of the Senate to control federal patronage. Although Monroe and his predecessors had frequently consulted Senators from the
states in which appointments were to be made, they had never regarded
senatorial suggestions as binding, nor had they invariably sought such
advice. In those states where factional contests were assuming an importance once accorded party rivalry, it was becoming more and more
essential that senators dominate federal patronage if they were to main-

tain their power. In 1821 Ninian Edwards complained to Adams that Illinois patronage was going to his political rival and Senate colleague, Jesse Thomas, who was a Crawford partisan and frequent critic of the administration. Edwards, a devotee of Calhoun, felt that his service in behalf of administration measures should be rewarded. When he suggested that the Illinois patronage at least be divided between himself and Thomas, Monroe informed him through Wirt that the President did not feel limited by senatorial recommendations. "The constitutional act of nomination is his," Wirt told Edwards firmly, "and he ought to be free, to nominate whom he pleases." If the President were bound by senatorial approval, the appointive power would cease to be an Executive function. Wirt also intimated that Monroe considered it proper for senators to wait until he consulted them before offering suggestions.[9]

The tendency of the senators to interfere with appointments and the President's determination to resist encroachment on the constitutional power of the executive led to a bitter controversy early in 1822 over the appointment of a postmaster in Albany after Solomon Southwick was removed for shortages in his accounts. Among the leading aspirants for the place was a former Federalist and veteran of the War of 1812, General Solomon Van Rensselaer, who had the endorsement of Calhoun and of a number of important congressmen including (so the applicant thought) Senator Rufus King. Under the terms of the act establishing the Post Office all appointments were made directly by the Postmaster General, who did not hold Cabinet rank. On the basis of these solid endorsements Postmaster General Return Jonathan Meigs determined in favor of Van Rensselaer, when Senator Martin Van Buren intervened objecting to both Van Rensselaer's Federalist background and his attachment to De Witt Clinton. While these allegations were correct, they scarcely seemed to justify the intensity of Van Buren's protest (he even persuaded Rufus King to join him in a plea to Monroe to delay the appointment), for he, too, had once been a Clintonian and had no hesitation about associating with Federalists. The suspicion that the New York Senator was interfering solely because he had not been consulted in advance was strengthened when he proposed Chancellor Joseph Lansing, generally thought to be too old and feeble to undertake the duties of the Albany postmastership. Faced by this unexpected political complication, Meigs referred the matter to Monroe. At a Cabinet meeting on January 5, 1822, a "warm discussion" followed when Crawford urged Monroe to grant Van Buren's request for a delay in making the nomination while additional names were proposed. When Wirt and Calhoun criticized Meigs (he had withdrawn from the meeting after stating his problem) for shifting the responsibility to the President, Adams defended the Postmaster General, reminding his colleagues that Postmaster General Gideon Granger had been forced to resign during the Madison administration for making an appointment unacceptable to the President. If Monroe were to find Van Rensselaer unsatisfactory then Meigs, if he failed to consult the President in advance, might suffer Granger's fate. Monroe did not commit himself during the meeting, but afterward he privately informed Smith Thompson, who had been pressing Van Buren's case, that he would not intervene, since Congress had given the Postmaster General full authority over all postal appointments. Van Buren, taking his defeat with ill grace, engineered resolutions in Albany condemning the choice. Monroe, however, remained unperturbed and kept Meigs in office.

The dispute over the Albany post office not only illuminated the senatorial attempt to control patronage but also marked the beginning of Van Buren's gradual drift into the Crawford camp. Although the New York Senator did not publicly endorse the Secretary of the Treasury until 1823, he actively organized congressional forces to combat the "Monroe heresy," as he described the President's policy of party amalgamation. Insisting that Monroe was diluting the principles of the old Jeffersonian party with the dogmas of Federalism, Van Buren assumed the task of reconstructing the old Republican party, an undertaking admirably adapted to his States' Rights views and his political ambitions. The New York Senator believed that parties were essential, not only as a convenient means of enabling politicians to obtain office but also to assist the people in assessing the qualifications and views of the candidates. How could the voters properly exercise their suffrages if all the candidates bore the same label? In revitalizing the party his principal tactic lay in exposing the so-called evil tendencies of the Monroe administration.[10]

II

The congressional session of 1821–1822 had been under way only a few weeks when two distinct groups made their appearance—the "radicals," who fostered economizing measures largely aimed at the War Department, and the "prodigals," who defended the administration's program.[11] Although *prodigal* did not become part of the American political vocabulary, *radical* was widely used until 1825 to describe the pro-Crawford forces in Congress. The term *radical,* according to John Taylor of Caroline, was adopted from a phrase describing the party formed in France after the Bourbon restoration to defend the charter granted by Louis XVIII against the attacks of the ultraroyalists. Taylor, himself a conservative Republican, thought of the Radicals as defending the federal Constitution from the efforts of the nationalists to subvert it in their own interests.[12] Van Buren meant much the same thing when he declared that the objective of the Radicals was the "resuscitation of the old democratic party." [13] By 1824 Radical was used exclusively to designate the Crawford element in Congress, but in its first application the term simply described that spectrum of opinion found among the Republicans most opposed to the nationalizing tendencies of the Monroe administration. Although the Radical faction was based on a solid core of Southern States' Rightists, it also included a strong contingent of Northerners whose extreme *laissez faire* economic views were later to play such an important role in the Jacksonian movement.[14] The Radicals secured an important victory at the beginning of the session, when Philip P. Barbour of Virginia was elected Speaker of the House by a narrow margin over the previous incumbent, John Taylor of New York. Barbour owed his victory not only to the support of the Crawfordites and the conservative Republicans but also to the determination of Van Buren to prevent the election of a Clintonian. Moreover, Calhoun, convinced that Taylor during the previous session had deliberately chosen committee members known to be hostile to the War Department, also exerted his influence to prevent his re-election.

Ordinarily the President remained aloof from contests over the speakership, but in view of the pressure brought to bear against Taylor by Calhoun and Secretary Thompson, who acted as Van Buren's agent, Adams appealed to the President to express a preference for the New Yorker. While it was true that Taylor was personally well-disposed to the Secretary of State, Adams also believed that Barbour would be far more hostile to the administration than Taylor had ever been. Adams admitted to Monroe that Taylor had made some undesirable committee appointments, but he explained that the New Yorker blamed these choices on his unfamiliarity with the views of the appointees. Adams also reminded the President that Taylor had been active in blocking efforts in New York to prevent Monroe's nomination in 1816. This was not the first occasion on which Monroe's intervention had been solicited, for several members of Congress had asked the President in

1819 if he wanted Clay replaced as Speaker in view of the Kentuckian's hostility to the administration. At that time Monroe had advised against a change, since it would make Clay's criticisms seem overly important and also his removal would be displeasing to the Westerners. Although Adams had then thought Monroe's decision wise, now that he had a personal interest at stake, he sought the President's intervention. Monroe, however, after thinking the matter over for a day, decided that it would be improper for him to interfere.[15] With the election of Barbour the conservative Republicans gained control of the House machinery for the first time since Nathaniel Macon had been supplanted as Speaker in 1807. Barbour, who later identified himself with Crawford, at once revealed his lack of sympathy toward the administration by appointing Madison's penny-pinching Secretary of War, William Eustis, to the chairmanship of the House Committee on Military Affairs. Equally displeasing to the administration was his choice of Jonathan Russell, probably Adams' bitterest enemy in Congress, as chairman of the House Committee on Foreign Affairs, which was now dominated by antiadministration members. Later in the session, when Calhoun complained of Barbour's appointments, Adams was quick to remind the Secretary of War of his responsibility for these developments: "Mr. Calhoun, you may thank yourself for it all. You, and you alone, made Mr. Barbour Speaker; and I trust you will not have forgotten how earnestly I entreated you merely not to prevent the re-election of Taylor, who had offered friendship and good will to the administration, and who would have kept his word." [16]

In spite of the vast amount of discussion in the House about extravagance and mismanagement in the War Department, little was done to reduce expenses. The economy campaign reached its peak when Ben Hardin, a Kentucky Republican of old-fashioned views, presented a report from the Committee on Retrenchment condemning both loans and internal taxes as a means of balancing the budget and recommending instead that governmental expenditures be reduced to the level of former administrations. The committee, truly conservative in character, also blamed the protective tariff for the shortage in government receipts, alleging that higher duties had resulted in a drastic shrinkage of imports. The machinery of the House ground to a halt a week later when Hardin's committee recommended that congressional salaries be cut. After this nothing further was heard about cutting the federal budget.[17]

Although Eustis was an ardent advocate of economy, his preoccupation with details made him lose sight of the larger issues. Consequently his committee approved an appropriation of $370,000 for fortifications but refused to include the fort on Dauphin Island which had been deleted in the previous session. The President, deeming this post vital to the protection of the Gulf coast and the approaches to New Orleans, promptly sent in a long special message reviewing the arguments in favor of the project. He reminded the House that by terminating construction at Dauphin Island it was ignoring the lessons derived from the War of 1812. In spite of the fact that the Dauphin Island fort was strongly endorsed by the Army Board of Engineers, Eustis stubbornly refused to restore it to the budget.[18] In May Congress had another taste of the President's firmness in adhering to his convictions, when he vetoed a bill providing for the collection of tolls on the Cumberland Road. It was on this occasion that the President submitted his long essay on the constitutional doctrines involved in the internal-improvements controversy, which remained almost the only issue not involved in the Presidential electioneering in progress.

The sharp separation of factional lines during the session proved of some advantage to the administration, since economizing became a partisan issue rather than a general program necessary to solve a critical national problem. Calhoun was able to check some of the most serious threats to his budget in the House with the help of his loyal supporters Joel Poinsett and George McDuffie. Calhoun's most serious defeat was engineered in the Senate, where Senator Thomas Hart Benton (assisted quietly by Martin Van Buren) managed to delete the appropriation for the government-operated Indian trading posts. The destruction of this agency in the interest of private fur traders eliminated an important element in the humanitarian and civilizing program contemplated by Monroe and Calhoun.[19]

Throughout most of the session Monroe was engaged in a sharp disagreement with the Senate, where the antiadministration forces, benefiting from Van Buren's leadership, were much better organized than in the House. The conflict between the President and the Senate over two minor military appointments was particularly bitter. This controversy arose over the interpretation of the act passed at the previous session reducing the Army by half. Under the terms of this law, the President had been required to assign commissions in the reduced force to officers holding the same rank in the old army. From a long list of appointees submitted in January the Senate had refused to confirm two officers—Nathan Towson, as a colonel in the newly established artillery regiment, and James Gadsen, as Adjutant General. The Senate action was intended both to harass Calhoun, who had selected the officers to be retained in the service, and also to give the President a lesson on the importance of the Senate's power over appointments. Since the chairman of the committee recommending the rejections was John Williams of Tennessee, a Crawford partisan, the list had been minutely scrutinized for flaws. The objection to the nominations was not based on the qualifications of the two officers, but rested on the technical ground that they were not eligible under the terms of the act reducing the Army. Not only was the committee report couched in offensive terms, but it went so far as to suggest the proper officers for the posts.[20] Indignant over this blatant attempt to check the appointive power of the executive, Monroe drafted a message defending his selections. Crawford alone among the Cabinet members defended the Senate and questioned the wisdom of sending a message which, he insisted, would only cause further irritation.[21] Monroe, undeterred by the comments of the Secretary of the Treasury, sent a sharply worded special message charging the Senate with attempting to restrict his constitutional power over appointments. He contended that in these two cases he had not been restricted by the provisions of the act requiring him to make appointments from existing ranks, since the nominations in question related to newly established positions. The issue was hopelessly confused when it was discovered that the passages from the War Department's copy of the official Army regulations, which Monroe quoted in his defense, did not appear in the printed copy used by the Senate committee. The Senate responded to Monroe's vigorous defense of his constitutional powers with a further rejection of the nominations. As long as Monroe remained in office these two posts were left vacant. Crawford, who had a hand in promoting the rejections, was disappointed when the controversy aroused less public interest than he had expected.[22]

After this episode Monroe made no effort to conceal his displeasure with Crawford, who professed surprise that the dispute over the Army appointments had quite "soured" the President.[23] When Crawford made this comment to Gallatin in June, he did not know that Monroe was so exasperated by the affair that he was seriously considering removing the Secretary of the Treasury. Among those Monroe consulted was Congressman Joel R. Poinsett, who agreed that the President was fully justified in removing Crawford, but he pointed out that the dismissal of the Secretary would probably facilitate his election to the Presidency by making him a martyr to executive rancor. Poinsett suggested that it might be better to wait until there was a public demand for Crawford's removal.[24] Later in the summer, when Crawford heard rumors that he might be dismissed, he wrote Monroe to inquire about their veracity. The President, who had decided not to remove Crawford, told the Secretary that the report was not correct. He took the occasion, however, to complain about the open hostility of Crawford's friends toward the administration. Denying any complicity with the opposition, the Secretary attributed the accusation to the misrepresentations of two men close to the President—he had Adams and Calhoun in mind. After receiving this explanation, Monroe asked Crawford to continue in the Cabinet.[25]

III

Before the session began, Monroe had expected an outcry over Andrew Jackson's recent conduct as Governor of Florida. Surprisingly, in spite of the violent denunciations of Jackson by the Richmond *Enquirer* and other papers, there was no repetition of the scenes following the Seminole War. Monroe had named him Governor of Florida early in 1821 in recognition of his past services and in gratitude for his resignation from the Army, since in the reduced force there was only one major general and this rank had been assigned to Jacob Brown, Jackson's senior in the service.[26] Aware of Jackson's impetuous habits, Monroe had accompanied the appointment with a cautionary letter. "Past experience," he warned the Governor, "shows that neither of us are without enemies. If you still have any, as may be presumed, they will watch your movements, hoping to find some inadvertent circumstance to turn against you. Be therefore on your guard." [27] To protect the administration from indiscretions arising from Jackson's penchant for playing favorites, Monroe carefully deprived the General of the territorial patronage—a restriction not pleasing to the new Governor. It is doubtful, however, that Jackson's choices would have been inferior to those made by the President. Since these appointments were temporary, pending the transfer of the province to the United States, when a regular territorial government would be instituted, Monroe had not screened the applicants carefully. Instead he yielded to pressure from old friends, who recommended candidates whose claims were based on need rather than on ability. Indeed, Monroe asked Jackson to house as many of them as he could in public buildings, for they were "literally poor."

The most questionable of his appointments was the elevation of Eligius Fromentin, a former Senator from Louisiana, whose reputation was dubious and whose knowledge of the law slight, to a federal judgeship.[28]

Jackson had been in Florida less than a month when his rash conduct risked a rupture with Spain and exposed the administration to unnecessary criticism.[29] First, he arrested the former Spanish Governor, José Callava, who had remained to turn over the province to American authorities, for failing to surrender documents needed in a lawsuit. Then, after refusing to acknowledge the writ of *habeas corpus* issued by Fromentin on Callava's behalf, Jackson became involved in an absurdly vituperative exchange of letters with the judge. However imprudent Jackson's conduct may have been, it was not without legal basis, for Congress had defined his authority in Florida as equivalent to that exercised by the Spanish governors except in matters involving revenue and the slave trade, which were placed under federal jurisdiction. While it was undeniable that he was not bound by Fromentin's writ, his arrest of Callava was open to question, since the former Spanish Governor, as an official Spanish agent, might have some claim to diplomatic immunity. Monroe, who was resting at Oak Hill, at first took a detached view of the affair, as another manifestation of Jackson's impetuousness. He agreed with Wirt, who had written him with concern about events in Florida, that "Jackson may have displayed some sign of zeal and warmth, and have exerted the Spanish powers too much in the Spanish way . . ." but he preferred to suspend judgment until investigation had established whether the Governor had overstepped his authority.[30] The Cabinet officers in Washington, however, felt less olympian, for they were exposed to the angry protests of the Spanish Minister and fully informed of the unfavorable reaction in the press. They considered the controversy so serious that Monroe came to Washington late in October for a week of Cabinet discussions.[31]

The problem presented by Jackson was no easier to resolve than had been the case in 1818, but the absence of Crawford made the process of agreement less strained. As usual Adams, who felt that the nation owed Jackson a debt of gratitude which could never be fully paid, wanted to uphold the Governor, even if this required reprimanding Fromentin. Monroe, however, was not responsive to the proposal. His patience had vanished after reading the press attacks, which seemed directed as much at him as at the Governor. He was understandably angered that Jackson's thoughtlessness had once again involved the United States in difficulties with Spain.[32] He was consequently not in-

clined to agree with the Secretary of State. Instead he approved a
solution akin to that reached after the Seminole War: Jackson and Fromentin had overstepped their respective spheres of authority (admittedly ill-defined), although both had acted in good faith. It was hoped
that this formula would disengage the administration without loosing
the imprecations of Jackson and his friends. In his annual message in
1821, Monroe attributed the "collision" between the Governor and
the judge to a misunderstanding of the act defining their powers and
affirmed his confidence in their integrity. He referred to the Callava
affair only in passing, noting that the failure of a Spanish official to
turn over the records of the province had resulted in "several incidents
of a painful nature." [33] The President's vague statement on this point
gave no indication of the strong stand taken by the administration in
responding to the protests of the Spanish Minister, who had been informed that Callava had no claim to diplomatic immunity, since the
incident occurred after the six-month period allotted in the treaty for
the transfer of Florida.[34]

Remembering the prolonged correspondence with Jackson after the
Seminole War, Monroe let Adams inform the Governor of the administration decision. Not until he received Jackson's welcome letter of resignation in November did the President write the Governor to thank
him for his services.[35] Although Monroe was careful to see that Jackson
received verbal assurances of the President's continued confidence,
the ex-Governor was angered by Monroe's failure to reprimand Fromentin. Moreover, Jackson nursed a suspicion that his enemies had persuaded Monroe to send him to a post where the difficulties were such
that he would only bring discredit on himself. In March 1822 Jackson
wrote the President complaining that the message had not done him
justice. As proof of his continued "friendship" Jackson enclosed a copy
of an abusive anonymous letter which asserted that the President was
jealous of Jackson because the latter had received more attention than
Monroe when they were together during the Presidential tour in 1819.
In a courteous reply Monroe assured the General that he was "utterly
incapable of doing an injustice to anyone intentionally and certainly . . .
an injury" to Jackson would be "among the last acts" of which he would
be capable. Although Jackson professed himself satisfied, and even
praised Monroe's essay on internal improvements the Tennessean remained convinced that Crawford had turned the President against
him.[36] Forgetting all the past favors Monroe had conferred on him,

Jackson became increasingly bitter. Never again did the President see anything but the angry and vindictive side of Jackson.

IV

During the winter Monroe had been subjected to a peculiarly unpleasant form of personal attack in the form of innuendoes that he was seeking a third term. Some of these reports even suggested that he would not hesitate to use military force to accomplish his ambition. John Randolph, who had been rehabilitated by the conservative Republicans now that States' Rights doctrines were so popular, excelled at this form of abuse, which was particularly common in Virginia. Certainly no one took these charges seriously—they were part and parcel of the electioneering over the succession—but they caused Monroe much distress.[37]

As the session drew to a close, the President, worn out by the strain of the constant attacks on the administration and sensitive to the personal criticism then current, became unusually short-tempered and impatient. This rare irritability led to his only display of temper toward Adams during seven years of almost daily association. Adams, although a major contender for the Presidency, had been subjected to relatively little criticism during the session. Administration foreign policy had met with wide approval, and the President's announcement in March of his intention to recognize a number of Latin American states had silenced some of the most outspoken critics of the State Department. No one had given much weight to Congressman John Floyd's attempts to prove that Adams was hostile to the interests of the West, because the status of Oregon had been left unsettled in the convention negotiated with England in 1818. As a by-product of the clamor over Oregon, Adams became involved in a bitter controversy with Congressman Jonathan Russell of Massachusetts.[38] The dispute originated in Floyd's request in January for the complete minutes and correspondence of the commissioners at Ghent. Since these documents were only remotely connected with the Oregon question, Adams realized that there was an entirely different motive behind the call for the Ghent records, most of which had previously been released. The request had been prompted by Russell, who blamed Adams for his failure to secure further diplomatic assignments after his return from Sweden. Russell was mistaken in this conclusion, for the President had decided not to reappoint him until he had established himself more securely as a political figure in the United States.[39] By engineering the publication of the minutes, Russell hoped to show that Adams had sponsored a proposal to permit Great Britain to navigate the Mississippi in return for concessions in the fisheries—a project Russell and Clay had first opposed, although ultimately all the commissioners had agreed to submit the proposition. The British had rejected the offer, but Russell hoped that the belated revelation would inflame the West against Adams and thereby advance Clay's candidacy. The Ghent documents proved disappointing when they were submitted in February, for they revealed only that the members of the commission had united in making the proposal to the British. They did not indicate that there had been a disagreement among the commissioners when the suggestion was first made. This information, as Russell knew, was contained in a letter he had written Monroe on February 11, 1815, commenting unfavorably upon Adams' willingness to sacrifice the interests of the West for the fisheries. Since Russell's letter with its embarrassing comments upon the motives of some of his colleagues had been marked private, Madison and Monroe had preferred not to place it on file in the State Department. In April Floyd specifically called for this letter unless the President felt that its publication would be "injurious to the public good." Russell, who had discovered that the original was not in the State Department, provided a "duplicate" at the request of the chief clerk of the Department. The "duplicate," as Adams immediately detected, bore every sign of having been composed long after the peace commissioners had returned home. It was only after reading Russell's duplicate that Monroe remembered the original, which he located among his personal papers. A comparison with Russell's recent copy revealed shocking discrepancies, not so much in the statement of facts as in the interpretation placed upon the events at Ghent.

With a complete vindication so readily at hand, Adams was dismayed by the President's reluctance to release either the original or the so-called duplicate. Monroe held back, feeling that publication would seem to make him a party to the Presidential electioneering. Undoubtedly Monroe's fatigue made him dread a controversy that might cast doubts on decisions made a decade earlier. When Adams pointed out that his report to Congress explaining the President's reasons for withholding the original letter and the "duplicate" would inevitably give rise to speculation about their contents, Monroe flared up: "Your *report....* 'Tis *my* report! It is not a report at all until I have accepted it." Controlling his temper with difficulty, Adams stiffly responded: "Sir, it is *your* report, to do what you please with it, when received; but so far as I understand the Constitution of this country it is my report to make, and I am the responsible person in making it." Tempers quickly cooled after Adams commented that he had never questioned the right of the President to decide what was to be reported. He only hoped that the President would allow him an opportunity to present his side to the public.[40]

Adams accepted Monroe's decision to notify Congress of the existence of the original letter, which would be placed in the files of the State Department. In his message Monroe also warned the House that the publication of Russell's letter would prompt replies from the other commissioners, which should be made public in fairness to them.[41] Now that he was aware that the President possessed the original letter, Russell saw to it that Floyd did not ask for its submission. Russell drafted a new version (much closer to the original), which he gave to Robert Walsh for publication in the Philadelphia *National Gazette*. Determined to rout his enemy, Adams arranged for a friendly congressman to introduce a resolution calling for the letters. When this resolve was passed over Floyd's objections, Adams drew up a report (carefully revised by George Hay at the President's request to eliminate the harsher passages) pointing out the more obvious discrepancies. The appearance of the letter completely discredited Russell, whose political career collapsed. Although Adams suspected Clay had a hand in the affair, the Kentuckian was unaware of Russell's plans. As soon as Clay saw the letters, he dissociated himself from his long-time admirer.[42]

V

Although Monroe was dismayed by the eruption of factionalism early in his second term, he did not alter his conclusions about the desirability—as well as the practicability—of eliminating party rivalry. There had never been, he told Madison in May, "such a state of things as has existed here during the last Session, nor have I personally ever experienced so much embarrassment and mortification. Where there is an open contest with a foreign enemy, or with an internal party, in which you are supported by just principles, the course is plain, and you have something to cheer and animate you to action, but we are now blessed with peace, and the success of the late war has overwhelmed the Federal party, so that there is no division of that kind to rally any persons together in support of the administration." [43] Attributing the numerous attacks on his policies to the fact that three of the candidates for the succession were Cabinet members, he reiterated his basic faith in the feasibility of a one-party system. As he explained:

We have undoubtedly reached a new epoch in our political career, which has been formed by the destruction of the federal party ... by the general peace, and the entire absence of all cause, as to public measures, for great political excitement, and, in truth, by the real prosperity of the Union. In such a state of things it might have been presumed that the movement would have been tranquil, marked by a common effort to promote the public good in every line to which the powers of the general government extended. It is my fixed opinion that this will be the result after some short interval, and that the restless and disturbed state of the Commonwealth, like the rolling of the waves after a storm, tho' worse than the storm itself, will subside, and leave the ship in perfect security. Surely our government may get on and prosper without the existence of parties. I have always considered their existence as the curse of the country, of which we had sufficient proof, more especially in the late war. Besides, how keep them alive, and in action? The causes which exist in other countries do not here. We have no distinct orders.

Madison sympathized with Monroe's aspirations, but he did not share this optimistic faith that parties could be completely eliminated. "There seems to be," he replied, "a propensity in free governments, which will always find or make subjects, on which human opinions and passions may be thrown into conflict. The most, perhaps, that can be counted on, and that will be sufficient, is, that the occasions for party contests ... will either be so slight or so transient, as not to threaten any permanent or dangerous consequences to the character and prosperity of the Republic." [44] Madison allocated to the party system a pragmatic function which Monroe, in stressing the ideological basis of party conflict, tended to overlook.

Another voice closely associated with both Madison and Monroe sounded quite another note, for Jefferson looked upon the party question not from the point of view of an elder statesman or a visionary but from the standpoint of personal involvement in the issues of the day, which nonetheless echoed the conflicts of the past. In a letter to Albert Gallatin on October 29, 1822, Jefferson expounded a distinctive view:

You are told indeed that there are no longer parties among us. that they are all now amalgamated. the lion and the lamb lie down together in peace. do not believe a word of it. the same parties exist now as ever did. No longer indeed under the name of Republicans and Federalists. The latter name was extinguished in the Battle of Orleans. those who wore it finding monarchism a desperate wish in this country, are rallying to what they deem the next best point, a consolidated government. altho this is not yet avowed (as that of monarchism, you know, never was) it exists decidedly, and is the true key to the debates in Congress, wherein you see many, calling themselves Republicans, and preaching the rankest doctrines of the old Federalists. one of the candidates is presumed to be of this party. the other a Republican of the old school, and a friend to the barrier of state rights, as provided in the constitution against the barriers of consolidation. . . .[45]

Small wonder that Van Buren, who was trying to revive what he called the old democratic party of Jefferson, found so much inspiration in his visit to Monticello in the spring of 1824.[46]

VI

In view of Monroe's experiences during the first session of the Seventeenth Congress, it is not surprising that his approach to the second session, which assembled in December 1822, was rather cautious. His message, which was one of the most diffuse and ill-organized of his Presidential papers, rambled loosely over a number of inconsequential topics and contained extensive sections of the self-congratulatory material so much disliked by Secretary Adams. During the desultory Cabinet discussions of the message, Adams had objected both to its length and to the trivial character of its contents. In particular he thought the lengthy justification of the importance of the military academy at West Point completely out of place. He saw no reason why Congress should be given a lecture about the problems of disciplining the young men at the academy. He withdrew his objections, however, when he learned that much of this material had been introduced at the request of Calhoun, who feared an attack on the academy, since there had been some criticism of its utility during the previous session. Most of the Cabinet members considered the President's remarks on the Greek revolution not only too lengthy but too extreme. Nonetheless, Monroe retained the passage in which he affirmed:

The mention of Greece fills the mind with the most exalted sentiments and arouses in our bosoms the best feelings of which our nature is susceptible.

Superior skill and refinement in the arts, heroic gallantry in action, disinterested patriotism, enthusiastic zeal and devotion in favor of public and personal liberty are associated with our recollections of ancient Greece. That such a country should have been overwhelmed and so long hidden, as it were, from the world under a gloomy despotism has been a cause of unceasing and deep regret to generous minds for ages past.

It was, after all, a safe topic directly appealing to popular enthusiasms and also one which would not involve the administration in acrimonious rebuttals. The only important alteration in the message was the deletion of a section forecasting a deficit for 1824 if imports continued to decline at the current rate. Both Adams and Calhoun considered the evidence upon which Crawford had based this conclusion insufficient.

Monroe reported only one development in foreign affairs—the negotiation of a treaty of commerce with France, the most substantial fruit of his long drive to establish full commercial reciprocity with all nations.[47] Although far short of the comprehensive agreement desired, it aroused little public interest and was ratified without dissent. Trade with France was slight, and Americans did not feel the same sensitivity about French commercial restrictions as they did in the case of England. Monroe had been seeking a treaty since the Bourbon restoration, when France imposed high protective duties on foreign manufacturers and levied discriminatory tonnage duties on non-French vessels. Monroe and Adams considered these levies contrary to the Convention of 1800, in which trade had been established on a most-favored-nation basis. In 1820, however, when the United States adopted retaliatory legislation imposing similar burdens on French commerce, France had protested that these measures contravened the clause in the Louisiana Purchase agreement admitting French ships to Louisiana on the most-favored-nation basis in perpetuity.

The path to an adjustment between the two nations seemed permanently blocked by France's refusal to accept the American contention that the application of the most-favored-nation provision was dependent upon the granting of equivalent concessions. Since France gave no advantages to American shippers, her merchants could not expect any from the United States. Although Adams and De Neuville began negotiations in 1820, they made little progress in view of the French Minister's insistence that France's rights in Louisiana be acknowledged and the bitter controversy he provoked over the seizure of the *Apollon,* a French ship engaged in smuggling. Although there was no doubt that the *Apollon* intended to use Amelia Island as a base for illicit trade, the American position was not entirely defensible, for the ship had been seized in Spanish waters. De Neuville, who had won considerable respect for his sensible conduct as a moderator during the negotiations with Onís, astonished both Adams and Monroe by the acrimonious character of his protests and his blustering threats of war unless the ship was released. The discussions between Adams and the French Minister became so embittered that a breach between the two nations seemed imminent. Adams, who felt that much of De Neuville's rage was artificially engendered to impede the conclusion of a trade agreement in which France had no real interest, was all for taking a firm line with the French Minister. Crawford, on the other hand, who was aware of Gallatin's interest in promoting a settlement to constitute a capstone for his long tenure as Minister to France, strongly objected to the harsh language used by Adams in his replies to De Neuville's notes. Monroe shared Adams' views that the French Minister's language had indeed been insulting and his conduct rude, but, since it appeared that the protests over the *Apollon* and the *Jeune Eugénie* (seized by an American patrol on suspicion of being a slaver) had not been undertaken on instructions from France, Monroe felt that it was to the advantage of the United States to reply in less violent terms. Consequently, the substance of Adams' notes was preserved, but the language was considerably toned down.[48]

Adams and De Neuville did not resume their negotiations until the federal courts dismissed the case against the *Apollon* and the *Jeune Eugénie* was released. In the spring of 1822, on the basis of new instructions from France which Gallatin was instrumental in promoting, a treaty was concluded providing for an even balance of discriminatory duties, which after a two-year period would be reduced gradually by one-fourth until they eventually disappeared. Adams was by no means pleased with this agreement, for he felt he could have obtained a much better settlement if Crawford and Gallatin had not interfered.[49] The administration was less successful, in spite of Gallatin's persistent efforts, in securing an indemnity for the depredations on American commerce committed during the Napoleonic era. These remained unsettled until Jackson's administration.[50] After the conclusion of the Treaty of Commerce, which was in many ways the result of Gallatin's success in persuading the French government to make some concessions to the United States, the Minister to France returned home to participate in the election of 1824 on Crawford's behalf.[51]

The only important specific recommendations in the President's message concerned domestic affairs. First, he endorsed an increase in the tariff to provide additional protection for American manufacturers. Second, he recommended an appropriation to repair the badly deteriorated surface of the Cumberland Road. This proposal was made necessary by his veto during the previous session of a bill authorizing the collection of tolls to maintain the road. He had rejected the bill on the grounds that Congress did not have the power to exercise control over a road entirely within the boundaries of a state. However, he considered it proper for Congress to provide funds to repair the road: "Surely if they had the right to appropriate money to make the road they have the right to appropriate it to preserve the road from ruin." [52]

The President's message did not produce any sharp reaction in Congress—even his references to internal improvements failed to elicit the usual ill-natured comments about the inconsistency of his views. With relatively little debate funds were appropriated to repair the Cumberland Road. Nor did the troubled issue of fortifications evoke the usual storm of protest from the economizers. Eustis' committee appropriated $500,000 for Monroe's favorite project, although firmly refusing to include the fort at Dauphin Island in the grant. In a Congress dominated by States' Rightists it is not surprising that the Monroe recommendations on the tariff did not meet a favorable response.

The administration was spared the bitter onslaught so characteristic of the previous session not because of any decline in the conflict between rival Presidential candidates but because the Presidential electioneering took a new turn. During the session of 1822–23 Crawford's followers were too deeply involved in defending the record of the Secretary of the Treasury to devise new attacks on the administration. Much of the session was occupied with an inquiry into Crawford's management of the Treasury during the Panic of 1819. This investigation had been set off by the publication late in January in the Washington *Republican and Congressional Examiner* of a series of letters signed "A. B.," in which the Secretary of the Treasury was charged with suppressing portions of public documents in a recent report to Congress in order to conceal irregularities in the relations between the Treasury and state banks.[53] Not until a year later was it known that the author of the letters was Senator Ninian Edwards of Illinois, an ardent Calhoun backer. The *Examiner* had been established in August 1822 as a Calhoun organ under the editorship of Thomas McKenney, former Superintendent of Indian Trade, whose post had been legislated out of existence during the congressional campaign against the War Department. An investigating committee (carefully chosen by Speaker Barbour to ensure Crawfordite control) discovered that there had indeed been excisions in the documents before they reached the printer, but accepted Crawford's explanation that he had been unaware of these deletions. Further charges by "A. B.," alleging that Crawford's acceptance of bank notes not redeemable in specie had led to a loss of federal funds, produced a second investigation which, like the first, found no culpability on the part of the Secretary of the Treasury. Although it was undeniable that the Treasury had accepted (contrary to law) state bank notes not redeemable in specie, there had apparently not been any financial loss to the government. At most Crawford had been guilty of generosity toward banks not redeeming in specie in order to prevent further failures. These investigations, by placing the Crawfordites on the defensive, eased the pressure on the administration.

VII

Shortly before Congress adjourned in March 1823 the pressures of Presidential electioneering involved Monroe in a little-publicized misunderstanding with Martin Van Buren. In late March Monroe had offered Secretary of the Navy Thompson, who enjoyed a considerable legal reputation, the associate justiceship of the Supreme Court left vacant by the death of Brockholst Livingston. Rather surprisingly, Thompson responded coyly, refusing to give an immediate answer and asking for time to consult his friends. Although puzzled by the reluctance of the Secretary of the Navy, Monroe agreed to defer the appointment until he should hear definitely from Thompson. What the President did not know was that Thompson, in the grip of a severe case of Presidential fever, had been trying to coax Van Buren, who was still publicly uncommitted, to endorse him as the choice of New York.[54] After receiving the President's offer Thompson wrote Van Buren, asking the advice of the New York Senator and indicating that he would not accept the post, since he thought the duties were too taxing. According to Thompson, the President (acting on the recommendation of the Secretary of the Navy) was willing to offer Van Buren the post if he were favorably disposed. This was most misleading, for Monroe had not been interested in Thompson's suggestion, for he wished to appoint a justice with greater legal background and reputation than Van Buren possessed. Unfortunately Van Buren took up Thompson's proposal enthusiastically, enlisting Rufus King to write Monroe on his behalf. When he failed to hear from the President, Van Buren had King approach Adams, who informed King that the President was holding the post open pending a definitive answer from Thompson.[55] After extracting the truth from Thompson, Van Buren asked that his name be withdrawn. Having antagonized the most powerful figure in New York politics, Thompson abandoned his Presidential aspirations and accepted the justiceship.[56] Thompson's clumsy attempt to secure Van Buren's endorsement cost him the friendship of the New York Senator, but it is doubtful that the episode affected Van Buren's attitude toward Monroe, for the New Yorker had already moved into the Crawford camp.

CHAPTER 29

PRESIDENTIAL POLITICS
AND DIPLOMACY

DURING THE summer of 1823, Monroe, contrary to his usual habit, did not rusticate at Oak Hill, but—much to the detriment of his health—lingered in the Capital until mid-August. He remained in the city to undertake with Secretary Adams a review of all pending diplomatic issues with Great Britain prior to drafting a series of new instructions for Rush. The nine dispatches to Rush drawn up by Adams ranged over the long-familiar territory of Anglo-American disputes: freedom of the seas, impressment, West Indian trade, the navigation of the St. Lawrence, the Northeast and Northwest boundaries, and such lesser but equally aggravating controversies centering around the fisheries and the admission of American consuls into British colonial ports. To expect all of these problems to be resolved was more than Monroe hoped for, but the events of recent years made the possibility of an amicable settlement of many long-standing differences more than wishful thinking. In any case, it was appropriate for an administration nearing its close not only to attempt a rapprochement with the nation's ancient antagonist but also at least to incorporate into the public record a comprehensive statement of the basic principles and aims of American foreign policy. To Adams this summary, presenting him as a vigorous defender of all the rights claimed by the nation for half a century, would be of singular benefit during the coming election. For Monroe, the instructions would serve as a final testimony of his dedication to the ideals established by his predecessors and since regarded as self-evident truths.

It was hoped that the negotiations contemplated in the new instruc-

tions would complete the work begun in the Convention of 1818, which
had successfully settled several major Anglo-American conflicts. The
negotiations resulting in the Convention of 1818 had originated in a
suggestion made by Castlereagh that the two governments set up a commission (similar to those established under the Treaty of Ghent) to
settle the dispute over the Columbia River region. This question had
been an irritant since the end of the war, when the United States sought
to recover Astoria, the American base for fur-trading operations in Oregon, which had been seized by the British. Castlereagh had proposed
establishing a commission when, after considerable pressure from Rush,
he had agreed to restore Astoria. Considering the Oregon question too
important to be handled by a commission, Monroe and Adams preferred direct negotiations, which might be broadened to include other
issues—notably those relating to the fisheries and to colonial trade. In
the instructions prepared for him in 1818, Rush had been ordered not
to introduce either neutral rights or impressment unless the British
indicated a willingness to meet American demands. In view of Rush's
youth and inexperience Monroe sent Gallatin, who was then Minister
to France, to London to participate in the negotiations, which commenced in July 1818. Undoubtedly the addition of the strongly Anglophobe Minister to France made the American negotiators more resist-
ant to concession than if Rush had acted alone.[1]

The most important controversy settled in the Convention of 1818
was the fisheries dispute, which had remained unresolved since the war,
when the British took the position that all previous agreements had
lapsed, although they had in fact imposed few restrictions on American
fishers. It is unlikely that an agreement on this point would have been
possible if Monroe (over the objections of the Secretary of State) had
not instructed Gallatin and Rush to abandon the traditional American
claim of a "right" to use the fisheries. Without defining the nature of
the American claim, the convention granted extensive privileges in
the fisheries "for ever." The negotiators were also successful in drawing
a line from the Lake of the Woods to the Rocky Mountains along the
49th parallel, but they could not agree to anything more precise in relation to Oregon than to permit the subjects of both nations to have
free access to the region. The commissioners also managed to dispose
of the bitterly disputed question concerning the slaves seized by the
British during the War of 1812 by agreeing to refer the controversy
to a friendly ruler for adjudication.[2] When the British, as might be expected, adamantly refused to make any concession in the West Indian

trade, Rush and Gallatin simply renewed the limited trade agreement of 1815 for ten years.

Most unexpectedly the British commissioners were willing to work out an understanding on impressment modeled on an American proposal made in 1816, when the United States had suggested restricting service on American merchant ships to native-born citizens and those already naturalized, if Great Britain would ban impressment. The British interest in reviving this proposition had been sparked by Rush's renewal of the offer early in 1818 (apparently acting on verbal instructions from Monroe). At that time Castlereagh had seemed favorably disposed, if British naval officers would be permitted to examine crew rosters for the purpose of registering protests. In view of the approaching negotiations, Rush had not pursued the matter. In taking up the American plan, the British commissioners added two new conditions: that the two powers exchange lists of naturalized citizens and that the agreement be subject to termination by either power on six months' notice. Considering the exchange of naturalization lists completely impractical, Gallatin and Rush referred the question to Washington. Monroe canvassed the proposal at several lengthy Cabinet sessions in October 1818, during which Adams and Crawford (as was so often the case) were diametrically opposed. Adams, who always preferred rigid adherence to well-established policy on these issues, opposed all concessions. Moreover, he felt that the six months' termination proviso simply meant that Britain could conveniently cancel the agreement in wartime just when it would be of the greatest value to the United States. Crawford and Wirt, on the other hand, sensibly contended that the only reason for the time limit was to make the agreement more palatable to the English public. Monroe finally decided to reject the provision relating to the examination of crew lists, since this involved accepting the right of search, and to request that the agreement be limited to a specific number of years rather than be subject to short-term cancellation. The subject was not discussed any further in London, since the convention had been completed long before Rush and Gallatin were informed of the President's decision.[3]

In spite of the significant concessions made by Great Britain, the Convention of 1818 aroused little interest in America, for it arrived when public attention was focused exclusively on the controversy over Jackson's conduct in Florida and the negotiations with Onís. The President, however, was highly gratified by the outcome of the negotiations and wrote Rush privately to express his satisfaction.[4] The Senate quietly ratified the treaty without a dissenting vote late in January 1819. Not until five years later, in the heat of the passions generated by the election of 1824, did the convention receive much attention, when Adams' opponents advertised the failure to obtain a settlement of the Oregon question as a characteristic betrayal of Western interests.[5]

II

In the summer of 1823, when Adams began drafting the new instructions for Rush, Great Britain was the only nation with which numerous unresolved conflicts were still pending. The ratification of the Florida treaty and a recent commercial treaty with France had settled the major grievances with those powers. In spite of the oppressive summer heat, with only an occasional swim in the Potomac for relaxation, the Secretary of State labored at the projected instructions and draft conventions with a relish engendered by his own love of diplomatic convolutions and his intimate familiarity with every detail of these much-debated issues. In view of Adams' knowledge and his skill as a writer, it is not surprising that Monroe, who read the voluminous outpourings of the Secretary of State with great care, made few changes. The issues and arguments were well-worn ones with which he was as familiar as the Secretary of State. With the exception of the instructions relating to the slave trade, no new concepts were developed. The Cabinet members were not much interested in these arid contests with Britain—only the proposals concerning the slave trade, which involved a departure from traditional policy, shook the secretaries out of their midsummer apathy.[6]

The first instruction to be completed (dated June 23) dealt with trade between the United States and the British West Indies, now virtually closed to American ships as a result of restrictions imposed by Great Britain after the War of 1812 and subsequent retaliatory acts adopted by the United States. The last of these measures (collectively known as the Navigation Acts) had been passed by Congress in 1820, closing American ports to all British vessels coming from ports in the British colonies in the Western Hemisphere unless carrying goods produced in the colony from which the ship had cleared. These laws, based on the assumption that the British colonies needed American produce far more than the United States required colonial staples, had indeed had a devastating effect upon the economies of the island colonies and had damaged British shipping interests. The Navigation Acts had not been framed in response to any widespread public demand—the British West Indian trade was not only slight (that with Cuba was much greater) but it also concerned a very limited segment of the American commercial community.[7] The controversy over the West Indian trade, which was not resolved until 1830 and then to the disadvantage of the United States, was a dispute in which principles were more significant than the practical interests involved. This question, which had been pending since the end of the Revolution, had assumed a symbolic importance rendering a realistic compromise impossible. Monroe's primary aim (and he was merely continuing the policy established by Washington) was to force Britain to admit American ships to West Indian ports on the same basis as British vessels, a policy fully supported by Congress during his administration. In no other area did the legislature so docilely accept Monroe's leadership. All the Navigation Acts had been framed under administration guidance with little reference to public opinion.[8] Thus, early in 1822, when the merchants of Norfolk and other Virginia towns engaged in this trade protested the loss of business as a result of the restrictive legislation, Presidential influence was sufficient to induce the House Committee on Commerce to continue the existing policy. The decision of the committee, which was chaired by Thomas Newton of the Norfolk district, was facilitated by the news that Parliament was about to modify the old colonial system to which the British attachment was as great as the American determination to destroy it. Although news of the result of the parliamentary discussion did not arrive before the end of the session, the President was given discretionary power to open American ports on a reciprocal basis if British restrictions were modified.[9]

The regulations approved by Parliament in the spring of 1822 opened specific colonial ports to American ships carrying certain enumerated commodities. Although this was a substantial concession in the light of British devotion to the old colonial system, it fell short of American demands. Since Monroe mistakenly considered the British modifications as presaging total surrender, he ignored Gallatin's plea (made in a rare private letter to the President) to accept a substantial concession rather than lose all by declining the current offer.[10] Monroe and Adams, after consulting Rufus King, the author of the law granting the President discretionary power to lift American restrictions, issued a proclamation opening American ports to British ships engaged in the colonial trade, but retaining discriminatory duties and tonnage charges. British shippers were little better off than before. Adams even attempted to persuade Monroe not to yield any ground at all until the British had completely reformed their colonial legislation. The British were understandably disappointed by this cool response to what they considered a generous favor of a kind never previously granted. In March 1823 Congress, acting in response to administration suggestions, confirmed the provisions of the President's proclamation and made the repeal of discriminatory duties dependent upon the elimination of all British intercolonial duties. It was to implement this legislation that Rush was now provided with a complete review of the American position.[11]

In view of the weight Monroe and Adams attached to the heritage of past diplomacy, it was inevitable that neutral rights and freedom of the seas would constitute the subject of one set of instructions. To accompany this dispatch Adams also carefully drafted a convention spelling out in detail the familiar American contentions. Among the most notable features of the convention were provisions abolishing privateering and guaranteeing the full immunity of private property (except contraband) on neutral vessels in wartime. If Monroe was fond of high-sounding phrases in his messages, the Secretary of State now found an opportunity to indulge a similar taste, for few Americans were more fanatically attached to an abstract concept of neutral rights and none accorded the issue a more sacred character than Adams. "This plan," Adams observed of his convention, "involves nothing less than a revolution of the laws of war—a great amelioration in the condition of man. Is it the dream of a visionary, or is it the great and practical conception of a benefaction to mankind?" Monroe, who shared the Secretary's ardor for the project, considered the convention of such great significance that he sent a copy to the American Minister in Russia in the hope that he might interest the Czar, who seemed to have a special affection for such advanced and grandiose schemes for the betterment of the world. The only member of the Cabinet to express a skeptical view was Crawford, who regarded Adams' lengthy review of the neutral-rights controversy as quite wasted, since Britain would never approve such a radical alteration in the rules governing the conduct of neutrals in time of war.[12]

Of all the documents prepared by Adams and the President during the summer, the most novel and the most thoroughly discussed was the draft of a convention to suppress the slave trade. Since the end of the war Castlereagh and then his successor, George Canning, to whom the issue was a matter of passionate concern, had sought to persuade the United States and other powers to adopt effective measures to render the general condemnation of the slave trade in the Treaty of Ghent a reality. In the past Monroe had rebuffed British proposals, since they had been predicated on the creation of an international patrol with authority to search the vessels of all nations. Although it was admitted that the slave trade could not be terminated except through the grant of a general power of search, American sensitivity on this point seemed to constitute an insuperable obstacle to an agreement. Indeed, the European powers proved equally reluctant to grant this right in view of British maritime practices during the Napoleonic conflict.[13] The intensity of American feeling was aptly expressed by Adams, when, in reply to the British Minister's query whether there was any greater evil than the slave trade, he retorted: "Yes, admitting the right of search by foreign officers of our own vessels upon the seas in time of peace: for that would be making slaves of ourselves." [14] Monroe shared this view, and in 1818 he had unhesitatingly rejected a proposal involving the right of search subject to the restriction that ships seized be adjudicated before an international commission.[15]

Monroe's decision at that time was entirely in harmony with American convictions. It is true that by 1818 there was a growing concern over the postwar boom in the slave trade. The traffic had been forbidden to American citizens since 1794, but many slavers, citizens or not, utilized the United States flag to screen their activities. Awareness of the involvement of citizens in the slave trade had led to a stiffening of the prohibitory legislation in 1818, when Congress imposed severer penalties upon those convicted and authorized the seizure of American ships involved in the slave trade. Earlier in the same session the Senate had approved a resolution urging cooperation with other powers to suppress the slave trade, without making specific recommendations. In the brief debate on this resolve it was apparent that many Senators feared that participation in international control would involve granting the right of search to foreign powers.[16] Without a clear indication from Congress or from the American public of a willingness to modify the traditional view of freedom of the seas, Monroe again rejected proposals made by Stratford Canning shortly after his arrival as Bagot's successor in 1819. On this occasion, however, the Cabinet was not unanimous. Both Secretary of the Navy Thompson and Crawford were inclined to permit a limited right of search, while Adams and Calhoun firmly resisted such a concession. Adams insisted that the British offer was motivated by nothing more than resentment at seeing Americans

profit in a trade from which British merchants were excluded. To
soften his refusal the President proposed that in the future squadrons
of both nations patrolling the African coast work closely together.
Unfortunately Monroe's offer had little value, for American patrolling
was intermittent. The British Minister continued to raise the issue
until Adams sharply complained that the United States was being
pressed too much on the subject.[17]

In continuing to exert pressure, Stratford Canning was hoping that
recent signs of a shift in American opinion as well as the disagreement
in the Cabinet might make Monroe amenable to international action.
In this assumption Canning was quite correct, for two forces at work
in the public arena were operating to produce a change in American
policy. The Northern antislavery elements and the largely Southern-
based American Colonization Society—groups usually antipathetic to
one another—had found a common ground in seeking to destroy the
slave trade. The colonizationists, although not primarily concerned
with the trade itself, hoped—as a by-product of more stringent measures
for the suppression of the traffic in slaves—to obtain federal aid in
establishing a colony in Africa for the resettlement of free Negroes.
The first step in the realization of this goal was taken in the spring
of 1819, when a bill sponsored by colonizationist Charles F. Mercer of
Virginia was passed appropriating $100,000 to found an agency to
provide for the return of Africans removed from captured slave traders.
In order to facilitate their return to Africa, the measure transferred
jurisdiction over Africans seized on slave ships from the state governments, which customarily sold them as slaves, to the federal government.[18]

Monroe, whose 1801 correspondence with Jefferson about colonization had recently been published by Mercer, was deeply sympathetic
with the aims of the Colonization Society. As he commented in a Cabinet
meeting several days after the passage of Mercer's bill, he was convinced that the legal obstacles to manumission and the ultimate
destruction of slavery would only be lifted when the "free blacks, who
lived by pilfering, corrupted slaves, and produced such pernicious
consequences . . ." were removed from the United States.[19] But
much as he approved of colonization, he did not think that he had
power under the Constitution to acquire territory in Africa, nor did
he feel that the loosely worded bill gave him authority to resettle free
Negroes in Africa, since it referred only to the return of Africans
captured on slave traders. When Monroe's conclusion, which was

approved by Adams, was formally endorsed by the Attorney General, the door seemed closed on federally sponsored colonization. Crawford, who was deeply committed to the aims of the Society, of which he was an active member, succeeded in persuading Wirt to modify his original opinion and in winning the President's consent to more effective federal action. With Wirt's approval Crawford secured Monroe's consent to support an interpretation of the clause permitting federal agents to provide for the comfort and protection of the captive by permitting the agents to hire free Negroes to build proper quarters to house the captives. Lest there be any misunderstanding, Monroe explained his interpretation of the bill in a special message in December 1819. Since this communication evoked no additional legislation, Monroe concluded that he had correctly grasped the intent of the legislators. During Monroe's administration the agents appointed to resettle captured Africans were invariably chosen from candidates named by the Colonization Society. With the indirect help of the administration the Colonization Society acquired title to Liberia from its own funds and then permitted the federal government to use the colony as a base for resettling captured Africans. In its early years the colony was largely sustained from funds allocated to the federal agents resident in Liberia. It was in gratitude to the President that the directors of the Society named the first settlement Monrovia.[20]

Either as a result of his rivalry with Crawford or from more general considerations, Adams was frankly contemptuous of the colonizationists, whom he regarded as either weak-minded visionaries, office-hunters or popularity-seekers. He placed Crawford in the last category, for Adams' dislike of his colleague made it impossible for him to ascribe any but selfish motives to explain the conduct of the Secretary of the Treasury.[21] Adams was not only opposed to Monroe's liberal interpretation of the law of 1819; he steadily held out for a rigid adherence to the established American position on neutral rights. In 1821 and 1822, when congressional committees were considering petitions advocating the granting of a limited right of search to suppress the slave trade, Adams used his influence to oppose such a grant, whereas Crawford lobbied in behalf of this concession. Crawford was successful in the contest, for the committees approved resolutions recommending that powers seeking to suppress the slave trade be accorded a restricted right of search.

Although neither committee report was brought to a vote, they indicated that a decided change was taking place in American public opinion. In 1823 the antislavery cause was further advanced when the House adopted Mercer's resolves recommending that the United States negotiate with the European powers to condemn the slave trade as a form of piracy.[22] This proposal, which was partially inspired by the constant efforts of Stratford Canning to alter American policy, had the advantage of making it unnecessary for the United States to make a specific grant of the right of search, for pirates were not subject to the protection of the flag of any nation. Adams, who foresaw renewed public opposition when it came to the point of actually allowing the British to search American vessels on the suspicion that they might be slavers, was far from pleased with Mercer's solution.[23] Monroe, who was in constant touch with Mercer, undoubtedly had indicated his approval before the resolution was proposed. Welcoming the opportunity to make a major concession on an issue to which the British attached so much importance, Monroe acted immediately to implement Mercer's resolution and thereby open the way for a general settlement of Anglo-American difficulties.[24]

The instructions (dated June 23) on the slave trade and the accompanying convention were framed in accordance with Mercer's resolution. The United States proposed that both nations condemn the slave trade as piracy, which would allow the search of suspected ships engaged in the slave trade without a direct granting of the right. All ships captured were to be tried by tribunals of the country to which the vessel belonged. The convention, the instructions to Rush and a note addressed to Canning precipitated a lengthy debate in the Cabinet, when Crawford objected to the inclusion in the note to Canning of elaborate arguments defending the American position on the right of search. It struck him as absurd to defend so vehemently a right which the nation was about to yield in a disguised form. Calhoun, who shared Adams' reluctance to depart from past usages, insisted that the United States was in fact abandoning a basic principle in allowing the British to capture slavers on the grounds that they were pirates. Although Monroe considered Adams' language unnecessarily offensive, he agreed that the administration must firmly uphold the traditional interpretation of freedom of the seas, but he wished to avoid offending the British, since this would jeopardize the chances of securing other American objectives. Consequently he instructed Adams to remove the most irritating passages from the note to Canning and to transfer them to Rush's instructions. This alteration would produce the same impact in America but be less offensive to the British.[25]

Apart from his reservations about Adams' note to Canning, Crawford fully approved the terms of the convention. Adams' reluctance to depart in any way from the established American position on neutral rights was strengthened at this time by his conviction that the agreement, if approved by Great Britain, would be used to prove his disloyalty to basic principles of American foreign policy. Later, when the treaty was subject to attack in the Senate on this very basis, he inevitably concluded that Crawford had been engaged in a Machiavellian plot to discredit him. In drawing this conclusion Adams was unjust to the Secretary of the Treasury, whose refusal early in 1824 to endorse the convention was unquestionably the result of the effects of the complete physical collapse he had suffered in September 1823.

The final set of instructions, which dealt with the outstanding boundary disputes, were approved by Monroe late in July 1823 with only minor changes. In these dispatches Adams instructed Rush to settle the Maine boundary dispute by direct negotiations in view of the inability of the joint commission established under the Treaty of Ghent to reconcile the American claim with the British determination to have a strip of northern Maine for a military road to the maritime provinces. Adams also reviewed in detail the background of the Oregon question, for political pressure from fur-trading interests and Presidential aspirants was forcing the administration to attempt to terminate the informal joint occupation arranged in the Convention of 1818. Senator Thomas Hart Benton, Representative John Floyd and a handful of congressmen were raising a noisy clamor that the President act to prevent the loss of Oregon (just as the nation had lost Texas) because of the indifference of the Secretary of State to Western interests. Although Rush was instructed to press for the fifty-first parallel as the northern boundary of Oregon, he was authorized to accept the forty-ninth as a minimum. Since the Oregon question was intimately linked with Russian expansion, the American Minister in St. Petersburg was instructed to persuade the Russians to confine their west-coast activities north of the fifty-fifth parallel.[26]

III

In spite of the resentment of the British Cabinet over Monroe's failure to agree to joint action in Latin America, the prospects for a general *rapprochement* seemed excellent early in 1824. Canning, for whom a closer understanding between the two nations was a cardinal objective of British policy, promptly accepted the slave trade convention with inconsequential modifications and appointed commissioners to negotiate with Rush on the other issues raised in Adams' instructions. To implement the slave trade convention Parliament promptly adopted measures necessary to classify the trade as piracy under international law.[27] In view of the unanimity of the House in approving Mercer's resolution, Monroe did not anticipate any serious difficulty when he submitted the treaty to the Senate on April 30, 1824.[28] To his chagrin and embarrassment, however, it was soon evident that such serious objections were being raised about permitting Britain to search American ships that the treaty was in jeopardy. The opposition to the treaty, organized primarily by John Holmes of Maine, Martin Van Buren and other partisans of the Secretary of the Treasury, was political—an attempt to depict Adams as willingly sacrificing a fundamental American right. Unable to muster enough votes to prevent ratification, the opponents of the treaty concentrated their efforts on promoting an amendment forbidding the exercise of the right of search except in African coastal waters.[29]

As soon as Monroe realized the strength and determination of the opposition, he moved rapidly to exert his influence in behalf of ratification without amendment. Asking Senator John Taylor of Caroline to delay the vote until he could prepare a supplementary message, the President submitted a vigorous plea for ratification on May 21. The nation, he reminded the Senators, had a commitment to ratify an agreement which it had initiated and which the British government had accepted with only minor modifications. He stressed the fact that no basic right had been conceded, for pirates had never enjoyed the protection of the flag. He specifically condemned the proposal to amend the treaty by confining the right of search to African waters as a restriction utterly incompatible with the objectives of the two powers. As a further prod to the Senate he attached copies of the House resolutions adopted during the previous session. All this was secondary, however, to his main argument: "It cannot be disguised that the rejection of this convention cannot fail to have a very injurious influence on the good understanding between the two governments. . . ." [30] The Senators remained impervious to Monroe's plea, ratifying the treaty with the restrictive amendment.[31]

Before the final vote was taken Monroe appealed to Crawford to intervene in behalf of the agreement of which he had previously been an ardent advocate. To Monroe's consternation, Crawford not only declined to exert his influence but also maintained that he had never approved the draft convention when it had been before the Cabinet.[32] Monroe was angered by the refusal of the Secretary of the Treasury, who was still incapacitated by illness, to restrain his followers, but he charitably attributed Crawford's assertion that he had never approved the treaty to the memory damage resulting from the Secretary's collapse.[33] Adams, however, never doubted for a moment that Presidential politics lay behind the sudden outcry over a treaty with which he was so closely connected. At this time Crawford's supporters were particularly bitter toward Monroe, for they interpreted his continued neutrality in the election as indicating a preference for Adams. Monroe, who had endured so much as a result of Crawford's Presidential ambitions, considered removing the Secretary on the grounds of physical incapacity, for it had been necessary for him to employ a facsimile signature for more than six months. Although there were considerable doubts about the constitutionality of the use of a facsimile, more favorable medical reports about Crawford's health induced the President to postpone action.[34]

Monroe's gloomy forebodings that the Senate amendments to the convention would prevent a general settlement with England proved correct, for Canning refused to accept the amended text. Like most English statesmen, he had been exasperated in the past by the American habit of altering treaties in the Senate, and in this case he felt fully justified in refusing to accept modifications in an agreement originally drafted by the United States. He felt, and with this view Monroe was in sympathy, that a commitment had been made and that it should be honored. Unfortunately, Canning's refusal to accept this modest gain closed the door permanently on Anglo-American cooperation in suppressing the slave trade.[35] Shortly after receiving the text of the treaty Canning suspended the discussions between Rush and the British commissioners. The negotiations had not advanced far, but the rejection of the treaty ended all immediate hope for a general understanding on the issues which had so long separated the two nations. A sincere attempt was made to settle the Maine boundary dispute, but agreement proved impossible since Rush lacked authority to accept the navigation of the St. Lawrence (the United States claimed this as a right) as compensation for granting the British a strip of northern Maine.[36] Like so many other Presidential policies during Monroe's last two years in office, the dream of a *rapprochement* with Great Britain was sacrificed to the ambitions of the rivals for the succession.

The labors of Monroe and Adams during the summer of 1823 yielded only one positive result—a treaty with the Czar delimiting Russia's sphere of activities on the Pacific coast.[37] In April 1824, Henry Middleton, the American Minister to St. Petersburg, acting on instructions similar to those sent Rush concerning American claims in the North West, concluded an agreement in which the Russians agreed to confine their operations north of 54′60″. In addition, the Russians, by recognizing the American position on freedom of the seas, abandoned their efforts to establish a *mare clausum* in the Pacific. Of somewhat lesser significance was the permission granted to American merchants to trade in the unsettled regions north of 54′60″ for ten years. In view of his recent disappointments, Monroe tended to attach undue importance to this agreement, which he felt proved that the Czar had "great respect" for the United States. Monroe considered it especially significant, since the treaty had been negotiated after the Russians had seen his message of December 1823, in which he had "expressed sentiments in regard to our principles and hemisphere adverse to those entertained by the holy alliance." [38] Not surprisingly, this agreement—which further protected America's claim to Oregon—was ratified by the Senate with only one dissenting vote.

CHAPTER 30

THE END OF
AN AGE

A LTHOUGH John Quincy Adams thought that future generations might regard the Monroe administration as the "golden
age" of the Republic, there was, in truth, little during his last
two years in office to suggest the autumnal peace and tranquility implied
by this term.[1] After 1822 it can justly be said that an "Era of Bad
Feelings" totally eclipsed the harmony evident during his first term.
As the election of 1824 approached, Monroe's policies were not only
subjected to a constant fire, but the electioneering also struck more and
more closely at the President. Monroe was incredulous, and at the same
time deeply hurt, that his personal integrity should be questioned in
view of his absolute neutrality during the contest. So strict was his
impartiality that he canceled a visit to James Barbour in the summer
of 1822 when he learned that Crawford would be there, fearing that a
sojourn at that time would be interpreted as indicating a preference
for the Secretary of the Treasury. For much the same reason Monroe
declined to attend a ball given by Secretary Adams in 1824 for General
Jackson on the anniversary of the battle of New Orleans.[2] The President's neutrality enraged Crawford and his backers, for they felt that
Monroe was obligated to endorse the candidacy of the Secretary of the
Treasury in repayment (as they believed) for Crawford's withdrawal
in Monroe's favor in 1816. The Crawfordites made no secret of their
conviction that the President's silence indicated that he preferred
Adams.[3] The rancor against him reached a peak late in 1823 after
Crawford became so seriously ill that he was incapable of discharging
the duties of his office for nearly a year.

In September 1823, when the Secretary of the Treasury was visiting James Barbour, he was stricken with a severe case of erysipelas which the local doctor treated with lobelia. The results of this medication (he was apparently given an overdose) were catastrophic—Crawford collapsed completely and his illness was then diagnosed as a massive stroke; for months he remained speechless, nearly blind and immobile.[4] The seriousnesss of his condition was carefully concealed from the public, for had the true state of his health been known he would never have received the nomination of the congressional caucus early in 1824. Not until September 1824 did he resume his duties in the Treasury, and even then his speech was still thick and hesitant, and his memory uncertain.[5] In spite of an illness so serious that friends doubted that he would ever completely recover, political pressures made it impossible for him either to resign from the Treasury or for Monroe to replace him in the Cabinet.[6] The President could not supplant the caucus candidate without making it seem that he was attempting to destroy Crawford's chances by publicizing the Secretary's incapacity. On the other hand the Georgian could not resign, for this would be to admit openly the gravity of his condition. Although he recovered sufficiently in March to supervise his campaign activities and attend one Cabinet meeting in April, he suffered a relapse in May during which, as he later admitted, he was at times quite "deranged." [7]

Of all Monroe's critics the most persistent, and certainly one of the most influential, was Thomas Ritchie of the Richmond *Enquirer*. Not only was Ritchie an ardent Crawfordite, but he, like so many Virginians, bore considerable animosity toward Monroe for the President's failure to accept the constitutional views advanced by the dominant States' Rightist element in Virginia. Thus, after praising the section of the President's message of 1823 dealing with Latin America, Ritchie saw no inconsistency in concluding his editorial with the observation that the "document completely disappointed" him. Why? Simply because Monroe had approved the protective tariff.[8] On April 9, 1824, the *Enquirer* published an extremely harsh letter from William Branch Giles, who still cherished a grudge against Monroe dating back to the Madison administration, accusing the President of disregarding the Constitution in order to exalt the power of the executive.[9] A month later "Virginius" charged that Monroe had adopted a nationalistic program solely out of a love of popularity. According to "Virginius," the President had surrounded himself with sycophantic advisers (all hostile to Crawford), who had deluded him about the true state of public opinion.[10] Equally embarrassing for Monroe was the publication of his correspondence with Jackson in 1816, when they had discussed the advisability of appointing Federalists to high office. The release of these letters had been engineered by the Crawfordites to discredit Jackson by showing his willingness to recommend the advancement of Federalists and to injure Monroe by demonstrating that as an advocate of party amalgamation he could not be considered a true Republican.[11]

II

The bitterness of the Crawfordites toward Monroe was a prime factor behind the attempt to discredit Ninian Edwards, the recently appointed Minister to Mexico. Edwards had been confirmed over the objections of Crawford's friends in the Senate, who maintained that the former Illinois Senator was the author of the "A. B." letters published in 1822. In his anxiety to obtain the post, Edwards had created the impression that he had not written these attacks on the Secretary of the Treasury, although he apparently never specifically denied his authorship. In March 1824 the Secretary of the Treasury submitted to the House a report (reputedly written by George Tucker of Virginia) which not only vindicated his conduct of the Treasury during the Panic of 1819 but also questioned the veracity of the evidence Edwards had given before a congressional committee during the previous session. The submission of the report had obviously been timed to coincide with Edwards' departure for Mexico—it was assumed he would be too far from the Capital to defend himself effectively. Edwards, who received a copy of the report just as he boarded the stage in Washington, managed to draft a defense which he mailed to the Speaker of the House from Wheeling. Renewing his charges against the Secretary of the Treasury, Edwards, to Monroe's consternation, admitted that he had indeed composed the "A. B." letters. To investigate the charges Clay named a committee under the chairmanship of John Floyd, who bore considerable personal rancor toward the Minister to Mexico.[12]

The identification of Edwards as "A. B." made it appear, as Crawford's friends had long contended, that Monroe had deliberately favored known enemies of the Secretary of the Treasury. Although Monroe had never asked Edwards directly whether he had written these letters, the President and the members of the Cabinet had been under the impression that he had no connection with them. Certainly, had Monroe known that the former Illinois Senator was "A. B.," he would never have appointed him to a major diplomatic post.[13] The President was so exasperated with Edwards and so anxious to prevent further friction with the legislature that he wanted to send a special messenger ordering the Minister to return at once to the Capital in order to be present for the anticipated congressional inquiry. Adams and Southard joined to persuade him merely to write and request Edwards to delay his journey until it was certain whether his presence would be required. As soon as the House committee sent the sergeant-at-arms to recall Edwards, Monroe informed the House in a special message of his action requesting the Minister to suspend his journey. Adams' conclusion that the House committee, in sending the sergeant-at-arms, was trying to create the impression that Edwards was fleeing from investigation was not entirely absurd. Since the whole matter had been completely explored the preceding year and all the necessary documents were available, there was no real need for Edwards to appear. Adams urged the President to resist pressure to force Edwards' resignation, for this would seemingly admit that the charges in the "A. B." letters were untrue.[14]

Floyd's committee, which did not complete its deliberations until after the session ended, once again exonerated the Secretary of the Treasury, conveniently ignoring the irregularities involved in accepting the notes of state banks not redeeming their notes in specie. Although the committee did not formally censure Edwards, Crawford's loyal supporter, John Forsyth, entered into the record at the final session a statement challenging the veracity of Edwards' testimony given under oath, since an inconsequential discrepancy had been exposed. The investigators also managed to create the impression (on very flimsy evidence) that Edwards had denied writing the "A. B." letters in order to win confirmation.[15] The doubt cast on Edwards' integrity, even though no specific charges were made against him, placed Monroe in a difficult position. The emissary had not been discredited, but enough questions had been raised about his character and conduct to render him an undesirable appointee. For two days after the committee report, Monroe and the Cabinet wrestled with the problem of whether Edwards should be asked to resign or be removed. The second of these Cabinet meetings—and this was truly unprecedented—lasted from eight in the morning until nine-thirty in the evening with only a break for dinner with the President. Monroe felt strongly that Edwards (if he failed to resign) should be removed to spare the administration further criticism. In the face of Adams' strong objections to dismissal, since the committee had not disproved the veracity of Edwards' charges, it was agreed at the end of the first day that Wirt, a close friend of the Minister, sound him out to see whether he contemplated resigning. On the following day, when Wirt reported that Edwards would shortly let the President have his decision, all hoped that he would voluntarily withdraw and relieve the administration of a painful dilemma. During the second day of meetings, at which the full report of the Floyd committee was read aloud, the secretaries discussed broad aspects of administration policy during the last seven years.

It was at this time that Monroe first revealed the depth of his resentment against Crawford for permitting his followers to attack administration measures. Monroe rightly felt that the Edwards affair would never have developed if Crawford and his friends had been content with the earlier congressional reports exonerating the Secretary of the Treasury. "The range of the discussion this day," Adams commented in his diary, "was over the whole of Mr. Monroe's administration and to the deadly opposition against it by Mr. Crawford's partisans, from the Seminole debates down to the ratification of the Slave-Trade Convention. The President said he thought Mr. Crawford had not sufficiently discountenanced this warfare. . . ." Late in the afternoon all were relieved when news of Edwards' resignation was received. The controversy did not quite end at this point, however, for the Crawfordites persuaded the managers of the Independence Day dinner held at the capitol to exclude Edwards, whereupon Adams, Calhoun, Southard and Wirt issued statements withdrawing their acceptances to the celebration.[16]

III

Among the more unpleasant aspects of the Edwards investigation were comments on Monroe's integrity in quite another context. In the course of testifying before the committee, Senator James Noble of Indiana (a dedicated Crawford backer) remarked that Edwards once told him that he had the President in his power through the means of Colonel Samuel Lane, the late Commissioner of Public Buildings. Although the topic was not pursued, the reference was familiar to all, for it had been discovered after Lane's death in 1822 that his accounts were short $20,000. The President was drawn into this affair because he had chosen Lane and William Lee (the Second Auditor of the Treasury) to administer the $20,000 appropriated in 1817 for furnishing the White House. The furniture fund had been managed by Lee and Lane without additional compensation. Since there was no official staff to operate the White House, Monroe also relied on Lane to handle transactions which were in a sense personal, involving goods and services used by the Monroes while living in the White House. When Monroe was out of town, Lane ordinarily paid bills without first consulting the President. Unfortunately Lane had been careless in his accounts. For example, a shipment of 1200 bottles of burgundy and champagne for use in the White House had been charged to the furniture fund until the error was detected by a Treasury clerk. Lane had also advanced money to Monroe's steward, who was later discovered to have been dishonest. Apparently Lane never pressed Monroe for payment; indeed, he rarely notified the President that a bill had been paid. Consequently, when Lane died suddenly, Monroe, whose own bookkeeping had been lax, was shocked to discover that he owed Lane $6,500 for disbursements made in his name—at least this was the figure that emerged from an examination of Lane's confused records. Although Monroe doubted that his debt was this large, he arranged to repay the full sum to Lane's executors.[17] Fortunately there were no deficiencies in the furniture fund, for all the shortages related to Lane's accounts for money received for the sale of public lots in the District of Columbia.

The investigation of Lane's affairs exposed to public view a confusing arrangement with the President for the use of Monroe's personal furniture in the White House until the arrival of items ordered in France. In the spring of 1817 Monroe sold his furniture to the United States on a probationary basis for $9,017.22 after it had been independently appraised. Against this credit he drew $6,000 from the furniture fund, which he used to defray the expenses of his northern tour. Since he later repaid this sum, the ownership of the furniture reverted to him. Again in 1819 another sale took place and Monroe drew from the furniture fund for a second time for the expenses of his western tour. Not until 1821 was the sale of the furniture processed through the Treasury Department. Prior to that date the arrangement had been a private agreement between Lane and the President. Since the manner in which the transaction was handled made it appear that Monroe had borrowed from the furniture fund using his personal property as collateral, his enemies made the most of the affair. In December 1822 John Cocke of Tennessee, who chaired a House committee investigating Lane's affairs, prepared a report so prejudicial to Monroe that the committee refused to accept it. In the following session, Cocke (a loyal Jacksonian) headed a second investigating committee, which was restricted to a scrutiny of Lane's public defalcations. When Cocke requested Monroe to appear before the committee he refused, telling the messenger that Cocke was a "scoundrel" and that he had no other answer to give.[18] Although unable to extend the scope of his inquiry, Cocke spoke at length in the House, reviewing Lane's transactions with Monroe and creating the impression that Monroe had benefited from Lane's laxity.[19] Forsyth and a number of other Crawfordites took the opportunity to add their own brand of commentary by affirming confidence in the President's integrity—but urging a full investigation to clear his name. All this, as well as the wide publicity given Cocke's speech in the press, distressed Monroe. As he complained to Samuel Gouverneur: "Every kind of malignant effort is made to annoy me, by men of violent passions, some of whom are very ignorant, and others little restrained by principle. I have pursued my system of policy steadily, relying on the support of the nation, and treating every attack of a personal nature with contempt and scorn. I shall persevere in this to the end of my term, and be happy, when I can retire, beyond their reach in peace to my farm." [20]

Shortly before his second term ended Monroe moved to vindicate his transactions with Lane. In a special message on January 5, 1825, Monroe invited an investigation of every aspect of his financial relations with the government throughout his career. The message was supported by two memoirs, the first of which dealt with his diplomatic accounts since 1794, on which he claimed a balance in his favor. The second memoir presented sufficient data concerning the furniture fund to leave no doubt that every cent could be accounted for. A House committee under Samuel D. Ingham, a Pennsylvanian well-disposed to Monroe, accepted the data relating to the furniture fund without question. Monroe considered this action sufficient justification for letting the sale of his furniture stand. A second committee examined his diplomatic accounts, reporting on the justice of his claim but without making a specific recommendation that he be reimbursed. The validation of the latter claim was to occupy a considerable portion of Monroe's activity after his retirement. Adams found all this prying into the President's private affairs humiliating. It was, he thought, as incongruous as to expect a "blooming virgin to exhibit herself naked before a multitude." [21]

IV

Although less personal in its implications, one of the more disagreeable episodes of the session of 1823–1824 was the conflict between Monroe and the Georgia delegation over administration Indian policy. This dispute, which was exacerbated by the devotion of the Georgians to the Secretary of the Treasury, had its roots in the incompatibility between Republican theory concerning the status and rights of the Indians and the pragmatic aims of the citizens of the states where the Indians still held large tracts of land. As President, Monroe sought to implement a general policy, originally formulated by Jefferson and Madison, looking forward to the ultimate civilization of the Indian. He explained his point of view in his first annual message in 1817, when he informed Congress that it was the duty of the nation to provide for the "preservation, improvement, and civilization of the native inhabitants. The hunter state can exist only in the vast uncultivated desert. It yields to the more dense and compact form and greater force of civilized population; and of right it ought to yield, for the earth was given to mankind to support the greatest number of which it is capable, and no tribe or people have a right to withhold from the wants of others more than is necessary for their own support and comfort." Monroe was much more advanced in his thinking on Indian affairs than most of his contemporaries. Believing, as he had stated in his annual message of 1817, that the Indians must be given individual plots of land if they were to be induced to abandon their nomadic habits, he instructed Governor Lewis Cass of the Northwest Territory to make such grants to those Indians declining to be moved west of the Mississippi.[22] The Senate, quite unmoved by these generous aspirations, struck out all grants in fee simple made in treaties negotiated with the Indians in 1817.[23]

In spite of the approbation of a civilizing policy by Monroe and his predecessors, little was done to advance this humanitarian program. In 1802 Congress had established an annual grant of $15,000 for this purpose, entrusting the disbursement to executive discretion. The money had been used for presents in the form of agricultural implements, livestock and looms, although no separate account had ever

been kept of its disposition. In May 1819, as a result of Monroe's recommendation, an annual sum of $10,000 was allocated for educational
purposes, which the President used to subsidize existing educational
institutions—about one-tenth of the funds expended on Indian education at this time were derived from this appropriation.[24]

In his second annual message, Monroe proposed a major revision of
federal Indian policy in order to prevent the inevitable extinction of
the Indians as white settlement advanced. To achieve the goal of
civilizing the Indians and of dissolving the communal ties which tended
to preserve the tribes as separate communities, he recommended the
adoption of comprehensive legislation guaranteeing the rights of the
Indians and making it possible for them to acquire individual title to
the land. In short, the President was advocating the abandonment of
the long-established custom of negotiating separate treaties with individual tribes in favor of a general system of federal laws governing
Indian affairs. Monroe's plan, which would give the national government an active role in promoting the adaptation of the Indians to a
sedentary way of life, met with little favor, for the suggestion that the
Indians be amalgamated into the white community was contrary to
the prejudices of most Americans. Even Jefferson found nothing to
approve in Monroe's proposal, for he believed that it was more in
harmony with the principles of the government to continue the policy
of removal—which, to his way of thinking, required only patience and
money. Monroe's recommendation, which was undoubtedly the only
practical way of protecting the rights of the Indians still living east of
the Mississippi, was ignored by Congress.[25] During the next few years,
as foreign affairs and the problems presented by the Panic of 1819 took
precedence, the Indian question receded into the background. Not until
his second inaugural did Monroe recur to the topic with a vigorous plea
for a comprehensive program to civilize the Indians.

In spite of his interest in direct federal action to promote Indian
adaptation to white civilization, the pressure of land speculators and
settlers compelled Monroe to continue the policy of removal begun
during the War of 1812. The process of removal had gone on so rapidly
in the Northwest Territory that Monroe reported in his annual message
of 1817 that virtually all Indian claims in Ohio had been liquidated
and the Indians moved west of the Mississippi. Within a few years
Indiana and Illinois were also largely vacated by the Indians. The
methods used by the territorial governors and Indian agents, who
were often closely allied with land speculators, do not bear close scrutiny

—bribery, intimidation, negotiations with tribal minorities or with groups which had no claim to the land were all common. In the Southwest the high-handed methods used by Jackson earned him a reputation as an outstanding negotiator of Indian treaties, for he always obtained the cession of vast tracts of land. His greatest success was the treaty negotiated at Fort Jackson when the Creeks—as punishment for attacking white settlements—were compelled to cede 23,000,000 acres of land. Few Americans were disturbed by the fact that the treaty had been obtained from friendly tribes, for the hostile ones had fled to Spanish Florida.[26] Only in the most flagrant cases were fraudulent treaties renegotiated. For the most part the Indians were either ineffective in their protests or simply accepted their fate. In any event, since it was accepted that the Indians must ultimately give up their nomadic life, the cessions could be defended as necessary to the advance of civilization.

The first effective resistance to removal was organized by the Indians of the Southwest, who had adopted an agricultural and sedentary way of life while preserving their communal social organization. Of these the most important, as well as the most advanced, were the Cherokees (they developed a written language in 1821) who held 10,000,000 acres of land in western Georgia. After the war, as Indian claims were rapidly liquidated elsewhere in the nation, the Georgians demanded that the United States fulfill the terms of the compact of 1802, under which Georgia had ceded her western lands to the federal government. In this agreement, the United States had promised to clear all Indian land claims if it could be done peaceably and on reasonable terms.

By 1820 land hunger in Georgia was so intense that Cherokee removal became a prime issue in state politics. As a result of state pressure, Monroe, in March 1820, requested Congress to provide funds to purchase the Cherokee lands.[27] It was not until 1822 that Congress, in response to a memorial from the Georgia legislature, appropriated the absurdly inadequate sum of $30,000. Negotiations with the Indians undertaken in October 1823 ended in failure, for the Cherokees absolutely refused to make any further cessions or to consider resettlement in the West. As a result of a successful self-improvement program, the Cherokees possessed a number of unusually capable and well-educated leaders, four of whom went to Washington in January 1824 to present their case to the President. In the official reply to the representations of the chiefs, which was delivered by Calhoun but in fact drafted by Monroe, the Cherokees were courteously urged to reconsider their decision and reminded of the impossibility of attempting to preserve a tribal mode of life in the midst of a civilized community. Again the Indians refused to contemplate removal. When Calhoun notified the Governor of Georgia that the Indians were inflexible, he received a furious reply denouncing the administration for failing to honor its obligations to Georgia and for accepting the Cherokee contention that they did not have to cede their lands if they did not want to do so. Far more embittered was the statement of the Georgia delegation in Congress, whose members not only accused the President of bad faith but also characterized his policy toward Georgia as "hypocritical" and "dishonorable." If the Indians would not leave peacefully, then, according to the Georgia congressmen, they must be removed by force, for they had no permanent claim to land which they held only as tenants at the will of the state.[28] The President, outraged by this assault, asked Crawford to secure its withdrawal. The Georgians, however, absolutely refused to modify their public declaration.[29]

Monroe responded to this intemperate onslaught in a special message to the Senate upholding the binding character of the agreement of 1802, which, as he pointed out, had been specific in stipulating that removal must be achieved peacefully and at a reasonable cost. Moreover, he defended the right of the Indians to control their lands: "Any attempt to remove them by force would, in my opinion, be unjust." He admitted, however, that it was impossible under the conditions of American society for the Indians to continue to survive as distinct communities within settled areas. Only by removing them to "lands equally good, and perhaps more fertile" in the West would they be able to preserve their communal way of life. Again he pled for congressional action to define the character of Indian rights so that when agreements were made they would be binding on all parties and not subject to modification on subsequent negotiation. Monroe now abandoned as impractical his earlier plan of amalgamating the Indian population with the white settlers on the basis of individual land ownership.[30] His new program was defined in detail in a special message on January 27, 1825, recommending the adoption of a systematic plan for resettling all Indians west of the Mississippi in territory set aside for them with permanent guarantees of Indian control. He also proposed that the region allocated to the Indians be separated from white settlement by a buffer zone from which the latter would be excluded. The plan was to be voluntary, for Monroe believed that a proper congressional guarantee of permanent title would be sufficient to persuade the Indians to relocate. His message was accompanied by a report from Calhoun, with whom the President worked closely on all matters of Indian policy, detailing arrangements for removing 80,000 Indians. In view of the popular attitudes of the day, which demanded removal but saw no merit in spending vast sums on the project or why potentially valuable lands should be closed to settlement, the plan was ignored. It did not even receive the courtesy of token study in either house.[31]

Monroe's last action in regard to Indian affairs was typical of the confusion and uncertainty characterizing federal programs for more than a quarter of a century. The day before his term ended Monroe submitted to the Senate an Indian treaty by which Creek Indians of Georgia surrendered their remaining lands. After it had been ratified, it was discovered that the treaty had been negotiated with a minority group within the tribe and under such fraudulent circumstances that Adams repudiated the agreement. In a new treaty the Creeks still lost their lands, but at least received a much larger sum in recompense than was then the rule. The Cherokee problem was finally resolved by Jackson, who permitted the forcible removal Monroe and later Adams stubbornly resisted.[32]

V

The tariff was one of the few issues raised during the session of 1823–1824 which did not lead to bitter partisan conflict. In his annual message Monroe had recommended that Congress undertake a "review of the tariff for the purpose of affording such additional protection to those articles which we are prepared to manufacture, or which are more immediately connected with the defense and independence of the country." [33] With Clay back in the speakership—he had been elected on his return to Congress by a large majority over Barbour, who had never been popular even with those who shared his conservative views—the Committee on Manufactures had been given a pro-tariff majority. Moreover, the protectionist element in the House was stronger than during the previous session, since the new House, chosen under the reapportionment based on the census of 1820, contained a larger representation from the middle states. The tariff issue followed sectional lines and consequently cut across rival Presidential factions. Even Van Buren voted for the tariff, which Southern Crawfordites condemned. Andrew Jackson, who was then in the Senate, also supported the bill, which raised duties on iron, raw wool and textiles. The majority was

close in both houses, but the protectionists secured a significant victory.
If not a triumph for the administration, it was at least a measure in
harmony with Monroe's nationalist point of view.[34]

The President and the public obtained some respite from the fury
of the Presidential campaign in the late summer of 1824, when General
Lafayette arrived on his first visit to America since the Revolution.[35]
As the members of all factions united to greet the hero of two revolutions with a thunderous welcome, there was a momentary revival of
the harmony of the first years of Monroe's administration. The public
demonstrations accorded the President in 1817 were re-enacted in behalf of Lafayette, whose appearance in the United States just on the
eve of the fiftieth anniversary of the Revolution touched deeply on
national sensibilities. During his year-long stay Lafayette, who was
universally greeted as the "Guest of the Nation," was entertained at
the expense of local dignitaries and town corporations, for it was known
that he was on the verge of ruin. Although Lafayette's journey had been
prompted by an invitation extended by both houses of Congress, his
tour was not a state visit—the General held no public office, having just
been defeated for re-election to the Chamber of Deputies by an ultra-
royalist candidate. Monroe's original apprehensions that conspicuous
official attention to such a prominent spokesman of liberalism might
evoke an unfavorable reaction among the members of the Holy Alliance
were eased when the General tactfully declined the offer of a public
vessel for his voyage to America. By landing in New York and lingering
for two months in the North before going to the Capital, Lafayette made
his visit seem less of a public function and more of a private concern.
Monroe was delighted to see his revolutionary comrade and friend,
on whom, he told Jefferson, time had "produced less waste of his form
. . . than it does on most men and none on his mind." [36]

Since it was desirable to prevent Lafayette's tour from assuming the
character of a state visit, he was welcomed in Washington at the capitol
by city officials, and then, after the usual ceremonies, escorted to the
White House, where he was received in the Oval Room. After welcoming the General, his son and Auguste Levasseur, who acted as Lafayette's
secretary, Monroe presented all three to the Cabinet members and
military and naval officers who had been invited to the White House.
Although the reception was formal, Monroe extended to Lafayette and
his companions an invitation to dine at the White House whenever
they wished, assuring the General that a place would always be laid for
him at the table as long as he remained in Washington. He regretted

that he was unable to lodge the General in the White House, but he had yielded to the claims of the people of the city, who wished to entertain the distinguished visitor. On the day after his arrival Lafayette break-fasted with the President and was later the guest of honor at a White House dinner party which included the Cabinet members, the justices of the Supreme Court and naval and military officers. On this occasion the casual rules of seating at Presidential dinners were altered to the extent of assigning the visitor a place at the President's right. Mrs. Monroe, who had been ill during much of the winter, presided at the dinner, impressing Auguste Levasseur with her remarkable beauty in spite of her sixty years. He found her both amiable and witty.[37]

Monroe's plans to entertain the General later in the month informally in Albemarle fell through, for the President had to return to the Capital before Lafayette arrived for his visit to Jefferson. Because of Lafayette's delay, Monroe was unable to be present at the public dinner in Charlottesville attended by Jefferson and Madison. Not until the sum-mer of 1825 did Monroe act as host to the Guest of the Nation, who spent several days at Oak Hill with President Adams.[38] Monroe went out of his way to assist Lafayette in realizing one of the principal ob-jectives of his journey—the enactment of a generous grant by Congress to relieve the burden of debt which had brought him to the verge of ruin. As soon as Monroe learned of his friend's distress (he too was in much the same position after a lifetime of public service) he used his influence to obtain a congressional appropriation. In line with the President's recommendations, Congress granted Lafayette the handsome sum of $200,000 plus a township of land in the West.[39]

When Lafayette returned to Washington for a longer visit in De-cember 1824 he was frequently seen at White House dinner parties and at the evening drawing rooms. During Lafayette's second sojourn in the Capital, Monroe (contrary to his usual rule) accepted an invitation to a public dinner in Williamson's Hotel tendered the General by Congress. With political jealousies discarded for the moment, the guests spontaneously rose to their feet when the President's health was toasted. Monroe was deeply touched by this demonstration and by the toast pledged by the guests: "Our respectability abroad and prosperity at home are the best eulogy of his administration." [40] Some weeks later Monroe accompanied the General to Thomas A. Cooper's benefit to see the celebrated actor in the *Taming of the Shrew*.[41] At the last drawing room of Monroe's administration, on February 9, 1825, the Guest of the Nation took second place to John Quincy Adams, who had been chosen President on the same day. In spite of a heavy snowstorm the White House was crowded as all Washington came to honor the President-elect and to bid farewell to the Monroes. Even Jackson appeared to congratulate the Secretary of State on his victory. Clay was also there—looking, according to Crawford's friends, "exultant" as he walked through the reception rooms with two "fashionable belles" hanging on his arms. William H. Crawford remained at home to receive an assemblage of admirers who chose to ignore the soiree at the White House.[42]

VI

When the electoral count had failed to produce a majority for any one of the four Presidential candidates, thus placing the final decision before the House, Monroe was no longer the target of such bitter criticism. The electioneering of the rival factions was just as fervid, but they shifted their activities to the halls of Congress, where each frantically sought to form coalitions to ensure a final victory. Until the House balloted on February 9, there was little attention to legislative matters and nothing of consequence was accomplished in either house. Although direct antagonism toward the executive was less in evidence, Monroe at Adams' request postponed appointments until after the House decision in order not to appear to be attempting to influence the outcome by the use of the patronage.[43] Sometime during the winter the long-suppressed irritation between Crawford and Monroe erupted in an angry scene over the efforts of the Secretary of the Treasury to obtain appointments for some of his friends. When the President failed to act on his recommendations, the Secretary came to the White House to press for prompt decision. The ensuing interview, as recalled by Secretary of the Navy Southard, was indeed stormy:

After sitting a few moments Mr. C. asked Mr. M. if he had as yet nominated those officers to the Sen. Mr. M. said that he had not. That he had found some difficulty among the numerous applicants to decide which would be the best . . . and had been requested by some members of Congress to delay a day or two to enable them to lay some information before him. Mr. C. then said in a very offensive manner, something like the following words—I wish you would not dilly-dally about it any longer, but have some mind of your own and decide it so that I may not be tormented with your want of decision. Mr. M. surprised at his tone and what he said looked at him and demanded to know if he came there to treat him with disrespect.

Mr. C. then raised his cane and said—You infernal scoundrel. Mr. M. seized the tongs and ordered him instantly to leave the room or he would chastise him and rung the bell for the servant. Mr. C. got up and moved towards the door of the room and when he had opened it turned round and said to him, You misunderstood me and I am sorry for what I said. Mr. M. said, well sir, if you are sorry let it pass. I think Mr. C. then asked him to shake hands with him in parting and he did so.[44]

Although formally reconciled, Crawford never again returned to the White House before the end of Monroe's term.[45]

In view of the cordial relations which had always existed between the President and the Secretary of State, it is not surprising that Adams discussed with Monroe his plans for forming a Cabinet. Following the custom of his predecessors, Adams wished to retain the incumbents— even including Crawford, who declined the offer, resigning on March 3. When Adams told Monroe that he planned to place Clay in the State Department, the President, apparently unaware of the significant role Clay had played in Adams' triumph in the House, at first raised no objection. Unfortunately, before he could warn Adams that this nomination would inevitably lead the public to conclude that a bargain had been made to ensure Adams' election, the Kentuckian had already accepted the appointment.[46] The President-elect also consulted Monroe about his inaugural address, which he read to the President except for those passages relating to Monroe's administration.[47]

In accordance with established tradition Monroe played a subsidiary role in the inauguration of his successor, honoring custom by accompanying Adams from his home to the Capitol for the ceremony and departing immediately afterward.[48] The inaugural ceremony was held in the House chamber, where Monroe and his family, sitting beside the justices of the Supreme Court in front of the Speaker's rostrum, listened to Adams read his address. In his speech Adams echoed many of Monroe's favorite themes, reiterating the credo of nationalism which had guided his predecessor and of which he so fully approved. In terms somewhat more restrained than those used by Monroe, Adams spoke at length of the blessings liberty had brought to the nation, of the peace and prosperity without parallel in the world enjoyed by the people under a free government and of the need to maintain a proper balance between the states and the federal government as the most effective means of preserving liberty. In his last annual message Monroe had not permitted himself the indulgence of reviewing the accomplishments of his eight years in office. This omission was rectified by Adams, who praised his predecessor for obtaining Florida by peaceful means, for extending the boundaries of the nation to the Pacific, for lowering taxes while at the same time reducing the national debt by sixty million dollars, for strengthening the defenses of the nation by the construction of a network of coastal defenses, for recognizing and encouraging the independence of the Latin American states and for advancing humanitarian efforts to suppress the slave trade. It was indeed gratifying to the retiring President to hear his successor pledge himself to be guided by the same goals on which the Monroe administration had been based. "The great features of its policy...," Adams declared, "have been to cherish peace while preparing for defensive war; to yield exact justice to other nations and maintain the rights of our own ... to discharge with all possible promptitude the national debt; to reduce within the narrowest limits of efficiency the military force; to improve the organization and discipline of the Army; to provide and sustain a school of military science; to extend equal protection to all the great interests of the nation; to promote the civilization of the Indian tribes, and to proceed in the great system of internal improvements within the limits of the constitutional power of the Union." On this last point he elaborated at some length, reminding the nation that Monroe had stressed the need for a comprehensive program in his first inaugural. In spite of his own private conviction that federal internal improvements were constitutional, Adams tactfully avoided contradicting his predecessor on this point, although clearly implying that his own conclusions were somewhat different.[49] After the ceremony Adams returned home, receiving congratulatory calls for two hours, and then joined the throng gathered at the White House to bid farewell to the retiring President. Although Monroe was anxious to leave the capital for the peace and quiet of Oak Hill, the illness of his wife prevented him from vacating the Executive Mansion for several weeks.[50]

CHAPTER 31

LAST YEARS

I T WAS with a sense of relief that Monroe turned over the reins of power to Adams on March 4, 1825. Not only did he welcome a release from the responsibilities of office, but he hoped that his wife, whose strength had not been adequate to the demands made upon her as First Lady, would regain her health in the serene atmosphere of Oak Hill. Moreover, as all Washington knew, he was on the brink of financial disaster. If he were to salvage anything from his estate, it was essential that he pay off the heavy debt accumulated in the two decades since his second mission to France. He was particularly concerned about providing for the welfare of his younger daughter's family, for Samuel L. Gouverneur, whose many fine personal qualities were esteemed by his father-in-law, was obviously not a worldly success. The transition to the life of a country gentleman and elder statesman proved easy for Monroe, who contentedly busied himself with his farm, his books, his private papers, and the pleasures of a purely domestic life surrounded by family and friends.[1] At Oak Hill he again was able to enjoy the outdoor pursuits he considered so important for his physical well-being. Until infirmities compelled him to move to New York in 1830, he rode on horseback every day the weather permitted. At sixty-seven Monroe was still vigorous, although his wasted frame and deeply lined face testified to the strain of recent years and to the effects of several severe illnesses since the end of the war.[2]

Except for a momentary temptation to let his friends nominate him for the governorship in 1825, Monroe avoided all political involvement of a partisan character.[3] Not only did his private affairs require steady attention, but he also made the unhappy discovery that any kind of political activity suggesting an affiliation with anti-Jackson forces reduced his chances of obtaining congressional reimbursement for claims dating as far back as his first French mission. In view of these circumstances, he unhesitatingly declined Adams' offer of membership on the mission sent to the Panama Congress in 1826 and he was equally firm in resisting suggestions that he accept the Vice-Presidential nomination on the Adams ticket in 1828.[4]

Adhering to the example set by Jefferson and Madison, Monroe did not attempt to influence the policies of his successor, nor, except in special cases, did he endorse applications for appointments. It was, he thought, quite appropriate for him to foster the case of Nicholas P. Trist (married to one of Jefferson's granddaughters), who desperately needed a federal appointment to support his family. Responding to Monroe's appeal, Adams awarded Trist a clerkship in the State Department.[5] Although they rarely corresponded and met only on a few occasions after 1825, Monroe and Adams cherished a warm regard for each other. On his first visit to Washington after his retirement, Monroe called on Adams even though he knew that the Jacksonians would regard his visit as proof that he was favoring Adams over Jackson in the election of 1828. It was, he felt, not only an act of courtesy to his successor that he should call but also an obligation to be fulfilled in view of the "friendly relation which had so long existed between us." Adams' appointment of George Hay to a federal judgeship was certainly as much a token of respect to Monroe as a recognition of Hay's unquestioned talents at the bar. Monroe, who had scrupulously refrained from appointing relatives to office, was deeply appreciative of this gesture. Monroe interested himself directly in seeking the lucrative New York postmastership for Samuel L. Gouverneur, writing both Adams and Postmaster General John McLean on behalf of his son-in-law. Adams was delighted when McLean honored Monroe's request, for he knew that this appointment would do much to ease the financial circumstances of the former President's family.[6]

At Oak Hill Monroe worked steadily to increase the return from his estate, which was then planted largely in wheat, rye and other grains, with a considerable portion used for grazing sheep. He continued regular rotation of his fields, planting some in clover, leaving others fallow and applying gypsum, which was then used by progressive farmers. He planned to add to his flock of sheep, for sheep-raising would more efficiently utilize the fine meadows. Ultimately he hoped to increase his flock to a thousand—there had been 360 in 1817. To better his sheep-herding Monroe asked Lafayette for advice and for literature on the subject. Lafayette, grateful for the aid Monroe had given him in obtaining a grant from Congress, happily complied, sending (in addition to two marble mantelpieces for the house) two sheep dogs—"*chiens de Brie*." To improve the facilities at Oak Hill Monroe constructed a mill, a distillery and a larger barn. The working force at Oak Hill at this time consisted of twenty slaves ranging in age between sixteen and sixty-five. As was the case on most Virginia plantations, there were another dozen either too young, too old or too infirm to work. The regular round of planting, shearing, fencing, threshing and all the manifold pursuits of a large plantation came directly under Monroe's supervision.[7]

Life at Oak Hill fell into the comfortable domestic routine of a Virginia plantation, rendered somewhat more subdued than was the rule by Mrs. Monroe's continuing illness and the preoccupation of the former President with his finances. The Hays usually lived at Oak Hill, where Eliza assumed the duties of household management. Indeed, her husband reported, she was so busy in the first year after Monroe's retirement that she had "walked, and worked and bustled off some thirty or forty pounds of flesh and (borrowing an idea from the P[resident]) has increased in value as she has diminished in size."[8] The Hays' only child, Hortensia, also lived at Oak Hill until 1829, when she married Nicholas Lloyd Rogers of Baltimore. Among the most frequent visitors at Oak Hill were Tench Ringgold and his family. Ringgold, a grandson of George Hay by his first marriage, was devoted to Monroe and labored valiantly to obtain the payment of the former President's claims.

The Gouverneurs, whose children were too young to make it convenient to undertake the long journey from New York, were rarely at Oak Hill. Fortunately Mrs. Monroe, who doted on her grandchildren, was well enough to go to New York for an extended visit with her younger daughter during the summer of 1825. Three years later Monroe accompanied his wife to New York for his first reunion with Maria since his retirement.[9] The Monroes were especially concerned about the Gouverneurs at this time, since it had been discovered in 1824 that Maria's eldest son (then slightly over two years old) was a deaf-mute. Consultation with leading physicians yielded only the discouraging report that the condition was incurable. Lafayette, who was in America when Monroe learned of his grandson's condition, undertook to inquire about the possibilities of treatment in France. On his return home, he reported that French doctors would not undertake to comment on the case without a personal examination. Should the Gouverneurs come to France, he offered to accommodate them. The voyage was never made, and James was enrolled in a special school. To the relief of the Gouverneurs their daughter Elizabeth (born in 1823) and a second son, Samuel L. Gouverneur (born in 1826), were completely healthy.[10]

From time to time old family friends and former political associates paused at Oak Hill. Since Monroe, unlike Jefferson, did not become a national monument in his lifetime, he was spared the constant incursions of foreign visitors and Americans seeking a glimpse of one of the Founding Fathers. To some extent Monroe discouraged calls from those still enmeshed in Presidential politics, for such visits could be interpreted as proof that he was seeking to influence the election of 1828. When such visitors were present, Monroe, although he obviously enjoyed their company and the opportunity to talk about his participation in the nation's history, cautiously avoided discussing current politics.[11] With family friends he was more relaxed. On one occasion when his guests were debating the merits of John Randolph of Roanoke, Monroe responded to an appeal for his opinion with more than usual frankness: "Well, Mr. Randolph is, I think, a capital hand to pull down, but I am not aware that he has ever exhibited much skill as a builder." [12] Apart from reticence on current politics, Monroe's visitors found him unchanged—modest, diffident, quiet and, as always, rather awkward in his movements. Egbert Watson, a young Virginian from Albemarle acting as Monroe's secretary at this time, was impressed by Monroe's unfailing courtesy and by his complete unselfishness, for he always considered the wishes and comfort of others before his own. Although Monroe talked freely to Watson, the young man, as he admitted many years later, did not find Monroe's recollections of the past, which were the chief subject of his conversation, of consuming interest. Watson, accustomed to a more youthful society on his father's plantation, found life at Oak Hill restricted. He admitted that the Hays did indeed talk quite enough, but in spite of the fact that their conversation was liberally interlaced with "my dears," they never seemed to agree on any subject.[13] Hortensia provided more pleasant companionship, but when she was away, Watson found little solace in beating Mr. Hay at backgammon or in assisting Mrs. Hay in caring for the greenhouse.[14]

The most notable visitors to Oak Hill were Lafayette and President Adams, who visited Monroe in August 1825. Late on August 6, President Adams, Tench Ringgold, the Guest of the Nation and his son, George Washington Lafayette, started out for Oak Hill in the President's carriage, which was followed by the General's secretary Levasseur and the President's son John riding in a two-seater gig and a carry-all for the servants and luggage. After an overnight stop at Fairfax Courthouse, the party rose at five and took the road to Oak Hill. They were six miles from Monroe's estate when the crosstree on Adams' carriage snapped. Although temporary repairs enabled them to continue, Ringgold and the General's son had to walk or take turns with Levasseur in John Adams' gig. It was a weary and disheveled group of travelers George Hay met as he rode out in search of the long-expected visitors. At Oak Hill Lafayette and his party were greeted by Monroe and Eliza Hay, who was acting as chatelaine during her mother's absence in New York. The only other guest was Dr. James W. Wallace (described by Adams as an "eccentric personage"), an old friend of the Monroes who had lived with them during the previous winter as a family physician. During Lafayette's two-day visit there was a constant stream of visitors, who appeared in droves in spite of heat so intense that Monroe and his guests were compelled to remain indoors until evening. On the ninth Monroe joined Lafayette and Adams at the public dinner in honor of the Guest of the Nation held under a canopy on the courthouse square of Leesburg. After dinner the party paused at the home of W. T. T. Mason, a relative of Dr. Wallace's, where to Adams' dismay a double christening had been arranged. With good grace he joined Monroe in standing sponsor to Mary Louise Mason, while the General filled the same role for Mary Lafayette Mason. After a sweltering night at Ludwell Lee's home (Belmont), where Adams and Monroe were quartered in the same bedchamber, Adams and the General headed for Washington, while Monroe rode home.[15]

Monroe and Lafayette met again two weeks later in Albemarle, during the General's farewell visit to Jefferson. This time Monroe was able to participate in the ceremonies honoring Lafayette, attending the dinner held in the Rotunda by the students and faculty of the University. It was on this occasion that Monroe saw Jefferson for the last time, when he and Madison went to see their old friend, now grown extremely frail. When Lafayette left Albemarle to return to Washington, Monroe accompanied him. The journey was broken by a visit to Montpelier and by dinners and balls in Culpeper and Warrenton. Chief Justice Marshall, who attended the Warrenton dinner, rode as far as Oak Hill with Monroe and Lafayette. Lingering only for the night at Oak Hill, the General departed for Washington the next morning. Although they corresponded frequently, this was the last time the two revolutionary comrades saw one another.[16]

II

During Monroe's retirement his friendship with Madison intensified. It was only when these two friends of four decades were together that Monroe's habitual gravity gave way to a more youthful and carefree manner.[17] When he was with Madison, Monroe seemed to recapture something of his youth, talking and laughing without restraint. There was indeed something of a boyish escapade in the ramble they took at Monticello during the summer of 1828 when Madison lost a pair of shoe buckles (no doubt of a long-vanished fashion), which Monroe promptly replaced as soon as he returned to Oak Hill.[18] Their reunions were frequent, for Monroe usually went to Charlottesville twice a year to attend the meetings of the Board of Visitors of the newly opened University of Virginia. Invariably he lingered for several days at Montpelier with Madison, who had been chosen Rector of the University after Jefferson's death in 1826. Until his health failed in 1830, Monroe was regularly present for the sessions of the Visitors and joined his colleagues in presiding over the annual July examinations administered by the faculty to the students.

Monroe's participation in the management of the University during the difficult early years was undertaken in part as a labor of love to the memory of Jefferson, who had devoted the last decade of his life to the establishment of the University. Although Monroe had been a member of the original board of Central College (the predecessor of the University) and had presided over the Masonic ceremonies held when the cornerstone of the first building was laid in October 1817, the demands of the Presidency prevented him from continuing as a board member. Reappointed after his retirement, he eagerly joined Madison, Joseph C. Cabell, Chapman Johnson (an old associate), and the other members of the Board of Visitors in making Jefferson's dream a reality.[19] The presence of three former Presidents on the Board was indeed remarkable, and (as John Adams observed) the "world will expect something very great and very new" from "such a noble triumvirate." [20] Much about the University was assuredly new, but during the early years it seemed to promise little that was great. Among the novelties introduced by Jefferson was a code of discipline enforced by the students. This radical experiment proved ill-suited to conditions at the University, for the students were too young and too undisciplined to operate such a code. Within six months after the University opened, the system broke down, as students disrupted classes, assaulted professors and rioted. In the face of these disorders, which brought threats of resignation from the professors, who had been recruited in Europe with great difficulty, a rigid set of rules under faculty enforcement was established. Monroe was not present at the Board meeting when the new disciplinary code was drafted, but he was placed on a committee with Chapman Johnson to draw up a new plan of government for the University.[21] Collecting data from other institutions—including West Point, which had experienced severe disciplinary problems—he submitted a report to the Board of Visitors in 1830.

Monroe began his report by observing that the government of a university was not unlike parental authority and must be so organized as to ensure that the students applied themselves to their studies, attended lectures and showed respect toward the professors. Moreover, they must be restrained from dissipation, drinking, gaming and frequenting taverns. Supervision of this kind could be given neither by the Board nor by the professors, for it tended to distract them from their primary task of teaching and preparing lectures. Monroe also felt that the custom of electing a chairman from the faculty to act as an administrative officer created friction among the professors. To improve the over-all operation of the University and establish a satisfactory system of discipline, Monroe recommended that two new officers be added to the staff. The first, to be called the president (he also suggested Superintendent or Warden), would be in charge of the operation of the University and be directly responsible to the Visitors. Although he would preside at faculty meetings, the president would have no direct control over the professors except through the action of the Visitors. The second official would be in charge of discipline and work under the direction of the president. Monroe suggested that this office might be combined with the post of military instructor, for the report envisaged an enlargement of the existing program of military instruction. Military training struck Monroe as one of the most effective ways of keeping the students occupied during their idle hours. His report was never acted upon by the Board of Visitors, for the finances of the University did not permit the addition of two new staff members. Moreover, Madison, who exercised a dominant influence on policy, had little enthusiasm for military training as a basic part of the curriculum.[22]

III

The management of Oak Hill, family concerns and the affairs of the University occupied much of Monroe's time, but his most intensive energies were directed toward lifting the debt of $75,000 which burdened his estate.[23] His financial plight—so serious by the end of his second term that a reduction of the scale of official entertaining had been necessary—had reached a critical state by 1825.[24] He feared that unless this debt were liquidated he might lose all his property. He believed he could obtain relief from the most pressing debts and save Oak Hill if he could obtain reimbursement for expenses (plus interest) dating back to his first mission to France, and if he could sell the Albemarle property at a fair price. The claims against the government had been left unsettled, since he could scarcely pass upon them while serving either as Secretary of State or as President. In the summer of 1825 his expectation of easing his burden received a major setback when he failed to sell his 3,500-acre estate in Albemarle. The offers for the property were so far below the valuation of $67,000 which appraisers had placed on Highland that he withdrew it from the market.[25] His need for money was so great, however, that he parted with 900 acres of the best land for twenty dollars an acre, even though this sale diminished the value of the residue. The proceeds from this sale were used to scale down the debt held by the Bank of the United States to $25,000.[26]

His failure to dispose of Highland made it necessary to rely primarily on congressional action to reimburse him for his unsettled claims.[27] On several occasions before his retirement Monroe had vaguely alluded to sums still due from past services, but the exact amount was not specified until January 1825, when, in a special message, he invited Congress to scrutinize all his financial transactions with the government since 1794. In response to his request, a House committee was appointed to obtain detailed information from the President. After receiving these data, which established the President's claim at $53,000, the committee reported the sum to the House without a specific recommendation. The facts Monroe had presented for consideration were indeed complex, relating to transactions of the past thirty years. First, he requested the payment of $2,750 to cover his salary from January 1, 1797, when he took leave of the French government until his departure from Bordeaux on April 20, 1797. This sum had not been allowed by the Washington administration on the grounds that his mission terminated with his recall. Monroe cited in justification the usual practice whereby returning Ministers were permitted to select the date for the official termination of their services. He also sought a reimbursement of $3,515 for contingent expenses during his first French mission. He had originally been allowed $110.71, much less than the sum granted to Rufus King during a similar time period in London. Monroe based the claim to the larger sum on the fact that he had been obliged to make unusual expenditures to assist Americans in France. The next claim was still more complicated. In 1803, when Monroe had gone to France the second time, Jefferson had not granted him an outfit, but Madison had recognized the validity of this claim in 1810. He now requested $4,555 to cover interest on the outfit (equivalent to a year's salary of $9,000) for the period 1803–1810. In short, he was seeking reimbursement for the money he might have made on the capital sum of $9,000 if it had been at his disposal for seven years prior to 1810. The largest figure in his statement was $10,000 for extraordinary expenses during his residence in England. His justification for this sum rested on the the contention that his sojourn in England, which had been extended to three years, had been intended originally as temporary and consequently he had been at much greater expense for living arangements than if he had arranged for a prolonged stay from the first. These sums, together with a number of lesser items, brought the total (with interest) to $53,000. The fact that diplomatic accounts often went unsettled for many years was not unusual, and most congressmen agreed that Monroe's official position had been an obstacle in the way of earlier action. Nor were these demands in themselves without precedent; however, many questioned the obligation of the government to pay interest on an account left unsettled by the claimant. In Monroe's case the interest, amounting to $30,266, constituted the larger portion of the claim.[28]

After Congress failed to reimburse him before adjourning in the spring of 1825, Monroe, pressing his granddaughter Hortensia into service as a copyist, began compiling more detailed evidence to bolster his claims. Aware of the importance of support from leaders hostile to the administration, for President Adams was unable to command a majority in Congress, Monroe turned to Andrew Jackson, sending him copies of the committee report and the relevant documents. He did this, he told the General, because he was "anxious that the subject be well understood in all its parts, and especially by those for whose good opinion I entertain the highest regard." He also sought the intervention of Postmaster General John McLean, a Jackson supporter, whose good offices would be invaluable. Although Jackson never seems to have interested himself in Monroe's claim, McLean, who owed his appointment to Monroe, did everything he could to foster the interests of the former President.[29]

Throughout the winter of 1825–1826, Monroe anxiously watched the progress of his claims from Oak Hill. The outlook at first seemed discouraging, for his accounts were referred to the Committee on Claims, which was notoriously unsympathetic to private claimants; but he took heart late in December after his friends secured the appointment of a select committee under the chairmanship of Samuel D. Ingham, a Pennsylvanian friendly to the former President. In order to mollify those who considered Monroe's demands excessive, Ingham prepared a report disallowing the items most certain to provoke objections. He not only eliminated the claim for interest on the outfit for the second mission to France, but he cut the over-all interest charges. The sums requested for contingent expenses on the various missions were also deleted. Ingham recommended that the former President be paid $29,513 in principal and interest in satisfaction of his claims against the United States.[30] Monroe was shown a copy of the report before it was submitted, but neither his protests nor the efforts of Samuel L. Gouverneur, who had gone to the capital to lobby in his father-in-law's behalf, persuaded Ingham to restore the omissions.[31] Ingham's revisions failed to satisfy the House, which enacted the bill only after eliminating all interest charges and fixing the total reimbursement at $15,900.

The hostility toward these claims was compounded of several elements. Many congressmen not only felt that Monroe had no right to expect interest on accounts so long unsettled but they were also uneasy at the prospect of establishing a costly precedent. Moreover, as Ringgold informed Monroe while the bill was pending, many Jacksonians and

Crawfordites, convinced that Monroe had favored Adams in 1824, were still inimical to him. To counteract these reports, Monroe at once penned a reply to Ringgold intended for general circulation among the members of Congress, asserting that he had remained impartial through the recent election. As he reminded Ringgold, he had never done anything to injure Crawford's chances, but on the contrary had continued the Secretary of the Treasury in office during his illness in spite of great pressure for his removal. As to Jackson, Monroe noted that he had always been one of the General's most constant admirers and that he had given the General his full support after the Seminole War during the public outcry over Jackson's conduct. In this letter he touched briefly upon the real reason behind his appeal to Congress—the desperate state of his finances.[32] Fortunately for Monroe, a kindlier disposition prevailed in the Senate, where Hugh L. White (a close associate of Andrew Jackson) restored the interest payment recommended by the Ingham committee. Yielding to the Senate's insistence upon the amendment, the House approved the payment of $29,513 the day before the session ended.[33]

Although he had been deeply preoccupied with his own concerns during the session, Monroe was not indifferent to Jefferson's similar plight. Late in 1825, Jefferson's personal finances were in such a state that he appealed to the legislature for permission to dispose of Monticello in a public lottery. Not merely content with commiserating with his old friend, whose embarrassments Monroe above all could appreciate, he urged his son-in-law to do everything he could to promote the sale of tickets in New York, if the lottery were authorized.[34]

Monroe did not by any means regard the bill enacted in the spring of 1826 as a final disposition of his accounts, in spite of the declaration that the payment was made in satisfaction of all his claims. If his need for money had not been so great, he would have declined the sum voted by Congress.[35] Although the appropriation relieved the most immediate pressures, the amount fell so far short of his anticipation that it was now all the more imperative to dispose of the residue of his Albemarle property. Hoping to force purchasers into competition with one another, he arranged to sell Highland at auction in July 1826. When none of the bids matched his minimum price, he withdrew it from the sale.[36] With great reluctance, he turned over all but 707 acres of Highland to the Bank of the United States to discharge his debt of $25,000. He considered the property worth much more than this, but the bankers were not so sanguine.[37] The board of the Washington branch of the Bank accepted the property only because it believed "it to be good policy to treat this distinguished citizen and old servant of the public, with liberality and indulgence. . . ." The only other course open to the Bank was to bring suit against a former President for the repayment of the loan. Undoubtedly Biddle's long friendship with Monroe smoothed the way for an arrangement somewhat contrary to the policies of the Bank, which did not consider Virginia real estate a sound investment.[38] From the sale of the slaves at Highland, Monroe realized $5,000, which was used to reduce his debt to John Jacob Astor.[39]

By the end of 1826 Monroe had paid off some of his larger obligations, but his affairs were still so precarious that he had no recourse but to seek full reimbursement of his accounts from Congress.[40] In renewing these efforts Monroe was motivated both by the need for money and by a determination to achieve public vindication. Always hypersensitive to criticism, he regarded the deletion of specific charges as a reflection on his integrity. Only when these items had been paid would his character be re-established. Until a further grant was made in 1831 the claims seldom left his thoughts, and when he alluded to them in his letters a querulous note was often apparent. He renewed his quest in November 1826 with a memoir in the *National Intelligencer*. After reviewing his public services, undertaken (as he constantly reiterated) in the face of serious personal sacrifices and only in response to irresistible public demand, he presented further verification for the sums rejected by Congress. Although not advanced as a basis for reimbursement, he also informed the public of the serious loss which he had suffered when he purchased a house in Paris in 1795 with the idea of selling it at cost to the United States as a permanent residence for American Ministers. His subsequent difficulties with the Washington administration, however, had frustrated this project. In selling the house he experienced a loss of $10,000, for the purchaser, taking advantage of Monroe's departure, never paid the balance. He also alluded, for the first time, to services he had rendered as Secretary of War by borrowing money over his own signature, an action which had not only relieved the government in a period of crisis but had also resulted in considerable savings on interest and other charges. With the parallel in mind of the compensation granted by Congress to Daniel D. Tompkins for similar arrangements, Monroe concluded by observing that these loans "ought not to be lost sight of in the consideration of claims which he deems just, when resting on their separate and intrinsic merits." His claims were bolstered by affidavits and letters from individuals familiar with the circumstances. Although John McLean, who arranged for the publication of the memoir, considered it a satisfactory justification for all Monroe's accounts, he nonetheless warned the former President that little could be expected from the Congress assembling in 1826, since its membership was the same as that of the preceding session. McLean only hoped that the following Congress, due to meet in 1827, would be more favorably disposed.[41]

In spite of McLean's optimism, two years elapsed before Monroe's case was again considered. This delay was a by-product of the bitter conflict between Jackson and Adams for the Presidency. Monroe, who was quite aware that the success of his claims depended on the good will of the Jacksonians, wanted to remain absolutely neutral during the election. Unfortunately the activities of his friends, many of whom were devoted to Adams, tended to implicate him in anti-Jackson activities. Early in 1827, Monroe was inadvertently drawn into the electioneering as a result of comments made by Samuel S. Southard, Adams' Secretary of the Navy, at a wine-drinking party. Southard, in the course of some critical references to Jackson, asserted that Monroe really deserved the credit for the victory at New Orleans, for the General had only departed from Mobile after imperative orders from Washington. The story reached Jackson in such a garbled form that he believed Monroe had been present during the discussion. Distinctly cool to Monroe since his tenure as Governor of Florida, Jackson was only too willing to believe John H. Eaton and other advisers who insisted that Monroe would stop at nothing to prevent his election.[42] The Jacksonians struck back in unsigned newspaper squibs suggesting that Monroe had neglected to supply the General with materials essential for the defense of the city and that New Orleans had been saved only because of the foresight and single-handed efforts of General Jackson. Much more disturbing than these anonymous articles was Hugh L. White's speech in January 1817 at a dinner in honor of Jackson. As the General listened, White informed the guests—and his remarks were widely printed in the newspapers—that the victory at New Orleans was solely Jackson's work, for the Secretary of War had neglected to send him both men and supplies. Gathering data from his own papers and recruiting Ringgold to examine War Department records, Monroe sent White a detailed statement showing the number of troops ordered to

New Orleans, and on hand when Jackson arrived. He admitted that the arms shipped down the Mississippi had not arrived in time, but this was by no means the fault of the War Department, which had dispatched them well in advance of the battle.[43] Monroe was understandably distressed by White's reply, conceding that the Secretary of War could not be blamed for the delay in the shipment of the arms but still insisting that there had actually been "a want of attention, or neglect, if you please, in not hastening the arms to Pittsburg in due time." [44] With his reputation at stake, Monroe was ready to publish the correspondence relating to the shipment of arms, but McLean and Ringgold dissuaded him, pointing out that this would indeed involve him in the electioneering against Jackson, which Ringgold felt had been Southard's objective from the beginning.[45] Certainly Southard and other Adams supporters were doing everything they could to enlist Monroe's support. In December, Southard and John Taliaferro proposed that Monroe accept the Vice-Presidential nomination on the Adams ticket, but Southard's enticement of a "pleasant employment and a handsome yearly income for the next four years" was not sufficient to induce him to agree.[46]

Monroe was again entangled in the electioneering when he and Madison were named electors on the Adams ticket in Virginia.[47] This action had been undertaken in spite of a letter from Monroe requesting that he not be chosen, since he intended to remain neutral. Madison, who also wished to avoid involvement in current political rivalries, was as distressed as his friend. The position of the two former Presidents became more and more awkward when the Adams committee failed to send them official notification. Both wished to withdraw, but felt that resigning before formal notification would imply personal criticism of those responsible. The fact that many Adams backers were friends of long standing made their situation particularly difficult. Unfortunately, the long delay gave currency to reports that they were endorsing Adams for re-election.[48] Not until the middle of February did Monroe receive official notification. Promptly resigning, he repeated his wish to remain neutral, reiterating his conviction that former Presidents should abstain from political activity except in great national emergencies. For his part, Madison rested his withdrawal on his complete retirement from the political arena. As he told Monroe, he preferred not to express himself on the probable usefulness of former chief executives in national crises, for success on the part of an ex-President might not be pleasing to the incumbent.[49] Until the election ended with Jackson's victory Monroe's claims were necessarily dormant.

Once the election was over Monroe and his friends renewed the campaign on his behalf. To win wider public support for his cause, Monroe had already arranged for the printing of 3,000 copies of his memoir of November 1825 to be distributed to political leaders, former associates and legislators.[50] In the meantime, friends in Albemarle circulated a petition recommending congressional action on the claims.[51] The petition went beyond Monroe's previous demands in proposing the payment of a commission on the loans negotiated in 1814. The petitioners made much of Monroe's impoverishment as a result of his unselfish devotion to the interests of the nation. The petition and memoir were turned over to a select committee under the chairmanship of Representative William Cabell Rives of Albemarle County—a Jacksonian and close friend of both Monroe and Madison. On February 11, 1829, the Rives committee recommended that Monroe be awarded $60,000, a figure which included the claims previously rejected plus $25,000 as a commission on the loans he had raised while Secretary of War. Several new claims were also allowed—most notably the sum of $2,423.52 to reimburse him for money advanced to Paine which had never been repaid. In spite of Rives' efforts, the report was postponed until the next session.[52] Monroe and his friends blamed this delay on Jackson's animosity toward the former President. This conclusion seemed verified when, shortly after his inaugural, Jackson removed George Hay's grandson, Charles Hay, who for many years had been Chief Clerk of the Navy Department. Monroe and George Hay found it difficult to believe Jackson's protestations that the removal had not been influenced by personal or political considerations. Monroe was even fearful that the President's wrath might extend to Samuel L. Gouverneur, whose family was dependent upon the income from the New York postmastership. His uneasiness on this score was augmented by Postmaster John McLean, a long-time Jackson admirer, who within a month after the inauguration told Monroe that the new incumbent in the White House was "deficient in requirement and capacity for the station he fills. He is influenced by those who are about him. His firmness is not that which arises from a mature investigation and enlightened conclusion, but of impulse." Gouverneur, perhaps because of his long friendship with Vice-President Calhoun, was spared for the moment.[53]

IV

When not supervising his farm or gathering data to substantiate his claims, Monroe spent much of his leisure in his library, which numbered nearly 3,000 volumes. Although Monroe did not have the scholarly inclinations of either Jefferson or Madison, he had read widely and collected a library which reflected his specific interests. It is striking that of the 500 titles known to have been owned by Monroe only fifty duplicate those found in Jefferson's much larger library. Most of Monroe's books, which were acquired during his residence in Europe, are those one might expect to find in the library of a man whose primary interests were political—collections of laws and public documents; books on economics, international law and political theory; as well as a substantial number of volumes devoted to history. Nor is it surprising, in view of his youthful predilections, that many of the titles were in French. Although Monroe, in contrast to Jefferson, never discussed scientific subjects in his letters, his library revealed an unexpectedly deep interest in natural history. Not only did he own such standard works as Buffon (in a thirty-volume edition) and Linnaeus, he also possessed such relatively exotic items as the works of Erasmus Darwin and Georges Cuvier. The historical works in his collection ranged from the standard Greek and Roman historians, through Rollin, Gibbon and Hume, to more recent works on European and American history. Although he bought relatively few books after 1810, among the later titles in his library were a translation of Carlo Botta's history of the American Revolution, published in 1821, and Edward Baines' work on the French Revolution, which appeared in 1819. The great productions of the Enlightenment were all present in complete editions—Bayle's dictionary, the *Encyclopédie,* the writings of Voltaire and Rousseau, as well as the works of Frederick the Great.[54]

In the comfort of his library, with ample leisure and his books at hand, Monroe began drafting a long-contemplated book on political theory to which he gave the cumbersome but descriptive title *The People the Sovereigns, Being a Comparison of the Government of the United States with those of the Republics Which Have Existed Before, with the Causes of their Decadence and Fall.*[55] The writing went slowly, for after a lifetime devoted to solving practical problems, he did not find it easy to explore abstract concepts. This work, only partially completed in a first draft, was designed to present "in a clear and distinct light the difference between the governments and people of the United States, and those in other countries, ancient and modern, and to show that certain causes which produced disastrous effects in them" were not operative in America. In short, he was attempting to answer the question why a government based on the sovereignty of the people could be expected to function permanently in the United States, whereas previous examples of such governments had ended in disaster. Although he considered the state of civilization to which a people had advanced an essential condition for the preservation of free institutions, he did not elaborate on this theme, since he was more concerned with the political factors involved. From this restricted point of view he concluded that the governments of Sparta, Athens and Carthage (he did not complete the section on Rome) had failed because they identified sovereignty with government. In order to establish enduring free governments nations must separate these two aspects of political power. Although he never finished his study, it was obvious that he believed that the United States had achieved this goal by dividing power between the state and federal governments. His political reflections, which owed a considerable debt to Rousseau, also revealed a familiarity with the Greek historians and Aristotle's *Politics*.

Monroe abandoned work on *The People the Sovereigns* in 1829 after hearing George Hay's unfavorable reaction to the manuscript. According to Monroe's secretary, who had made a copy of the President's draft, Hay had bluntly observed: "I think your time could have been better employed. If the framers of our Constitution could have had some work, from a modern standpoint, on the Constitutions of Greece and Rome, it might have been of value to them. I do not think yours is of practical value now." Hay suggested instead that Monroe write a history of his own times, which would be much more interesting and valuable to posterity. Monroe, delighted with the idea, at once began work on an autobiography, which remained a major occupation until shortly before his death.[56]

Age had not modified Monroe's habit of reticence. Still very much bound by the attitudes current in his youth, he composed a work (he only carried it to 1805) which does no more than depict the public events in which he participated. Written in the third person, it offers little that cannot be found in official records. There are few anecdotes, only a handful of references to his private life, no glimpses behind the scenes and no revealing portraits of the great men of his day.

V

Monroe rendered his last public service as a member of the Virginia constitutional convention which met in Richmond in October 1829.[57] He was not the only elder statesman to attend, for Madison, John Marshall and Governor William Branch Giles, and John Randolph of Roanoke were also present. Characteristically, Monroe, whose health was poor, had agreed to serve as a delegate from the Loudoun—Fairfax district only because he considered it his duty to use his influence to help resolve the crisis generated by the conflict over constitutional reform. His physical condition certainly rendered the trip inadvisable, but Monroe was not inclined to give in to his physical failings. Since late in 1828, when he had been severely injured in a fall from his horse, he had been quite infirm. Nonetheless, he had attended the July meeting of the Board of Visitors in Charlottesville, in spite of being further weakened by a bout of fever in the spring. In view of the state of his health, it was felt necessary for Eliza Hay to accompany her father to Richmond to see that he was properly looked after. Other considerations apart, the prospect of working with Madison on a new state constitution was irresistibly appealing to Monroe. After his arrival in Richmond, he was so buoyed up by the occasion that he was convinced that the journey had benefited his health.[58] It was apparent to all, however, that the emaciated and feeble former President was rapidly failing. Madison, although a decade older than Monroe, was much more vigorous.

The constitutional convention had been summoned by a reluctant state legislature after decades of agitation by the leaders of the underrepresented western counties. Only western threats to dismember the state had compelled the eastern politicians to yield to the demand for constitutional reform—long recommended by Jefferson as necessary to achieve basic structural changes in the state government. Although the greatest conflict in the convention raged over the equalization of representation by apportioning it on the basis of white population, the question of suffrage extension and the reorganization of the gubernatorial office also produced sharp disagreement. The eastern leaders opposed reform because they feared that an enlargement of the suffrage accompanied by an apportionment based on white population would ultimately threaten the existence of slavery. Of the 450,000 slaves in the state in 1829, only 50,000 resided west of the Blue Ridge. Eastern resistance to reform was not related to an immediate threat of a transfer of power, for the approval of the white basis would still leave the eastern counties securely in control of the legislature, but it rested on the apprehension that the future growth of the western counties would eventually give that region a preponderance in population. Monroe and Madison, fearful that failure to reach an agreement satisfactory to the West might lead to secession, went to the convention determined to endorse compromise measures. In taking this stand they alienated themselves from both the reformers and the conservatives. So great was the attraction of having a former President as a delegate in the convention that the voters of Loudoun had chosen Monroe, although it was known that he did not endorse the reform program which was highly popular in the county.[59]

It was natural that the delegates, recalling the Virginia ratifying convention of 1788, should wish to elevate one of the elder statesmen to the post of President of the convention. The honor fell to Monroe, when Madison and Marshall (approached first as seniors in age) declined.[60] Monroe, who was nominated by Madison, accepted the honor in spite of his feebleness, for the office was not expected to be strenuous. Most of the business would be transacted in the Committee of the Whole under the chairmanship of other members. While the delegates entertained the greatest respect for Monroe, about whom the aura of revolutionary military service still lingered, he did not arouse the degree of reverence stirred by Madison—the last surviving member of the Virginia Convention of 1776, which drafted the first state constitution, and the most celebrated member of the Philadelphia Convention. Madison spoke but twice during the convention, exerting his greatest influence as chairman of the committee on representation. Giles, so crippled that he could not stand without crutches, was still an active force in state politics. In the convention, he emerged as one of the most intransigent spokesmen for the established order. John Marshall, who usually endorsed compromise measures, was considerably less influential, for his Federalist past and his nationalist judicial orientation had not endeared him to his fellow Virginians. John Randolph added his shrill voice in opposition to any reform tending to reduce the power of the eastern counties. So great was the interest in the views of Madison, Monroe and Marshall that the official reporter of the convention regularly noted how they voted, even where there had not been a roll call.

For two months, until his health failed, Monroe regularly attended the sessions, speaking on several occasions in defense of compromise measures. In the hope of reconciling the conflicting parties, Monroe and Madison endorsed a proposal distributing representation in the lower house on the basis of white population, but permitting the Senate to rest on a formula acknowledging the rights of slaveowners. To answer the argument that this arrangement was contrary to the principles of free government, Monroe reminded the delegates that during the Revolution, which had been fought to establish these same principles, slavery had not been regarded as an impediment to the cause. Moreover, he pointed out that the three-fifths clause of the federal Constitution was a further indication that property in the form of slaves had been accepted as a basis of representation. Monroe, who had long been committed to a program seeking the ultimate elimination of slavery by colonizing free Negroes in Africa, argued—as a secondary reason for the adoption of the compromise—that it was essential to preserve the unity of the state in order to obtain federal assistance for the realization of this long-range goal of emancipation. These comments, as well as his remark "I am satisfied, if no such thing as slavery existed, that the people of our Atlantic border, would meet their brethren of the west, upon the basis of a majority of the free white population," exasperated the conservatives, but scarcely deserved Giles' condemnation as irrelevant.[61] On November 16, when Monroe arose to speak again, he begged the delegates to be patient, since his "faculties for debate, always humble, have been impaired by long disuse . . . and have, of late years, been yet further impaired by bodily infirmity." Once more he urged compromise to prevent the state from splitting apart. Although the combined prestige of Madison and Monroe was not sufficient to ensure the adoption of the compromise, which at least had the merit of providing for a periodic redistribution of representation, they were able to prevent a complete conservative victory. The eastern leaders accepted a measure which bypassed the question of the basis of representation by assigning a fixed number of Delegates and Senators to each section without providing for reapportionment. This arrangement, which postponed the conflict to a later date, was approved by a vote of 59 to 47 with Monroe and Madison in the negative.[62]

In line with his attempt to reconcile the warring factions on apportionment, Monroe adopted a moderate position on the question of enlarging the suffrage. He agreed with the reformers that the right to vote ought to be extended, but he insisted that a minimal land-ownership requirement be retained. These convictions were also endorsed by Madison. These two old friends seem to have disagreed on only one major point: the mode of electing the governor. Both wished to see his term lengthened and his powers increased, but Monroe did not join Madison in advocating popular election. Monroe, whose opinions were shared by the majority, preferred to continue the existing practice of legislative election, which he felt led to the selection of far abler men than would be the case if direct popular election were established. If the governor were chosen by statewide elections, he predicted that the Old Dominion would inevitably be riven by factional strife.[63]

When his health gave way early in December, Monroe was obliged to resign, although the work of the convention was far from completed. Continued illness detained him in Richmond for nearly a month before he left for Oak Hill by way of Washington to take advantage of the easier steamboat route and to gratify Tench Ringgold, who had been laboring to restore friendly relations between Monroe and President Jackson.[64] Encouraged by a conversation in which Jackson had spoken sympathetically of Monroe's plight, Ringgold arranged for the two men to meet at a dinner party in January. Seemingly all went well, and Ringgold made a point of assuring two of Jackson's confidants, John H. Eaton and W. H. Lewis, that Monroe had always been well disposed to the President, whose conduct he had defended after the Seminole War. Undoubtedly, it was hoped that the *rapprochement* would remove the obstacles which had hitherto impeded the settlement of the ex-President's claims. The encounter, however, produced no immediate benefits.

VI

Early in March 1830, a House committee under the guidance of Charles F. Mercer, of whose friendship there could be no doubt, reintroduced Rives' report.[65] To Monroe's disappointment, this report, which apparently did not have Jacksonian endorsement, was postponed until the next session. All the efforts of his friends and the personal pressure exerted in Washington by Samuel L. Gouverneur were unavailing.[66] Although the conflict between Jackson and Calhoun, which erupted in the spring of 1830, does not seem to have influenced the decision to delay action on Monroe's claims, the bitterness it evoked threatened to block approval in the future. In May (just a week before the session ended), Jackson sent Calhoun a copy of a letter from Crawford to John Forsyth, reviewing at length the 1818 Cabinet discussions over the Seminole War and singling out Calhoun as the arch-villain in the movement to censure the General. Crawford, who had written the letter in response to Van Buren's prompting, also maintained that both Monroe and Calhoun had been aware at the time of the Cabinet meetings that Jackson had offered to take the posts on his own responsibility in a letter written to Monroe on January 6, 1818. Crawford, who was careful to point out that he had never read the letter until after the Cabinet discussions, seemed to imply that Monroe and Calhoun had first connived to let Jackson think that he had tacit approval to seize the posts and then conspired to condemn him. Jackson's fury over these revelations cannot be attributed to his discovery of a well-guarded secret, for as early as 1818 he had been perfectly aware of Calhoun's opinion and had raised the matter with the South Carolinian in 1828 in a discussion which terminated amicably. Since that date, however, Calhoun's role in the Eaton affair had completely alienated the President, enabling Van Buren and others, who were anxious to eliminate Calhoun as a Presidential candidate, to play on Jackson's easily inflamed sensibilities.[67]

As soon as he read Crawford's letter, Calhoun hastened to Oak Hill to verify his recollection that he had not known about Jackson's letter of January 6, 1818, until after the Cabinet discussions over Jackson's conduct. In spite of the disagreeable matter at hand, Monroe thoroughly enjoyed the visit from his former Secretary of War. It was with obvious reluctance, however, that he agreed to allow Calhoun to gather material to repudiate Crawford's allegations. He knew that participation in the controversy would jeopardize his claims, but he could not withhold his consent on an issue which was not only vital to Calhoun's future, but one which also reflected on the events of his Presidency. In granting Calhoun permission to secure information from other Cabinet members, Monroe asked him not to publish the material until the story became known through other sources. Monroe felt that premature action would create the impression that the Vice-President was responsible for launching an attack on Jackson.[68] To refresh his own memory Monroe wrote Wirt, who confirmed the fact that the letter had not been discussed in the Cabinet prior to the decision on Jackson's conduct in Florida. When Calhoun showed Crawford a letter from Monroe con-

firming this version, the former Secretary of the Treasury at once wrote
his old chief insisting that the letter of January 6 had indeed been
known to Calhoun, although he admitted Monroe had apparently forgotten about it at that time. As proof of the veracity of his recollections,
Crawford relied on the testimony of a "tenacious" and "accurate"
memory. All the other members of the Cabinet concurred with Monroe
except for Crowninshield, who had not been present on the day Jackson's letter had first been produced in the Cabinet.[69]

The Calhoun–Jackson controversy receded into the background in
the face of the personal tragedy which overwhelmed Monroe in the
summer of 1830. His own health continued to be good, although he had
not felt strong enough to go to Charlottesville for the July meeting
of the Board of Visitors. Still, he managed to ride every morning and
then rested in bed during the heat of the day. He resumed work on
his autobiography, which he hoped to complete by the end of the year.[70]
Yet family cares increasingly deprived him of the tranquility he so much
desired. In June, it was apparent that George Hay, on whom he had
so long relied for counsel in both private and public concerns, was so
ill that recovery seemed doubtful. Eliza accompanied her husband to
Washington for treatment, but she had been there only a few weeks
when she was summoned to Baltimore to assist at her daughter's confinement and then remained to nurse her through a bout of scarlet
fever. With nerves strained by sickroom cares, Eliza quarreled with
her son-in-law in July. Although Monroe felt that his daughter was in
the right, he tried to patch up the misunderstanding.[71] When Tench
Ringgold took his grandfather to the springs in August, Eliza was too
exhausted to accompany her husband. On his way home, George Hay
became so ill in Albemarle that his wife was summoned to his side,
but did not reach him before his death on September 21. On her return
to Oak Hill with his body, further tragedy awaited Eliza. Mrs. Monroe,
whose health had shown some improvement in September, had suffered
a relapse during Eliza's absence. Her condition was so alarming that
Monroe had at once written to summon Maria to Oak Hill. Just after
this letter had been posted and within hours after Eliza's return, Mrs.
Monroe died on September 23.[72]

Monroe was prostrated by the blow. Egbert Watson, then visiting
Oak Hill, long remembered the "touching grief manifested by the
old man on the morning after Mrs. Monroe's death, when he sent for
me to go to his room, and with trembling frame and streaming eye

spoke of the long years they had spent happily together, and expressed his conviction that he would soon follow her." Mrs. Monroe was buried at Oak Hill in a vault in which Monroe ultimately expected to join her.[73]

Monroe was so shaken by his wife's death that his daughters decided that it was impossible for him to continue living at Oak Hill. In October, he and Eliza went to New York to live with the Gouverneurs, and here he remained until his death.[74] The pain of his loss still haunted him in New York. In a letter to James Brown, whose wife had also recently died, Monroe unburdened himself:

We have both suffered, the most afflicting calamity that can befall us in this life, and which, if time may alleviate it, it cannot efface. After having lived, with the partner of your [illegible], in so many vicissitudes of life, so long together, and afforded to each other comforts which no other person on earth could do, as both of us have done, to have her snatched from us, is an affliction which none but those who feel it, can justly estimate.[75]

In late December 1830, Monroe, now too ill to leave his room, was once again deeply preoccupied with the Jackson–Calhoun embroglio. In order to assist the former Secretary of War, who could not defer the publication of his defense any longer, Monroe drew up a statement summarizing his recollections of the disputed Jackson letter.[76] Calhoun, however, did manage to hold back the publication until the House— the principal obstacle in the way—approved Monroe's claims. His pamphlet appeared in February 17, 1831, two weeks after the House granted the former President $30,000.[77]

This sum had been awarded, not because Congress was convinced about the validity of Monroe's case but simply because of public pressure to relieve the distress of a distinguished public servant. Monroe had reopened the question of his unsettled accounts in November 1830, when, swallowing his pride, he wrote to remind the Speaker of the House of the bill postponed from the last session. Once again he reviewed the losses occasioned by his services to the nation. For the first time he recounted the story of the advance made to Napoleon before the ratification of the Louisiana Purchase treaty. He did not present it as the basis of a claim, but to provide another example of the personal financial risks he had been willing to assume in executing public responsibilities.[78] Reinforced by a petition from Albemarle and one from

New York City, the bill was taken up by the Committee of the Whole in January. The opposition was led by Lewis Williams of North Carolina, a member of the Committee on Claims and one of Calhoun's most inveterate opponents. Williams saw no reason why Congress, which had already dealt "generously" and "justly" with the former President, should be expected to relieve the financial embarrassments of an individual simply because he had once held high office. After all, Monroe had known the compensation before he accepted the many posts he had held during his career. Why, Williams asked, should Monroe, who had received $400,000 in salary (more than any other public figure in the United States) from the federal government, expect further payment? Although Mercer and others defended the justice of Monroe's claims, they rested their case primarily upon the fact that the former President, now living on the charity of relatives, was nearly destitute.[79] Monroe's friends brought every possible pressure to bear on the House. Gouverneur and Silas Burrows, a wealthy New York merchant, descended on Washington to lobby in Monroe's behalf, while John McLean worked to win over the Ohio delegation. Curiously, the Virginians in Congress were quite unsympathetic to the plight of their fellow citizen. Not only were they deeply committed to Jackson, but they still held a grudge against Monroe for the nationalist policies he had adopted during his Presidency.[80] A compromise bill was finally worked out allowing him $30,000 (less than half the sum recommended by the committee) for "public losses and sacrifices." Far short of the vindication Monroe desired, the bill at least granted him the balance deleted from the measure approved in 1826.

VII

The congressional grant enabled Monroe to pay off most of his obligations, but he decided nonetheless to dispose of Oak Hill. Not only did his health make it impossible for him to live there, but apparently Samuel Gouverneur did not feel that he could assume the management of the estate. Monroe, perhaps not fully realizing how ill he was, talked of using the proceeds to purchase a house in New York and ease the strain on his daughter's cramped household.[81] Before selling the home he loved so much, he planned a final visit. Undoubtedly the members of his family did not share his optimism on this score, for he was gradually growing weaker and so wracked by an incessant cough that he

could not rest properly. When Adams saw him in April 1831, he felt
that Monroe would never again leave his room. Although the former
President was alert and anxious to discuss the recent revolutions in
Europe, Adams cut his visit short when he realized that the effort of
speaking drained Monroe's strength.[82] In May Monroe made his will,
dividing his estate equally between his two daughters, except for the
provision that Maria be paid $6,000 out of the total, for in 1809 he
had given Eliza "Ashfield," for which he had paid that amount. When
the projected sale of Oak Hill fell through the family was much relieved, for—as Tench Ringgold noted—the news that his beloved estate
had not been sold would greatly ease the mind of "the good old man"
in his last days. Indeed Ringgold felt that Monroe's life might be saved
if he could be taken to Oak Hill—in a litter if necessary.[83]

Confronted by the limitations of age and illness, Monroe notified
Madison in April (the last letter to his old friend) that he could no
longer serve on the Board of Visitors. His greatest regret in resigning,
he assured Madison, was the knowledge that they would never meet
again. Madison, now over eighty and understanding the gravity of
Monroe's illness, was saddened by the news. "The pain I feel," he wrote
in reply, "associated as it is with the recollections of the long, close,
and uninterrupted friendship which united us, amounts to a pang
which I cannot well express, and which makes me seek for an alleviation
in the possibility that you may be brought back to us in the wonted
degree of intercourse." Hopefully, he asked if Monroe might not come
to Albemarle when he made his last visit to Oak Hill.[84] To this query
Monroe made no reply; he was much too ill to write. All hope for his
recovery was abandoned as his friends and relatives did everything they
could to make his last days free from worry. In spite of their best efforts,
they were unable to spare him further involvement in one of the most
acrimonious political controversies stemming from his administration.
In June, barely three weeks before he died, a letter arrived from John
Rhea, the aged former congressman from Tennessee and devoted Jacksonian, asking Monroe if he remembered that he had authorized Rhea
early in 1818 to give verbal instructions to Jackson to seize Florida.
Gouverneur was appalled by the letter, but (and Wirt agreed) he felt
he must show it to his father-in-law lest failure to deny the statement
later be used to substantiate this fantastic story. On June 14, after
Monroe was shown the letter, he signed a deposition denying Rhea's
allegation.[85] The signature on this document was the last time Monroe

put pen to paper. On July 4, 1831, shortly after three in the afternoon he died peacefully, fully conscious, and, as Ringgold told Madison, resigned to his fate.[86]

Monroe's funeral, the most elaborate staged in New York up to that time, was held on July 7, when his body was taken by a guard of honor from Samuel L. Gouverneur's residence to the City Hall and placed on a platform draped in black. After President William Duer of Columbia University delivered the eulogy, funeral services were held in St. Paul's Episcopal Church. Then, as church bells tolled throughout the city and minute guns were fired at Fort Columbus, a vast procession composed of civic officials, state legislators, members of the Bar, consuls, members of the Cincinnati, and citizens accompanied the cortege up Broadway to the Second Street Cemetery. After the coffin was placed in the Gouverneur vault, the ceremony concluded with three volleys fired over the grave by the guard of honor.[87]

Throughout the nation Monroe's passing was marked by commemorative observances. In nearly every city and town, a day of mourning was observed, church bells tolled, eulogies were delivered, and memorial resolutions adopted by the citizens. President Jackson ordered all military posts and naval vessels to set aside a day to honor the late President by firing minute guns from noon to sunset and ending with a twenty-four-gun salute. Monroe's death moved the nation, not because the achievements of his administration were then valued so highly but rather because the people saw in his death the passing of one of the last heroes of the revolutionary generation. The fact that Monroe, like Jefferson and John Adams, died on the Fourth of July, called to mind all the more sharply his association with the struggle for independence. Everywhere the press and eulogists lauded his military exploits during the Revolution to the exclusion of his later career. Almost nothing was said of his Presidency and little about the rest of his public service apart from his role in the Louisiana Purchase.[88] Only John Quincy Adams, who delivered the Boston eulogy, attempted to break through the conventional rhetorical platitudes and view Monroe's career as a whole. He saw in Monroe's public service a lifetime dedicated to strengthening the nation and establishing it securely on republican principles.[89] Thus for Adams, Monroe's contributions to the cause of the Union during the Confederation Congress were as significant as his youthful military service; the acquisition of Florida and the extension of the boundaries of the United States to the Pacific as noteworthy as the Louisiana Purchase. No one, he proclaimed, had done

more than Monroe to expand the limits of the United States and foster
the security of the nation—a work Monroe began in the Confederation
Congress when he defeated the Jay–Gardoqui resolves, continued
through the Louisiana Purchase, and completed in the Transcontinental Treaty. All was not unqualified praise, for Adams frankly
recalled the more controversial aspects of Monroe's career—the first
mission to France, the rejected treaty, his stand on internal improvements. Allowing for the excessive hyperbole which he deemed essential
to the occasion, Adams' summation of Monroe's Presidency made a
fitting epitaph:

There behold him for a term of eight years, strengthening his country for
defence by a system of combined fortifications, military and naval, sustaining
her rights, her dignity and honor abroad; soothing her dissensions, and
conciliating her acerbities at home; controlling by a firm though peaceful
policy the hostile spirit of the European Alliance against Republican South
America extorting by the mild compulsion of reason, the shores of the
Pacific from the stipulated acknowledgement of Spain; and leading back
the imperial autocrat of the North, to his lawful boundaries, from his
hastily asserted dominion over the Southern Ocean. Thus strengthening and
consolidating the federative edifice of his country's Union, till he was
entitled to say, like Augustus Caesar of his imperial city, that he had found
her built of brick and left her constructed of marble.[90]

ABBREVIATIONS

AC	*Annals of Congress*
Adams, *Memoirs*	John Quincy Adams, *Memoirs*
AECPEU	Archives Etrangères, Correspondence Politique, Etats-Unis
AHA	American Historical Association
AHR	*American Historical Review*
ASPFR	*American State Papers, Foreign Relations*
Autobiography	James Monroe, *Autobiography*
Bemis, *Adams*, I	Samuel Flagg Bemis, *John Quincy Adams and the Foundations of American Foreign Policy*
Boyd, *Jefferson*	*Papers of Thomas Jefferson*, ed. by Julian P. Boyd
Bull. NYPL	*Bulletin of the New York Public Library*
Cong. Globe	*Congressional Globe*
Enquirer	Richmond *Enquirer*
F.O. 5	Great Britain, Foreign Affairs, Ser. 5
Intelligencer	Washington *National Intelligencer*
JM	*Writings of James Monroe*, ed. by S. M. Hamilton
Jour. CC	*Journals of the Continental Congress*
LC	Library of Congress
Md. Hist. Mag.	*Maryland Historical Magazine*
MHS	Massachusetts Historical Society
Monroe Foundation	James Monroe Memorial Foundation, Fredericksburg, Virginia
Monroe, LC	Monroe Papers, Library of Congress
Monroe, NYPL	Monroe Papers, New York Public Library
MVH	*Mississippi Valley Historical Review*
NA	National Archives
NYHS	New-York Historical Society
NYPL	New York Public Library
Pa. Mag.	*Pennsylvania Magazine of History and Biography*
PHS	Historical Society of Pennsylvania
Proc. Am. Ant. Soc.	*Proceedings of the American Antiquarian Society*
Proc. MHS	*Proceedings of the Massachusetts Historical Society*

Richardson, *Messages*	*Messages and Papers of the Presidents,* ed. by James D. Richardson
U.Va.	University of Virginia
Va. Mag.	*Virginia Magazine of History and Biography*
VSL	Virginia State Library
WMQ	*William and Mary Quarterly*

NOTES

1. The Washingtons settled at "Ferry Farm," near Fredericksburg. George's father, Augustine, died in 1743 leaving an estate in excess of 10,000 acres and at least forty-nine slaves. See Douglas Southall Freeman, *George Washington* (7 vols., New York, 1948–57), I, 48–74; Irving Brant, *James Madison* (6 vols., New York, 1941–66), I, 30–31.

2. The holdings of the Monroe family on Monroe's Creek were in the neighborhood of 1,100 acres. When Monroe was born most of this property was divided betweeen two branches of the family. One branch, descended from the eldest son of the settler, held 640 acres; the second branch, descended from a younger son (it was to this branch that James Monroe belonged), resided on a tract of approximately 500 acres which had been originally patented by Thomas Mountjoy in 1691. This estate may have entered the possession of the Monroe family by marriage; the widow of the settler (Andrew Monroe) married Edward Mountjoy. For a detailed study of Westmoreland land grants see David W. Eaton, *Historical Atlas of Westmoreland County* (Richmond, 1942), 46, 62.

3. James Monroe, *Autobiography* (Syracuse, 1959), 21. [Hereinafter cited as *Autobiography*.] Monroe began this work after his retirement from the Presidency and was not able to complete it before his death. It is of minimal value to biographers, since it is largely official in nature and cites official documents rather than relying on private recollections. For a complete genealogy of the Monroe family see Brooke Payne and George Harrison King, "The Monroe Family," *WMQ*, ser. 2, XIII (1933), 231–41. They correct many serious errors made by previous investigators. The statement about his ancestors in Monroe's *Autobiography* touches directly on one of the unresolved questions concerning the origins of the Monroe family. Monroe simply declared that the family was founded in America by Andrew Monroe, who migrated from England after the execution of the king and after serving in the Cavalier army. Monroe derived his information from a cousin who had visited Scotland and established that the Virginia Monroes were connected with

the Monroe family of Fowlis (*Autobiography*, 22). However, subsequent investigators discovered that there was an Andrew Monroe resident in Maryland about 1642 whose name appears on a deed in 1648 listing his residence as Appomattox in Virginia. After this date his name disappears from the Maryland records and that of Andrew Monroe appears in the Westmoreland records. If this is the same person, then Andrew Monroe was in the colony before the battle of Preston (in which Andrew Monroe of Katewell served) and again after the battle which took place on August 17, 1648. King and Payne believe that these are the same person. They conclude that Andrew moved from Maryland to Virginia in 1648, and after April 1648 (when his name appears on a deed) returned to Scotland, serving in August in the battle of Preston, and then returned to Virginia, where in 1650 he took up land. This solution has the advantage of reconciling family tradition with the problem presented by the Maryland records. It is, however, open to several objections, although none completely refute the conclusion made by Payne and King. First, when in Maryland, Andrew Monroe was involved with Richard Ingle, which connects him with the Puritan element, thus making it rather unlikely that he would return to Scotland to serve in the Cavalier army. Second, the records of Northumberland County (to which Westmoreland then belonged) contain an oath of loyalty to the Commonwealth drawn up on April 11, 1652, and signed by various residents of the county, including Andrew Monroe (original is in Westmoreland County Deeds and Orders, 1650–52, VSL; it is reprinted in *Va. Mag.*, XLIX, 33–36). This would indicate that there was an Andrew Monroe whose support of the royalist cause was so well known that he was required to take an oath of loyalty. If he had been a supporter of Richard Ingle, would his signature have been necessary? The Andrew Monroe who resided in Maryland was unable to write and always signed with his mark (*Archives of Maryland*, IV, 384; Monroe Johnson, "Maryland Ancestry of James Monroe," *Md. Hist. Mag.*, XXIII (1928), 194). It is uncertain whether the Andrew Monroe living in Virginia could sign his name; his signature (along with five others) on the oath of loyalty is recorded in the hand of a clerk. All the other signatories either wrote themselves or signed by a mark. In view of these discrepancies, I prefer to leave the matter as Monroe stated it, since he was citing a recently verified family tradition. In regard to Monroe's father there is a problem of lesser importance. Hugh Blair Grigsby referred to Monroe's father as a "carpenter," and in the late nineteenth century Lyon G. Tyler discovered a bond in the King George County records apprenticing Spence Monroe as a "joiner" to Robert Walker. From this Tyler concluded that Spence was probably active as a builder—it was not unknown for men who classed themselves as "gentlemen" to be described as "carpenters" or "joiners." However, the evidence that the Spence Monroe listed in the King George records is the same as the Spence living in Westmoreland is only presumptive. It is true that the two counties are adjacent and that the Monroes had connections in King George; it is equally true that Spence was not an uncommon first name in the Monroe family. See Lyon G. Tyler, "James Monroe," *WMQ*, ser. 1, IV (1895–96), 272–5.

4. *Autobiography*, 22; Eaton, *Westmoreland*, 22; William Meade, *Old Churches, Ministers and Families of Virginia* (2 vols., Philadelphia, 1857), II, 161; Albert J. Beveridge, *Life of John Marshall* (4 vols., New York, 1916–19), I, 37. Exact dates of Marshall's attendance are not known; he was two years older than Monroe.

5. Monroe's mother, who is not mentioned in Spence's will, apparently died some years earlier. Birth dates of the other children are not known. Apparently Elizabeth was the eldest; she married William Buckner and resided at "Mill Hill" in Caroline County. Joseph Jones Monroe was the youngest son and was born about 1770 (Monroe in a letter to Jefferson, Jan. 16, 1790, Jefferson Papers, MHS, speaks of his brother as still a minor). Joseph Jones Monroe married three times, living in Albemarle and Northumberland Counties until after the War of 1812, when he moved to Missouri, where he died in 1824. Andrew Monroe moved to Albemarle, dying at Milton in 1826. For additional details see Payne and King, *loc. cit.*, 236–37. Monroe was deeply attached to his brothers and sister. The lack of material success of his brothers was a source of disappointment and made it necessary for him to aid them constantly.

6. *DAB*.

7. *Autobiography*, 22; Dumas Malone, *Jefferson and His Times* (3 vols., New York, 1948–   ), I, 51, 59–60.

8. The following account of events in Virginia during 1774–1776 is taken from J. J. Eckenrode, *The Revolution in Virginia* (Boston, 1916); Malone, *Jefferson*, I, 180ff.; David J. Mays, *Edmund Pendleton* (2 vols., Cambridge, Mass., 1952), II, *passim*.

9. Eaton, *Westmoreland*, 15–18.

10. For general conditions at William and Mary and for the specific details here cited see "Journal of the President and Masters of William and Mary College, May, 1775–November, 1775," *WMQ*, ser. 1, XV (1935), 1–14, 134–42.

11. The only record of this event is in Theodorick Bland, Jr., *The Bland Papers* (2 vols., Petersburg, 1840–43), I, xxiii. The exact figures were 230 muskets, 301 swords and 18 pistols. Mazzei does not mention this episode in his memoirs.

12. Monroe to Jefferson, Sept. 9, 1780, Stanislaus Murray Hamilton (ed.), *Writings of James Monroe* (7 vols., New York, 1898–1903), I, 9. [Hereinafter cited as *JM*.] The exact date of Monroe's enlistment cannot be ascertained; in his autobiography he stated it was January 1776, but it was probably later, since he was still carried on the bursar's books at the college through March; *Autobiography*, 22. J. F. Mercer was not related to Hugh Mercer. The family of the former was of Irish origin; Hugh Mercer had emigrated from Scotland after the failure of the Jacobite uprising of 1748 and had settled in Fredericksburg about 1760, where he practiced medicine. He was a friend of Washington and a man of some influence. His death at Princeton prematurely ended a promising military career.

13. I can find no authority for the statement of previous biographers that Monroe served in the company of Capt. William Washington, a kinsman of George Washington. This statement was based upon the fact that at Trenton Monroe did serve briefly in Washington's company, but only as a volunteer—as he clearly states in his autobiography. Monroe's service with Thornton is based on his autobiography and on a letter he wrote to Thornton's son-in-law, George Coleman, Jan. 17, 1809, *Tyler's Quarterly*, IX, 247–48.

14. The Third Virginia became part of the continental line on Feb. 13, 1776. There is no reference to Monroe in Gen. Lewis' orderly book, but the Third Virginia is mentioned; see *Orderly Book of that Portion of the American Army Stationed at or Near Williamsburg, Va., under the Command of General Andrew Lewis, from March 18, 1776 to August 28, 1777,* ed. by Charles Campbell (Richmond, 1860).

15. There are no really good descriptions of Monroe by his contemporaries and almost no casual references to him before 1790; the above description is largely inference based upon substantial later accounts and upon traits revealed in his correspondence. See portrait of Monroe painted about 1780–85 and reproduced in *Autobiography,* 30.

16. The Ninth was commanded by Col. Issac Reed; Mercer was promoted in June, but Weedon did not join the Third until Aug. 13, possibly while the regiment was en route to Long Island. See C. S. Flagg and W. O. Waters, "Bibliography of Musters and Pay Rolls," *Tyler's Quarterly,* XX, 185.

17. Capt. John Chilton to _____, N.Y., Sept. 13, 1776, *Tyler's Quarterly,* XII, 91. Chilton was a member of the Third Virginia and wrote several interesting and informative letters from New York, which I have drawn upon heavily in the following account of the skirmish at Harlem Heights. The Third arrived several days before the Ninth. Flagg and Waters, *op. cit.,* XX, 185.

18. John Chilton to _____, Morris's Height Camp, Sept. 17, 1776, *Tyler's Quarterly,* XII, 92; Freeman, *Washington,* IV, 180–90. In this account of the defense of Manhattan I have relied upon Freeman's detailed narrative.

19. There are some discrepancies in the various accounts of this engagement, as Freeman points out in his *Washington,* IV, 190ff. The exact position of various regiments on the heights is not known, and both Capt. Chilton and Capt. Gustavus Wallace, who wrote letters immediately after the engagement, give the impression that the flanking movement was ordered before Knowlton's skirmish, but Freeman— using fuller sources—puts Knowlton's action prior to the flanking movement; I have followed him. Since Wallace and Chilton (their letters are in *Tyler's Quarterly,* XII, 90–96) were with their companies in the engagement, it is possible they were not familiar with the precise sequence of events. The bugle call is well authenticated, but curiously neither Chilton nor Wallace mentions it.

20. Freeman, *Washington,* IV, 200, fn. 154, states that Monroe volunteered, but I find no evidence to support this; he was regularly attached to Thornton's company, and in his autobiography he does not speak of volunteering at Harlem as he did at Trenton. I assume that Freeman's statement is based on the incorrect assumption that he was regularly in William Washington's company, and therefore he concluded that Monroe must have volunteered here, since he was clearly with Thornton. The other two companies were those of Capts. John Ashby and Charles West.

21. *Autobiography,* 23.

22. George Weedon to John Page, Morris's Heights, Sept. 20, 1776, Weedon Papers, Chicago Historical Society. George Weedon to John Page, White Plains,

Oct. 26, 1776, *ibid.* Monroe's participation is inferred from the fact that Capt. Thornton was in this engagement.

23. In the account of the operations at White Plains and the retreat into New Jersey I have again followed closely Freeman's excellent and detailed account; Freeman, *Washington,* IV, 204–302.

24. *American Archives, Military Affairs,* 5th ser., III, 515–16, 1401–2. These are the only two muster rolls of the Third which have been preserved. The Third's military career ended at Charleston in 1780 when it surrendered to the British.

25. Monroe, *Autobiography,* 24. This figure was nearly correct; according to a return cited in Freeman, *Washington,* IV, 268–73, Washington's army numbered 3,442 rank and file present and fit for duty on Dec. 1—a return which was not available to Washington, who had reported to Congress a week earlier that he had 5,410 actives. Actually, in the confused state of affairs he had no way of knowing the exact size of his forces.

26. Two other smaller detachments, composed largely of militia, were to cross at and below Trenton, but since they were unable to carry out their assignments, they can be eliminated from consideration.

27. Monroe left a detailed account of his participation in the attack on Trenton in his autobiography. In this narrative he stated that he had crossed the river at Coryell's Ferry, 10 miles up the river from McKonkey's. In view of the location of this ferry—it is quite far from the junction of the two roads—and Monroe's statement that they proceeded about a half-mile from the ferry to the crossroads, I have not followed him on this point. This error, understandable at the distance of a half-century, when he wrote his account of Trenton, probably arose from the fact that he convalesced for ten days after being wounded at Trenton in the home of Mr. Coryell, and he later associated Coryell's Ferry with the one at which he had crossed. In none of the accounts of the battle of Trenton is Coryell's Ferry mentioned as a crossing point. Monroe's own account of his movements corresponds much more accurately with the assumption that he crossed at McKonkey's, where all the other troops crossed. For narratives of the battle of Trenton see Freeman, *Washington,* IV, 216ff., and Alfred H. Bill, *The Campaign of Princeton, 1776–1777* (Princeton, 1948).

28. Monroe did not clearly state on which road he was stationed, and I have assumed it was in the direction of Trenton.

29. *Autobiography,* 25; W. W. H. Davis, "Washington on the West Bank of the Delaware, 1776," *Pa. Mag.,* IV (1880), 52–53.

30. In addition to Capt. Washington and Monroe, only two enlisted men were wounded at Trenton and none killed. Monroe was moved to Wyncoop's after staying ten days at the home of Lewis S. Coryell, also of Bucks County; see Monroe, *Autobiography.* Concerning his stay at the Wyncoop's, there is a tradition in that family that Monroe fell in love with Wyncoop's daughter, but since she was already engaged did not return his affection. This seems to rest upon too slender a thread to be accepted. It is told in W. P. Cresson, *James Monroe* (Chapel Hill, 1946), 31.

CHAPTER 2

AIDE TO LORD STIRLING

1. Monroe to Maj. John Thornton, Fredericksburg, July 3, 1777, *Tyler's Quarterly,* IX, 247–8.

2. August 11, 1777, Washington Papers, LC.

3. August 12, 1777, *Tyler's Quarterly,* IX, 247.

4. Freeman, *Washington,* IV, *passim;* for Stirling see George H. Danforth, *The Rebel Earl* (Dissertation, Columbia U., 1955). Monroe did not become a permanent member of Stirling's staff until Nov. 20, 1777, although his actual service began on a temporary basis late in August 1777. See John C. Fitzpatrick, *Writings of George Washington* (39 vols., Washington, 1931–44), X, ii, and *Autobiography,* 27.

5. *Autobiography,* 29.

6. Lee to Monroe, July 18, 1780, Charles Lee, *Lee Papers* (4 vols., New York State Historical Society, *Collections,* 1871–74), III, 429.

7. Rupert Hughes, *George Washington* (3 vols., New York, 1926–30), III, 397–400.

8. General Orders, Fitzpatrick, *Washington,* X, 88.

9. *Autobiography,* 27.

10. Peter S. DuPonceau (he had Americanized his first name) to _____, Philadelphia, June 18, 1836, *Pa. Mag.,* XL (1916), 179. This letter is of an autobiographical nature. The biographical details are from *DAB.*

11. P. S. DuPonceau to Monroe, April 11, 1778, DuPonceau Papers, PHS.

12. It is often stated that Monroe assisted Lafayette off the field after he had been wounded—an honor also assigned to many others. Monroe does not mention this in his autobiography (or any other place), and I am inclined to agree with Louis Gottschalk, *Lafayette Joins the American Army* (Chicago, 1937), App. IV, 339–40, in regarding all such claims as spurious. It was only a flesh wound and apparently not incapacitating. When Lafayette visited the U. S. in 1824–25 he limped slightly, and this was attributed to his wound—actually the limp came from an improperly set broken leg that occurred many years after Brandywine.

13. Freeman, *Washington,* IV, 490–519; I do not find any evidence for the statement, Cresson, *Monroe,* 34, that Stirling's brigade was involved at Chew House; this seems to have been Maxwell's brigade, which originally was part of the reserves; Stirling's own account, written that day after the battle, does not mention the siege of the Chew House and implies his reserves did not advance that far. See Lord Stirling to _____, Oct. 5, 1777, printed in part in *American Art Association Sale Catalogue* of Jan. 22, 1926, clipping in MS. Division NYPL.

14. Danforth, Rebel Earl, 240–41.

15. Hughes, *Washington,* III, 244; Freeman, *Washington,* IV, 549ff. Monroe does not mention the Conway Cabal in his autobiography. After Germantown there

is a gap until 1780. Apparently Monroe planned to review the events leading to Lee's disgrace and put off writing about this period until he could check other accounts; unfortunately he never found time to fill in this blank. For a thorough examination of the question see Bernhard Knollenberg, *Washington and the Revolution* (New York, 1941). Knollenberg discounts the existence of any plot against Washington.

16. Excellent accounts of the winter at Valley Forge will be found in Alfred Hoyt Bill, *Valley Forge* (New York, 1952) and Freeman, *Washington,* IV, 564–633.

17. Bill, *Valley Forge,* 101.

18. DuPonceau to _____, June 13, 1836, *Pa. Mag.,* XL, 180.

19. *Ibid.,* 180.

20. Hughes, *Washington,* III, 326.

21. Accounts of the celebration will be found in Bill, *Valley Forge,* 189–92; Hughes, *Washington,* III, 334–37; Freeman, *Washington,* V, 1–2. The quotation is from Freeman.

22. DuPonceau, *loc. cit.,* 181–2.

23. Monroe to DuPonceau, Camp, May 7, 1778, Rives Papers, LC.

24. Freeman, *Washington,* V. 5, 15–17.

25. Monroe to Washington, June 28, 1778, Monroe, *Writings,* I, 1. Monroe in dating this letter added to the date "4 o'clock" without specifying A.M. or P.M. Consequently the interpretations of it have been somewhat confused. Cresson, *Monroe,* 42, incorrectly assumes that it was written at 4 A.M., while on a scouting expedition before the battle. The context of the letter in relation to the course of the battle leaves no doubt but that it was written at four in the afternoon. Freeman, *Washington,* V, 32, fn. 60, also assigns the letter to 4 P.M.

26. Freeman, *Washington,* V, 31–33; Christopher Ward, *The War of the Revolution* (2 vols., New York, 1952), II, 584–86.

27. Freeman, *Washington,* V, 39; Hughes, *Washington,* III, 397–400. As noted above in fn. 15, Monroe did not cover this period in his autobiography.

28. Monroe to Mrs. Prevost, Oct. 31, 1778, Monroe Papers, NYPL.

29. McHenry Journal, Emmett Collection, NYPL.

30. Monroe to Mrs. Prevost, Nov. 8, 1778, printed in Matthew L. Davis, *Memoirs of Aaron Burr* (2 vols., New York, 1837), I, 184–86. The identification of the young lady as Miss Nannie Brown as the basis of a story that she was cruelly jilted by Monroe cannot be substantiated. See Cresson, *Monroe,* 515, fn. 8.

31. *Tyler's Quarterly,* IX, 246.

32. This account of Monroe's movements during the winter of 1778–79 is based on his letter to Charles Lee, Aylett's Warehouse, June 15, 1779, *JM,* I, 2. This letter is undated and Hamilton assigned the date 1780 to it, but internal evidence makes it clear that the correct date is 1779. See also Monroe to Stirling, Sept. 18, 1782, William H. Duer, *Life of William Alexander, Lord Stirling* (New York, 1847), 251; *Autobiography,* 29.

33. For details of this interesting scheme, which stemmed largely from the Laurenses' strong antislavery views and was not conceived as a measure of desperation, see David Duncan Wallace, *Life of Henry Laurens* (N.Y. 1915), 448–53.

34. Hamilton to Laurens, Middle Brook, May 22, 1779, *Proc. MHS,* LVIII (1924–25), 220.

35. May 30, 1779, *JM,* I, 20–21, fn.

36. *Autobiography,* 29.

CHAPTER 3

POLITICAL APPRENTICESHIP

1. Monroe to Jefferson, Sept. 9, 1780, *JM,* I, 8–9; Monroe also alluded to these private disappointments in a letter to Lord Stirling, Sept. 10, 1782, Duer, *Stirling,* 250. However, he did not give any details. Since Monroe had inherited his father's estate it seems unlikely that this referred to either his brothers or sister. The fact that his expectations in his private fortune were affected seems to point to Jones. One possible explanation is that Monroe, who undoubtedly had long regarded himself as his uncle's heir, was abruptly removed from that status when a son was born to his uncle. This event, late in his uncle's life, must have been unexpected. The exact date of the birth of Joseph Jones, Jr., is not known, but in 1794 he was old enough to accompany Monroe to France to be educated abroad. From references in Monroe's letters the boy would seem to have been in his mid-teens, thus 1779 would be a likely birth date. Perhaps Monroe at first felt that his uncle would no longer be concerned with his career. If this was the cause of his distress, he clearly had recovered by early 1780 and his uncle continued actively to advance his career. There is no suggestion that his disappointment resulted from a rejected suit.

2. Jan. 30, 1787, Julian P. Boyd (ed.), *The Papers of Thomas Jefferson* (16 vols., Princeton U. Press, 1950–   ), XI, 97.

3. *Autobiography,* 31; Monroe to Jefferson, Sept. 9, 1780, *JM,* I, 8–11.

4. Jefferson to Skipwith, Aug. 3, 1771, Boyd, *Jefferson,* I, 76–80.

5. March 7, 1780, printed in George Morgan, *The Life of James Monroe* (Boston, 1921), 74–75; the original is in the Monroe Foundation, Fredericksburg.

6. Jefferson to Monroe, June 10, 1780, Boyd, *Jefferson,* III, 431.

7. Monroe to Jefferson, Cross Creek, June 26, 1780, *JM,* I, 3–7; Jefferson to the President of Congress, June 28, 1780, Boyd, *Jefferson,* III, 25–26.

8. Monroe to George Hay, May 2, 1819, Monroe Papers, LC. In this letter Monroe spoke of remaining with DeKalb two months, but his service was shorter than this. Had he been with DeKalb for two months he would have been present at the battle of Camden on Aug. 16, which he does not mention in his letters or in his autobiography.

9. Monroe to Jefferson, Sept. 9, 1780, *JM,* I, 9–11.

10. Monroe to Jefferson, June 18, 1781, *JM,* I, 11.

11. Joseph Jones to James Madison, Nov. 5, 10, 1780, excerpted in *Henkels Sale Catalogue,* #694 (Washington–Madison sale), 64.

12. Oct. 1, 1781, *JM,* I, 13.

13. Monroe to Jefferson, June 18, 1781, *JM,* I, 11–12; Boyd, *Jefferson,* III, 341 fn.

14. Monroe to Jefferson, Oct. 1, 1780, *JM,* I, 14.

15. *Ibid.,* I, 12–14; Jefferson to Monroe, Oct. 5, 1781, Jefferson to Franklin, Oct. 5, 1781, Boyd, *Jefferson,* VI, 126–128.

16. It has been frequently stated that on Nov. 11, 1782, Monroe attended a peace ball held in Fredericksburg to celebrate the defeat of Cornwallis. According to the legend Washington, Steuben, D'Estaing and deGrasse were also present. David M. Matteson in his "Fredericksburg Peace Ball," *Va. Mag.,* XLIX, 152–56, has conclusively shown that Washington was not in Fredericksburg on this date; he did attend a ball there in 1784 and this seems to be the source of the error.

17. Monroe to Washington, Aug. 15, 1782, *JM,* I, 19–22; *Autobiography,* 33.

18. Apr. 15, 1782, *Proc. MHS,* Ser. 2, XIX (1905), 150.

19. May 11, 1782, *JM,* I, 15–17.

20. May 20, 1782, Boyd, *Jefferson,* 184–86, 187 fn.; Malone, *Jefferson,* I, 394–95. Edmund Randolph was one of those to whom Monroe showed this letter. See Randolph to Madison June 1, 1782, printed in *Henkels Sale Catalogue,* #694 (Washington–Madison sale), 156.

21. June 28, 1782, *JM,* I, 117–18.

22. [Marshall] to [Monroe], Apr. 17, 1783, Monroe Papers, NYPL; Albert Beveridge, *Life of John Marshall* (4 vols., New York, 1916–19), I, 209.

23. *Journals of the Council of State of Virginia* (5 vols., Richmond, 1931), III, 104.

24. Beveridge, *Marshall,* I, 165–72, 179.

25. *Autobiography,* 33; Deed of Sale, June 22, 1783, Monroe Foundation, Fredericksburg.

26. This figure is based on Monroe's statement to N. P. Trist, Feb. 8, 1828 (Trist Papers, LC), and can be verified in Willard R. Jillson, *Old Kentucky Entries and Deeds* (Louisville, 1926) and in his *The Kentucky Land Grants* (Louisville, 1925).

27. Brant, *Madison,* II, 338–41.

28. June 26, 1782, printed in *George Rogers Clark Papers,* ed. by James Alton James in Vol. XIX of the *Collections* of the Illinois State Historical Library (Springfield, Ill., 1924), 68–69.

29. Jan. 5, 1783, printed in *ibid.,* 178–80.

30. Jan. 5, 1783, printed in *ibid.*

31. He last attended on Oct 21, 1783, *Journals of the Council of State of Virginia*, III, 297.

32. *Autobiography*, 33–34.

CHAPTER 4

THE CONFEDERATION CONGRESS

1. In this chapter, I have relied heavily on Edmund Cody Burnett, *The Continental Congress* (New York, 1941), for background material.

2. *Ibid.*, 590–93; Samuel Dick to Thomas Sinnickson, Mar. 18, 1784, *Letters of Members of the Continental Congress*, ed. by Edmund Cody Burnett (8 vols., Washington, D.C., 1936) [hereinafter cited as Burnett, *Letters*], VII, 472.

3. Monroe to _____, Feb. 25, 1785, printed in *The Month at Goodspeed's*, XXX, no. 5–6, 126–27; Beverley Randolph to Monroe, May 14, 1784, Monroe, LC.

4. Monroe to Jefferson, May 14, 1784, *JM*, I, 26; list of books sold to James Monroe [May 10, 1784], Boyd, *Jefferson*, VII, 230.

5. May 8, 1784, Boyd, *Jefferson*, VII, 234.

6. Burnett, *Continental Congress*, 591; Boyd, *Jefferson*, VI, 406, fn.; *Journals of the Continental Congress* [hereinafter cited as *Journals CC*], XXV, 836, Dec. 23, 1783; Thomas Jefferson, *Autobiography*, in Paul Leicester Ford, *The Writings of Thomas Jefferson* [hereinafter cited as Ford, *Jefferson*] (10 vols., New York, 1892–99), I, 77–81.

7. Burnett, *Continental Congress*, 598–602; Monroe to Gov. Harrison, May 14, 1784, Burnett, *Letters*, VII, 527.

8. *Journals CC*, XXVII, 444–45, May 27, 1784; Monroe to Jefferson, May 20, 1784, *JM*, I, 26–29.

9. Jefferson, *Autobiography*, in Ford, *Jefferson*, I, 81.

10. Monroe to Jefferson, [May] 25, 1784, *JM*, I, 29; Burnett, *Continental Congress*, 605–7.

11. Jefferson to Madison, Apr. 25, 1784, Boyd, *Jefferson*, VII, 19.

12. Feb. 1784; quoted in Kate Mason Rowland, *The Life of George Mason* (2 vols., New York, 1892), II, 68–70.

13. *Journals CC*, XXVII, 428–539, May 25–June 2, 1784; Burnett, *Continental Congress*, 608–10; Thomas Stone to Monroe, n.d., and Monroe to Gov. Benjamin Harrison, June 11, 1784, Burnett, *Letters*, VII, 552, 628–29.

14. Monroe to Jefferson, June 1, 1784, *JM*, I, 31–32; Burnett, *Continental Congress*, 609–12, 638.

15. Beveridge, *Marshall*, I, 179–82.

16. *Autobiography*, 38; Monroe to Jefferson, June 1, July 20, 1784, *JM*, I, 37–38.

17. Oct. 10, 1784, Ridley Papers, MHS.

18. Monroe to Gen. Gates, Schenectady, Aug. 19, 1784, Emmett Coll., NYPL.

19. To Jefferson, Aug. 9, 1784, *JM*, I, 39; Boyd, *Jefferson*, VII, 392, fn. 1, reads "rusing" instead of "running," but in my opinion running is the correct reading of the original.

20. George Clinton, *Public Papers,* ed. by Hugh Hastings (10 vols., Albany, 1904), VIII, 338–39.

21. *Autobiography,* 39; Brant to Monroe, Nov. 29, 1784, in William Stone, *Life of Joseph Brant-Thayendenega* (2 vols., New York, 1838), II, 245–47.

22. *Autobiography,* 39–40.

23. To Jefferson, Nov. 1, 1784, *JM*, I, 42.

24. *Autobiography,* 41; *Journals CC,* XXVII, 641.

25. Monroe to Gov. Harrison, Oct. 30, 1784, *JM*, I, 39–40; John Tyler to Monroe, Nov. 26, 1784, in Lyon G. Tyler, *Letters and Times of the Tylers* (3 vols., Richmond, 1884–96), III, 9; R. H. Lee to George Washington, Nov. 20, 1784, PHS; John Marshall to Monroe, Dec. 2, 1784, Monroe, LC; J. F. Mercer to Madison, Nov. 12, 1784, Burnett, *Letters,* VII, 610; Brant, *Madison,* II, 355–60.

26. To Jefferson, Nov. 1, 1784, *JM*, I, 42–43.

27. Dec. 14, 1784, *JM*, I, 53–54.

28. Grayson to Madison, *ca.* December 1785, Burnett, *Letters,* VIII, 264; R. H. Lee to Monroe, Oct. 17, 1785, *ibid.,* VIII, 238.

29. Monaghan, *Jay,* 273–74.

30. *Autobiography,* 41. The committee was not an important one, but it was an honor to be included in such distinguished company. The boundary dispute was settled by direct negotiations and the committee never rendered any service. Monroe's other commitments forced him to resign on May 15, 1786. Burnett, *Letters,* VIII, 11 fn.

31. Marshall to Monroe, Dec. 2, 1784, Monroe, LC; Jones to Monroe, Dec. 4, 1784, Monroe Foundation, Fredericksburg, Va.

32. Monroe to Madison, Dec. 14, 1784, *JM*, I, 60.

33. Monroe to Madison, Feb. 1, Mar. 6, 1785, and Monroe to Jefferson, Dec. 14, 1784, *JM*, I, 56–63; Samuel Hardy to Gov. P. Henry, Aug. 28, 1785, Burnett, *Letters,* VIII, 203–4; Monroe to _____, Feb. 20, 1785, *The Month at Goodspeed's,* XXX (February 1959), 5–6, 127.

34. The report is in Monroe's hand, *Journals CC,* XVII, 705–6, Dec. 23, 1784.

35. *Ibid.,* XXVII, 656–67, Dec. 3, 1784.

36. Monroe to Jefferson, Nov. 1, 1784, *JM*, I, 42–43; *Journals CC,* XXVIII, 59–60, Feb. 11, 1784.

37. Monroe to Jefferson, Apr. 12, 1785, *JM*, I, 67–74.

38. The report is in Monroe's hand and his letter to Jefferson, Apr. 12, 1785 (*JM*, I, 68–69), makes it clear that the report was substantially his work. The other

members were Pinckney, W. S. Johnson, John Lawrence and King: *Journals CC,* XXVIII, 418–21, June 2, 1785. The text of the report is reprinted in *JM,* I, xliii–xlvi.

39. Jefferson to Monroe, June 17, 1785, Boyd, *Jefferson,* VIII, 232–33; Jefferson's report is in *ibid.,* VI, 393–400; see also *ibid.,* VII, 203.

40. Monroe to _____, Feb. 20, 1785, *The Month at Goodspeed's,* fn. 33.

41. *Journals CC,* XXVIII, 200–4, Mar. 28, 1785; Burnett, *Continental Congress,* 634–36.

42. June 16, 1785, *JM,* I, 84–85.

43. Monroe to Jefferson, Aug. 15, 1785, and Monroe to Madison, July 26, 1785, *JM,* I, 97–98, 103–5; Madison to Jefferson, James Madison, *Writings,* ed. by Gaillard Hunt (9 vols., New York, 1900–10) [hereinafter cited as Hunt, *Madison*], II, 180; Burnett, *Continental Congress,* 633–36.

44. Brant, *Madison,* II, 376; Madison to Monroe, Hunt, *Madison,* II, 147.

45. To Jefferson, Apr. 12, 1785, *JM,* I, 69.

46. Payson Jackson Treat, *The National Land System, 1785–1820* (New York, 1910), 28–39; R. King to E. Gerry, May 8, 1785, Monroe to Madison, May [8], 1785, Grayson to Washington, May [8?], 1785, Burnett, *Letters,* VIII, 113, 115, 118; Burnett, *Continental Congress,* 622–25; *Journals CC,* XXVIII, 327, 335–39, May 3–5, 19, 1785; *Journals CC,* XXVIII, 294–95, Apr. 23, 1785; Brant, *Madison Nationalist,* 342–52; Malone, *Jefferson,* I, 278–79; Treat, *National Land,* 36, 38–39.

47. Monroe to Jefferson, Jan. 19, 1786, *JM,* I, 112–13; Monroe to William Short, Jan. 23, 1786, Short Papers, LC.

48. Burnett, *Continental Congress,* 652–53; Monroe to Jefferson, Jan. 19, 1786, *JM,* I, 117–18.

49. *Journals CC,* XXX, 251–54, May 10, 1786.

50. To Jefferson, May 11, 1786, *JM,* I, 127.

51. Jefferson to Monroe, July 9, 1786, Boyd, *Jefferson,* X, 112–13.

52. Burnett, *Continental Congress,* 631, 685.

53. Monroe to Jefferson, July 16, 1786, *JM,* I, 141.

54. *Journals CC,* XXIX, 657–58, Aug. 25, 1785. Monroe's committee modified a previous committee report (Monroe served on this earlier committee, of which Elbridge Gerry was chairman) which had required Jay to report to Congress on all proposals made by Gardoqui, *ibid.,* XXIX, 561, July 20, 1786.

55. *Ibid.,* XXVII, 705–6, Dec. 23, 1784.

56. To Madison, July 12, 1785, *JM,* I, 94.

57. On the negotiations see Frank Monaghan, *John Jay* (New York, 1935), 255–61; Samuel F. Bemis, *Pinckney's Treaty* (New Haven, 1960), 66–101; Burnett, *Continental Congress,* 654–58; M. A. Otero, "American Mission of Gardoqui" (Ph.D. dissertation, University of California, Los Angeles, 1949).

58. To Madison, May 31, 1786, *JM,* I, 132.

59. Monroe to Patrick Henry, Aug. 12, 1786, *JM,* I, 144–45; Bemis, *Pinckney's Treaty,* 84, states that this conference took place in the spring, but Monroe is quite specific in his letter.

60. See fn. 58, *supra.*

61. King to Elbridge Gerry, June 4, [1786]; Burnett, *Letters,* VIII, 380–82.

62. King to Monroe, July 30, 1786, *ibid.,* VIII, 402; Monroe to Jefferson, Aug. 19, 1786, *JM,* I, 153.

63. *Journals CC,* XXXI, 467–84, Aug. 3, 1786.

64. Monroe to Henry, Aug. 12, 1786, Monroe to Madison, Sept. 3, 1786, *JM,* I, 148–49, 161–62. Only a few persons at this time were aware of the interest in a monarchy; Monroe knew nothing of these plans until many years later. See memorandum of a conversation between Jefferson and Monroe made by Nicholas P. Trist, Jan. 7, 1826, Trist Papers, LC. On the subject of monarchy in general see Richard Krauel, "Prince Henry of Prussia and the Regency of the United States, 1786," *AHR,* XVII (1911), 44–51; Louise B. Dunbar, *A Study of "Monarchical" Tendencies in the United States from 1776–1801* (Urbana, Ill., 1923), Chap. IV; Burnett, *Letters,* VIII, 459 fn. In 1786 the discussions dealt with the possibility of offering Prince Henry of Prussia the post of regent; he seems to have actually been sounded out.

65. Monroe to Madison, Aug. 10, 1786, *JM,* I, 143.

66. This summary of Monroe's speech is based upon the preamble to the resolutions he submitted to Congress on Aug. 29, since brief notes kept by William S. Johnson indicate that he elaborated on the same points in his speech. Burnett, *Letters,* VIII, 437.

67. Monroe to Madison, Aug. 14, 1786, Madison to Monroe, Aug. 17, 1786, *JM,* I, 151–53.

68. Burnett, *Letters,* VIII, 440–41; *Journals CC,* XXXI, 576–93, Aug. 29, 1786.

69. Monroe to Jefferson, July 16, 1786, Monroe to P. Henry, Aug. 12, 1786, *JM,* I, 141, 148.

70. Monroe to Washington, Aug. 20, 1786, Lambert Cadwalader to Monroe, Burnett, *Letters,* VIII, 446–47; Arthur St. Clair to Monroe, Aug. 20, 1786, printed in William Henry Smith, *Life and Public Service of Arthur St. Clair* (2 vols. Cincinnati, 1882), II, 559–603. Cadwalader may have supported Monroe in the Committee of the Whole, but he voted against Monroe's proposition on the final ballot. See Monroe to Madison, Sept. 12, 1786, *JM,* I, 162.

71. Monroe to Jefferson, Jan. 19, 1786, Burnett, *Letters,* VIII, 284–85 fn., 442 fn.

72. *Journals CC,* XXXI, 574–96, Aug. 29, 1786.

73. *Ibid.,* XXXI, 596–622, Aug. 30–Sept. 2, 1786.

74. *Ibid.,* XXXI, Aug. 29, 1786; Monroe to Madison, *JM,* I, 163–64.

75. Jefferson, July 16, 1786, *JM,* I, 142.

76. Memorandum by King, Sept. 1786, Charles King, *Life and Correspondence of Rufus King* (6 vols., New York, 1894–98), I, 126–27.

77. Aug. 16, 1786, Burnett, *Letters,* VIII, 469.

78. Monroe to Madison, Sept. 3, 1786, *JM,* I, 160–61; *Journals CC,* XXXI, 697.

79. Monroe to Madison, Oct. 7, 1786, Burnett, *Letters,* VIII, 476.

80. Madison to Monroe, Nov. 30, 1786, Madison, LC. Monroe may have been in Richmond in November and discussed the Mississippi question with members of the legislature. Madison wrote him on Oct. 30, 1786, urging him to come to Richmond. See Gaillard Hunt, *Writings of James Madison* (9 vols., New York, 1900–10), II, 276.

81. Aug. 12, 1786, *JM,* I, 149.

82. Monroe's letters to Madison have not survived, but Madison's replies of March 19 and May 13, 1786 (Hunt, *Madison Writings,* II, 233–242), leave no doubt as to Monroe's views; for comments about a general convention see Grayson to Madison, March 22, 1786, Burnett, *Letters,* VIII, 333.

83. Aug. 16, 1786, Burnett, *Letters,* VIII, 430.

84. Timothy Bloodworth to Gov. Richard Caswell, Sept. 4, 1786, Rufus King to John Adams, Oct. 2, 1786, Monroe to Madison, Oct. 2, 1786, *ibid.,* VIII, 462, 475; *Journals CC,* XXXI, 770, Oct. 11, 1786.

85. Oct. 12, 1786, *JM,* I, 169.

CHAPTER 5

LAWYER AND FARMER, 1786–1790

1. Monroe to Jefferson, Oct, 12, 1786, *JM,* I, 169.

2. Stephen Mix Mitchell to W. S. Johnson, Feb. 21, 1786, Burnett, *Letters,* VIII, 309.

3. May 28, 1786, Gratz Collection, PHS.

4. Monroe to Joseph Jones, Mar. 2, 1786, Monroe Foundation, Fredericksburg, Va.

5. Jones to Monroe, [1785], in *ibid.* For the Kortright family see John Austen Stevens, Jr., *Colonial New York: Sketches Biographical and Historical, 1768–1784* (New York, 1867), 140; Clarence Winthrop Bowen, *History of Woodstock, Connecticut* (6 vols., Norwood, Mass., 1926), III, 254, 260.

6. Gerry to Monroe, June 11, 1787, *New England Genealogical and Historical Quarterly,* XLIX (1895), 435.

7. Dec. 18, 1786, Boyd, *Jefferson,* X, 612.

8. Monroe to Jefferson, July 27, 1787, *JM,* I, 173.

9. Jones to Monroe, Dec. 7, 1786, Monroe, LC.

10. Monroe to Jefferson, Jan. 19, Oct. 12, 1786, *JM,* I, 119, 169.

11. Jones to Monroe, [March 1786], March 25, 1786, Mercer to Monroe, April 6,

1786, Monroe Foundation, Fredericksburg, Va.; Jones to Monroe, Feb. 9, Mar. 14, Apr. 15, 1786, Monroe, LC; Monroe to Jefferson, July 27, 1787, *JM,* I, 173.

12. Jones to Monroe, Apr. 30, 1786, Monroe, LC; Monroe to Jefferson, May 11, 1786, *JM,* I, 129.

13. Monroe to [Madison], Feb. 6, 1787, Monroe, NYPL.

14. Monroe to Jefferson, Aug. 19, 1786, July 27, 1787, *JM,* I, 158, 173.

15. April 13, 1787, Monroe Foundation, Fredericksburg, Va.

16. Monroe to ———, April 4, 7, 19, 1788, University of Virginia; Monroe to Madison, Oct. 13, Dec. 6, 1787, *JM,* I, 176, 179.

17. Monroe to [Madison], Feb. 6, 1787, Monroe, NYPL; Madison to Monroe, April 30, 1787, Edward Carrington to Monroe, Apr. 18, 1787, Monroe, LC; Monroe to James Hunter, June 17, 1787, University of Virginia.

18. Monroe to Jefferson, July 27, 1787, *JM,* I, 173.

19. *Ibid., JM,* I, 174; Monroe to his wife, fn. 15 *supra;* John Taliaferro to Monroe, May 4, 1786, Monroe Foundation, Fredericksburg, Va.

20. William Armstrong Crozier, *Virginia County Records: Spotsylvania County, 1721–1800* (New York, 1905), 456.

21. J. Jones to Monroe, Mar. 3, 1787, Monroe, LC; John Dawson to Madison, Apr. 15, 1787, MHS, *Proceedings,* ser. 2, XVIII (1903), 457.

22. Carrington to Monroe, May 1, 1787, Monroe Papers, William and Mary College; Madison to Monroe, Apr. 19, 1787, Hunt, *Madison Writings,* II, 355.

23. Jefferson to Madison, Jan. 30, 1787, Boyd, *Jefferson,* XI, 97. Jefferson used almost the same expression in referring to Monroe in a letter to W. T. Franklin, May 7, 1786, *ibid.,* IX, 466.

24. July 27, 1787, *ibid.,* XI, 631. Passages in italics are in cipher in the original.

25. Madison to Washington, Mar. 18, 1787, Hunt, *Madison Writings,* II, 354.

26. E[dmund] R[andolph] to Madison, Mar. 22, Apr. 4, 1787, Madison, LC.

27. J. Dawson to Madison, Sept. 25, 1787, Department of State, Bureau of Rolls, *Documentary History of the Constitution of the United States* (5 vols., Washington, D.C., 1894–1905), IV, 295. [Hereinafter cited as *Doc. Hist. of Const.*]

28. Madison to Monroe, May 23, 1787, Madison, LC.

29. *Journal of the House of Delegates of Virginia . . . [1787–1788],* 40, 61, Nov. 17, Dec. 3, 1787; Monroe to Madison, Dec. 6, 1787, *JM,* I, 178–79.

30. *Journals of the House of Delegates . . . [1787–1788],* 98, Jan. 1, 1788; Monroe to Jefferson, Apr. 10, 1788, *JM,* I, 189.

31. Monroe to Madison, Oct. 13, 1787, *JM,* I, 176.

32. W. Grayson to W. Short, Nov. 10, 1787, Burnett, *Letters,* VIII, 678; Monroe to Madison, Oct. 13, 1787, *JM,* I, 176; G. L. Turberville to Madison, Dec. 11, 1787, Madison, NYPL.

33. Madison to Jefferson, Apr. 22, 1788, Hunt, *Madison Writings,* V, 121.

34. *Autobiography,* 49–50; Monroe to Jefferson, Apr. 10, 1788, *JM,* I, 189; the

account of the election in Spotsylvania is taken from John Taliaferro to S. L. Gouverneur, Apr. 8, 1844, Gouverneur Papers, NYPL.

35. Monroe to Jefferson, Apr. 10, 1788, *JM,* I, 188.

36. Printed in *JM,* I, Appendix I, 307–43.

37. Pamphlets relating to the Constitution are reprinted in Paul Leicester Ford, *Pamphlets on the Constitution of the United States . . .* (New York, 1888).

38. Jones to Madison, Oct. 29, 1787, Madison, LC.

39. Excellent accounts of the convention are to be found in Beveridge, *Marshall,* I, 356–480; Brant, *Madison,* III, 193–228; David John Mays, *Edmund Pendleton* (2 vols., Cambridge, Mass., 1952), II, 217–73; the debates are to be found in Jonathan Elliot, *Debates in the Several State Conventions on the Adoption of the Federal Constitution* (5 vols., Philadelphia, 1836).

40. Quotes are from Monroe to Jefferson, July 12, 1788, *JM,* I, 185; descriptions are based on Beveridge, *Marshall,* I, 367–76.

41. Brant, *Madison,* III, 277.

42. Monroe's speeches, like most of the others, are badly reported; he does not seem to have supplied written versions to the reporter. Marshall's recollection in 1832 that Monroe and Grayson did so is clearly incorrect in Monroe's case. See Thomas H. Bayley's Memorandum on a Conversation with John Marshall in 1832, Virginia State Library.

43. Elliot, *Debates,* III, 207–22.

44. *Ibid.,* 311–12.

45. *Ibid.,* 334–40, 344.

46. A. Stuart to John Breckinridge, June 19, 1788, Breckinridge Papers, LC; Robert Breckinridge to James Breckinridge, July 2, 1788, Breckinridge–Marshall Papers, Filson Club, Louisville, Ky.; Madison to Washington, June 13, 1788, Hunt, *Madison Writings,* 179 fn. Stuart in his letter listed six doubtful members—P. Carrington (Marshall), Wm. Ronald (Powhatan), Wm. Fleming (Botetourt), Rice Bullock, H. Marshall (Fayette) and R. Breckinridge (Fayette), all of whom voted to ratify. Another list of eleven doubtful delegates (including only three listed by Stuart—Carrington, Marshall and Ronald) appears in [John Scott], *The Lost Principle; or the Sectional Equilibrium. . . . by "Barbarossa"* (Richmond, 1860), 235–37. Scott gives no source.

47. Elliot, *Debates,* III, 488–90.

48. *Ibid.,* 630–31, 652, 656–63.

49. July 12, 1788, *JM,* I, 185–86.

50. Oct. 26, 1788, *JM,* I, 195; Monroe to Jefferson, Feb. 15, 1789, *JM,* I, 199; Edgar Woods, *Albemarle County in Virginia* (Charlottesville, 1901), 279–80.

51. Monroe to Madison, Oct. 26, 1788, *JM,* I, 194.

52. Henry Lee to Washington, Sept. 13, 1788, *Doc. Hist. of Const.,* V, 50; E. Carrington to H. Knox, Dec. 20, 1788, cited in David Matheson, "The Organization of the Government under the Constitution," *History of the Formation of the*

Union under the Constitution (Washington, D.C., 1941), ed. by the Constitutional Sesquicentennial Commission, Sol Bloom, Director General, 194–95.

53. Carrington to Knox, fn. 52 *supra*. Writers with a strong federalist bias have perpetuated this erroneous view. See Beveridge, *Marshall*, II, 45–52.

54. *Journals of the House of Delegates . . .* [*1788–1789*], 31, Nov. 14, 1788.

55. R. H. Lee to John Jones, Oct. 15, 1788, James Curtiss Ballagh, *Letters of Richard Henry Lee* (2 vols., New York, 1914), II, 478–79.

56. On Nov. 17 and 20, 1788; see *Acts of the Virginia Assembly, 1788, 1789*.

57. E. Carrington to Madison, Oct. 24, Nov. 9, 1788, Madison, LC; Washington to Benjamin Lincoln, Nov. 14, 1788, Fitzpatrick, *Washington*, XXX, 125.

58. E. Carrington to Madison, Nov. 18, Madison, LC; David Humphrey to Jefferson, Nov. 19, 1788, Jefferson, LC.

59. To Madison, fn. 63 *infra*.

60. Mays, *Pendleton*, II, 274; Edmund Randolph to Madison, Nov. 21, 1788, Madison, LC.

61. [George Nicholas] to Madison, Jan. 2, 1789, *Doc. Hist. of Const.*, V, 139; Jones to Madison, Nov. 21, 1788, Madison, LC.

62. E. Carrington to Madison, Nov. 26, 1788, Madison, LC.

63. J. Jones to Madison, Dec. 14, 1788, Madison, LC.

64. Feb. 15, 1789, *JM*, I, 199.

65. Brant, *Madison*, III, 241.

66. Alexander White to Madison, Dec. 4, 1788, E. Carrington to Madison, Dec. 19, 1788, Madison, LC.

67. To James Higginbotham, [1788], *WMQ*, ser. 1, IX, 124–25.

68. George Lee Turberville, Dec. 12, 1788, Madison, NYPL; Brant, *Madison*, III, 239–40; E. Carrington to Henry Knox, Feb. 16, 1789, Matheson, Origin of Fed. Govt., *loc. cit.*, 194; Richmond, Va. *Virginia Independent Chronicle*, Jan. 28, 1789.

69. Benjamin Johnson, Jr., to [Madison], Jan. 19, 1789, Rives Papers, LC; Brant, *Madison*, III, 240.

70. Brant, *Madison*, III, 241–42.

71. Monroe to Jefferson, Feb. 15, 1789, *JM*, I, 199. For the election returns see Brant, *Madison*, III, 242.

72. Monroe to Madison, Apr. [26], 1789, *JM*, I, 201.

73. *Ibid.*

74. Monroe to Madison, June 15, 1789, *JM*, I, 202.

75. Monroe to Madison, July 25, 1790, *JM*, I, 216.

76. Monroe to Madison, July 19, Aug. 12, 1789, *JM*, I, 203, 206; Monroe to ———, Johns Deposit, University of Virginia.

77. Monroe to Madison, Oct. 26, 1788, *JM*, I, 195.

78. June 27, 1792, *JM*, I, 234–35.

79. Brant, *Madison*, II, 341.

80. Mays, *Pendleton*, II, 288; *Autobiography*, 51, 55.

81. Dec. 14, 1789, Ford, *Jefferson*, V, 137.

82. See Boyd, *Jefferson*, XVI, 167–76.

83. Sarah N. Randolph, *Domestic Life of Thomas Jefferson* (New York, 1871), 205.

84. It was submitted formally on Feb. 12; see Boyd, *Jefferson*, XVI, 167–78; Monroe to Jefferson, Jan. 16, 1790, *ibid.*, XVI, 110.

CHAPTER 6

SENATOR AND PARTY LEADER, 1790–1794

1. Jefferson to W. Short, Apr. 27, 1790, Ford, *Jefferson*, V, 164; Malone, *Jefferson*, II, 324–25. Jefferson's opposition to Walker contributed to the bitterness Walker later manifested toward him.

2. Monroe to Jefferson, July 3, 18, 1790, *JM*, I, 210, 214.

3. To Short, Sept. 30, 1790, Coolidge Papers, MHS.

4. Monroe to Jefferson, Oct. 20, 1790, *JM*, I, 217.

5. Nov. 3, 1790, *Tyler's Quarterly*, V, 192.

6. Monroe to Jefferson, Oct. 20, 1790, *JM*, I, 217–18.

7. Jefferson to ———, Jan. 11, 1790 [correct date is 1791], Jefferson, LC; Monroe to James Lyle, Nov. 19, 1790, *Va. Mag.*, 221–22; Monroe to Jefferson, Nov. 26, 1790, *JM*, I, 219.

8. Brant, *Madison*, III, 324–25. It is not certain whether Monroe accepted, but it seems likely that Mrs. Monroe remained in New York for most of the winter.

9. Roy Swanstrom, The United States Senate, 1789–1801 (Ms. Ph.D. thesis, University of California, Berkeley, 1958), 390–430.

10. *AC*, 1C1S, Senate, Dec. 8, 1790.

11. *Ibid.*, Senate, Jan. 31, Mar. 3, 1791.

12. R. H. Lee to Monroe, Jan. 15, 1791, Ballagh, *Lee*, II, 541.

13. *AC*, 1C1S, Senate, Jan. 13, 20, 1791.

14. *Ibid.*, Feb. 20, 1791; Swanstrom, Senate, 525–38; George Clinton to Monroe, Feb. 16, 1791, Monroe, LC.

15. Draft of speech in Monroe's hand, n.d., Monroe, NYPL.

16. J. Jones to Monroe, Jan. 27, 1791, Monroe, LC.

17. Monroe to Jefferson, Jan. 16, 1790, Coolidge Papers, MHS; same to same,

Mar. 29, 1791, *JM*, I, 221–22; Jefferson to Monroe, Apr. 17, 1791, Ford, *Jefferson*, V, 317–18. Joseph was at Edinburgh at the same time Jefferson's son-in-law Thomas Mann Randolph was also studying there.

18. Monroe to Madison, July 25, 1790, *JM*, I, 215.

19. Text of resolutions may be conveniently found in Henry Steele Commager, *Documents in American History* (2 vols., fifth ed., New York, 1949), I, 155.

20. Jan. 24, 1791, Monroe, LC.

21. Jefferson to Monroe, July 10, 1791, Ford, *Jefferson*, V, 352; Madison to Jefferson, May 12, June 27, 1791, Hunt, *Madison Writings*, VI, 51–53.

22. June 17, 1791, *JM*, I, 223.

23. These essays, which have not previously been identified as written by Monroe, were published on Nov. 14 and 24 and Dec. 12, 1791, in the *National Gazette*. Number 1 appeared in *Dunlap's American Daily Advertiser*. A draft of the first essay and a portion of the second are in Monroe Foundation, Fredericksburg, Va. See also J. Jones to Monroe, Nov. 28, 1791, in the same collection.

24. Aratus #1.

25. Aratus #2.

26. Jefferson to Monroe, July 10, 1791, Ford, *Jefferson*, V, 351.

27. Monroe to [John Breckinridge?]; Breckinridge Papers, LC.

28. Memorandum by Rufus King, n.d.; King, *Life of King*, I, 419–21.

29. Malone, *Jefferson*, II, 400–1; Jefferson to Short, Nov. 9, 1791, Ford, *Jefferson*, V, 389; Monroe to _____, n.d., Rives Papers, LC; *Executive Journals of the Senate*, 2C1S, 93, Dec. 30, 1791.

30. Mason to Monroe, Jan. 30, 1792, Monroe, LC.

31. Malone, *Jefferson*, II, 402–3.

32. Jefferson, *Anas*, Mar. 9, 1792, Ford, *Jefferson*, I, 182–3; Jefferson to Monroe, Apr. 11, 1792, *ibid.*, V, 503; Monroe to Jefferson, Apr. 11, *JM*, I, 227.

33. *AC*, 2C1S, Senate, Feb. 9–23, 1792.

34. Madison to Jefferson, June 12, 1792, Madison, LC.

35. Jefferson to Martha J. Randolph, Mar. 22, 1792, Jefferson to T. M. Randolph, May 17, 1792, Jefferson, LC.

36. Monroe to Madison, June 27, 1792, *JM*, I, 235.

37. Monroe to Jefferson, June 17, 1792, *JM*, I, 230–32.

38. Monroe to Jefferson, June 17, 1791, *JM*, I, 223; Monroe to Gov. Beverley Randolph, June 16, 1791, Gratz Coll., PHS.

39. Monroe to Jefferson, July 25, 1791, Monroe to Madison, June 27, 1792, *JM*, I, 225, 133; for an account of the various committees see footnotes in Boyd, *Jefferson*, II, 305, 322.

40. June 23, 1792, Ford, *Jefferson*, VI, 93–94.

41. To Jefferson, June 17, 1792, *JM*, I, 237–38.

42. Burr to Monroe, Sept. 10, 1792, Monroe, LC.

43. For an extensive account of these essays see Philip M. Marsh, *Monroe's Defense of Jefferson and Freneau Against Hamilton* (Oxford, Ohio, 1948); Malone, *Jefferson,* II, 453–55.

44. For more details and a somewhat more favorable view of Beckley see Noble E. Cunningham, Jr., "John Beckley: An Early American Party Manager," *WMQ,* ser. 3, XIII (1956), 40–52, and Philip M. Marsh, "John Beckley, Mystery Man of the Early Jeffersonians," *Pennsylvania Magazine of History and Biography,* LXXII (1948), 54–69.

45. On the Reynolds affair see Nathan Schachner, *Alexander Hamilton* (New York, 1946), 365–68; John C. Miller, *Alexander Hamilton* (New York, 1959), 334–42.

46. For the exposure which took place in 1797 see Chapter IX.

47. Smith and Willett to Monroe and Madison, Sept. 30, 1792, Monroe Foundation, Fredericksburg, Va.

48. For references to these activities see Monroe to Madison, Sept. 18, 1792, *JM,* I, 241, and John Dawson to Monroe, Oct. 19, 1792, Monroe, NYPL.

49. Monroe to Madison, Oct. 9, 1792, *JM,* I, 242–45; Madison to Monroe, Oct. 11, 1792, Madison, LC.

50. A copy of the reply in Monroe's hand dated Oct. 19 and signed by both is in Monroe, LC.

51. Jabez D. Hammond, *History of Political Parties in the State of New York* (2 vols., Syracuse, 1852), I, 51–55.

52. *AC,* 2C2S, Senate, *passim;* Monroe to Jefferson, Nov. 21, 1792, *JM,* I, 247; Malone, *Jefferson,* III, 19; Jefferson to T. M. Randolph, Nov. 2, 1792, Ford, *Jefferson,* VI, 127–28.

53. Brant, *Madison,* III, 379–80; Monroe to Madison, May 18, 1792, *JM,* I, 255.

54. To Jefferson, May 5, 1793, *JM,* I, 251–53.

55. To Jefferson, May 28, 1793, *JM,* I, 257–59.

56. See fn. 54 *supra.*

57. To Jefferson, June 27, 1793, *JM,* I, 262–65.

58. John Dawson to Monroe, July 12, 1793, Monroe, NYPL.

59. July 14, 1793, Ford, *Jefferson,* VI, 346.

60. Jefferson to Madison, June 28, 1793, *ibid.,* VI, 326.

61. Brant, *Madison,* III, 375–79.

62. For a summary of the Genet affair see Freeman, *Washington,* VII, 100–6; Malone, *Jefferson,* III, 114–31; Alexander DeConde, *Entangling Alliances: Politics and Diplomacy Under Washington* (Durham, N.C., 1958), Chaps. 7–9; and William Frederick Keller, American Politics and the Genet Mission (Ms. PhD. thesis, University of Pittsburgh, 1951).

63. Some weeks previously Genet had told Jefferson that he intended appealing to the people. Jefferson to Monroe, June 28, 1793, Ford, *Jefferson*, VI, 323.

64. This report is printed in *ibid.*, I, 237–41, as part of the Anas. In his report Jefferson wrote that Genet had told Dallas that he would "appeal from the President to the people."

65. Freeman, *Washington*, VII, 108–9; Malone, *Jefferson*, III, 132–33; Jefferson, Anas, Aug. 6, 1793, Ford, *Jefferson*, I, 256.

66. For a detailed account of the whole campaign see Harry Ammon, "The Genet Mission and the Development of American Political Parties," *Journal of American History*, LII (March 1966), 725–41.

67. Jefferson to Madison, July 7, 1793, Ford, *Jefferson*, VI, 238–39; Madison to Jefferson, Aug. 5, 1793, Hunt, *Madison Writings*, VI, 139.

68. Aug. 12, 1793, *JM*, I, 271.

69. Monroe to Madison, May 18, 1793, *JM*, I, 254. Taylor's pamphlet cannot be identified and it is impossible to say whether it was published. At one time it was incorrectly believed to be a work entitled *Examination of Late Proceedings in Congress Respecting the Official Conduct of the Secretary of the Treasury*. This pamphlet, published in the spring of 1793, has been attributed to John Beckley and Monroe by Edmund and Dorothy Smith Berkeley, "The Piece Left Behind," *Va. Mag.*, LXXV (1967), 174–80. They have conclusively shown that Beckley was one of the authors, but the degree of Monroe's involvement is by no means certain. The evidence they present is indirect, and I have found nothing in the Monroe papers or contemporary correspondence hinting that he wrote such a pamphlet. In any case Monroe did not show a strong interest in fiscal matters.

70. Madison to Jefferson, Aug. 27, 1793, Hunt, *Madison Writings*, VI, 179.

71. Aug. 23, 1793, Emmett Collection, NYPL; the printed version in *JM*, I, 272–73, contains several minor errors.

72. Madison to Jefferson, Aug. 27, 1793, Hunt, *Madison Writings*, VI, 179.

73. Brant, *Madison*, III, 381.

74. A copy of the draft Madison sent Jefferson on Sept. 2 is printed in Hunt, *Madison Writings*, VI, 192, fn. 1.

75. Brant, *Madison*, III, 381.

76. To Jefferson, Sept. 2, 1793, Hunt, *Madison Writings*, VI, 195.

77. Madison to Archibald Stuart, Sept. 1, 1793, *ibid.*, VI, 188–90; Monroe to Jefferson, Sept. 3, 1793, *JM*, I, 273–75.

78. For the texts see Richmond, *Virginia Gazette and General Advertiser*, Sept. 25, Oct. 2, 1793. The Staunton resolutions were also issued in broadside form. A copy may be found in the Virginia Broadsides, Library of Congress. The final resolve of the Staunton resolutions differed somewhat from that of Caroline, being far more moderate in its references to Genet, and was obviously a modification made by the Francophile Monroe.

79. Madison to Jefferson, Aug. 27, 1793, Hunt, *Madison Writings*, VI, 179.

80. See Philip M. Marsh, "James Monroe as 'Agricola' in the Genet Controversy, 1793," *Va. Mag.*, LXII (1954), 472–76 and Harry Ammon, "Agricola versus Aristides: James Monroe, John Marshall and the Genet Affair in Virginia," *ibid.*, LXXIV (July 1966), 312–20.

81. Fn. 66 *supra*.

CHAPTER 7

MINISTER TO FRANCE

1. Madison to [Jefferson], copy, Mar. 2, 1794, Madison, LC; Monroe to Jefferson, Mar. 3, 1794, *JM*, I, 281; Monroe to [R. R. Livingston], February 10, 1794, Livingston Papers, NYHS; Monroe to _____, Apr. 30, 1794, Hornor Papers, PHS; New York, *Diary*, Mar. 6, 1794.

2. Monroe to Jefferson, Mar. 16, 1794, *JM*, I, 286–89.

3. Monroe to Madison, Mar. 7, 1794, Cannaroe Papers, PHS.

4. Monroe to _____, Apr. 30, 1794, Hornor Papers, PHS; Brant, *Madison*, III, 395 ff.

5. Monroe to Jefferson, Mar. 3, 1794, *JM*, I, 281–83; *AC*, 3C1S, Senate, Jan. 24, 1794; Freeman, *Washington*, VII, 151.

6. Monroe to Jefferson, Mar. 3, 1794, *JM*, I, 282–83; King, *Rufus King*, I, 532; *AC*, 3C1S, Senate, Feb. 28, 1794.

7. *AC*, 3C1S, Senate, Mar. 24, 28, 1794; Mathew Lyon to Monroe, Mar. 5, 1816, Monroe, NYPL.

8. Maria Knox to Monroe [February 1794], Monroe, NYPL; Monroe to Jefferson, Mar. 3, 1794, *JM*, I, 281.

9. Richard Hildreth, *The History of the United States of America* (6 vols., New York, 1880), IV, 486–88.

10. Monroe to _____, Apr. 30, 1794, Hornor Papers, PHS.

11. May 4, 1794, *JM*, I, 293; *AC*, 3C1S, Senate, Apr. 28, 1794.

12. *AC*, 3C1S, Senate, May 5–6, 1794; Isaac S. Harrell, *Loyalism in Virginia* (Durham, N.C., 1926), 160–73; Memorandum of Rufus King, May 6, 1794, King, *Rufus King*, I, 535–36.

13. T. T. Dwight, May 6, 1794, Seth Ames, *Works of Fisher Ames* (2 vols., Boston, 1854), I, 148.

14. Monroe to Jefferson, Mar. 16, 1794, *JM*, I, 289.

15. Monroe to Washington, Apr. 8, 1794, *JM*, I, 292.

16. Apr. 9, 1794, Fitzpatrick, *Washington*, XXXIII, 320; Freeman, *Washington*, VII, 166–67.

17. Apr. 16, 1794, Gratz Collection, PHS.

18. Account of debates in a memorandum of Rufus King, Apr. 17–18, 1794, 2, King, *Rufus King,* I, 521–22. In spite of the rule of secrecy in the Senate, the proceedings seem to have been well known. There is a copy of King's memorandum in the Hamilton Papers, LC.

19. The President was much annoyed at this reference to Jay's report, which was in the files of the State Department, and seems to have thought Randolph had been responsible for letting Monroe see it. Randolph to Washington, Apr. 19, 1794, Washington Papers, LC.

20. *Executive Journals of the Senate,* 3C1S, 152, Apr. 19, 1794; Monroe to _____, Apr. 23, 1794, Gratz Collection, PHS.

21. Joseph Fauchet, *Mémoire sur les Etats Unis D'Amerique,* ed. by Carl Ludwig Lokke in American Historical Association, *Annual Report for 1936* (Washington, 1938), I, 105–7.

22. Jay to Washington, Apr. 30, 1794, John Jay, *Correspondence,* ed. by Henry P. Johnston (4 vols., New York, 1890), IV, 9–10.

23. Brant, *Madison,* III, 400; Monroe to Jefferson, May 26, 1794, *JM,* I, 296–98.

24. Monroe to Jefferson, May 26, 1794, *JM,* I, 298.

25. Monroe to Madison, May 26, 1794, Monroe to Jefferson, May 27, 1794, *JM,* I, 299–300; Davis, *Memoirs of Burr,* I, 408–9.

26. Freeman, *Washington,* VII, 171. Monroe's name was not on the lists drawn up by Knox, Hamilton and Randolph and submitted to the President. These lists are in the Washington Papers, LC.

27. *Executive Journal of the Senate,* 3C1S, 157, May 28, 1794. There was no rollcall; presumably Monroe received the courtesy of an unopposed confirmation.

28. A[aron] B[urr] to Monroe, May 30, 1794, Monroe, LC.

29. To Jefferson, May 26, 1794, *JM,* I, 297–98.

30. May 16, 1794, Monroe, LC.

31. July 3, 1796, Ford, *Jefferson,* VII, 88.

32. June 1, 1794, *JM,* I, 302.

33. Monroe to Joseph Monroe, June 16, 1794, to Joseph Jones, Oct. 27, 1796, in Monroe Foundation; Jones to Monroe, Mar. 26, 1795, Monroe, LC; Jones to Madison, Nov. 4, 1794, Madison, LC.

34. Monroe to Jones, Oct. 27, 1796, Monroe Foundation.

35. Monroe Account Book, 1794–1801, Monroe, LC; Monroe to Madison, Sept. 2, [1794], *JM,* II, 37; Hulbert Footner, *Sailor of Fortune: the Life . . . of Commodore Barney. . . .* (New York, 1940), 196–97.

36. Dated June 10, 1794, reprinted in *JM,* II, 2–9 and in *American State Papers, Foreign Relations* [hereinafter cited as *ASPFR*], I, 668–69. The editor of the *ASPFR* seems to have taken the letter from Monroe's *View* (see Ch. 9, fn. 40) since the same passages are in italics.

37. Monroe Account Book, 1794–1802, Monroe, LC; Monroe to Randolph, Aug. 15 [should be August 11], 1794, *JM*, II, 16; Footner, *Barney*, 196–97.

38. Fauchet to Minister of Foreign Affairs, May 5, 1794, AHA, *Annual Report* (1903), II, 333.

39. Beverly W. Bond, Jr., *Monroe Mission to France, 1794–1796* in *Johns Hopkins University Studies in Historical and Political Science,* Ser. XXV, Nos. 2 and 3 (Baltimore, 1907), has long been the standard Monograph, but it is now dated. The basic facts are generally correct, but Bond's sources were limited to printed documents and the Monroe papers. The best recent study, although deficient on the French aspect, is to be found in Alexander DeConde, *Entangling Alliances: Politics and Diplomacy Under George Washington* (Duke University Press, 1958); Samuel Flagg Bemis, "Washington's Farewell Address; A Foreign Policy of Independence," *American Historical Review,* XXXIX (1933), 254–56, presents a fresh interpretation; Albert H. Bowman, "Struggle for Neutrality: A History of Diplomatic Relations Between the United States and France, 1790–1801" (Unpub. Ph.D. thesis, Columbia University, 1954) makes full use of unpublished archival material. For French policy the following works are especially useful: Bernard Fay, *The Revolutionary Spirit in France and America* (New York, 1927); George Lefebvre, *The Thermidorians and the Directory* (New York, 1931); A. Aulard, *The French Revolution* (4 vols., London, 1910); E. Wilson Lyon, "The Directory and the United States," *AHR,* XLIII (1937), 513–32, has useful suggestions but is largely concerned with the period after Monroe's departure.

40. *Autobiography,* 57–61; Albert Mathiez, *After Robespierre* (New York, 1931), 19–20; Monroe to Randolph, Feb. 12, 1795, *JM*, II, 196–97.

41. Monroe to Madison, Sept. 2, [1794], Monroe to Randolph, Aug. 25, 1794, Feb. 12, 1795, *JM*, II, 32, 38–40, 195–96; *Autobiography,* 60–62; Memoir on the reception of Monroe, Thermidor, Year II, Archives des Affaires Etrangères, Correspondence Politique, Etats-Unis [hereinafter cited as AECPEU], v. 41, f. 280.

42. *Autobiography,* 64; *View, JM,* III, 391 fn.; Monroe to Madison, Sept. 2, 1794, *JM*, II, 40.

43. *JM*, II, 13–15; Joshua Barney to his brother, Dec. 21, 1794, in Bernard Mayo, "Joshua Barney and the French Revolution," *Maryland Historical Magazine,* XXXVI (1941), 359.

44. *JM*, II, 33 fn.

45. Letter of Barney cited fn. 43 *supra.*

46. *Autobiography,* 65.

47. Monroe to Madison, Sept. 2, 1794, *JM,* II, 40.

48. Madison to Monroe, Dec. 4, 1794, *JM*, II, 210 fn.

49. Jay to Washington, Sept. 13, 1794, Washington Papers, LC; Jay to Hamilton, Sept. 14, 1794, Henry P. Johnston (ed.), *Correspondence and Public Papers of John Jay* (4 vols., New York, 1890), IV, 114.

50. Brown to Monroe, Dec. 5, 1794, Monroe, LC.

51. Dec. 2, 1794, *ASPFR*, I, 689–90. When Monroe received this on Feb. 9, 1795, he dispatched a lengthy defense on Feb. 12, 1795, *JM*, II, 193–205.

52. Dec. 5, 1794, *ASPFR*, I, 690.

53. Washington to Jay, Dec. 18, 1794, Fitzpatrick, *Washington*, XXXIV, 60–61.

54. Monroe to Randolph, Aug. 25, 1794, *JM*, II, 32–33; *Autobiography*, 65–67.

55. *JM*, II, 41–49.

56. To Randolph, Sept. 15, 1794, *JM*, II, 202.

57. Randolph to Monroe, July 30, 1794, *ASPFR*, I, 699, Monroe to Randolph, Nov. 7, 1794, Monroe to Committee of Public Safety, Oct. 18, 1794, *JM*, II, 88–90, 99.

58. Dec. 2, 1794, *ASPFR*, I, 690.

59. Monroe to Randolph, Feb. 12, 1795, *JM*, II, 202.

60. Monroe to Randolph, Oct. 16, 1794, *JM*, II, 73–75; Monroe to Commissary of Foreign Affairs, Sept. 20, 1794, AECPEU, v. 41, f. 432; Buchot to Monroe, Sept. 23, 1794, Monroe Foundation; Randolph to Monroe, July 2, 1795, Monroe, LC.

61. Buchot to Monroe, Sept. 14, 1794, Monroe, LC; Monroe to the consuls, June 8, 1795, copy in French, AECPEU v. 44, f. 60; Monroe to Sec. of State, July 6, 1795, *JM*, II, 317–21.

62. Copy of the list of May 15, 1796, is in Monroe, NYPL, and that of Apr. 24, 1796, is in Monroe, LC. At this time there were about 150 Americans in Paris.

63. To Sec. of State, Aug. 1, 1795, Monroe to the Commissary of the Marine, Aug. 30, 1795, *JM*, II, 331–32, 343–46.

64. Monroe to Randolph, Dec. 2, 1794, *JM*, II, 152; the report is printed in *ASPFR*, I.

65. Printed in *JM*, II, 88–96; see also Monroe to Randolph, Nov. 7, 1794, *JM*, II, 98–99.

66. Lefebvre, *Thermidorians*, 84ff; Monroe to Randolph, Nov. 7, 1794, Monroe to Madison, Nov. 30, 1794, *JM*, II, 102–3, 136–37; *View*, *JM*, III, 392–93.

67. Monroe to Randolph, Nov. 7, 1794, *JM*, II, 101–3.

68. In AECPEU, v. 42, f. 18–30 dated October 3, 1794. The report is unsigned but Bowman, Struggle for Neutrality, 234–47, ascribes it to Otto; Monroe to Randolph, Nov. 7, 1794, *JM*, II, 103.

69. It is impossible to date this interview precisely, since Monroe rarely dated his conferences. See Monroe to Randolph, Dec. 2, 1794, *JM*, II, 147.

70. Sept. 25, 1795, *ASPFR*, I, 678.

71. Gardoqui to Monroe, Sept. 9, 1794, Monroe Foundation; Gardoqui to Monroe, Oct. 7, 1794, Monroe, LC; Committee of Public Safety to Monroe, Nov. 13, 1794, Monroe to Randolph, Nov. 20, 1794, Monroe to Madison, Nov. 30, 1794, all in *JM*, II, 109–12, 118–21, 137–38.

72. Monroe to Randolph, Nov. 20, 1794, enclosing a copy of the note, *JM*, II, 121–26; Monroe to Madison, Dec. 7, 1799, *JM*, III, 167.

73. Monroe to Madison, Nov. 30, 1794, *JM*, II, 138.

74. To Randolph, Nov. 20, Dec. 2, 1794, *JM*, II, 121–22, 149–51.

75. Order of the Committee of Public Safety, 25th Brumaire [Nov. 15, 1794], AECPEU, v. 42, f. 212–13; Miot to Monroe, Nov. 24, 1794, *ASPFR*, I, 689. This was confirmed in January by a decree of the Convention.

76. On trade in general see Lefebvre, *Thermidorians*, 84–95. Histories of France during this era do not contain any references to the United States or to Monroe. Of all the diplomatic problems facing France, that presented by the United States was one of the least significant.

77. DeConde, *Entangling Alliances*, 354; A. L. Burt, *The United States, Great Britain and British North America from the Revolution to the Establishment of Peace after the War of 1812* (New York, 1961), 208–9. Burt considers that the Monroe mission was looked upon as insurance in the event of a rupture with Britain.

CHAPTER 8

THERMIDORIAN FRANCE

1. Monroe to Randolph, Aug. 15, 1794, *JM*, II, 16; on general conditions in France see works cited Ch. VII, fn. 39, *supra*.

2. To Jefferson, Sept. 7, 1794, to Madison, Nov. 20, 1794, *JM*, II, 49–52, 131–36.

3. Monroe to Randolph, Oct. 30, 1795, Monroe to Jefferson, Nov. 18, 1795, *JM*, II, 379–97, 410–21.

4. Monroe to Randolph, Oct. 16, 1794, *JM*, II, 69ff.

5. New York *Herald*, Feb. 28, 1795. The editor identified Monroe as the author.

6. Madison to Monroe, Mar. 11, 1795, Madison, LC.

7. Monroe to Randolph, May 17, 1795, *JM*, II, 260–61.

8. Mathiez, *After Robespierre*, 86–90.

9. Pierce Butler to Madison, Jan. 5, 1795, Madison, LC.

10. *Autobiography*, 73–74. He particularly distrusted James Swan, a Bostonian long resident in Paris and then a French purchasing agent.

11. Morris' house was on the rue de la Roi, now 101 rue de Richelieu; for description and plans of the Folie see Lucius Wilmerding, Jr., "James Monroe and the Furniture Fund," *New-York Historical Society Quarterly*, XLIV (April 1940), 133–34, and *James Monroe Public Claimant* (Rutgers University Press, 1960), by the same author, 97–101; G. Thoüiy to Monroe, Dec. 2, 1795, Monroe Foundation. The original furniture is in the Monroe Law Office, Monroe Foundation, Fredericksburg, Virginia. Replicas are in the White House.

12. T. H. Perkins, MS Diary, June 18, 1795, MHS.

13. Thomas G. Cary, *Memoir of Thomas Handasyd Perkins* (Boston, 1856), Perkins Diary, [Mar. 28, 1795], 76.

14. Madison to Monroe, Apr. 6, 1795, Madison, LC; Monroe to Madison, Aug. 1, 1796, Rives Papers, LC; Jefferson to John Edwards, Jan. 22, 1797, Ford, *Jefferson,* VII, 112; Edwards to Monroe, Apr. 20, 1798, Monroe, LC; Memo of Rufus King, Aug. 19, 1796, C. King, *Rufus King,* II, 77–80; William Theobald Wolfe Tone, *Life of Theobald Wolfe Tone* (2 vols., Washington, D.C., 1826), I, 282.

15. Benjamin P. Kurtz and Carrie C. Autrey (eds.), *Four New Letters of Mary Wollstonecraft and Helen M. Williams* (University of California Press, 1937), *passim;* John Alger, *Englishmen in the French Revolution* (London, 1889), 89–93; James Leslie Woodress, *A Yankee's Odyssey; the Life of Joel Barlow* (Philadelphia, 1958), 129, 142ff.

16. Washington to Randolph, July 24, 1795, Fitzpatrick, *Washington,* XXXIV, 247.

17. W. T. Tone, *Life of Tone,* II, 23, 24, 29. Tone had a U.S. passport issued under a false name.

18. Cary, *T. H. Perkins,* Perkins Diary, March 14, 1795, 61.

19. Moncure D. Conway, *Life of Thomas Paine* (2 vols., New York, 1908), II, 116–20; Monroe to the Committee of General Surety, Nov. 1, 1794, Monroe to Randolph, Nov. 7, 1794, *JM,* II, 96, 107–8.

20. Monroe to Madison, Jan. 20, 1796, *JM,* II, 440–41. Monroe also lent Paine over $1,000, which was never repaid; see Wilmerding, *Monroe,* 103. This restriction on writing did not apply to non-American topics, for Paine wrote *Agrarian Justice* and his *Decline and Fall of the English System of Finance* while with Monroe. See Alfred Owen Aldridge, *Man of Reason: The Life of Thomas Paine* (New York, 1959), 240–41. Monroe attempted to send Paine to America in 1795 by using him as a courier, but the Committee would not grant him permission to leave, since he was still a member of the Convention. Bowman, Struggle for Neutrality, 213.

21. W. T. Tone, *Life of Tone,* II, 348.

22. Conway, *Paine,* II, 155–56, 239; Paine to the Directors, Dec. 1796, AECPEU, v. 46, f. 425.

23. Monroe to Thomas Pinckney, Aug. 11, 1828, Monroe, NYPL; Monroe to Rufus King, Jan. 7, 1796, clipping from sale catalog in MS Division, NYPL; Monroe to Madison, July 5, 1796, *JM,* III, 20–21; Enoch Edwards to Monroe, July 21, 1796, Monroe, LC; Conway, *Paine,* II, 166ff.

24. Monroe to Madison, July 5, 1796, *JM,* III, 27.

25. [Benjamin Vaughan] to Monroe [1796], Monroe Foundation.

26. See AECPEU, v. 41, f. 432, v. 43, f. 228; Buchot to Monroe, Sept. 23, 1794, Monroe Foundation.

27. *Autobiography,* 70–71; André Maurois, *Adrienne: The Life of the Marquise de Lafayette* (New York, 1961), 258.

28. Jefferson to Mrs. Church, n.d., in Sarah N. Randolph, *Domestic Life of Thomas Jefferson* (New York, 1871), 253; Cary, *T. H. Perkins,* 85; Monroe to Jefferson, July 30, 1796, *JM,* III, 41. Hamilton has the name incorrectly as Simm.

29. Monroe to Madison, Jan. 20, 1796, *JM,* II, 445–46.

30. Monroe to Jefferson, Sept. 7, 1794, June 27, 1795, *JM,* II, 212, 312; Baron Hyde de Neuville, *Mémoires et Souvenirs* (3 vols., Paris, 1890).

31. Monroe to Joseph Jones, Sept. 15, 1795, Monroe Account Book, 1794–1802, Monroe, LC.

32. *Autobiography,* 102–3; T. H. Perkins Diary, July 4, 1795, MHS.

33. S. Higginson to Pickering, Oct. 14, 1796, Pickering Papers, MHS; Monroe to _____, Mar. 26, 1798, *Bulletin of the New York Public Library,* IV (1900), 41–43; Monroe to Madison, July 5, 1796, *JM,* III, 19–20; Enoch Edwards to Monroe, Apr. 20, 1798, Monroe, LC; W. M. Morris to Monroe [1798], Monroe Foundation; New York *Herald,* Sept. 17, 1796.

34. *Autobiography,* 86–87; Footner, *Barney,* 199–200; Mathiez, *After Robespierre,* 49, 92, 114.

35. Monroe to Jones, Sept. 15, 1795, Aug. 1, 1796, Monroe Foundation; Randolph to Monroe, Feb. 5, 1795, Monroe, LC; Monroe to Jefferson, July 30, 1796, *JM,* III, 47.

36. Monroe Account Book, 1794–1802, Monroe, LC; Monroe to Jefferson, July 30, 1796, *JM,* III, 41, 47; E. Gerry to Monroe, Nov. 2, 1795, Monroe, LC.

37. Monroe to Governor Robert Brooke, Aug. 20, 1795, Monroe to Secretary of War, Apr. 11, 1796, Monroe, LC.

38. Monroe to Secretary of State, Jan. 13, 1795, *JM,* II, 168–69.

39. Monroe to Randolph, Dec. 18, 1795, *JM,* II, 154–61; Monroe to Madison, Dec. 18, 1795, *ibid.,* II, 152–54; quote is from letter to Randolph, *ibid.,* II, 160.

40. Monroe to Committee of Public Safety, Dec. 27 [correct date is Dec. 26], 1794, *JM,* II, 162–63; draft, *JM,* II, 162, fn. 1.

41. Jay to Monroe, Nov. 28, 1794, Monroe to Jay, Jan. 17, 1795, *JM,* II, 180–81.

42. Jay to Monroe, Feb. 5, 1795, *ASPFR,* I, 517; Monroe to Secretary of State, Mar. 17, 1795, *JM,* II, 229–34.

43. Monroe to Secretary of State, Apr. 14, 1795, *JM,* II, 238–42; Monroe did not show his correspondence with Jay to the Committee, as Bond, *Monroe Mission,* 34, asserts.

44. Hichborn to Monroe, Mar. 31, 1795, *JM,* II, 243 fn. 1; John Trumbull, *Autobiography,* ed. by Theodore Sizer (New Haven, 1953), 184–85. Trumbull maintained that Monroe (through Hichborn) requested him to leave Paris because his presence was objectionable to the French government. Trumbull refused to do so unless directly requested by French officials.

45. Madison to Monroe, Mar. 26, 1795, Madison, LC; Monroe to [Madison], June 3, 1795, Rives Papers, LC; Monroe to Madison, July 26, Oct. 24, 1795, *JM,* II, 330, 402.

46. Bond, *Monroe Mission,* 65–66; Monroe to Secretary of State, Oct. 4, 1795, *JM,* II, 368–78; Barlow to Monroe, May 24, 1796, Monroe, LC.

47. Bond, *Monroe Mission,* 65–66, expresses the opinion that the French were sincere in this offer, but he does not cite any evidence. Monroe to [W. Short], May 4, 1795, draft, Monroe, LC; Monroe to Committee of Public Safety, Jan. 25, 1795, Monroe to Short, May 30, 1795, Monroe to Secretary of State, Mar. 6, June 13, 1795, *JM,* II, 218–19, 228, 284, 288; Monroe to [Madison], June 3, 1795, Rives Papers, LC.

48. Monroe to _____, Sept. 18, 1795, Gratz Coll., PHS.

49. Monroe to Madison, Sept. 8, 1795, *JM,* II, 347–55.

50. Oct. 23, 1795, Rives Papers, LC.

51. M. A. Gauvain [he acted as Monroe's secretary in 1795], Statement of Monroe's Treatment in France, Apr. 2, 1797, Monroe, LC.

52. Rochambeau to Tench Coxe, Feb. 6, 1796, enclosed in Coxe to Washington, June 14, 1796, Washington Papers, LC.

53. R. R. Livingston to Monroe, July 10, 1795, Melancthon Smith to Monroe, Aug. 6, 1795, Monroe, LC; Randolph to Monroe, Apr. 7, July 14, 1795, *ASPFR,* I, 701–9.

54. For Delacroix's report of Jan. 16, 1796, see DeConde, *Entangling Alliances,* 427–48; James A. James, "French Opinion As a Factor in Preventing War Between France and the United States, 1795–1800," *AHR,* XXX (1924), 44.

55. Fay, *Revolutionary Spirit,* 394–404; Sydney Seymour Biro, *The German Policy of Revolutionary France* (2 vols., Harvard University Press, 1795), II, 483–513, had some interesting comments upon foreign policy of the Directory in general. As noted earlier, there is almost nothing about Franco-American relations in the standard treatments of the Revolution; it was not only a minor problem, but French leaders never grasped the economic possibilities offered by American trade.

56. Joseph Fauchet, *Mémoire sur les Etats Unis D'Amérique,* ed. Carl Ludwig Lokke in American Historical Association, *Annual Report for 1936* (Washington, 1938), I, 83–119, but especially 113–19. There is some disagreement about the precise influence of this report. Lokke (and this writer agrees with him) does not consider Fauchet's *Mémoire* to have guided French policy, but Bemis, "Washington's Farewell Address," *AHR,* XXXIX, 259, and E. Wilson Lyon, "The Directory and the United States," *AHR,* XLIII, 514–32, regard it as the basis of policy under the Directory. Fauchet did advise the Directors to do everything possible to promote a Republican victory, but he clearly condemned either coercion or saber-rattling as the proper means.

57. Monroe to Secretary of State, Feb. 16, 1796, *JM,* II, 455–56; Monroe to Madison, May 7, 1796, Madison, LC.

58. Monroe's original letter dated Feb. 17, 1796, is in AECPEU, v. 45, f. 144; observations on Monroe's Letter in *ibid.,* v. 45, f. 146.

59. Feb. 27, 1796, *JM,* II, 460–61; DeConde, *Entangling Alliances,* 427ff.

60. Memo in Monroe Account Book, 1794–1801, dated Mar. 8, 1796, Monroe, LC.

61. Delacroix to Monroe, Mar. 11, 1796, *ASPFR*, I, 732–33. For details of minor issues see Bond, *Monroe Mission*, 59ff. This note and Monroe's reply of Mar. 15 and 20 are not the original notes written on those dates. Monroe permitted Delacroix to take his note back, when, upon receiving Monroe's reply, Delacroix realized that he had taken an untenable position on some matters. Delacroix then submitted a new note (but under the original date) and Monroe drew up a new answer using his original dates. Monroe had even sent his first reply on its way to the Secretary of State but was able to recall it; Monroe to Secretary of State, May 2, 1796, *JM*, II, 491. Monroe omitted from his *View* that portion of his letter of May 1 relating to this return and redrafting of notes. This passage was also deleted in *ASPFR*. See *JM*, II, 490, fn. 1. Monroe's reply of March 15, to Delacroix is in *JM*, II, 467–81.

62. Feb. 10, 1794, Livingston, NYHS.

63. Tazewell to Monroe, May 19, 1796, Monroe, LC; Hamilton to Wolcott, June 9, 1796, Lodge, *Hamilton*, VIII, 403; Monroe to Madison, July 5, 1796, Rives Papers, LC.

64. Printed in *JM*, II, 484–88.

65. Quote is from Monroe to Madison, Sept. 1, 1796, *JM*, II, 53.

66. Pickering to Monroe, June 13, 1796, *ASPFR*, I, 737.

67. Hamilton to Wolcott, June 15, 1796, Wolcott to Hamilton, June 17, 1796, Hamilton to Washington, June [23], 1796, Hamilton Papers, LC. Other letters relating to the Cabinet conferences will be found in the Washington Papers, LC.

68. Pickering, Wolcott and McHenry to Washington, July 2, 1796, Pickering Papers, MHS; Monroe's letter to Logan is in *JM*, III, 6–7, incorrectly dated June 24, 1796; the original of this letter is in the Washington Papers, LC. The enclosure is printed as Monroe to Jefferson, June 23, 1795, *JM*, II, 292–304. Copies of this letter were sent to Jefferson, Burr, Beckley and R. R. Livingston. The enclosure seems never to have been published.

69. See fn. 53 *supra;* Washington to Pickering, July 8, 1796, Fitzpatrick, *Washington*, XXXV, 127; apparently Washington, who was at Mount Vernon, was unaware of the delay. He did not arrive in Philadelphia until Aug. 21; it is interesting to note that Pickering's dispatch to Monroe is dated August 22. See Freeman, *Washington*, VII, 399–400.

70. August 10, 1796, Fitzpatrick, *Washington*, XXXV, 174.

71. Pickering to Washington, July 29, 1796, Washington Papers, LC. Pickering repeated the same arguments to John Adams, Sept. 2, 1796, Adams Papers, MHS.

72. Monroe, *View, JM*, III, 426.

73. Delacroix to Monroe, July 7, 1796, *ASPFR*, I, 739; Monroe to Minister of Foreign Affairs, July 14, 1796, *JM*, III, 27–32.

74. This document printed in *JM*, III, 11–16, is entitled "Exposition of the Actual State in which the Majority of the House Found Itself and which Induced Many Members to Vote for the Treaty." Original (not in Monroe's hand) and a French translation are in Monroe, LC. I infer it was not submitted since no copy is to be found in AECPEU; see also Memo in Monroe Account Book, 1794–1802, dated July 16, 1796, Monroe, LC.

75. Monroe to Secretary of State, Aug. 4, 1796, *JM*, III, 48–51; Monroe to Secretary of State, Aug. 27, 1796, Delacroix to Monroe, Oct. 7, 1796, *ASPFR*, I, 742–45.

76. Shepard Bancroft Clough, *France: A History of National Economics, 1789–1939* (New York, 1939), 56–57.

77. To Madison, Sept. 1, 1796, Monroe, *View*, *JM*, III, 52, 442.

78. Otto to Monroe, Mar. 20, 1797, quoted in Lyon, "Directory and the U.S.," *AHR*, XLIII, 517; *Autobiography*, 140.

79. To Madison, Jan. 1, 1796 [should be 1797], Rives Papers, LC.

80. *ASPFR*, I, 747.

81. Pickering to P. Wingate, Apr. 12, 1797, Pickering Papers, MHS.

CHAPTER 9

A DIPLOMAT RETURNS

1. Monroe to Madison, Jan. 8, 1797, *JM*, III, 66; *Autobiography*, 142.

2. Wiliam Spence Robertson, *Life of Miranda* (2 vols., Chapel Hill, 1929), I, 54–59, 158, 180ff.

3. Prevost to Miranda and replies, Mar. 29–Apr. 1, 1797, Monroe, LC; Miranda to Hamilton, Apr. 1, 1797, Hamilton Papers, LC.

4. Gallatin to his wife, June 28, 1797, Henry Adams, *Life of Albert Gallatin* (New York, 1943), 186; *Greenleaf's New York Journal*, July 1, 1797.

5. Gallatin to his wife, June 30, 1797, Adams, *Life of Gallatin*, 187; New York *Herald*, July 8, 1797.

6. Hamilton to Monroe, July 5, 1797, Henry Cabot Lodge, ed., *Works of Alexander Hamilton* (Federal ed., 12 vols., New York, 1904), VII, 448–50.

7. [James Thomson Callender], *History of the United States for 1796....* (Philadelphia, 1797), 218ff. Originally this was published in numbers; the Reynolds correspondence is in No. 5.

8. Gelston's minutes of the conference, July 11, 1797, Gratz Coll., PHS.

9. The dinner was on the fourteenth; New York *Daily Advertiser*, July 15, 1797.

10. July 17, 1797, Lodge, *Hamilton* (Federal), VII, 456–58. Venable wrote separately in a similar vein.

11. Hamilton to Monroe [July 17, 1797] and Monroe's reply, *ibid.*, VII, 458–63.

12. Hamilton to Monroe, July 22, 1797, *ibid.,* VII, 471–74.

13. Relevant letters are in *ibid.,* VII, 472–79.

14. Madison to Monroe, Oct. 19, 1797, Madison, LC.

15. Madison to Jefferson, Oct. 20, 1797, Madison, LC.

16. July 6, 1797, *JM,* III, 66–67.

17. July 17, 1797, Monroe, LC.

18. July 19, 1797, *JM,* III, 70–73.

19. July 24, 1797, *JM,* III, 73 fn. 1. Jefferson thought he detected the hand of Hamilton in this letter. Memo in Jefferson's hand, Aug. 24, 1797, Jefferson Papers, LC.

20. *JM,* III, 84, fn. 1.

21. Both are dated July 31, 1797, *JM,* III, 74–85.

22. To John Dawson, Apr. 19, 1798, Monroe, NYPL, to Jefferson, Dec. 25, 1797, *JM,* III, 89.

23. To E. Gerry, May 30, 1797, Adams, MHS.

24. Gerry to Monroe, Apr. 4, 1797, Monroe, LC.

25. *Greenleaf's New York Journal,* Aug. 8, 1797; Pickering to Washington, Aug. 9, 1797, *JM,* III, 384 fn. 1. There are a number of items containing unfavorable comments on Monroe in the Pickering Papers, MHS.

26. Washington to Pickering, Aug. 29, 1797, Fitzpatrick, *Washington,* XXXVI, 18.

27. John Nicholas to Monroe, Sept. 20, 1797, Monroe, LC.

28. Monroe to Madison, Sept. 24, 1797, *JM,* III, 86.

29. Madison to Monroe, Feb. 5, 1797, Madison, LC.

30. William Wirt to Mrs. Mary Ellis, Apr. 12, 1797, Wirt Papers, MdHS.

31. Monroe to Madison, Nov. 22, Dec. 7, 1799, Monroe to Jefferson, Jan. 27, 1798, *JM,* III, 97, 159–60; [Baron de Montlezun], *Souvenirs des Antilles, Voyages . . . aux Etats Unis. . . .* (2 vols., Paris, 1818), I, 97.

32. Monroe to Jefferson, Feb. 12, 1798, *JM,* III, 102.

33. Monroe to Jefferson, Jan. 27, 1798, *JM,* III, 97; Monroe to John Mason, Jan. 17, 1797, Johns Deposit, UVa.

34. John Breckinridge to Monroe, Aug. 12, 1798, Monroe, NYPL; Monroe to Jefferson, Nov. 15, 1798; Monroe to Madison, July 13, 1799, *JM,* III, 143–44, 157; Monroe to _____, Oct. 29, 1801, Gratz Coll., PHS.

35. Edmund Randolph to Monroe, Monroe NYPL; Jefferson to Monroe, Feb. 8, Mar. 8, 1798, Ford, *Jefferson,* VII, 198, 216; Monroe to Jefferson, Feb. 25, June 17, 1798, *JM,* III, 105, 129. William Wirt also considered correct party affiliation essential to success at the bar in Richmond; Wirt to Dabney Carr, Mar. 25, 1803, Wirt Papers, MdHS.

36. Monroe to Gen. Hull, Mar. 26, 1801, *Bulletin NYPL,* IV (1900), 46; E.

Edwards to Monroe, June 10, 1798, Monroe, LC; Monroe to Madison, June 8, 1798, Rives Papers, LC; Monroe to Edwards, Feb. 12, 1798, *JM*, III, 98–100.

37. Dawson to Monroe, Apr. 5, 1798, Edwards to Monroe, June 10, 1798, Monroe, LC; Monroe to Madison, June 24, 1798, *JM*, III, 136–38; Jefferson to Monroe, Apr. 5, 1798, Ford, *Jefferson*, VII, 232.

38. Monroe to Madison, Dec. 7, 1799, *JM*, III, 160. Only one item was published in the New York *Gazette*, June 20, 1798. See William Lee to Monroe, Feb. 10, 1801, Monroe, NYPL.

39. July 23, 1797, Monroe, LC.

40. Full title is *A View of the Conduct of the Executive in the Foreign Affairs of the United States, Connected with the Mission to the French Republic During the Years 1794, 5, 6. By James Monroe Late Minister Plenipotentiary to the Said Republic Illustrated by His Instruction and Other Authentic Documents.* Philadelphia, 1798, B. F. Bache, pp. lxvi, 407; Preface is reprinted in *JM*, III, 383–457.

41. Monroe to Madison, Sept. 24, 1797, *JM*, III, 86; Jefferson to Madison, Aug. 3, 1797, to Monroe, Oct. 25, 1797, Ford, *Jefferson*, VII, 164–67, 177–78.

42. *JM*, III, 457.

43. Boston *Columbian Centinel,* Jan. 6, 1798.

44. Monroe to Jefferson, Feb. 12, 1798, *JM*, III, 102.

45. March 25, 1798, Monroe, LC.

46. Dec. 27, 1797, Ford, *Jefferson*, VII, 182.

47. Pickering to Washington, Jan. 20, 1798, Wolcott to Washington, Jan. 20, 1798, both in *JM*, III, 385 fn.

48. See *JM*, III, 385 fn.

49. Monroe to Jefferson, Feb. 19, 1798, *JM*, III, 104.

50. Boston *Columbian Centinel,* Mar. 7, 1798.

51. Monroe to Jefferson, Mar. 26, 1798, *JM*, III, 107.

52. Adams reply of May 8, 1798, is in Adams, *Works*, IX, 190; Monroe to Madison, June 24, 1798, *JM*, III, 136.

53. Fitzpatrick, *Washington*, XXXVI, 204–370.

54. *Ibid.,* 208, 209, 211, 222.

55. Monroe to Jefferson, July 12, 1797, *JM*, III, 70; Jefferson to Madison, Aug. 3, 1797, Ford, *Jefferson*, VII, 165–66; Madison to Jefferson, Aug. 5, 1797, Madison, LC. Malone, *Jefferson*, III, 304, suggests that Monroe's advice was unsolicited, but the letter seems to indicate that he had already discussed the topic with Jefferson in Philadelphia.

56. Monroe to Jefferson, Sept. 5, 1797, *JM*, III, 85.

57. Jefferson to Monroe, Sept. 7, 1797, Ford, *Jefferson*, VII, 172–73.

58. Monroe to Jefferson, [Oct. 20], 1797, Jefferson Papers, LC.

59. John Taylor to Jefferson, Feb. 15, 1799, *John P. Branch Papers of*

Randolph Macon College II (1902), 280; Malone, III, 335–56; Adrienne Koch and Harry Ammon, "The Kentucky and Virginia Resolutions," *WMQ*, Ser. 3, V (1948), 152–53.

60. W. C. Nicholas to Monroe, Jan. 13, 1798 [should be 1799], Monroe, NYPL; Jefferson to W. C. Nicholas, Aug. 26, 1799, Jefferson Papers, LC; same to same, Sept. 5, 1799, Andrew L. Lipscomb and Albert Berg, eds., *Writings of Thomas Jefferson* (20 vols., Washington, D.C., 1900–04), X, 130–31.

61. Monroe to Madison, Nov. 22, 1799, Madison, LC; Jefferson to Madison, Nov. 22, 1799, Ford, *Jefferson,* VII, 400.

62. Monroe to G. W. Erving, Apr. 4, 1800, Monroe to Madison, June 24, 1798, *JM,* III, 139, 172.

63. Dec. 10, 1797, Rives Papers, LC.

64. To Jefferson, Apr. 14, 1798, June 1798, *JM,* III, 118, 130.

65. To Jefferson, Feb. 12, 1798, *JM,* III, 101.

66. To Jefferson, Nov. 16, 1798, *JM,* III, 149–52.

67. Monroe to Jefferson, June 1798, *JM,* III, 134–35; Samuel Terrell to Garritt [*sic*] Minor, Dec. 5, 1797, Watson Papers, UVa.; E. Carrington to Pickering, Dec. 29, 1797, Pickering Papers, MHS.

68. John Taylor to Jefferson, Feb. 15, 1799, Jefferson Papers, LC; Robert Gamble to Pickering, July 12, 1798, Pickering, MHS.

69. Jefferson to Monroe, May 21, 1798, Lipscomb and Berg, *Jefferson,* X, 39–40; Madison to Monroe, June 9, 1798, Madison, LC; Monroe to Jefferson, June 1798, *JM,* III, 129; Jefferson to Monroe, Jan. 23, 1799, Jefferson to John Taylor, Jan. 24, 1799, Ford, *Jefferson,* VII, 319–21, 322.

70. P. N. Nicholas to Monroe, Oct. 13, 1799, Monroe, NYPL; Monroe to Madison, Dec. 7, 1799, III, 160–62; Henry H. Simms, *Life of John Taylor* (Richmond, 1932), 85–86; James Thomson Callender, *Prospect Before Us* (Richmond, 1800), 140; *Greenleaf's New York Journal,* Dec. 18, 1799; Richmond *Virginia Gazette and General Advertiser,* Dec. 10, 1799. There were two votes for Madison and one for John Stewart, the clerk of the House who was removed in favor of William Wirt.

CHAPTER 10

GOVERNOR OF VIRGINIA

1. Richmond *Enquirer,* May 2, 1806.

2. *Statutes at Large for Virginia, from October Session 1792 to December Session 1806* ... (3 vols., Richmond, 1835) ed. by Samuel Shepherd, II, 28–29. A lump sum of £2000 (slightly over $9,000) was divided among the councillors according to the number of sessions attended. The council chose one of its members to preside in the absence of the governor; technically he was lieutenant governor, although no such office was established by the state constitution.

3. St. George Tucker, *Blackstone's Commentaries* ... (5 vols., Philadelphia, 1833), I, Appendix C, 122–24. The essays written by Tucker and added as appendices constitute a uniquely valuable source on the political institutions of Virginia.

4. The Virginia constitution in *Federal and State Constitutions and Organic Laws* ... *of the United States* (7 vols., Washington, D.C., 1909), ed. by Francis Newton Thorpe, VII, 3813ff.

5. Jefferson to James Barbour, Jan. 12, 1812, Barbour Papers, NYPL.

6. Jefferson to Barbour, Jan. 22, 1812, *ibid.*

7. Monroe to Pendleton, Mar. 5, 1800, *Proc. MHS*, XLII (1908), 325. Letter of William Munford, Richmond *Virginia Argus*, Feb. 12, 1802.

8. Richmond *Enquirer*, June 25, 1805.

9. Dec. 1, 1800, *JM*, III, 221.

10. *Ibid.*, III, 221–25; *Acts Passed at a General Assembly ... of Virginia: Begun* [*Dec. 7, 1801*] ... (Richmond, n.d.), 15–16.

11. Dec. 6, 1801, *JM*, III, 306–7.

12. *Ibid.*, III, 318.

13. Dawson to Monroe, Jan. 19, 1800, NYPL; Journals of the Council, *passim*, VSL.

14. Journals of the Council, Dec. 7, 1802, VSL.

15. W. H. Cabell to J. Cabell, Dec. 14, 1802, Cabell Papers, U.Va. John White was the other councillor removed.

16. Reminiscences of John Tyler, 1858, quoted in Tyler, *Life of Tylers*, I, 219; Alexander Wilbourne Waddell, *Richmond, Virginia, in Old Prints* (Richmond, 1932), 23–31.

17. Report of Richard Adams *et al.* to Clerk of the House of Delegates, Jan. 10, 1800, Executive Papers, VSL; Monroe to Madison, Aug. 14, Sept. 9, Nov. 7, 1800, *JM*, III, 201, 203, 220.

18. *Acts Passed at a General Assembly ... of Virginia: Begun* [*Dec. 4, 1797*] ... (Richmond, 1798), 12.

19. Journals of the Council, May 2, 1801, VSL; Monroe to Clarke, Oct. 5, 1801, Executive Letter Book, VSL.

20. Journals of the Council, Apr. 6, 1801, VSL; Monroe to Clarke, June 20, 1801, *JM*, III, 195–98.

21. Message of Dec. 6, 1802, *JM*, III, 363; S. T. Mason to Monroe, May 15, 1800, Executive Papers, VSL. Monroe had hoped to engage Lamotte, a cannon founder he had secured for the federal government while Minister to France.

22. Various letters, Jan. 1800, Executive Letter Book, VSL; Journals of the Council, Feb. 11, Mar. 25, Sept. 15, 1801, Feb. 21, 1802, VSL; Monroe to S. T. Mason, May 25, 1801, Executive Letter Book, VSL.

23. *Acts Passed at a General Assembly ... of Virginia: Begun* [*Nov. 8, 1796*] ... (Richmond, 1797), 4–7.

24. Message of Dec. 6, 1802, *JM*, III, 362–63.

25. May 9, 1800, Executive Letter Book, VSL.

26. Message of Dec. 1, 1800, *JM*, III, 222; Journals of the Council, May 23, 1801, Feb. 6, 1801, VSL; Message of Dec. 1, 1800, *JM*, III, 223; Monroe to Martin Mims, July 12, 1802, Executive Papers, VSL.

27. Message of Dec. 6, 1802, *JM*, III, 363; Martin Mims to Monroe, Nov. 18, 1802, Executive Papers, VSL.

28. Wood entered a protest when Monroe ignored a recommendation from a county court. Journals of the Council, July 26, 1800, VSL.

29. Journals of the Council, Oct. 30, 1802, VSL.

30. John Koontz raised the problem of Federalist control in a letter to Monroe, July 19, 1800, Executive Papers, VSL; Journals of the Council, July 26, 1800, VSL; Monroe to the Clerk of Northumberland County, Aug. 19, 1801, Executive Letter Book, VSL.

31. Mar. 23, 1801, Executive Letter Book, VSL.

32. Monroe to Jefferson, May 4, 1801, *JM*, III, 282.

33. S. T. Mason to Monroe, May 23, 1800, Monroe, LC; John Dawson to Monroe, Mar. 6, 1800, Monroe, LC; Monroe to Jefferson, May 4, 23, 1801, *JM*, III, 282–87.

34. May 29, 1801, Ford, *Jefferson*, VIII, 59.

35. Dawson to Madison, Nov. 28, 1799, Madison, LC; Circular letter to county courts, Mar. 28, 1800, Executive Letter Book, VSL; Richard Claiborne to Monroe, May 20, 1800, *Calendar of Virginia State Papers*, IX, 111–12; Monroe to Jefferson, Jan. 4, 1800, *JM*, III, 169; Dawson to Monroe, Mar. 28, 1800, Monroe, NYPL.

36. Monroe to Madison, May 15, 1800, Monroe, NYPL; Monroe to Jefferson, May 25, 1800, *JM*, III, 179–80; Jefferson to Monroe, May 26, 1800, Monroe, LC.

37. Jefferson to Monroe, Apr. 13, 1800, Lipscomb, *Jefferson*, XIX, 119. Monroe to Jefferson, May 25, 1800, *JM*, III, 179.

38. Monroe to Jefferson, Apr. 23, 26, 1800, *JM*, III, 173, 176.

39. May 4, 1800, Monroe, NYPL.

40. Monroe to Edmond Genet, July 30, 1800, *JM*, III, 195.

41. Monroe to Peter Carr, Aug. 19, 1800, Carr-Cary Papers, U.Va.; Jefferson to Monroe, May 13, 1799, Monroe Foundation. The boy was named James Spence Monroe.

42. Monroe to Madison, Aug. 13, Sept. 9, 1800, *JM*, III, 200, 294; Monroe to Maj. Thomas Newton, July 28, 1800, Executive Letter Book, VSL.

43. Monroe to Maj. Thomas Newton, Aug. 25, 1800, Monroe to Superintendent of Quarantine at Jordan's Point, Aug. 26, 1800, Monroe to George Hay, Aug. 26, 1800, Executive Letter Book, VSL.

44. This account of Gabriel's revolt is based primarily on Monroe's message to the legislature, Dec. 5, 1800, *JM*, III, 234–44; the Executive Letter Book and the

Journals of the Council, VSL; and on Herbert Aptheker, *American Negro Slave Revolts* (New York, 1963), 219–30.

45. Dr. McClurg [mayor of Richmond] to Monroe, Aug. 10, 1800, Executive Letter Book, VSL. McClurg had received a letter from Petersburg reporting rumors but without any substantiating evidence. McClurg had then formed a special patrol for Richmond and notified Monroe, but no further action was taken at that point. Undoubtedly, the rumors arose from Gabriel's activities.

46. Monroe to Col. John Nivison, May 12, 1802, *JM*, III, 346.

47. Quotes are from J. T. Callender to Jefferson, Sept. 13, 1800, Jefferson, LC. Callender was reporting hearsay, since he was then in prison.

48. Although whites were suspected of complicity, no proof was ever produced. Monroe to Gov. Dayton of S.C., Oct. 21, 1800, Executive Letter Book, VSL. See petition of the inhabitants of Nottaway, Jan. 16, 1802, Executive Papers, VSL; and Monroe to the General Assembly, Jan. 25, 1802, Executive Letter Book, VSL.

49. Message of Dec. 5, 1800, *JM*, III, 241.

50. Sept. 15, 1800, *JM*, III, 208.

51. Journals of the Council, VSL.

52. Monroe to Jefferson, Sept. 22, Dec. 30, 1800, Monroe to Madison, Nov. 7, 1800, *JM*, III, 209, 219, 249; Monroe to Madison, Sept. 29, 1800, Rives Papers, LC.

53. Monroe to the Council, Sept. 27, 28, 1800, Executive Letter Book, VSL.

54. Monroe to Col. Thomas Newton, Oct. 5, 1800, *ibid*.

55. Monroe to Col. Alexander Quarrier, Oct. 11, 1800, *ibid*.

56. Monroe to Jefferson, Sept. 15, 1800, *JM*, III, 209.

57. Malone, *Jefferson*, III, 480; Journals of the Council, Sept. 18, Oct. 3, 1800; Monroe to Madison, Oct. 8, 1800, *JM*, III, 215; Aptheker, *Negro Revolts*, 222.

58. Monroe to Capt. William Austin, Dec. 27, 1800, Executive Letter Book, VSL; Monroe to McClurg, Dec. 27, 1800, *JM*, III, 247–48.

59. *JM*, III, 243.

60. Quoted in Malone, *Jefferson*, III, 480.

CHAPTER 11

REPUBLICANISM TRIUMPHANT

1. John Beckley to Monroe, August 26, 1800, John Tyler to Monroe, August 14, 1800, Monroe, NYPL.

2. W. C. Nicholas to John Breckinridge, Oct. 22, 1800, Breckinridge Papers, LC; Monroe to Madison, Nov. 3, 1800, Madison, LC; Pierce Butler to Monroe, Nov. 27, 1800, Monroe, NYPL; Pinckney to Jefferson, Nov. 22, 1800, *JM*, III, 245, fn. 1.

3. Monroe to Jefferson, Apr. 23, 1800, *JM*, III, 173.

4. Monroe had already received a letter from Hugh Williamson of New York (Nov. 6, 1800, Monroe, LC) warning him of this danger.

5. Monroe to Madison, Nov. 6, 1800, Madison to Jefferson, Oct. 21, 1800, David Gelston to Madison, Nov. 21, 1800, Rives Papers, LC.

6. Madison to Monroe, Nov. 10, 12, Madison, LC; Burr to John Taylor, Oct. 23, 1800, Washburn Papers, MHS; Brant, *Madison*, III, 22–25.

7. John Preston to John Breckinridge, Dec. 28, 1800, Breckinridge Papers, LC.

8. Monroe to Jefferson, Dec. 30, 1800, *JM*, III, 248–49.

9. Same to same, Jan. 6, 1801, *JM*, III, 254.

10. Monroe to Madison, Jan. 27, 1801, *JM*, III, 257; Richmond *Virginia Argus*, Feb. 6, 1803.

11. Monroe to Col. John Hoomes, 8 P.M., Feb. 14, 1801, *JM*, III, 259; Monroe to the senators from Virginia, Feb. 18, 1801, Executive Letter Book, VSL.

12. Jefferson to John Taylor, June 1, 1798, Ford, *Jefferson*, VIII, 263.

13. *AC*, 14C2S, House, 793–800, Jan. 30, 1817. Thomas Ritchie considered Randolph's statement sufficiently important to publish a denial in the *Enquirer*.

14. "J. M. to the People," Mar. 31, 1799, in Richmond *Virginia Argus*, Apr. 12, 1799; *ibid.*, May 9, 1800.

15. Dec. 29, 1799, Monroe, LC.

16. Monroe to Madison, May 15, 1800, Monroe, NYPL.

17. Feb. 14, 1801, Monroe, LC.

18. Feb. 11, 1801, *ibid.*

19. Monroe to _____, Feb. 12, 1801, *ibid.*

20. Richmond *Virginia Gazette and General Advertiser*, May 18, 1805; Monroe to Jefferson, Mar. 3, 1801, *JM*, III, 261.

21. Feb. 23, 1801, endorsed "confidential," Monroe, LC.

22. W. C. Nicholas to Madison [1801], draft, Nicholas to Jefferson [1801], draft, Nicholas Papers, LC.

23. Mar. 3, 1800, *JM*, III, 262–63.

24. Jefferson to Monroe, Mar. 7, 1801, Ford, *Jefferson*, VIII, 8–10.

25. Monroe to Jefferson, Mar. 18, 1801, *JM*, III, 269–74.

26. Giles to Jefferson, Mar. 16, 1801, quoted in Dice Robins Anderson, *William Branch Giles* (Menasha, Wisc., 1914), 177.

27. Monroe to Jefferson, Apr. 30, 1801, draft not sent, *JM*, III, 282, fn. 1; same to same, May 4, 1801, *ibid.*, III, 280–81.

28. To Monroe, Apr. 17, 1801, Monroe, LC.

29. Monroe to Jefferson, Dec. 21, 1801, *JM*, III, 324; Jefferson to Monroe, May 9, 1802, Monroe to [Madison], draft, Mar. 11, 1802, Monroe, NYPL.

30. Monroe to Jefferson, Mar. 23, 1801, Sept. 28, 1801, *JM*, III, 275, 301.

31. To Jefferson, Apr. 25, 1801, *JM*, III, 342–43.

32. Monroe to [Madison], May 23, 1801, Monroe, NYPL; Madison to Monroe, May 6, 1801, James Madison, *Letters and other Writings*. . . . (4 vols., Phila., 1865), II, 172; see Charles A. Jellison, "That Scoundrel Callender," *Va. Mag.*, LXVI (1959), 294–306.

33. Monroe to Jefferson, June 1, 1801; Monroe to Madison, June 6, 1801, *JM*, III, 289–90; Monroe to Madison, June 14, 1801, photostat from original in Morristown National Park.

34. Jefferson to Monroe, July 15, 1801, Ford, *Jefferson*, VIII, 164; Monroe to Jefferson, July 26, 1802, *JM*, III, 356; Richmond *Examiner*, July 5, 1803; Richmond *Virginia Gazette and General Advertiser*, July 20, 1803. An attempt to silence Callender by means of a libel suit brought against him by George Hay proved unsuccessful. *Examiner*, Dec. 15, 22, 1802, Jan. 12, 1803.

35. Monroe to Jefferson, Jan. 18, 1801, *JM*, III, 257; Monroe to Capt. Quarrier, July 8, 1801, Executive Letter Book, VSL.

36. *Acts Passed at a General Assembly . . . of Virginia: Begun [Dec. 1, 1800] . . .* (Richmond, n.d.), 24.

37. Monroe to Jefferson, June 15, 1801, *JM*, III, 292–95; he does not explain why he waited six months before writing Jefferson on this matter; Jefferson to Monroe, Nov. 24, 1801, Ford, *Jefferson*, VIII, 104.

38. To Monroe, June 3, 1802, Executive Papers, VSL.

39. Christopher Gore to Jefferson, Oct. 10, 1802, *ibid.* According to Gore the company was having difficulty with Negroes recently brought in from Jamaica and Nova Scotia; George Goosley to Monroe, June 9, 1802, Executive Papers, VSL; he offered $300 for each slave, agreeing to sell them in Havana.

40. See Executive Correspondence, VSL, for January 1802; Monroe to the Speakers of the General Assembly, Jan. 16, 1802, *JM*, III, 329.

41. See Executive Letter Book, March 1802, VSL; To the mayor of Norfolk, Mar. 17, 1802, *ibid.*

42. Monroe to Gervais Storrs and Joseph Selden, May 3, 1802, Monroe to Grief Green, May 4, 1802, *ibid.*; John B. Scott to Monroe, Executive Papers, VSL; To Col. John Nivison, May 12, 1802, *JM*, III, 344.

43. May 17, 1802, *JM*, III, 348.

44. May 11, 1802, Executive Papers, VSL; see Executive Papers and Executive Letter Book, VSL, June 1802.

45. Journals of the Council, VSL, May–June 1802; Monroe to the mayor of Norfolk, May 25, 1802, Executive Letter Book, VSL.

46. John Clarke to Monroe, May 22, 1802, George Goosley to Monroe, June 5, 1802, Executive Papers, VSL; Monroe to Martin Mims, July 12, 1802, Executive Letter Book, VSL.

47. Journals of the Council, VSL, Jan. 26, 1802; Monroe to the General Assem-

bly, Jan. 26, 27, 1802, *JM*, III, 330–34; *Journals of the House of Delegates* [*1801–1802*], 49, 79, 81–84.

CHAPTER 12

THE LOUISIANA PURCHASE

1. *Autobiography*, 153; Monroe to Jefferson, Jan. 7, 1803, Monroe, LC.

2. S. T. Mason to Monroe, Dec. 10, 1802, Jefferson to Monroe, Dec. 11, 1802, Monroe, LC; S. Pleasants, *et al.*, to Monroe [n.d.] and Monroe's draft reply [n.d.], Monroe, NYPL.

3. Jan. 10, 1803, Ford, *Jefferson*, VIII, 188.

4. William Plumer to Daniel Plumer, Jan. 15, 1803, Plumer Papers, LC; *Executive Journals of the Senate*, I, 436, Jan. 12, 1803.

5. Jan. 13, 1803, Ford, *Jefferson,* VIII, 190–92.

6. *Ibid.,* VIII, 192.

7. Monroe to _____, Mar. 2, 1803, Monroe, NYPL; [Joseph Jones] to [Madison], n.d., Madison Papers, LC; *Autobiography*, 154; Wilmerding, *Monroe, Claimant*, 37.

8. Madison to _____, Mar. 3, 1803, Samuel Coleman to Madison, Apr. 9, 1803, Madison, LC; Brant, *Madison*, IV, 110.

9. E. Wilson Lyon, *Louisiana in French Diplomacy* (University of Oklahoma Press, 1934), 162–64.

10. Sept. 20, 1803, *JM*, IV, 75–76.

11. Lyon, *Louisiana*, 180–81.

12. Quoted in *ibid.*, 202.

13. *Ibid.*, 183.

14. Monroe to Madison, Feb. 22, 1803, *JM*, IV, 2.

15. *AC*, 7C2S, 1905–2110.

16. Monroe to _____, Mar. 2, 1803, Monroe, NYPL.

17. Monroe to Madison, Mar. 7, 1803, Rives Papers, LC; Madison to Monroe, Feb. 28, 1803, Madison Papers, LC; *Autobiography*, 154–55.

18. Monroe to Madison, Apr. 9, 1803, Rives Papers, LC; Monroe to senators from Virginia, May 25, 1803, *JM*, IV, 32; *Autobiography*, 154–55; Monroe to [Joseph Jones], June 8, 1803, Monroe Foundation, Fredericksburg.

19. The account of the Louisiana Purchase in Henry Adams, *History of the United States During the Administrations of Jefferson and Madison, 1801–1817* (8 vols., New York, 1890), has become a classic and still remains the fullest discussion of all aspects of the Louisiana question. However, Adams' dislike of all the parties involved results in a number of misstatements. His account has been modified by the more recent work of Lyon, *Louisiana,* Brant, *Madison,* IV, and George Dangerfield, *Chancellor Robert R. Livingston of New York, 1746–1813* (New York,

1960). Brant and Dangerfield disagree over Livingston's merits as a diplomat. Dangerfield presents Livingston's faults honestly and is remarkably fair in his treatment of Monroe. Arthur P. Whitaker, *The Mississippi Question, 1795–1803* (New York, 1934) is all-important for background material.

20. Quoted in Dangerfield, *Livingston*, 358. The letter was delivered by Benthalou, who was hastening to meet his wife.

21. Monroe to Madison, Apr. 15, 1803, not sent, *JM*, IV, 9; Skipwith to Monroe, June 8, 1829, Monroe, NYPL.

22. See Livingston to Monroe, Apr. 27, 1802, Monroe, NYPL.

23. Dangerfield, *Livingston*, 359–60.

24. Quote is from Livingston to Talleyrand, Apr. 12, 1803, cited in Brant, *Madison*, IV, 127–28 (Dangerfield, *Livingston*, does not cite this letter); Monroe to Madison, Sept. 17, 1803, Rives Papers, LC; Monroe to Madison, Dec. 17, 1803, *JM*, IV, 119.

25. Lyon, *Louisiana*, 214; Dangerfield, *Livingston*, 359–61. Dangerfield bases his account on that in François de Barbé-Marbois, *Histoire de la Louisiane* (Paris, 1829). Marbois, however, does not explain why he waited for two days after receiving Napoleon's instructions before calling on Livingston—was he in fact waiting for Monroe to arrive in Paris?

26. Dangerfield, *Livingston*, 361–63.

27. Monroe to Livingston, Apr. 13, 1803, Monroe to Madison, Apr. 15, 1803, *JM*, IV, 8–9; Dangerfield, *Livingston*, 366.

28. Quote is from Monroe to Madison, Sept. 17, 1803, Rives Papers, LC. Dangerfield, *Livingston*, 363, Lyon, *Louisiana*, 217, and other writers on the negotiations give the date of the dinner as April 12. Although it does not materially affect the sequence of events, it should be noted that this dinner took place on the thirteenth. Monroe again and again states that Marbois saw Livingston the day after his arrival in Paris, *i.e.*, Marbois called on April 13. See Monroe to Madison, Apr. 15, 1803, *JM*, IV, 10. The confusion about the date arises from the fact that Livingston's letter is dated "April 13, 1803, midnight," *AC*, 7C1S, 1129, and it has always been taken for granted that he wrote it in the early hours of the thirteenth; whereas in fact he wrote in the early hours of the fourteenth describing the events of the evening of the thirteenth. That it is the thirteenth is also clear from Livingston's reference to Monroe's spending the day with him reading his papers. Monroe arrived too late on the twelfth to go through the correspondence. In this letter there is also another one of those ambiguities, or more accurately contradictions, about dates which are strewn so liberally through Livingston's letters at this time: Livingston refers to an interview with Talleyrand on the *twelfth* at which the proposal to sell Louisiana was made, when obviously he is referring to the interview of the eleventh about which he had already written Madison. The fact that the dinner was on the thirteenth is also confirmed by a letter from Livingston to King, Apr. 13, 1803, *Proceedings of the American Antiquarian Society*, n.s., LII, 497–98. In this letter there is a postscript dated April 14 in which Livingston noted that he was called to confer with Marbois "last night."

29. Apr. 13, 1803, *AC*, 7C2S, 1128–32.

30. Monroe to Madison, Apr. 15, 1803, *JM*, IV, 9–12; endorsed not sent. In citing this letter Dangerfield used the text printed in *State Papers and Other Correspondence Bearing on the Purchase of the Territories of Louisiana*, 57C2S, HR Docs. #4. This edition omits the endorsement and hence Dangerfield leaves the impression that Monroe was the first to complain, whereas, Livingston first stated his grievances.

31. Monroe to Madison, May 14, 1803, Rives Papers, LC.

32. Monroe to Madison, Aug. 11, 1803, Rives Papers, LC; Monroe left a detailed account of the last stages of the negotiations between Apr. 27 and May 2, 1803, which is printed in *JM*, IV, 12–19. I have followed this journal closely.

33. Undated Memorandum by Monroe, *JM*, IV, 500.

34. Lyon, *Louisiana*, 227.

35. Monroe to Livingston, Apr. 30, 1803, quoted in Dangerfield, *Livingston*, 368.

36. Monroe Journal, May 1, 1803, *JM*, IV 16.

37. Lyon, *Louisiana*, 223–24; Monroe Journal, May 1, 1803, *JM*, IV, 16.

38. For details of their conclusions on this point see: Dangerfield, *Livingston*, 367–68; Isaac Joslin Cox, *The West Florida Controversy, 1798–1813* (Baltimore, 1918), 84ff.; Brant, *Madison*, IV, 145–51; Monroe to Madison, May 18, June 19, 1803, Monroe to Livingston, n.d., endorsed not sent, *JM*, IV, 24–29, 41–43; opinion on Louisiana sent to Madison by Monroe and Livingston, June 19, 1803, *JM*, IV, 503–9.

39. Quoted in Lyon, *Louisiana*, 225–26.

40. To Madison, Apr. 27, 1809, Rives Papers, LC.

41. July 29, 1803, *AC*, 7C2S, 1166.

42. *Autobiography*, 159–60; Monroe to Baring Bros., Mar. 6, 1806, Monroe to Lafayette, Mar. 16, 1806, *JM*, IV, 425–30.

43. Monroe to Jefferson, Sept. 30, 1803, *JM*, IV, 75–6.

44. *Autobiography*, 156–61; Cambacérès to Monroe, Apr. 17, 1803, Paul Benthalou to Monroe, Jan. 24, 1824, Monroe, NYPL.

45. Monroe to Madison, May 14, 1803, Rives Papers, LC.

46. Dangerfield, *Livingston*, 390.

47. John Quincy Adams, *Memoirs*, ed. by Charles Francis Adams (12 vols., Philadelphia, 1874–77), V, 432–34, 444–45, Nov. 20, Dec. 3, 1821.

48. Dangerfield, *Livingston*, 376–77.

49. These letters to King are in *Proceedings of the American Antiquarian Society*, n.s., LII, 396–402.

50. Dangerfield, *Livingston*, 377–78.

51. *JM*, IV, 31–33; this was sent under cover of a letter to Madison, who

was to use his discretion whether it should be forwarded. Monroe to Madison, June 8, 1803, Rives Papers, LC.

52. *JM,* IV, 33.

53. Dangerfield, *Livingston,* 379.

54. Monroe to Madison, Nov. 25, 1803, *JM,* IV, 102–3.

55. Dangerfield, *Livingston,* 331–33; Lyon, *Louisiana,* 159–61.

56. Quoted in Brant, *Madison,* IV, 137.

57. Dangerfield, *Livingston,* 351, 379; fn. 52 *supra.*

58. See Lyon, *Louisiana,* 192–207; Brant, *Madison,* IV, 121–33; Dangerfield, *Livingston,* 369–71.

59. Monroe to Madison, July 11, 1804, Rives Papers, LC; the printed version of this letter in *JM,* IV, 184, is misdated May 6, 1804; the original is clearly dated July 11.

60. Monroe to Madison, June 8, 1803, *JM,* IV, 34–36; *Autobiography,* 168–69.

61. Jefferson to W. C. Nicholas, Sept. 7, 1803, Ford, *Jefferson,* VIII, 247 fn.; Jefferson to J. C. Breckinridge, August [18], 1803, Breckinridge, LC.

62. *Autobiography,* 169–70; Monroe to Madison, June 8, 1803, *JM,* IV, 34; Livingston to Madison, Sept. 17, 1803, Madison, LC.

63. Monroe to Madison, Aug. 15, 31, 1803, *JM,* IV, 61, 72; Livingston to Monroe, Sept. 7, 1803, copy, Madison, LC.

64. Livingston to Monroe, Sept. 11, 1803, copy, Livingston to Madison, Sept. 17, 1803, Madison, LC; Monroe to Livingston, Oct. 9, 1803, *JM,* IV, 78–92.

65. Brant, *Madison,* IV, 156–57.

66. For details see *ibid.,* IV, 213–29 and Dangerfield, *Livingston,* 380–85.

67. Skipwith to Madison, Feb. 21, 1804, Consular Corres., LC.

68. Dangerfield, *Livingston,* 384.

69. Monroe to Livingston, Oct. 29, 1803, *JM,* IV, 94–5.

70. To Madison, Aug. 18, 1804, Rives Papers, LC.

71. Monroe Journal, *JM,* IV, 18–19; Monroe to Madison, Dec. 16, 1804, *JM,* IV, 290–91.

72. Livingston to Madison, Sept. 18, 1803, Rives Papers, LC.

73. Oct. 15, 1803, quoted in Brant, *Madison,* IV, 153.

74. Monroe to Charles Pinckney, July 5, 1803, NA.

75. Monroe to Madison, June 19, July 20, 1803, *JM,* IV, 37–8, 45–6; *Autobiography,* 172.

76. Memorandum by Monroe, June 24, 1803, *JM,* IV, 39, fn. 2; *Autobiography,* 172–73.

77. Monroe to Madison, July 19, 1803, NA.

1. *Autobiography*, 185–86.

2. *Ibid.*, 185–86; Monroe to Madison, July 26, Aug. 31, Nov. 6, 24, 1803, *JM*, IV, 52, 69–70, 96–101.

3. Bradford Perkins, *The First Rapprochement, England and the United States, 1795–1805* (Philadelphia, 1955), 132–3, and *The Prologue to War: England and the United States, 1805–1812* (U. of California, 1961), 8–11; Steven Watson, *The Reign of George III* (London, 1960), 414–15.

4. Monroe expressed these opinions on many occasions; see Monroe to Madison, Nov. 16, 25, 1803, and Monroe to Jefferson, Mar. 15, 1804, *JM*, IV, 97, 103, 155.

5. Monroe to Madison, July 1, 1804, *JM*, IV, 218.

6. Monroe to Madison, Nov. 25, 1803, *JM*, IV, 103; same to same, Oct. 21, 1803, NA.

7. Perkins, *First Rapprochement*, 173.

8. Dec. 26, 1803, Hunt, *Madison*, VII, 77 fn.

9. Sept. 25, 1804, *JM*, IV, 255.

10. To Madison, July 1, 1804, *JM*, IV, 218–20; Brant, *Madison*, IV, 172–75.

11. Monroe to Madison, July 26, 1803, *JM*, IV, 54; same to same, Mar. 18, 1804, Rives Papers, LC.

12. Monroe to Madison, Sept. 18, 1804, Rives Papers, LC.

13. Monroe to Hawkesbury, Nov. 28, 1804, Monroe to Madison, Oct. 21, 1803, Erving to Monroe, Nov. 5, 1803, NA.; Monroe to Madison, Dec. 15, 1803, *JM*, IV, 112–13.

14. To Madison, Jan. 9, 1804, *JM*, IV, 131; Madison to Monroe, Mar. 6, 1804, Hunt, *Madison*, VII, 168.

15. To Madison, Mar. 3, 1804, *JM*, IV, 151.

16. To Jefferson, Mar. 15, 1804, *JM*, IV, 158–59.

17. Jessie Benton Fremont, *Souvenirs of My Time*, quoted in Morgan, *Monroe*, 262.

18. To Jefferson, Mar. 15, 1804, to Madison, Apr. 26, 1804, *JM*, IV, 156–58, 171–72.

19. Monroe to Madison, Mar. 12, 1804, Rives Papers, LC.

20. Monroe to [Joseph Jones], Mar. 12, June 3, 1804, Monroe Foundation; Monroe to Madison, Nov. 25, 1803, Monroe to Jefferson, Mar. 15, 1804, *JM*, IV, 105–6, 161; Monroe to Madison, Dec. 15, 1803, Thomas Swann to Madison, May 6, 1804, Madison, LC; Monroe to [Joseph Selden], July 15, 1804, J. M. Forbes to Monroe, Aug. 27, 1805, Monroe, LC. Monroe's debt was at least $10,000.

21. Jones to Madison, Jan. 7, June 16, 1804, Madison Papers, LC; Madison to Jones, July 14, 1804, NYPL; Monroe to Madison, Jan. 10, 1806, *JM*, IV, 391.

22. Madison to Monroe, Apr. 15, 1804, Hunt, *Madison*, VII, 141–42; Monroe to Madison, Apr. 26, May 3, 1804, *JM*, IV, 173–75.

23. Perkins, *First Rapprochement*, 175.

24. Madison to Monroe, Jan. 5, 1804, Hunt, *Madison*, VII, 79–114; Monroe to Madison, Sept. 8, 1804, *JM*, IV, 248; Brant, *Madison*, IV, 172–75; A. L. Burt, *The United States, Great Britain and British North America from the Revolution to the Establishment of Peace after the War of 1812* (New York, 1961), 227–28.

25. Monroe to Madison, June 3, 1804, *JM*, IV, 193–96.

26. Monroe to Madison, June 10, 1804, Rives Papers, LC; same to same, June 28, 1804, *JM*, IV, 306–7; Dangerfield, *Livingston*, 386–90; Monroe to Madison, June 10, 1804, Rives Papers, LC.

27. Monroe to Madison, Aug. 7, 1804, *JM*, IV, 229–35; to Madison, Sept. 14, 1804, Rives Papers, LC.

28. Monroe thought highly of Purviance, a Baltimorean who had been his secretary on his first mission to France. Purviance's illness (apparently a mental illness of a melancholic nature) prevented him from exercising the duties of his office. George W. Erving was obliged to fill in. Erving to Monroe, Dec. 10, 1804, Apr. 16, 1805, Monroe, LC; Monroe to Erving, Mar. 12, 1805, Monroe, NYPL.

29. Monroe to Madison, Aug. 10, 1804, *JM*, IV, 236–38.

30. Detailed discussion of all aspects of the Spanish negotiations will be found in Isaac Joslin Cox, *The West Florida Controversy, 1798–1813* (Baltimore, 1918) and in Henry Adams, *History*, II, *passim*. The latter, as was his rule, was in evident hostility toward Monroe as the spokesman of Republican policy.

31. Monroe to Madison, Nov. 16, 1803, *JM*, IV, 96; Brant, *Madison*, IV, 159.

32. Brant, *Madison*, IV, 260; Monroe to Madison, Dec. 16, 1804, *JM*, IV, 278–97.

33. Monroe to Talleyrand, Nov. 8, 1804, *JM*, IV, 266–74.

34. Livingston to Monroe, Nov. 12, 1804, Monroe, LC; Monroe to Livingston, Nov. 13, 1804, *JM*, IV, 274–76.

35. *Autobiography*, 178–80, 208–9; Adams, *History*, II, 305.

36. Hunt, *Madison*, VII, 141.

37. Monroe to Madison, Dec. 16, 1804, *JM*, IV, 294–6; Monroe to Fulwar Skipwith, July 21, 1823, *Bull. NYPL*, VI (1902), 257.

38. Monroe Journal of negotiations in Spain, Apr. 22, 1804, NA.

39. *Ibid.*, Feb. 10, 1805.

40. Brant, *Madison*, IV, 198, 203–5, 291; Cox, *West Florida*, 129; Madison to Monroe, Oct. 26, 1804, Monroe, LC.

41. Monroe to Madison, Dec. 16, 1804, quote is from Pinckney to Monroe, Nov. 18, 1804, Monroe, LC; *Autobiography*, 210.

42. *Autobiography*, 211.

43. Jefferson to Monroe, Jan. 8, 1804, Ford, *Jefferson*, VIII, 289.

44. Monroe to Madison, May 26, 1805, Rives Papers, LC.

45. On Pinckney's character see *DAB;* Pinckney prepared a summary of the negotiations for Madison (Mar. 18–May 20, 1805, NA) which is far inferior to that kept by Monroe and reveals his inadequacies; Pinckney to Monroe, May 28, 1805, Monroe, NYPL.

46. Monroe to Madison, Jan. 27, 1805, Rives Papers, LC; Monroe Journal of negotiations, Mar. 30, 1805, NA.

47. To Madison, Jan. 27, 1805, Rives Papers, LC; Henry Adams, *History*, III, 30, is incorrect in stating that Monroe received this letter in February.

48. *AC*, 8C2S, 1364–73.

49. Monroe Journal of negotiations, Jan. 30, 1805, *et seq.*, NA.

50. Jan. 31, 1805, *AC*, 8C2S, 1373–74.

51. Monroe Journal of negotiations, Feb. 2, 1805, NA.

52. Cox, *West Florida*, 122.

53. Monroe and Pinckney to Cevallos, Feb. 5, 1805, *AC*, 8C2S, 1374–78.

54. Cevallos to Monroe and Pinckney, Feb. 10, 16, 1805, *ibid.*, 1378–87.

55. Monroe and Pinckney to Cevallos, Feb. 18, 1805, *ibid.*, 1387.

56. Monroe Journal of negotiations, Feb. 18, 1805, NA.

57. Monroe to Armstrong, Feb. 26, 1805, Monroe, NA.

58. Monroe and Pinckney to Cevallos, Feb. 15, 26, 1805, *AC*, 8C2S, 1393–1403.

59. Monroe and Pinckney to Cevallos, Mar. 8, 16, 1805, *ibid.*, 1414–22, 1427.

60. Armstrong to Monroe, Mar. 12, 1805, Monroe, NYPL; Monroe to Armstrong, Mar. 27, 1805, NA.

61. Armstrong to Monroe, Apr. 5, 1805, Monroe, NYPL.

62. Monroe Journal of negotiations, Mar. 25, 1805, NA; Monroe and Pinckney to Cevallos and reply, Mar. 30, 1805, *AC*, 8C2S, 1428.

63. Monroe and Pinckney to Cevallos, Apr. 9, 1805; Cevallos to Monroe and Pinckney, Apr. 9, 1805, and their reply, Apr. 12, 1805, *AC*, 8C2S, 1432–6.

64. Monroe Journal of negotiaions, Apr. 13, 1805, NA.

65. Notes are in *AC*, 8C2S, 1435–51.

66. May 12, 1805, *ibid.*, 1451–52; Monroe Journal of negotiations, May 8–14, 1805, NA.

67. May 15, 1805, *AC*, 8C2S, 1454.

68. Brant, *Madison*, IV, 262–64, harshly condemns Monroe and Pinckney for failing to present the alternative sent them by Madison in instructions of July 8, 1804 (*ASPFR*, II, 680); however, Madison's dispatch does not seem to have reached the emissaries until negotiations were well advanced. Monroe never mentioned

receiving it in his letters, although he notes receiving instructions of Apr. 14 and Oct. 26, 1804, which reached him after he arrived in Madrid. Monroe did not always specifically acknowledge instructions, but when he departed from them he usually explained his reasons. There is a very strong probability that Madison's letter of July 8 arrived in England long after he had departed for Spain. Purviance, who acted as chargé, wrote Monroe on Oct. 19, 1804 (NA), that he had received dispatches from Washington dated as late as July 20. Purviance suffered a mental collapse after Monroe left London, and the affairs of the legation were obviously in a great state of confusion. When Purviance wrote Monroe on Oct. 19 he clearly did not know what to do with the recently arrived dispatches. On Mar. 12, 1805, Monroe (letter is in NYHS) wrote Purviance acknowledging the receipt of a letter of Dec. 10, which was the first letter received from Purviance since he had been in Spain. On Nov. 14, 1804 (NA), Purviance wrote informing Monroe that Mr. Bankhead (a distant relation of Monroe's from Westmoreland, who acted as private secretary to the emissaries during the final stages of the negotiations) would bring recently arrived dispatches to Monroe. Bankhead apparently did not reach Madrid until sometime in March, for Monroe referred to a Mr. Preble on Mar. 1, 1805 (in a letter to Armstrong, NA), who had been acting as his secretary. If the July 8 dispatch arrived at this point (and indications are that it did not), then Monroe and Pinckney did not regard them as mandatory, but apparently interpreted them to mean that this alternative was to be stated at the beginning of the negotiations as a possible solution. Perhaps they decided (assuming they had the July 8 instructions) that nothing could be gained by presenting them. It is noteworthy that Madison never queried Monroe or Pinckney about this matter. Apparently, he did not place great importance on the proposal.

69. July 6, 1805, *Bull. NYPL,* IV (1900), 50–1.

70. The public letter is dated May 23, 1805, NA; the private letter of May 23, 1805 is in Rives Papers, LC; Armstrong to Monroe, May 4, 1805, NA.

71. Brant, *Madison,* IV, 263.

72. Jefferson to Madison, Sept. 18, 1805, Rives Papers, LC.

73. Charles E. Hill, "James Madison," in Bemis, *American Secretaries of State,* III, 56–9.

74. Jefferson to Madison, Oct. 11, 1805, Ford, *Jefferson,* VIII, 380 n.

75. Adams, *History of the U.S.,* III, 130–36; Harry Ammon, "The Election of 1808 in Virginia," *WMQ,* 3rd Ser., XX (1963), 33–40.

76. Randolph to Monroe, Mar. 20, 1806; Taylor to Monroe, Feb. 27, 1806; Nicholson to Monroe, May 5, 1806, Monroe, LC.

77. Madison to Monroe, Mar. 10, 1806, Rives Papers, LC; Monroe to Armstrong, Mar. 11, 1806, *JM,* IV, 427.

78. Jefferson to Monroe, Jan. 8, 1804, Ford, *Jefferson,* VIII, 288; Monroe to Jefferson, Mar. 15, 1805, July 8, 1806, *JM,* IV, 153, 477; Monroe to Madison, June 30, 1805, NA.

79. Monroe to Madison, Jan. 10, 1806, *JM,* IV, 392–3.

80. June 15, 1806, *JM*, IV, 456–7.

81. Jefferson to Monroe, Mar. 16, 1806, Monroe, LC; May 4, 1806, Ford, *Jefferson*, VIII, 447.

82. Adams, *History*, III, 370–88.

CHAPTER 14

THE REJECTED TREATY

1. Monroe to Madison, Aug. 6, 1805, Monroe to Jefferson, Oct. 6, 1805, *JM*, IV, 303, 329. In this chapter I have made extensive use of A. L. Burt, *The United States, Great Britain and British North America from the Revolution to the Establishment of Peace after the War of 1812* (New York, 1961) and Bradford Perkins, *Prologue to War: England and the United States* (University of California, 1961).

2. Monroe to John Armstrong, Aug. 26, Sept. 2, 1804, *JM*, IV, 31–34; Monroe to Madison, Aug. 20, 1805, NA; Adams, *History*, III, 43–47.

3. Monroe to Lord Mulgrave, Sept. 23, 1805, *JM*, IV, 333.

4. Monroe to Jefferson, Oct. 6, 1805, Monroe to Madison, Dec. 11, 1805, *ibid.*, IV, 344–51, 376.

5. Monroe to Jefferson, Sept. 26, Oct. 6, 1805, Monroe to Madison, Oct. 18, 1805, *ibid.*, IV, 334–58; Perkins, *Prologue*, 177–80; Brant, *Madison*, IV, 297–99.

6. Monroe to Madison, Oct. 18–25, 1805, *JM*, IV, 361–62.

7. *Ibid.*, IV, 352 fn.

8. Monroe to Madison, Nov. 22, 1805, *Bull. NYPL*, IV (1900), 54–55.

9. Perkins, *Prologue*, 16–19.

10. Monroe to Madison, Jan. 28, 1806, *JM*, V, 45, fn. 12.

11. Feb. 2, 1806, *ibid.*, IV, 403.

12. Perkins, *Prologue*, 114–15.

13. To Madison, Feb. 12, 1806, *JM*, IV, 411–14.

14. To Madison, Mar. 11, 1806, *JM*, V, 39, fn. 2.

15. He made this limitation quite clear in a letter to Armstrong, Mar. 11, 1806, *JM*, IV, 428.

16. Jefferson to Levi Lincoln, June 25, 1806, Ford, *Jefferson*, VIII, 456.

17. Burt, *British North America*, 233; Perkins, *Prologue*, 104–5; Monroe to James Bowdoin, June 20, 1806, *JM*, IV, 472–73.

18. Perkins, *Prologue*, 109–13.

19. Monroe to Madison, June 9, 1806, *JM*, IV, 447.

20. June 15, 1806, *ibid.*, IV, 456–57.

21. [May 18, 1806], *ibid*, IV, 437–39.

22. Brant, *Madison*, IV, 297–301, 314–15, 368; Adams, *History*, III, 396.

23. Fox to Anthony Merry, Apr. 7, 1806, *Instructions to the British Ministers to the United States, 1791–1812*, ed. by Bernard Mayo, AHA, *Annual Report for 1936*, III, 221.

24. Monroe to Madison, Apr. 29, June 9, 1806, *JM*, IV, 433, 445–47.

25. Apr. 29, 1806, *JM*, IV, 432–33.

26. Quotes are from John Randolph to Monroe, Mar. 20, 1806, and Joseph Nicholson to Monroe, May 5, 1806; see also James M. Garnett to Monroe, Mar. 19, 1806, John Taylor to Monroe, Feb. 27, 1806; all in Monroe Papers, LC.

27. Jefferson to Monroe, May 4, 1806, Ford, *Jefferson*, VIII, 447–48; Wirt to Monroe, June 10, 1806, Monroe, LC; quote is from John Beckley to Monroe, July 13, 1806, Monroe, NYPL.

28. Monroe to Jefferson, June 15, 1806, endorsed not sent, *JM*, IV, 455–57; quote is from Monroe to Jefferson, July 8, 1806, Monroe, LC. This last letter is entirely different from the letter of July 8 which he sent, which is printed in *JM*, IV, 477.

29. Monroe to Jefferson, July 8, 1806, *JM*, IV, 477.

30. Monroe to Randolph, June 16, 1806, *JM*, IV, 460–67; Larkin Smith first raised the presidential issue in a letter to Monroe, June 7, 1805, Monroe, NYPL.

31. Nov. 12, 1806, *JM*, IV, 485–89.

32. Perkins, *Prologue*, 116.

33. *Ibid.*, 121–22; Adams, *History*, III, 406.

34. Perkins, *Prologue*, 16–18, 122.

35. Monroe to Lord and Lady Auckland, Dec. 11, 1806, Pinkney to Monroe, [Jan. 10, 1807], Monroe, NYPL; quote is from Pinkney to Monroe, Nov. 14, 1806, *JM*, IV, 454, fn. 1.

36. Quoted in Daniel C. Gilman, *James Monroe* (New York, 1855), 99. Lord Holland's observation belies Henry Adams' assertion, *History*, III, 408, that Monroe was under Pinkney's influence; all indications are that the reverse was the case.

37. Lady Elizabeth Holland, *Journal* (2 vols., New York, 1909), II, 202, 209. Feb. 12, Mar. 2, 1807.

38. Watson, *George III*, 453.

39. *AC*, 10C1S, 2452–65; Perkins, *Prologue*, 117–18.

40. Perkins, *Prologue*, 106–7; Jefferson to Monroe, May 4, 1806, Ford, *Jefferson*, VIII, 449.

41. Monroe and Pinkney to Madison, Sept. 11, 1806, Madison to Monroe and Pinkney, Nov. 28, 1806, *AC*, 10C1S, 2485–91, 2505.

42. Watson, *George III*, 436–40; Perkins, *Prologue*, 17–18.

43. Monroe and Pinkney to Madison, Nov. 11, 1806, *AC*, 10C1S, 2496–503.

44. Nov. 8, 1806, *ibid.*, 2503.

45. Nov. 11, 1806, *ibid.,* 2496–503.

46. Quoted in Perkins, *Prologue,* 129.

47. *AC,* 10C1S, 2519.

48. Madison to Monroe and Pinkney, Feb. 3, 1806, *ibid.,* 2539–45.

49. Text of treaty is in *ibid.,* 2523–33; Perkins, *Prologue,* 124–32.

50. Monroe and Pinkney to Madison, Jan. 3, 1807, *AC,* 10C1S, 2507–23.

51. Jan. 11, 1807, *JM,* V, 2.

52. To Monroe, Feb. 22, 1807, Monroe, LC.

53. Jefferson to Monroe, May 4, 1806, Ford, *Jefferson,* VIII, 450; Wilkinson to Col. Mercer, Jan. 6, 1808, Cadwalader Coll., PHS.

54. Perkins, *Prologue,* 135; decision to reject the treaty was made Feb. 2, 1807, Jefferson, *Anas,* in Ford, *Jefferson,* I, 406–07.

55. Burt, *British North America,* 202–4.

56. Mar. 4, 1807, *JM,* V, 64, fn. 1; Monroe to Giles, Apr. 20, 1807, *JM,* V, 4–7.

57. Joseph Nicholson to Monroe, Apr. 12, 1807, John Randolph to Monroe, May 30, 1807, Monroe, LC.

58. Jefferson to Monroe, Mar. 31, 1807, Ford, *Jefferson,* IX, 35–7.

59. Jefferson to Monroe, May 29, 1807, Monroe, LC.

60. June 1, 1807, *JM,* V, 5, fn. 1.

61. Mar. 22, 1808, *JM,* V, 27–34.

62. Watson, *George III,* 444–46; Perkins, *Prologue,* 184–5, 197–202.

63. Monroe and Pinkney to Canning, July 24, 1807, Monroe and Pinkney to Madison, Oct. 10, 1807, *AC,* 10C1S, 2643–52; for a full discussion of the last phases of the negotiations, see Perkins, *Prologue,* 189ff.

64. The pertinent documents are in *AC* 10C1S, 2627ff.

65. Monroe to Canning, Sept. 7, 1807, Canning to Monroe, Sept. 23, 1807, Monroe to Madison, Oct. 10, 1807, *ibid.,* 2633–63; Perkins, *Prologue,* 195.

CHAPTER 15

A QUARREL AND A RECONCILIATION

1. Monroe to Madison, Dec. 13, 1807, *JM,* V, 20.

2. Alexander McRae to Monroe, Dec. 22, 23, 1807, Monroe, NYPL.

3. See undated memorandum in Monroe's hand in an account book dated 1794–1800 (Monroe, LC), which contains a statement of the reasons for his dissatisfaction.

4. For a full account of the election and the background of the Old Republican

movement, see Harry Ammon, "The Election of 1808 in Virginia," *WMQ*, 3rd Ser., XX (Jan. 1963), 33–56.

5. Mathew Clay to Monroe, Feb. 24, 1808, Monroe, LC.

6. Memoir of W. A. Burwell, LC; Protest of John Randolph *et al.*, Feb. 27, 1808, in Richmond *Virginia Argus*, Mar. 11, 1801; *Enquirer*, Jan. 28, 1808; John Quincy Adams, *Memoirs*, ed. by Charles Francis Adams (12 vols., Philadelphia, 1874–77), I, 504–6, Jan. 20–23, 1808; Brant, *Madison*, IV, 422–29; Anderson, *Giles*, 123–24.

7. Proceedings of the Executive Council of Virginia, 1806–1808, July 9, Dec. 12, 1808, pp. 150, 261, VSL.

8. William Wirt to Monroe, Feb. 8, 1808, Monroe, LC; Alexander McRae to Monroe, Dec. 31, 1807, Monroe, NYPL.

9. "Powhatan," "A. B." [George Hay], *Enquirer*, Jan. 19, Feb. 23, 1808. There seems to have been no serious effort to coordinate the Clinton and Monroe campaigns. An attempt was made to persuade Clinton to accept second place on the Monroe ticket, but this fell through. E. C. Stanard to Monroe, Feb. 19, 1808, Monroe, NYPL.

10. *Enquirer*, Jan. 23, 26, 1808; "Hortensius" [George Hay], *ibid.*, Jan. 30, 1808. The Madison caucus was directed by James Barbour, Thomas Ritchie and Robert B. Taylor. The official notice of the caucus planned for Jan. 28 appeared in *ibid.*, Jan. 16, 1808.

11. *Ibid.*, Jan. 26, Sept. 30, Oct. 25, 1808.

12. Jefferson to Monroe, Feb. 18, 1808, Ford, *Jefferson*, IX, 177.

13. Monroe to _____, July 15, 1808, Monroe to Hay, April 29, 1808, *JM*, V, 52–62; Monroe to [L. W. Tazewell], Sept. 25, 1808, Monroe, LC.

14. L. W. Tazewell to Monroe, Oct. 8, 1808, Monroe, LC.

15. Feb. 18, 1808, Ford, *Jefferson*, IX, 178.

16. Jefferson to Monroe, Mar. 10, 1808, *ibid.*, IX, 180 fn.; the other letters in this exchange are in *ibid*, IX, 176–84 and *JM*, V, 24–35.

17. Monroe to Jefferson, Apr. 18, 1808, *JM*, V, 51.

18. Pertinent letters are in Madison Papers, LC; Rives Papers, LC; and *JM*, V, 27–37.

19. Madison Papers, LC.

20. This paper survives in incomplete files in LC and VSL. It was never very successful and expired as a Federalist organ in 1811. See also John Taylor to Monroe, July 27, 1811, Monroe, LC.

21. Ammon, "Elec. of 1808," *WMQ*, XX, 47–48.

22. *Ibid.*, 47–50.

23. *Enquirer*, June 3, 21, 22, 1808.

24. Printed in *ibid.*, Sept. 30, 1808, from the *Spirit of '76*, Sept. 24, 1808; see also Monroe to Tazewell, Sept. 25, 1808, draft, Monroe, LC.

25. Oct. 18, 1808.

26. Reprinted from *Spirit of '76* in New York *American Citizen,* Oct. 26, 1808. None of the Richmond papers seem to have printed it.

27. *Virginia Argus,* Nov. 1, 1808.

28. Returns are from *ibid.,* Nov. 8, 11, 17, 25, 1808.

29. Ammon, "Elec. of 1808," *WMQ,* XX, 53–5.

30. Monroe to Jefferson, Jan. 18, 1809, *JM,* V, 90–2; Creed Taylor to [Richard Brent], draft, Jan. 28, 1809, Creed Taylor Papers, U.Va.

31. Jefferson to Monroe, Jan. 28, 1809, Ford, *Jefferson,* IX, 292–94. A proposal to send a special mission, which was made in the House by D. R. Williams of South Carolina, was rejected. Two of Jefferson's strongest supporters, J. G. Jackson and J. W. Eppes, opposed it. It is doubtful that this proposal had any connection with Monroe's suggestion. *AC,* 10C Extra Session, 1096–1124, Jan. 11, 1809.

32. Nicholas to Samuel Smith, Apr. 3, 1811, Smith Papers, LC. Many years later James G. Jackson (Mrs. Madison's brother-in-law) maintained that Madison intended to appoint Monroe. See Jackson to Monroe, Mar. 11, 1819, Monroe, LC, and *Letters on the Richmond Party* (Washington, D.C., 1823), 22.

33. Monroe to Sir Francis Baring, Oct. 15, 1809, *Bull. NYPL,* V (1901), 380.

34. Monroe to _____, Apr. 6, 1808, Monroe to Hay, Apr. 29, 1808, *JM,* V, 47, 52; Jefferson to Madison, Mar. 30, 1809, Rives Papers, LC.

35. Monroe to William Short, Feb. 11, 1811, Short Papers, LC.

36. Mrs. Eliza Trist to Mrs. Mary Gilmer, Sept. 1, 1808, Gilmer Papers. U.Va.

37. Monroe to [Stephen Pleasanton], May 22, 1815, Pleasanton Papers, U.Va.

38. Wirt to Mrs. Wirt, Sept. 11, 1809, Wirt Papers, MdHS.

39. Monroe to Hay, Feb. 28, 1810, Monroe, NYPL.

40. Dec. 18, 1807, quoted in Anne Hollingsworth Wharton, *Social Life in the Early Republic* (Philadelphia, 1902), 136.

41. Mar. 30, 1809, Rives Papers, LC.

42. Monroe to Taylor, Jan. 8, 1809, *JM,* V, 87–90; L. W. Tazewell to Monroe, Jan. 26, 1809, Monroe, NYPL; Monroe to James Bowdoin, Jan. 17, 1809, *Coll. MHS,* ser. 7, no. 6, 451–53; Taylor to Monroe, Jan. 15, 1809, Monroe, LC.

43. *Enquirer,* Oct. 24, 1809.

44. Jefferson to Madison, Nov. 30, 1809, Ford, *Jefferson,* IX, 265–67; Brant, *Madison,* V, 164.

45. Monroe to Hay, Nov. 30, 1809. *Bull. NYPL,* V (1901), 431–33; J. M. Garnett to Randolph, Dec. 19, 1809, Randolph-Garnett Transcripts, LC.

46. Monroe to Charles Everett, Dec. 5, 28 [both letters are incorrectly dated Sept. in *JM*], 1808, Monroe to Richard Brent, Dec. 25, 1809, *JM,* V, 103–4, 110–13; Everett to Monroe, Dec. 11, 1809, Monroe, NYPL.

47. Randolph to J. M. Garnett, Dec. 25, 1809, Randolph-Garnett Transcripts, LC.

48. L. W. Tazewell to Monroe, Feb. 13, 1811, Monroe, LC. In this discursive

letter Tazewell gives the impression that Monroe had been approached before he ran for the legislature.

49. New York *Gazette and General Advertiser*, May 17, 1810; New York *Evening Post*, May 19, 1810; J. H. Nicholson to Gallatin, May 21, 1810, Gallatin Papers, NYHS; Brant, *Madison*, V, 131, 159.

50. Perkins, *Prologue*, 239–43; Brant, *Madison*, V, 126–40, 163–67.

51. Richmond *Enquirer*, Apr. 10, 1810.

52. Monroe to Richard Brent, Feb. 25, 1810, *JM*, V, 116–20; for details about Monroe's accounts see Lucius Wilmerding, Jr., *James Monroe, Claimant* (Rutgers U. Press, 1960).

53. Monroe to Taylor, Sept. 10, 1810, *JM*, V, 138.

54. To Madison, May 25, 1810, Ford, *Jefferson*, IX, 275–76.

55. Sept. 10, 1810, *JM*, V, 124–50.

56. Monroe to Randolph, June 15, 1810, U.Va.

57. Quoted in Brant, *Madison*, V, 166.

58. Randolph to J. M. Garnett, Sept. 28, Oct. 10, 1810, Garnett to Randolph, Oct. 23 [1810], all in Randolph-Garnett Transcripts, LC; Randolph to Monroe, Aug. 28, 1810, Monroe, LC.

59. *Journals of the House of Delegates [of Virginia] 1810–1811 . . . , passim;* Monroe to Jefferson, Dec. 24, 1810, *JM*, V, 159; Monroe to John Taylor, Jan. 23, 1811, Washburn Papers, MHS.

60. Quotation is from Jefferson to Monroe, Jan. 25, 1811, Monroe, LC.

61. L. W. Tazewell to Monroe, Dec. 30, 1810, Monroe to Tazewell, Jan. 15, 1811, Monroe, LC; *Enquirer*, Dec. 4, 1810.

62. Samuel Smith to _____, May 6, 1811, draft, Smith Papers, LC. It may have been expected that Monroe would be elected governor in December, for the death of Cyrus Griffin (the incumbent judge) had long been expected and Tyler had indicated a wish for the post in May, 1810. The fact that Griffin did not die until Dec. 14 made it impossible to execute this plan. The evidence is presumptive rather than conclusive. See Tyler to Jefferson, May 12, 1810, in Lyon G. Tyler, *Letters and Times of the Tylers* (3 vols., New York, 1884–96), I, 171–72, 244–47; Jefferson to Madison, May 25, 1810, Ford, *Jefferson*, IX, 275. Timothy Pickering recalled the whole transaction nearly twenty years later. He then described Tyler's appointment as characteristic Republican political maneuver. Pickering to John Marshall, Jan. 24, 1826, Pickering Papers, MHS.

63. Chapman Johnson to Monroe, Jan. 12, 1811, Monroe to Johnson, Jan. 14, 1811, *JM*, V, 164–65, fn. 1; both letters were printed in the *Enquirer*, Jan. 17, 1811, the day after Monroe was elected governor.

64. Letter to Taylor is in *JM*, V, 121–50; see also Monroe to Tazewell, Jan. 15, 1811, Monroe, LC.

65. Jan. 12, 1811, quoted in William Cabell Bruce, *Life of John Randolph of Roanoke* (2 vols., New York, 1922), I, 348.

66. Randolph to J. M. Garnett, Feb. 26, 1811, Randolph-Garnett Transcripts, LC; Randolph to Monroe, Jan. 14, 15, 1811, Monroe to Randolph, draft, Feb. 11, 1811, all in Monroe, LC.

67. For efforts to reconcile Randolph, see Monroe to Randolph, Feb. 13, 1811, *JM*, V, 169–72, and Randolph to Monroe, Mar. 2, 1811, Monroe, LC. In the gubernatorial election 129 votes were cast for Monroe, 57 for G. W. Smith (who was later chosen Monroe's successor), and 10 were scattered for other candidates. Since there was no roll call it is impossible to comment on the nature of the opposition. Richmond *Enquirer,* Jan. 17, 1811.

68. Taylor to Monroe, Jan. 31, 1811, Monroe, LC; Adams, *Memoirs,* V, 456, Dec. 20, 1821.

69. Letters are in *JM*, V, 178–84.

70. Taylor to Monroe, Mar. 21, 1811, Tazewell to Monroe, Mar. 17, 1811, Monroe, LC.

71. To Madison, Mar. 23, 1811, *JM*, V, 181–83.

72. Mar. 26, 1811, quoted in Brant, *Madison,* V, 285.

73. Monroe to Madison, Mar. 29, 1811, *JM*, V, 183.

74. Brant, *Madison,* V, 284–86; Adams, *History,* V, 371–74.

75. See *Enquirer,* Apr. 26, May 10, 31, June 7, July 16, 1811; Hay to Monroe, Apr. 22, 1811, Monroe Foundation.

76. Anderson, *Giles,* 171; Monroe to Joseph J. Monroe, Dec. 6, 1811, *JM*, V, 194–95; Brant, *Madison,* 300–9.

77. Quote is from Monroe to Jefferson, Apr. 3, 1811, *JM*, V, 185.

78. Jefferson to Madison, Apr. 7, 1811, Rives Papers, LC; Jefferson to Monroe, May 5, 1811, Ford, *Jefferson,* IX, 323.

CHAPTER 16

SECRETARY OF STATE

1. To Albert Gallatin, Mar. 29, 1811, Gallatin Papers, NYHS.

2. Elbridge Gerry, Jr., *Diary,* ed. by Claude G. Bowers (New York, 1927), 154, July 2, 1813.

3. William Lowndes to his wife, Dec. 7, 1811, Harriet H. Ravenel, *Life and Times of William Lowndes* (New York, 1901), 90; Tazewell to Monroe, Jan. 17, 1812, Monroe, LC.

4. Diary of Mrs. Seaton, Jan. 2, 1813, in Josephine Seaton, *William Winston Seaton* (Boston, 1871), 90–91.

5. Ravenel, *Lowndes,* 101, 130–31; Monroe to J. J. Monroe, Dec. 6, 1811, *JM*, V, 195; Foster to the Foreign Minister, Apr. 24, 1812, F.O. 5, V. 85.

6. Dec. 1, 1815, Mary Boardman Crowninshield, *Letters,* ed. by Francis Boardman Crowninshield (Cambridge, 1905), 29–30.

7. *National Intelligencer,* July 8, 1812; Seaton, *W. W. Seaton,* 86; Dolley Madison to E. Coles, May 12, 1813, [Lucia B. Cutts], *Memoirs and Letters of Dolly [sic] Madison* (New York, 1886), 91.

8. Monroe to _____, May 3, 1814, draft, Monroe, NYPL. The cottage still stands at Oak Hill.

9. Monroe to Joseph Monroe, Dec. 6, 1811, Monroe to Jefferson, Aug. 9, 1812, *JM,* V, 195, 216; Monroe to George Hay, July 17, 1812, Hay to Monroe, July 3, 1812, Monroe, NYPL; quote is from Monroe to Emily [Monroe], July 26, 1812, in *ibid.;* Monroe to Madison, Aug. 14, 1812, Rives Papers, LC. His sister Elizabeth Buckner died in 1812. Monroe to Madison, Sept. 30, 1812, Rives Papers, LC.

10. Monroe to Jefferson, Aug. 9, 1812, *JM,* V, 216.

11. The best accounts of Monroe's service as Secretary of State are in Julius W. Pratt, "James Monroe," in Bemis, *American Secretaries of State,* III, 201–81; Brant, *Madison,* V, *passim;* Adams, *History, passim;* Bradford Perkins, *Prologue to War* (University of California Press, 1961), which contains many new insights, is especially valuable. Roger H. Brown, *The Republic in Peril* (New York, 1964) and Theodore Clarke Smith, "War Guilt in 1812," *Proc. MHS,* LXIV (1932), 319–45, are significant commentaries on the events just prior to the declaration of war.

12. Monroe to Taylor, June 13, 1812, *JM,* V, 205ff.

13. Brant, *Madison,* V, 265–87; Perkins, *Prologue,* 248–52.

14. Brant, *Madison,* V, 256–58.

15. Translation quoted from Adams, *History,* VI, 51–53; original of June 30, 1811, in AECPEU, v. 65.

16. Sérurier to the Foreign Minister, July 5, 1811, *ibid.,* v. 65; Brant, *Madison,* V, 330; Adams, *History,* VI, 55–56.

17. Wellesley to Foster, Apr. 10, 1811, in Bernard Mayo, ed., *Instructions to the British Ministers in the United States, 1791–1812,* AHA *Annual Report,* 1936, III, 310–22.

18. Foster to Wellesley, July 2, 1811, F.O. 5, v. 76.

19. Foster to Wellesley, Aug. 5, 1811, F.O. 5, v. 76.

20. Adams, *History,* VI, 24–39.

21. Foster to Wellesley, July 5, 1811, F.O. 5, v. 76.

22. Sérurier to the Foreign Minister, July 10, 1811, translated in Adams, *History,* VI, 58.

23. Sérurier to the Foreign Minister, July 20, 1811, AECPEU, v. 65; Adams, *History,* VI, 59–63; Brant, *Madison,* V, 334–48.

24. Foster to Wellesley, July 12, 18, Aug. 5, 1811, F.O. 5, v. 76.

25. Brant, *Madison,* V, 337–39.

26. Monroe to Madison, Aug. 5, 11, [1811], Rives Papers, LC; Brant, *Madison,* V, 347–48.

27. Foster to Wellesley, Sept. 16, 19, Dec. 20, 1811, F.O. 5, v. 76–77.

28. Cipher dispatch, Foster to Wellesley, Nov. 5, 1811, F.O. 5, v. 77; there are two letters of this date of which only one is in cipher. See also Foster to Wellesley, Nov. 9, 1811, *ibid.*

29. Quote is from Brant, *Madison,* V, 365.

30. Monroe to Joseph J. Monroe, Dec. 6, 1811, Monroe to Charles Everett, Dec. 7, 1811, *JM,* V, 196–97.

31. Perkins, *Prologue,* 296–97.

32. Richardson, *Messages,* I, 483, Nov. 5, 1811.

33. Perkins, *Prologue,* 346–52; Brown, *Republic in Peril,* 44–51; Smith, "War Guilt in 1812," *Proc. MHS,* LXIV, 319–45.

34. Perkins, *Prologue,* 356; Ravenel, *Lowndes,* 90, 101.

35. For a thorough and fascinating account of the War Hawks see Bernard Mayo, *Henry Clay: Spokesman of the Old West* (Boston, 1937).

36. *AC,* 12C1S, 374–77, Nov. 29, 1812; Brant, *Madison,* V, 376–91; Adams, *History,* VI, 123–33.

37. Perkins, *Prologue,* 354–57, 361–62.

38. *Ibid.,* 360–63; Adams, *History,* VI, 157–68; Brant, *Madison,* V, 398–402; *AC,* 12C1S, 1822–28.

39. *JM,* V, 191–93. The letter is not dated but was written after Congress met.

40. Foster to Wellesley, Nov. 21, 23, 25, 1811, F.O. 5, 77. Quote is from dispatch of Nov. 25.

41. Foster to Wellesley, Nov. 21, 23, Dec. 28 (in cipher), 1811, Feb. 2, 1812, F.O. 5, 77, 84.

42. See the excellent accounts of the Henry affair in Samuel Eliot Morison, *By Land and By Sea* (New York, 1953) and Perkins, *Prologue,* 368–72.

43. Monroe to Jefferson, Mar. 9, 1812, *JM,* V, 199–200.

44. Clay to Monroe, Mar. 15, 1812, Hopkins, *Clay,* I, 637.

45. Foster to Wellesley, Apr. 1, 1812, F.O. 5, 85; Brant, *Madison,* V, 422–23.

46. Sérurier to Bassano, Mar. 23, 1812, quoted in Adams, *History,* VI, 193–95.

47. Brant, *Madison,* V, 427–28.

48. Monroe to Joseph Gales, Apr. 3, 1812, Monroe, NYPL; Perkins, *Prologue,* 387; *National Intelligencer,* Apr. 7, 1812; Joseph Gales, "Recollections of the War of 1812," *ibid.,* Aug. 8, 1857.

49. Brant, *Madison,* V, 434–35, 449, established that this and the other editorials were written by Monroe.

50. *National Intelligencer,* Apr. 28, May 5, 7, 1812.

51. Perkins, *Prologue,* 390.

52. For the best account of events in Florida see Pratt, "Monroe," *loc. cit.,* III, 238–62; Brant, *Madison,* V, 442–48; Adams, *History,* III, 237–43; Brooks, *Bor-*

derlands, 8–14, 22–23; Isaac J. Cox, "Border Mission of General George Mathews," *MVH*, XII (1925), 309–33. Adams, as might be expected, suggests that Madison and Monroe encouraged Mathews, but repudiated him when the news arrived at an inconvenient time. Brant, on the other hand, minimizes administration involvement. However, he does feel that Monroe should have replied to Mathews' letter in order to check his impetuosity. Brooks, Pratt and Cox take the view that Mathews acted in excess of his instructions, but that the administration knew generally what he was doing. Since Secretary of State Robert Smith had encouraged revolutionary activities in West Florida through his agents, Mathews was merely following an earlier example. However, Mathews behaved imprudently in operating quite so openly and giving the impression that an invasion rather than a revolution was in progress.

53. Pratt, "Monroe," *loc. cit.*, III, 262.

54. Foster to Castlereagh, May 28, June 6, 8, 1812, F.O. 5, v. 86; Brant, *Madison*, V, 266–74; Perkins, *Prologue*, 400–2.

55. Sérurier to Bassano, May 27, 1812, AECPEU, v. 67; Brant, *Madison*, V, 462–69; Pratt, "Monroe," *loc. cit.*, III, 260–62. Monroe may have written the editorial on May 30.

56. Richardson, *Messages*, I, 504.

57. On the authorship of this report, see Carl Wiltse, "Authorship of the War Report of 1812," *AHR*, XLIX (1943–44), 253–69; the report is in *AC*, 13C1S, HR, 1546–54.

58. Brant, *Madison*, V, 466–74.

59. Monroe to Taylor, June 13, 1812, *JM*, V, 208.

60. Brant, *Madison*, V, 476–77, asserts that Monroe lobbied to restrict the war to a naval operation. This conclusion is based on a portion of a letter to Gallatin, June 1, 1812, Gallatin Papers, NYHS, of which the upper half is missing. It is so ambiguously worded that I do not feel Brant's conclusion, which contradicts everything else Monroe said and did at this time, is correct. There is no echo of such a consideration in Monroe's letter to John Taylor of Caroline, June 13, 1812, *JM*, V, 207.

61. Brant, *Madison*, V, 477.

62. Foster to Castlereagh, June 20, 23, 1812, F.O. 5, v. 86; Richmond *Enquirer*, June 2, 1812.

63. Brant, *Madison*, V. 477–48; *AC*, 13C1S, 267–97; Perkins, *Prologue*, 410–15.

64. Foster to Castlereagh, June 20, 23, 1812, F.O. 5, v. 86; Monroe to Russell, June 26, 1812, *JM*, V, 212; Brant, *Madison*, VI, 33–34; Perkins, *Prologue*, 415–16.

65. Sérurier to the Minister of Foreign Affairs, June 19, 23, July 12, 1812, AECPEU, v. 67.

66. For details see Adams, *History*, VI, 254–57; Perkins, *Prologue*, 323–38.

67. Brant, *Madison*, VI, 59; Pratt, "Monroe," *loc. cit.*, III, 253.

68. Foster to Castlereagh, Aug. 10, 20, 24, 1812, F.O. 5, v. 87; Brant, *Madison*, VI, 61–3, 71.

CHAPTER 17

THE NATION IN PERIL

1. Adams, *History*, VI, 419; Monroe to Hay, July 9, 1812, *Bull. NYPL*, VI (1902), 210; James Barbour to Monroe, July 13, Sept. 1, 1812, Monroe, LC.

2. Monroe to Madison, Sept. 2, 4, 8, 10, 12, 1812, Madison to Monroe, Aug. [misdated, should be Sept.] 8, 1812, Rives Papers, LC; Monroe to Clay, Sept. 17, 1812, Monroe to Jefferson, June 7, 1813, *JM*, V, 221–23, 260.

3. Geo. Hay to Monroe, Oct. 9, 15, Nov. 1, 1812, John Minor to Monroe, Oct. 25, 1812, all in Monroe, NYPL.

4. Sept. 9, 1812, Monroe, LC.

5. James Barbour to Monroe, June 23, 1812, Dearborn to Monroe, July 30, 1812, Zebulon Pike to Monroe, Aug. 28, Sept. 4, 14, 1812, George Izard to Monroe, May 26, July 15, Sept. 8, 1812, Monroe to [Izard], Sept. 1, 1812, all in Monroe, NYPL; Clay to Monroe, July 22, Aug. 12, 25, 1812, Izard to Monroe, Oct. 31, 1812, Monroe, LC.

6. Eustis to Madison, Dec. 3, 1812, Rives Papers, LC; Brant, *Madison*, VI, 120–21.

7. Monroe to _____, Oct. 16, 1812, *Bull. NYPL*, VI (1902), 211; A. J. Dallas to [Madison], Sept. 19, 1812, in George M. Dallas, *Life and Writings of Alexander J. Dallas* (Philadelphia, 1871), 128.

8. *AC*, 12C2S, 562.

9. Monroe to Crawford, Dec. 3, 1812, *JM*, V, 227; Monroe to Madison, Sept. 2, 1812, Rives Papers, LC. Monroe was more than willing to accept the office, and Gallatin's comment that Monroe shrank from the post does not seem to be correct. Apparently Gallatin was not told the reason why Monroe did not receive the appointment. See Monroe to Jefferson, June 7, 1813, *JM*, V, 264; Gallatin to Madison, Jan. 4, 7, 1813, Rives Papers, LC; Brant, *Madison*, VI, 127.

10. This report was current in Washington during the winter. Sérurier to Bassano, Jan. 8, 1813, AECPEU, v. 70; Baker to Castlereagh, Dec. 19, 1812, F.O. 5, v. 88; Abijah Bigelow to his wife, Dec. 22, 1812, *Am. Ant. Soc. Proc.*, XI, 347.

11. Report is dated Dec. 23, 1812, *JM*, V, 227–35; for the bill see *AC*, 12C2S, 1322–25.

12. "Notes on an Idea of a Plan of Campaign for 1813," *JM*, V, 235–37.

13. Gallatin to Madison [Jan. 4, 1813], Crawford to Madison, June 6, 1813, Rives Papers, LC.

14. Gallatin to Madison, Jan. 7, 1813, Rives Papers, LC.

15. To Madison, Apr. 7, 1811, Rives Papers, LC.

16. Morgan Lewis to Madison, Apr. 8, 18, 1811, Rives Papers, LC; Foster's comment is in Foster to Wellesley, July 18, 1811, F.O. 5, v. 76.

17. Sérurier to Bassano, Jan. 8, 1813; Nathaniel Burwell to his wife, Dec. 20, 1812, Burwell Papers, LC; Crawford to Monroe, Sept. 8, 1812, Monroe, LC; Brant, *Madison,* VI, 125–26.

18. Adams, *History,* VI, 429; Brant, *Madison,* VI, 128.

19. Armstrong to Ambrose Spencer, Jan. 25, 1813, photostat, NYHS.

20. Quote is from Monroe to Jefferson, June 7, 1813, *JM,* V, 262–63.

21. Monroe to Madison, Feb. 25, 1813, *ibid.,* V, 244–48. I have based my account of this affair on this letter and on one to Jefferson cited above, fn. 20. Brant, *Madison,* VI, 204–6 challenges Monroe's version and maintains that Monroe with-drew his name, thus exonerating Armstrong. He bases his argument on the con-tention that Monroe's letter of Feb. 25, which exists only in draft form in Monroe's papers, was deliberately planted by Monroe in his papers at some later date in order to alter the record in a manner unfavorable to Armstrong. Brant bases his case on the fact that there is another letter written by Monroe bearing the same date which requests that the President not bring up the subject of a military appoint-ment with Armstrong. It so happens that this second letter opens with a reference to Mrs. Monroe's indisposition, which was preventing him from seeing the President early in the morning. The draft letter also uses a similar statement, and from this Brant infers that they could not have been written on the same date; he asserts that Monroe merely used the phrase to begin his later doctored version. However, this is by no means positive. It is equally likely that the shorter letter, which re-quested the President to say nothing to Armstrong, was written in the expectation that Monroe would be able to see the President later in the day. The second letter, which exists only in draft (and the fact that the original is not to be located is by no means proof that such a letter was never sent), was written when Monroe realized his wife's illness was going to prevent him from leaving the house at all. The second letter explained why he had written earlier to request that the matter be dropped. It is a rather confused letter of the kind so typical of Monroe's cor-respondence when he was in a hurry.

To further support his contention that Monroe's letter of Feb. 25 was actually written later, Brant points out that in a letter written by Gallatin to Madison on April 22, Gallatin expressed his disapproval of Armstrong's intentions of going to the northern theater in a manner which seemed to indicate that this was the first he had heard of the plan. In his letter of Feb. 25 Monroe speaks of the President as having mentioned Armstrong's proposal and then presents his arguments against permitting the Secretary of War to become *de facto* field commander. To my mind this is not conclusive evidence against Monroe for it is quite possible that Gallatin, who was not as deeply involved in the question of military arrangements as Monroe, may not have been informed of Armstrong's intention until later; Gallatin certainly was not fully informed about the reasons why Monroe did not become Secretary of War at that time.

There is still another item lending support to the authenticity of Monroe's letter of Feb. 25. In *JM,* V, 293, Hamilton prints a letter to Madison written on Sept. 25, 1814. In this letter Monroe gave his reasons for wishing to become permanent Secretary of War. Among other reasons, he noted that if he held the post on an acting basis for a second time, it might be assumed that he shrank from the responsibility. In footnote 1 on the same page Hamilton prints a portion of a draft of this letter which Monroe deleted from the letter as sent to Madison. In this draft Monroe specifically stated that Armstrong "excluded me from the command of the northern army in the last campaign." Monroe deleted this and other references to the conflict between him and Armstrong in his final version of the letter. This seems a strong indication that events as described in the letter of Feb. 25 were correctly stated.

22. Brant, *Madison*, VI, 156–59.

23. Monroe to Jefferson, June 7, 1813, *JM*, V, 259.

24. Apr. 15, 1813, *ASPFR*, III, 695–700; the confidential paragraphs are in *JM*, V, 255 fn. 1; Monroe to commissioners, June 23, 1813, *ibid.*, V, 367–68.

25. Pratt, "Monroe," *loc. cit.*, III, 269–70; Gallatin to Monroe, May 2, 8, 1813, Monroe, LC; Monroe to Gallatin, May 5, 6, 1813, Monroe to Bayard, May 6, 1813, *JM*, V, 252–59.

26. To Gallatin, Apr. 23, 24, 1813, Gallatin Papers, NYHS.

27. Fred L. Engelman, *Peace of Christmas Eve* (New York, 1962), 30.

28. Brant, *Madison*, VI, 190–91; Monroe to the commissioners, Aug. 5, 1813, *JM*, V, 368–70.

29. Brant, *Madison*, VI, 179–87; Monroe to Jefferson, June 16, 28, 1813, *JM*, V, 268–73.

30. *AC*, 13C1S, 170–307, June 10–21, 1813.

31. *ASPFR*, III, 608–612, July 12, 1813.

32. Glenn Tucker, *Poltroons and Patriots* (2 vols., New York, 1943), I, 242–58; Adams, *History*, VII, 150–59.

33. Tucker, *Poltroons*, II, 413–20; quote is from Monroe to Crawford, draft, [1814], Monroe, LC; Brant, *Madison*, VI, 207–21.

34. Randolph to Josiah Quincy, Aug. 30, 1813, quoted in Bruce, *Randolph*, I, 347.

35. Monroe to Madison, Apr. 13, 1813, Rives Papers, LC; Brant, *Madison*, VI, 168.

36. Monroe to Madison, July 16, 18, 1813, Rives Papers, LC; Armstrong to Madison, July 19, 1813, Madison, LC; Armstrong to Monroe, July 20, 1813, Monroe, LC; Reminiscences of James Taylor, typescript, pp. 51–60, Filson Club, Louisville, Ky.; Brant, *Madison*, VI, 206–7.

37. Quoted in Brant, *Madison*, VI, 207.

38. Monroe to Hay, Mar. 11, 1814, *Bull. NYPL*, VI (1902), 216; Monroe to Taylor, Dec. 23, 1815, *Proc. MHS*, XLII (1908), 335; Adams, *Memoirs*, VI, 4–5, Jan. 2, 1822.

39. Monroe to Madison, Dec. 27, 1813, Rives Papers, LC; the original as printed in *JM*, VI, 238–41, contains a number of errors; Armstrong to _____, Dec. 29, 1813, photostat, NYHS.

40. Memo by Rufus King, January 1814, C. King, *Life of R. King*, V, 317.

41. Memo by John W. Taylor, Jan. 12, 1814, Taylor Papers, NYHS.

42. Armstrong to C. K. Gardner [August 1819], Gardner Papers, New York State Library, Albany; Madison to Armstrong, June 2, 1814, photostat, NYHS.

43. Views respecting the rejection of the mediation of Russia, memo in Monroe's hand, n.d., *JM*, VI, 277–81.

44. Adams, *History*, VII, 396–97; Brant, *Madison*, VI, 238–41; J. J. Astor to Monroe, Apr. 30, May 24, June 1, 1814; Pinkney resigned abruptly rather than conform to a recent act of Congress requiring the Attorney General to live in the Capital.

45. Brant, *Madison*, VI, 242; *ASPFR*, III, 700–1; the confidential paragraphs are in James A. Bayard, "Papers," *AHR Annual Report*, 1913, II, 263–65.

46. Brant, *Madison*, VI, 266–68; Gallatin and Bayard to Monroe, May 6, 1814, Monroe, LC; Monroe to the plenipotentiaries, June 27, 1814, *JM*, V, 371–72; Pratt, "Monroe," *loc. cit.*, III, 272.

47. *AC*, 13C2S, 1946–47, Apr. 4, 1814; Adams, *History*, VII, 70, 367–69, 373–77; Brant, *Madison*, VI, 248–49.

48. Monroe to Madison, Apr. 10, 1814 Rives Papers, LC; Brant, *Madison*, VI, 255.

CHAPTER 18

THE CAPITAL INVADED

1. Izard to Monroe, May 24, June 3, 1814, Monroe, LC; quote is from Izard's letter of June 3. A complaint was also received from Henry Dearborn, June 3, 1814, Monroe, NYPL, among others.

2. William Dawson to Monroe, June 2, 1814, *Bull. NYPL*, VI (1902), 246. Dawson writing from Bermuda warned of the expedition being gathered for an invasion of the Chesapeake. See also Monroe to Jefferson, Dec. 21, 1814, *JM*, V, 303; William Jones to R. M. Johnson, Oct. 31, 1814, *AC*, 13C3S, 1568–70; Brant, *Madison*, VI, 250–83; quote is from Armstrong to Peter B. Porter, July 16, 1814, photostat, NYHS, original in PHS.

3. Brant, *Madison*, VI, 285–90; Adams, *History*, VIII, 123; recollections of Tench Ringgold in a letter to Monroe, Oct. 10, 1827, Monroe LC. The report of the House Committee on the capture of Washington barely hints at Armstrong's failure to organize defenses. *AC*, 13C3S, 1518–50.

4. Draft in Madison, LC.

5. Monroe to Crawford, June 25, 1814, Monroe, LC; quote is from Monroe to [Madison], July 3, 1814, *JM*, V, 284–87. Brant, *Madison*, VI, 272, considers the letter of July 3 to Madison, which exists only in draft, as having been written later but conveniently predated to put Monroe on record as approving the rechartering

of the Bank of the United States. He bases his contention on the fact that Monroe later in the year expressed disapproval of the bank. This is by no means conclusive, since Monroe, like most Republicans, thoroughly disliked the idea of the bank and had long regarded it as unconstitutional. Only reluctantly in the face of the financial difficulties besetting the government did Madison and other Republicans accept its necessity; Jefferson continued to oppose a recharter. There is additional proof that Monroe in the summer of 1814 was inclined to favor a bank. In the Monroe Foundation in Fredericksburg there is a letter from Spencer Roane to Monroe, Mar. 3, 1816, in which Roane refers to the fact that Monroe had approved granting a charter in 1814. Roane, like many Virginia Republicans, was absolutely opposed to a federal bank.

6. The best account of the invasion is that to be found in Adams, *History,* VIII, 120–48; Tucker, *Poltroons,* II, 501–84, uses much new material; see also *AC,* 13C3S, 1515–1738, for report of committee on capture of the city.

7. Tucker, *Poltroons,* II, 520–21.

8. Monroe to Armstrong, Aug. 18, 1814, *JM,* V, 289; Armstrong to Monroe, Aug. 18, 1814, Monroe, LC.

9. Monroe to Madison, Aug. 21, 1814, *JM,* V, 289–90; same to same, 11 P.M. [Aug. 21, 1814], Rives Papers, LC; Monroe to [Winder], Aug. 20, [1814], Letters Rec'd, War Dept., NA; Brant, *Madison,* VI, 291.

10. See Adams, *History,* VIII, 139–44; Brant, *Madison,* VI, 298–305; Tucker, *Poltroons,* II, 536–44. Adams judges Winder harshly, but Tucker and Brant are less condemnatory. He was faced by an impossible situation. Adams, relying on Armstrong's *Notices on Adams' Eulogy of Monroe* (Washington, 1832), tends to place entirely too much blame for the defeat on Monroe. Monroe, in his only comment on the battle, written two weeks later, speaks of himself as having formed the line and disposed the troops at Bladensburg. Neither he nor his contemporaries (apart from Armstrong) considered him responsible for the defeat. Monroe to George Hay, Sept. 7, *Bull. NYPL,* VI (1902), 218.

11. Tucker, *Poltroons,* II, 570–75; Wharton, *Social Life,* 163; quote is from Brant, *Madison,* VI, 307.

12. [Monroe's] Notes Respecting the Burning City in 1814, *JM,* V, 373–74.

13. Quote is from *ibid.;* Brant, *Madison,* VI, 309–11; Monroe to George Hay, Sept. 7, 1814, *Bull. NYPL,* VI (1902), 218.

14. Brant, *Madison,* VI, 312–18; Adams, *History,* VIII, 162; DAB; Ambrose Spencer to Armstrong, Jan. 17, 1815, photostat, NYHS. Monroe did not interfere with the operation of the War Department. The basis for this charge was the fact that in 1813 when Armstrong was in the north, Madison asked Monroe to supervise routine War Department affairs. When Armstrong returned to Washington, he found current correspondence in the State Department, where it had been moved for convenience.

15. Monroe to Taylor, Dec. 23, 1815, *Proc. MHS,* XLII (1902), 335.

16. This account is based on a draft letter to Madison, Sept. 25, 1814, *JM,* V, 293. Brant, *Madison,* VI, 330–31, believes this was written much later and predated

in order to alter the record by establishing that he had not refused to serve in the War Department in 1812. As proof of his contention, Brant cites a letter of Secretary Jones written on Sept. 25 in which he states that Monroe would be Secretary of War. Hence, he argues that Monroe had no basis for such a letter as that of Sept. 25. However, it is equally probable that Jones was told of Monroe's appointment only after the President had received Monroe's letter and finally decided to nominate him.

17. This seems to have been seriously considered. See Monroe to _____, Dec. 2, 1814, *Bull. NYPL*, VI (1902), 219; Morgan Lewis to Monroe, Sept. 11, 1814, George Hay to Monroe, Nov. 27, 1814, Monroe, LC.

18. Tompkins to Madison, Oct. 6, 8, 1814, Rives Papers, LC.

19. Brant, *Madison*, VI, 329, 346.

20. Adams, *History*, VIII, 165–73; Monroe to Winder, Sept. 8, 1814, War Department, NA; there are many letters in War Department files relating to defense arrangements.

21. Monroe to Hay, Mar. 5, 1815, *Bull. NYPL*, VI (1902), 223.

22. Adams, *History*, VII, 384, VIII, 264, 283.

23. Adams, *History*, VIII, 263–86; *AC*, 13C3S, 1502–16.

24. Adams, *History*, VIII, 267–81; Anderson, *Giles*, 199–200; *Niles' Register*, VII, 181–82, Nov. 26, 1814.

25. Adams, *History*, VIII, 283–85.

26. Wilmerding, *Monroe Claimant*, 106–07; Tench Ringgold to Monroe, Jan. 18, 1827, Monroe, LC.

27. Dallas to _____, Sept. 7, 1814, Monroe, LC; Monroe to Jefferson, July 25, Oct. 10, Dec. 21, 1814, *JM*, V, 288, 299, 305; Jefferson to Monroe, Sept. 24, Oct. 16, 1814, Ford, *Jefferson*, VIII, 488, 492–94.

28. Monroe to Madison, May 4, 1815, Rives Papers, LC.

29. Brant, *Madison*, VI, 338–39, 350; Adams, *History*, VIII, 254; Monroe to Madison, Jan. 26, 1815, Rives Papers, LC.

30. Jesup to Monroe, Dec. 31, 1814, War Department, NA.

31. Monroe to Swartwout, Jan. 11, 1815, *ibid;* Tench Ringgold's minutes of conversation between Monroe and Swartwout, Jan. 10, 1815, Monroe, NYPL.

32. Monroe to Madison, Jan. 19, 1815, Rives Papers, LC; see also Monroe to _____, Dec. 2, 1814, *Bull. NYPL*, VI, 219; Hay to Monroe, Nov. 27, 1814, Monroe, LC.

33. Monroe to Swartwout, Jan. 13, 1815, Swartwout Papers, NYPL. A copy was sent to Gen. King.

34. Monroe's first letter was written on Sept. 5, 1814. This letter and others of later date to the same effect are all in War Department, NA; for details on Jackson's operations see John Spencer Bassett, *Life of Andrew Jackson* (2 vols., N.Y., 1911), I, 127–81.

35. Oct. 21, 1814, Jackson Papers, LC.

36. Bassett, *Jackson*, I, 162–64; Monroe to Jackson, Dec. 7, 1814, *JM*, V, 301–2. On the original of this letter in the Jackson Papers, LC, there is a note by Jackson asserting that this letter was written to shift the blame to him for the shortage in supplies in New Orleans, by laying stress on the fact that he was delaying in Mobile. Jackson felt that Monroe, aware that Jackson had not been properly supported in New Orleans, had expected him to be defeated, and was guaranteeing that the blame would fall on the general for failing to go promptly to New Orleans. This note was probably added to the letter in 1827.

37. Monroe's first order for shipments of arms was issued on November 2. There is much correspondence about these shipments in War Department, NA, when Monroe later tried to ascertain whether they arrived or not. It is not exactly clear why they were delayed. See Lt. Col. George Bomford to Monroe, Feb. 4, 1815; John Morton to Capt. A. R. Woolley; Capt. J. Morton to Monroe, Dec. 7, 1814, all in NA. The affair was revived again in 1827 when Jackson's supporters, as part of the electioneering, raised charges that the administration had failed to support him adequately at New Orleans. Monroe was deeply hurt and again attempted to find out exactly what had happened to the arms. However, the relevant papers relating to the Ordnance Department at Pittsburgh could not be located. The matter was further complicated by the recollections of Gen. Thomas Jesup that when he had arrived in New Orleans in 1816 he had learned that there was a large quantity of arms in the arsenal, but that Jackson, who had ordered the commanding officer of the arsenal to go to Fort St. Philip, was unaware of them. Monroe to Hugh L. White, Feb. 9, 1827, *JM*, VII, 110; Tench Ringgold to Monroe, Sept. 30, 1827, Monroe, NYPL; T. S. Jesup to Monroe, Oct. 7, 1827, Monroe, LC; G. Bomford to Monroe, Nov. 1, 1827, *ibid.*

38. James Brown to Jackson, Feb. 20, 1815, *Louisiana Historical Quarterly*, 83–4; *National Intelligencer*, Feb. 16, 1815, contains correspondence relating to this.

39. Monroe to DuPonceau [June 27, 1816], DuPonceau to Monroe, June 17, July 2, 1816, Monroe, LC.

40. Brant, *Madison*, VI, 333–35.

41. Monroe to J. Q. Adams, Mar. 13, 1815, *JM*, V, 376.

42. Feb. 22, 1815, *JM*, V, 321–25.

CHAPTER 19

PEACE AND POLITICS

1. Feb. 22, 1815, *JM*, V, 321–25.

2. Monroe to Madison, Feb. 22, 1815, Rives Papers, LC.

3. Adams, *History*, IX, 86.

4. John Minor to Monroe, Mar. 2, 1815, Monroe, LC; note in Monroe's hand, ca. 1815, filed with 1827 papers, Monroe, vol. 35, LC; William Lee to Monroe, Apr. 30, 1815, Monroe, NYPL; Hugh Mercer to James Preston, May 25, 1815, Preston Papers, VHS.

5. Dallas, *Life of A. J. Dallas,* 136, 401, 413; Madison to Monroe, Apr. 10, 1815, Monroe, LC; A. J. Dallas to Monroe, Mar. 13, Aug. 28, 1815, Monroe, LC; Monroe to Madison, Apr. 11, 1815, Rives Papers, LC.

6. Monroe to Madison, Apr. 30, May 4, 11, 1815, Rives Papers, LC; Dallas to Madison, May 12, 1815, *ibid.;* Madison to Monroe, n.d. [ca. May, 1815], Madison, LC; Monroe to Madison, May 5, 1815, draft, Monroe, LC.

7. Mar. 12, 1815, Monroe Foundation, Fredericksburg.

8. The consultation took place through the agency of Nicholas Biddle, who was sent a sealed letter for Dr. Wistar, which did not contain the patient's name. The illness was of long standing, since Dr. Rush and Dr. Physick had been consulted in 1811. George Hay to N. Biddle, Jan. 25, Mar. 25, 1815; Biddle to Hay, Mar. 31, 1815, copy, all in Biddle Papers, LC; Rush to Monroe, June 1, 1811, Benjamin Rush, *Letters,* ed. by L. H. Butterfield (2 vols., Princeton, 1951), II, 1082.

9. Monroe to Hay, Mar. 2, July 15, 1815, *Bull. NYPL,* VI, 221–22. Monroe to Madison, June 3, 1815, Rives Papers, LC.

10. Quote is from Monroe to _____, Mar. 10, 1816, Johns Deposit, U.Va.; see also Monroe to _____, Jan. 3, 1814, NYPL; Monroe to _____, July 24, 1816, Monroe, LC; the Loudoun property was now Monroe's, for he had inherited the balance of the tract from his cousin, Joseph Jones, Jr., who died in 1808.

11. Monroe to Richard Rush, Aug. 25, 1815, Gratz Coll., PHS.

12. Quote is from Monroe to Hay, Jan. 12, 1815, *Bull. NYPL,* VI, 220; Monroe to Stephen Pleasanton, Aug. 4, 14, Sept. 17, 1815, Johns Deposit, U.Va; Monroe to [George W. Campbell?], Sept. 6, 1815, *ibid.;* Monroe to Madison, Aug. 12, Sept. 19, 1815, Rives Papers, LC.

13. Monroe to Madison, Oct. 8, 1815, Rives Papers, LC.

14. Monroe to the Peace Commissioners, Apr. 10, 1815, *JM,* V, 377–80; Monroe to Madison, June 27, 1816, *JM,* V, 336–37; Brant, *Madison,* VI, 395, 398, 407; Monroe to Madison, July 16, Aug. 14, 1816, Rives Papers, LC; Adams, *History,* IX, 87.

15. Monroe to Madison, Mar. 24, 26, Apr. 3, 8, 22, 1815, Monroe to Baker, Apr. 1, 1815, Baker to Monroe, Apr. 3, 1815, Rives Papers, LC; Madison to Monroe, Mar. 26, St. George Tucker to Monroe, Apr. 2, 1815, Monroe, LC; Monroe to Joseph Gales, n.d., Augustus Neale to Monroe, Sept. 5–25, 1815, Monroe, NYPL; Perkins, *Castlereagh,* 126, 166.

16. Perkins, *Castlereagh,* 1–2.

17. In the account of the Rush-Bagot Agreement I have relied primarily on *ibid.,* 24–44; Burt, *Brit. North Am.,* 388–95, and E. A. Cruikshank, "The Negotiations of the Agreement for the Disarmament on the Lakes," *Proceedings of the*

Royal Society of Canada, Ser. 2, XXX (1936), 151–84. The latter is particularly valuable, since it contains extensive selections from the official documents.

18. Brant, *Madison,* VI, 397–98.

19. *Ibid.,* VI, 409; Monroe to Madison, June 29, 1816, Rives Papers, LC; Madison to Monroe, July 2, 1816, copy, Madison Papers, LC.

20. Brant, *Madison,* VI, 408–09; Madison to Monroe, July 19, 1816, Madison Papers, LC.

21. Rush to C. J. Ingersoll, Oct. 9, 1816, Ingersoll Papers, PHS; Monroe to Madison, July 26, Aug. 14, 1816, Rives Papers, LC.

22. Quote is from Monroe to Madison, Aug. 31, 1816, Rives Papers, LC; Madison to Monroe, Aug. 28, 1816, Monroe, NYPL.

23. Monroe to Madison, Dec. 2, 1816, Rives Papers, LC; Brant, *Madison,* VI, 411.

24. Adams, *Memoirs,* V, 136–37, June 2, 1820; Louisa Adams to John Adams, Jan. 2–7, 1820, Adams Papers, MHS.

25. Monroe to Hay, July 15, 1813, Oct. 17, 1815, *Bull. NYPL,* VI, 213, 224–25. Hay seems to have believed that Jefferson was not in favor of Monroe as Madison's successor. On many occasions Hay spoke slightingly of Jefferson to John Quincy Adams. Adams, *Memoirs,* VI, 349, May 23, 1824.

26. Monroe to _____, McGregor Coll., U.Va.; Monroe to Madison, Apr. 23, 1815, Hay to Monroe, Jan. 6, 1815, Monroe, LC; Hay to Monroe, Mar. 12, 1815, Monroe Foundation; Joseph Wheaton to Madison, Apr. 28, 1815, Madison, LC.

27. Expressions of this view were made by Nicholas Biddle to Jonathan Roberts, Dec. 14, 1815, Biddle, LC; Joseph Nicholson to Wm. Pinkney, Mar. 2, 1816, LC; John Reid to D. M. Farney, Mar. 12, 1816, NYPL; Wm. Pinkney to Monroe, Jan. 13, 1817, Washburn Papers, MHS; "Curtius," *Intelligencer,* Apr. 9, 1816.

28. Monroe to Charles Everett, Dec. 16, 1815, *Tyler's Quarterly,* V (1923), 12; Monroe to [Samuel B. Pleasanton], Jan. 24, 1816, Monroe-Pleasanton Papers, U.Va.; Hay to Monroe, July 9, 1815, Monroe, LC; Hay to Monroe, Nov. 25, 1815, Monroe Foundation; *Letters on the Richmond Party,* 30–32.

29. Roane to Barbour, Feb. 12, 1816, *Bull. NYPL,* X, 170.

30. Monroe to Jefferson, Oct. 22, 1816, Monroe to [Nicholas], Nov. 17, 1816, NYPL; *Letters on the Richmond Party,* 31.

31. Ambler, *Ritchie,* 63–64; Richmond *Enquirer,* Feb. 20, Mar. 30, 1816.

32. James Barbour, Armistead Mason, James Pleasants, Jr., Thomas Newton and Wm. H. Roane to Gov. Hugh Nelson, Feb. 9, 1816, Barbour Papers, NYPL.

33. J. R. Betts to Van Buren, Jan. 19, Feb. 5, Mar. 17, 1816, Van Buren Papers, LC; Peter B. Porter to Monroe, Mar. 25, 1816, Monroe, LC. See also the excellent account by Robert V. Remini, "New York and the Presidential Election of 1816," *New York History,* XXXI (1950), 308–23. I have drawn extensively on his article.

34. Remini, "Election of 1816," *loc. cit.,* 319.

35. Jonathan Roberts, "Memoirs," *Pa. Mag.,* LXII (1938), 398; There is some ambiguity about Gallatin's position, but Crawford certainly thought Gallatin preferred him. See Crawford to Gallatin, May 10, 1816, Gallatin, NYHS. See also Bolling Hall to C. J. Ingersoll, Dec. 15, 1815, Ingersoll Papers, PHS; Philadelphia *Aurora,* Feb. 26, 1816; Bemis, Adams, I, 244, Pierce Butler to Monroe, Sept. 27, 1816, Monroe, LC. According to Jonathan Roberts, "Memoirs," *Pa. Mag.,* LXII (1938), 361, Monroe felt Gallatin in leaving the Treasury in 1813 had deserted the government at a critical time.

36. Remini, "Election of 1816," *loc. cit.,* 320–21; Crawford to Gallatin, May 10, 1816, Gallatin Papers, NYHS; *National Intelligencer,* Mar. 14, 1816. There is some discrepancy between the figures for the vote and the number attending. Although five absentees left proxies, only 119 votes were cast out of 123 attending; apparently some present did not vote. Remini believes that thirteen Crawfordites defected. In his estimate he includes a number of Representatives, who supposedly preferred Crawford but yielded to the state party leaders who wished Monroe to be nominated.

37. Remini, "Election of 1816," *loc. cit.,* 319; *National Intelligencer,* Feb. 24, Mar. 2, 1816.

38. Albany *Advertiser,* Aug. 16, 1816; *National Intelligencer,* Apr. 9, May 23, June 6, July 6, 1816; Shaw Livermore, Jr., *The Twilight of Federalism . . . 1815–1830* (Princeton University, 1962), 34.

39. Armistead T. Mason to John Mas, Feb. 18, 1817, *WMQ,* XXIII (1915), 239; James C. Jewett to Gen. Dearborn, Feb. 5, 1817, *ibid.,* XVII (1908), 144; Clay to [Caesar A. Rodney], Feb. 22, 1817, Hopkins, *Clay,* II, 316.

40. Monroe to Jackson, Dec. 14, 1816, *JM,* V, 342; Jonathan Roberts to N. Biddle, Jan. 30, 1817, Biddle Papers, LC.

41. Richard Rush to C. J. Ingersoll, Jan. 4, 1817, Ingersoll Papers, PHS; *AC,* 13C3S, 1932, Act of Mar. 3, 1815.

42. Jackson to Monroe, Nov. 12, 1816, Jackson, *Corres.,* II, 265; Sullivan to Monroe, July 10, 1817, Monroe, LC.

43. Dec. 14, 1816, *JM,* V, 344–46.

44. Monroe to Jefferson, Feb. 23, 1817, *JM,* VI, 2–4.

45. Crawford to Gallatin, Mar. 12, 1817, Gallatin Papers, NYHS.

46. Wiltse, *Calhoun,* I, 139–40; Shelby to Monroe, Apr. 7, 1817, Monroe, LC; Monroe to Jackson, Mar. 1, 1817, *JM,* VI, 5; Adams, *Memoirs,* IV, 72–4, Apr. 4, 1818.

47. Wiltse, *Calhoun,* I, 144, 173; Bemis, *Adams,* I, 252.

48. Wiltse, *Calhoun,* I, 143; Hammond, *New York Politics,* I, 410; Benjamin F. Butler to his wife, May 7, 1823, Butler Papers, NY State Library, Albany; Bemis, *Adams,* I, 251–52.

49. Richard Rush to John Adams, Jan. 7, 1817, *Pa. Mag.,* LXI (1937), 159; Monroe to Adams, Mar. 6, 1817, *JM,* VI, 15.

50. Crawford to Gallatin, Mar. 12, 1817, Gallatin Papers, NYHS; Adams, *Memoirs*, IV, 130, Sept. 30, 1818.

51. Adams, *Memoirs*, IV, 388, June 4, 1819.

52. Adams, *Memoirs*, IV, 470, Dec. 6, 1819.

53. Perkins, *Castlereagh*, 211.

54. Adams, *Memoirs*, IV, 14, Oct. 30, 1817.

55. G. W. Sullivan, *Public Men*, 257; John P. Kennedy, *Life of William Wirt* (2 vols., New York, 1872), I, 15, 74–87; Adams, *Memoirs*, IV, 82, Apr. 28, 1818; Wirt to Hugh Nelson, Mar. 27, 1818, Wirt Papers, MdHS; Wirt to his wife, Nov. 13, 1817, *ibid.*

56. Adams, *Memoirs*, IV, 310, Mar. 25, 1819.

57. B. W. Crowninshield to Monroe, June 16, 1818, *Proc. MHS*, LXII (1929), 49; Crowninshield to Monroe, Sept. 22, 1818, Gratz Coll. PHS; Monroe to Crowninshield, Dec. 18, 1818, draft, NYPL.

58. Monroe to Madison, Oct. 5, 1818, Madison Papers, LC; Adams, *Memoirs*, IV, 132–33, Oct. 15, 1818.

59. Adams, *Memoirs*, IV, 136, Oct. 19, 1818.

60. Smith Thompson to Van Buren, Nov. 3, 18, 1818, Van Buren Papers, LC; John Rodgers to Monroe, Oct. 24, 1818, Gratz Coll., PHS.

61. Adams, *Memoirs*, VI, 173–75, Aug. 15, 1823. Southard's wife was related to the Taliaferro family of Virginia, to which Monroe was connected through Joseph Jones.

62. Hammond, *New York Politics*, I, 303, 361, 390–91, 561; Louisa C. Adams to John Adams, Dec. 1, 12, 1822, Adams Papers, MHS; William Plumer to William Plumer, Jr., Feb. 15, 1822, Plumer Papers, LC; *National Intelligencer*, Feb. 19, 1818, Mar. 3, 1821; Adams, *Memoirs*, V, 326, Mar. 10, 1821, S. L. Gouverneur to Monroe, Apr. 21, 1823, Monroe Foundation, Fredericksburg.

CHAPTER 20

THE ERA OF GOOD FEELINGS: IDEAL

1. Boston *Columbian Centinel*, July 12, 1817.

2. To B. Henry, Nov. 27, 1816, draft, Biddle Papers, LC.

3. May 22, 1823, Hunt, *Madison*, IX, 135.

4. *National Intelligencer*, Mar. 5, 1817; Van Deusen, *Clay*, 116; Clay to James Barbour, Mar. 3, 1817; Hopkins, *Clay Papers*, II, 320.

5. Brooks, *Borderlands*, 125–26; Bagot to Castlereagh, Mar. 11, 1817, F.O. 5, v. 121.

6. William Wirt, *Letters of a British Spy* (Baltimore, n.d.), 109 (1021).

7. Wirt to [Dabney Carr], Oct. 12, 1819, Wirt Papers, MdHS.

8. To S. L. Gouverneur, Aug. 8, 1831, John C. Calhoun, *Letters, AHA Annual Report for 1899,* II, 198.

9. Monroe to Hay, Aug. 5, 1817, *Bull. NYPL,* VI (1902), 230.

10. E. Williams to W. E. Williams, Mar. 17, 1817, O. H. Williams Papers, MdHS.

11. Rush to C. J. Ingersoll, Jan. 4, 1817, Ingersoll Papers, PHS.

12. *National Intelligencer,* Apr. 23, 1817.

13. Monroe to Jackson, Dec. 14, 1816, *JM,* V, 342–48; Jackson to Monroe, Nov. 12, 1816, John Spencer Bassett and J. F. Jameson, eds., *Correspondence of Andrew Jackson* (6 vols., Washington, D.C., 1926–33), II, 265.

14. Harry Ammon, "James Monroe and the Era of Good Feelings," *Va. Mag.,* LXVI (1958), 390–91; Livermore, *Federalism,* 160–67, has an excellent account of the publication of these letters.

15. Apr. 13, 1816, Monroe, LC.

16. Samuel Eliot Morison, *Life and Letters of Harrison Gray Otis* (2 vols., New York, 1913), II, 201–3.

17. On Washington's tour, see Freeman, *Washington,* VI, 240ff.; for a full, semiofficial account of the tour see Samuel P. Waldo, *A Narrative of a Tour of Observation Made During the Summer of 1817* . . . (Hartford, Conn., 1820).

18. To [Richard Rush], July 14, 1817, Gratz Coll., PHS.

19. *National Intelligencer,* June 4, 1817; Monroe to Hay, Aug. 5, 1817, *Bull. NYPL,* VI (1902), 227.

20. Robert Walsh to F. W. Gilmer, June 3, 1817, Gilmer Papers, U.Va.

21. Monroe to Hay, Aug. 5, 1817, cited *supra,* fn. 19.

22. Waldo, *Tour,* 61.

23. Morison, *Otis,* II, 207; Christopher Gore to Jeremiah Mason, June 22, 1817; G. S. Hilliard, ed., *Memoir, Autobiography and Correspondence of Jeremiah Mason* (Cambridge, Mass., 1873), 157–58; Monroe to Jefferson, July 27, 1817, *JM,* VI, 27–28.

24. Boston *Columbian Centinel,* July 5, 1817; *Niles' Weekly Register,* July 12, 1817; Ralph Waldo Emerson to Ed. B. Emerson, July 23, 1817, Ralph L. Rusk ed., *Letters of Ralph Waldo Emerson* (6 vols., Columbia University, 1939), I, 39–40.

25. See fn. 18 *supra.*

26. *Niles' Weekly Register,* July 12, 1817; Boston *Columbian Centinel,* July 5, 1817; R. W. G. Vail, "Notes on the History of the Early American Circus," *Am. Ant. Soc. Proc.,* XLIII, 180.

27. *Niles' Weekly Register,* July 19, 1817; Edward T. Channing, *An Oration Delivered on [July 4, 1817]* . . . *in Boston* (Boston, 1817).

28. Boston *Columbian Centinel,* July 9, 1817.

29. July 10, 1817, Monroe, LC.

30. Turner, *Plumer*, 282–85.

31. *National Intelligencer,* July 31, 1817.

32. July 27, 1817, Rives Papers, LC.

33. Monroe to Hay, Aug. 5, 1817, cited *supra* fn. 19.

34. Crawford to Gallatin, Oct. 27, 1817, Gallatin Papers, NYHS; Clay to Jonathan Russell, Aug. 18, 1817, Hopkins, *Clay,* II, 372.

35. Mason to Rufus King, July 24, 1817, C. King, *Life of R. King,* VI, 79–80; for the reaction of the Federalists, see Livermore, *Federalism,* 47–68.

36. Harrison Gray Otis to Isaac Parker, Dec. 29, 1818, Otis Papers, MHS; George Sullivan to Monroe, Jan. 15, 1820, Monroe, LC.

37. June 25, 1819, quoted in Livermore, *Federalism,* 56.

38. Morison, *Otis,* II, 203.

39. *JM,* VI, 163.

CHAPTER 21

THE ERA OF GOOD FEELINGS: REALITY

1. Jonathan Roberts to Biddle, Jan. 30, 1817, Biddle Papers, LC.

2. Crawford to Albert Gallatin, Mar. 12, 1817, Gallatin Papers, NYHS.

3. Rufus King to _____, Jan. 3, 1818, C. King, *Life of R. King,* VI, 95.

4. Adams, *Memoirs,* IV, 119, July 18, 1818.

5. *Ibid.,* IV, 72, Apr. 4, 1818.

6. James Stirling Young, *The Washington Community, 1800–1828* (Columbia U. Press, 1966), 128–30, 163–78; White, *Jeffersonians,* 45–59.

7. Roger H. Brown, *The Republic in Peril* (New York, 1964), *passim.*

8. This is contrary to the usual view that Monroe was a mild figure content to ride out the storms of his administration without making a significant attempt to influence the course of events. This view, which has been widely accepted by historians, springs from unfamiliarity with the inner workings of the Monroe administration. Most typical of this view are George Dangerfield, *The Era of Good Feelings* (New York, 1952), 97, 100, and his *Awakening of American Nationalism* (New York, 1965), 22; White, *Republicans,* 38; Young, *Washington Community,* 187. For a different view, closer to the approach I have adopted, see Stuart Gerry Brown, *The American Presidency; Leadership, Partisanship, and Popularity* (New York, 1966), 7–12, 70–74, 230.

9. Adams, *Memoirs,* IV, 457, Nov. 6, 1819.

10. *Ibid.,* V, 199, Nov. 12, 1820.

11. *Ibid.,* IV, 450–53, Nov. 27, 1819.

12. Henry Clay to Amos Kendall, Jan. 8, 1820, Hopkins, *Clay*, II, 752.

13. Crawford to Gallatin, July 24, 1819, Gallatin Papers, NYHS.

14. Adams, *Memoirs*, IV, 31, 212, Dec. 26, 1817, Jan. 6, 1819; White, *Republicans*, 5, 101–6, 212.

15. Adams, *Memoirs*, IV, 66–70, Mar. 18–28, 1818; Crawford to Monroe, Mar. 22, 1818, Monroe, LC.

16. Adams, *Memoirs*, IV, 450–53, Nov. 27, 1819.

17. Young, *Washington Community*, 131–33.

18. Adams, *Memoirs*, IV, 6, Sept. 20, 1817; *National Intelligencer*, Sept. 8, 12, 19, 1817.

19. Adams, *Memoirs*, VI, 431, Nov. 20, 1824.

20. *Ibid.*, V., 199, Nov. 12, 1820.

21. *Ibid.*, V, 200, Nov. 12, 1820.

22. Richardson, *Messages*, II, 11–20, Dec. 2, 1817.

23. *AC*, 15C1S, 445, 512, Dec. 12, 24, 1817.

24. *Ibid.*, 21, Dec. 9, 1817.

25. *AC*, 15C1S, 451–60, Dec. 15, 1817.

26. Dec. 22, 1817, *JM*, VI, 46.

27. Madison to Monroe, Dec. 27, 1817, Hunt, *Madison*, VIII, 430–437.

28. Adams, *Memoirs*, IV, 30–31, Dec. 24, 1817.

29. *AC*, 15C1S, 1373, Mar. 13, 1817.

30. *Ibid.*, 1374, Mar. 13, 1817.

31. Van Deusen, *Clay*, 118–23; Monroe was apparently conscious that the question of using fatigue parties to construct roads presented a special problem, but he was unable to resolve it successfully in his essay on internal improvements (see *infra*, fn. 34). His chief argument seems to have been that they were not constructed or improved roads, like the Cumberland Road, but traces through the woods made by cutting down trees and using logs for causeways, but otherwise unimproved. See Harrison, Internal Improvements, 259, cited *infra*, fn. 32.

32. *AC*, 15C1S, 1385–89, 1678, Mar. 18, Apr. 3, 1817; Risjord, *Old Republicans*, 197–203; the only full account of the internal improvements issue is in Joseph Hobson Harrison, Jr., The Internal Improvement Issue in the Politics of the Union, 1783–1825 (Ph.D. dissertation, University of Virginia, 1954), on which I have drawn extensively in this summary.

33. Crawford does not seem to have reported; Harrison, *op cit.*, 456–59.

34. Text of the essay is in *JM*, VI, 216–84.

35. Adams, *Memoirs*, IV, 462, Dec. 2, 1819.

36. *AC*, 15C1S, 1875, May 6, 1822.

37. Harrison, Internal Improvements, 632–45; Risjord, *Old Republicans*, 239–243.

38. The internal improvements issue was complicated by the fact that in Congress there were three groups: those who believed Congress had the power to construct internal improvements, and hence would not agree to an amendment; those who believed Congress had the power, if state consent were first obtained; those who denied that Congress had the power. To some extent these three polarized each other. It is not clear that there was ever an absolute majority willing to vote for an extensive program.

39. *AC,* 15C1S, 1402, Mar. 17, 1818.

40. Whitaker, *Lat. Am. Ind.,* 218–20.

41. *AC,* 15C1S, 1464–646, Mar. 24–28, 1818.

42. Adams, *Memoirs,* IV, 70, 78, Mar. 28, Apr. 10, 1818.

43. Apr. 28, 1818, *JM,* VI, 49.

44. *Intelligencer,* May 9, 30, 1818.

CHAPTER 22

THE WHITE HOUSE

1. The term "White House" was used in James Fenimore Cooper, *Notions of the Americans* (2 vols., New York, 1963), originally published in 1838; Talbot Hamlin, *Benjamin Henry Latrobe* (New York, 1955), 302, fn. 35. Latrobe designed the portico.

2. Adams, *Memoirs,* IV, 16–22, Nov. 7–23, 1817.

3. *Ibid.,* IV, 263–70, Feb. 17–20, 1819; Monroe once canceled a planned visit to Madison because the British Minister was there at the time, Monroe to Madison, Oct. 18, 1817, *JM,* VI, 29–30.

4. Adams, *Memoirs,* IV, 314, Mar. 29, 1819.

5. *Ibid.,* IV, 16, Nov. 7, 1817.

6. *Ibid.,* IV, 295, Nov. 13, 1819.

7. Samuel L. Southard to Rebecca Southard, Dec. 22, 1822, Southard Papers, Princeton University Library.

8. Adams, *Memoirs,* IV, 45, 188, Jan. 30, Dec. 11, 1818.

9. *National Intelligencer,* Dec. 17, 1817.

10. Letter of Mrs. Wm. Seaton, 1818, in Anne Hollingsworth Wharton, *Social Life in the Early Republic* (Philadelphia, 1902), 185.

11. Adams, *Memoirs,* IV, 45–46, 188–92, Dec. 12, 1817, Jan. 22, 1818.

12. Louisa C. Adams to John Adams, Jan. 22, 1818, Adams Papers, MHS.

13. Adams, *Memoirs,* IV, 189, Dec. 12, 1818; Louisa C. Adams to John Adams, Dec. 25, 1818, Adams Papers, MHS.

14. Adams, *Memoirs,* IV, 479–81, Dec. 19, 20, 1819.

15. *Ibid.*, IV, 482–93, Dec. 22–29, 1822.

16. Daniel D. Tompkins to his wife, Feb. 24, 1818, Tompkins Papers, New York State Library, Albany.

17. The above paragraphs are based on the following: Louisa Adams' diary letter to John Adams, Jan. 1, Mar. 2, 1818, Apr. 16, May 3, 1820, Adams Papers, MHS; Sophia Otis to Mrs. Wm. F. Otis, Jan. 6, [ca. 1819], Otis Papers, MHS; Baron Axel Klinkowström, "Letters," *American Scandinavian Review*, XIX (1931), 394–402; *National Intelligencer*, Jan. 2, 1817; Cooper, *Notions of the Americans*, 11, 56, 183, and *passim;* Wharton, *Social Life*, 185.

18. Adams, *Memoirs*, IV, 264, Feb. 17, 1819.

19. *Ibid.*, IV, 493, Dec. 31, 1819; Louisa C. Adams to John Adams, Feb. 17, 1819, Adams Papers, MHS; Rufus King to Christopher Gore, Dec. 1, 1820, C. King, *Life of R. King*, VI, 364.

20. Cooper, *Notions of the Americans*, II, 53–55; S. L. Southard to Rebecca Southard, Dec. 22, 1822, Princeton University Library; Louisa C. Adams to John Adams, Jan. 8–18, 1819, Adams Papers, MHS.

21. Louisa C. Adams to John Adams, Jan. 7, 1818, Mar. 20, 1820, Adams Papers, MHS.

22. Otis to his wife, Jan. 27, 1821, Otis Papers, MHS; Elijah Mills to _____, [Jan. or Feb.], 1819, *Proc. MHS*, ser. 1, XIX, 31.

23. Louisa C. Adams to John Adams, Jan. 8, 1817, Adams Papers, MHS.

24. C. J. Ingersoll to Richard Rush, Feb. 8, 1823, in William M. Meigs, *Life of Charles Jared Ingersoll* (Philadelphia, 1897), 118; Jefferson to Monroe, Apr. 8, 1817, Monroe, LC; Monroe to Jefferson, Apr. 23, 1817, *JM*, VI, 21–22.

25. Jefferson to Monroe, Feb. 21, 1823, Ford, *Jefferson*, XII, 276; Louisa C. Adams to John Adams, Dec. 3–12, 1822, Adams Papers, MHS; Abner Lacock to Monroe, June 4, 1821, Monroe, LC.

26. William Wirt to Laura Wirt, May 23, 1820, Wirt Papers, MdHS.

27. Louisa C. Adams to John Adams, Feb. 22, 1819, Feb. 22, 1820, Adams Papers, MHS; Mrs. Henry Dearborn to H. A. S. Dearborn, Feb. 23, 1823, MHS; *National Intelligencer*, Feb. 24, 1821.

28. Louisa C. Adams to John Adams, March 15, 1818, Adams Papers, MHS; James Schouler, *History of the United States of America* (7 vols., New York, 1880–1913), III, 219.

29. Joseph Lancaster to Robert Vaux, Jan. 27, 1819, Vaux Papers, PHS.

30. Adams, *Memoirs*, IV, 30, Nov. 10, 1817, VI, 403, July 31, 1824; Baron Klinkowström to _____, Feb. 12, 1819, *loc. cit.*, 396; Elijah Mills to _____, Feb. 9, 1822, *Proc. MHS*, ser. 1, XIX, 34–35.

31. Joseph C. Cabell to Fulwar Skipwith, June 19, 1811, Causten Pickett Papers, LC.

32. Payne and King, "Monroe Family," *loc. cit.*, 237.

33. Nicholas Biddle to Mrs. Hay, Feb. 11, 1818, Biddle Papers, LC; Burr Powell to Monroe, Jan. 16, 1831, Monroe, LC.

34. Adams, *Memoirs*, V, 15, Mar. 9, 1820; Louisa C. Adams to John Adams, Dec. 10–20, 1818, Louisa C. Adams to Charles F. Adams, Mar. 7, 1822, Adams Papers, MHS; "Hay Family," *Tyler's Quarterly*, VIII (1926), 277.

35. Quote is from Louisa C. Adams to John Adams, Mar. 7, 1820, Adams Papers, MHS; Mrs. Wirt to William Wirt, Dec. 4, 1822, Wirt Papers, MdHS.

36. John Quincy Adams to Louisa C. Adams, Aug. 2, 1821, Louisa C. Adams to John Quincy Adams, Aug. 9, 1821, Adams Papers, MHS.

37. Mrs. S. H. Smith to Mrs. Kirkpatrick, Apr. 23, 1820, S. H. Smith Papers, LC.

38. Samuel L. Gouverneur to Monroe, Dec. 6, 1822, Monroe Foundation, Fredericksburg.

39. Louisa C. Adams to John Adams, Mar. 10, 1820, Adams Papers, MHS; Wharton, *Social Life*, 188; Monroe to Madison, May 3, 1820, Madison Papers, LC.

40. Boswell R. Hoes to John B. Larner, Nov. 4, 1911, McGregor Coll., U.Va.

41. Monroe to George Hay, Sept. 6, 1818, Monroe Foundation, Fredericksburg; Monroe to Robert Swartwout, Oct. 27, 1819, Swartwout Papers, NYPL.

42. Monroe to Jefferson, May 3, 1820, *JM*, VI, 119.

CHAPTER 23

SPAIN AND HER COLONIES: THE PROBLEM

1. In this chapter I have made extensive use of the three major works dealing with Spain, Latin America and the United States: Brooks, *Borderlands;* Bemis, *Adams,* I, and Arthur P. Whitaker, *The United States and the Independence of Latin America, 1800–1830* (Baltimore, 1941).

2. Bemis, *Adams,* I, 372.

3. Whitaker, *Independence of Latin America,* 42–85, 193–242.

4. *Ibid.,* 227–30; Rush to Monroe, Apr. 24–30, 1814, Monroe, LC.

5. Whitaker, *Independence of Latin America,* 232–36.

6. May 26, 1820, *JM*, VI, 132.

7. Bemis, *Adams,* I, 307; Monroe to Madison, Nov. 24, 1817, *JM*, VI, 32–33.

8. *JM*, VI, 31; Adams, *Memoirs*, IV, 13–15, Oct. 25, 1817.

9. Richardson, *Messages,* II, 11–20. No operations were undertaken at Galveston, since the piratical establishment did not continue.

10. Adams, *Memoirs*, IV, 30–31, Dec. 24, 1817.

11. To Ingersoll, Dec. 2, 1817, Ingersoll Papers, PHS.

12. Adams, *Memoirs,* IV, 31–32, Dec. 26, 1817; Wiltse, *Calhoun,* I, 155–56; Monroe to Jackson, Dec. 28, 1817, Monroe, NYPL.

13. Quote is from Jackson to Monroe, Dec. 20, 1817, Monroe, NYPL; see also Monroe to Jackson, Aug. 4, Sept. 27, Oct. 5, Dec. 2, 1817, Jackson to Monroe, Oct. 22, 1817, John Rhea to Jackson, Dec. 24, 1817, Jan. 7, 1817 [should be 1818], all in Jackson Papers, LC.

14. Bassett, *Jackson Correspondence,* II, 345–46.

15. Monroe to Adams, Mar. 11, 1830, Monroe to Calhoun, May 19, 1830, *JM,* VII, 209, 217.

16. July 5, 1830, Monroe, LC.

17. Calhoun to Monroe, May 26, 1830, Jan. 21, 1831, Monroe, LC; Monroe to Calhoun, [Jan. 27, 1831], draft, *JM,* VII, 218; Monroe to Wirt, May 30, 1830, Wirt Papers, MdHS.

18. Cited in Richard R. Stenberg, "Jackson's Rhea Letter Hoax," *Journal of Southern History,* II (1936), 481, fn. 4. Stenberg's article exhaustively examines the evidence and concludes that Monroe never gave Rhea any instructions for Jackson.

19. Adams, *Memoirs,* IV, 194, Dec. 17, 1818. Monroe's silence in relation to Jackson's letter of Jan. 6 was quite deliberate. In a draft of his letter to Jackson of Dec. 21 (Monroe, NYPL) he specifically referred to the letter of January 6; however, in the letter as sent he deleted this reference. Later, in 1831, Monroe himself confused the copy with the letter sent (see Adams to Monroe, Feb. 16, 1831, Monroe, LC), as did Cresson, *Monroe,* 316–17. In order to understand the references in Monroe's letter of Dec. 21, it is necessary to read his letter of Oct. 20, 1818; both are in *JM,* VI, 74, 84–86.

20. Jackson to Rhea, Apr. 23, 1821, copy, Jackson Papers, LC; *JM,* VII, 234–36; Stenberg, *loc. cit.,* II, *passim.*

21. S. L. Gouverneur to F. P. Blair, June 15, 1832, T. L. Smith to S. L. Gouverneur, Nov. 4, 1832, Gouverneur Papers, NYPL; Wiltse, *Calhoun,* II, 431, fn. 49.

22. Monroe to Calhoun, Jan. 30, 1818, Meriwether, *Calhoun,* II, 104.

23. Adams, *Memoirs,* IV, 35–38, Jan. 6–12, 1818.

24. Crawford to Monroe, [Jan.] 1818, Monroe, LC.

25. Richardson, *Messages,* II, 23–25; New York *Evening Post,* Jan. 12, Feb. 3, 1818.

26. Notes in Monroe's hand, Jan. 15, 1818, Adams, MHS; for a full discussion of this complex boundary question, see Brooks, *Borderlands,* 92–95, and Bemis, *Adams,* I, 309–12.

27. Feb. 12, 1818, Adams, MHS.

28. Adams, *Memoirs,* IV, 51, Jan. 31, 1818; Perkins, *Castlereagh,* 287.

29. Bemis, *Adams,* I, 309–10; quote is from undated memorandum cited, *ibid.,* I, 309.

30. Brooks, *Borderlands*, 135–37.

31. Memo in Monroe's hand, n.d. but ca. May, 1818, Adams Papers, MHS; Adams, *Memoirs*, IV, 91–92, May 13, 1818.

32. Adams, *Memoirs*, IV, 103–7, June 26, 1818.

33. *Ibid.*, IV, 107, July 8, 1818; Monroe to Adams, July 8, 9, 1818, Adams Papers, MHS.

34. Dangerfield, *Good Feelings*, 138, accepts without question Adams' statements, but Bemis, *Adams*, I, 316, is more cautious and does not comment directly on Monroe's attitude in these discussions; see Adams, *Memoirs*, IV, 108–14, July 15–20, 1818; on the subsequent controversy between Jackson and Calhoun, see the excellent summary in Wiltse, *Calhoun*, II, 76–81.

35. Monroe to Adams, July 20, 1819 [should be 1818, date was inserted by Adams], Adams Papers, MHS; Adams, *Memoirs*, IV, 114–19, July 20–28, 1818; Calhoun to [Monroe], Aug. 1, 1818, Monroe, NYPL. Monroe's draft of the note to Onís does not seem to have been preserved, although the covering letter dated July 17, 1818, is in Adams Paper, MHS. The letter indicates his unwillingness to approve Jackson, but does not suggest repudiation.

36. July 19, 1818, *JM*, VI, 54–61.

37. Monroe to Calhoun, Sept. 9, 1818, draft, Monroe, NYPL; Monroe to Jackson, Oct. 20, 1818, *JM*, VI, 74–75.

38. Jackson to Monroe, Nov. 15, 1818, copy, Jackson Papers, LC.

39. Dec. 21, 1818, *JM*, VI, 85–87.

CHAPTER 24

SPAIN AND HER COLONIES: THE SOLUTION

1. Bemis, *Adams*, I, 317–21.

2. *Ibid.*, I, 324; Adams, *Memoirs*, IV, 130ff.

3. Monroe to Adams, Nov. 20, 1818, Adams Papers, MHS; Bemis, *Adams*, I, 323–35.

4. Richardson, *Messages*, II, 248–49.

5. Adams, *Memoirs*, IV, 164, Nov. 7, 1818.

6. Whitaker, *Lat. Am. Ind.*, 167–71, 239–43; although appointed in the spring of 1817 the commissioners did not sail until late in the year. The reason for delay was not because of Adams' orders, as Brooks, *Borderlands*, 87, suggests, but the illness of Rodney's son. See Randolph Campbell, Henry Clay and the Emerging Nations of Spanish America (dissertation, University of Virginia, 1966), 51–56; Henry M. Brackenridge was the Secretary of the mission. For a detailed account of the mission, see William F. Keller, *The Nation's Advocate: Henry Marie Brackenridge and Young America* (U. of Pittsburgh, 1965), Ch. 14 and 15.

7. Adams, *Memoirs,* IV, 164–69, Nov. 7, 9, 1818; Monroe to Jefferson, Nov. 23, 1818, *JM,* VI, 85.

8. *National Intelligencer,* Nov. 20, 1818; J. W. Eaton to Jackson, Nov. 20, 1818, Jackson Papers, LC.

9. Bemis, *Adams,* I, 326–27; Bemis calls this dispatch the greatest state paper in Adams' diplomatic career. Jefferson was unstinting in his praise of this dispatch, which he called one of the ablest state papers he had ever seen; he urged Monroe to have it translated into French for American ministers to circulate in Europe. Jefferson to Monroe, Jan. 18, 1819, Ford, *Jefferson,* XII, 113.

10. Richmond *Enquirer,* Dec. 22, 1818, Jan. 7, Feb. 13, 1819; Adams, *Memoirs,* IV, 227, Jan. 23, 1819; George Hay to Monroe, Feb. 12, 1819, Monroe, LC.

11. *AC,* 15C1S, 515ff., Jan. 12–Feb. 8, 1819; Louisa Adams to John Adams, Feb. 4, 1819, Adams Papers, MHS; Adams, *Memoirs,* IV, 239–43, Feb. 3, 1819.

12. Crawford to Gallatin, July 24, 1819, Gallatin Papers, NYHS; Wiltse, *Calhoun,* I, 177; *AC,* 15C2S, 1165, Feb. 13, 1819.

13. King to Jeremiah Mason, Feb. 7, 1819, C. King, *Life of R. King,* VI, 205.

14. Adams, *Memoirs,* IV, 219, Jan. 15, 1819.

15. For a detailed account of the boundary negotiations, see Bemis, *Adams,* I, 330–33 and the relevant maps at the end of the volume.

16. Adams, *Memoirs,* IV, 266–70, Feb. 19, 1819; Brooks, *Borderlands,* 161.

17. Adams, *Memoirs,* IV, 270, Feb. 20, 1819.

18. Quote is from Adams, *Memoirs,* IV, 290, Mar. 9, 1819; Bemis, *Adams,* I, 336–37; Brooks, *Borderlands,* 175–78.

19. Adams, *Memoirs,* IV, 65, 187, 193, Mar. 22, Dec. 8, 16, 1818; Louisa Adams to John Adams, Mar. 11, 1820, Adams Papers, MHS.

20. Adams, *Memoirs,* IV, 205, Jan. 2, 1819.

21. Whitaker, *Lat. Am. Ind.,* 256–59.

22. *Ibid.,* 262–63.

23. Mar. 24, 1819, *JM,* VI, 92–102.

24. Whitaker, *Lat. Am. Ind.,* 215–21, 243–46, 275–304.

25. Adams, *Memoirs,* IV, 408–16, Aug. 11–21, 1819; appointment papers, National Archives; Harold A. Bierck, Jr., "Spoils, Soils, and Skinner," *Md. Hist. Mag.,* XLIX (1954), 21–40; Charles C. Griffin, "Privateering from Baltimore During the Spanish American War of Independence," *ibid.,* XXXV (1940), 1–25. Eventually 45 persons were convicted of piracy in 1820; the President, after deliberating with the Cabinet, pardoned all but ten. Adams, *Memoirs,* V, 1921, 55–56, 63–66, Mar. 14, 31, Apr. 11–12, 1820.

26. Joseph E. Agan, "Corrêa da Serra," *Pa. Mag.,* XLIX (1925), 23–25; Rush to Madison, June 14, 1817, copy, Monroe, LC; Rush to Monroe, June 21, 1817, Monroe, LC; Adams, *Memoirs,* IV, 327, April 8, 1819.

27. Robert Walsh to F. W. Gilmer, Oct. 17, 1819, Gilmer Papers, U.Va.

28. C. A. Rodney to Monroe, Sept. 19, 1820, Monroe, LC.

29. Agan, *loc. cit.*, 33–42; Monroe to Adams, Aug. 11, Sept. 25, 29, 1820, Adams Papers, MHS; Monroe to Jefferson, Aug. 23, Nov. 15, 1820, *JM*, VI, 152–59; Adams, *Memoirs*, V, 176, 180, Sept. 19, 26, 1820.

30. *National Intelligencer*, Mar. 31–July 30, 1819; Monroe to Adams, June 14, July 5, Aug. 2, 3, 1819, Adams Papers, MHS; Clay to Joseph Gales, July 19, 1819, Hopkins, *Clay*, II, 700; Wiltse, *Calhoun*, I, 180; Samuel Lane to John W. Taylor, Aug. 10, 1819, Taylor Papers, NYHS; Adams, *Memoirs*, 402, 405, July 17, Aug. 9, 1819.

31. Adams, *Memoirs*, IV, 405–412, Aug. 10–17, 1819.

32. *Ibid.*, IV, 435–67, Nov. 10–Dec. 5, 1819.

33. *Ibid.*, IV, 461, Dec. 3, 1819.

34. Richardson, *Messages*, II, 54–62, Dec. 7, 1817.

35. Adams, *Memoirs*, IV, 496–97, Jan. 8, 1820, V, 24–25, Mar. 18, 1820.

36. *Ibid.*, V, 17, Mar. 10, 1820.

37. *Ibid.*, V, 28–35, Mar. 21–23, 1820; Richardson, *Messages*, II, 69.

38. *AC*, 16C1S, 1719–1820, Apr. 3–4, 1820.

39. Adams, *Memoirs*, V, 66, Apr. 12, 1820.

40. *Ibid.*, V, 74, Apr. 25, 1820; Bemis, *Adams*, I, 353; *AC*, 16C1S, 2230, May 10, 1820.

41. Adams, *Memoirs*, V, 98–105, May 6–9, 1820.

42. *Ibid.*, V, 126–27, May 20, 1820.

43. May 1820, *JM*, VI, 119–23. Monroe wrote to Jackson in a similar vein, May 23, 1820, and to Gallatin, May 26, 1820, *JM*, VI, 126–53.

44. The four were James Brown (Clay's brother-in-law), R. M. Johnson, John Williams of Tennessee and William A. Trimble of Ohio; Adams, *Memoirs*, V, 171, 285, Feb. 12, 19, 1821; Bemis, *Adams*, I, 352–53.

45. Adams, *Memoirs*, V, 288, Feb. 22, 1821.

46. *Ibid.*, V, 268, Feb. 11, 1821; *AC*, 16C2S, 1070–92, Feb. 9–10, 1821; Whitaker, *Lat. Am. Ind.*, 332–33; Van Deusen, *Clay*, 128–30.

47. Bemis, *Adams*, I, 356–58; Whitaker, *Lat. Am. Ind.*, 343–60.

48. Bemis, *Adams*, I, 359; Richardson, *Messages*, II, 116–18.

49. Monroe to Garnett, Mar. 29, 1822, and Garnett's statement of Apr. 1, 1822, *JM*, VI, 203–15.

50. To Jefferson, Mar. 14, 1822, to Madison, May 10, 1822, *JM*, VI, 213, 285.

51. Monroe to William Thornton, May 18, 1822, Thornton Papers, LC.

52. Adams, *Memoirs*, V, 494–96, Apr. 20–22, 1822.

53. *Ibid.*, V, 492, Apr. 19, 1822, VI, 24, June 20, 1822.

54. *Ibid.*, V, 514, May 2, 1822, VI, 25–26, June 20, 1822; Madison to Monroe,

May 6, 1822, Hunt, *Madison,* IX 91–92; Monroe to Madison May 10, 1822, *JM,* VI, 284–86.

55. Adams, *Memoirs,* VI, 122–30, Jan. 9–12, 1823. No minister reached Mexico during the Monroe administration. When Jackson declined, he appointed Ninian Edwards, who had to resign in 1824 before going to Mexico because of the exposure of his authorship of the "A.B." letters attacking Crawford's management of the Treasury. In January 1823, Monroe named J. B. Prevost chargé to Peru, but later withdrew his name in the face of Senate opposition.

56. Adams, *Memoirs,* VI, 23, June 19, 1823; Whitaker, *Lat. Am. Ind.,* 388–89.

57. Whitaker, *Lat. Am. Ind.,* 410–20.

CHAPTER 25

THE POLITICS OF SLAVERY

1. Throughout this section I have drawn extensively on the extended study of Glover Moore, *The Missouri Controversy, 1819–1821* (Lexington, Ky., 1953).

2. Spencer Roane to Barbour, Dec. 29, 1819, *WMQ,* X (1901), 7; Beveridge, *Marshall,* IV, 323–26.

3. To J. J. Crittenden, Feb. 6, 1820, quoted in Mrs. Chapman Coleman, *Life of John J. Crittenden* (2 vols., Phila., 1871), I, 41.

4. Wiltse, *Calhoun,* I, 195–96; Moore, *Missouri Compromise,* 95, 123–24, 235; Dangerfield, *Good Feelings,* 230–31.

5. Hay to Monroe, Dec. 24, 1819, Monroe, LC; these essays appeared over the signature "An American," in December 1819 and January 1820.

6. Taken from a draft in possession of S. L. Gouverneur and printed in *Congressional Globe,* 30C2S, Appendix, 67. The draft of the veto message and other important documentary material relating to the Missouri Compromise were printed in this issue of the *Globe* in connection with the debates over the organization of the Oregon Territory.

7. Adams, *Memoirs,* IV, 498–99, Jan. 8, 1820.

8. Monroe to Hay, Jan. 10, 1820, Monroe, NYPL.

9. Monroe to Barbour, Feb. 3, 1820, *WMQ,* X (1901), 9; Madison to Monroe, Feb. 10, 1820, Hunt, *Madison,* IX, 21–23.

10. *AC,* 16C1S, 363–67, Feb. 3–7, 1820.

11. Charles Yancey to Barbour, Feb. 9, 1820, *WMQ,* X (1901), 75–76; Barbour to Madison, Feb. 10, 1820, Madison, LC.

12. To William King, Feb. 9, 1820, quoted in Moore, *Missouri Compromise,* 235, fn. 73. William King was a half-brother of Rufus King and a resident of Maine. He was urging both John Holmes (also from Massachusetts) and Hill to seek a compromise to ensure the admission of Maine, *ibid.,* 197.

13. Ammon, "Richmond Junto," *Va. Mag.*, LXI (1963), *passim.*

14. Monroe to Madison, Feb. 5, 1820, Rives Papers, LC; Monroe to Jefferson, Feb. 7, 1820, *JM*, VI, 114; Madison to Monroe, Feb. 10, 1820, Hunt, *Madison*, IX, 21–23.

15. H. Clay to Leslie Combs, Feb. 5, 1820, Hopkins, *Clay*, II, 774.

16. For an excellent analysis of the political implications of the conflict, see Livermore, *The Twilight of Federalism*, 88–112.

17. Burwell Bassett to Monroe, Feb. 9, 1820, Charles Everett to Monroe, Feb. 9, 1820, all in Monroe Foundation, Fredericksburg, Va.; other letters are in *WMQ*, X (1901), 7ff.; Richmond *Enquirer*, Feb. 10, 1820.

18. Everett to Monroe, Feb. 20, 22, [1820], Monroe, NYPL; Hay to Monroe, *Bull. NYPL*, X (1906), 175.

19. Monroe to Roane, Feb. 15, 1820, draft, Monroe, NYPL, also printed in *Cong. Globe*, 30C1S, App., 67, where it is dated Feb. 16; Hay to Monroe, Feb. 17, 1820, Monroe, LC.

20. Roane to Monroe, Feb. 16, 1820, *Bull. NYPL*, X (1906), 175.

21. Hay to Monroe, Feb. 17, 1820, Monroe, LC.

22. Printed in *Cong. Globe*, 30C1S, App., 66, together with Hay to Monroe, Feb. 16, 1820.

23. To Peachy R. Gilmer, Feb. 17, 1820, Gilmer Papers, VSL.

24. Moore, *Missouri Compromise*, 100ff.; *AC*, 16C1S, 1566–88, Feb. 29–Mar. 2, 1820. Of the fourteen Northerners who voted to eliminate restriction, five changed their votes on the final ballot; the other nine had always opposed restriction. The final passage of the bill was facilitated by the absence of several members. This was sufficient to reverse a vote of 91–82 for restriction to a vote of 90 to 87 to eliminate the restrictive clause.

25. Adams, *Memoirs*, IV, 530, Feb. 23, 1820.

26. Adams, *Memoirs*, V, 5–9, Mar. 3, 1820. The written opinions, which were placed on file in the State Department, have vanished. They could not be located in 1848, when a search was made for them during the debates on the Oregon Territory, although an entry was found in the State Department showing that they had been deposited. Calhoun, who denied the power of Congress to restrict slavery in territories during the debates of 1848, had no recollection of the President having called for written opinions. *Cong. Globe*, 30C1S, App., 57.

27. Monroe to Madison, Feb. 19, 1820, Rives Papers, LC; Madison to Monroe, Feb. 23, Hunt, *Madison*, IX, 24–26.

28. Monroe to Jefferson, May 1820, *JM*, VI, 121–22.

29. *National Intelligencer*, Dec. 28, 1819.

30. Smith Thompson to Van Buren, Jan. 3, 28, Apr. 9, Van Buren Papers, LC; Adams, *Memoirs*, V, 57–61, Apr. 6–9, 1820; Clay to Jonathan Russell, Apr. 10, 1820, Hopkins, *Clay*, II, 82; _____ Bayley to [Monroe?], Apr. 10, 18, 20, 1820,

Monroe, LC; *National Intelligencer*, Apr. 8, 10, 11, 1820; Richmond *Enquirer*, Apr. 11, 14, 1820.

31. "Virginius," Richmond *Enquirer*, Nov. 7, 1820.

32. Charles S. Sydnor, "The One Party Period of American History," *AHR*, LI (1946), 442.

33. Lynn W. Turner, *William Plumer* (Chapel Hill, 1962), 310–15.

34. Moore, *Missouri Compromise*, 153; *AC*, 16C2S, 1147–63, Feb. 14, 1824.

35. Monroe to Madison, Nov. 16, 1820, *JM*, VI, 160; Moore, *Missouri Compromise*, 128–41; Adams, *Memoirs*, V, 201–03, Nov. 13–15, 1820.

36. Moore, *Missouri Compromise*, 147–54.

37. *Ibid.*, 139–40.

38. Monroe to Madison, Feb. 17, 1821, Rives Papers, LC; Biddle to Monroe, Feb. 27, 1821, in *Cong. Globe*, 30C1S, App., 65; the three who changed their votes were Samuel Moore, Thomas J. Rogers and Daniel Urdree. See *AC*, 16C2S, 1116, 1239, Feb. 12, 26, 1821, and Moore, *Missouri Compromise*, 107, 153, 167.

39. Moore, *Missouri Compromise*, 150–64.

CHAPTER 26

POLITICS OF RETRENCHMENT

1. See the excellent study by Murray N. Rothbard, *The Panic of 1819; Reaction and Policies* (Columbia University Press, 1962), No. 605 in *Columbia University Studies in the Social Sciences*, 1–23.

2. Richardson, *Messages*, II, 61, Dec. 7, 1819.

3. Risjord, *Old Republicans*, 208–11; Rothbard, *Panic of 1819*, 170-72.

4. Richardson, *Messages*, II, 74–75, Nov. 14, 1820.

5. *Ibid*, II, 78; Rothbard, *Panic of 1819*, 24–30; it is quite possible that this plan was originated by Langdon Cheves, see Cheves to Crawford, Oct. 16, 1820, Monroe, LC.

6. Ralph C. H. Catterall, *The Second Bank of the United States* (University of Chicago, 1902, repr. 1960), 58–60.

7. *Ibid.*, 460; Walter Buckingham Smith, *Economic Aspects of the Second Bank of the United States* (Harvard University Press, 1953), 105.

8. The absence of a scholarly biography of Crawford makes it difficult to assess his role as Secretary. Although much had been written about the Second Bank, there is almost nothing relating to the public sector of the Bank's operations. Smith, cited fn. 7 *supra*, provides the best information on this aspect. Esther Rogoff Taus, *The Banking Functions of the United States Treasury* (Columbia U. Press, 1943; repr. 1967), has very little on this period. However, she notes (p. 31) that

Crawford set a precedent followed by later Secretaries in redeeming federal securities before their due date in order to relieve a money stringency. However, this took place in the spring of 1824, when Crawford was ill. The negotiations were handled by the President and Biddle. Biddle to Monroe, May 28, 1824, Monroe, LC; Biddle to Thomas Cadwallader, May 26, 1824, Gratz Coll., PHS.

9. Rothbard, *Panic of 1819*, 123–27.

10. Adams, *Memoirs*, IV, 499, Jan. 8, 1820; quote is from Monroe to Biddle, Oct. 26, 1819, Biddle Papers, LC.

11. Crawford to Gallatin, July 24, 1819, Gallatin Papers, NYHS; Thomas Payne Govan, *Nicholas Biddle: Nationalist and Public Banker* (U. of Chicago Press, 1959), 60; Bray Hammond, *Banks and Politics in America* (Princeton U., 1957), 301–6.

12. White, *Republicans*, 68–70.

13. Richardson, *Messages*, II, 60; Treasury Report of Dec. 12, 1819, in *Niles' Weekly Register*, Dec. 18, 1819.

14. Adams, *Memoirs*, IV, 500, Jan. 8, 1820.

15. Crawford to Gallatin, July 24, 1819, Gallatin Papers, NYHS.

16. Reports of Dec. 1, 1820, in *Niles' Weekly Register*, Dec. 9, 1820, Jan. 6, 1821. It is interesting to note that the Treasury reports became more detailed after 1821. The report for 1822 not only contained expenses and receipts up to Sept. 30 and an estimate for the fourth quarter, as had previous reports, but it also contained a statement for 1821, which had not been the case in earlier reports. The reports may be most conveniently located in *ibid.*

17. Richardson, *Messages*, II, 106, Dec. 3, 1821; Adams, *Memoirs*, V, 331, 451, Mar. 19, Nov, 23, 1821. Apparently Monroe was not able to make it a regular practice for the Secretary of the Treasury to show him the annual report before submitting it to Congress. The issue arose again in 1824, when relations were very strained between Monroe and Crawford as a result of the election of 1824. *Ibid.*, VI, 438–39, Dec. 10, 1824.

18. Risjord, *Old Republicans*, 231–32.

19. Wiltse, *Calhoun*, I, 149–50, 165–70, 200–6; *AC*, 16CiS, 2575.

20. Wiltse, *Calhoun*, I, 119–25; Risjord, *Old Republicans*, 193–97.

21. Adams, *Memoirs*, V, 331, Mar. 19, 1821.

22. *Ibid.*, V, 237–42, 262, Jan. 18, 19, 24, Feb. 5, 1821.

23. Adams, *Memoirs*, V, 331–32, Mar. 19, 1821.

24. *Ibid.*, V, 331–32, Jan. 9, 1821.

25. Rufus King to A. J. King, Jan. 19, 1821, C. King, *Life of R. King*, VI, 378.

26. *Ibid.*, V, 324, Mar. 9, 1821.

27. Wiltse, *Calhoun*, I, 236; Robert V. Remini, *Martin Van Buren and the Making of the Democratic Party* (Columbia University Press, 1969), 22.

28. Adams, *Memoirs,* V, 291–308, Feb. 23, Mar. 1, 1821.

29. Canning to Fazekerley, Nov. 14, 1820, Stanley Lane-Poole, *Life of Strat-ford Canning* (2 vols., London, 1888), I, 317; Washington *National Intelligencer,* Aug. 16, Dec. 7, 1819.

30. Canning to Planta, Mar. 8, 1821, *ibid.,* I, 318.

31. Quote is from Adams, *Memoirs,* V, 317–18, Mar. 5, 1821; *National Intelligencer,* Mar. 6, 1821; James Hall to Robert G. Wirt, Mar. 10, 1821, Wirt Papers, MdHS.

32. Richardson, *Messages,* II, 73–80.

CHAPTER 27

AN AMERICAN SYSTEM

1. Whitaker, *Lat. Am. Ind.,* 260–65.

2. Monroe to Adams, May 18, 1821, Adams Papers, MHS.

3. *JM,* VI, 365.

4. In this chapter I have made extensive use of Dexter Perkins, *The Monroe Doctrine, 1823–1826,* Vol. XXIX in *Harvard Historical Studies* (Cambridge, 1927), the finest study of the subject, fair and judicious in its conclusions; Whitaker, *Latin American Independence,* 429–563, which supplements Perkins; Samuel Flagg Bemis, *John Quincy Adams,* I, 363–408, which is on the whole balanced in its assessment of responsibility but unintentionally gives undue importance to Adams; Bradford Perkins, *Castlereagh and Adams: England and the United States, 1812–1823* (U. of Cal., 1964), 305–47, which offers important insights into the basis of British policy. Also useful is Edward Howland Tatum, Jr., *The United States and Europe 1815–1823* (New York, 1967, reissue of 1936 ed.). The pertinent documents are to be found in *JM,* VI, 324ff.; in Worthington C. Ford, "Genesis of the Monroe Doctrine," *Proc. MHS,* 2nd Ser., XV (1901–2), 373–436 (the text is of little value, since Ford's object was to give all credit to Adams for the authorship of the doctrine); and in William R. Manning (ed.), *Diplomatic Correspondence of the United States Concerning the Independence of the Latin-American Nations* (3 vols., New York, 1925).

5. B. Perkins, *Castlereagh,* 314–20.

6. Bemis, *Adams,* I, 382.

7. Monroe to Jefferson, Oct. 16, 1823, *JM,* VI, 323–25.

8. Oct. 24, 1823, *JM,* VI, 391–93.

9. D. Perkins, *Monroe Doctrine, 1823–1826,* 98; T. R. Schellenberg, "Jeffersonian Origins of the Monroe Doctrine," *Hispanic American Review,* XIV, 1–31, presents the evidence in detail but overstresses Jefferson's influence on Monroe and ignores fact that the idea was a commonplace; Whitaker, *Latin American Independence,* 102–5, 415–19.

10. Oct. 30, 1823, *JM*, VI, 394.

11. See Monroe's letters to Madison, Dec. 26, 1823, Rives Papers, LC, and to Rush, Dec. 16, 1823, Gratz Coll., PHS.

12. Adams, *Memoirs*, VI, 185, Nov. 15, 1823.

13. *Ibid.*, VI, 166–81, Nov. 7, 1823.

14. Bemis, *Adams*, I, 384–85.

15. *Ibid.*, I, 386; the draft reply to Tuyll and Monroe's revisions are printed in Ford, "Monroe Doctrine," *Proc. MHS*, 2nd. Ser., XV, 378–80.

16. Adams' memo is in Monroe Papers, NYPL; B. Perkins, *Castlereagh,* 311.

17. Adams, *Memoirs*, VI, 185, Nov. 13, 1823.

18. Whitaker, *Latin American Independence,* 430; B. Perkins, *Castlereagh,* 311–13.

19. Adams, *Memoirs*, VI, 185–87, Nov. 12–15, 1823.

20. *Ibid.*, VI, Nov. 16–18, 187–91; Rush's dispatches are in *JM*, VI, 386–88, but were received on Nov. 16, not on Nov. 19 as Hamilton states; see Adams, *Memoirs*, VI, 187, Nov. 16, 1823; Louisa C. Adams, diary extract, Nov. 30, 1823, in a letter to George W. Adams, Dec. 12, 1823, Adams Papers, MHS.

21. Draft and revisions are printed in Ford, "Monroe Doctrine," *Proc. MHS,* 2nd Ser., XV, 384–88; the final version is in *JM*, VI, 405–8; Adams, *Memoirs*, VI, 187–93, Nov. 17–21, 1823; John A. Logan, Jr., *No Transfer: an American Security Principle* (Yale U. Press, 1961), 167–70.

22. Monroe to Jefferson, June 2, 1823, *JM*, VI, 310; Jefferson to Monroe, June 11, 1823, Ford, *Jefferson,* X, 257.

23. Adams, *Memoirs*, VI, 194, Nov. 21, 1823.

24. *Ibid.*, VI, 197, Nov. 22, 1823.

25. *Ibid.*, VI, 198, Nov. 24, 1823.

26. Adams first saw this portion of the message on November 24 and used it, as he specifically states, as the basis of his reply to Tuyll, which he showed the President on November 25 just before the Cabinet met. *Ibid.*, VI, 198–99, Nov. 24–25, 1823.

27. The note is dated Nov. 16, 1823; D. Perkins, *Monroe Doctrine,* 85–86.

28. Dec. 17, 1823; Gratz Coll., PHS.

29. Adams, *Memoirs*, VI, 208, Nov. 26, 1823.

30. *Ibid.*, VI, 202–8, Nov. 26, 1823.

31. Barbour to Madison, Dec. 2, 1823, Madison Papers, LC.

32. Text is in Ford, "Monroe Doctrine," *Proc. MHS,* 2nd Ser., XV, 405–9; Bemis, *Adams*, I, 394–95; *Memoirs*, VI, 199–212, Nov. 25–27, 1823.

33. Bemis, *Adams*, I, 395.

34. Richardson, *Messages,* II, 209, 218–19.

35. Adams, *Memoirs,* VI, 226, Dec. 4, 1823; the report appeared in the *National Intelligencer,* Dec. 4, 1823.

36. Monroe to Adams, Dec. 3, 1823, Adams Papers, MHS; Bemis, *Adams,* I, 396–98; B. Perkins, *Castlereagh,* 338.

37. Adams, *Memoirs,* VI, 226, Dec. 4, 1823.

38. The text of the secret instructions was printed for the first time in Bemis, *Adams,* I, Appen. 2, 577–79.

39. Gratz Coll., PHS.

40. Whitaker, *Latin American Independence,* 516.

41. D. Perkins, *Monroe Doctrine, 1823–1826,* analyzes at length the reaction at home and abroad.

42. Dec. 30, 1823, Monroe, NYPL.

43. D. Perkins, *Monroe Doctrine, 1823–1826,* 154–60, 186–92; Whitaker, *Latin American Independence,* 555–60.

44. D. Perkins, *Monroe Doctrine, 1823–1826,* 162–84; B. Perkins, *Castlereagh,* 339–45.

45. Madison to Barbour, Dec. 5, 1823, Hunt, *Madison,* IX, 161–63.

46. Bemis, *Adams,* I, 405, fn. 64. The House resolution was prompted by rumors that Britain had suggested joint action to check intervention. Romulus M. Saunders to Bartlett Yancey, Dec. 31, 1823, *North Carolina Historical Review,* VI (1931), 440. Monroe preferred to refuse the request rather than oppose the passage of the resolution. Monroe to Adams, Dec. 23, 1823, Adams Papers, MHS.

47. *AC,* 18C1S, 1014, Jan. 20, 1824.

48. D. Perkins, *Monroe Doctrine, 1823–1826,* 146–47; Whitaker, *Latin American Independence,* 539–40.

CHAPTER 28

THE WAR OF THE GIANTS

1. "Virginius," Nov. 7, 1820.

2. See Wiltse, *Calhoun,* I, chap. 16–17; Risjord, *Old Republicans,* 228–55; Remini, *Van Buren,* 12–43.

3. Carl Russell Fish, *The Civil Service and the Patronage* (Cambridge, 1904), *Harvard Historical Studies,* XI, 66–70; *AC,* 15C1S, 623, 2214, April 20, May 9, 1820.

4. Adams, *Memoirs,* V, 18–19, May 15, 1820.

5. *Ibid.,* VII, 424, Feb. 7, 1828; James Schouler, *History of the United States of America* (7 vols., 1880–1913), III, 175.

6. Crawford to Monroe, June 12, 1820, Gratz Coll., PHS.

7. Adams, *Memoirs,* VII, 425, Feb. 7, 1828; Madison to Monroe, Dec. 28, 1820, Hunt, *Madison,* IX, 43; Jefferson to Madison, Nov. 19, 1820, Rives Papers, LC; Monroe employed the law in November to remove an official whose accounts were deficient by not reappointing him. See Monroe to [Walker Jones], draft, Nov. 24, 1820, Monroe, NYPL.

8. Adams, *Memoirs,* IV, 497, Jan. 8, 1820.

9. Quote is from Wirt to Edwards, Jan. 11, 1821, in White, *Republicans,* 127–28.

10. Adams, *Memoirs,* V, 479–84, Jan. 4–7, 1822; Remini, *Van Buren,* 18–25, has a full account of the conflict over this appointment.

11. John Floyd to James McDowell, Jan. 4, 1821, McDowell Papers, U.Va. Louisa Catherine Adams used the same terms in a letter to John Adams, Jan. 29, 1821, Adams Papers, MHS.

12. *AC,* 18C1S, 559, April 22, 1824. Apparently the term was originally used derisively, but later it seems to have been accepted by Crawford's supporters. Remini, *Van Buren,* 38. The term *Radical* does not seem to have been used in France at this time; apparently Taylor derived his usage from the current press accounts in the United States.

13. Quoted in Risjord, *Old Republicans,* 230.

14. *Ibid.,* 229; Remini, *Van Buren,* 23.

15. Adams, *Memoirs,* IV, 471, Dec. 6, 1819; V, 431–37, Nov. 30–Dec. 2, 1821.

16. Quote is from *ibid.,* V, 523, May 8, 1822; see *ibid.,* V, 474, Jan. 2, 1822.

17. *AC,* 17C1S, 1551, 1623, April 15, 20, 1822.

18. *AC,* 17C1S, 1540, April 13, 1822; Richardson, *Messages,* II, 119–26.

19. Wiltse, *Calhoun,* I, 232, 251–52.

20. *AC* 17C1S, Senate Executive Proceedings, 470–510, Jan. 22–Apr. 30, 1822. The political character of this rejection can be judged from the fact that the executive proceedings, which were ordinarily not made public, were immediately released. In view of the petty character of the factional conflicts of this era it should be noted that both Towson and Gadsden were on intimate terms with Jackson. However, there is no evidence that this was an anti-Jackson move. For the association of the officers with Jackson see Bassett, *Jackson,* I, 289; Sam Houston to Jackson, Feb. 4, 1827, Jackson, *Correspondence,* VI, 492; [Gadsden] to [Jackson], April 10, 1822, Jackson Papers, LC.

21. Adams, *Memoirs,* V, 486–88, April 8–12, 1822; Richardson, *Messages,* II, 129–36, April 13, 1822. Gadsden kept his former post and Towson was made Paymaster General.

22. Crawford to Gallatin, June 26, 1822, Gallatin Papers, NYHS.

23. *Ibid.*

24. Poinsett to Monroe, May 10, 1822, Monroe, LC.

25. Since none of these letters has been preserved, this account is based on Adams' summary of Monroe's statement to the Cabinet; Adams, *Memoirs,* VI, 390, June 21, 1824.

26. *Ibid.,* V, 321, Mar. 8, 1821.

27. May 23, 1821, *JM,* VI, 185.

28. Quote is from *ibid.* Fromentin was a former French priest who had come to the United States during the Revolution and married into a Maryland family. He later emigrated to Louisiana, where he practiced law. After the Restoration he left his wife to return to France to seek a church office. Failing in this, he came back to Louisiana. See William F. Keller, *The Nation's Advocate: Henry Marie Brackenridge and Young America* (U. of Pittsburgh, 1956), 278. Fromentin's Maryland connection may have been with the Winder family; see William H. Winder to Monroe, Nov. 24, 1821, Monroe, LC.

29. For a full account of the affair in Florida see Bassett, *Jackson,* I, 294–321. Bassett called this the "least credible [*sic*] episode" in Jackson's national career. The relevant documents are in *AC,* 17C1S, pp. 2295–578.

30. Monroe to Wirt, Oct. 7, 1821, Monroe, LC.

31. Adams, *Memoirs,* V, 365–77, Oct. 22–30, 1821.

32. *Ibid.,* V, 452, Dec. 18, 1821.

33. Richardson, *Messages,* II, 103–4, Dec. 3, 1821.

34. Adams to Joaquin de Anduaga, Nov. 2, 1821, Adams, *Writings,* VII, 183–89; Adams, *Memoirs,* V, 453, Dec. 18, 1821.

35. Monroe to Jackson, Dec. 31, 1821, *JM,* VI, 207; Adams, *Memoirs,* V, 472, Jan. 2, 1822.

36. Jackson to Monroe, July 26, 1822, draft, Jackson Papers, LC; Bassett, *Jackson,* I, 319–21.

37. Randolph's speech is not in the *Annals* (few speeches were carefully reported at this time), but it is mentioned in P. N. Nicholas to F. W. Gilmer, March 6, 1822, Gilmer Papers, U.Va.; Charles Yancey to Monroe, Oct. 27, 1821, William and Mary College Library.

38. For details of this complex affair see Bemis, *Adams,* I, 498–507, and Adams, *Memoirs,* V, 497–526.

39. Adams, *Memoirs,* IV, 74, April 4, 1818.

40. *Ibid.,* V, 508, April 30, 1822. Italics in original.

41. Richardson, *Messages,* II, 139, May 4, 1822.

42. Clay to Martin D. Hardin, June 23, 1822, Clay to Russell, July 9, 1822, Clay to Gales and Seaton, Nov. 22, 1822, all in Hopkins, *Clay,* III, 238–39, 252–56.

43. May 1822, *JM,* VI, 286–91.

44. May 18, 1822, Hunt, *Madison,* IX, 97.

45. Gallatin Papers, NYHS.

46. Remini, *Van Buren*, 59.

47. For a detailed account of Franco-American relations see Richard Aubrey McLemore, *Franco-American Relations, 1816–1836* (Louisiana State University Press, 1941), and Bemis, *Adams*, I, 448–56.

48. Monroe to Adams, July 12, 24, 27, Aug. 18, 1821, Adams, MHS; Adams to Monroe, July 25 (two letters of the same date), 1821, Crawford to Monroe, July 20, 1821, Monroe, LC; Crawford to Gallatin, May 13, 1821, Gallatin Papers, NYHS; Adams, *Memoirs*, V, 336–423, Mar. 26–Nov. 28, 1821.

49. Adams, *Memoirs*, VI, 27, June 21, 1822.

50. McLemore, *Franco-American Relations*, 28–35.

51. Gallatin was nominated for the Vice-Presidency on the Crawford ticket by the congressional caucus, but the opposition of Virginia leaders, who considered him responsible for perpetuating Hamiltonian policies in the Treasury, forced his withdrawal from the ticket before the election.

52. Richardson, *Messages*, II, 185–95, Dec. 3, 1822; Adams, *Memoirs*, VI, 99–110, Nov. 12–27, 1822.

53. For an account of the "A. B." affair see Wiltse, *Calhoun*, I, 258–63 and *passim*.

54. See Remini, *Van Buren*, 33–35; Smith Thompson to Van Buren, Mar. 17, 1823, Van Buren Papers, LC.

55. Smith Thompson to Van Buren, Mar. 25, 1823, Rufus King to Van Buren, April 28, 1823, Van Buren Papers, LC; S. L. Gouverneur to Monroe, April 12, 1823, Monroe Foundation.

56. Van Buren to Smith Thompson, April 15, 1823, Thompson to Van Buren, April 25, 1823, Van Buren Papers, LC; Thompson to Monroe, May 31, 1823, Monroe, LC; Monroe to Thompson, July 16, 1823, De Coppet Coll., Princeton. Monroe also considered John C. Spencer, a highly esteemed lawyer and son of Ambrose Spencer. However, he apparently ruled Spencer out on the ground of age—he was only thirty-five. See letter of S. L. Gouverneur cited fn. 55 *supra*.

CHAPTER 29

PRESIDENTIAL POLITICS AND DIPLOMACY

1. Perkins, *Castlereagh*, 259–82; Bemis, *Adams*, I, 279–98; Burt, *Brit. North Am.*, 399–412.

2. This issue was not finally resolved until 1826, when the two nations signed a convention providing for an indemnity to the United States of $1,204,960. Bemis, *Adams*, I, 293.

3. Adams, *Memoirs*, IV, 147–50, Oct. 29–30, 1818.

4. Mar. 7, 1819, *JM*, VI, 89–90.

5. Perkins, *Castlereagh*, 277–78.

6. Bemis, *Adams*, I, 410–12. An extensive account of all these controversies is in *ibid.*, I, 408–536.

7. *Ibid.*, I, 457; see also F. Lee Benns, *The American Struggle for the British West Indian Carrying-Trade* in *University of Indiana Studies*, X, No. 56 (March 1923), 53, 70–71; Perkins, *Castlereagh*, 231–32.

8. Benns, *West Indian Trade*, 68–70; Adams, *Memoirs*, IV, 495, 503–4, Jan. 3–13, 1820.

9. Adams, *Memoirs*, V, 519, May 7, 1822; Benns, *West Indian Trade*, 75–81.

10. Gallatin to Monroe, Feb. 4, 1822, Gallatin, *Writings*, III, 232.

11. Bemis, *Adams*, I, 458; Benns, *West Indian Trade*, 82–89, 92–98; Perkins, *Castlereagh*, 237.

12. Adams, *Memoirs*, VI, 164–67, July 18, 25, Aug. 1, 1823; Bemis, *Adams*, I, 436–37.

13. C. K. Webster, *The Foreign Policy of Castlereagh* (2 vols., London, 1931), II, 453–63; Bemis, *Adams*, I, 413.

14. Adams, *Memoirs*, VI, 37, June 22, 1822.

15. *Ibid.*, IV, 151–52, Oct. 30, 1818.

16. *AC*, 15C1S, 107, Jan. 12, 1818, and Appendix, 2574. This is the first resolution to be approved in either house. It has been incorrectly stated that a joint resolution was approved in 1817 proposing the cession of a limited right of search (see Bemis, *Adams*, I, 414–15). This error stems from Frank K. Klingberg, *The Anti-Slavery Movement in England* (New Haven, 1926), 166, which is cited by Bemis, *Adams*, I, 415, fn. 10. On February 11, 1817, a House committee chaired by Timothy Pickering made a report favoring the use of federal funds to remove free Negroes to Sierra Leone or for the purchase of a colony, if the first proposal was impractical. Attached to the report was a proposed joint resolution putting the recommendation in the form of a resolve and urging negotiations with European powers to terminate the slave trade. Nothing was said about the right of search. Attached to the report is a note that it was never called up, and hence the resolves were not acted upon. The text of this report is to be found in House Report #283, 27C3S (1843), 211–12. The Report of 1817 is technically numbered House Document #77, 14C2S, but is not included in any official publication prior to 1843.

17. Adams, *Memoirs*, V, 216–23, Dec. 23–30, 1819; Stratford Canning to George Canning, June 6, 1823, quoted in Hugh B. Soulsby, *Right of Search and the Slave Trade in Anglo-American Relations, 1814–1862* (Baltimore, 1931), 29.

18. L. P. Staudenraus, *African Colonization Movement, 1816–1865* (Columbia University Press, 1961), 29–30, 50–51.

19. Adams, *Memoirs*, IV, 292, Mar. 12, 1819.

20. *Ibid.*, IV, 436, Nov. 18, 1818; Staudenraus, *Colonization*, 52–55, 57–62; Richardson, *Messages*, II, 63–65, Dec. 17, 1819.

21. Adams, Memoirs, IV, 292–93, Mar. 12, 1819.

22. *AC,* 16C2S, HR, 1064–71, Feb. 9, 1821; *AC,* 17C1S, HR, 1535–38, April 11, 1822; Adams, *Memoirs,* VI, 428, Nov. 10, 1824; Soulsby, *Right of Search,* 29.

23. Adams, *Memoirs,* VI, 140, 362, June 4, 1823, May 27, 1824.

24. Soulsby, *Right of Search,* 26–30. Gallatin made this point in a private letter to Monroe, Feb. 4, 1822, Gallatin, *Writings,* III, 232.

25. Adams, *Memoirs,* VI, 148–51, June 19–20, 1823; Bemis, *Adams,* I, 428–29.

26. For a full account of these involved issues see Bemis, *Adams,* I, 471–74, 482–552.

27. Bemis, *Adams,* I, 433.

28. Richardson, *Messages,* II, 241; Adams, *Memoirs,* VI, 317, May 3, 1824.

29. Adams, *Memoirs,* VI, 338, May 18, 1824. John Holmes and Van Buren led the fight.

30. Richardson, *Messages,* II, 243–47.

31. Senate proceedings are in *Niles' Register,* June 12, 1824. The Senators opposing the treaty did not have a sufficient majority to defeat it, but were able to muster enough votes to prevent the administration from securing the two-thirds vote needed to approve the passages under attack. Rufus King maintained that the success of those hostile to the treaty was partly due to the fact that Southerners had been aroused by speeches in Parliament hailing the treaty as a step toward the total destruction of slavery. Adams, *Memoirs,* VI, 329, May 14, 1824.

32. Adams, *Memoirs,* VI, 345, May 21, 1824.

33. *Ibid.,* VI, 344–45, 356, 428, May 21, 25, Nov. 10, 1824; Van Buren to _____, draft, May 26, 1824, Van Buren Papers, LC; Bemis, *Adams,* I, 434–35.

34. Wirt to Monroe, July 5, 1824, Adams Papers, MHS; James Anderson to Monroe, Aug. 7, 1824, Monroe Foundation; Adams, *Memoirs,* VI, *passim;* Wiltse, *Calhoun,* I, 262–64.

35. Monroe to Adams, May 20, 1824, Adams Papers, MHS; Canning to Rush, Aug. 27, 1824, *ASPFR,* V, 364–65; Harold Temperley, *The Foreign Policy of Canning, 1822–1827* (London, 1925), 495–96.

36. Rush to Adams, Aug. 12, 1824, *ASPFR,* V, 533–58; Bemis, *Adams,* I, 463–64, 475–76.

37. Bemis, *Adams,* I, 517, 523–27.

38. Monroe to Madison, Aug. 2, 1824, *JM,* VII, 32–33.

CHAPTER 30

THE END OF AṄ AGE

1. Adams, *Memoirs,* VI, 196–97, Nov. 22, 1823.

2. *Ibid.,* VI, 228–29, Jan. 6–8, 1824.

3. Washington *Republican,* Feb. 5, 1824, referring to a story in the Washington

Gazette (a Crawford paper); Romulus Saunders to Bartlett Yancey, April 3, 1822, *North Carolina Historical Review,* VIII (1931), 438; Addington to Canning, Aug. 2, 1824, F.O. 5, v. 186; Monroe to John Taylor of Caroline, May 12, 1823, Washburn Papers, MHS.

4. On Crawford's illness see Wiltse, *Calhoun,* I, 277–78; Remini, *Van Buren,* 43, 67. The Richmond *Enquirer,* Sept. 26, 1823, described his illness as a bilious attack. There is some disagreement about the treatment which led to his collapse— it may have been an overdose of calomel. The fact that he was bled twenty-three times while in Virginia can scarcely have been beneficial; see Romulus Saunders to Bartlett Yancey, Dec. 31, 1823, *North Carolina Historical Review,* VIII (1931), 441.

5. Tobias Watkins to John Q. Adams, Sept. 14, 1824, Adams Papers, MHS. Except for one appearance in April, Crawford did not attend a Cabinet meeting after his illness began until Nov. 10, 1824; Adams, *Memoirs,* VI, 428. According to Adams his eyesight, speech and memory were still impaired.

6. Wirt to Monroe, July 5, 1824, Adams Papers, MHS; Adams, *Memoirs,* VI, 355, May 24, 1824; John McLean to John W. Taylor, Taylor Papers, NYHS.

7. Romulus Saunders to Bartlett Yancey, Dec. 10, 1824, *North Carolina Historical Review,* VIII (1931), 447.

8. *Enquirer,* Dec. 6, 1823.

9. Giles' letter, dated Mar. 10, 1824, was widely reprinted.

10. *Enquirer,* May 14, 1824.

11. Washington *Republican,* May 12, 1824. These letters were widely reprinted.

12. For a summary of the Edwards affair see Wiltse, *Calhoun,* I, 291–93; Edwards' letter to the Speaker, April 6, 1824, is in *AC,* 18C1S, April 19, 1824. Adams identified Tucker as the author of Crawford's report; Adams, *Memoirs,* VI, May 21, 1824.

13. Monroe to Wirt, Sept. 27, 1824, *JM,* VII, 37; Monroe to Daniel P. Cook, draft, April 27, 1826, Monroe, LC; Wirt to Monroe, May 1, 1826, Monroe, LC.

14. Adams, *Memoirs,* VI, 296–306, April 19–24, 1824.

15. Report is in *AC,* 18C1S, 2770–916. Forsyth was not a member of the committee.

16. Adams, *Memoirs,* VI, 388–98, June 21–22, July 1–3, 1824.

17. This account is based on Lucius D. Wilmerding, Jr., "James Monroe and the Furniture Fund," *New-York Historical Society Quarterly,* XLIV (1960), 133–49.

18. Adams, *Memoirs,* VI, 287, April 10, 1824.

19. May 13, 1824, *AC,* 18C1S, 2608.

20. Quote is from Monroe to Samuel L. Gouverneur, April 29, 1824, Monroe, NYPL; see also Monroe to _____, May 19, 1824, Monroe LC; Washington *Republican,* April 14, May 13, 1824.

21. Adams, *Memoirs,* VI, 289, April 11, 1824.

22. Dec. 2, 1817, Richardson, *Messages,* II, 16.

23. Annie H. Abel, "History of Indian Consolidation West of the Mississippi," *AHA Annual Report,* 1906, I, 288.

24. George D. Harmon, *Sixty Years of Indian Affairs . . . 1789–1850* (Chapel Hill, 1941), 160–65.

25. Richardson, *Messages,* II, 46, Nov. 16, 1818; Jefferson to Gallatin, Nov. 24, 1818, Ford, *Jefferson,* XI, 104–5.

26. See R. S. Cotterill, *The Southern Indians, The Story of the Civilized Tribes Before Removal* (Norman, Okla., 1954), and Abel, "Indian Consolidation," *loc. cit.,* I, 326–29.

27. Richardson, *Messages,* II, 68, Mar. 17, 1820; Adams, *Memoirs,* V. 21, Mar. 13, 1820.

28. Wiltse, *Calhoun,* I, 293–94; Cotterill, *Southern Indians,* 215–19; Abel, "Indian Consolidation," *loc. cit.,* I, 322–26; address of Georgia delegation is in *AC,* 18C1S, 462–71.

29. Monroe to James Barbour, Mar. 14, 16, 1824, *Bull. NYPL,* VI (1902), 26.

30. Richardson, *Messages,* II, 234–36, Mar. 30, 1824.

31. Ibid., II, 280–83; Wiltse, *Calhoun,* I, 296–97.

32. Cotterill, *Southern Indians,* 219–22. It is not clear to what extent Monroe was aware of the fraud involved in the negotiations. He later admitted that he had some doubts about the treaty, but he had considered it his duty to submit it. Monroe to S. L. Southard, Aug. 16, 1825, McGregor Collection, U.Va.

33. Richardson, *Messages,* II, 215–16, Dec. 2, 1823.

34. Edward Stanwood, *American Tariff Controversies in the Nineteenth Century* (2 vols., New York, 1904), 197–221; Risjord, *Old Republicans,* 246–48.

35. For documents relating to Lafayette's tour, see Edgar Ewing Brandon (ed.), *Lafayette: Guest of the Nation* (3 vols., Oxford, Ohio, 1950–58), I, 28.

36. Quote is from a letter of Oct. 18, 1824, *JM,* VII, 41; Adams, *Memoirs,* VI, 378–79, June 10, 1824; Lafayette to Monroe, May 10, 1824, Monroe, LC.

37. Brandon, *Lafayette,* II, 24–29, 46–47; Auguste Levasseur, *Lafayette in America* (2 vols., New York, 1829), I, 168–69.

38. Monroe to Jefferson, Oct. 18, 1824, *JM,* VII, 41; Lafayette to Monroe, Nov. 12, 1824, Monroe, LC; Adams, *Memoirs,* VII, 40, Aug. 6, 1825.

39. Monroe made a general recommendation in his annual message, but suggested the specific sum privately to friendly congressmen. Monroe to J. R. Poinsett, Dec. 13, 1824, Lafayette to Monroe, Dec. 23, 1824, Monroe, LC; Brandon, *Lafayette,* II, 170–72. Some congressmen, such as Clay, who voted for the grant, considered the sum excessive. Adams, *Memoirs,* 440, Dec. 12, 1824.

40. Quoted from account in *National Intelligencer* reprinted in Brandon, *Lafayette,* II, 180–81; Adams, *Memoirs,* VI, 457–58, Jan. 1, 1825.

41. Adams, *Memoirs*, VI, 500, Feb. 7, 1825.

42. Quotes are from Smith, *Washington Society*, 182–87; Cooper, *Notions of the Americans*, II, 183–84.

43. Adams, *Memoirs*, VI, 477–509, Jan. 24–Feb. 11, 1825; Adams to Monroe, Feb. 3, 1825, Monroe, LC.

44. To Samuel L. Gouverneur, Sept. 3, 1831, Southard Papers, Princeton.

45. S. L. Gouverneur to Southard, Sept. 4, 1831, *ibid.* Gouverneur confirmed Southard's account in this letter. Neither was apparently present at the conference; presumably Monroe told them about the quarrel.

46. Adams, *Memoirs*, VI, 508–9, Feb. 11, 1825; Memo in Monroe's hand dated Feb. 11, 14, 1825, photostat, Monroe, LC; Monroe to Adams, Mar. 3, 1825, Adams, MHS.

47. Adams, *Memoirs*, VI, 512, Feb. 25, 1825.

48. *Ibid.*, VI, 518–19, Mar. 4, 1825; *National Intelligencer* account reprinted in Richmond *Enquirer,* Mar. 8, 1825.

49. Richardson, *Messages*, II, 294–99.

50. Adams, *Memoirs*, 527–28, Mar. 9, 1825.

CHAPTER 31

LAST YEARS

1. Monroe to C. J. Ingersoll, April 25, 1827, Ingersoll Papers, PHS.

2. Brant, *Madison*, VI, 460; description by Egbert Watson cited in Gilman, *Monroe*, 186–88.

3. Monroe to S. L. Gouverneur, Nov. 2, 1825, Monroe, NYPL; S. L. Gouverneur to Monroe, Nov. 13, 1825, William and Mary College Library. When it was again suggested that he run in 1827, Monroe promptly declined. Monroe to James McIlhany, January 1827, *JM,* VII, 90–91.

4. Monroe to James Barbour, Oct. 20, 1826, *JM,* VII, 86; S. L. Southard to Monroe, Dec. 16, 1827, John Taliaferro to Monroe, Dec. 15, 1827, Monroe, LC.

5. Monroe to S. L. Southard, Oct. 6, 1828, Southard Papers, Princeton; Southard to Monroe, Oct. 28, 1828, Monroe, NYPL; Monroe to N. P. Trist, Aug. 13, 1828, Trist Papers, LC.

6. Monroe to [Smith Thompson], Sept. 12, 1828, photostat, PHS; John McLean to Monroe, Sept. 13, 19, 1828, Monroe to McLean, Sept. 29, 1828, J. Q. Adams to Monroe, Jan. 17, 1829, Monroe, LC.

7. Memo of sheep at Oak Hill, 1817, Monroe Foundation, Fredericksburg; Monroe to Lafayette, May 30, 1826, Lafayette to Monroe, Nov. 28, 1826, Monroe to S. L. Gouverneur, June 25, 1825, Aug. 16, 1826, all in Monroe, NYPL; a list of

appraisement of the late James Monroe's property at Oak Hill, Jan. 22, 1836, Monroe Foundation, Fredericksburg.

8. George Hay to S. L. Southard, Mar. 13, 1828, Southard Papers, Princeton.

9. Monroe to S. L. Gouverneur, Dec. 21, 1825, Monroe, NYPL; George Hay to S. L. Southard, Aug. 13, Sept. 10, 1825, Southard Papers, Princeton; Monroe to Madison, May 13, Aug. 5, 1828, *JM*, VII, 167–78, 277; Monroe to Joseph H. Swift, Sept. 12, 1828, photostat in LC from original in the West Point Library.

10. Monroe to S. L. Gouverneur, July 31, Dec. 21, 1824, Feb. 9, 1825, April 10, 1829, Lafayette to Monroe, Dec. 27, 1824, June 29, 1828, all in Monroe, NYPL; Lafayette to Monroe, June 17, 1829, Monroe, LC; S. L. Gouverneur to Monroe, June 15, 1826, Monroe Foundation, Fredericksburg. James Monroe Gouverneur died in an asylum on Apr. 14, 1865. See Boswell R. Hoes to John B. Larner, Nov. 4, 1911, McGregor Collection, U.Va.

11. Gilman, *Monroe,* 186–88.

12. *Ibid.,* 190.

13. Egbert Watson to Daniel M. Railey, Aug. 1, 1828, typescript, U.Va.

14. Egbert Watson to Daniel M. Railey, Feb. 25, 1829, typescript, U.Va.

15. Adams, *Memoirs,* VII, 40–43, Aug. 6–10, 1825; Robert D. Ward, *An Account of General La Fayette's Visit to Virginia, in the Years, 1824–'25 . . .* (Richmond, Va., 1881), 108.

16. Ward, *La Fayette's Visit to Virginia,* 110–17.

17. Gilman, *Monroe,* 194.

18. Monroe to Madison, Aug. 5, 1828, *JM*, VII, 177.

19. Philip Alexander Bruce, *History of the University of Virginia, 1819–1919* (5 vols., New York, 1920–22), I, 167, 188–91; Madison to Monroe, Sept. 20, 1825, Monroe, LC.

20. Quoted in Brant, *Madison,* VI, 450.

21. Bruce, *University of Virginia,* II, 298–30. Bruce, accepting the recollections of a former student, states that Monroe participated in the meeting of the Board of Visitors held in the Rotunda on October 3, 1825, immediately after the riots, when both students and faculty were summoned before the Visitors. However, the manuscript minutes of the Visitors (U.Va.) do not list Monroe as among those present. Evidence based on his correspondence indicates that he was then at Oak Hill. Monroe apparently did not attend any meetings until 1826. Monroe to S. L. Gouverneur, Aug. 16, Sept. 5, 1826, Monroe, NYPL.

22. Monroe's draft report and a copy are in Monroe, NYPL. He sent it to Madison in 1830. Monroe to Madison, July 2, 1830, *JM*, VII, 214–15. Bruce does not mention the report in his *History of the University of Virginia.* The University continued the practice of electing the chief administrative officer from the faculty until the beginning of the twentieth century, when the office of president was established.

23. This figure represents an estimate based on various statements made by Monroe. His principal debts were: $43,000 originally held by the Bank of Columbia but later transferred to the Bank of the United States; $16,600 to banks in Virginia; $9,000 to John Jacob Astor; $3,500 to individuals. There was also a large debt (the exact sum was never stated) held by Baring Brothers, the English banking firm. Monroe to N. P. Trist, April 25, 1827, Trist Papers, LC; Monroe to _____, June 30, 1826, Cannaroe Papers, PHS; Monroe to Lafayette, Nov. 30, 1826, Monroe to S. L. Gouverneur, Jan. 20, 1826, Monroe, NYPL.

24. His indebtedness was then rumored to be $40,000. See William Plumer to William Plumer, Jr., Apr. 5, 1824, Plumer Papers, LC; Adams, *Memoirs,* VI, 442, Dec. 16, 1824.

25. Monroe to _____, April 2, 1823, Monroe, LC; appraisal by Hugh Nelson and John Watson, Jan. 31, 1823, Monroe, LC; Jefferson thought this a fair valuation, Jefferson to Madison, Feb. 21, 1823, Monroe, LC. The estate was broken down as follows: 2,000 acres of "mountain land," $25 an acre; 1,500 acres at $10 an acre; the buildings and stock bringing the total to $67,000. Monroe was handicapped in selling the land by his immediate need of money, which did not permit him to sell it on long terms. Monroe to N. P. Trist, Oct. 1, 1827, Trist Papers, LC.

26. Monroe to _____, Nov. 6, 1825, Monroe LC; Monroe to C. J. Ingersoll, April 25, 1827, Ingersoll, PHS. This debt, originally held by the Bank of Columbia, was taken over by the Bank of the United States, when Monroe retired.

27. I have relied on Wilmerding, *James Monroe, Public Claimant,* in discussing these claims, although not entirely agreeing with his critical judgment of Monroe.

28. Wilmerding, *Monroe, Claimant,* 53–75.

29. Monroe to Jackson, July 3, 1825, *JM,* VII, 57; Monroe to McLean, Aug. 7, 1825, *JM,* VII, 59–60; Monroe to S. L. Gouverneur, Dec. 2, 1825, Monroe, LC; there are many letters in Monroe, LC, from McLean expressing his concern.

30. Monroe to S. L. Gouverneur, Dec. 21, 1825, Monroe, NYPL; S. L. Gouverneur to Monroe, Washington, Feb. 26, 1826, Monroe, LC; Wilmerding, *Monroe, Claimant,* 81–82.

31. Monroe to [Joseph Brooke?], Mar. 15, 1826, *JM,* VII, 70–78. Monroe to [S. D. Ingham], May 17, 1826, draft; Monroe, LC.

32. Ringgold to Monroe, May 4, 1826, Monroe, NYPL; Monroe to Ringgold, May 8, 1826, *JM,* VII, 80–84.

33. *Register of Debates,* 19C1S, 763, 846, 852, 1188–91, 1628–31, 2688.

34. Monroe to S. L. Gouverneur, Feb. 15, 1826, Monroe, NYPL; Monroe to Jefferson, Feb. 13, 23, 1826, *JM,* VII, 67–70.

35. Monroe to S. L. Gouverneur, Aug. 16, 1826, Monroe, NYPL.

36. Monroe to S. L. Gouverneur, June 15, 1826, Monroe Foundation, Fredericksburg; Monroe to S. L. Gouverneur, June 1, July 12, 1826, Monroe, NYPL.

37. Monroe to S. L. Gouverneur, Mar. 19, 1827, Monroe, NYPL; Monroe to

Thomas Newton, Feb. 26, 1827, *JM*, VII, 113. The Bank declined Monroe's original proposal that it accept in payment of his debt 940 acres of land valued at $20 per acre and an additional 600 valued at $10 per acre. The Bank agreed that Monroe should receive any balance in excess of his debt after the land was sold; apparently it did not bring in a surplus when it was sold by the Bank in 1828. Monroe to S. L. Gouverneur, Mar. 19, 1827, Monroe, NYPL; Monroe to C. J. Ingersoll, April 25, 1827, Ingersoll Papers, PHS. The remaining 707 acres of land which Monroe owned in Albemarle were mortgaged to the Bank of Richmond. Monroe to S. L. Gouverneur, Jan. 11, 1828, Monroe, NYPL. One of the rare specimens of Mrs. Monroe's handwriting is found on the conveyance to the Bank of the United States, dated Mar. 22, 1827, Autograph Coll., PHS.

38. Thomas Swann to Nicholas Biddle, Dec. 7, 1826, Biddle Papers, PHS.

39. Monroe to N. P. Trist, May 28, 1828, Trist Papers, LC; Monroe to S. L. Gouverneur, Jan. 18, 1828, Monroe, NYPL.

40. Monroe was particularly pressed for money at this time for he had to aid S. L. Gouverneur, who was in financial difficulties and threatened with suit for fraud. The circumstances are not clear, but the suit was dropped; New York *Evening Post,* Dec. 12, 1826; Monroe to Gouverneur, Aug. 21, 1828, Monroe Foundation, Fredericksburg.

41. Wilmerding, *Monroe, Claimant,* 86–87. The memoir, entitled "The Memoir of James Monroe, Esq., relating to his Unsettled Claims upon the People and Government of the United States," is in *JM*, VII, 243–309; McLean to Monroe, Nov. 11, 1826, Monroe, LC.

42. John H. Eaton to Jackson, Jan. 27, Feb. 4, 1827, Memo in Jackson's hand, [Feb.–Mar. 1831], Jackson Papers, LC; John McLean to Monroe, Feb. 1, 1827, Monroe, LC; Tench Ringgold to Monroe, Feb. 10, 1827, S. L. Southard to Monroe, Feb. 11, 1827, Monroe Foundation, Fredericksburg; Monroe to Southard, July 9, 1827, Southard Papers, Princeton.

43. Monroe to Hugh L. White, Jan. 26, Feb. 9, 1827, *JM*, VII, 93–112; Tench Ringgold to Monroe, Jan. 10, Feb. 4, 1827, Monroe, LC.

44. Hugh L. White to Monroe, Jan. 29, 1827, Monroe, LC.

45. Ringgold to Monroe, Sept. 30, 1827, Monroe, NYPL; Ringgold to Monroe, Oct. 10, 1827, McLean to Monroe, Nov. 15, 1827, Monroe, LC.

46. Quote is from S. L. Southard to Monroe, Dec. 16, 1827, Monroe, LC; John Taliaferro also wrote (Dec. 15, 1827, Monroe, LC) asking Monroe to be Adams' running mate.

47. S. D. Ingham to Monroe, Jan. 4, 1828, Gratz Coll., PHS; S. D. Ingham to Monroe, Feb. 1828, Monroe, LC.

48. J. C. Cabell to Madison, Jan. 12, 1828, Madison to Monroe, Jan. 23, Feb. 5, 1828, Madison Papers, LC; Monroe to Madison, Jan. 18, 29, Feb. 15, 1828, *JM*, VII, 144–52.

49. Monroe to Judge Brooke, Feb. 21, 1828, *JM,* VII, 153–54; Madison to Monroe, Feb. 5, 1828, Madison Papers, LC.

50. Monroe to [N. P. Trist], ca. 1828, Trist Papers, LC; James P. Preston to Monroe, Mar. 23, 1828, C. J. Ingersoll to Monroe, April 20, 1828, Monroe, NYPL; Monroe to Hugh Nelson, Jan. 27, 1829, *JM,* VII, 189–92.

51. David Michie to Monroe, Dec. 9, 1828, Monroe, NYPL. The proposal to circulate a petition had been discussed with Monroe in 1827, but postponed until Monroe could assemble further documentation. Monroe to S. L. Gouverneur, Mar. 19, 1827, Monroe, NYPL.

52. Wilmerding, *Monroe, Claimant,* 93–110.

53. Monroe to S. L. Gouverneur, Mar. 30, Apr. 10, 1829, Monroe, NYPL; McLean to Monroe, April 4, 1829, Jackson to George Hay, Apr. 19, 1829, Monroe, LC. Reasons for Charles Hay's removal were never explicitly stated but Adams implies that political considerations were involved. Adams, *Memoirs,* VIII, 131, Apr. 6, 1829. For Gouverneur's association with Calhoun see "Calhoun-Gouverneur Correspondence, 1823–36," *Bull. NYPL,* III, 324–38.

54. Gordon W. Jones, *The Library of James Monroe* (Bibliographical Society of the University of Virginia, Charlottesville, Va., 1967).

55. Lafayette to Monroe, Feb. 24, 1825, Monroe, LC; the manuscript is in Monroe, NYPL. His grandson, Samuel L. Gouverneur, published it in 1867.

56. Gilman, *Monroe,* 192–93; Hay obviously had a low opinion of the work, for he told Adams that Monroe had written a "dissertation on government which nobody would read." Adams, *Memoirs,* VIII, 131, April 6, 1829. The manuscript autobiography is in Monroe, NYPL. In 1959 it was edited and published by Stuart Gerry Brown.

57. For accounts of the convention see Charles Henry Ambler, *Sectionalism in Virginia from 1776 to 1861* (Chicago, 1910); Hugh Blair Grigsby, *The Virginia Convention of 1829–30. A Discourse Delivered Before the Virginia Historical Society at Their Annual Meeting . . . Dec. 15, 1853* (Richmond, 1854); Brant, *Madison,* VI, 460–67.

58. Monroe to Wirt, Oct. 24, 1828, Monroe to Adams, Dec. 17, 1828, Monroe to Madison, Mar. 20, June 25, Sept. 10, 1829, *JM,* VII, 182–206; Tench Ringgold to Monroe, Dec. 29, 1829, Monroe to Madison, Oct. 4 1829, Monroe, NYPL.

59. Monroe to S. M. Edwards, April 6, 1829, *JM,* VII, 194–95; S. M. Edwards to Monroe, April 14, 1829, Monroe, LC; Brant, *Madison,* VI, 461–62. Later, however, public resolutions were adopted in Loudoun criticizing Monroe's stand. Burr Powell to Monroe, Nov. 27, 1829, Monroe, NYPL.

60. Monroe to Madison, Oct. 4, 1829, Monroe, NYPL.

61. *Proceedings and Debates of the Virginia State Convention of 1829–30* (Richmond, 1830), 148–51, 236–37, Nov. 2, 9, 1829.

62. Ambler, *Sectionalism,* 162–63.

63. *Ibid.*, 168–70; *Debates, Convention of 1829*, 439–82, Nov. 21–26, 1829.

64. *Debates, Convention of 1829*, 620, Dec. 12, 1829; Monroe to [James Barron], Jan. 11, 12, 18, 1830, William and Mary Library; Ringgold to Monroe, Dec. 29, 1829, Monroe, NYPL.

65. Wilmerding, *Monroe, Claimant*, 110–11. Mercer increased the amount recommended the previous year to $68,000 to provide for interest since the earlier report.

66. S. L. Gouverneur to Monroe, May 31, 1830, Monroe, NYPL.

67. See detailed account of this letter above in Chapter 23. See also Wiltse, *Calhoun*, II, 76–81. The relevant correspondence involved in the renewal of this conflict in 1830 is printed in Richard C. Crallé (ed.), *The Works of John C. Calhoun* (6 vols., New York, 1857), VI, 349–445.

68. Letters from Monroe to Calhoun are in *JM*, VII, 207ff.; Calhoun's letters are in Monroe, LC; Monroe to S. L. Gouverneur, May 17, 1830, Monroe, NYPL; Monroe to Wirt, May 30, 1830, Wirt Papers, MdHS.

69. Crawford to Monroe, July 5, 1830, Calhoun to Monroe, Jan. 21, 1831; Monroe, LC.

70. Monroe to S. L. Gouverneur, June 9, 1830, Monroe, NYPL; Monroe to Madison, July 2, 1830, *JM*, VII, 213.

71. Monroe to S. L. Gouverneur, June 6, 9, 1830, Monroe, NYPL; Monroe to Gouverneur, Aug. 11, 1830, Monroe, LC. The causes of the quarrel are not clear, but as a result Eliza was determined that Ashfield (the estate given her by her father) should be left to Hortensia in such a way that Rogers would not be able to control it. Monroe to Mrs. Hay, July 2, 1830, Monroe Foundation, Fredericksburg.

72. Monroe to S. L. Gouverneur, Sept. 23, 1830; entries in day book of Joseph Hawkins, overseer at Oak Hill, give dates of death; both are in Monroe, NYPL. The exact nature of Mrs. Monroe's illness is not known, although it was of a chronic character. For many years she had suffered from convulsions which left her unconscious. In 1826, she had been badly burned when she fell into the fireplace during a convulsion (she had been alone in the room at the time). Monroe to S. L. Gouverneur, Dec. 29, 1826, Monroe, NYPL.

73. Gilman, *Monroe*, 195.

74. Monroe to N. P. Trist, Nov. 11, 1830, Trist Papers, LC.

75. Dec. 9, 1830, Johns Deposit, U.Va.

76. Adams to Southard, Feb. 9, 1831, Southard Papers, Princeton; Monroe to Wirt, Feb. 4, 1831, Wirt Papers, MdHS; Monroe's statement [Jan. 27, 1831] is in *JM*, VII, 218.

77. Wiltse, *Calhoun*, II, 96; *Register of Debates*, 21C2S, 614. Although the Senate did not approve the measure until March 2, the issue never seems to have been in doubt. Edward Livingston used the occasion to reassert his brother's claim

for sole credit for the Louisiana Purchase, but he voted for Monroe's claim. *Register of Debates*, 21C2S, 329–33, Mar. 2, 1831.

78. Wilmerding, *Monroe, Claimant,* 111–19.

79. *Register of Debates,* 21C2S, 426–49, 614, Jan. 7, Feb. 4, 1831.

80. Adams, *Memoirs,* VIII, 260, Dec. 30, 1830; Monroe to S. L. Gouverneur, Jan. 9, 1831, John McLean to Gouverneur, Jan. 3, 1831, Monroe, NYPL. Burrows, a friend of Gouverneur's, was a rather eccentric and erratic figure. He was also on good terms with Nicholas Biddle, whom he was helping to advance the cause of the Bank of the United States. On Jan. 7, 1831, Burrows wrote Monroe asking his views about the renewal of the charter. Monroe replied on Jan. 20 with a strong endorsement of the Bank, stressing its importance both in regulating the currency and in lending money to the United States. This letter was published several months after Monroe died. Govan, *Biddle,* 147ff., 190–96; *Niles' Register,* Oct. 1, 1831, 82–83.

81. Monroe to John H. Cocke, Apr. 15, 1831, U.Va.; Monroe to Madison, Apr. 11, 1831, *JM,* VII, 231.

82. Adams, *Memoirs,* VIII, 360, Apr. 27, 1831.

83. Copy of will dated May 16, 1831, Monroe, LC; Ringgold to S. L. Gouverneur, June 13, 1831, Monroe, NYPL. The exact size and disposition of his estate has not been traced. The Gouverneurs retained Oak Hill until 1855. It may have been in connection with the division of the estate that they borrowed $16,000 on Oak Hill in 1837 (Mrs. Hay left for Europe the following year and remained there until her death). See Loudoun County Deeds, Book 4I, 150–53, photostat, U.Va. According to Edward Coles, who was in New York in 1832, the Gouverneurs were very secretive about the size of the estate, but he believed that the only reason they were able to salvage anything was the decsion of Baring Brothers not to press for the repayment of the loan made to Monroe many years before. Coles to Dolley P. Madison, New York, Feb. 22, 1832, *WMQ,* 2nd ser., VII (1927), 39.

84. Monroe to Madison, Apr. 11, 1831, and Madison's reply, Apr. 27, 1831, are in *JM,* VII, 231–34.

85. J. Rhea to Monroe, June 3, 1831, Monroe, LC; S. L. Gouverneur to Wirt, June 11, 1831, copy, Wirt to Gouverneur, June 16, 1831, Monroe, LC. Wirt's letter is printed in part in *JM,* VII, 234, fn. 1. The deposition is in *JM,* VII, 234–36. The affair did not end at this point. A year after Monroe's death, when wide publicity was given to Rhea's version, Gouverneur published Monroe's deposition, and was promptly removed from his postmastership. Wiltse, *Calhoun,* II, 431, fn. 49; there are letters relating to this action in the Gouverneur Papers, NYPL.

86. Ringgold to Madison, July 7, 1831, Madison Papers, LC.

87. *Niles' Weekly Register,* July 23, 1831. In 1858, Monroe's remains were removed to Richmond by the state of Virginia for reburial in Hollywood Cemetery. Governor Henry A. Wise's plan of reburying Jefferson and Madison at the same place was never executed. [Udolpho Wolfe (ed.)], *Grand Civic and Military*

Demonstration in Honor of the Removal of the Remains of James Monroe . . . from New-York to Virginia (New York, 1858).

88. The contemporary press was full of such accounts; those relating to Virginia are in the Richmond *Enquirer,* July 12–27, 1831.

89. John Quincy Adams, *The Lives of James Madison and James Monroe* (Buffalo, N.Y., 1850). There are many editions of this work. The life of Monroe consists of Adams' eulogy (delivered Aug. 25, 1831) with an appendix summarizing Monroe's administration year by year. The life of Madison was composed in the same manner.

90. *Ibid.,* 293–95.

BIBLIOGRAPHY

A. Manuscripts
B. Public Documents: Manuscript
    1. United States
    2. Foreign
    3. State
C. Public Documents: Printed
D. Newspapers
E. Contemporary Writings
F. Books and Articles

A. MANUSCRIPTS

Library of Congress.
    Biddle Papers; Breckinridge Papers; Consular Correspondence; Jackson Papers; Jefferson Papers; Madison Papers; Monroe Papers; Plumer Papers; Randolph-Garnett Transcripts; Rives Papers; Smith Papers; Thornton Papers; Van Buren Papers; Washington Papers.
Massachusetts Historical Society.
    Adams Family Papers; Coolidge Papers; T. H. Perkins Diary; Pickering Papers; Ridley Papers; Washburn Papers.
New-York Historical Society.
    Gallatin Papers; Livingston Papers; John W. Taylor Papers.
New York Public Library.
    Barbour Papers; Emmet Collection; Gouverneur Papers; Madison Papers; Monroe Papers; Swartwout Papers.
Pennsylvania Historical Society.
    Cannaroe Papers; Gratz Collection; Hornor Papers; Ingersoll Papers; Vaux Papers.

Alderman Library, University of Virginia.

Gilmer Papers; Johns Deposit; McDowell Papers; Pleasanton Papers; Creed Taylor Papers; Watson Papers.

Other Collections.

Thomas H. Bayley Memorandum on a Conversation With John Marshall, Virginia State Library, Richmond; Breckinridge-Marshall Papers, Filson Club, Louisville, Ky.; Butler Papers, New York State Library, Albany; Gardner Papers, New York State Library; Monroe Papers, Monroe Foundation, Fredericksburg, Va.; Southard Papers, Princeton University Library; James Taylor Reminiscences, Filson Club; Weedon Papers, Chicago Historical Society; O. H. Williams Papers, Wirt Papers, Maryland Historical Society, Baltimore, Md.

B. PUBLIC DOCUMENTS: MANUSCRIPT

1. *United States.*

Records of the State Department, War Department, Treasury Department, Navy Department and Office of the U.S. Attorney General, all in National Archives, Washington, D.C.

2. *Foreign.*

France: Archives des Affaires Etrangères, Correspondance Politique, Etats-Unis, photostats, Library of Congress. Cited as AECPEU.

Great Britain: Public Records Office, Foreign Affairs, Series 5. Cited as F.O. 5. Photostats, Library of Congress.

3. *State.*

Executive Papers, Executive Letter Book, Journals of the Governor's Council, all in Virginia State Library, Richmond, Va.

C. PUBLIC DOCUMENTS: PRINTED

American Archives. . . . Edited by Peter Force, fifth Series, *Military Affairs.* 3 vols., Washington, D.C., 1848–53.

American State Papers, Foreign Relations. Edited under the authority of Congress by Walter Lowrie and Mathew St. Clair Clark. 6 vols., Washington, D.C., 1832–59. Cited as *ASPFR.*

American State Papers, Military Affairs. Edited under the authority of Congress by Walter Lowrie and Mathew St. Clair Clark. 7 vols., 1832–61.

Annals of Congress, 1789–1824. 38 vols., Washington, D.C., 1832–61. Cited as *AC.*

Archives of Maryland, vol. 4, *Judicial and Testamentary Business of the Provincial Court, 1637–1650.* Edited by William Hand Brown. Baltimore, 1887.

Campbell, Charles., ed. *Orderly Book of That Portion of the American Army Stationed at or near Williamsburg, Va.,, under the Command of General Andrew Lewis, from March 18, 1776 to August 28, 1777.* Richmond, Va., 1860.

Commager, Henry Steele, ed. *Documents in American History.* 2 vols., 5th ed., New York, 1949.

Congressional Globe. Washington, D.C., 1834–77.

Documentary History of the Constitution of the United States. Department of State, Bureau of Rolls. 5 vols., Washington, D.C., 1894–1905.

Elliot, Jonathan. *Debates in the Several State Conventions on the Adoption of the Federal Constitution.* 5 vols., Philadelphia, 1836.

Fauchet, Joseph. *Mémoire sur les Etats Unis d'Amérique.* Edited by Carl Ludwig Lokke. AHA, *Annual Report,* I, 1936, 83–123.

Journals of the Continental Congress. Edited by Worthington C. Ford *et al.* 34 vols., Washington, D.C., 1904–37.

Journals of the Council of State of Virginia. 5 vols., Richmond, 1931.

Manning, William R., ed. *Diplomatic Correspondence of the United States Concerning the Independence of the Latin-American Nations.* 3 vols., New York, 1925.

Mayo, Bernard, ed. *Instructions to the British Ministers to the United States, 1791–1812.* AHA, *Annual Report,* III, 1936.

Proceedings and Debates of the Virginia State Convention of 1829–30. Richmond, 1830.

The Register of Debates in the Congress of the United States. 14 vols., Washington, D.C., 1825–37.

Richardson, James Daniel, ed. *Messages and Papers of the Presidents, 1789–1897.* 11 vols., Washington, D.C., 1875–1893.

Thorpe, Francis Newton, ed. *Federal and State Constitutions and Organic Laws . . . of the United States.* 7 vols., Washington, D.C., 1909.

United States Senate. [Compilation of] *Reports of the Committee of Foreign Relations of the United States Senate, 1789–1901.* 8 vols., Washington, 1901.

United States Senate. *Executive Journals.*

Virginia General Assembly. *Acts* [various dates].

Virginia House of Delegates. *Journals* [various dates].

D. NEWSPAPERS

Albany, N.Y., *Advertiser.*

Baltimore, Md., *Niles' Weekly Register.*

Boston, Mass., *Columbian Centinel.*

New York, N.Y., *American Citizen; Daily Advertiser; Diary; Evening Post; Gazette and General Advertiser; Greenleaf's New York Journal; Herald.*

Philadelphia, Pa., *Dunlap's American Advertiser; National Gazette.*

Richmond, Va., *Enquirer; Examiner; Spirit of '76; Virginia Argus; Virginia Gazette and General Advertiser; Virginia Independent Chronicle.*

Washington, D.C., *National Intelligencer.*

E. CONTEMPORARY WRITINGS

Adams, John Quincy. *The Lives of James Madison and James Monroe.* Buffalo, N.Y., 1850.

————. *Memoirs.* Edited by Charles Francis Adams. 12 vols., Philadelphia, 1874–77.

————. See Worthington C. Ford., ed.

Ames, Fisher. *Works of Fisher Ames. With a Selection from his Speeches and Correspondence.* . . . Edited by Seth Ames. 2 vols., Boston, 1854.

Ballagh, James Curtiss, ed. *Letters of Richard Henry Lee.* 2 vols., New York, 1914.

Bassett, John Spencer, ed. *Correspondence of Andrew Jackson.* 7 vols., Washington, D.C., 1928–35.

Bayard, James A. *Papers, 1796–1815.* AHA, *Annual Report,* II, 1913.

Bigelow, Abijah. "Letters." *Proc. Am. Ant. Soc.,* XL (1930), 305–406.

Bland, Thordorick, Jr. *The Bland Papers.* 2 vols., Petersburg, Va., 1840–43.

Boyd, Julian P., ed. *Papers of Thomas Jefferson.* 17 vols., Princeton, N.J., 1950–.

Brown, Everett S. *The Missouri Compromises and Presidential Politics 1820–1825 from the Letters of William Plumer, Junior.* St. Louis, Mo., 1926.

Burnett, Edmund C., ed. *Letters of Members of the Continental Congress.* 8 vols., Washington, D.C., 1921–36.

Butterfield, L. H., ed. *Letters of Benjamin Rush.* 2 vols., Princeton, N.J., 1951.

Calhoun, John C. See Richard C. Crallé, Robert Meriwether, eds.

"Calhoun-Gouverneur Correspondence." *Bull. NYPL,* III (1899), 324–28.

[Callender, James Thomson]. *History of the United States for 1796.* . . . Philadelphia, 1797.

————. *Prospect before Us.* Richmond, Va., 1800.

Channing, Edward T. *An Oration Delivered on [July 4, 1817].* . . . Boston, 1817.

Chilton, John. "Letters." *Tyler's Quarterly of History and Genealogy,* XII (1930), 90–6.

Clark, George Rogers. *Papers.* Edited by James Alton Pease. In Illinois State Historical Library, *Collections,* XIX, Springfield, Ill., 1924.

Clay, Henry. See James F. Hopkins, ed.

Clinton, George. *Public Papers.* Edited by Hugh Hastings. 10 vols., Albany, N.Y., 1904.

Cooper, James Fenimore. *Notions of the Americans.* Intro. by Robert E. Spiller. 2 vols., New York, 1963.

Crallé, Richard C., ed. *The Works of John C. Calhoun.* 6 vols., New York, 1857.

Crowninshield, Mary B. *Letters of Mary Boardman Crowninshield, 1815–1816.* Edited by Francis Boardman Crowninshield. Cambridge, Mass., 1905.

[Cutts, Lucia B.] *Memoirs and Letters of Dolly Madison . . . Edited by Her Grandniece.* New York, 1886.

Emerson, Ralph Waldo. *Letters.* Edited by Ralph L. Rusk. 6 vols., Columbia University, 1939.

[de Montlezun, Baron]. *Souvenirs des Antilles, Voyages en 1815 et 1816 aux États Unis.* . . . 2 vols., Paris, 1818.

de Neuville, Hyde, Baron. *Mémoires et Souvenirs.* 3 vols., Paris, 1890.

Fearon, Henry Bradshaw. *Sketches of America: A Narrative of a Journey . . . through . . . America.* . . . London, 1819.

Fitzpatrick, John C., ed. *Writings of George Washington.* 39 vols., Washington, D.C., 1931–44.

Ford, Paul Leicester, ed. *Pamphlets on the Constitution of the United States.* . . . New York, 1888.

———. *Writings of Thomas Jefferson.* 10 vols., New York, 1892–99.

Ford, Worthington C., ed. *Writings of John Quincy Adams.* 7 vols., New York, 1913–17.

Gerry, E., Jr. *Diary of Elbridge Gerry, Jr.* Edited by Claude G. Bowers. New York, 1927.

Hamilton, Alexander. See Henry Cabot Lodge, ed.

Hamilton, Stanislaus Murray, ed. *Writings of James Monroe.* 7 vols., New York, 1898–1903. Cited as *JM.*

Hilliard, G. S., ed. *Memoir, Autobiography, and Correspondence of Jeremiah Mason.* Cambridge, Mass., 1873.

Holland, Elizabeth, Lady. *Journal (1791–1811).* Edited by the Earl of Ilchester. 2 vols., New York, 1909.

Hopkins, James F., and Hargreaves, Mary W. M., eds. *The Papers of Henry Clay.* 2 vols., University of Kentucky, 1959–.

Hunt, Gaillard, ed. *The Writings of James Madison.* 9 vols., New York, 1908.

Jackson, Andrew. See John Spencer Bassett, ed.

Jay, John. *Correspondence and Public Papers.* Edited by Henry P. Johnston. 4 vols., New York, 1890.

Jefferson, Thomas. See Julian Boyd, Paul L. Ford, A. Lipscomb, eds.

"Journal of the President and Masters of William and Mary College, May, 1775–November, 1775." *WMQ,* Ser. 1, XV (1935), 1–14, 134–42.

King, Charles. *Life and Correspondence of Rufus King.* 6 vols., New York, 1894–98.

Klinkowström, Axel, Baron. "Letters." *The American-Scandinavian Review,* XIX (1931), 394–402.

Lee, Charles. *Papers* in New-York Historical Society, *Collections.* 4 vols., New York, 1871–74.

Lee, Richard Henry. See James Curtiss Ballagh, ed.

Letters on the Richmond Party. Washington, D.C., 1823.

Levasseur, Auguste. *Lafayette in America....* 2 vols., New York, 1829.

Lipscomb, A., and Berg, Albert, eds. *Writings of Thomas Jefferson.* 20 vols., Washington, D.C., 1900–1904.

Livingston, Robert R. "Letters." Edited by Edward Alexander Parson. *Proc. Am. Ant. Soc.,* N.S., LII (1942), 363–407.

Lodge, Henry Cabot, ed. *Works of Alexander Hamilton.* Federal ed., 12 vols., New York, 1904.

Madison, James. See Gaillard Hunt, ed.

Meriwether, Robert L., ed. *The Papers of John C. Calhoun.* 3 vols., University of South Carolina Press, 1959–.

Monroe, James. See Stanislaus M. Hamilton, ed.

———. *Autobiography.* Edited by Stuart Gerry Brown. Syracuse, N.Y., 1959.

———. "Letters." *Bulletin of the New York Public Library,* IV (1900), 41–61; V (1901), 371–82, 431–33; VI (1902), 210–30, 247–57. Cited as *Bull. NYPL.*

———. "Letters." *Proc. MHS,* XLII (1908), 318–47.

———. *The People the Sovereigns, Being a Comparison of the Government of the United States with those of the Republics, Which Have Existed Before with the Causes of their Decadence and Fall.* Edited by S. L. Gouverneur. Philadelphia, 1867.

———. *A View of the Conduct of the Executive in the Foreign Affairs of the United States, Connected with the Mission to the French Republic During the Years 1794, 5, 6.* . . . Philadelphia, 1798.

Roberts, Jonathan. "Memoirs of a Senator from Pennsylvania." Edited by Philip S. Klein in *Pa. Mag.,* LXII (1938), *passim.*

Rush, Benjamin. See. L. H. Butterfield, ed.

Saunders, Romulus S. "Letters to Bartlett Yancey." *North Carolina Historical Review,* VI (1930), 427–62.

Sullivan, William. *Public Men of the Revolution.* Philadelphia, 1847.

Trumbull, John. *Autobiography.* Edited by Theodore Sizer. New Haven, Conn., 1953.

Tucker, St. George, ed. *Blackstone's Commentaries.* . . . 5 vols., Philadelphia, 1803.

Waldo, Samuel P. *A Narrative of a Tour of Observation Made During the Summer of 1817.* . . . Hartford, Conn., 1820.

Washington, George. See John C. Fitzpatrick, ed.

F. BOOKS AND ARTICLES

Abel, Annie Heloise. "The History of Events Resulting in Indian Consolidation West of the Mississippi." AHA, *Annual Report,* I, 1906, 233–450.

Adams, Henry. *History of the United States during the Administrations of Jefferson and Madison, 1801–1817.* 8 vols., New York, 1890.

Adams, Henry. *Life of Albert Gallatin.* New York, 1943.

Agan, Joseph Eugene. "Corrêa da Serra." *Pennsylvania Magazine of History and Biography,* XLIX (1925), 1–43.

Aldridge, Alfred Owen. *Man of Reason: The Life of Thomas Paine.* New York, 1959.

Alger, John G. *Englishmen in the French Revolution.* London, 1889.

———. *Paris in 1789–94.* London, 1902.

Ambler, Charles Henry. *Sectionalism in Virginia from 1776 to 1861.* Chicago, 1910.

———. *Thomas Ritchie: A Study in Virginia Politics.* Richmond, 1913.

Ammon, Harry. "Agricola versus Aristides: James Monroe, John Marshall and the Genet Affair in Virginia." *Va. Mag.,* LXXIV (1966), 312–20.

———. "The Election of 1808 in Virginia." *WMQ,* ser. 3, XX (Jan. 1963), 33–56.

———. "The Genet Mission and the Development of American Political Parties." *Journal of American History,* LII (1966), 725–41.

———. "The Richmond Junto, 1800–1824." *Va. Mag.,* LXI (1953), 395–418.

———. "James Monroe and the Era of Good Feelings." *Va. Mag.,* LXVI (1958), 387–398.

Anderson, Dice Robins. *William Branch Giles: A study in the Politics of Virginia and the Nation from 1790 to 1830.* Menasha, Wis., 1914.

Aptheker, Herbert. *American Negro Slave Revolts.* New York, 1963.

Aulard, A. *The French Revolution, A Political History.* 4 vols., London, 1910.

Bassett, John Spencer. *Life of Andrew Jackson.* 2 vols., New York, 1911.

Bemis, Samuel Flagg. *American Foreign Policy and the Blessings of Liberty and Other Essays.* New Haven, 1962.

———, ed. *American Secretaries of State. . . .* 10 vols., New York, 1928.

———. *John Quincy Adams and the Foundations of American Foreign Policy.* New York, 1949. This is the first volume of a two-volume study of John Quincy Adams. Cited as Bemis, *Adams,* I.

———. *Pinckney's Treaty.* New Haven, 1960.

———. "Washington's Farewell Address: A Foreign Policy of Independence." *AHR,* XXXIX (1933), 254–66.

Benns, F. Lee. *The American Struggle for the British West India Carrying-Trade, 1815–1830.* In *Indiana University Studies,* X, no. 56.

Berkeley, Edmund, and Dorothy Smith. "The Piece Left Behind." *Va. Mag.,* LXXV. (1967), 174–80.

Beveridge, Albert J. *Life of John Marshall.* 4 vols., New York, 1916–19.

Bierck, Harold A., Jr. "Soils, Spoils, and Skinner." *Maryland Historical Magazine,* XLIX (1954), 21–40.

Bill, Alfred Hoyt. *Valley Forge.* New York, 1952.

———. *The Campaign of Princeton, 1776–1777.* New York, 1948.

Biro, Sydney Seymour, *The German Policy of Revolutionary France.* 2 vols., Cambridge, Mass., 1957.

Bond, Beverly W. *The Monroe Mission to France, 1794–1796.* In *Johns Hopkins University Studies in History and Political Science,* ser. XXV, nos. 2, 3 (Feb., Mar., 1907).

Bowen, Clarence W. *History of Woodstock, Connecticut.* 6 vols., Norwood, Mass., 1926–30.

Bowman, Albert H. A History of Diplomatic Relations Between the United States and France. (Ph.D. Thesis, Columbia University, 1954).

Brandon, Edgar Ewing, ed. *Lafayette: Guest of the Nation.* 3 vols., Oxford, Ohio, 1950–58.

Brant, Irving. *James Madison.* 6 vols., New York, 1941–1961.

Brooks, Philip Coolidge. *Diplomacy and the Borderlands: The Adams-Onis Treaty of 1819.* In *University of California Publications in History,* XXIV (1939).

Brown, Roger H. *The Republic In Peril.* New York, 1964.

Brown, Stuart Gerry. *The American Presidency: Leadership, Partisanship, and Popularity.* New York, 1966.

Bruce, Philip Alexander. *History of the University of Virginia, 1819–1919.* 5 vols., New York, 1920–22.

Bruce, William Cabell. *John Randolph of Roanoke.* 2 vols., New York, 1922.

Burnett, Edmund Cody. *The Continental Congress.* New York, 1941.

Burt, A. L. *The United States, Great Britain and British North America From the Revolution to the Establishment of Peace After the War of 1812.* New York, 1961.

Callahan, J. Morton. *Neutrality on the American Lakes and Anglo-American Relations.* In *Johns Hopkins University Studies in History and Political Science,* ser. XVI, nos. 1–4 (Jan.–April, 1898).

Campbell, Randolph. Henry Clay and the Emerging Nations of Spanish America, 1815–1829. Ph.D. Dissertation, University of Virginia, 1966.

Cary, Thomas G. *Memoir of Thomas Handasyd Perkins.* Boston, 1856.

Catterall, Ralph C. H. *The Second Bank of the United States.* University of Chicago, 1902. Repr. 1960.

Clough, Shepard Bancroft. *France: A History of National Economics, 1789–1939.* New York, 1939.

Coleman, Mrs. Chapman. *Life of John J. Crittenden.* 2 vols., Philadelphia, 1871.

Conway, Moncure D. *The Life of Thomas Paine.* 2 vols., New York, 1918.

Cotterill, R. S. *The Southern Indians: The Story of the Civilized Tribes Before Removal.* University of Oklahoma Press, 1954.

Cox, Isaac Joslin. "Border Mission of General George Mathews." *Mississippi Valley Historical Review,* XII (1925), 309–33.

——. *The West Florida Controversy, 1798–1813.* Baltimore, 1918.

Cresson, W. P. *James Monroe.* Chapel Hill, N.C., 1946.

Crozier, William Armstrong. *Virginia County Records: Spotsylvania County, 1721–1800.* New York, 1905.

Cruikshank, E. A. "Negotiations of the Agreement for Disarmament of the Great Lakes." *Royal Society of Canada, Proceedings,* 3d. ser., XXX, ser. 2, 151–85.

Cunningham, Noble E., Jr. "John Beckley: An Early American Party Manager." *WMQ,* ser. 3, XIII (1956), 40–52.

Dallas, George M. *Life and Writings of Alexander James Dallas.* Philadelphia, 1871.

Danforth, George H. The Rebel Earl. Ph.D. Thesis, Columbia University, 1955.

Dangerfield, George. *Awakening of American Nationalism.* New York, 1965.

——. *Chancellor Robert R. Livingston of New York, 1746–1813.* New York, 1960.

——. *Era of Good Feelings.* New York, 1952

Davis, Matthew L. *Memoirs of Aaron Burr with Miscellaneous Selections from his Correspondence.* 2 vols., New York, 1858.

Davis, W. W. H. "Washington on the West Bank of the Delaware, 1776." *Pa. Mag.,* IV (1880), 52–53.

DeConde, Alexander. *Entangling Alliances: Politics and Diplomacy Under Washington.* Durham, N.C., 1958.

Duer, William H. *Life of William Alexander, Lord Stirling.* New York, 1847.

Dunbar, Louise B. *A Study of "Monarchical" Tendencies in the United States from 1776 to 1801.* In *University of Illinois Studies in the Social Sciences,* X, no. 1. Urbana, Ill., 1923.

Eaton, David W. *Historical Atlas of Westmoreland County.* Richmond, Va., 1942.

Eckenrode, J. J. *The Revolution in Virginia.* Boston, 1916.

Edwards, Ninian W. *Life and Times of Ninian Edwards.* Springfield, Ill., 1870.

Engelman. *Peace of Christmas Eve.* New York, 1962.

Fay, Bernard. *The Revolutionary Spirit in France and America.* New York, 1927.

Fish, Carl Russell. *The Civil Service and the Patronage. Harvard Historical Studies,* XI, Cambridge, Mass., 1904.

Flagg, C. A., and Walters, W. O. "Bibliography of Musters and Pay Rolls." *Va. Mag.,* XX (1912), 52–68, 181–94, 267–81.

Footner, Hulbert. *Sailor of Fortune: The Life of . . . Commodore Barney. . . .* New York, 1940.

Ford, Worthington C. "Genesis of the Monroe Doctrine." *Proc. MHS,* 2d ser., XV (1901–1902), 373–436.

Freeman, Douglas Southall. *George Washington.* 7 vols., New York, 1948–57.

Gilman, Daniel C. *James Monroe.* New York, 1885.

Gottschalk, Louis. *Lafayette Joins the American Army.* University of Chicago, 1937.

Govan, Thomas Payne. *Nicholas Biddle: Nationalist and Public Banker.* University of Chicago, 1959.

Gray, Denis. *Spencer Perceval.* Manchester University Press, 1963.

Griffin, Charles C. "Privateering from Baltimore During the Spanish American War of Independence." *Maryland Historical Magazine,* XXXV (1940), 1–25.

Grigsby, Hugh Blair. *The Virginia Convention of 1829–30, a Discourse Delivered before the Virginia Historical Society at Their Annual Meeting...Dec. 15, 1853.* Richmond, 1854.

Hamlin, Talbot. *Benjamin Henry Latrobe.* New York, 1955.

Hammond, Bray. *Banks and Politics in America from the Revolution to the Civil War.* Princeton, 1957.

Hammond, Jabez D. *History of Political Parties in the State of New York.* 2 vols., Syracuse, N.Y., 1952.

Harmon, George Dewey. *Sixty Years of Indian Affairs, Political, Economic and Diplomatic, 1789–1850.* Chapel Hill, N.C., 1941.

Harrell, Isaac S. *Loyalism in Virginia.* Durham, N.C., 1926.

Harrison, Joseph Hobson, Jr. The Internal Improvement Issue in the Politics of the Union, 1783–1825. Ph.D. Dissertation, University of Virginia, 1954.

Hildreth, Richard. *History of the United States of America.* 6 vols., New York, 1880.

Hughes, Rupert. *George Washington.* 3 vols., New York, 1926–30.

James, James A. "French Opinion as a Factor in Preventing War between France and the United States, 1795–1800." *AHR,* XXX (1924), 44–55.

Jellison, Charles A. "That Scoundrel Callender." *Va. Mag.,* LXVI (1959), 294–306.

Jillson, Willard Rouse. *The Kentucky Land Grants: A Systematic Index to All the Land Grants Recorded in the State Land Office at Frankfort, Kentucky, 1784–1924.* Filson Club Publication no. 33, Louisville, Ky., 1925.

——. *Old Kentucky Entries and Deeds.* Filson Club Publication no. 36, Louisville, Ky., 1926.

Johnson, Monroe. "Maryland Ancestry of James Monroe." *Maryland Historical Magazine,* XXIII (1928), 193–95.

Keller, William Frederick. American Politics and the Genet Mission, 1793–1794. Ph.D. Dissertation, University of Pittsburgh, 1951.

——. *The Nation's Advocate: Henry Marie Brackenridge and Young America.* Pittsburgh, 1956.

Kennedy, John P. *Life of William Wirt.* 2 vols., New York, 1872.

King, George Harrison. See Brooke Payne.

Klingberg, Frank K. *The Anti-Slavery Movement in England.* New Haven, Conn., 1926.

Knollenberg, Bernhard. *Washington and the Revolution.* New York, 1941.

Krauel, Richard. "Prince Henry of Prussia and the Regency of the United States, 1786." *AHR,* XVII (1917), 44–51.

Lane-Poole, Stanley. *Life of Stratford Canning.* 2 vols., London, 1888.

Lefebvre, Georges. *The Thermidorians and the Directory.* New York, 1964.

Livermore, Shaw, Jr. *The Twilight of Federalism.* Princeton, 1962.

Logan, John A., Jr. *No Transfer: An American Security Principle.* Yale University Press, 1961.

Lyon, E. Wilson. "The Directory and the United States." *AHR,* XLIII (1938), 514–32.

———. *Louisiana and French Diplomacy.* University of Oklahoma Press, 1934.

Malone, Dumas. *Jefferson and His Time.* 3 vols., New York, 1948–.

Marsh, Philip M. "James Monroe as 'Agricola' in the Genet Controversy, 1793." *Va. Mag.,* LXII (1954), 472–76.

———. "John Beckley, Mystery Man of the Early Jeffersonians." *Pa. Mag.,* LXXII (1948), 54–69.

———. *Monroe's Defense of Jefferson and Freneau against Hamilton.* Oxford, Ohio, 1948.

Matheson, David. "The Organization of the Government Under the Constitution." In *History of the Formation of the Union under the Constitution.* Washington, 1941. Edited by the Constitutional Sesquicentennial Commission, Sol Bloom, Director General.

Mathiez, Albert. *After Robespierre: The Thermidorian Reaction.* New York, 1931.

Matteson, David M. "Fredericksburg Peace Ball." *Va. Mag.,* XLIX (1941), 152–56.

Maurois, André. *Adrienne, the Life of the Marquise de Lafayette.* New York, 1961.

Mayo, Bernard. *Henry Clay: Spokesman of the Old West.* Boston, 1937.

———. "Joshua Barney and the French Revolution." *Md. Hist. Mag.,* XXXVI (1941), 359.

Mays, David John. *Edmund Pendleton.* 2 vols., Cambridge, Mass., 1952.

McLemore, Robert A. *Franco-American Diplomatic Relations 1816–1836.* Louisiana State University, 1941.

Meade, William. *Old Churches, Ministers and Families of Virginia.* 2 vols., Philadelphia, 1857.

Meigs, William M. *Life of Charles Jared Ingersoll.* Philadelphia, 1897.

Miller, John C. *Alexander Hamilton.* New York, 1959.

Monaghan, Frank. *John Jay.* New York, 1935.

Moore, Glover. *The Missouri Controversy, 1819–1821.* Lexington, Ky., 1953.

Morgan, George. *Life of James Monroe.* Boston, 1921.

Morison, Samuel Eliot. *By Land and by Sea.* New York, 1957.

———. *The Life and Letters of Harrison Gray Otis.* 2 vols., New York, 1913.

Nolan, J. Bennett. *Lafayette In America Day by Day.* In *Historical Documents, Institut Français de Washington,* vol. 7., Baltimore, 1934.

Otero, Michael A. The American Mission of Diego de Gardoqui, 1785–1789. Ph.D. Dissertation, University of California, Los Angeles, 1948.

Payne, Brooke, and King, George Harrison. "The Monroe Family," *WMQ,* Ser. 2, XIII (1933), 234–41.

Perkins, Bradford. *Castlereagh and Adams: England and the United States, 1812–1823.* University of California, 1964.

———. *The First Rapprochement, England and the United States, 1795–1805.* Philadelphia, 1955.

————. *The Prologue to War: England and the United States, 1805–1812.* University of California, 1961.

Perkins, Dexter. *The Monroe Doctrine, 1823–1826. Harvard Historical Studies,* vol. XXIX. Cambridge, 1927.

Pratt, Julius W. "James Monroe," See Bemis, *American Secretaries of State,* III, 201–281.

Randolph, Sarah N. *Domestic Life of Thomas Jefferson.* New York, 1871.

Ravenel, Harriet H. *Life and Times of William Lowndes.* New York, 1901.

Remini, Robert V. *Martin Van Buren and the Making of the Democratic Party.* Columbia University, 1967.

————. "New York and the Presidential Election of 1816." *New York History,* XXXI (1950), 308–23.

Risjord, Norman K. *The Old Republicans: Southern Conservatism in the Age of Jefferson.* Columbia University, 1965.

Robertson, William Spence. *Life of Miranda.* 2 vols., Chapel Hill, N.C., 1929.

————. "The Recognition of the Hispanic American Nations by the United States." *Hispanic American Historical Review,* I (1918), 239–69.

Rothbard, Murray N. *The Panic of 1819: Reactions and Policies.* Columbia University, 1962.

Schachner, Nathan. *Alexander Hamilton.* New York, 1946.

Schellenberg, T. R. "Jeffersonian Origins of the Monroe Doctrine." *Hispanic American Review,* XIV (1934), 1–31.

Schouler, James A. *History of the United States.* 7 vols., New York, 1880–1913.

[Scott, John]. *The Lost Principle; or the Sectional Equilibrium. . . . By "Barbarossa."* Richmond, 1860.

Seaton, Josephine. *William Winston Seaton.* Boston, 1871.

Simms, Henry H. *Life of John Taylor.* Richmond, 1932.

Smith, Theodore Clarke. "War Guilt in 1812." *Proc. MHS,* LXIV (1932), 319–45.

Smith, Walter Buckingham. *Economic Aspects of the Second Bank of the United States.* Harvard University, 1953.

Smith, William Henry. *Life and Public Services of Arthur St. Clair.* 2 vols., Cincinnati, 1882.

Soulsby, Hugh B. *The Right of Search and the Slave Trade in Anglo-American Relations, 1814–1862.* Baltimore, 1931.

Stanwood, Edward. *American Tariff Controversies in the Nineteenth Century.* 2 vols., New York, 1903.

Staudenraus, P. J. *African Colonization Movement, 1816–1865.* Columbia University, 1961.

Stenberg, Richard R. "Jackson's Rhea Letter Hoax." *Journal of Southern History,* II (1936), 480–96.

Stevens, John Austen, Jr. *Colonial New York: Sketches Biographical and Historical, 1768–1784.* New York, 1867.

Stone, William. *Life of Joseph Brant-Thayendenega.* 2 vols., New York, 1838.

Swanstrom, Roy. *The United States Senate, 1787–1801.* Ph.D. Dissertation, University of California, 1959.

Tatum, Howland, Jr. *The United States and Europe, 1815–1823.* New York, 1946. Repr. 1967.

Taus, Esther Rogoff. *The Banking Functions of the United States Treasury, 1789–1941*. New York, Columbia University, 1943. Repr. 1967.

Taussig, F. W. *Tariff History of the United States*. New York, 1892. Repr. 1967.

Temperley, Harold. *The Foreign Policy of Canning, 1822–1827*. London, 1925.

Tone, William Theobald Wolfe. *Life of Theobald Wolfe Tone*. 2 vols., Washington, 1826.

Treat, Payson Jackson. *The National Land System, 1785–1820*. New York, 1910.

Tucker, Glenn. *Poltroons and Patriots*. 2 vols., New York, 1943.

Turner, Lynn W. *William Plumer of New Hampshire, 1759–1850*. Chapel Hill, N.C., 1962.

Tyler, Lyon G. "James Monroe." *WMQ*, ser. 1, IV (1895), 272–74.

———. *The Letters and Times of the Tylers*. 3 vols., Richmond, 1884–96.

Vail, R. W. G. "Notes on the History of the Early American Circus." *Proceedings of the American Antiquarian Society*, XLIII (1934), 116–85.

Van Deusen, Glyndon G. *The Life of Henry Clay*. New York, 1937.

Waddell, Alexander Wilbourne. *Richmond, Virginia, in Old Prints*. Richmond, Va., 1932.

Wallace, David Duncan. *Life of Henry Laurens*. New York, 1915.

Ward, Christopher. *The War of the Revolution*. 2 vols., New York, 1952.

Watson, J. Steven. *The Reign of George III, 1760–1815*. Oxford University, 1960.

Webster, C. K. *The Foreign Policy of Castlereagh*. 2 vols., London, 1931.

Wharton, Anne Hollingsworth. *Social Life in the Early Republic*. Philadelphia, 1902.

Whitaker, Arthur P. *The Mississippi Question, 1795–1803*. New York, 1934.

———. *The United States and the Independence of Latin America*. Baltimore, 1941.

White, Leonard. *The Jeffersonians: a Study in Administrative History, 1801–1829*. New York, 1951.

Wilmerding, Lucius, Jr. *James Monroe, Public Claimant*. Rutgers University, 1960.

———. "James Monroe and the Furniture Fund." *New-York Historical Society Quarterly*, XLIV (1960), 133–49.

Wiltse, Charles M. "Authorship of the War Report of 1812." *AHR*, XLIX (1943–44), 253–69.

———. *John C. Calhoun*. 3 vols., New York, 1944–51.

[Wolfe, Udolpho, ed.] *Grand Civic and Military Demonstration in Honor of the Removal of the Remains of James Monroe ... from New-York to Virginia*. New York, 1858.

Woodress, James Leslie. *A Yankee's Odyssey: the Life of Joel Barlow*. Philadelphia, 1958.

Woods, Edgar. *Albemarle County in Virginia*. Charlottesville, Va., 1901.

Young, James Sterling. *The Washington Community, 1800–1828*. Columbia University, 1966.

INDEX